1,300

Critical Evaluations

of

Selected Novels and Plays

1,300
Critical Evaluations
of
Selected Novels and Plays

OFFPRINTS OF ALL THE NEW MATERIAL FROM THE
12-VOLUME REVISED EDITION OF *MASTERPLOTS*

Edited by
FRANK N. MAGILL

Volume Four
Rob - Z
1935 - 2578
Index

SALEM PRESS
Englewood Cliffs

R
809.924
M194o
1978
V.4

LIBRARY OF CONGRESS CATALOG CARD NUMBER: 78-55387

Complete Set: ISBN 0-89356-043-X
Volume 4:   ISBN 0-89356-047-2

Some of the material in this work also appears in *Masterplots*, Revised Edition (1976).

PRINTED IN THE UNITED STATES OF AMERICA

LIST OF TITLES IN VOLUME FOUR

LIST OF TITLES

1,300 CRITICAL EVALUATIONS OF SELECTED NOVELS AND PLAYS

ROBIN HOOD'S ADVENTURES

Type of work: Folk tales
Author: Unknown
Type of plot: Adventure romance
Time of plot: Thirteenth century
Locale: England
First published: c. 1490

Robin Hood, the legendary outlaw, is a folk hero who has been celebrated in ballad and tale since the Middle Ages. The first collection of ballads dealing with his exploits, published about 1490, tells of Robin Hood's courage, skill at archery, and daring deeds in support of the poor. Although known chiefly as a children's hero today, Robin has served as the prototype for a great many heroes of romantic fiction.

Robin Hood's Adventures is without doubt one of the best-loved stories of all time. It has the elements which make for entertaining reading: romance, adventure, the stage of history, and lofty characters. As a work of prose fiction, however, it is quite unusual in one respect: comparatively few have actually read the book, whereas millions have heard about the story. Those who have not read the original have nevertheless come to know and love the characters of the Robin Hood legend through the countless other versions of the story in prose, fireside tales, motion pictures, and more recently television.

The Robin Hood story itself goes back well into the Middle Ages. Legends developed about a "good" outlaw who protected and supported the poor while he stole from the rich. Early legends did not center on one bandit, however. There appear to have been several similar heroes of this type who were eventually coalesced into the character of Robin Hood, Earl of Huntingdon, as he appears in this story. Whether or not the prototypes of Robin Hood were real, as some historians believe them to have been, is a moot point. It is the legend and not the reality of the story which has excited people for centuries.

Although the first recorded reference to Robin Hood occurred in the writings of the Scottish historian John of Fordun, died c. 1384, the first known compilation of prose and poetry of the Robin Hood legend came in 1490 with the publication of *TheLytel Geste of Robin Hood,* by Wynkyn de Worde, a noted British printer. If there were records for best sellers in those days, certainly this tale would have been high on the list. It proved so popular that this version appeared again several decades later and has been reprinted and retold for centuries. It was used as a basis for works of later novelists such as Sir Walter Scott in *Ivanhoe* and more recently on film in successful movie and television adaptations of the story.

Its popularity has exceeded even these genre, however, and is represented in songs, children's toys and costumes, and even games. Playing Robin Hood is a fantasy game popular with children, somewhere below war, and cops and robbers. To the English especially, Robin Hood is a great hero. He and King Arthur are the most revered characters in British legends, and their popularity has spread and continues to thrive throughout the world.

Although *Robin Hood's Adventures* would hardly be classed as one of the great works of world literature, it is so entertaining that it may be read with delight over and over again. It is truly a case of the overall story being more important to its popularity than any of the individual elements of the work. The reader can forgive a lack of in-depth character analysis when he is made to feel as if he were riding through Sherwood Forest by Robin Hood's side.

The story line of the tale is quite simple: the underdog, Robin Hood, fights oppression and injustice in the form of the Sheriff of Nottingham and Prince John, to protect the poor and rally them around the good, but absent, King Richard I. Robin Hood represented an early attempt to personify *noblesse oblige*. He was a highborn man who helped the unfortunate. He did not condescend in his assistance, however, because he lived and worked among the poor in Sherwood Forest. By contrast, Prince John was a blatant representation of a powerful, oppressive leader. By persecuting Robin Hood, he inadvertently encouraged Robin's followers. King Richard, his brother, represents the colorful "good king" who was fighting in the Holy Land during the Third Crusade to overthrow the Moslems.

While this narrative makes for entertaining reading and is the basic plot outline for many works, it is quite far removed from historical fact. As the legends grew about Robin Hood, the actual historical events surrounding the reigns of Richard and John became blurred. In reality, Richard was rarely seen in England after he became king. He preferred traveling and fighting in other countries. And John was not a particularly bad leader, merely unlucky. He was called John Lackland because he had the unfortunate habit of losing English territories to the French. For this reason he became very unpopular, and hence has had a bad reputation down through the centuries. Adding up the elements of John's unpopularity, Richard's swashbuckling image, and the possibility of real Robin Hood-type bandits exisiting in the period surrounding the signing of the *Magna Carta,* the legend has been expanded so that the historical truth has been buried in a good story. If one reads *Robin Hood's Adventures* as escapist literature, the facts may not matter, but one should bear in mind that the tale is not historically accurate.

History aside, the book is entertaining reading material. It has a sense of adventure that can be appreciated by almost anyone and has enough plot to keep the interest of the reader in the less adventurous moments. Its characterizations are weak, however. They are too black-and-white to be true reflections of life. One must realize, though, that in the fifteenth century, English literature had not developed into its later sophisticated form and that the novel had the added handicap of being based on preconceived characters and events.

To have changed dramatically the nature of one of the central characters would have been to violate the reader's trust, even if the author had wished to do so. This work and *The Once and Future King,* written at a much later date, were polished versions of popular legends and as such could not deviate from tradition without destroying the value of the story. So one should approach *Robin Hood's Adventures* as one would approach a light-hearted film: sit back, relax, and enjoy it.

Patricia Ann King

ROBINSON CRUSOE

Type of work: Novel
Author: Daniel Defoe (1660-1731)
Type of plot: Adventure romance
Time of plot: 1651-1705
Locale: An island off the coast of South America, and the Several Seas
First published: 1719

Like many famous stories, Robinson Crusoe *is more known than read. The tale of the shipwrecked sailor who survives, rescues a servant (Friday), and eventually "civilizes" the island before being rescued, is universally familiar. Crusoe's adventures as a castaway actually occupy a modest portion of the book. The real story is that of a man who survives and prospers, whatever the environment, through hard work, intelligence, tenacity, and faith in his Protestant God.*

On the surface an exotic novel of travel and adventure, *Robinson Crusoe* functions primarily as Defoe's defense of his bourgeois Protestantism. Crusoe's adventures—the shipwrecks, his life as a planter in South America, and his years of isolation on the island—provide an apt context for his polemic. A political dissenter and pamphleteer, Defoe saw his enemies as the Tory aristocrats whose royalism in government and religion blocked the rise of the middle class. Further, like Swift in *Gulliver's Travels,* Defoe in his novel viewed England as religiously and politically corrupt. Each author was intent upon bringing about a moral revolution, using his hero as an exemplum. Gulliver, however, represents a moral failure, whereas Crusoe's adventures reveal his spiritual conversion, a return to the ethics and religion of his father. As one critic has said, "We read it [*Robinson Crusoe*] . . . in order to follow with meticulous interest and constant self-identification the hero's success in building up, step by step, out of whatever material came to hand, a physical and moral replica of the world he had left behind him. If *Robinson Crusoe* is an adventure story, it is also a moral tale, a commercial accounting and a puritan fable."

Significantly, Crusoe's origins are in northern England, in York, where he was born in the early part of the seventeenth century and where his father had made a fortune in trade. He is of the solid middle class, that class which was beginning to come to political power during the early eighteenth century, when Defoe published his book. Crusoe's father is an apologist for the mercantile, Puritan ethic, which he tries without success to instill in his son. As Crusoe says, "mine was the middle state," which his father "had found by long experience was the best state in the world, the most suited to human happiness, not exposed to the miseries and hardships, the labour and sufferings of the mechanick part of mankind, and not embarrassed with the pride, luxury, ambition and envy of the upper part of mankind." Its virtues and blessings were those of "temperance, moderation, quietness, health [and] society."

Yet his father's philosophy, which is designed to buy man happiness and pleasure in both this life and the next, fails to persuade the young Crusoe, who finds nothing but boredom amidst the comforts of the middle class. He longs to go to sea, to follow a way of life which represents the antithesis of his father's. He seeks the extremes of sensation and danger, preferring to live on the periphery rather than in the secure middle where all is mundane and sure. Crusoe's decision to become a sailor is an act of adolescent rebellion, yet it is also very much in the tradition of Puritan individualism. Not content with the wisdom of his class, the young man feels it is necessary to test himself, to discover himself and his own ethic.

Even after the first stage in his adventures, which culminates in Crusoe's amassing a modest fortune in South America, he refuses to follow his father's ethic and settle down. Intent on his own "inclination," as he says, he leaves his plantation and once again takes up the uncertain life of sea trade. It is at this point in the narrative that Crusoe is shipwrecked, abandoned alone on a tropical island without any hope of rescue.

Crusoe's first response to his isolation and the prospect of living the rest of his life alone is one of despair. Yet his instinct to survive remains dominant, and he sets to the task not only of staying alive but also of creating a humane, comfortable society. One of the first things he does is to mark time, to make a calendar. Despite all his efforts, however, to continue his own life and environment, he falls ill and it is at this point that he realizes his complete vulnerability, his absolute aloneness in the universe. Stripped of all his illusions, limited by necessity to one small place, Crusoe is thrown back upon himself, confronted by an immense emptiness. He asks desperately: "What is this earth and sea of which I have seen so much? Whence is it produced? And what am I and all the other creatures, wild and tame, human and brutal? Whence are we?"

All these questions predate Crusoe's religious conversion, the central and most significant act of the novel. His answer to the questions is that all creation comes from God and that the state of all creation, including his own, is an expression of the will of God. Upon this act of faith, he rebuilds not only his own life but also his own miniature society which reflects in its simplicity, moderation, and comfort the philosophy his father had taught. Further, his faith brings him to an acceptance of his own life and station, an acceptance that he was never able to make before: "I acquiesced in the dispositions of Providence, which I began now to own and to believe ordered everything for the best." And later, after two years on the island. he says, "It was now that I began sensibly to feel how much more happy this life I now led was, with all its miserable circumstances, than the wicked, cursed, abominable life I led all the past part of my days; and now I changed both my sorrows and my joys; my very desires altered, my affections changed their gusts, and my delights were perfectly new from what they were at my first coming."

Once the overwhelming question of the novel—"Whence are we?"—has been answered, the rest of the narrative and Crusoe's adventures justify, to his aristocrat readers, his religious faith and middle-class Puritan ethic. Besides this justification there remains the glorification of the self-reliant and self-directing man; he was a man unfamiliar to Defoe's readers, a new man who was beginning to appear on the fringes of the power structure and who was about to demand his place in a society that was evolving toward a new political structure that we now recognize as middle-class democracy.

David L. Kubal

RODERICK HUDSON

Type of work: Novel
Author: Henry James (1843-1916)
Type of plot: Psychological realism
Time of plot: The 1870's
Locale: Chiefly Rome, also Florence and Switzerland
First published: 1876

In this early novel, Henry James presents themes and character types that were to be central to all his works. Most notable is the "international theme": the clash between the innocent, energetic, even vulgar American and the beautiful, complex, sometimes decadent European milieu. Also in Roderick Hudson, *James develops the character of the artist whose talents and passions carry the possibilities of both brilliant creativity and tragic self-destruction.*

This novel opened one of the richest and most complicated careers in American literature. Themes and devices which James was to employ over and over again are used in *Roderick Hudson* for the first time.

Roderick Hudson may, of course, be viewed as a signal achievement of American literary independence, as a reflection of the clash between the old world and the new, or as a story of the corruption of innocence by decadence. It is also important to note that *Roderick Hudson* has an artist as its central character. The novel asks what it takes for an American artist to survive as a creative talent. For James, always self-conscious in his role as an artist, and especially an American artist, this was a pressing question. So James's first novel, then, may be considered in many ways as a catalogue of temptations, temptations which must be resisted if an artist is to survive and succeed.

It is Roderick's egoism and self-absorption that are ultimately fatal. In order to develop his talent he must be exposed to the cultural experiences of the civilizations of Europe. At the same time, his selfishness makes him vulnerable to the temptation of Christina Light, and especially to the temptation of possessing her. Plunging into relationships in Europe separates Roderick from the healthy, stabilizing American influence of Mary Garland.

James argues that unless an American artist is able to preserve a certain simplicity and honesty, qualities associated with American civilization, he will be distracted and finally destroyed as a talent by European decadence. At the same time it is clear from Rowland Mallet's experience, and the experiences of others like him in later works by James, that creative accomplishment also requires a sense of daring and risk. The unwillingness or inability to take those risks also dooms talent.

In *Roderick Hudson,* then, it is balance and poise which are crucial for artistic survival. One may also conclude that *Roderick Hudson* is not merely a prescription for survival in general, but expresses James's strategy and hope for himself and reveals those temptations he felt were dangerous for his own development.

RODERICK RANDOM

Type of work: Novel
Author: Tobias Smollett (1721-1771)
Type of plot: Picaresque romance
Time of plot: Eighteenth century
Locale: England
First published: 1748

Influenced by Le Sage's Gil Blas, *Tobias Smollett's first novel is a vigorous picaresque in which he sends his intrepid hero, Roderick Random, on a series of adventures which include such disparate settings as London high society and the naval battle of Cartagena. Smollett's narrative is strident and inventive, his caricatures are vivid and hilarious, and his prose is strong and direct.*

Roderick Random is without doubt among the most adventure-ridden episodic novels of the eighteenth century. Innumerable incidents befall Roderick as he roams in every conceivable direction on land and sea, driven by necessity and survival. It is, then, a novel written in the best picaresque tradition with a hero who is at once roguish and (to a point) virtuous, resilient in the face of adversity yet often despairing, honorable in some matters but underhanded in a great many others. He is by turns whimsical, deliberate, sensitive, vengeful, petulant, gracious, and whatever else Smollett finds occasion for him to be. Structurally *Roderick Random* also fits easily into the picaresque tradition, not only in the obvious influence of Le Sage's *Gil Blas,* noted by Smollett in his preface, but also in its plot deficiencies. There are several such weaknesses—most of them sudden, unconvincing turns in the narrative —which betray the picaresque fondness for overemphasizing action and character.

Today the novel is most often read for two things: its glittering wit and its caustic social satire. There are many delightful touches in the book (the repartee of Miss Snapper, for example) which show off Smollett's comic skills and these, added to the author's ribaldry, make for great fun at times. But perhaps the most engaging parts of the novel are its scenes of London life: the card sharps, the wags, the floozies and fops, the poverty, the stench, the cruelty. We meet every imaginable species of human creature from prissy lords and lavender-trousered ship captains to lascivious priests and penitent whores. As a result Smollett depicts not just the sins of a sin-worn world but also the need to match good nature with plain animal cunning. Part of the controlling idea in *Roderick Random* is that education is best obtained, albeit harshly, not in schoolrooms but in city streets.

This theme is a favorite of eighteenth century British fiction. Fielding's *Tom Jones,* published just a year after *Roderick Random,* is a well-known reiteration of it; Tom, like Roderick, lacks wisdom and self-control (the age would have called it prudence), hence, he is repeatedly victimized by individuals with a crueler nature than his own. In Smollett's book we see the same pattern: a young man with a basically "good nature" (to echo Fielding) forced into a world of duplicity where his kindness and trust are manipulated by others. Thus the "knavery of the world," as Smollett dubs it, everywhere demands that the hero learn to be worldly-wise; the difficulty is to do this without destroying one's fundamental goodness. Often we see Roderick on the verge of such destruction. He is ungracious to his faithful friend Strap; he is at times unconscionably cruel in his schemes for revenge; he gravitates too easily toward unsavory rakes (Banter is a good example) and is himself tainted with affectation. But the point is that he remains good at heart and in the end is "rewarded" with Narcissa much as Tom Jones, having gained *prudentia,* is allowed to possess "Sophia."

It can be said, then, that the novel employs its main character as a moral *exemplum* for preaching and illustrating the traditional values of the age, among them temperance, virtue, fortitude, and honesty. It can also be said that the book's emphasis on sensibility reinforces the efficacy of human goodness, for if the reader is moved to applaud virtue and hate vice, to upbraid the hero's ingratitude despite his attractiveness, then Smollett has in large part proved his point.

Even a quick reading of the novel makes it plain how much Smollett relies on the theme of disguise to develop not only the concept of prudence but also a number of other concerns. One notable example is clothing imagery (it abounds in the book) in such scenes as Beau Jackson's appearance before the medical examiners. Wildly costumed as an old duffer, Jackson is a literal application of the adage that "the clothes make the man." He is found out, naturally, and thereby Smollett prepares us for one of the dominant themes of the novel. Simply, that theme argues that pretension, subterfuge, and hypocrisy are all penetrable. With experience and a sharp eye an individual can see through them.

The question to be asked, then, is: "What individual?" And the answer usually offered up by eighteenth century writers is: "The satirist." It is a commonplace observation that the satirist strips away the coverings of things, that after creating disguises for his characters he tears them away in order to reveal what lies beneath. In the case of Smollett this is unquestionably so. The clothing imagery fits well with his satiric purposes, for everywhere his intent is to bare our moral as well as our physical natures. Also, an understanding of this commonplace in part elucidates Smollett's dislike of "Romance" and other such writings. His attack on romance in the preface owes much to the satiric spirit which prevailed in the Augustan age, for there are few modes so different in philosophy as the romantic and the satiric. Romances—or "novels" as they were often called in Smollett's day—are in a sense departures from this world; they are fantasies, unrealities, idealizations. Satire, on the other hand, is fully committed to the world as it is;

thus, it both eschews the improbable and dissolves the apparently real in order to plummet life's deepest recesses.

It should also be mentioned that *Roderick Random,* Smollett's first novel, is interesting simply for its biographical and historical inclusions. Smollett was himself a surgeon, therefore as one might expect the book offers plenty of commentary on eighteenth century medical practices. He also served in the Royal Navy as a surgeon's mate, was present at the disastrous attack upon Cartagena (this is discussed at length in the novel), and so had a first-hand knowledge of seamanship as well as medicine. Lastly, the story of Molopoyn, which occurs near the end of the book, is a thinly disguised account of Smollett's endeavors to promote his tragedy, *The Regicide.*

David B. Carroll

ROGUE HERRIES

Type of work: Novel
Author: Hugh Walpole (1884-1941)
Type of plot: Historical chronicle
Time of plot: 1730-1774
Locale: England
First published: 1930

Rogue Herries is the first novel in a tetralogy which traces in detail the story of an English family over a period of two hundred years, concentrating largely upon domestic morals and manners. The novels grow in complexity as new generations appear and succeed one another, but Walpole keeps the narrative under control by relating the action to the descendants of the original, notorious Rogue Herries.

Rogue Herries, like the other installments of the Herries chronicle, is an ambitious effort on the part of Hugh Walpole. In addition to offering a work that conforms to the criteria of a "traditional" novel—characterized by memorable characters and a well-constructed plot—he incorporates features that have become indicative of his own personal style.

Most prominent in *Rogue Herries* is the youthfulness and enthusiasm of its tone. The major characters, while differing in other ways, share a common zest for life. Francis, in the midst of his curious moods and mysterious motivations, loves drinking, cock-fighting and bull-baiting with other high-spirited men, and he relishes taking his horse Mameluke out into the countryside. David, Francis' son, who is tame in nature compared to his father, comes to love the valley and mountains that make up Borrowdale where the Herries family lives; it is an organic fusion—David becoming a part of everything around him—that characterizes him throughout his life. Sarah Denburn, David's wife, enthusiastically joins forces with David to find a means of escape from her uncle so that she might partake of the full life she envisions as David's mate. It is Walpole's design to have this zest for life identify his positive characters, while lethargy, as seen in Uncle Pomfret and Aunt Janice, identifies the negative personalities.

The malevolent characters that exist in the novel, as well as in most of Walpole's works, demonstrate that the author sees a continuous conflict in the universe between good and evil forces. This theme is apparent in the stormy relationship between Francis Herries and his wife Margaret, the former representing evil, the latter good, if docility can be defined as "good"; in the tragic execution of Mrs. Wilson, resulting from the people of Grange's ill-founded supposition that she was a witch and caused the death of her friend, Hannah Mounsey; and, again, in the tenuous relationship between Francis and Mirabell Starr, with Francis' devoted love identifying the good, and Mirabell's incapacity to love after the death of her young man, Harry, representing the evil. Behind much of this war between good and evil, Walpole places the influence

of the sensational—supernatural forces—as a prime cause. Witches, war-
locks, and magic spells are shown to play an influential role in the minds and
the lives of characters in this and in other Walpole novels.

Even though the novel concerns itself with a prevailing theme of good
versus evil, presents a consistent backdrop of actual historical events, and
offers many subplots—the development of David and the story of Sarah
Denburn, to name only two—the story is primarily about one person. It is
the story of Francis Herries, the "rogue," and his search for self-identity.
Through reports from many different viewpoints, including this own, Francis'
actions appear rather impetuous and largely uncontrolled. Walpole makes the
chaotic nature of the elder Herries more apparent by employing a "doubles"
device. In this case, the orderly, even-tempered personality of David counter-
balances the disordered tempestuousness of his father. There are other
"doubles" in the novel—for example, Sarah's vivacity counters David's reserve—but none are so clearly outlined as the pattern involving Francis and
David. At the same time, Francis frequently questions the motives that prompt
his behavior, although offering no substantial answers; he recognizes his imperfections, but he cannot find cures for them. In fact, the only near-resolution
in the quest for self-realization that drives Francis on remains quite obscure.
Somehow, in Mirabell Starr he finds the embodiment of his visionary "great
white horse" and, consequently, fulfillment in his life. Walpole supplies no
clear reason why Mirabell should serve such a vital function. Perhaps it is
because she is Francis' first true love or because her gipsy ways exert some
magical influence upon him. The reader's imagination is the final judge in
this matter, this very easily being Walpole's design from the beginning.

In spite of the questions left unanswered, *Rogue Herries* is a substantial
accomplishment as a novel. Walpole's attention to careful plot and character
development, the lively narrative pace, and his devotion to detail in physical
and topographical setting and their influence upon the story, make the first
volume of the Herries chronicle fine reading.

THE ROMAN ACTOR

Type of work: Drama
Author: Philip Massinger (1583-1640)
Type of plot: Tragedy of intrigue
Time of plot: First century
Locale: Rome
First presented: 1626

The Roman Actor *depicts the degeneracy of imperial Rome under the tyrant* Domitian. *In contrast to the general corruption stands Paris, the actor, who is the most original and impressive element in the play. Unfortunately, Massinger's awkward double plot focuses most of the attention on Domitian, a much less interesting personality, while Paris is only occasionally forced into the central action.*

The Roman Actor was licensed on October 11, 1626, by Sir Henry Herbert, who had become Master of Revels three years earlier. In 1629 the play was published in quarto as acted at Blackfriars by the King's Men. The play takes its source material from Dio Cassius and Suetonius, and Massinger interspersed that with his own inventive episodes. Perhaps herein lies the problem. For as masterful as Massinger was with plot development, The Roman Actor displays little of his artistry in that respect. Within the first act of the play, he introduces two plots: one centering on the nature of tyranny as it emerges in Domitian's quest to be placed above the law and looked upon as divine, particularly as he maneuvers to acquire the hand of Domitia; and the other focusing on Paris as he supports the value of the actor's profession. It is not until Act III that Massinger attempts to combine the two plot lines in a semblance of interaction. Because of the incompatibility of the two themes, the play remains highly episodic, though the situations posed have dramatic value. This characteristic makes The Roman Actor atypical of Massinger's high abilities.

The play should not be discounted, however, for it has several qualities worth examining. One of these is in the character of Paris. In the Elizabethan period the actor was looked upon as a vagabond and a rogue. The art of acting was admired, but to act for a living was disgraceful. Yet, actors were popular in Court circles, and it was a common practice to give parties in their honor. The actor had suffered the same in Roman times. Actors were branded *infami;* and if they were Roman citizens, they lost their civil rights. Like their Elizabethan counterparts, their entertainments were a favorite diversion for the Emperors. To Paris, the actor, falls the task of defending the theater of Rome, and by inference, the theater of Massinger's time.

Another positive element of The Roman Actor is its contribution to the development of a type of problem play from the earlier Kydian revenge tragedy. In The Roman Actor the play is set against a background of revenges to which the plot is eventually linked; thus, not pure intrigue but the collaboration of circumstance and character becomes the main force of the play. Life is viewed more as a balanced whole in which there is no dominance of evil or good within a person's character, and the revenge is noted for both the justice it metes out and the harm and cruelty it creates in both a social and personal sense. This characteristic is somewhat evident even in Domitian.

Massinger in *The Roman Actor* uses several devices popular in the dramatic writing of the period. One was the concept of metaphorically viewing the world as a stage—a concept that goes back as far as Democritus, in whose *Fragment* it is written, "The world's a stage, life a play./You come, you look, you go away." The metaphor was made most famous earlier in Massinger's own dramatic period by Jacques's lines in William Shakespeare's play, *As You Like It*—"All the world's a stage,/And all the men and women merely players." In Act I when Aretinus tells Paris that he speaks too boldly and wonders if he thinks he is on stage, Paris responds, "The whole world being one [a stage]/This place is not exempted. . . ." Technically, Massinger represents the whole world in *The Roman Actor* with the Roman Empire, the world outside the Roman Empire evidenced by the wars from which Domitian returns, and the spirit world suggested by the character of the Soothsayer and the apparance of the apparition in Act V.

Another device popular among Elizabethan dramatists that appears in *The Roman Actor* is the use of the play-within-a-play. Here we have not one but three, each masterfully introduced and having a specific thematic or dramatic meaning. The final play which Domitian orders, *The False Servant,* contributes to a startling close—a technique Massinger developed to a fine art.

In the dedicatory message of the 1629 quarto, Massinger called *The Roman Actor* "the most perfect birth of my Minerva." Among other things, Massinger's defense of theater through the character of Paris, his contribution to the development of a new dramatic offshoot of the Kydian tragedy of revenge, his adept use of popular dramatic devices, and the *coup de théâtre* of the play-within-a-play would seem to make *The Roman Actor* perfect. It is, however, the slow development of the first three acts that places the blemish on that perfection.

THE ROMANCE OF A SCHOOLMASTER

Type of work: Novel
Author: Edmondo de Amicis (1846-1908)
Type of plot: Social criticism
Time of plot: Nineteenth century
Locale: Italy
First published: 1876

There is little romance in The Romance of a Schoolmaster. *The novel portrays an elementary schoolteacher in the Italian provinces during the second half of the nineteenth century. Emilio must contend with low pay, pettifogging enemies, low social status, and a weak cultural background. Amicis postulates socialism as a solution to these evils, but it is his careful, detailed rendering of the physical world and moral landscape of his times that makes the novel memorable.*

Edmondo de Amicis was known primarily as a prose stylist; he was famous for his books of travel and for his ability to picture a landscape with words. Despite his great popularity at the end of the nineteenth century, however, his reputation has now all but disappeared. His later works were written under the influence of Zola; his powers of observation were particularly suited to the naturalistic style. The plots of his novels were loosely constructed, and *The Romance of a Schoolmaster* is no exception; its plot is little more than a slender thread connecting a number of scenes in the schoolmaster's life. The book is written in a somber style, unlike the buoyant mood of his early works. Amicis did not investigate the historic causes of the conditions he exposed; he simply showed what they were, attempting to paint the situation so as to call public attention to the evils that he felt must be changed.

The class structure in the schoolmaster's town is mercilessly shown, as is the lack of concern among the population for genuine education or culture. Individuals who cling precariously to bits of social status are shown to be the cruelest to those below them on the social scale. Nearly everyone, it seems, can manage to feel superior to the poor schoolmaster. The title is more ironic than not; neither the style of the work nor the story of Ratti's existence suggests anything noble or romantic about his life.

The inner motives of Amicis' characters are sometimes obscure; he possesses more interest in accurately portraying the milieu than in analyzing *why* people act as they do. There is a minimum of dramatic power in the novel; the scenes are artfully multiplied until the reader is almost overwhelmed by the depressing picture of the pitiful schoolmaster's existence. The descriptions of lower class life and the social conditions are written with earnestness and conviction. The novel has definite historical interest and its author will continue to hold a minor place in European literature.

THE ROMANCE OF LEONARDO DA VINCI

Type of work: Novel
Author: Dmitri Merejkowski (1865-1941)
Type of plot: Historical romance
Time of plot: 1494-1519
Locale: Italy and France
First presented: 1902

The royal courts, the Vatican, the quiet countryside, the studios of artists, an alchemist's workshop, and many other scenes serve as a backdrop for the story of the later years of the famed painter and thinker, Leonardo da Vinci. More than a fictionalized biography, it is also the history of a culture, for Merejkowski has depicted the religious and political struggles of the age as well as its adventure, romance, and bravado.

Any lesser figure than Leonardo would have been swallowed up in the mass of historical detail with which Merejkowski fills his fictionalized biography of the great Florentine artist. Certainly, the detail amassed, the scholarship and authenticity of scene, is impressive. But the reader never feels that he knows Leonardo as an individual. Perhaps this is not the fault of the novelist, for Leonardo was one of the most secretive of men. He had few close friends, was essentially a thoughtful, lonely individual, and trusted almost nobody. Yet, the greatness of the artist and thinker does emerge from these pages, even if the man stands somewhat aloof.

The other characters in the novel, whether famous (such as Cesare Borgia) or not so famous, emerge much more fully. Merejkowski's interpretation of the famous Monna Lisa Gioconda may or may not be historically accurate, but she does emerge as a fascinating individual. Monna Cassandra, the sorceress, is perhaps the best realized character; but more important are the figures who wield power. Power and its uses is a theme which runs through the novel. Leonardo, as an artist, was forced to bow before the possessors of power, whether he liked it or not. He knew that these men were inferior to himself, yet had to court their favor.

It was a turbulent time and Merejkowski has captured the excitement that filled the air. He meticulously dramatizes the intrigue and jealousies and the violence of the period, but he also presents the excitement of the intellectual reawakening of the society. The book is long and the style is somewhat ponderous, but the men and women rise above these shortcomings.

THE ROMANCE OF THE FOREST

Type of work: Novel
Author: Mrs. Ann Radcliffe (1764-1823)
Type of plot: Gothic romance
Time of plot: Seventeenth century
Locale: France and Savoy
First published: 1791

The Romance of the Forest is one of the classic gothic novels, adhering in every particular to the formula, largely developed by Mrs. Radcliffe, which has endured in popular fiction to the present. Adeline is the typical threatened heroine, the Marquis de Montalt the usual aristocratic villain, Theodore Peyrou, the stalwart hero, and Pierre de la Motte the brooding, ambiguous father figure.

The historical importance of this novel cannot be exaggerated. Together with Walpole's *The Castle of Otranto,* Ann Radcliffe's novel established the legitimacy of the Gothic romance, that strange amalgam of French chivalry and Demonic terror that dominated popular fiction well into the middle of the nineteenth century. The earlier French romances of the seventeenth and eighteenth centuries stressed manners and tender passions. The Gothic romance grafted these themes to the new interest in medieval terrors and the supernatural. From Scott to Balzac, the "Gothic" maintained its hold on writers who wanted to appeal to popular taste. Even in America writers such as Poe and Hawthorne took its qualities into account.

The Romance of the Forest not only influenced the fiction that was to follow, but also made a profound impression on the lyrical and "nature" poets of the Romantic movement—not to mention Romantic rebels such as Byron. The remorse ridden Pierre de la Motte anticipates Byron's heroes *Manfred* and *Cain* (as well as Charlotte Brontë's Rochester and Emily Brontë's Heathcliffe).

Perhaps the single most impressive legacy of this rather pedestrian entertainment, however, is its descriptive passages, its way of creating atmosphere and tone in long and detailed accounts of the setting, the immediate backdrop to the "mysterious" actions. The description of the abbey ruins near the forest of Fontanville not only establishes the proper awe and sublimity required by the story, it also demonstrates the evocative power of Nature itself—a lesson not forgotten by the young Coleridge and Wordsworth, who saw in this kind of descriptive writing the crude archetype of their own meditative poetry. *The Romance of the Forest* can be ridiculed for its contrived plotting and for the easy way it settles for rational solutions to the mysterious problems it poses. But finally it is one of those strange works in the history of literature that performs transitional and suggestive functions of a significance far beyond its intrinsic value.

ROMANCE OF THE THREE KINGDOMS

Type of work: Novel
Author: Lo Kuan-chung (c. 1320-c. 1380)
Type of plot: Historical romance
Time of plot: Third century
Locale: China
First transcribed: Fourteenth century

Using official history as well as oral traditions in composing this great dynastic romance, Lo Kuan-chung permanently fixed the popular image of the period of the Three Kingdoms, beginning with the rise of the Yellow Turban rebels under the last emperors of the Eastern Han dynasty and ending with the unification of China under the first Chin emperor. Romance of the Three Kingdoms *has been the most popular book in China for centuries.*

Romance of the Three Kingdoms is an imaginative reconstruction of a familiar past enriched by folk tradition. It has the grand design of an epic. The compact structure is well matched with the author's pioneering experiment in a colloquial style, plain diction, simple syntax, and rapid narrative. The story begins at a crisis in history. It is a lively representation of an era full of conflicts, culminating in the Battle of Red Cliff. It was by the victory of this battle that Chu-ko Liang, the central figure of the action, established the miraculous power balance of the three kingdoms.

He is at once a diplomat, a statesman, and a strategist. The fascinating portrait of such a versatile character is further touched with the mystery of his innate modesty. He is also known as a prophet and a priest who can work miracles precisely because his personality is so simple and serene. He lived the life of a poet-recluse when Liu Pei visited him three times at his idyllic hut. He became Liu Pei's prime minister and soon defeated Ts'ao Ts'ao at Red Cliff with the alliance of Sun Ch'üan, thus founding the Kingdom of Shu Han. To the other characters of the novel such achievements would seem impossible. The motivation behind his action has also attained a purity of epic height. Unlike almost all the active characters in the novel, he is free from the desire for fame, wealth, or power, and is thus free to devote his whole self to Liu Pei and his cause.

Ts'ao Ts'ao is always the caricature of a hypocrite in Chinese folk tradition. In the novel, however, he is also a sensitive poet as well as an unpredictable ruler. His ambition and extravagance have made him more or less a clown on the capricious wheel of fortune. Kuan Yü is a tragic hero whose courage and prowess are well-matched by his long streak of good luck. When his physical strength decreases with age, he acts with increasing arrogance to sustain his self-image. Ts'ao Ts'ao is a romantic admirer of his great heart and his unshakable loyalty to Liu Pei, while Chu-ko Liang has to evaluate his ability realistically. Both of them often humor him like a child. His downfall has proved to be a fatal blow to the Shu Han Kingdom, in whose cause Chu-ko Liang died a martyr. It takes such an active and perfect character as Chu-ko Liang to realize fully the folk saying that man proposes and God disposes. Still, his human endeavor itself has become an immortal part of destiny.

THE ROMANTIC COMEDIANS

Type of work: Novel
Author: Ellen Glasgow (1874-1945)
Type of plot: Humorous satire
Time of plot: 1920's
Locale: Richmond, Virginia
First published: 1926

The Romantic Comedians *presents the age-old problem of an old man who marries a young girl. More particularly, Glasgow symbolizes in her two main characters the struggle between two diverse eras in American culture. Judge Gamaliel Bland Honeywell stands for the faded Victorianism of the American South in the last third of the nineteenth century, while Annabel represents the first Southern generation after World War I.*

Ellen Glasgow has been largely overlooked by students of American literature. Her output was prodigious, and her penetrating analysis of the social history of Virginia from 1850 to 1930, her insight into the position of women, her brilliant use of ironic characterization are qualities that set her apart from the mass of popular novelists of the first third of the century and necessitate a reevaluation of her work.

It was Glasgow's colleague, James Branch Cabell, who first called her a social historian; reviewing *Barren Ground,* he said that her books, taken collectively, were a "portrayal of all social and economic Virginia since the War Between the States." Other critics and Glasgow herself accepted the label; despite its accuracy, the phrase "social historian" is too narrow for the wide range of Glasgow's talents and has been partially responsible for the present neglect of her work. She has also suffered from commentary by antagonistic male critics. Never one to accept a "woman's role," Glasgow often attacked those whose writing or person she did not admire. This penchant, as well as her creation of less-than-admirable male characters, has led to some highly questionable commentary about both her life and work. As late as 1971, one critic commented on her "anti-maleness," and then went on to contradict himself: "She continued to pursue the male of her own species with glee." Such unmeasured statements have not helped Glasgow's literary reputation.

Properly, Glasgow should be seen as an early member of the Southern Literary Renaissance. In 1931 she helped to organize a conference of Southern writers at the University of Virginia, attended by William Faulkner, Sherwood Anderson, and Allen Tate, among others. She was always interested in her native Virginia and wrote perceptively about various epochs and social classes. If her view is often an ironic one, it nevertheless helps the reader to see the love-hate relationship that she had with the South. She judges, but with a sympathetic voice.

The Romantic Comedians comes just after the more famous *Barren Ground* and is, like Glasgow's succeeding work (*They Stooped to Folly*), a novel of manners. Like all such works, *The Romantic Comedians* depends for much of its impact on tone and point of view, for neither plot nor characters are unique. The novel relies on the reader's knowledge of similar situations and characters in making its ironic commentary. From the outset, the narrator directs the reader's attitudes. Characters' names satirically reveal inner traits: "Bland Honeywell," "Upchurch," "Bredalbane," "Lightfoot." We see the Judge as a slightly ridiculous figure, interested in the outward demonstration of his grief and unable to understand correctly his own emotions: " 'I am a bird with a broken wing,' he sighed to himself. . . ." This romantic outward show of grief over his dead wife lacked sincerity, for simultaneously, he ". . . felt an odd palpitation . . . where his broken wing was helplessly trying to flutter." The narrator's voice is unmistakable, and Glasgow shows herself to be in the great tradition of Jane Austen and George Eliot, two other ironic critics of society.

Judge Honeywell is portrayed as a man of a bygone era, unable to understand or adjust to new ideas, yet somewhat naïvely excited by the prospect of Annabel's youth and beauty. He has firm beliefs which nevertheless do not alter his self-interested actions. His most endearing characteristic is his willingness to forgive Annabel, but this too he carries to excess, needlessly accepting the guilt for her unhappiness.

But not only Judge Honeywell is satirized; all of the characters are shown to be romantic or a bit ridiculous. Annabel is deluded by imagining that ultimate personal happiness is attainable and of primary importance. Her amoral attitude does, however, cut through the hypocrisy and moral sham of people like her mother and Amanda Lightfoot. Annabel asserts that perfect ladies "lie as perfectly as they behave." Edmonia Bredalbane carries her "scandalous" behavior to an extreme which, even in its refreshing lack of convention, is shown to be silly. Glasgow reverses the generally accepted roles in the relationship of the Judge and his twin sister; here the woman is emancipated and the man tied by convention.

The theme of the novel is voiced by Mrs. Upchurch who muses on "the popular supersitition that love and happiness are interchangeable terms." She notes that both old and young, old-fashioned and modern, are "enslaved" by this illusion. The Judge, Amanda, Annabel, Dabney—"all this company of happiness-hunters appeared to be little better than a troupe of romantic comedians." This attitude seems to be the view of the narrator as well, but Mrs. Upchurch is not always the narrator's mouthpiece. In fact, Mrs. Upchurch's pragmatic morality, which shifts radically depending on the situation, is as often laughed at as the Judge's unyielding system. But Mrs. Upchurch has a more realistic view of life than any other character.

Glasgow displays skill not only in the consistency of her tone but also in her use of images to suggest character. The Judge always thinks of Annabel in terms of nature—"fields and streams," "tall wind-blown grasses," the "April mist" in her eyes. But these very qualities in Annabel—her "natural" freedom and amorality—doom their marriage; wild nature cannot become domestic and maternal. As their relationship deteriorates, he begins to think of her in terms of images of light without heat: she lacks the warmth he craves. She is like "the fire at the heart of an opal"; her head is like "November leaves in the sunlight"; after she runs off with Dabney she looks alive "not as a flower, but as a jewel."

Although the point of view is most often centered in Judge Honeywell's consciousness, the narrator sometimes inserts commentary to make her attitude more obvious. Usually this is unobtrusive but occasionally it becomes an affectation of style or a violation of the convention already established. An example would be the phrase, "like most lawyers and all vestrymen" in beginning a comment on the Judge. In general, though, Glasgow's ironic tone is consistent, pungent, and entertaining. The female characters—including the dead Cordelia—each represent a distinctive way of dealing with the role assigned to women in the South of the 1920's. These aspects make Glasgow more than a social historian and suggest a higher place for her in the hierarchy of American letters.

Margaret McFadden-Gerber

THE ROMANTIC LADIES

Type of work: **Drama**
Author: Molière (Jean Baptiste Poquelin, 1622-1673)
Type of plot: Comedy of manners
Time of plot: Seventeenth century
Locale: Paris
First presented: 1659

The Romantic Ladies *is an example of the literary work which, although initially directed at a particular topical issue, becomes a permanent relevant work of art because of the universality inherent in its theme and presentation. Intended to mock a Parisian social faction that engaged in an artificial, ultra-sentimental verbal style,* The Romantic Ladies *is a biting satire on all social and cultural pretensions and affectations.*

The Romantic Ladies was first performed only one year after the author's permanent establishment in Paris; it was an enormous success and secured his reputation as the capital's foremost dramatist. *The Romantic Ladies* is significant as a curious blend of the particular and the universal: the play not only ridicules a specific group in the Parisian society of Molière's day, but also satirizes human foibles which are common to every time and place.

In the second quarter of the seventeenth century, there grew up in Paris, in reaction to the prevalent coarseness of manners in French society, a group known as the *précieux*. This group centered around the literary salon of Mme. de Rambouillet, and was devoted to the cultivation of dignified speech and manners and the study, discussion, and patronage of literature. What began as a sort of cultural club under the guidance of Mme. de Rambouillet, however, evolved into a fad distinguished only by its absurdity in the hands of her successors. These later *précieux,* who met to gossip and act out scenes from popular romantic novels, spoke in a highly affected style which became for a time the rage in salons all over Paris. It was the craze led by this later circle that Molière lampooned in *Les Precieuses ridicules* (frequently translated as *Two Precious Damsels Ridiculed*). Mme. de Rambouillet herself, realizing that Molière's barbs were not aimed at her but at her successors, was one of the play's ardent admirers, and invited Molière to stage three performances at her home.

Given the specificity of the target of the play's ridicule, it is easy to imagine its success with Molière's contemporaries. They understood all the references and recognized the follies of the characters from their firsthand observations. They laughed at Cathos' and Magdelon's assumption of romantic pseudonyms ("The names Polyxene and Aminte are far more graceful, you must agree") and their avowal to live their lives as romantic heroines; they sympathized with down-to-earth Gorgibus and his bewilderment in the face of his daughter's and niece's "gibberish" ("No doubt about it; they're over

the edge"). It is important to examine the reason that audiences have continued to laugh over this play for more than three centuries. The answer lies
in the universality of Molière's comedy. The impulse toward preciosity is
not exclusively a seventeenth century French phenomenon, but rather a constitutional weakness common to all people. Every time and place has its
précieux because the desire for distinctiveness and novelty of expression seems
to be part of human nature. Thus it is that we laugh at Cathos and Magdelon,
at Mascarille and Jodelet, even as we recognize that some of their folly and
affectation is within us all.

Molière found the perfect vehicle for making audiences laugh at human
folly in plays such as *The Romantic Ladies.* In the development of this
highly successful style, he drew heavily upon two sources: traditional French
farce and Italian *commedia dell'arte*; using and creatively transforming features from each, he molded the unique brand of dramatic comedy for which
he is famous. The use of masks, for example, dating back to ancient times,
had been revived in the Italian drama and was in turn adopted by the French
neoclassicists. These masks were used to characterize various types, including
scheming valets, jealous husbands, unscrupulous liars, misers, prudes, braggarts, coquettes, libertines, and pedants; figures such as Harlequin, Pantaloon,
and Scaramouch are still familiar. Molière developed his own character types,
based on old stock figures, which came to be his trademark; the two most
famous were Sganarelle and Mascarille. He became a master of the device
of the mask, and the art of reliance upon gesture and posture rather than
facial expression to convey meaning reached its highest point in his plays.
After expanding, modifying, and exploring all the theatrical possibilities of
masks, however, Molière went on to do what the *commedia dell'arte* never
attempted: he depicted through his characters all the social relationships and
class conditions within French society, exposing the vices of high and low
alike with his wit.

In an early play such as *The Romantic Ladies,* however, the masks are
still of standard farcical types. In the play's original performances, Molière
himself played Mascarille, wearing a mask, while Jodelet, a widely popular
slapstick comedian, performed under his own name, wearing the white
powder mask for which he was famous. The figures of Mascarille and Jodelet
—valets who have a talent for parading about passing for what they are not
(in this case, noblemen)—represent the folly of affectation and falseness.
They are the agents through which Molière ridicules the representatives of
the *précieux,* Cathos and Magdelon; they are brought to humiliation through
their gullible acceptance of the valets' deception. The message in *The Romantic Ladies* is basically the same as in all of Molière's plays: excess,
whether of vice or virtue, leads to a downfall. Molière was a constant and
thorough observer of life, and his observations all led him to the conclusion
that whenever a person becomes dominated by a single passion, idea, or

obsession, his common sense will be overridden and ill consequences will follow. Thus, the two young ladies in this play have been carried away beyond all the bounds of reason by their passion for romances, and they are easily duped by their prospective husbands' scheme.

The plot in *The Romantic Ladies,* as in all of Molière's comedies, is minimal; it is merely a vehicle to allow characters their full comic play, which is Molière's primary purpose. Molière was a master of all the verbal laugh-getting devices, including double entendre, echo-dialogues, and malapropisms, but above all he was the supreme farceur; some fine examples of traditional, rollicking French farce in this play include Mascarille's entrance with the sedan-chair bearers; the drubbing of the valets by La Grange and Du Croisy; and Jodelet's stripping of his countless layers of garments. For this reason, a play such as *The Romantic Ladies* must be seen performed for full effect; to appreciate it fully merely by reading it would be impossible. Molière's greatness lies in his ability to fuse astute criticism of the follies and absurdities of human behavior with unsurpassed comedy. Ironically, perhaps his greatest and most lasting tribute came from one of his contemporaries who, in a malicious attempt to slander him, called Molière "the first jester of France."

Nancy G. Ballard

THE ROMANY RYE

Type of work: Novel
Author: George Henry Borrow (1803-1881)
Type of plot: Simulated autobiography
Time of plot: Nineteenth century
Locale: England
First published: 1857

In The Romany Rye. *George Borrow continues the quasi-autobiographical adventures of the scholar-gipsy he introduced in* Lavengro. *The novel follows the usual picaresque pattern, as Lavengro wanders about encountering a series of curious characters and odd situations. Although unevenly written,* The Romany Rye *offers a vivid, detailed view of lower-class life and marginal society in nineteenth century England.*

George Borrow's *The Romany Rye* is the sequel to *Lavengro.* In both books the narrator, a man of wide-ranging interests whose adventures are based on those of the author himself, is the same eccentric intellectual who must become a tinker to make a living. Lavengro's poverty, however, gives him access to an area of nineteenth century existence which generally remained a mystery to English readers. His life among the gipsies, particularly, held a deep fascination for the middle class: dark, perhaps with an unrecognized sexual attraction, their lives which were migratory had no seeming pattern. The gipsies, moreover, were purported to have special powers which drew Lavengro to them, seeking their knowledge and experience.

The popularity of *Lavengro* and the *Romany Rye* was also a part of a new interest in the underside of life. Like Dickens' novels and the perceptive sociological observations of Henry Mayhew's *London Labour and the London Poor* (1851-1864), Borrow's two books, even though in fictive disguise, informed their Victorian audience of life on the road with such eccentric character studies as those of Belle and the Petulengros. Borrow's subject matter also included events from everyday life in rural England. Lavengro's adventure at the fair, the bartering for the horse, and the attendant atmosphere broadened the experience of the average urban reader.

To add further interest, together with Lavengro's conversations about religion and language, Borrow wove into his narration the story of his hero's love for Belle, and his loss of her when she migrates to America. As in Matthew Arnold's great poem, "The Scholar Gypsy," published a few years before *The Romany Rye,* therefore, we are left with a solitary traveler, a man of learning who for his own reasons remains alone, outside respectable society, seeking his own personal truth, although too old now to make the journey to India.

As a work of literature, both *Lavengro* and *The Romany Rye* suffer from several artistic weaknesses. One reviewer's description of the novel as "a collection of bold picaresque sketches" points the way to the basic structural flaw in the work: the plot is not sufficient to give the characters space to develop, while at the same time the characterizations are not strong enough to compensate for the inadequate storyline. Even viewed separately as vignettes, the various scenes display a wide variance in quality; those in which the author digresses into philological discussions, for example, or indulges in tirades against Catholicism, are invariably unsuccessful, while scenes such as those depicting the fight with the Flaming Tinman or presenting the old apple-woman of London Bridge are excellent and enjoyable sketches. Borrow's style is likewise uneven, and ranges from writing that is tiresome, verbose, and clichéd, to passages vigorous and colorful enough to hold their own among the finest specimens of nineteenth century prose.

ROME HAUL

Type of work: Novel
Author: Walter D. Edmonds (1903-   )
Type of plot: Regional romance
Time of plot: 1850
Locale: Erie Canal
First published: 1929

Rome Haul is a vivid, accurate view of life on the Erie Canal during that brief period in America when transport by canal flourished as the dominant mode of long-range hauling. There is poignancy and passion in the lives of people like Dan and Molly, Mrs. Gurget and Sol, and even Gentleman Joe Calash, who lived on the canal before the railroads destroyed its free, picturesque life.

Although Walter Edmonds had published several short stories, *Rome Haul* was his first novel, and it was quite successful with readers and critics. In an opening note Edmonds describes the fun he had in writing it and how easily the writing progressed; however, he does not discuss the great amount of research he had done in preparation for this book.

Edmonds was already somewhat familiar with canal life, for he had lived in a small town on the Black Canal, and canal life had always fascinated him. When he left the area to go to Harvard, his memories of the canal remained with him. To authenticate his account of the Erie Canal, he scrupulously studied records, listened to canal legends, and talked to the boatmen. This careful and thorough research is reflected in the realistic and minute detail of scene and action in *Rome Haul*. This is one of the strongest points of his writing, but he is also skilled in creating natural, vigorous dialogue which adds to the reality of the canal atmosphere.

Although Edmonds says that, in writing the book, he lost his earlier interest in quaintness of the characters and began to see them as real people, a Dickensian touch remains—Dan Harrow is a farmer, Fortune Friendly is a would-be minister, and the enormously fat Mrs. Gurget, with her extreme fondness for rum noggins, immediately reminds one of the unforgettable Sairey Gamp of *Martin Chuzzlewit*. Edmonds, however, does not rely as heavily on caricature as does Dickens.

The plot is the major weakness of the novel, for it is quite loose in spots, and as a narrative the structure is weak, a fault Edmonds corrects in his most famous novel, *Drums Along the Mohawk*. However, any lack of literary distinction in *Rome Haul* is amply compensated by the sense of lusty life within it.

ROMEO AND JULIET

Type of work: Drama
Author: William Shakespeare (1564-1616)
Type of plot: Romantic tragedy
Time of plot: Fifteenth century
Locale: Verona, Italy
First presented: c. 1595

This famous story of star-crossed lovers, one of Shakespeare's most popular, is his great youthful tragedy. The play is passionate, witty, rapid, intensely lyrical, and romantically beautiful. Romeo and Juliet are personifications of young love; they are also the innocent victims of an angry, foolish society, embodied in the feuding families, and a malevolent providence that uses their deaths to force the feuding factions to reconciliation.

One of the most popular plays of all time, *Romeo and Juliet* was Shakespeare's second tragedy (after *Titus Andronicus* (1594), a failure), written during his first transitional period. Consequently, the play shows the sometimes artificial lyricism of early comedies such as *Love's Labour's Lost* (c. 1594) and *A Midsummer Night's Dream* (1595) while its character development predicts the direction of the playwright's artistic maturity. In his usual fashion, he bases his story on common sources: Masuccio Salernitano's *Novellino* (1476), William Painter's *The Palace of Pleasure* (1566-1567), and, especially, Arthur Brooke's poetic *The Tragical History of Romeus and Juliet* (1562). Shakespeare reduces the time of the action from the months it takes in Brooke to a few compact days.

In addition to following the conventional five-part structure of a tragedy, Shakespeare also employs his characteristic alternation, from scene to scene, between taking the action forward and retarding it, often with comic relief (as when the ribald musicians follow the "death" scene in Act 4, scene 5), to heighten the dramatic impact. Although in many respects the structure recalls that of the *de casibus* genre (dealing with the fall of powerful men), its true prototype is Boethian tragedy as employed by Chaucer in *Troilus and Criseyde*—a fall into unhappiness, on the part of more or less ordinary people, after a fleeting period of happiness. The fall is caused both traditionally and in the play by the workings of fortune. Insofar as *Romeo and Juliet* is a tragedy, it is a tragedy of fate rather than of tragic flaw. Although the two lovers have weaknesses, it is not their faults, but their unlucky stars, that destroy them. As the friar comments at the end, "A greater power than we can contradict / Hath thwarted our intents."

Shakespeare succeeds in having the thematic structure closely parallel the dramatic form of the play. The principal theme is that of the tension between the two houses, and all the other oppositions of the play derive from that central one. Thus, romance is set against revenge, love against hate, day against night, sex against war, youth against age, and "tears to fire." Juliet's soliloquy in Act 3, scene 2 makes it clear that it is the strife between her family and Romeo's that has turned Romeo's love to death. If, at times, Shakespeare seems to forget the family theme in his lyrical fascination with the lovers, that fact only sets off their suffering all the more poignantly against the background of the senseless and arbitrary strife between the Capulets and Montagues. For the families, after all, the story has a classically comic ending; their feud is buried with the lovers—which seems to be the intention of the indefinite fate that compels the action.

The lovers, of course, never forget their families; their consciousness of the conflict leads to another central theme in the play, that of identity. Romeo questions his identity to Benvolio early in the play, and Juliet asks him, "Wherefore art thou Romeo?" At her request he offers to change his name and to be defined only as one star-crossed with her. Juliet, too, questions her identity, when she speaks to the nurse after Romeo's slaying of Tybalt. Romeo later asks the friar to help him locate the lodging of his name so that he may cast it from his "hateful mansion," bringing a plague upon his own house in an ironic fulfillment of Mercutio's dying curse. Only when they are in their graves, together, do the two lovers find peace from the persecution of being Capulet and Montague; they are remembered by their first names only, an ironic proof that their story had the beneficial political influence the Prince wishes at the end.

Likewise, the style of the play alternates between poetic gymnastics and pure and simple lines of deep emotion. The unrhymed iambic pentameter is filled with conceits, puns, and wordplays, presenting both lovers as very literate youngsters. Their verbal wit, in fact, is not Shakespeare's rhetorical excess but part of their characters. It fortifies the impression we have of their spiritual natures, showing their love as an intellectual appreciation of beauty combined with a pure physical passion. Their first dialogue, for example, is a sonnet divided between them. In no other early play is the imagery as lush and complex, making unforgettable the balcony speech in which Romeo describes Juliet as the sun, Juliet's nightingale-lark speech, her comparison of Romeo to the "day in night," which Romeo then develops as he observes, at dawn, "more light and light, more dark and dark our woes."

At the beginning of the play Benvolio describes Romeo as a "love-struck swain" in the typical pastoral fashion. He is, as the cliché has it, in love with love (Rosaline's name is not even mentioned until much later). He is sheer energy seeking an outlet; sensitive appreciation seeking a beautiful object. Both Mercutio and the friar comment on his fickleness. But the sight of Juliet immediately transforms Romeo's immature and purely erotic infatuation to true and constant love. He matures more quickly than anyone around him realizes; only the audience understands the process, since Shakespeare makes Romeo as introspective and verbal as Hamlet in his monologues. Even in love, however, Romeo does not reject his former romantic ideals. When Juliet comments, "You kiss by th' book," she is being astutely perceptive; Romeo's death is the death of an idealist, though not of a foolhardy youth. He knows what he is doing, his awareness growing from his comment after slaying Tybalt, "O, I am Fortune's fool."

Juliet is equally quick-witted, and also has early premonitions of their sudden love's end. She is made uniquely charming by her combination of girlish innocence with a winsome foresight that is "wise" when compared to the superficial feelings expressed by her father, mother, and Count Paris. Juliet, moreover, is realistic as well as romantic. She knows how to exploit her womanly softness, making the audience feel both poignancy and irony when the friar remarks, at her arrival in the wedding chapel, "O, so light a foot / Will ne'er wear out the everlasting flint!" It takes a strong person to carry out the friar's stratagem, after all; Juliet succeeds in the ruse partly because everyone else considers her weak both in body and will. She is a subtle actress, telling us after dismissing her mother and the nurse, "My dismal scene I needs must act alone." Her quiet intelligence makes our tragic pity all the stronger when her "scene" becomes reality.

Shakspeare provides his lovers with effective dramatic foils in the characters of Mercutio, the nurse, and the friar. But the play remains forever that of "Juliet and her Romeo."

Kenneth John Atchity

ROMOLA

Type of work: Novel
Author: George Eliot (Mary Ann Evans, 1819-1880)
Type of plot: Historical romance
Time of plot: 1492-1498
Locale: Italy
First published: 1863

Romola. *George Eliot's foray into historical fiction, is the story of a thoroughly good woman, Romola, and a thoroughly wicked man, Tito Melema. Both are fascinating, complex figures, and their delineation compensates for the complicated, somewhat unwieldy plotting that results from Eliot's extreme attention to historical and atmospheric detail.*

Following the trend for historical novels, George Eliot decided that the Florence of Savonarola would make a good setting for a novel. She studied details of Florentine history, setting, and costume at the British Museum and during a trip to Italy in 1861. But, although the research was meticulous, it is as a vivid study of personalities that *Romola* now interests readers, rather than as a documentation of a period in history. The picture of Tito's egoism is presented with chilling accuracy. Perhaps the book lacks the spontaneity of Eliot's English stories, but it remains a fascinating study of selfishness and the lengths to which rationalization can stretch.

Tito Melema arrives in Florence on the day that Lorenzo the Magnificent died, in 1492. The reader is aware of the historical importance surrounding the date, but Tito is concerned only with himself. Unscrupulously, he uses his beauty and intelligence, and the gems entrusted to him by his guardian, to make his way in Florentine society. Skillfully, George Eliot analyzes his thoughts, as he persuades himself that his actions are justified. He commits one crime after another, against good people, against justice, against basic morality; but always he clears himself in his own mind. Once his thoughts are bent in a particular direction, he proceeds heedlessly, regardless of whom he destroys. In a sense, he forms a parallel with Savonarola, a man whose mind warped to believe that he is acting out the will of God. Seldom have psychological and moral analyses been so devastatingly combined.

Another theme running through the novel is that of female intellectual powers. This was a prominent theme in many of Eliot's books, together with a distrust of physical beauty. Tessa represents animal nature, while Romola stands for spiritual and mental aspirations; Tito finds that he must choose between the two. Although he is physically attracted to Tessa, his ambition leads him to Romola. The world, it appears, belongs to youth and strength, to the beautiful and ambitious. But George Eliot's rigorous morality and intellectual toughness penetrate beneath the façades which most of the characters, and particularly Tito, use to further their interests. All, good and despicable, are stripped of pretensions. Perhaps goodness and intelligence do not always triumph over superficial beauty and unscrupulousness, but, George Eliot implies, this is no reason for men to accept that fact. At the very least, humanity should aspire to something better.

A ROOM WITH A VIEW

Type of work: Novel
Author: E. M. Forster (1879-1970)
Type of plot: Social comedy
Time of plot: Early 1900's
Locale: Florence, Italy, and Surrey, England
First published: 1908

A Room with a View, *like all of Forster's early fiction, takes a satirical view of "the underdeveloped heart." Set in Italy, a locale that Forster uses to suggest another, more emotive style of life, the novel tells the story of Lucy Honeychurch's growth as a feeling human being, largely because of her involvement with the emotional, volatile George Emerson.*

Forster's novel is a play of opposites which struggles toward a practical synthesis, fit for his ordinary human characters. On the one hand, the medieval or the ascetic, which is imaged as a "room" without a "view," and connected to Cecil Vyse and the English in general, is opposed on the other by the Greek world, one of passion and fruition, or a "view" without a "room," related to the Emersons. Each perspective, when taken separately, seems a whole knowledge; when they are seen in conjunction, they appear as half-knowledges; but when they are synthesized, as they are in the marriage of Lucy Honeychurch and George Emerson, they form a truth, a truth tempered to man's capabilities.

It is clear that Forster himself leans toward the passionate exuberance of the Greek world and its Dionysiac element; he realizes, however, that man cannot tolerate that intensity for long. Therefore he values the medieval, but only insofar as it teaches the necessity of boundaries.

The plot of *A Room with a View* is designed to educate Lucy and George to the wisdom of a balance between the two extremes. At the beginning Lucy is restrained, locked in her own "room" without a sense of possibility, while George is a passionate romantic, possessed of an expansive "view," but without discipline, a "room." In the last chapter we find Lucy and George spending their honeymoon in Florence, secure in their room overlooking the vibrant street scene. Having left the restraints of England yet refusing to continue on to Greece with the Alans, they have achieved a harmony in Italy. Lucy has given George the necessary sense of limit, while he has awakened her to the possibilities of emotion. It is a comic scene, celebrating the ordinary suffused with passion.

RORY O'MORE

Type of work: Novel
Author: Samuel Lover (1797-1868)
Type of plot: Adventure romance
Time of plot: 1798
Locale: Southern Ireland
First published: 1837

Although flawed as a historical novel, Rory O'More *lives in its atmosphere of the stirring days of the rebellion of 1798; in its ferocious lampoons of soldiers, magistrates, and collectors; in the terrible and tragic realities of Irish peasant life; and in the pleasant idyl of its love story.*

In this novel, Samuel Lover combines the Irish raciness of Maria Edgeworth with the historical sense of Sir Walter Scott. The result is a sprightly romp through a period in Irish history when its destiny was briefly involved with that of Napoleon. Had Bonaparte activated his plan to attack England by supporting Irish independence, the history of Britain might have been significantly altered; the Irish question, after all, has haunted British politics to the present day.

The historical theme is treated seriously by Lover, and it provides the basis for the plot, but what is chiefly memorable about his work is the humorous speech and dialogue of his characters. Their words are energetic, colorful and always earthy. Even Rory, the hero of the novel, has a touch of the poet and orator in him: "In throth the counthry would be 'quite' enough if they'd let us be 'quite;' but it's gallin' and aggravatin' us they are at every hand's turn, and puttin' the martial law on us, and callin' us bad names, and abusin' our blessed religion."

Rory is a not-so-distant cousin of Handy Andy, Lover's most famous and beloved creation, a hero with a great talent for doing the wrong thing and a genius for escaping the consequences of his own blunders. Rory is shrewder than Handy Andy, but he has the same impish quality. Lover was primarily a humorist and entertainer, but he managed in *Rory O'More* to be true to his comic genius without vulgarizing his political principles. The novel combines comedy and politics into very fierce satire. The "Collector" for example, is ridiculed for advancing from beggar to tax collector simply by pleasing the local parson. The whole Protestant establishment is satirized in this acid sketch, but Rory tells it all with understatement and ingenuous friendliness: "Oh . . . the parson . . . he's a decent man enough."

ROSMERSHOLM

Type of work: Drama
Author: Henrik Ibsen (1828-1906)
Type of plot: Social drama
Time of plot: Middle nineteenth century
Locale: Small coastal town in western Norway
First presented: 1887

Rosmersholm *was written between Ibsen's social plays and the psychological, symbolic works of his last phase. While the play's context is social, the real action occurs within* Johannes Rosmer and his female friend, Rebecca West. *As they gradually come, through a series of searing personal revelations, to understand their real feelings toward each other and their real, if indirect, responsibility for the death of Rosmer's wife, they are finally driven to a double suicide.*

Rosmersholm is literally the home of Rosmer, but in keeping with the temper of the play, the title actually signifies a spiritual homecoming for Johannes Rosmer. His life, both personal and political, was stormy. Almost without realizing it, he found himself associated with unpopular political causes and movements by his friendship with Brendel and Mortensgard. In a similar vein, his relationship with Rebecca West, after Beata's suicide, further alienated him from the conventional mainstream. Former friends and colleagues—notably Rector Kroll—deserted him, foresook him, and betrayed him. His admission of religious lapse only exacerbated the situation. When all of his life seemed to tumble about him like a house of cards. Rosmer sought reassurance by asking Rebecca to make the ultimate sacrifice of her life. But at the decisive moment, Rosmer elected to join her in suicide. In so doing, Rosmer found his home—his spiritual home, Rosmersholm—which had formerly eluded him.

In reality, Rosmer only toyed with politics. He did not have the committed revolutionary's dedicated zeal; he was not willing or capable of the self-sacrifice involved in giving himself over to a cause. His loyalties were divided between public issues and personal gratification. In the end, he chose the latter, an important decision signifying a shift in Ibsen's focus and emphasis. Ibsen's earlier work had dealt with social issues of consequence to masses of people. *Rosmersholm* is a transitional piece which marks a change from social issues to personal and individual concerns which characterized Ibsen's later dramas.

Still, *Rosmersholm* is a politically charged play, for Rosmer's social ostracizing is more a consequence of his political philosophy than of his presumed unconventional life style. In fact, the latter is attributed to the former, and much of the action in the play revolves around political philosophy and meetings with notorious political figures, creating an onus from which even Rebecca is not exempt. The liberal-versus-conservative argument

is, of course, the fulcrum of the conflict, with the issue of the so-called emancipated woman—Rebecca—serving as a microcosm of the entire macrocosm of
the dispute. Rosmer's loyalties are thus ground between the Scylla of public
principle and the Charybdis of personal passion. Ibsen offers the only logical
possible solution to the dilemma: in effect, a mutual suicide pact. The inevitability of this conclusion is not clear from the start; it only emerges in
the unfolding of the play. As a consequence of such subtlety, the dramatic
dimensions of *Rosmersholm* are enhanced to tragic proportions, making the
play, despite its ambivalent stance, a genuine classic of its kind.

ROUGHING IT

Type of work: Record of travel
Author: Mark Twain (Samuel L. Clemens, 1835-1910)
Type of plot: Travel sketches and autobiography
Time of plot: Mid-nineteenth century
Locale: The West
First published: 1872

The organization of this American picaresque novel is episodic, even chaotic at times. However, Twain's rollicking humor, vivid descriptions of places like the silver mining camps and frontier Carson City, Nevada, and colorful encounters with impressive characters such as Slade the Terrible, an outlaw, and Brigham Young, the Mormon leader, make this long, personal narrative an entertaining book and a solid indication of the young Twain's blossoming talent.

The book begins with an engrossing account, lasting several chapters, of the stage coach trip west from St. Joseph, Missouri. The obvious authenticity of the adventure makes it fascinating even to a modern reader, and a hundred years ago readers must have found the richness of detail and description of even more interest. The account of the life and career of the desperado Slade reads like a tall tale, yet it is told in a most convincing manner, as are most of the stories that fill the long, but never dull book.

The Mormons gradually occupy, in the early chapters, an ever-larger place in the narrative. It is obvious that, for the author, they possessed a strange fascination. Brigham Young, the patriarch of the Mormon empire, emerges as a powerful, dynamic individual, a man of integrity and forceful personality, and a man who is able to strike the fear of God into his fellow Mormons. At the same time, the chapter dealing with the Mormon leader's problems with his many wives and children is highly amusing. Often Twain's humor is a kind of irony without comment, and all the more effective for the sly manner with which he slips it into the narrative. He uses this device frequently in the section dealing with the Mormons and Brigham Young.

The description of Nevada's capital, Carson City, places it as a rough-and-ready little community. The book is rich in detail; Twain never lost sight of the fact that his descriptions would be new and even startling to his readers. Where a less skillful writer might have merely sketched in a scene, Twain draws a complete picture, yet wastes no words. The scene of the escaped tarantulas in the bunk house at night is a masterpiece of vivid comic writing. And the description of unspoiled Lake Tahoe conveys the original beauty of the place with such power that the reader who has seen it a century later feels the tragedy of the change; this is an ironic effect that Twain could not have anticipated when he wrote the book.

The continuing descriptions of prospecting for gold in Nevada, writing for different newspapers in the West, and living in San Francisco are vivid, often exciting, and frequently amusing. The latter part of the narrative, the description of the trip to Hawaii and the long journey home by way of Panama might not be of as much interest to the more well-traveled modern reader, who has been educated about the world through twentieth century media, as to Twain's contemporaries, but the account is never dull, and the people Twain meets along the way are often wildly entertaining. Twain's gift for characterization was blossoming here, in portraits such as that of Hank Erickson, and soon he would be branching out into full-fledged fiction writing. *Roughing It,* a book worth reading for its own merits, was also a learning experience for a writer preparing to compose some of the greatest books in American literature.

ROXANA

Type of work: Novel
Author: Daniel Defoe (1660-1731)
Type of plot: Picaresque romance
Time of plot: Eighteenth century
Locale: England and Europe
First published: 1724

Roxana, *Defoe's last novel, resembles his earlier fiction, especially* Moll
Flanders, *in its picaresque structure, its realistic picture of eighteenth century
London low life, and its vigorous prose.* Roxana, *however, is much more
complicated and ambiguous than her predecessors, and the novel concludes on a
note of irresolution that is unusual for Defoe.*

Roxana, Or, The Fortunate Mistress was the last novel in Daniel Defoe's
series of great fictional works written between 1719 and 1724, which included
Robinson Crusoe (1719), *Moll Flanders* (1722), and *A Journal of the
Plague Year* (1722). Like its predecessors, it reflected the author's preoccupation with economic individualism and middle-class values as well as his
dissenting Protestant orientation; like them, it was written in Defoe's characteristically robust style. At the same time, this last of the author's great prose
works is unique, as it departs from the earlier novels to some degree in its
point of view, its thematic variations, and its plot structure.

In *Roxana,* as in all his works of fiction, Defoe is preoccupied with his
characters' struggles for economic independence; Roxana, like Robinson
Crusoe and Moll Flanders, is faced with poverty and starvation, but through
her ambition, practicality, and shrewd business sense she overcomes tremendous obstacles, eventually to amass a fortune. Roxana and her predecessors
are fiercely individual entrepreneurs who succeed on their own terms and owe
their hard-won security to no one but themselves. In order to stress their
independence, Defoe typically isolates his heroes and heroines in some drastic
way—Crusoe by shipwrecking him on a deserted island; Moll and Roxana by
making them social outcasts as a result of their criminal careers. From these
dire circumstances he then shows how sheer necessity operates to make his
characters act as they do.

When he decided to create a heroine like Roxana, who is driven to a variety
of criminal activities when she and her five children are abandoned by a
worthless husband, Defoe had more than ample evidence upon which to draw;
it was during his age that modern urban civilization had first devised large
police forces, detective networks complete with organized informant systems,
and a complex court system for handling the huge newly evolved criminal
population. Not only in his fiction, but in countless journalistic pieces and
pamphlets, Defoe argued passionately for the repeal of inhumane debtor's
laws, which he recognized as the cause of so much crime and injustice. As he

argued in one eloquent plea, "Necessity will make us all Thieves." At least partly connected with this intense social concern was Defoe's Protestant background. While he did not believe in the religious tenets of Puritanism, he inherited its conception of human existence as a continual struggle, its habit of viewing everyday events as charged with potential moral significance, and its tendency toward introspection.

In *Roxana,* Defoe's social conscience and ethical underpinnings combine to produce a unique, and in many ways brilliant novel, which is difficult to classify. The work resembles on the surface a picaresque tale, and does indeed share many features with other works of that category. In other essential points, however, *Roxana* is radically different from a traditional picaresque narrative, most significantly in the depth of its characterizations and in the implications of its plot. Whereas a *picaro* is primarily the tool through which his creator presents a series of comic episodes for the purpose of satirizing society and human folly, Defoe's heroine is a multi-dimensional individual. Roxana is revealed as a woman shaped by her environment and constantly striving to get the better of it. Also in contrast to the *picaro,* whose misadventures never pose a serious threat to his life, Roxana's danger is very real; she need only be apprehended to run the risk of hanging. Roxana's fears and pains, pleasures and ambitions, make her a very human and sympathetic heroine. This quality of realism is further heightened by Defoe's distinctive style, which shows all the influences of his journalist's profession. He has a reporter's eye for detail, and he crowds his scenes with particulars, all described in plain, straightforward prose; his objective, unadorned language creates a powerful effect of verisimilitude. Defoe always insisted that his fictions were not "romances." Although a romantic spirit breathes through many parts of this novel, Defoe's social and moral orientation, coupled with his wonderful capacity for "lying like the truth," place *Roxana* far beyond the realm of typical eighteenth century romances.

There is a strongly autobiographical flavor to all of Defoe's novels, which results largely from the author's close identification with his main characters; in its beginning sections, *Roxana* is no exception. But then a curious thing begins to happen. As Defoe develops Roxana's character—which he modeled closely on the actual careers of several real-life criminals—she begins to act in ways of which he cannot approve, and he loses his sympathy and close imaginative identification with her. This shifting sympathy, which occurs repeatedly throughout the novel, results in a curious vacillation on the author's part between admiring and approving of his heroine, and being deeply shocked at her behavior. The basic reason for Defoe's ambivalence toward Roxana lies in the fact that in this novel, the same basic theme used in *Moll Flanders*— that of the innocent woman being corrupted by the pressures of poverty—is carried to much greater lengths. Moll is to be forgiven because she abandons her life of crime once she has gained sufficient wealth to be independent; but

Roxana continues her illicit activities long after the demands of economic necessity are met.

Roxana also differs from its author's other works in the relative tightness of the plot, which is particularly unified by the threat of possible exposure and consequent ruin for the heroine. This threat is reinforced so often, and the daughter is so persistent a presence in the later narrative, that exposure seems, indeed, the only natural conclusion to which the plot can proceed—but it does not. Defoe is not willing to have his heroine hanged, any more than he can in right conscience allow her to live happily ever after; and it is from this conflict between sympathy and justice that much of the dramatic tension in the novel is generated. The solution to which Defoe resorts at the end of the novel solves not only the problem of plot, but that of the author's shifting attitude toward Roxana and of the difficult moral problem posed in the theme as well. In an insightful psychological twist, he imposes Roxana's punishment in the form of haunting guilt over her daughter's murder and consuming fear that her evil past will be revealed. Thus Roxana at the end of the novel suffers the fate of Tantalus; surrounded by wealth and friends, she can never enjoy them; her peace is poisoned, as she realizes that the simple pleasures of her friend the Quaker woman are forever unattainable for herself.

Nancy G. Ballard

RULE A WIFE AND HAVE A WIFE

Type of work: Drama
Author: John Fletcher (1579-1625)
Type of plot: Romantic comedy
Time of plot: c. 1600
Locale: Spain
First presented: 1624

Although the moral assumption of the play—the absolute dominance of masculine authority—may seem absurd to a modern audience, its tightly knit, fast-moving, adroitly manipulated comedy remains amusing up to the present day. The main plot, the taming of Margarita by Leon, is carefully balanced against the subplot, the gulling of Michael Perez by Estifania, and the two plots, united by dramatic irony, reinforce each other admirably.

Rule a Wife and Have a Wife is an assured piece of work by a mature craftsman of comedy. A popular play up to our own century, it succeeds through a well-paced and smoothly functioning plot that allows the humor to arise out of the basic situation rather than from farce, witty lines, or an overabundance of puns. Fletcher's knitting together of main plot and subplot is very skillful; the question of who owns and commands the elaborately furnished town house (which comes to serve as a symbol of the wealth and power all strive for) generates much of the later action of the play.

But more interesting to us today, perhaps, than the comic machinations are the attitudes and values common to the age that the work reveals. Most obvious of these is the "taming of the shrew" motif expressed by the title and by the major action. Margarita is a comic figure because she does not behave the way a woman is supposed to behave; not only does she enjoy the company and embraces of numerous men, but, more reprehensibly, she attempts to "rule" them with her ascendant will. This situation is corrected by Leon, an indigent gentleman who, having cheated Margarita out of control of her fortune by marrying her under false pretenses, finally gets her to kneel contritely before him and humbly beg his pardon for "my base self, disobedience, my wantonness, my stubbornness." The socially approved form of obedience, that is, man over women, has been reestablished (and at the same time, presumably, Margarita's insatiable lusts have somehow been dissolved by her husband's assertive self-righteousness).

Almost equally striking is the degree to which deception and fraud provide dramatic force in the play. All the main characters pretend to be what they are not in order to gain their ends: Margarita, by marrying, hopes to appear to the prying and censurious world a virtuous woman; Leon, by feigning stupidity and submissiveness, hopes to gain wealth and power; and both Perez and Estifania hope to gain wealth and security. The winners, of course, are the most ingenious deceivers. In comparison with Leon and Estifania, such a traditional cheat as Cacafogo, the rich usurer, is outclassed, beaten at his own game. The Duke, another minor leaguer, attempts two cheats, the commissioning of Leon and his own wound, but these are easily turned against him by the greater skill of his adversary. Virtue and plain dealing are clearly not sufficient for success in the world of Fletcher's comedy.

The question of why deception is so necessary is answered easily enough: only through deception can one escape from poverty. Leon has consumed his time and art searching out the subtleties of women so that he may marry a rich one, and is naturally resentful that Perez has apparently succeeded so easily and so hugely where he has failed. Perez and his wife, for their part, get along splendidly when they can eat in the arbors and cool their wine in the running fountain, but when they are forced to live in a miserable hovel, where the bed is "no bigger than a basket," love soon goes out the window: "we lie like butter clapt together, and sweat ourselves to sauce immediately." In his rage at discovering the cheat, he is fully prepared to kill Estifania. The contrast between poverty and wealth is a powerful motif in this play: when Leon is ordered off to the wars, for instance, he insists on taking his newly acquired hangings, plate, and jewels along with him, so that he can be assured of his belongings, if not his wife.

None of these motifs—the subjugation of women, the importance of deception, the frantic efforts to acquire wealth—are made explicit by Fletcher, who, after all, is primarily interested in providing dramatic entertainment; but they nevertheless imbue the play with a dark underglaze that makes it an appropriate comic counterpart to the often fetid tragedies of the age.

R. U. R.

Type of work: Drama
Author: Karel Čapek (1890-1938)
Type of plot: Social criticism
Time of plot: The future
Locale: An unnamed island
First presented: 1921; published in 1920

Karel Čapek's provocative science-fiction play R. U. R. *gave the world a new word:* robot. *Although the play may seem simplistic compared to today's speculative fiction, the problem of loss of soul in a mechanistic world continues to be vital, and Čapek's early delineation of this question remains disturbing and prophetic.*

Karel Čapek was born in Bohemia in 1890. He attended the University at Prague and later continued his studies at Berlin and Paris. Together with his brother Josef he wrote plays, several of which are available in translation and which received moderate success with English-speaking audiences. Čapek's career was not confined solely to drama. He worked as a novelist and was also for a limited time a political activist. Through his political interests he became acquainted with Thomas Mazaryk, with whom he worked to help activate a sense of Czechoslovakian unity after the 1918 revolution. Čapek retained his awareness of socio-cultural problems in his literary works, as can be seen in his play *R.U.R.* (Rossum's Universal Robots).

Čapek's concept of the future as seen in this play is a frightening one. His view of a world dependent upon mechanical devices is a disturbing look into the future which has appeared frequently in modern works of "speculative fiction." Particularly well-known in this genre are such novels as George Orwell's *1984* (1949), and Aldous Huxley's *Brave New World* (1932), as well as the works of such currently popular authors as Isaac Asimov and Ray Bradbury.

Čapek may correctly be grouped with the genre because of techniques common to his works which mark the genre as a whole. First, speculative fiction and plays deal exclusively with the possible future, that is, the future which can be projected from the factual present. Second, the literature in this genre is almost always concerned either directly or indirectly with the moral implications of advanced technology and its possible applications. Third, speculative fiction is obsessed with the human condition and human limitations which may or may not be capable of correctly utilizing and controlling the technology which it created.

In *R.U.R.* Čapek explores a period at some indefinite future point which is strikingly similar to modern society (as seen by Čapek about 1920) in all aspects, except that this society has created and become dependent upon robots. Čapek places the action upon an island, the location of which remains undefined. By limiting his action to such a confined space, the author attempts to make the action of the play more plausible, though the device does not consistently work smoothly. It makes elaborate stratagems necessary whereby information such as the worldwide revolt of robots becomes a trite dilemma rather than news of a revolution which threatens the world and all human life.

As Čapek elaborates on the idea of the soul, however indirectly, he implies that it is a human characteristic rather than a human creation. Yet at the close of the play the audience or reader sees two robots become capable of emotion and mutual love, an action which negates Čapek's implied premise, that humanity cannot be replaced because no one can instill a soul into a mechanical device. His play ends with the symbolic exit of a robot pair, the wire and plastic Adam and Eve, and the curtain falls with a deafening thud on the remains of Rossum's factory. Čapek's play is an interesting exercise in speculative fiction, but it is not equal to the strenuous gymnastics through which he forces his characters, human as well as robot. It remains interesting as an example of twentieth century Czechoslovakian drama.

THE SAINT

Type of work: Novel
Author: Antonio Fogazzaro (1842-1911)
Type of plot: Religious romance
Time of plot: Late nineteenth century
Locale: Italy
First published: 1905

Antonio Fogazzaro was deeply committed both as a literary artist and as a believing Catholic. The Saint is the product of both impulses. In it he sought to express his concerns about the tensions in the Church of his time. The result is a moving, serious chronicle of a devoted yet discontented priest, Benedetto, who tries to impress an intransigent clergy with the moral and spiritual needs of his people.

Antonio Fogazzaro, one of the great authors of the period of Italian history known as the *risorgimento,* was a native of Vicenza, Italy. Like his contemporary Giovanni Verga, he successfully combined reminiscences of his homeland with modern realism, and themes of local culture with universal themes, thus creating a new type of literature popular in Italy around the turn of this century. Fiction of this type is still read and studied in Italy, but unfortunately it has never been as popular elsewhere because of its strong regionalistic flavor and concern with highly specific national issues.

The Saint was the third novel in the trilogy in which Fogazzaro expressed his deepest intellectual and religious concerns; it followed *Piccolo mondo antico* (*The Patriot,* 1896), perhaps the author's finest novel, and *Piccolo mondo moderno* (*The Man of the World,* 1900), sometimes translated as *The Sinner.* The main character of *The Saint,* the pious monk Benedetto, preaches for the reformation of the Church and is in turn forced to leave his monastery because members of the local clergy do not want their corruption revealed to the people. The monk devotes all his energies to the poor, until a vision compels him to seek an audience with the Pope and warn him of the four great sins of the modern day Church which must be overcome if it is to survive. (It is interesting to note that Fogazzaro himself requested an audience with Pius X and was refused.) Benedetto's temptations and turns of fortune parallel the history of the Modernist movement within the Italian Church which the author supported. The Church was not only hostile to the movement, as might be expected, but condemned *The Saint* as well; its condemnation, however, did not deter a wide audience from admiring it and being influenced by its arguments. The author himself was deeply affected by the Church's criticism of his book. While many of the leaders of the Modernist movement eventually left the Church, Fogazzaro, a devout believer, was unable in right conscience to do so; his later works, which all fall far short of the trilogy in emotional power and literary merit, even reveal a softening of his views on reform.

The inspiration for *The Saint* was rooted in the author's deep love for the Catholic Church; ironically, this love was also responsible for both the power and depth of the novel and for its artistic weaknesses. The work is moving and powerful in those places where Fogazzaro's inner conflicts are played out through the narrative; the dramatization of the conflicting demands of man's reason and his mystical nature, the clash between the old faith and new scientific thought, and the gulf between the clergy and the laity provide the story with its energy. At the same time, Fogazzaro's ambitious attempt to create a believable character of transcendent spiritual qualities, who raises himself from a life of dependence on earthly pleasures to a life of sainthood, is unsuccessful. Benedetto is not a convincing figure. He lacks human frailties to the extent that neither author nor readers can really identify with him. Yet it was the same deep rooted feeling for the Church which produced the novel, that made Fogazzaro even attempt the characterization which proved to be beyond his means. As it turned out, it is the struggling, tormented, and very human figures of the earlier novels, rather than the saint, who are the most memorable of the author's creations.

ST. PETER'S UMBRELLA

Type of work: Novel
Author: Kálmán Mikszáth (1847-1910)
Type of plot: Humorous romance
Time of plot: Second half of nineteenth century
Locale: Hungary
First published: 1895

Kálmán Mikszáth was a country squire, lawyer, magistrate, journalist, member of parliament, and novelist, but his forte was undoubtedly his superb storytelling, surpassed in Hungary only by Maurus Jókai. St. Peter's Umbrella, his first novel, is a delightfully humorous story of the adventures, problems, and relationships provoked by a semi-magical red umbrella that almost seems to have a life of its own.

Sometimes called the Hungarian Mark Twain, Kálmán Mikszáth established his fame as a short story writer before he turned to writing novels, the first of which was *Szent Péter esernyöje (St. Peter's Umbrella)*. Like much of Mark Twain's work, the novel reveals a bittersweet, pessimistic-optimistic dichotomy in Mikszáth's attitude toward the human condition. Although wanting to believe in essential human goodness, Mikszáth was empirically convinced that human flaws and failings were innate and ineradicable. Thus, the well-meaning priest becomes party to a heretical superstition about the umbrella. So, too, the otherwise inoffensive brothers and sister of Pál Gregorics become greedy vultures who begrudge Gyury a share of his father's estate.

Yet, for all this, *St. Peter's Umbrella* is not a Dickensian tale of unrelieved gloom but a light-hearted fable with the makings of a modern legend—literary rather than folk, in its origins, for it does not stem from the ethnic lore of Hungary. The unifying factor in the story is the umbrella, a symbol of protection from inclement weather. And as the plot unfolds, the umbrella gains additional symbolic significance: it mysteriously appears in Glogova, bringing good fortune. It becomes even more intriguing as the object of Gyury's search. Hence, the umbrella is the very stuff from which fable and legend are made. In fact, throughout the novel, Mikszáth follows the conventions of Hungarian fables, and consequently invests the story with an air of authenticity.

Indeed, the aura of authenticity in *St. Peter's Umbrella* is so strong that the improbable coincidences are often overlooked. How likely is it that a passerby would place an umbrella over an untended baby in a rainstorm? How likely is it that a putative corpse being buried on a rainy day by a priest with an umbrella should prove to be very much alive? How likely is it that Gyury would find the widow of Jónás Müncz? How likely is it that Gyury would find a lost earring (so small and so insignificant an object, although the mayor had ordered the town crier to announce its loss), which coincidentally belonged to Veronica Bélyi, sister of the priest who possessed the umbrella for

which Gyury was searching? How likely is Gyury's falling in love with Veronica? It is a tribute to Mikszáth's storytelling powers that the reader never
asks such questions, enjoying the fable on its own mythic terms.

ST. RONAN'S WELL

Type of work: Novel
Author: Sir Walter Scott (1771-1832)
Type of plot: Social criticism
Time of plot: Early nineteenth century
Locale: Scotland
First published: 1824

St. Ronan's Well *is a bitter and scathing satirical novel. The members of idle society at a watering place are easily recognizable individuals, probably modeled after superficial admirers of Scott's work; his own experiences may be reflected in Francis Tyrrel's lack of success in Lady Penelope's circle. What is unusual in this novel is the fact that the good intentions of the sympathetic characters are partly responsible for the final tragedy.*

St. Ronan's Well was not favorably received by the critics of its day; in fact, following publication of the novel, Scott's reputation fell considerably. The unpopularity of the novel may be partly attributed to the fact that the scene of *St. Ronan's Well* is not Scott's customary historical setting, but rather a contemporary setting, a fashionable watering place. This change no doubt upset many of his readers. In an introduction attached to *St. Ronan's Well,* Scott defended the setting of his book on the neoclassical basis that it helped him in the imitation of life. The setting, he argued, allowed him to portray contemporary figures. Unfortunately, this argument was not persuasive.

Another problem in the novel was that Scott was forced by his publisher to eliminate a key section. Clara, the aristocratic lady, had been seduced prior to the opening scene of the book. Despite the fact, however, that the seduction was only reported, and not described, Scott's publisher balked. Scott is reported to have objected that if the woman had not been an aristocrat, but had been a working girl, the publisher would never have called for a change. Nevertheless, Scott surrendered to the pressure and rewrote more than twenty pages of *St. Ronan's Well* in order to try to account for the change in motivation. He was not entirely successful, and his "imitation of life" suffered.

There were also other weaknesses apparent in *St. Ronan's Well.* Since Scott did not choose a historical theme, there was little historical conflict to give resonance to the plot. Thus, the conflict between the brothers, the death of Clara, and the disguises and intrigues, seem nakedly melodramatic. Also, though Scott was able to draw some interesting and accurate Scottish and English types, he was not able to portray that variety of social types to which his audience had become accustomed in the Waverley series.

On the positive side, however, Scott's use of dialect in *St. Ronan's Well* is less forced and unnatural than in the historical romances. Meg Dods, for example, speaks a fluent Scots, interesting and readable. Since she was a contemporary, Scott did not have to make her language "poetic" or lace it with archaic, figurative expressions.

SAKUNTALA

Type of work: Drama
Author: Kalidasa (c. sixth century)
Type of plot: Exotic romance
Time of plot: Golden Age of India
Locale: India
First presented: c. sixth century

Kalidasa has been termed the Shakespeare of India, and Sakuntala *is usually considered his best play.* Sakuntala, *the beautiful daughter of a Brahman and a nymph, meets King Dushyanta in a Sacred Grove. They fall in love and subsequently marry. An incidental insult to a holy man by Sakuntala results in a curse of forgetfulness being laid on Dushyanta. Love finally triumphs when fate intervenes to lift the spell and reunite the lovers.*

The story of Sakuntala stems from an ancient Hindu legend, recounted in Book I of the *Mahabharata*. When Kalidasa dramatized this well-known legend, he was not presenting an unfamiliar tale, but artfully retelling an old one. His method is a familiar one in Western culture. Ancient Greek dramatists and playgoers, for example, shared a common mythos just as Kalidasa and his audience did. Greek writers had the *Iliad* and the *Odyssey* for their sources; Indian writers went to the two great Hindu epics, the *Mahabharata* and the *Ramayana,* for theirs. And in both the West and the East, writers usually adhered to the main storyline of the original, but varied the plot structure slightly and added subplots and details of psychological insight.

The advantages of working within an accepted cultural framework are immediately evident. The audience instantly recognizes the story, correctly identifies allusions in it, and knows with certainty the story's place in the larger mythological context, freeing the writer from lengthy description and explanation to concentrate on intricacies of plot and the characters' spiritual and psychological development. This close formal correspondence between East and West makes Kalidasa's play eminently accessible to Western readers.

But there are crucial differences, too. The most obvious, of course, is material: the content of the two mythologies is vastly different. But even more important is a subtle and complex difference in dramaturgy. Aristotelian Western drama places top priority on plot (imitation of action); characterization, setting, and other embellishments are subordinate to the action which advances the plot. Sanskrit drama, however, emphasizes *rasa* (a dominant emotion or flavor, a "sympathy"). It imitates emotion; the action is thus subordinated to the progressive evocation of an emotional state. Hence, priorities are shifted from action to feeling, from an accumulation of episodes to a series of moods, a movement from plot to dominant emotion.

And in *Sakuntala,* the dominant emotion is love, in all its varieties and flavors. Thus Sakuntala fares badly at the hands of the gods and of human beings in order to intensify the depiction of her emotional state, to bring out in stark relief the multifaceted depths of her love. Sakuntala's love—its intensity, its depth, its breadth—is what *Sakuntala* is all about. The play examines an emotional state so compelling that it overwhelms all other considerations.

Herein lies the core of Sanskrit drama at its best in Kalidasa's masterpiece: feeling takes precedence over rationality. The Western reader must therefore adjust to the Hindu scale of dramatic values instead of imposing Western standards upon a non-Western play. The rewards of reading *Sakuntala* in the appropriate cultural context are well worth the effort.

SALAMMBÔ

Type of work: Novel
Author: Gustave Flaubert (1821-1880)
Type of plot: Historical romance
Time of plot: Third century B.C.
Locale: Carthage
First published: 1862

Salammbô *is a monumental description of Carthage while that city-republic was still a great power. Into this novel Flaubert put five years of study about Carthage during the Punic Wars. Character analysis is scant and the plot little more than animated history, but critical opinion accords it a distinguished place because of its faithful picture of the people and the times.*

Gustave Flaubert wrote *Salammbô* with the most painstaking care and eye for historical accuracy. He visited the ruins of Carthage and many of the other sites that appear in the novel, and he read widely on the history of the city and its wars; incidents he reports are frequently taken from the historical record. His main source is evidently the Greek historian Polybius, whom he used not only for the broad movement of events but for minor points concerning dress, customs, and details of ordinary life.

The style of *Salammbô* is luxuriant and heavily pictorial. Flaubert, a master of prose craftsmanship, elegance, and balance, nevertheless achieves the stylistic "agility" he declared as his aim. The exactness of architectural, military, and social details reveals a literary technician working conscientiously within the limits of his sources. Images of physical horror as well as naturalistic description of hair, sweat, and flesh counterbalance the richly exotic imagery.

Among scenes of extraordinary vitality are those describing the feast at Hamilcar's gardens, with its richly detailed pictures of the palace, the kitchens, and the courses of the banquet itself; Salammbô's first appearance before the barbarian hosts; Mathô's stealthy visit to Salammbô's bedside and his seizure of the Tanit veil; Taanach and the ritual of the python; and the deaths of Mathô and Salammbô. Yet in each scene Flaubert attempts to create a romantic, not a realistic, image of Carthage. The details, densely assembled into opalescent imagery, are intended to be picturesque and florid, a delight for the senses instead of the mind. The author treats romance as poetry; his plot—heroic to the point of self-parody—is only incidental, a vehicle to provide different settings. What matters is the language: its color, tone, nuance. On the basis of its technical achievements, *Salammbô* is an important early contribution to nineteenth century aestheticism. In its experiments with prose-poetry and impressionism, the novel is part of a French tradition that includes Gautier's *Mademoiselle de Maupin* (1835), Rimbaud's *Une Saison en Enfer* (1873), and Huysmans' *À rebours* (1884); in English aestheticism, *Sal-*

ammbô is a forerunner of Pater's *Marius the Epicurean* (1885) and Wilde's *Salomé* (1893).

For readers familiar with Flaubert's masterpieces of psychological realism, *l'Education sentimentale* (1869) and *Madame Bovary* (1857), the exotic romanticism of *Salammbô* may appear to be uncharacteristic of the author. Yet the different effects of these novels are calculated. With his usual precision, Flaubert pinpointed the central difference between *Madame Bovary* and *Salammbô* as the difference between the major characters. He termed his heroine Salammbô a maniac controlled by a fixed idea; in contrast; Emma Bovary is simply a woman agitated by thronging passions. Another difference between the novels, more important perhaps for the modern reader, is the strangely timeless quality of *Salammbô*. While *Madame Bovary* is rooted in everyday life, in the trivialities of provincial France of the nineteenth century, the tragedy of *Salammbô* somehow rises above the mesh of particulars—despite Flaubert's insistence on accuracy.

SAMSON AGONISTES

Type of work: Drama
Author: John Milton (1608-1674)
Type of plot: Heroic tragedy
Time of plot: c. 1100 B.C.
Locale: Palestine
First published: 1671

Although Samson Agonistes *was not designed for the stage, the author modeled his work on Greek tragedy because he found it "the gravest, moralest, and most profitable of all other poems." Milton opens his play during Samson's imprisonment, and, although Biblical accounts of Samson's youth are mentioned, the episodes which make up most of the play and shape Samson's decision to destroy both the Philistines and himself, are the author's own creation.*

Since *Samson Agonistes* was published in the same volume with *Paradise Regained* just three years before Milton's death, tradition has ascribed its composition to the late years of his life and has marked the drama as the last of his three great poems. More recently, however, various theories have placed the date of the work as far back as the 1640's. Generally, support for the earlier date of composition is related to the critical opinion that the artistry of *Samson Agonistes* is of a lower order than that of *Paradise Lost* and *Paradise Regained.* In other words, by placing *Samson Agonistes* at a greater chronological distance from the other poems, it is easier to support a theory that it is an inferior work of art. It is certain from manuscript evidence, that as early as the 1640's Milton had planned a series of five Samson plays; so it is by no means impossible that at least a first draft of *Samson Agonistes* was written at that time. Hence, though the traditional view that *Samson Agonistes* belongs to the end of Milton's canon is still widely held, whether the drama was written just before publication or nearly thirty years earlier, we do know that it was initially conceived long before it appeared.

Perhaps the origin of the view that *Samson Agonistes* is inferior to Milton's other major poems lies in Dr. Johnson's criticism of its tragic form. Ever since he said that the play had a beginning and an end but no middle, critics have been addressing themselves to the problem of viewing the poem as a classical Greek tragedy. It was Milton himself who set the stage for later arguments by prefacing the poem with an essay discussing Aristotle's concept of tragedy and extolling classical tragedy as "the gravest, moralest, and most profitable of all other Poems." By hearkening back to the ancients as his models rather than his own Elizabethan predecessors, he hoped to reëstablish the "classical" pattern of tragedy, purging the abuses into which the genre had fallen through the English habit of mixing comedy and low-born persons into the plot of a tragic play. The difference between Milton and the ancients is also established in the prefatory essay, however, when he says that *Samson Agonistes* was never meant for the stage. Those who have sided with Dr. Johnson have found that in spite of Milton's attempt to follow the classical pattern, the play is flawed by the static and lifeless quality they see in the central episodes.

What the drama lacks, however, is not life, but action. All the famous acts of the protagonist have occurred either in the past or do occur outside the range of our vision. Samson's actions as the hero of the Israelites and his subsequent fall are over before the poem begins, and his final triumph over the Philistines takes place off stage. But if there is no physical action during the episodes with Manoa, Dalila, and Harapha, there is a great deal of psychological action. These episodes function both to provide us with the background of Samson's present dilemma and to reveal the progressive revitalization of Samson's need to fulfill his God-appointed role as the hero and deliverer of his people. Further, the three episodes may be seen as temptations to his faith, fortitude, and patience. The action of the drama then can be seen as the psychological process by which Samson meets and overcomes these temptations. Through these episodes which some have found dramatically empty, Samson moves from despair to courage and on to the final heroic act of self-sacrifice. Dr. Johnson's critical mistake was perhaps in not accepting inner conflicts and resolutions as "action."

Beyond the structural problems that complicate *Samson Agonistes'* claim to being a tragedy, there is an additional difficulty arising from the basic difference in theological perspective between Milton and his Greek counterparts. The question here is whether it is indeed possible to write such a thing as "Christian" tragedy. Is it possible, within Milton's view of man and God where even the Fall is "fortunate," to have an ultimately tragic event? One of the paradoxes in the drama then is that while the play does end with death, the death is victorious. In a sense, the real tragedy has already taken place before we see Samson, "eyeless in Gaza." Samson has already fallen, and the fall was precipitated by *hubris,* the classic flaw of excessive pride. Samson's death finally results from a conscious willful act, not the immediate result of a flaw or an act of the indifferent Fates; through his death Samson triumphs over his enemies and fulfills his destiny. But this victorious tragedy, too, has parallels among the classics. Certainly the Oedipus cycle presents the similar pattern of a protagonist who falls first through a flaw and then later, in a tragedy resulting from the first fall, transcends the disaster of death with a spiritual victory.

But granting the classical parallels to Milton's poem, we are left with the more substantial issue of fitting tragedy into Milton's Christian view of history. Critics are quite right to say that tragedy is not ultimately possible for a Christian hero in a Christian universe. That is not to deny, however, that tragedy may exist in human terms. Thus, on one level the deaths of Samson and Christ are tragic, but the paradox of the Christian faith is that he who loses his life shall find it; human tragedy is then transformed into a final victory. Though individual tragedies can exist, they are ultimately subsumed in the larger cosmic framework of the divine design. That is, they become a part of a larger pattern in which death is followed by resurrection. Hence, we can see Milton's tragic poem as the union of a Biblical theme and a classical literary form, just as *Paradise Lost* was the union of the classical epic form and the Christian vision of creation.

Timothy E. Bollinger

SANCTUARY

Type of work: Novel
Author: William Faulkner (1897-1962)
Type of plot: Psychological melodrama
Time of plot: 1929
Locale: Mississippi and Memphis, Tennessee
First published: 1931

Sanctuary *is a harsh, brutal, sensational novel of the rural South in the late 1920's. The kidnaping of a Southern belle, Temple Drake, by Popeye, a Northern gangster, offers a plot spine for Faulkner's observations on the collapse of the old Southern moralities and ideals in the face of the amoral, depersonalized, mechanistic modern world.*

The sensationalism stemming from the lurid violence and carnality of *Sanctuary* helped make it a best seller in 1931 and the first of Faulkner's novels to reach a wide audience. Faulkner himself once claimed that the work was a potboiler written to make money. Despite his disclaimer, however, *Sanctuary* has since come to be considered an important continuation of the Faulknerian themes of the disillusionment and despair which results from a discovery of the pervasive reality of evil, and the subsequent spiritual collapse which follows the discovery.

This drama of innocence and corruption, a theme which Faulkner also traces in *The Sound and the Fury,* in *Sanctuary* is delineated through the characters of Horace Benbow, Temple Drake, and Popeye. Benbow had been represented earlier by Faulkner in *Sartoris* (1929) as a naïve idealist and worshiper of spiritual purity and beauty in women. His illusions are shattered in *Sanctuary,* first by the realization that his marriage to Belle Mitchell has grown dull and routine, and then by the recognition that Little Belle, to whom he had transferred all his ideals concerning women, is actually no different than Temple Drake, or women generally. The conviction of Goodwin and his death at the hands of the mob undermine Benbow's idealistic beliefs in justice and mankind, just as his new contacts with moral and social hypocrisy, with perverted lust and cruelty, and with the blatant force of evil in the world take away his unrealistic idealizations of life.

Benbow discovers the fact of evil generally, but Temple Drake merely responds to the evil already inherent in her nature. This is what Benbow learns when he speaks to Temple at Miss Reba's. Her rape by Popeye and her subsequent moral degradation has only released in Temple the carnality that her virginity and background had previously checked. She is fascinated by and almost proud of her new moral role, once she has lost her innocence.

Neither good nor evil, Popeye's actions and personality are perverted beyond any moral scope. His sterile, pointless cruelties only emphasize the meaningless which Benbow comes to see in the universal order of things. In a world where the innocent are burned by mobs, where the guilty die for the wrong crimes, where public morality is more corrupt than that of a brothel, and where faded traditions are used to veil moral deterioration—in such a world a creature like Popeye not only belongs but makes sense. There is no meaning in Popeye's actions, just as there is no meaning—as Benbow learns —in the "logical pattern" of evil, or life as a whole. That there is no meaning, for Benbow underscores Faulkner's despairing view of the spiritual condition of modern man.

SANDFORD AND MERTON

Type of work: Novel
Author: Thomas Day (1748-1789)
Type of plot: Didactic romance
Time of plot: Late eighteenth century
Locale: England
First published: 1783-1789

Thomas Day utilizes the form of the novel in Sandford and Merton *to present the same basic theory of education espoused by Rousseau in* Émile. *Tommy Merton is the devitalized, headstrong, unreliable product of an artificial, pampered upbringing. Harry Sandford, a farmer's son, is healthy, kindly, and stable. Not surprisingly, Harry's examples and encouragement finally educate Tommy to life's true values and ready him for a promising manhood.*

So deeply influenced by Rousseau's theories of natural education was Thomas Day that he conducted living experiments with adopted children. That sounds somewhat grotesque, but the "experiments" were motivated by very human feelings as well as philosophical curiosity. Day longed for a wife with natural sensibilities, so he adopted two girls, aged eleven and twelve, and brought them up in ways calculated to develop their instincts and natural personalities. The most agreeable of the two was to become his wife. Day subjected the girls to ridiculous tests—such as dropping hot sealing wax on their bare arms in order to teach them to be fearless and tough. Day, along with Rousseau, believed that if children experienced the conditions found in "the noble state of nature"—such as courage, endurance, compassion, honesty—while being protected from the corrupting influence of social institutions, they would develop sense as well as sensibility. Neither of the girls became Day's wife. Some traits, Day discovered, were simply uneducable.

Sandford and Merton provided a happier method for indicating Day's theories. In this fiction he was able to control all the variables, and indeed, Tommy Merton does develop all the natural instincts that his effeminate and undisciplined home had almost stifled completely. With Harry Sandford's example, as a person and doer of good and sensible deeds, Tommy gradually bcomes a paragon of all the virtues Day had hoped his own wards—or at least one of them—might realize in her own person.

Harry's primary virtue is a kind of worldly sincerity, and Mr. Merton's hopes for Tommy are realized when his own son develops into the same straight-thinking as well as generous lad represented by Harry Sandford. It is here that Rousseau's ideas about the natural man coincide with a traditionally English appreciation of the straightforward manliness of the common English yeoman.

SANINE

Type of work: Novel
Author: Mikhail Artsybashev (1878-1927)
Type of plot: Philosophical romance
Time of plot: 1906
Locale: Russia
First published: 1907

Influenced by the moral attitudes prevalent in Russia after the abortive 1905 revolution, Mikhail Artsybashev celebrates an intensely individualistic, even hedonistic morality in Sanine. *The hero of the novel, Vladimir Petrovitch Sanine, lives his philosophy openly, and this brings him into continual conflict with the conformist society around him.*

Although written seventy years ago, *Sanine* seems to be a modern novel; it anticipates later movements, both social and literary. When Ivanovna declares that life has no meaning and Sanine asserts that existence is absurd, their conversation suggests the despair prevalent in many existential novels of the mid-twentieth century. The passionate passages that unite a cult of sexuality with a love of nature suggest the novels of D. H. Lawrence. This is the book of an immature writer, particularly when the characters proclaim that they must *"Live!,"* but in many respects it was ahead of its time, a forerunner of the frank, rebellious novels that began to appear around the world in the 1920's.

Sanine was written with an intensity obviously born of conviction. There are many vividly written passages and scenes of startling dramatic power, such as the episode in the cave between Yourii and Sina and the death of Semenoff. The book is crowded with young people, and the characterizations are clear and precise; all of them ring true. It is easy to believe that the young intellectuals of Russia experienced such disillusionment and moral confusion in the early years of the century.

Sanine deals with many issues that arise with every generation: the conflicts of the young with elders, the rejection of old values by the young, and the angry rebellion of youth against established institutions. Other issues dealt with in the novel later became common subjects in novels, including the conflict between convention and desire, the frustration of political activity and idealistic ambitions, the double standard that existed between men and women, and the bondage of a dying Christian religion. Psychologically, too, the author broke new ground in this novel. He admits, as few writers of his day did, that women, as well as men, have sexual feelings. And he explores the outer reaches of despair, approaching, at times, the novels of Dostoevski in intensity. Perhaps the most daring part of the book, for the decade in which it was written, is the suggestion that an attraction exists between Sanine and his sister, Lida. However, although the novel is both frank and angry, it never goes beyond the bounds of taste. It is flawed by an occasionally shrill tone, but it is an important and effective view of a critical period of Russian history, and of the young people who a decade later were to be caught up in the storm of revolution.

SAPPHO

Type of work: Novel
Author: Alphonse Daudet (1840-1897)
Type of plot: Naturalism
Time of plot: Nineteenth century
Locale: Paris
First published: 1884

Alphonse Daudet paints a realistic, if surprisingly delicate picture of Bohemian life in mid-nineteenth century Paris by tracing the experiences of Jean Gaussin, a young art student, as he becomes a part of this fascinating yet destructive society which in the end makes him its captive.

Often classed as a naturalist, Alphonse Daudet has in his work none of the pessimistic determinism one finds in Émile Zola and many other naturalists who based their fiction upon scientific theories and principles. In *Sappho,* the best-known of his Parisian novels of manners, Daudet's writing is realistic, impressionistic, and occasionally humorous or even moralistic. The Bohemian atmosphere of the half-world of Paris in the late nineteenth century is closely observed and vividly described. Some of his physically and morally decayed characters might well have posed for posters by Toulouse-Lautrec or sat at café tables near Van Gogh's famed absinthe drinker. The easy morality of the artists in Paris is suggested by Fanny Legrand's having been a mistress to the sculptor who used her to model for his statue of Sappho and by her having also lived with the poet La Gournerie. The famous composer de Potter's mistress, now a fifty-year-old painted horror, was formerly "celebrated in the world of love for her cynical licentiousness, her cutting remarks and horse-whipping of men."

In one striking scene, Daudet symbolizes the plight of young Jean Gaussin as he joins this immoral Parisian world. As Jean, with Fanny in his arms, reaches the fourth floor of his house, he realizes he is "carrying a woman no longer . . . [but] something horrible which was stifling him, which all the time he was trying to drop, to throw down in anger. . . ." Until the end of the novel he is alternately excited and repelled, angered and disgusted by the woman who educates him sexually. He does not delude himself that he is in love with Fanny as he is with Irène. For this reason he never understands Fanny's love for him since he looks upon himself as simply the latest in the series of men in her life. Daudet published *Sappho* a quarter-century before Sigmund Freud's *Three Contributions to the Theory of Sex* (1910), but in his characterization of both Jean and Fanny he shows an intuitive under-standing of the sexual nature of men and women such as Freud was to gain only through medical case studies.

SAPPHO

Type of work: Drama
Author: Franz Grillparzer (1791-1872)
Type of plot: Romantic tragedy
Time of plot: Sixth century B.C.
Locale: The island of Lesbos
First presented: 1818

Franz Grillparzer uses the unsubstantiated legend that Sappho committed suicide because she was spurned by a young man named Phaon as a starting point for this play. The conflict within Sappho between the demands of love and genius probably reflects the fact that the author himself believed, as a result of personal experience, that the two conflicting forces were incompatible.

Grillparzer's *Sappho* is one of a series of German works dealing with the problems of the artist personality, ranging from Goethe's *Torquato Tasso* to Thomas Mann's *Doctor Faustus*. The theme had special significance for the nineteenth century, when Romanticism developed the concept of the artist as separate from society, exalted and, in a sense, cursed.

Grillparzer's life was not happy and the difficulty he experienced in living as an artist provides some of the underlying impulse of the play. Sappho falls from her calling as an artist when she attempts to grasp life in its ordinary sense, represented by the handsome but unremarkable Phaon. Her tragedy has really taken place before the play begins; it is in the course of the drama that the implications of her abdication manifest themselves. As she enters, she has committed herself to descend from the heights of her art into the warm and comfortable valley of human life. It is a descent from the lofty heights of the spirit to the level of the senses and the body.

It is not to be taken as a mark against her character that, in this realm, she becomes a petty, vengeful woman—trying to act in this realm, she is completely out of her element, as Phaon instinctively realizes. He could adore Sappho, the poetess, but her attempts to fashion a love relationship are futile; she is too great, too far beyond him, and his love falls instead upon an utterly simple, naïve slave girl. Melitta is lovable precisely because she is on the same level as Phaon, and Sappho learns that it is impossible for her to regain the childlike simplicity of ordinary mortals. Her grasping for personal fulfillment as a private person places her in opposition to the will of the gods, who have bestowed on her the poetic gift. Having forsaken her proper world of art and unable to function in the alien world of everyday life, having offended the gods by her rejection of their gift, she can only achieve reconciliation and atonement in death.

SARAGOSSA

Type of work: Novel
Author: Benito Pérez Galdós (1845-1920)
Type of plot: Historical romance
Time of plot: 1808-1809
Locale: Spain
First published: 1874

Saragossa *is one of a series of novels by Pérez Galdós which covers the period of Spain's wars with Napoleon. Here the story of the second siege of Saragossa is presented as a historic example of Spanish patriotism. The author deftly interweaves the moving love affair between Augustine de Montoria and Mariquilla with the panoramic events of the siege.*

Hopefulness and despair, triumph and suffering—all the human emotions which surface during battles for bare existence within a besieged city are skillfully juxtaposed against the tender but tormenting sentiments of a forbidden love affair in Pérez Galdós' *Saragossa.* The parallel plots dramatize familiar themes often used in earlier works of literature such as the *Nibelungen* tales and *Romeo and Juliet.* Pérez Galdós employed this technique to develop fictional characters that are as true to life as the historical and geographical descriptions that form the backdrop of his historical novel.

Many historians have noted the unusual fury with which the Spanish people fought Napoleon's legions even after some of their leaders had deserted them. In *Saragossa,* the reader is exposed in a personal way to this fury, stemming from the resentment of Spanish commoner and aristocrat alike toward the imposition of French ideas on Spanish culture—even the noted statue of Saragossa's famed Virgin of Pilar has a sign reading "The Virgin of Pilar doesn't want to be French."

The reader is moved quickly into the adventure by the skilled narration, which starts when four men reach Saragossa's gates after having traveled across the country for days, fording streams, scaling hills, and traversing woods. They enter the city gates just as the clock tower strikes ten, on the evening before Napoleon's troops close in to begin the assault on the city's outer ramparts. One of the four volunteers, aristocratic Augustine, develops a romantic interest in classically beautiful Mariquilla, daughter of miserly Candiola. During the following months of siege, thousands of fanatic peasants, priests, merchants, and nobles engage in a bloody combat with the assaulting French, who find that Spain is astonishingly different from other European theaters of war. But Augustine also effects his trysts with Mariquilla even as her beloved, miserly father sleeps several rooms away.

The tragic climax of the siege as well as love affair is not surprising, but still well handled by Pérez Galdós, who drew his characters from the typical Aragonese of the early 1880's. The personalities are interesting both for their authenticity and the fast-paced action into which they are thrust. But constantly looming over them is the personality of the ancient, embattled city of Saragossa, so vividly drawn, and so indelible in the reader's memory.

SATANSTOE

Type of work: Novel
Author: James Fenimore Cooper (1789-1851)
Type of plot: Historical romance
Time of plot: 1751-1758
Locale: New York State
First published: 1845

Satanstoe, or, The Littlepage Manuscripts *combines the social criticism of Cooper's later life with his talents as a romanticist. This is the first of the "Littlepage" novels, a trilogy that traces the fortunes of the Littlepage family through four generations as their status as landed gentry is challenged by those who, in Cooper's opinion, would destory true democracy in the interest of economic leveling.*

To James Fenimore Cooper, who always felt himself to be a passionate advocate of democracy, property rights were vital to the democratic system. His most emphatic statements on the subject were made in a series of essays entitled *The American Democrat* (1938) where he said: "As property is the base of all civilization, its existence and security are indispensable to social improvement." And in the 1830's he felt its "existence and security" were in grave jeopardy. In the 1840's the situation, in Cooper's view, became even worse and stimulated "The Littlepage Trilogy," the first of which is *Satanstoe*.

The initiating events were a series of "Anti-Rent Wars" which took place in upper New York State from 1839 to 1846. The issue involved attempts by the rich descendants of early Dutch settlers to collect long neglected rent payments from tenant farmers who held their land through perpetual or long term leaseholds. The tenants reacted strongly, even violently, against what they felt to be a grossly unfair arrangement, eventually winning the right to purchase their lands outright. Although Cooper felt the long-term leasehold system to be archaic and inefficient, he saw the anti-rent agitation as a threat to the rights of property itself and so he fought against this latest evidence of "leveling" with the only weapon he had, his pen.

It was Cooper's intention in the Littlepage Trilogy to follow a single family of landed gentry through four generations largely by concentrating on biography and realism rather than emphasizing plot and action. The three novels trace the family's fortunes from the establishment of the estate (*Satanstoe*), through the beginnings of social unrest and agitation (*The Chainbearer,* 1845), and ending with the contemporary anti-rent controversy (*The Redskins,* 1846). This chronicle thus establishes, in Cooper's view, the validity of the landed gentry position by demonstrating their long-term superiority.

In each of the novels the issue of property rights and natural aristocracy versus forced equality and unmitigated majority rule is argued at great length, and these arguments represent one of the important debates in our nation's

history. But, unfortunately, Cooper was never able to integrate successfully his ideas into the action of the stories; the rhetoric remains just that,
argument for the sake of argument. And since each novel in the trilogy is
increasingly polemical, each is artistically inferior to its predecessor.

Therefore, *Santanstoe* remains the best of the Littlepage Trilogy because
its rhetoric is the most muted. To be sure it lacks the action, intensity, and
firm plotting of many earlier Cooper novels. Except for a few incidents, such
as the almost disastrous sleigh ride on melting ice, *Satanstoe* is a very leisurely,
almost aimless book. The pleasures of the novel reside in the careful, accurate
description of mid-eighteenth century life among the landed gentry—social
customs, manners, rituals, tastes, courting behavior, life styles—all presented
with a gentle, ironic humor. The most evident quality of this society is a
sense of security derived from a fixed social order and a stable environment.
The disruption of this security, only hinted at in *Satanstoe*, was to be the
subject of the subsequent novels as well as the bane of Cooper's later years.

SATIROMASTIX

Type of work: Drama
Author: Thomas Dekker (c. 1572-1632?)
Type of plot: Satirical romance
Time of plot: c. 1100
Locale: England
First presented: 1601

In Satiromastix *three plots are mixed together in a rather confusing manner.
The play was hastily composed by Thomas Dekker as a satirical answer to his rival,
Ben Jonson. Their stage quarrel had been initiated by Jonson in his play* Poetastor,
*which mocks both Dekker and his associate John Marston. Although Dekker's
response is probably inferior as drama, his caricature of Jonson is sharp, brilliant,
and severe.*

The story of Dekker's *Satiromastix* and its companion piece *Poetaster* by
Ben Jonson is part of the "stage quarrel," or War of the Theatres, of 1600.
In that year the professional outdoor theaters of Elizabethan England found
themselves in competition with two boy actor companies, The Children of
the Chapel Royal and The Children of St. Paul's Chapel. These two companies gave indoor evening performances, using lighting and elaborate stage
effects. They charged high prices for tickets and attracted a sophisticated,
wealthy audience.

The managers of the children's companies looked to the professional companies for writers. Jonson wrote at least part of the time for the children's
companies. *Poetaster* was one of these satiric, comic plays and was performed
by the Children of the Chapel Royal at Blackfriars'. Always a spirited person,
Jonson had had a falling out with Dekker and attacked him in the play
through the character Demetrius Fannius. Jonson pictures Demetrius as the
epitome of ignorance, lowness, and poverty, and as a man who would write
slanderous material against anybody if paid for it. *Satiromastix* appeared in
1601 at the Globe Theatre and at Saint Paul's as an answer to *Poetaster.*

Poetaster is considered the better of the two plays, but Dekker triumphs in
successfully using Jonson's characters for his own purposes. Demetrius Fannius becomes a moderate, tempered in all things by a sense of fairness, and
Horace (Jonson) becomes a vain, lying, temperamental sycophant. Jonson
never answered *Satiromastix* and the "battle" ended.

Whereas *Poetaster* is defended as an *ars poetica, Satiromastix* is criticized
for its imbalances, since four-fifths of the action is subplot. The stringy main
plot is also highly artificial and rigid. Imbalance and lack of unity are charges
also made against Dekker's *The Honest Whore.* Although *Satiromastix* is
effective satire, it has been labeled "a potpourri not well-blended."

THE SATYRICON

Type of work: Fictional miscellany
Author: Gaius Petronius Arbiter (?–A.D. c. 66)
Type of plot: Social criticism
Time of plot: First century
Locale: Italy
Earliest extant printed version: 1664

This vast work of Petronius is extant only in a fragment comprising books 15 and 16. The Satyricon *is a miscellany of anecdotes, longer stories, and parodies of literary forms and rhetorical conventions. By turns comic, ribald, and satiric, the work describes Roman life at the time of Nero with an incisive style that is both realistic and ironical.*

The Satyricon is a mere fragment of an extremely complex medley of stories that, in the complete version, perhaps were part of a mock-epic prose romance. Attached to the manuscript of *The Satyricon,* which was discovered in 1663 at Trau in Dalmatia, was a scribe's note describing the contents as taken from the "fifteenth and sixteenth books." If this information is correct, the original work must have been enormously long. For centuries, scholars have disputed the purpose, scope, and meaning of the whole work. Not even the name of the author is accepted for certain. By tradition, *The Satyricon* is attributed to Gaius Petronius—better known as Petronius Arbiter, the *elegantiae arbiter* of the court of Nero. Tacitus' famous description (*Annals,* xvi) of the death of Gaius Petronius seems to correspond well with the reader's perception of the writer of such a book: a refined voluptuary, clever but cynical, practical, sophisticated in his knowledge of the pleasures and vices of ancient Rome. Apart from Tacitus' brief account concerning Petronius, we know nothing for certain about the origin or reception of his book. And the fragment that remains has often been misinterpreted.

One major problem in reading *The Satyricon* in English is that many translations, particularly those of the nineteenth and early twentieth centuries, are corrupt. Some translators, because of prudery, have cut from the text whole portions that they consider offensive. Others have interpolated sections that are clearly not Petronius'; these additions, for the most part, err in the opposite direction: they are passages of deliberately and crudely obscene material that surpass in indelicacy the author's refined erotic language. For our time, the great translation of *The Satyricon* is by William Arrowsmith, whose vigorous, honest, and sensitive version closely approximates the qualities of the Latin original. (Readers of Latin may examine with confidence the modern scholarly editions by Alfred Ernout and E. T. Sage, or the older but still useful edition by W. D. Lowe.) But the reader must be cautioned about poor English translations that markedly alter the content or mis-construe the tone of the Petronius model. These inadequate translations, for the most part, cut out all or most of the poetical selections. A simple test to determine whether or not a given translation is faithful to the source is to check Eumolpus' long verse passage entitled "The Civil War"; accurate translations will include the whole passage, although the poem, allusive and rhetorically pompous, may seem tedious to some readers.

In its context, Eumolpus' poem may either imitate or parody heroic style. Petronius delights to parody conventions of language or literary form. The title of his work has been variously translated as "medley" (from *satura,* a mixed dish) or as "satyr-book" (from *saturika,* that is, concerned with satyrs and hence lecherous). From the fragment that we possess, *The Satyricon* may be taken in both senses, as a Roman "satire"—a *farrago* of mixed stories using a multitude of styles—and as a book of comic-erotic adventures pleasing to satyrs. Within the main plot concerning the adventures of Encolpius are interwoven many stories or parts of stories, in the manner of popular Greek tales (or of their imitated Roman counterparts, of which Apuleius' early second century *The Golden Asse* is a famous example). The most remarkable of the stories is Eumolpus' "The Widow of Ephesus," a cynical narrative that has served many later writers and dramatists including—to choose English authors — George Chapman and Christopher Fry. Although Eumolpus' story may be extracted from the plot as a perfect short piece, in the context of the action (Encolpius, Gito, and Eumolpus are aboard the ship of their enemies Lichas and Tryphaena), the anecdote takes on additional ironical meanings. Similarly, the stories that abound within stories of *The Satyricon* acquire richer tones of irony, satire, or comedy, depending upon the context at the moment. Petronius' chief device is parody, either to amuse or ridicule, and the stories furnish ample subjects for literary and social burlesques.

Although *The Satyricon* belongs to the genre of Menippean satire— a mixture of verse with prose, philosophy with low comedy, romance with realism—the word *satire,* as it is commonly understood, should not be applied to the book. Troubled by Petronius' outspoken and often coarsely erotic subject matter, some prudish commentators have attempted to apologize for the work on the grounds of its supposed moral satire. To be sure, the picture of Roman manners and morals that the author provides is one of vulgarity and excess. But Petronius is by no means a Christian moralist— nor, for that matter, a moralist in the stamp of Juvenal. Far from ridiculing the corruption of contemporary morals, he approaches his subject with amused tolerance. Even the great scene of Trimalchio's banquet, widely regarded as a keen satire upon Roman debauchery, may be seen in a different light as a comic burlesque upon vulgar ostentation. Surely, the tone of Petronius' irony is sprightly rather than censorious. If the author has a moral argument to demonstrate, he skillfully conceals it.

Similarly, any notion that *The Satyricon* is intended as a social satire—one concerned with the degradation of Roman culture—must be examined cautiously in terms of Petronius' moral ambivalence. Although his major characters are clearly homosexual (some are less clearly bi-sexual) and parasitical, they are not treated as objects of ridicule; instead, they are shown as amusing rogues, foolish or crafty, successful or unfortunate. The main character, Encolpius (whose name is roughly translated as "the crotch") is easily misled, especially by the guiles of his homosexual partner, the sixteen-year-old, narcissistic Gito; Encolpius is cheated and abused by his rival for Gito's affections, the devious Ascyltus; another rival is the old pederast, Eumolpus, the poet. In the world of *The Satyricon,* homosexual intrigues are taken as a norm and are treated casually. As a youth Trimalchio, we learn, began to earn his fortune through his sexual compliance with his master. To be even-handed, Petronius treats heterosexual relations with the same casual tolerance. His women are as sexually assertive as the men. Quartilla, Tryphaena, Circe, Chrysis, Corax—all are aggressive, earthy, lusty types quite the equal of their lovers. Yet the reader should not conclude from the evidence of Petronius' story that he judges Roman society harshly. Rather, he takes men and women as he finds them, observes their habits with cool, realistic detachment, and—in the section dealing with obscenity, following the Circe episode —refutes the charges that his book is obscene. The matter, of course, rests ultimately with the reader, who may regard Petronius' fragment either as a work of social criticism or of mock-epic romance.

Judged from the second point of view, *The Satyricon* describes the fortunes of Encolpius, who has apparently aroused the wrath of the sex-god Priapus. Throughout the book, the god's vengeance pursues his hapless victim. Against his will, Encolpius must take part in the orgy of Quartilla, priestess of the cult of Priapus; with Circe he is humiliated by his impotence. Always he tries to free himself from blame, but only manages to offend Priapus more seriously (as when he kills a pet goose sacred to the god). Encolpius' adventures may be understood as a parody of Odysseus' in the Homeric epic. Just as Odysseus outraged the god Poseidon and suffered from mistreatment as a consequence, so Encolpius apparently is tormented by Priapus. If the comparison drawn from the fragment is apt, the complete *Satyricon* must have been a prose mock-epic of great scope and richness, in our time recalling Joyce's *Ulysses* (1922). Modeled upon *The Odyssey,* both books parody heroic and literary conventions; are replete with puns, verbal games, and innovative stylistic techniques; and, through myth and symbolic action, finally create their own moral universe.

Leslie B. Mittleman

THE SCARLET LETTER

Type of work: Novel
Author: Nathaniel Hawthorne (1804-1864)
Type of plot: Psychological romance
Time of plot: Early days of the Massachusetts Colony
Locale: Boston
First published: 1850

The Scarlet Letter is Hawthorne's masterpiece and his most profound explora-
tion of sin, alienation, and spiritual regeneration. The novel traces the effects—
social, moral, psychological, and spiritual—of Hester Prynne's adulterous relation-
ship with the Reverend Arthur Dimmesdale on four people: the lovers themselves,
their daughter, Pearl, and Roger Chillingworth, Hester's husband.

Since it was first published in 1850, *The Scarlet Letter* has never been out
of print, nor indeed out of favor with literary critics. It is inevitably included
in listings of the five or ten greatest American novels. Considered the best of
Nathaniel Hawthorne's writings, it may also be the most typical—the strongest statement of his recurrent themes, an excellent example of his craftsmanship.

The main thematic emphasis in *The Scarlet Letter,* as in most of Hawthorne's work, is on sin and its effects upon both the individual and society.
It is frequently noted that Hawthorne's preoccupation with sin springs from
the Puritan-rooted culture in which he lived, and from his awareness of two
of his own ancestors who had presided over bloody persecutions during the
Salem witchcraft trials. It is difficult for us, in our more permissive century,
to conceive of the heavy import which seventeenth century New Englanders
placed upon transgression of the moral code. As Yvor Winters has pointed
out, the Puritans, believing in predestination, viewed the commission of *any*
sin as evidence of the sinner's corruption and foreordained damnation. However, the harsh determinism and moralism of those early years had softened
somewhat by Nathaniel Hawthorne's day; furthermore, he had worked out,
perhaps during the twelve years he spent in contemplation and semi-isolation,
his own notions about man's will and his nature. Thus *The Scarlet Letter*
proves him closer to Paul Tillich than to Cotton Mather or Jonathan Edwards.
Like Tillich, Hawthorne saw sin not as an *act* but as a *state*—that which
modern existentialists refer to as alienation, and which Tillich describes as a
three-fold separation from God, other men, and self. This alienation needs
no fire and brimstone as consequence; it is in itself a hell.

There is a certain irony in the way in which this concept is worked out
in *The Scarlet Letter.* Hester Prynne's pregnancy forces her sin to public
view, and she is compelled to wear the scarlet "A" as a symbol of her adultery.
Yet although she is apparently isolated from normal association with "decent"

folk, Hester, having come to terms with her sin, is inwardly reconciled to God and self; and she ministers to the needy among her townspeople, reconciling herself with others until some observe that her "A" now stands for "Able." On the other hand, Arthur Dimmesdale, her secret lover, and Roger Chillingworth, her secret husband, move freely in society and even enjoy prestige, Dimmesdale as a beloved pastor, Chillingworth as a respected physician. But Dimmesdale's secret guilt gnaws so deeply inside him that he views himself with scorn as a hypocrite, and he is unable to make his peace with his God or to feel at ease with his fellow man. For his part, Chillingworth has permitted vengeance so to permeate his spirit that his alienation is absolute; he refers to himself as a "fiend," unable to impart forgiveness or change his profoundly evil path. His is the unpardonable sin—unpardonable not because God will not pardon, but because his own nature has become so depraved that he cannot repent or accept forgiveness.

Hawthorne clearly distinguishes between sins of passion and those of principle. Finally even Dimmesdale, traditional Puritan though he is, becomes aware of the difference:

> We are not, Hester, the worst sinners in the world. There is one worse than even the polluted priest! That old man's revenge has been blacker than my sin. He has violated, in cold blood, the sanctity of a human heart. Thou and I, Hester, never did so.

Always more concerned with the consequences than the cause of sin, Hawthorne anticipated Sigmund Freud's theories of the effects of guilt to a remarkable extent. Hester, whose guilt is openly known, grows through her suffering into an extraordinarily compassionate and understanding woman, a complete person who is able to come to terms with life—including sin. Dimmesdale, who yearns for the relief of confession, but hides his guilt to safeguard his role as pastor, is devoured internally. Again like Freud, Hawthorne recognized that spiritual turmoil may produce physical distress. Dimmesdale's well-being diminishes, and eventually he dies from no apparent cause other than continual emotional stress.

The Scarlet Letter reflects a number of Hawthorne's shorter works. Dimmesdale reminds one of Young Goodman Brown who, having once glimpsed the darker nature of mankind, must forevermore view humanity as corrupt and hypocritical; and of Parson Hooper in "The Minister's Black Veil," who continues to perform the duties of his calling with eloquence and compassion, but is forever separated from the company of men by the veil which he wears as a symbol of secret sin. Chillingworth is essentially like Ethan Brand, the limeburner who found the unpardonable sin in his own heart: "The sin of an intellect that triumphed over the sense of brotherhood with man and reverence for God, and sacrificed everything to its mighty claims!"

Hawthorne's craftsmanship is splendidly demonstrated in *The Scarlet Letter*. The structure is carefully unified, with three crucial scenes at the beginning, middle, and end of the action taking place on the scaffold. The scarlet "A" itself is entwined into the narrative repeatedly, as a symbol of sin or of shame, as a reminder of Hester's ability with the needle and her Ableness with people, and in Dimmesdale's case, as evidence of the searing effects of secret guilt. Several times there is forewarning or suggestion which is fulfilled later in the book: for example, notice is made that Pearl, the impish child of Hester and Dimmesdale, seems to lack complete humanity, perhaps because she has never known great sorrow; at the end of the story, when Dimmesdale dies, we are told that, "as [Pearl's] tears fell upon her father's cheek, they were the pledge that she would grow up amid human joy and sorrow, nor forever do battle with the world, but be a woman in it."

Hawthorne's skill as symbolist is fully in evidence. As one critic has noted, there is hardly a concrete object in the book that does not do double duty as a symbol: the scarlet letter; the sunlight which eludes Hester; the scaffold of public notice; the armor in which Hester's shame and Pearl's elfishness are distorted and magnified—the list could go on indefinitely. The four main characters themselves also serve as central symbols in this, the greatest allegory of a master allegorist.

Sally Buckner

THE SCHOOL FOR HUSBANDS

Type of work: Drama
Author: Molière (Jean Baptiste Poquelin, 1622-1673)
Type of plot: Social satire
Time of plot: Seventeenth century
Locale: Paris
First presented: 1661

The School for Husbands, *Molière's first full-length play, was a great popular success and a favorite of Louis XIV. Utilizing a famous Roman play for its basic plot, the playwright created a piquant, high-spirited comic view of Parisian society in his day.*

Molière created something new in comedy. Farce, satiric comedy, and didactic comedy all had been known before Molière, but he invented a kind of comedy that rests on a double vision, of the right and wrong together, of the normal and abnormal side by side. He saw not only that affectation is, as Fielding said later, the true source of the ridiculous, but he also saw moral issues behind the comedy. Molière did not consider his comedies as literature; they were written to be performed, and no more. *The School for Husbands* was a great success when it was first performed, and it is both funny and filled with insights into the human condition.

The plot of *The School for Husbands* goes back ultimately to the Roman comic playwright Terence, with incidents which may be traced to Boccaccio, Lope de Vega, and others. The brothers Ariste and Sganarelle bring up two girls to be their wives. Sganarelle, the jealous taskmaster, originally played by Molière, is the one who is deceived by his tricky protégée, whereas the older but kindly Ariste reaps the reward of happiness. Some of Molière's enemies said that the play was prurient and indecent by its suggestions, as well as irreligious because of its attitude toward marriage. But the fun is aimed less at institutions than at foolish individuals.

Much of the humor in *The School for Husbands,* as in most of Molière's plays, comes from an incongruous mixing of the intellectual or mechanical— today we might say the fake—with the spontaneous and genuine. Theories of marriage, theories on how to control wives, can only be laughable because human nature cannot be ruled by theory. The characters in the play seem to be observing themselves, even commenting upon their own follies by their action and wit, and by a certain overplaying of their attitudes. The characters seem to recognize that they are foolish and to revel in the realization.

The School for Husbands marks great progress in Molière's development as an artist. As in his earlier plays, he draws heavily both on the Italian *commedia dell'arte* form and on the traditions of French farce; thus the comic situation of a young heroine kept under lock and key by a jealous, tyrannical guardian who is inevitably duped by his charge, was hardly new in 1661. But in Molière's hands the play far surpasses its antecedents in quality and subtlety; the stock comic characters and standard plot achieve thematic significance as integrated elements of the play as a whole, which is inspired by the playwright's social and moral vision. *The School for Husbands* also exhibits Molière's growing sophistication in matters of style and structure. He had already shown his mastery of the twelve-syllable rhymed couplet (Alexandrine) form in *The Romantic Ladies;* and in *The School for Husbands* his highly polished verse raises the play above the level of simple farce, suggesting the serious intent beneath its comic surface. Likewise, Molière constantly reiterates the theme of duality and contrast through the use of the double plot framework of a pair of brothers and a pair of sisters, producing continuous parallels, antitheses, and dramatic ironies for full comic effect.

THE SCHOOL FOR SCANDAL

Type of work: Drama
Author: Richard Brinsley Sheridan (1751-1816)
Type of plot: Comedy of manners
Time of plot: Eighteenth century
Locale: London
First presented: 1777

> The School for Scandal *contains elements of Restoration comedy—notably, its humor without its bawdiness—as well as the usual sentimentalism of the comedy of sensibility. There are two plots: Lady Sneerwell's love for Charles Surface and her scandalous tales about Lady Teazle and the latter's relations with Joseph Surface, and Sir Oliver Surface's tests to discover the worthier of his two nephews.*

Three plays of the eighteenth century have established themselves permanently in world theater, and they were written within four years of one another by a pair of Irishmen; they are Goldsmith's *She Stoops to Conquer* and Sheridan's *The Rivals* and *The School for Scandal.* Statesman, orator, wit, and almost incidentally playwright, Sheridan was known in his day as one of the most brilliant and versatile of men. His plays were all written before he was thirty, after which he devoted himself primarily to politics, which he considered the true gentleman's calling. Sheridan's chief ambition is reputed to have been no more than to be the foremost gentleman of his time and to shine in the finest society. Because he knew the society of the day so well, he was able to satirize it in his comedies with unusual brilliance.

His introduction to society was in Bath. He did not try to attract attention to himself by being different from other people; he thought it would be more subtly humorous to be just like everybody else. He did everything that was being done by the best people, only he took care to do each thing better than it could be done by anybody else in England. At the age of twenty-one, he eloped with Miss Elizabeth Ann Linley, a singer, the most beautiful girl in England. He had never earned money and had no profession, and he could think of no better way to earn a lot of money than by writing a play. So, at the age of twenty-three, he wrote *The Rivals.* Taking the traditional materials of the theater of the day, he put them together better than anybody else; the plot and characters were familiar, but the dialogue that held them together was brilliant. Two years later, he surpassed his first triumph with *The School for Scandal,* a more firmly built and mature play, wittier—if not quite as humorous or warm—than *The Rivals.*

The School for Scandal is composed of two plays, called earlier "The Slanderers" and "The Teazles," which Sheridan joined together. Occasionally, the joints that hold the play together might be noticeable, but the wit and satire, and the triumph of the screen scene, far outweigh any minor flaws. The scandal scenes and the Lady Teazle seduction plot are reminiscent of Restoration comedy, as are the witty servant, Trip, and the dialogue. One of the Surface brothers is a sentimental hero, a rake reformed, at the same time that the other is a satiric presentation of the man of sentiment in eighteenth century drama. The Charles-Maria love affair and Sir Oliver, the benevolent and sentimental old gentleman, and Rowley, the faithful family servant, are true to the sentimental comedy prevalent since the day of Steele. Various scenes of the first three acts frequently represent simultaneous action, occasionally confusing to the audience. But the screen scene weaves together all of the different threads of the complicated plot in a dazzling piece of theater. Sheridan, despite his reputation for procrastination and irregularity, labored diligently to polish the lines and wit of the play. He scribbled at the end of the final page: "Finished at last, thank God!"

The School for Scandal was given for the first time May 8th, 1777. People passing the theater were startled by a sudden roar or shout which seemed far too great to have come from the audience in the theater. It was the applause which greeted the falling of the screen in the fifth act. Sheridan's triumph was complete. The play made a fortune and the king came to see it.

In writing *The School for Scandal,* Sheridan allowed himself none of the license which the Restoration dramatists had allowed themselves. Although the wit was pointed, it avoided the suggestiveness and malice in which previous comedies had indulged, and the antics of Lady Sneerwell and her friends probably would have been more earthily scandalous if Congreve had written the play. Nevertheless, it is impossible not to note the influence of Congreve in the characterizations, the situations, and the dialogue of the play. True to his philosophy, Sheridan took the standard forms and perfected them to a level beyond the reach of anybody else, bringing the comedy of manners to its highest perfection. *The School for Scandal* may very well be the most popular comedy in the English language, revived frequently as a costume piece or in an updated costume and decor, and always winning appreciation for its wit and characterization and intriguing plot. The dialogue, especially of characters such as Snake and Lady Sneerwell, sounds amazingly modern to twentieth century ears, and the parts of Lady Teazle and Charles Surface remain superb acting roles, as coveted today as they were two hundred years ago.

The idea of a "scandalous college" occurred to Sheridan some five years before he wrote the play, in connection with his own experiences in Bath. In *The School for Scandal,* Sheridan takes on the fashionable poseurs of the day and reveals them for what they are, exposing their shallowness and pettiness and the lack of real intelligence behind their backbiting and gossip. Seldom has scandal-mongering and petty gossip been rendered more entertaining than in this play. The difference between fake sentiment, as illustrated by Joseph Surface, and the real thing, though unexpressed, is perfectly illustrated by Charles Surface in the auction scene and the reconciliation at the end of the play between Charles and his uncle. But hypocrisy is not the main theme of the drama, as, for example, in *Tartuffe*; it is but one of many targets for Sheridan's satire. The inability of society gossips to love is sharply contrasted with the genuine love that exists between Maria and Charles.

The end of Sheridan's life was filled with disasters. The new theater at Drury Lane, in which he owned a large share, burned, and in 1812 his seat in Parliament was lost to him. Ill health, debt, the forgetfulness of friends, and other troubles weighed upon him and hastened his end. When he died in 1816, his country suddenly recognized the importance of his achievements and gave him an almost royal funeral, with burial in the Poets' Corner of Westminster Abbey.

Bruce D. Reeves

THE SCHOOL FOR WIVES

Type of work: Drama
Author: Molière (Jean Baptiste Poquelin, 1622-1673)
Type of plot: Social satire
Time of plot: Seventeenth century
Locale: France
First presented: 1662

The School for Wives was the most successful of Molière's plays during his own lifetime. Although based on a common comedic subject, the play also echoes Molière's own situation—he was married to a beautiful actress half his age—and this probably helps to account for the greater depth of characterization, especially in the innocent girl, Agnès, and her foolish, sad guardian, Arnolphe.

The School for Wives was probably the most popular success of Molière's controversial career. Molière himself played Arnolphe, the middle-aged theorist of marriage, and Armande, his bride of less than a year, was the ingenue, Agnès. Although the motif of the play is an old one and appears in Italian and Spanish tales, it is a fact that the problem of the ardent middle-aged lover and the bride half his age whom he has trained from girlhood, was Molière's own. Perhaps this is why when in the last act Arnolphe pleads with the girl for her love, the comedy seems to drop away, exposing an agonized and aging man speaking desperate and moving words. The play is very funny, but it rings with truth and psychological realism beneath the humor and absurdity.

The School for Wives was Molière's first five-act comedy in verse, and generally its tone is realistic; the farcical action is confined, for the most part, to the servants. Although influenced by the traditional French farce and the Italian *commedia dell'arte,* the play is essentially a comedy of character, with an overlay of the comedy of manners. The theme is the old one that love conquers all and that the heart will always understand its own desires and will recognize the heart and soul destined to be joined with it. In an age of arranged marriages and subsequent philandering, Molière's conviction that marriage should be based on love would have been radical if it had not been integrated into the absurdities of the comedy.

The subsidiary theme of the play is that a young woman has a right to decent education commensurate with her intelligence and curiosity, and that any attempt to keep her ignorant is in contempt of her privileges as a human being. At the beginning of the play, Arnolphe sympathetically presents his position: he is so exasperated by feminine coquetry that he feels the only safety is in marrying a fool. His greatest mistake is in carrying his attitude to ridiculous and wrongheaded extremes. With the single-mindedness of a pedant, he constructs a complete scheme for rearing the girl in a convent from the age of four, so that she will be entirely untrained in the ways of the world.

His pride in his scheme warns the audience of his eventual and inevitable downfall.

The play is witty and amusing, but contains a surprisingly small amount of action. Mostly, it consists of speeches, many of them long and drawn out; the audience hears about the action more than it witnesses it. But to Molière's contemporaries, such a comedy was subject to certain rules of decorum; all violent action was banned from the stage and the audience's imagination filled in what was necessary. But, although the play is often static, it is never dull; *The School for Wives* is one of Molière's most delightful comedies.

Agnès is one of the most fascinating characters in any Molière comedy; if she sins, it is through lamblike ignorance and innocence, and her gradual awakening is a marvel of character portrayal. The revelation of her slowly developing temperament, all the stronger for its innocence and naïveté, is as touching as it is charming. At the same time, the pedant's personality undergoes a transformation, for he finds that he discovers, in spite of himself, the true nature of love. He, who had dismissed love and all of the accompanying nonsense as beneath him, finds that he is hopelessly in love with the girl he created. He has no choice but to eat his words and suffer the consequences of his stupidity and blindness. His awkward gropings toward the manners and words of love become both his own punishment and the delight of the audience.

The moral point of the play rests in the fact that Arnolphe deliberately sought to confine a human being, to unnaturally limit her development. Under the pretense of keeping her "simple," he made her into a charming freak. The struggle is between the spontaneous and the rigid, a struggle which lends itself perfectly to comedy. The more Arnolphe treats life mechanically, the more his efforts backfire, for life reacts spontaneously to make the outcome of his elaborate schemes the opposite of his intentions. Always, in Molière's plays, Nature is held up as the better guide than authority; human nature and human emotions must be allowed to take their own course. It is always the extreme position which causes unhappiness and eventual disaster. If human beings would avoid going off on absurd hobbyhorses, life would be smoother and more joyous for everybody concerned. But, of course, it would be duller, for it is this all-too-human tendency of men to embrace extreme points of view and absurd attitudes that provides Molière with his most brilliant comic creations.

Molière uses several clever devices to enliven his essentially simple plot. One is the fact that Arnolphe has taken the name of de la Souche. This allows Horace to make him the confidant of successive attempts to get Agnès out of old de la Souche's clutches. The complications of this misunderstanding are both absurd and hilarious. Another delightful and clever contrivance is the grotesque scurry of the denouement. The final scene of Act V is filled with rapid-fire patter in which Chrysalde and Oronte, Horace's father, newly arrived on the scene with a person called Enrique, who has spent the last fourteen years in America, explain to all concerned that the rustic Agnès is actually Chrysalde's niece and the daughter of this Enrique. Enrique is a perfect and totally implausible *deus ex machina,* standing by dumb as a fish until just before the curtain falls to remark in three lines that he has no doubts about the identity of his daughter and consents to her marrying Horace. It is a daring and absurd conclusion to the play, but it provides the necessary happy ending for the young lovers, and leaves Arnolphe sadder but wiser.

There is much excellent comedy in *The School for Wives,* the frenzy of Arnolphe, the leg-pulling by Chrysalde, an absurd notary babbling in legal jargon, the saucy maid Georgette, and the irony of the old lover trying to win the girl he tried to lock away from all eyes but his own. Chrysalde, in particular, is a satirist with a sense of humor, who tries with a long merry tirade to laugh Arnolphe out of his obsession. The contrasts and contradictions of human behavior provide the basic, and often subtle, humor of the play, but Molière is never above farce, as in the opening scene when Alain and Georgette first refuse to let their master through the gate and then quarrel about which of them is to do it. As is often the case in Molière's comedies, as well as in real life, the people in the play assume different guises, they adopt different faces as they need them, they remove their masks and then invent new ones. The cloak of politeness falls, and the chaos beneath is hilariously revealed.

Bruce D. Reeves

THE SCORNFUL LADY

Type of work: Drama
Authors: Francis Beaumont (1585?-1616) and John Fletcher (1579-1625)
Type of plot: Comedy of manners
Time of plot: Early seventeenth century
Locale: London
First presented: 1613-1617

The Scornful Lady *was the most popular of Beaumont and Fletcher's comedies during the Restoration period, because it playfully combined a number of famous theatrical ingredients. The main plot, Elder Loveless' pursuit of the sophisticated and independent Lady, has strong elements of the battle of the sexes; the subplot, the gulling of a usurer by a young prodigal who repairs his ruined fortune by marriage to a rich and beautiful widow, was to become a hearty commonplace of English comedy.*

The team of Beaumont and Fletcher left behind a rich legacy. While they were living, they enjoyed immense popularity—a popularity that surpassed even Shakespeare's. Court records kept of performances indicate that for every one of Shakespeare's plays, ten of Beaumont and Fletcher's were being given. *The Scornful Lady* shared in this popularity. Not only was *The Scornful Lady* a hit with the Elizabethan audiences and twentieth century critics, it was also, and perhaps more importantly, a hit with the audience of the Restoration period. John Dryden in *An Essay of Dramatic Poesy* (1668) revealed just how popular when he wrote, "Their plays are now the most pleasant and frequent entertainments of the stage; two of theirs being acted through the year for one of Shakespeare's or Jonson's." Although some of the comedies of the Beaumont and Fletcher canon underwent alterations, *The Scornful Lady* remained unscathed and was produced between 1660 and 1719 at least twenty-seven times.

Beaumont and Fletcher in *The Scornful Lady* set the stage for a number of techniques that were to be used frequently in Restoration comedy. When the Elder Loveless feigns death in *The Scornful Lady,* he prepares the way for the frequently-used stock situation of Restoration comedy in which a lover pretends a physical ailment in order to gain the sympathy of a servant or mistress. The disregard for morality; the concept of marriage as imprisonment for men, and a release from chastity for women; and wit, in the form of quick repartee and double entendre that appeared in Restoration comedy had a precedent set in *The Scornful Lady.* It is perhaps the spicy flavor of the wit of *The Scornful Lady* that made it most popular.

It would appear that the only characteristic of *The Scornful Lady* that was not borrowed by the Restoration comedy was its setting, which has little of the local color, attention to realistic details, and allusions to contemporary people and places found in the comedy of manners written by the Restoration

2020 The Scornful Lady/BEAUMONT and FLETCHER

dramatists. That the Restoration dramatists borrowed as much as they did is a boon to the reader of today. If it had not been for *The Scornful Lady,* we might not today be able to read and enjoy that famous china closet scene in William Wycherley's *The Country Wife.*

THE SCOTTISH CHIEFS

Type of work: Novel
Author: Jane Porter (1776-1850)
Type of plot: Historical romance
Time of plot: 1296-1305
Locale: Scotland, France, England
First published: 1810

Porter's desire in The Scottish Chiefs. Or. The Life of Sir William Wallace *was to write the story of a great national hero who was also a Christian hero. Today the goodness and nobility of William Wallace may seem overdrawn, but the story moves with vigor and momentum.*

Historically inaccurate and filled with diction extravagant by modern standards, *The Scottish Chiefs* is nonetheless a work of interest today, for it vividly portrays the political and military milieu of late thirteenth century and early fourteenth century Scotland. Jane Porter studied much literature about Sir William Wallace, Scotland's national hero, beginning with the heroic couplets written about him by Blind Henry the Minstrel in the fifteenth century. She used the information thus gathered to create a fast-paced medieval romance focusing on Wallace's life. The emphasis in the novel is on Wallace's military exploits in defense of Scotland and on his chivalry.

In a series of plots and counterplots, battles and retreats, Porter pictures Wallace as a military genius. With the help of other Scottish chiefs and their families and patriotic common folk, the young man thwarts the English who would rule Scotland. He knows when to run from the enemy, as evidenced in his decisions to hide in trees, behind waterfalls, and among crags and thickets in the deep glens. He also knows how to fight. His troops, although greatly outnumbered, win several battles because of his tactical strategy and his ability to inspire a fervor for justice in his soldiers. Notable among his successes is the defeat of thirty thousand Englishmen under Lord Warden by five thousand Scots.

Besides military prowess, Sir William possesses other virtues characteristic of the medieval knight. He is merciful to his enemies. When, for example, his armies invade the English countryside, he restrains them from murdering the people and laying waste the land; he insists that the soldiers merely replace goods taken by the English from Scotland. Wallace is also protective of women. Not only does he twice rescue Lady Helen, first from de Soulis and then from de Valence, but also, to maintain the honor of Helen's family, he suffers in silence the lies which her stepmother tells about him.

All in all, Porter's Wallace is an exemplary man, no discredit to the real Wallace, to whom Scots still pay homage.

THE SEA OF GRASS

Type of work: Novel
Author: Conrad Richter (1890-1968)
Type of plot: Regional romance
Time of plot: 1885-1910
Locale: The Southwest
First published: 1936

The Sea of Grass, *a sweeping drama of the cattle-grazing country in America at the end of the nineteenth century, conveys vividly the atmosphere of the space and freedom of the West. The novel is unusual in its championing of the large landholders over the homesteaders. Indeed, Colonel Jim Brewton stands as a kind of epic hero in the book, the last of a dying breed in the face of the petty encroachments of civilization.*

The Sea of Grass is a very good "Western," as well as a significant contribution to the naturalistic tradition in American literature. Employing an almost Homeric mode of narration and description, Richter develops a view of the relationship between land and human personality which is quite reminiscent of Norris and Steinbeck.

In addition to the three main characters, there is the New Mexico prairie itself, which assumes an almost personal presence in the novel. The moral quality of the Colonel, Lutie, and Brock is revealed as they each establish their own particular relation to "the sea of grass." In the Colonel, long grappling with and empathy for the land have produced immense courage, endurance, and directness. Lutie's own vitality and courage are, when tested by the range, found to spring from shallower sources. She must impose her own designs on frontier reality in order to survive psychologically. Ultimately she cannot endure and escapes to "civilization," the essential qualities of which are embodied in Brice Chamberlain. Brock, who in effect has two fathers, is destroyed by his inability to resolve the conflict between nature (Colonel Brewton) and civilization (Judge Chamberlain).

This conflict is also played out in the struggle between the Cross B and the nesters. Chamberlain, with his cultivated abstractions, pictures the Colonel as merely greedy. In fact, the old pioneer wishes to protect the land from despoliation by the rootless, opportunistic farmers. He refuses to sympathize with their very real plight simply because he knows that the land bears them no such sympathy. The drought which drives them away proves the absurdity of Chamberlain's political machinations and vindicates the Brewton ethic of Stoic patience.

Richter envisions nature as a beautiful yet terrifying Presence which radically determines human destiny. In the novel, he communicates this view by giving the tale overtones of Greek epic poetry. The narrator, Hal Brewton, sings of a forgotten age of heroes. Like Homer, he repeats certain key poetic formulae again and again. Colonel Brewton, though a plain citizen, is really a New Mexico king, and Lutie his venerated queen. Like classical myth, the plot of *The Sea of Grass* moves in great temporal circles, with new sons emerging to assume the old roles in the same fate-controlled drama.

THE SEA WOLF

Type of work: Novel
Author: Jack London (1876-1916)
Type of plot: Adventure romance
Time of plot: 1904
Locale: Pacific Ocean, Bering Sea
First published: 1904

The plot of The Sea Wolf *becomes progressively unbelievable, but this defect is overcome by the visceral description of shipboard life and the energetically written action scenes. The conflict between the erratic, dangerous, animalistic captain, Wolf Larsen, and the delicate, civilized, sympathetic Maud Brewster assumes an almost allegorical quality.*

The Sea Wolf, published in 1904, is still an exciting yarn; it can also be read as an allegory of the deepest hopes and fears of an age. The hopes were that mankind was becoming more spiritual, that his moral fiber was becoming stronger, his institutions enlightened, and his tastes elevated. The fears were that man's animal nature might frustrate his aspirations and that he might slip backward into a bestial state where his violence, greed, and lust would make a shambles of civilization. Such hopes and fears were a culmination of people's preoccupation with the theories of Charles Darwin (referred to by Wolf and Humphrey), who had shown man to be a product of evolution and a creature of nature.

Jack London was well prepared to write about this tension between man's upward and downward possibilities. Raised in a knockabout way in the San Francisco Bay area, he was on his own at fifteen, a drinking man and oyster pirate by sixteen, and a crewman on a sealing ship at seventeen. He knew the seamy side of life. He was also an avid reader, a man capable of strong romantic attachments, and a worker for social and economic justice. He aspired to a finer life.

In the novel Wolf Larsen represents the primitive and feral in man and Maud Brewster the spiritual. They stand, as Humphrey observes, at opposite ends of the ladder of evolution; both tug at him. Humphrey rejects Wolf's philosophy that life is a meaningless and brutal struggle, but he is toughened in body and mind by Wolf's harsh regimen. Maud's beauty and idealism fill Humphrey with love, tenderness, and chivalric courage. We may conclude that London was hopeful about man's future. Amoral Wolf's fierce vitality slowly ebbs. Ethereal Maud, brought at last to safety by Humphrey, unites with him in a chaste embrace. In this symbolic union Humphrey as modern man rejects the cruel and brutish and dedicates himself to what is saving and civilized.

THE SEAGULL

Type of work: Drama
Author: Anton Chekhov (1860-1904)
Type of plot: Impressionistic realism
Time of plot: Nineteenth century
Locale: Russia
First presented: 1896

The Sea Gull *was based on a seemingly trifling incident in the playwright's life. One afternoon Chekhov saw his friend, Ilya Levitan, the landscape painter, shoot a flying seagull. Later, feeling scorned by the woman he loved, Levitan threw the dead bird at her feet and threatened to kill himself.* The Sea Gull *is perhaps the most elaborate and realistic analysis of the life of the artist ever presented in dramatic form.*

The first production of *The Seagull* on October 17th, 1896, was a total disaster. The critics dismissed it as inept and even absurd and Chekhov, who had fled the theater before the final curtain, accepted their verdict. But one audience member, critic-playwright Vladimir Nemirovich-Danchenko, did not agree and determined to mount a second production of the play. Danchenko, who was at that time organizing the Moscow Art Theatre with Constantine Stanislavski, convinced his partner that the new Chekhov play had great potential and then talked the playwright into allowing *The Seagull* a second chance. Their production of the play in 1898 was an enormous artistic, critical, and commercial success and led to that collaboration of playwright and theater which established the Moscow Art Theatre as one of the world's greatest, and stimulated the writing of Chekhov's last three dramatic masterpieces, *Uncle Vanya* (1899), *The Three Sisters* (1901) and *The Cherry Orchard* (1904).

But, for all of the controversy provoked by the play, it is the most conventional of Chekhov's major plays. *The Seagull* is structured around romantic triangles—Arkadina-Trigorin-Nina, Konstantin-Nina-Trigorin, and, to a lesser extent, Masha-Konstantin-Medvedenko—activated by spite and jealousy, composed of incidents characteristic of popular melodrama—a failed suicide, a seduction and abandonment, a dead child, a successful suicide—and climaxed by an "obligatory scene" in which the main characters meet and resolve their conflicts in a face-to-face confrontation.

Chekhov's handling of this "orthodox" plot, however, is revolutionary and previews the formula he perfected in his last three masterworks. Konstantin's two suicide attempts and the melodramatic consequences of Nina's affair with Trigorin happen offstage. Chekhov "deformalizes" the play by undercutting the most intense moments with trivial details and apparently arbitrary bits of stage business—small talk, irrelevant comments and interjections, unexpected comical gestures, characters standing with their backs to the audience, and a game of "Lotto" while Konstantin prepares his suicide.

These deviations from traditional techniques are not merely novel stage gimmicks, however, but reflect Chekhov's basic dramatic and thematic purposes. He was not interested in theatrical action or excitement as such, but in the *effects* such incidents have on his people. Reality, he felt, does not consist of a series of dramatic climaxes, but is, rather, a mundane process of day-to-day living in which the crucial events happen unobtrusively in the background. The important thing, therefore, is to explore and dramatize their continuing effects on the characters. Thus, even in the last plays, Chekhov does not abandon conventional dramatic structure but mutes it in order to concentrate on what he believed to be more important: real people living real lives.

The Seagull does, however, differ thematically from his later plays; it is the work in which Chekhov makes his definitive statement about the nature of creativity and the role of the artist in society. As both a practicing physician and a creative artist, Chekhov had experienced great difficulty in reconciling the objective, practical world of medicine with the subjective, aesthetic environment of literature and theater. He had already analyzed the problem extensively in his fiction—notably in "A Boring Story" (1889), "The Grasshopper" (1892), and "The House with an Attic" (1896), but *The Seagull* was his final, comprehensive exploration of the subject. Thus, it has a thematic clarity and rhetorical directness that differentiates it from its successors.

This is not to say that *The Seagull* is more simple or obvious than the other works. The four major characters are exceedingly complicated; their relations to one another are subtle, ambiguous, and contradictory, and, although they are given ample opportunity to dramatize these complexities, it is for the audience to attempt the synthesis. Moreover, as completely individualized as the characters are, they embody basic attitudes toward life and art which are crucial to a final understanding and appreciation of the play.

Konstantin Treplev has three roles that he cannot reconcile—son, lover, and creative artist. His feelings about his mother are deep and ambivalent; he passionately craves her affection, yet he finds himself in an unequal competition with her; he desperately wants her to approve his creative efforts, yet consciously advocates artistic notions that are antithetical to hers; he is fully aware of her egotism, pettiness, selfishness, and cruelty, yet he clings to a vision of her as a tender, considerate young mother.

Konstantin's relationship to Nina is equally unrealistic. At best theirs was an adolescent boy-girl flirtation; there is no indication that she has ever been "serious" about him. In the early scenes of the play, as Konstantin tries to court her, she puts him off. But Konstantin cannot see this; he insists on projecting his romantic fancies onto her and feels betrayed when she fails to respond. His sentimental longing for her is not unlike Masha's crush on him, and he has no more chance with Nina than Masha has with him.

As an artist Konstantin has two functions in the play: he is both a creative writer striving to find his own personal voice and a representative of the "Symbolist Movement." Thus, Chekhov can use him to comment on this literary fashion while also developing his unique story. Although she speaks as much out of vindictiveness as conviction, Arkadina's comments about Konstantin's play—"decadent raving," "pretensions to new forms"—echo opinions Chekhov expressed in his own correspondence. Yet Konstantin is completely sincere in his advocacy of the new forms, and thus represents a perennial artistic type, the "avant gardist" who seeks to revolutionize the arts by finding "new forms," not realizing, as Konstantin finally does, that form without content is pointless.

One of the many ironies in the play is the fact that the "rival" writers, Konstantin Treplev and Boris Trigorin, have the same problem: they have no real direction and nothing to say. If Treplev is the abstract writer who, in an effort to capture "essences" in his writing, loses all humanity, Trigorin is the "slick" writer whose vision cannot go beyond the everyday lives of his trivial characters. He is in a permanent rut and he knows it. Commercial success and the adulation of Arkadina and Nina are meaningless to him because he is honest enough to know that his work is frivolous when compared to that of truly serious writers.

Writing has, for Trigorin, almost become an unsatisfying but necessary compulsion. He carries his notebook with him and is constantly jotting notes until we get the feeling that he only observes, never lives. When the dead seagull is presented to him, he makes notes for a story. Trigorin then acts out his story with Nina; life copies art and both are bereft of real intensity. Perhaps his affair with Nina is not merely a casual seduction, but a vain attempt at direct experience. Trigorin would be a villain were he not so weak; he arouses contempt and pity, not anger. Like Konstantin, he needs others to support his deflated ego, but, unlike his rival, he lacks the strength even to kill himself.

Arkadina is a more complex figure than she seems at first glance. She, too, is an artist, but, as a performer, she has no interest in the opinion of posterity, nor, for that matter, does she have much interest in any aspect of the future. She sees herself as a beautiful young actress and clings tenaciously to that image in the face of reality. Of course, her casual dismissal of time reveals an obsession with it. Arkadina is deeply insecure and very much afraid of age, sickness, poverty, and death. This fear shows in her suppression of all references to such things; her hostility toward her sick older brother, Sorin; her jealousy and fear of the truly young, especially Nina; her apparent flightiness; her domineering treatment of all underlings, including Trigorin; her stinginess; and, most of all, her attitude toward Konstantin. He is right in his belief that the major reason for her hostility toward him is that he "makes" her a middle-aged woman.

It is, however, through Nina, the "seagull" of Trigorin's unwritten short story, that Chekhov makes his definitive statement about creativity, and it is in her climactic interview with Konstantin that the major issues of the play are resolved. Although their external situations differ, they have both reached the crucial points in their artistic careers: they know what they can and must do if they are to realize their potentials.

Even though some of his stories have been published, Konstantin has received neither the critical acclaim nor the personal satisfaction he desires, and he understands why: his search for "new forms" has led him into an artistic cul-de-sac: "good literature," he muses, "is not a question of forms new or old, but of ideas that must pour freely from the author's heart." Konstantin's basic problem is that he has nothing to say "from the heart" and he knows it.

But if Konstantin has not been stimulated by success, Nina has been hurt, but not defeated, by failure. She is almost ready to realize herself, but one final obstacle remains: she must get rid of her obsessive identification with the seagull of Trigorin's story. Therefore, Nina has returned to Sorin's estate, not to see Konstantin as he desperately hopes, but to complete the purgation of this obsession by returning to its place of origin. To remain identified with the dead bird is to accept defeat; to free herself from it is to free herself from Trigorin's personal influence and his destructive attitudes. As she talks to Konstantin, she visibly shakes off the last vestiges of these pernicious influences. She has gone from the stagestruck girl of the first act, who viewed acting as a way to "fame, resounding fame," to the mature woman who understands that the essential thing is the creative act itself: "One must know how to bear one's cross, and one must have faith," she proclaims; "when I think of my calling I do not fear life."

Because Konstantin has no such "calling," he is plunged into the final despair by her visit. Frustrated by his attempts to reach his mother, convinced that he will never write anything of value, all hopes for his relationship with Nina dashed, Konstantin kills himself. Nina, on the other hand, begins her life as a complete woman and a committed actress—to become, perhaps, a great one.

Keith Neilson

THE SECOND MRS. TANQUERAY

Type of work: Drama
Author: Arthur Wing Pinero (1855-1934)
Type of plot: Social criticism
Time of plot: The 1890's
Locale: London and Surrey, England
First presented: 1893

Arthur Wing Pinero took the common Victorian theme of the fallen woman and the well-made play formula, and, by adding some candor in the dialogue and some satirical jibes at middle-class propriety, put together a play that seemed radical and daring when first produced. Seen from a modern viewpoint these innovations seem more contrived than iconoclastic, but the historical importance of The Second Mrs. Tanqueray *is undeniable.*

The Second Mrs. Tanqueray is one of the best examples in theatrical history of the play whose time has come. Written a few years earlier it is doubtful that it would have gained a production or, if it had, that it would have met with anything but hostility and commercial failure. Presented even a few years later, after the early works of George Bernard Shaw and his realistic contemporaries, it is unlikely that its "iconoclasm" would have set it apart or that it would have enjoyed the "instant masterpiece" status accorded it by many of the best critics. But in 1893, some of the Victorian moral rigidity began to give way to the more casual Edwardian life style, and the influence of the new Continental theater was first being felt. The moment was ripe for a play that seemed to challenge Victorian social and moral postures, but which did not, finally, repudiate those attitudes and values.

Later critics, however, have been more harsh in their appraisals. The most serious shortcoming of the play is that, seen from a modern perspective, the play is too serious for a conventional "well-made-play," but lacks true depth because Pinero failed to pursue the moral and psychological implications of the characters and situations to their logical conclusions. In other words, Pinero had the material for a potentially important serious play, but, for reasons of personal taste or commercial wariness, backed off and imposed a contrived but socially conventional conclusion to his play. Or, to be specific, is the suicide of the heroine, Paula Tanqueray, which resolves the action of the play, the inevitable result of her character and circumstances, or is it simply a means by which Pinero sentimentally extricates himself from a situation too morally ambiguous for Victorian audiences to accept?

If the suicide can be justified, it must be seen as the result of an accumulation of factors: Paula's disillusionment with Aubrey and the realization that, although he loves her, he neither respects her nor considers her morally fit to associate with his daughter; her boredom with the rural life at "Highercoombe" and recognition of the fact that she will never be accepted by

Aubrey's friends; her discovery that she has outgrown her old world, but has no new one to enter; lingering pain over her earlier breakup with Hugh Ardale which is renewed by his return; her loss of Ellean's potential love; and, finally, her own feeling that she is getting old and will soon have nothing left. Aubrey vows another "fresh start," but Paula knows better.

However, although we can "explain" the motivation behind Paula's actions, her behavior is not always dramatically convincing. She is too naïve and eager for a woman of the world in her dealings with Ellean; her haughty and self-defeating handling of Mrs. Cortelyon seems artificial; her treatment of Aubrey frequently seems arbitrary and unnatural; and her moralistic decision to confess her previous affair with Ardale to her husband cannot be justified. Thus, the suicide is not the only problem decision in the play. In spite of some powerful and probing characterization, Paula's behavior too often seems to be necessitated by the shape of the plot rather than the nature of the character.

Other characters also suggest complexities greater than those usually encountered in "well-made-plays." How much of Aubrey's love for Paula is genuine emotion and how much of it is rooted in an idealistic, moralistic desire to "save" and uplift a lost soul? How much influence does his deceased first wife have on the Tanqueray household and especially on Ellean? And what about the relationship between Aubrey and his daughter? Is it completely within the normal father-daughter pattern? None of these provocative suggestions, however, is followed through. They remain tantalizing hints on the edge of the action, clues to character depths and complexities which are never explored.

Thus, however good *The Second Mrs. Tanqueray* may be, the reader constantly feels that it could have been much better. But it is probably too much to expect Pinero to be an English Ibsen. Perhaps it is sufficient to say that, along with Henry Arthur Jones, he brought a new seriousness to the British theater and that, because of their lead, a new period of intense creativity was ushered onto the English stage.

THE SECOND SHEPHERD'S PLAY

Type of work: Drama
Author: Unknown
Type of plot: Social satire and devotional mysticism
Time of plot: The Nativity
Locale: Bethlehem and surrounding country
First transcribed: Fifteenth century manuscript

This drama belongs to that group of mystery plays which make up the Wakefield cycle. Within the cycle is a group of extraordinarily fine works, including The Second Shepherd's Play, *which were probably written in the fifteenth century by one anonymous dramatist known only as the "Wakefield master."* The Second Shepherd's Play, *the best farce among the mystery plays and a fine example of popular humor, is an early masterpiece of realism.*

The Second Shepherd's Play is one of the most excellent of the Medieval mystery plays. Unlike the Medieval morality play, which was allegorical in method and restricted to a few topics concerning salvation, the mystery play evidences much greater range in subject matter and characterization. Although originally limited to the dramatization of Biblical events, mystery plays increasingly treated stories from Scripture and Church history with a good deal of latitude. The primary aim of this form of drama was, of course, the elucidation of Biblical and traditional wisdom for the laity, but, by a process of development, there emerged from the mystery play the elements of Renaissance drama. In this evolutionary process, a group of plays called the Towneley cycle was very important and, of the Towneley plays, the most influential was *The Second Shepherd's Play.*

The mystery play had its origin in a part of the Mass for Easter called the *Quem quaeritis* (Whom do you seek?). The *Quem quaeritis* was sung antiphonally and was the forerunner of liturgical innovations which used dialogue, adapted from Scripture, to enliven the worship. As the dialogues expanded, they were moved out of the Mass proper, where they were perhaps becoming a distraction, to other services like Matins. When the practice was extended to Christmas and other feasts, the range of subjects and the scope of the dialogues were correspondingly amplified.

Eventually the dialogues began to incorporate materials irrelevant, sometimes inappropriate, to the liturgy and gradually these rudimentary plays were removed from the Church to the courtyard and finally to the marketplace and out of clerical control. Responsibility for the productions was assumed by the civil authorities and delegated to appropriate guilds (for example, the Noah plays were assigned to the shipbuilders.) There followed a slow process of secularization, although Biblical themes survived into the sixteenth century.

Early in the fourteenth century, it became customary to perform the plays on the feast of Corpus Christi. Many towns, especially in the north of

England, developed cycles of plays covering the whole range of Biblical history. The largest extant group is the York Cycle, but there were impressive collections at Norwich, Coventry, Newcastle, Chester, and elsewhere.

The Wakefield Cycle was the most impressive largely because of the enormously talented contributions of a gifted playwright known only as the Wakefield master. Sometimes called the Towneley Cycle, because the manuscript was long at Towneley Hall in Lancashire, this group of plays developed in three parts. The first part is a series of rather simple plays, some of which seem to have been borrowed from the York Cycle. The second part is a group of plays which were incorporated into the cycle in the early fifteenth century. The third part, added before mid-fifteenth century, was the work of the Wakefield master, who contributed several plays in a characteristic nine-line stanza and revised several others. *The Second Shepherd's Play* is the most distinctive of the master's additions.

The historical importance of *The Second Shepherd's Play* is in its departure from the devotional thrust of the mystery play. It is true that the mystery play had long accommodated extraneous secular material as it developed into a more elaborate dramatic structure. It is even true that the humor, in the situation and in language, had frequently become coarse. What is striking about *The Second Shepherd's Play* is basically a matter of proportion and individual talent. In this play, the secular component completely overwhelms the Biblical. Although the focus of the play is on the nativity and it concludes with a devout pageant, the intrigues among the shepherds, which dominate most of the play, are only tangentially related to the nativity and are hugely entertaining in their own right.

In many mystery plays the action moves quickly and easily between devotion and vulgar farce. *The Second Shepherd's Play* is more neatly divided and better controlled. The first part of the drama deals with the experiences of the shepherds, particularly with the conniving of Mak and his wife Gill. The dialogue of the three shepherds, as they complain of their lot, is full of cynical, comic reflections on their human situation. The plot of this section is simply the duping and their discovery of it. The tone is lighthearted, no great harm is done, and all is an excuse for good-humored repartee. The stanza of nine lines of different lengths accommodates short set speeches as well as rapid, witty interchanges.

The second part of the play, by way of great contrast, involves the shepherds in gift-giving in the Christmas tableau. Ostensibly it is only connected to the first part by the presence of the same shepherds. Yet, there are some surprising continuities. Despite the seriousness of the event, the poet maintains the same light touch and sensitivity to the more mundane concerns of mankind. The tone, however, does not interfere with the solemnity of the Scriptural occasion and the appropriate decorum. Rather, the pageant gains a vitality all too often lacking in religious representations.

In addition, there is another connection between the two plots insofar as the story of Mak is a sort of secular parody of the nativity. In the farcical plot, the shepherds do not give their gifts willingly but are conned out of them. When they finally approach the cradle, it is surrounded by the duplicitous Mak and Gill rather than Joseph and Mary, and the cradle contains not the Lamb of God but a real sheep. Thus, the main events of the play are a playful, but ultimately not a blasphemous, secularization of the Christmas story. The Wakefield master has infused the nativity into a pedestrian comedy and then transferred the joyous vitality of the farce to the serious conclusion. The result is that the mold of the mystery play has been stretched so far that *The Second Shepherd's Play* shares more with the kind of comedy that is to come in the Renaissance than it does with its Medieval liturgical antecedents and neighbors.

Edward E. Foster

THE SECRET AGENT

Type of work: Novel
Author: Joseph Conrad (Józef Teodor Konrad Korzeniowski, 1857-1924)
Type of plot: Psychological realism
Time of plot: 1880's
Locale: London
First published: 1907

In plot and situation, The Secret Agent *anticipates the modern thriller, but Conrad's view of man as an alienated individual as well as a social animal invests the novel with a significance beyond that of simple entertainment. In a side street of Soho, Conrad has gathered some of his most interesting and unusual figures. Realistically presented, these people are surveyed through a veil of irony which enhances rather than mars the total effect of the novel.*

Despite the absence of tropical seas or isolated jungle outposts, Conrad's usual settings, this novel is highly representative of his gift for framing tales of eerie adventure in a context combining psychological depth and the exotic.

On the surface it seems a political novel because of its concern with anarchists, mysterious foreign embassies, and terrorist bombings. But in fact, it records the isolated existence of a "stranger," the secret agent Verloc, doing his job of sabotage in what Bertolt Brecht was to call "The Jungle of Cities." London is as fiercely remote as the Congo. Even without the agonized conscience of a Kurtz (the tormented hero of Conrad's greatest novella, *The Heart of Darkness*), Verloc is a totally alienated human being living in the midst of a vast and indifferent city. Like a primitive jungle, London suffocates and oppresses, according to Verloc, who sees the city as a hateful place.

Verloc marries a native of this jungle, and she finally stabs him in a frenzy of revenge. Outraged by Verloc's responsibility for her brother's death, Winnie releases the retribution of nature. But she herself becomes the victim of Ossipon's greed.

Both the police and the anarchists are lost in a fog of corruption and misconceived duty. The novel is a profound statement of modern dehumanization and alienation. If Verloc, passive in life as in death, is the novel's central protagonist, then the "Professor" is its chief symbol. A seer figure, he wanders through the novel madly challenging the world by covering his person with dynamite. A walking bomb, the Professor is immune to arrest. Literally isolated, he is without compassion. In response to the "madness and despair" of Winnie's suicide, he intones the following: "Everybody is mediocre. Madness and despair! Give me that for a lever, and I'll move the world."

SEJANUS

Type of work: Drama
Author: Ben Jonson (1573?-1637)
Type of plot: Political tragedy
Time of plot: First century
Locale: Ancient Rome
First presented: 1603

Both of Ben Jonson's Roman tragedies (Sejanus *and* Catiline) *display his ability to create an illusion of living history. Both are well-constructed, both have strong characterizations, and both are written in firm, powerful verse; but both also have a certain hardness and lack of warmth that diminishes their effectiveness. Of the two,* Sejanus *is, perhaps, the more consistent in tone. The world of* Sejanus *is evil and terrifying; although good men open and close the play, wickedness is in power from beginning to end.*

Sejanus was a dismal failure on stage, and Sejanus' dismemberment was later used by Jonson as a metaphor of the play's failure—dismembered by audience and critics. The play is meaningful today because of its portrayal of Roman totalitarianism. Its frightful atmosphere reminds us of *1984*: a world of fear and danger where one can speak only in whispers and innuendos, where all are under suspicion, where one is even afraid lest he speak in his sleep. *Sejanus* shows the abuse of human dignity, the manipulative skills of ruthless politicians, the perversion of human relationships, and the complete paralysis of society; life is a frenzied movement, for to stay still is to perish. Sejanus' daughter is raped by the hangman because a virgin cannot be put to death—this is Jonson's epitome of a world gone mad, where all reason is lost.

The greatness of the play does not lie in character portrayal, for Tiberius is the only character with complexity. Sejanus has no richness to his personality; he is not an interesting villain. The good characters, such as Lepidus and Arruntius, function primarily as choral commentators, comparing the past with the present; they are either ineffectual or impotent. Rather, our interest is drawn to the contest between two supreme Machiavellians, Tiberius and Sejanus, and to Jonson's suggestion that a corrupt and decadent society will inevitably produce a Tiberius and a Sejanus.

Two traditional conventions inform the play—the motif of the revolving Wheel of Fortune and the classical idea of *hubris*. Together they cause Sejanus' fall. He falls when he is at the summit of success; his decline begins in Act III when he suggests to Tiberius the marriage to Livia. These two somewhat contradictory ideas are suggested within the play: that Sejanus' fall was fated because everyone will eventually fall; and that Sejanus' pride, in his desire to become a god, caused his fall.

The great pessimism of *Sejanus* lies in the knowledge that Sejanus' downfall will lead to neither a personal renewal nor a cleansing of the state. Rome without Sejanus will be no less corrupt than Rome with him.

THE SELF-TORMENTOR

Type of work: Drama
Author: Terence (Publius Terentius Afer, c. 190-159 B.C.)
Type of plot: Social comedy
Time of plot: Fourteenth century B.C.
Locale: The countryside near Athens
First presented: 163 B.C.

Although primarily a playwright who aimed his works at the aristocratic elite, Terence wrote comedies which, even today, remain quite amusing and provocative: In The Self-Tormentor *Terence once again borrowed and refined a play of his predecessor, Menander, which emphasized the perennial topic of the sexual precocity of the young as it conflicts with the authority and propriety of the old.*

The Self-Tormentor was the third drama by Terence, and as a comedy of intrigue it has a more complicated plot than any other surviving Roman play. Adapted from a play by Menander of the same title, this one uses a closely-woven double romance that apparently was Terence's own contribution. Like his play *The Brothers,* it is a "problem" drama dealing with two opposed systems of upbringing, neither of which works. Is harshness or leniency best in handling a son, particularly a son past puberty? This drama would suggest that neither has any effect on young men experiencing their sexual maturation.

This play's humor derives mainly from the reactions of Menedemus and Chremes, as their respective sons, aided by the slave Syrus, outmaneuver them at every turn. The romances are almost incidental to the game of fooling father. The highly intricate plot revolves around the attempt of both sons to have a mistress (or a mistress-made-wife) and trick their fathers into supporting them. The assumption is that the sexual needs of youth must be met however they can, with a minimum of compromise on the part of young men and a maximum of compromise by the old. Terence was in his middle twenties when he wrote the play, and it seems clearly intended to appeal to youthful audiences at the Megalensian games.

The chief irony is that Menedemus, who proved most intractable to his son's affair at first, becomes the most reconciled to it; while Chremes, who offers smug advice and feels himself to be on top of the situation, becomes the real dupe and is furious at his predicament. While Menedemus tries to work out a viable relationship with his son, Chremes is deluded into thinking his own delinquent son is innocent. In the end Menedemus is allowed to have the last word. The implicit moral is that a flexible moderation between strictness and tolerance is best in rearing a son.

SENSE AND SENSIBILITY

Type of work: Novel
Author: Jane Austen (1775-1817)
Type of plot: Comedy of manners
Time of plot: Nineteenth century
Locale: England
First published: 1811

*To Jane Austen there were people of sense and people of fine sensibility, but little
sense. In this novel of early nineteenth century English life she makes it quite clear
that she admires men and women of sense. Although the dialogue of this early novel
may seem stilted at times and the characters overdrawn, they combine to give a
clear picture of the manners of upper- and middle-class English society of that
period.*

Except for the behavior of Marianne Dashwood and John Willoughby,
Jane Austen's characters have nearly impeccable manners. They are the
upper-middle class whose time is spent in decorous leisure, in visiting, out-
ings, and dinner parties. Voices are modulated, amenities observed, and social
station respected. Yet, underneath this exquisite exterior, emotions of the
most primitive kind are hidden. From the beginning of the novel, avarice and
lust threaten to break through the restraints of the agreed-upon rules and
create chaos—a disorder both social and moral.

The plot is set in motion by the greed of Fanny and John Dashwood, leaving
his step-mother and half-sisters vulnerable to the likes of John Willoughby.
Willoughby himself is forced to deny his real feelings for Marianne because he
has no money, and must, therefore, marry into it. Mrs. Ferrars attempts to
choose her sons' brides using her wealth to bend them to her will. In short, the
passionate lives of the young are smothered by those who hold the purse.
Colonel Brandon's ward, seduced and abandoned by Willoughby, is an apt
example of what happens to the innocent in a culture whose morality is
based on land and money and where class determines identity and value.

Through the prudential efforts of Elinor Dashwood and Colonel Brandon,
the social fabric is kept intact, tragedy averted, and the comic spirit permitted
to emerge. Still, if sanity and harmony are restored at the novel's conclusion
with the weddings of the Dashwood sisters, the resolution barely compensates
for the emotional deprivation of Marianne, Willoughby, and even Elinor. The
sisters' marriages are certainly ones of sense; yet, they lack a dimension of
human experience, a sensibility to the possibilities of passion, which is forbidden by a rigid system of manners, uninformed by love or compassion.

A SENTIMENTAL EDUCATION

Type of work: Novel
Author: Gustave Flaubert (1821-1880)
Type of plot: Naturalism
Time of plot: Nineteenth century
Locale: France
First published: 1869

Frederic Moreau's sentimental education centers on his unconsummated love affair with Mme. Arnoux, a rich businessman's wife. As his ardor for her increases, so does his experience in the world around him. His education is completed when he almost—but not quite—fulfills his romantic desire. The 1848 revolution forms the background for Frederic's experiences and relates his private actions to the larger public events.

A Sentimental Education, considered by some critics to be Flaubert's masterpiece, was without question one of the most influential French novels of the nineteenth century. Perhaps closer to Flaubert than any other of his works, drawing largely from autobiographical material, and a rewriting of a novel by the same title which he wrote two decades earlier, the book was his effort to produce a moral history of the men of his generation. In this novel, Flaubert's concern is with the organic growth of a personality, with the unfolding and discovery of the self. Education has for Flaubert the almost existential meaning of becoming oneself through action. At the beginning of the book, the protagonist, Frederic Moreau, is little more than a potentiality, an empty page upon which experience has yet to leave its mark. It is only as Frederic confronts the world and is forced to make choices and to react among other people that he blossoms into a complicated and tormented human being. Always, the conflict is between the man that was and the man that is about to be; the time sequence in the novel is poised between past and future, between the raw youth and the man of experience, sadder and wiser, but not necessarily better.

The question facing Frederic, particularly after he has moved to Paris, is whether he should become a man of the world, successful in love and business, a man of action conventional in his behavior and opinions, or whether he should become a spectator of life, an outsider who remains aloof from the vanity of action and struggles to translate his ideal vision into an artistic form. It is the same question that Flaubert, himself, faced: to be a man-of-the-world, with all of his superficialities and conventions, or a man of art no longer of the real world. At the beginning, by necessity, Frederic stands on the sidelines, watching. He has not been able to enter into society, knows few people, and has little money, so he watches the activity of others. This static quality is stressed by the repetition of verbs such as "he watched," "he contemplated," "he admired," and "he dreamed." Frederic seems to be a wallflower at a great and glorious ball. But then two events thrust him into the stream of action: love and the inheritance of a fortune from his uncle. And then his real education begins.

Love is almost a pattern for all of the lessons of life, according to the point of view expressed in this novel; and education, in the sense of "education for living," synonymous with "sentimental education." Thus, the romantic or sentimental education of the hero assumes symbolic proportions. It is love—the many aspects of love, both sacred and profane—that opens up the world for Frederic Moreau. At first, his vision of love is very ideal and pure, but gradually it becomes more earthbound and physical, and he loses both his innocence and his idealism.

"I know nothing more noble," Flaubert once wrote, "than the contemplation of the world," and this novel provides such an opportunity for the reader. *A Sentimental Education* views the world in all of its complexity, the sordid as well as the beautiful, the painful as well as the ideal; in it, Flaubert presents with consummate skill his vision of the human condition, a view that many of his contemporaries considered shocking and disgusting, but from which generations have subsequently derived an ironic, profound pleasure.

The heart of the novel is the love affair between Frederic and Madame Arnoux, a relationship based upon the affair between the young Flaubert and one Elisa Schlesinger, the wife of a well-known music publisher, who is the prototype for the art dealer M. Arnoux. The real-life relationship continued, off and on, for many years, and was one of the central influences in the author's life. There is no doubt that the scene of Frederic's reunion with the white-haired Madame Arnoux had its counterpart in real life. Just as Madame Arnoux is a portrait of Madame Schlesinger, so Frederic is a self-portrait of the author. The principal difference is that Flaubert acted upon his dreams and learned to discipline himself in order to realize those ambitions. While Frederic is the ancestor of all of the anti-heroes of modern literature, Flaubert, himself, transcended the parts of himself that he gave to his hero, and found in his literary vocation the strength that Frederic never was able to discover in himself.

It is said that all of the characters in the novel, from Frederic's friends, to the Marshal, the famous courtesan, to the many minor characters who fill out the spectacular picture of Parisian society, are based on real individuals known by Flaubert. It is certain that the background events are all carefully based on history, and were researched to assure their authenticity. The 1848 revolution in particular was carefully studied, but Flaubert devoted as much care in describing an operation or a factory as in writing about a revolution. He allowed himself no license in the matter of background or historical facts. But, where a lesser novelist might have let the tumultuous events of his background overpower the human story of his protagonists, Flaubert carefully kept a balance between the different parts of the novel. Thus, the historical events provide a counterpoint highlighting the personal adventures of his hero.

To a modern reader, perhaps the most fascinating aspect of *A Sentimental Education* is this detailed portrait of French society at the time leading up to the *coup d'etat* of 1851. The endless evenings of petty conversation in restaurants and fashionable salons, the bickering and plotting over finances, the quarreling over politics, the scheming of writers and artists to achieve notoriety and attention in periodicals: all of it is vividly drawn. Frederic wanders among the rich and well-known, as well as among the student class and the less rich, absorbing the lessons that the world around him has to offer. Flaubert's meticulous, graceful style renders the scene sharply, even when his protagonist is most acutely suffering. The novel gives the illusion of shapelessness, but it is actually carefully constructed. It is both a view of a society in the throes of change and a portrait of a human being discovering his own potentialities.

Bruce D. Reeves

A SENTIMENTAL JOURNEY

Type of work: Novel
Author: Laurence Sterne (1713-1768)
Type of plot: Novelized autobiography
Time of plot: 1760's
Locale: France
First published: 1768

Sterne called his book A Sentimental Journey Through France and Italy, *but the title of this unconventional mixture of autobiography, travel impressions, and fiction is misleading, because he died before writing the Italian segment. Sentimental, as the title implies, outrageous and eccentric in its humorous effects, the novel entertains the reader with delightful accounts and observations of whatever enters the author's mind.*

Both in form and apparent subject, *A Sentimental Journey* follows in the tradition of the "grand tour" novel. The assemblage of scenes and persons, the escapades on the road, the cultural adjustments required of an Englishman abroad, the things to be learned and the places to be visited—this was common, enjoyable reading matter for an eighteenth century audience.

However, Sterne's "grand tour" sports a delightful touch of irreverence. Its hero, Yorick, is not a typical young gentleman matriculating into a peripatetic finishing school but a low-key picaro buffeted by impulse and whimsy. Thus his "travelling" is apparently random. Unplanned, untimed, it accords perfectly with his sole principle, which, it seems, is to have no principle whatever except obedience to natural affections, his growing sensibility, and his often unseemly passion. He prefers *filles de chambre* to cathedrals, a pretty face to a gallery portrait. With a free-flowing nature, then, he does not seek improvement through a travel plan; he prefers to stumble over it in following his heart. And the point made by Sterne is this: a benevolent nature, trusted to, rarely errs in promoting human goodness.

"Sentiment" and a host of attendant words such as "good nature," "sensibility," and "affections" were all terms with particular significance in Sterne's day. The so-called "doctrine of sensibility," popularized by the late seventeenth century Latitudinarian divines, urged an inherent goodness in man, a "sense" of moral absolutes which expresses itself in acts of charity and social benevolence. Championed philosophically by the third Earl of Shaftesbury (in his *Characteristicks of Men, Manners, Opinions, Times,* 1711) and in fiction by Henry Fielding, this emphasis on good nature ran counter to the often equally influential tradition represented by Thomas Hobbes (*Leviathan,* 1651) and Bernard Mandeville (*The Fable of the Bees,* 1714), a tradition which urged self-interest as the basis of all human action. These are the two forces which collide in *A Sentimental Journey* as Sterne explores what it means to be a good man.

The glance at Hobbes we see revealed in several characters: the huge oaf who purposefully blocks the view of a dwarf, the postilion who thrashes his horses, and even Yorick himself at the start of the novel when he refuses charity to a monk. Yet this "natural" cruelty—as Hobbes would have it—is set against the virtues of a larger number of characters: the old French officer who assists the dwarf, the mourner who laments his dead animal, and of course the enlightened Yorick whom later we see guiding the unfortunate Maria. On the one hand Sterne recognizes only too well man's divided nature, in which good and evil are deeply intertwined, yet on the other hand he wants to insist that the "deeper affections," the "eternal fountain of our feelings," as Yorick says, are a primary impulse of inordinate strength.

Beneath the surface, *A Sentimental Journey* is something of an allegory, a type of metaphorical trek in which Yorick (hence the reader) discovers the primacy of human feeling. It is a journey into sentiment. It is a discovery of sentiment. It is a travel not just through space and time but into sensibility itself, which is the common bond of all humanity. True, the book is an outrageous comedy—and it is wise not to forget this. Its famous ending ("When I stretched out my hand, I caught hold of the fille de chambre's—") and the mixed motives of its characters should remind us that Sterne wrote for delight as much as for instruction. But the comedy ought not to obscure a more serious intent in the book. There is a delicate line separating love from lust, Sterne argues, if only because the "web of kindness" has "threads of love and desire . . . entangled with the piece." The temptation, too often, is to rent the whole web (as Yorick says) by drawing out the former, with the result that man becomes merely heartless and cold. Instead, one ought to excuse occasional moral lapses in the interest of fostering greater love, for it is love alone that characterizes man in his best moments. This is the main point of Sterne's delightful Aristophanic fragment on the town of Abdera: there literature succeeds in making the most profligate town devoted to Cupid. It is equally the point of Yorick's amorousness and of his belief that, once rekindled at Love's flame, he is all generosity and good will again. It underlies his celebration of freedom (in volume II), La Fleur's Casanovan conquests, the Count de B's encomium on the fair sex, and, unforgettably, the French officer's noble lesson that mutual toleration teaches us mutual love.

One might also say that it underlies Sterne's prose style inasmuch as we, like Yorick, are sentimental travelers. The associative drift of the narrative precludes expectation; it demands instead that the reader allow himself to be taken wherever his sensibility wishes to go. Simply, the novel demands to be read less with the head and more with the heart. Many of the scenes, for example, are unabashed tearjerkers. And clearly Sterne plays on our elementary sense of justice—our *feeling* for what is right and wrong—in order to score his points. In an intriguing way, then, *A Sentimental Journey* is not merely about a grand tour but is itself a grand tour. It is an education in the consistency of human nature, not its diversity. It is, like Euripides before Abdera, Sterne before the world.

David B. Carroll

SEVEN AGAINST THEBES

Type of work: Drama
Author: Aeschylus (525-456 B.C.)
Type of plot: Classical tragedy
Time of plot: Remote antiquity
Locale: Thebes in Boeotia
First presented: 467 B.C.

In Seven Against Thebes, *the only surviving play from a trilogy about the House of Oedipus, the deaths of Eteocles and his brother, Polynices, sons of Oedipus and grandsons of Laius, culminate three generations of violence, bloodshed, and agony which arose from Laius' ingratitude to Pelops. Although not as great as Aeschylus' later masterpieces,* The Oresteia *and* Prometheus Bound, *it represented a new depth and intensity in his work.*

Seven Against Thebes was first produced as part of a Theban trilogy in 467 B.C., with which Aeschylus won first place in the Athenian drama competition. By then he had been writing tragedies for more than thirty years. Almost single-handedly he had fashioned an important art form out of the drama with his technical improvements and his gift for stirring dramatic poetry. Aeschylus was a very prominent playwright at that time, and younger men, such as Sophocles, were building on his achievements. Although *Seven Against Thebes* is a mature work, Aeschylus' finest triumphs were still to come—plays such as *Prometheus Bound* and *The House of Atreus* trilogy.

Unfortunately, the two other plays in this Theban series have not survived. Apparently they dealt with the legends of Laius and Oedipus, the grandfather and father of Eteocles and Polynices. *Seven Against Thebes* shows Aeschylus grappling with the theme of the blood curse. Laius was cursed because of his gross ingratitude to Pelops. Oedipus was cursed because he slew his father Laius and married his mother Jocasta; and he in turn cursed his sons Polynices and Eteocles for begrudging him food. This is the background for the fratricidal strife between the two, and for Eteocles' headstrong desire to fight his brother in the play.

With Aeschylus a family curse is something almost palpable, a presence that hovers over a clan and works its doom. Each member of the family has free will, but that will is part of a whole that heads passionately for disaster. We see this in Eteocles, a forerunner of the tragic hero; in Polynices; and in Antigone as she resolutely defies the edict of the Theban council by marching off to bury Polynices. Their fates are chosen, willed by themselves in full knowledge of the consequences, and yet they fit a broad pattern of calamity in the Theban dynasty.

Seven Against Thebes falls into three sections, which diminish progressively in length. The first part handles Eteocles' preparations for battle, the second tells of the war's end and shows the mourning for the sons of Oedipus, while the third deals with Antigone's rebellion against the edict.

In the first section we watch Eteocles in action as an effective leader in defending Thebes. His military address to the troops, his means of getting information about the enemy plans from seer and spy, the way he quells the panicky prayers of the Theban matrons, the type of men he chooses to defend the city gates, and his own willingness to fight, all point to an excellent general. If his right to rule Thebes is questionable, there is no doubt about the quality of his leadership in defending Thebes.

He is manly, disdainful of women who endanger the city through fright and weakness. Eteocles is not impious, for he sees the value of masculine piety in war, but he feels that men should rely chiefly on their own strength. However, there is a barrier between him and heaven—the curse his father laid on him. He knows that he is doomed, but he takes every precaution to save Thebes. The patriotism of Aeschylus shines through the character of Eteocles. If it were not for his willful sin of fratricide, Eteocles might have been an authentic tragic hero.

The second section merely underscores the idea of the blood curse, announces the Theban victory, and shows the mourning for Eteocles and Polynices. In the final section, with Antigone's defiance of the city elders, we realize that the family curse has not ended. Antigone is making a new crisis in burying her outcast brother. There is an echo of the brothers' feud in the way she leaves with Polynices' body while Ismene, following the edict, exits with the corpse of Eteocles.

It is significant that we see the conflict between the brothers from the Theban point of view—from inside the city. The attackers are depicted as evildoers, as boastful, impious adventurers largely, each intent on sacking and burning the city and carrying off the women as slaves. We can understand the panic of the Theban chorus. Aeschylus knew from his experience in the Greek and Persian wars how it felt to be assaulted by vast foreign troops who wanted to enslave one's homeland. He lived in a heroic era and his dramas convey the grandeur of Periclean Athens.

Among other things, *Seven Against Thebes* is a rousing martial poem with a wide variety of poetic and rhetorical techniques. There is the military pep talk, the dithyrambic invocation of the gods, invective, choral odes, antithesis in choosing defenders, the dirge, stichomythia in the mourning of Antigone and Ismene, and debate between Antigone and the herald. From a poetic point of view the play is a *tour de force*.

This drama is usually seen as a prelude to *The House of Atreus (The Oresteia)*, in which Aeschylus again took up the theme of the blood curse and created his greatest dramas. *Seven Against Thebes* is a finished work by itself, yet if it is not of the highest quality, that is because we have the later plays of Aeschylus and the finest plays of Sophocles and Euripides to use for comparison.

James Weigel, Jr.

THE SEVEN WHO FLED

Type of work: Novel
Author: Frederic Prokosch (1908-   )
Type of plot: Exotic romance
Time of plot: c. 1935
Locale: China
First published: 1937

Frederic Prokosch sketches the adventures of seven Europeans set adrift to brave an alien East in seven separate stories, vaguely unified by a prologue and epilogue. These Europeans are fleeing more than a revolutionary disturbance when they join a Chinese caravan for their flight across central Asia. Purposeless and disillusioned, they are running away, not only from themselves but from Europe itself, the shaper of their barren and frustrated lives.

Frederic Prokosch won international fame with *The Asiatics,* his first novel, which was translated into seventeen languages. His subsequent works were praised by such writers as W. B. Yeats and Thomas Mann. He has been credited with inventing the "geographical novel" in which sensuality is mingled with irony and mystery. Albert Camus said that he "conveys a fatalistic sense of life half-hidden beneath a rich animal energy." His novels have a breadth of canvas and an inclusiveness which is more characteristic of European than American fiction, and many of his readers have not realized that he is an American. His poetry has received wide acclaim and a number of awards.

In *The Seven Who Fled,* Prokosch lays before the reader a reminder of *The Bridge of San Luis Rey* type of plot, bringing together varied individuals experiencing dangers in an exotic setting. But there is more to this Harper Prize-winning novel than the strange, surreal landscape writhing with humanity. Beyond the hallucinatory images of the prose there is a concern with fundamental issues, with life and death. The episodic tale is told in a series of flashbacks; memory plays a vital role in the lives of these desperate, trapped people. Longings for past and future are united in the crisis of the present.

Gradually, the portraits of the seven Europeans are filled in. They are not all admirable people, but they are very human. Prokosch's vision of life is grim; his people struggle, but are doomed. Yet, at times, there is a strange victory in their damnation, a kind of transcendence for some of them. Nothingness, Prokosch implies, waits like a lover for all mortals. Death becomes in these tales an almost sexual consummation.

The characters suffer extremes of physical and emotional conditions. Stranded two thousand miles from the Caucasus and two thousand miles from Shanghai, they have no choice but to flee, but most of them find that they are helpless. As the events of their lives slow down, the actual pace of living seems to accelerate. A Balzacian vitality and lusty power pervades the descriptions of the low life encountered by the unfortunate seven.

The country itself, China and its borders, dominates the book. One of the characters comments that a landscape is a spiritual thing, a constant longing, a reflection of what is everlasting in human beings. One feels that the terrible deserts and mountains, the earth, the snows, all will remain after the seven Europeans are long forgotten. It is a gloomy message, but is unforgettably presented through dramatic scenes and dreamlike descriptions.

The gradual breaking down of the British explorer Layeville from the hardships of desert and mountains dominates the first half of the novel. His suffering, both mental and physical, his slowly ripening resignation, linger with the reader long after the book is put down. The other most vividly portrayed character in the first two hundred pages of the book is the half-mad Russian, Serafimov. A romantic, passionate man, he is tormented by memories and frustrations. He always felt that there were two people at war in him: a sly fellow and a wild one. He repeats to himself, "I'll survive," but his despair soon overwhelms him. He becomes a man obsessed, torn by an irrational hatred for another man. A strange, violent, almost homo-erotic obsession grows between the huge Russian and the small Belgian, Goupillière. As their ardent fears and hates mount, the reader realizes that one of them must inevitably destroy the other.

Serafimov's obsession also includes the middle-aged prostitute Tastin, who desperately attempts to use her feminine wiles on the men who straggle to her door. Also an exile from Russia, she is caught in the web of the struggle for survival, doomed never to escape its sticky embrace.

The two Germans, Hugo Wildenbruch and Joachim von Wald, form another strange and passionate friendship, torn by an almost Dostoevskian perversity. The young Joachim, like the others, seems to be as drawn to death as he is repelled by it. Like the Frenchman de la Scaze, the geologists are filled with a longing for danger, pain, extremity—"to be captured by *reality!*" The wealthy and bored de la Scaze is thrilled even by the prospect of being tortured.

Monsieur de la Scaze wrote one day, as he waited for some change in his condition, that life can only be seen as tragic by a thoughtful and sensitive person. He divided evil into four types, pondering these with a perverse pleasure, only to change his mind and declare that evil cannot be explained at all. His thoughts centered not on his young wife, sent away because of the danger, but on his own past. Like the others, he found himself unable to act rationally, or even at all. He wallowed in a mire of aimless reflections and tangled memories, and in vague observations of the strange world around him.

What had most impressed de la Scaze in all of China was its lack of pity. There was no room for pity in a place where the struggle for life was so intense. No longer sheltered by his wealth from the realities of existence, he was shocked by the self-centeredness of most people. But Dr. Liu, the

Chinese protector of Madame de la Scaze, told her that we all live on our own invisible pavilions, protecting ourselves as much as possible from the stress of naked existence. It was no surprise to this elderly Chinese merchant that men are selfish. He would have been amazed if they were not.

Olivia de la Scaze finally fled from the sinister Dr. Liu, sailing downriver toward the sea, passing an almost mythical Chinese landscape. A lyric beauty, a sense of tragedy, seems to flow across the page as the boat carries the young Spanish beauty to her destiny. At its best, Prokosch's style possesses a supple elegance which can transmit the immediate texture of an experience. At its worst, it becomes verbose and rather soft and flabby.

Unfortunately, a degree of posturing weakens the tone of the book. One might argue that the characters are all extremes, not like the normal mass of humanity. That the seven Europeans are consumed with their crazy rivalries, are egoistic and incapable of understanding their situation, is partly the theme of the novel, but they are too passive to be altogether successful as either symbols or heroes.

Bruce D. Reeves

THE SEVEN WHO WERE HANGED

Type of work: Novel
Author: Leonid Andreyev (1871-1919)
Type of plot: Social criticism
Time of plot: Early twentieth century
Locale: Russia
First published: 1908

Although the bulk of Leonid Andreyev's writings are abstract and symbolic, his reputation today is based primarily on a handful of realistic works, the most notable of which is The Seven Who Were Hanged. *In this novel, written as a polemic against capital punishment, the writer shows us the minds of the seven as they face their own mortality with courage, compassion, and understanding as well as fear, hostility, and bitterness.*

Andreyev's acknowledged thesis is developed by tracing the fates of five condemned revolutionaries and two condemned peasant murderers. Some of these individuals suffer greatly as they wait for their death, others scarcely comprehend what is happening to them, and some rise above their fate. Andreyev's point is that such punishment, however dealt with, is inhuman and wrong. Although the novel is virtually plotless, his slice-of-life technique, closely akin to the naturalism of Frank Norris and Theodore Dreiser, his American contemporaries, produces a powerful and compelling narrative.

Andreyev's novels and plays all tend to convey a relentless mood of despair; *The Seven Who Were Hanged* is scarcely an exception. Its pessimism is relieved by the subdued, almost Tolstoyesque, style and a pervading ironic sympathy for a suffering humanity. The apparently objective approach and the detailed attention to facts suggests the influence of Andreyev's background as a barrister and as a law and crime reporter. It is not surprising that he was a friend and disciple of Gorky, the leader of the Russian realist school of fiction.

The pathetic and grotesque feebleminded peasant, Yanson is, in some respects, the most vividly drawn and memorable of the characters. Certainly, he is the least sympathetic personality, although Andreyev skillfully makes the reader understand the crime being committed against even this vicious, stupid murderer. Sergey Golovin, young and healthy, with his routine of exercises, is the most charming person in the book, but he, too, gradually yields to the terrors of approaching death. Tanya Kovalchuk is perhaps the warmest and kindliest character, and the wisest. She realizes that the important consideration is not the cause of their death or the fate of their executioners, but that they, themselves, are ready to die, for "there is nothing more terrible than death." And, "when thousands kill one," she says, "it means that the one has conquered." Andreyev penetrates with deep psychological insight the changing emotions of the condemned seven, who "see both death and life at the same time."

SEVENTEEN

Type of work: Novel
Author: Booth Tarkington (1869-1946)
Type of plot: Humorous romance
Time of plot: Early twentieth century
Locale: Small Midwestern town
First published: 1916

Seventeen is the hilarious story of William Sylvanus Baxter, just seventeen, who is in love with Miss Pratt, a summer visitor in the neighborhood. The adolescent antics of a small-town Lothario are beguiling and utterly harmless, and the mischievous antics of Jane, William's pesky younger sister, are foolish and delightful.

One reviewer of *Seventeen,* after its first publication in 1916, suggested that the only person who would not like or appreciate the book would be a seventeen-year-old. Even though the book is nearly half a century old, the story of youthful love is not. Booth Tarkington depicts the situation with skill and humor. He portrays William Sylvanus Baxter as a love-struck seventeen-year-old whose life for one summer, at least, revolves around the rather silly and childish Lola Pratt. Tarkington's humor is sympathetic and understanding and because he does not take his hero seriously, the book remains light and funny. Seventeen is an age of portentous seriousness and extreme self-consciousness, not only for William Baxter, but for most boys his age, then and now. Tarkington knows this well and capitalizes upon the traumas of male adolescence. His sense of timing is perfect and he uses his humor at exactly the right moment to achieve the maximum effect. For example, when Mr. Parcher is suffering from listening to the meaningless and saccharin conversations between "little boy Baxter" and Miss Pratt, William's description of his flame as "My Baby Talk Lady" is the last straw, causing him to explode and send volumes of Plutarch flying across the room.

The novel is full of all the characters necessary to make a believable situation comedy. On the one hand, there is the obnoxious and menacing little sister, Jane, to act as William's chief antagonist. Then there are his parents who seem to thwart his every attempt to appear grown-up and independent to his friends. Mrs. Baxter, true to form for a mother, understands her son better than anyone else and realizes that youngsters do strange things which they "get over" in time. In the end, she tries to make life easier for him by making his father's dress clothes conveniently available to William for Lola's farewell party. There are times, though, when she appears to William to be unsympathetic and completely against him. William's peers are all sketches of simple, believable buddies who are all after the same thing—Lola Pratt. There is a camaraderie among them in their attempts to share her for the summer, which seems to them the best possible arrangement under the circumstances. Genesis, the old hired hand, presents a different type of problem for William Baxter, whose relationship to the black man is one of the aspects of the story which date it.

On the whole, *Seventeen* provides light entertainment for the young reader. There are no complicated literary techniques, (apart from Miss Pratt's rather ridiculous speeches), and the story is a straightforward, humorous, and an accurate study of a boy in his teens.

SHADOWS ON THE ROCK

Type of work: Novel
Author: Willa Cather (1873-1947)
Type of plot: Historical chronicle
Time of plot: Late seventeenth century
Locale: Quebec, Canada
First published: 1931

> Shadows on the Rock *is a very human story about a little-known segment of North American history, the early colonies in Canada. Cather makes the unfamiliar setting come alive through her detailed descriptions of the customs, habits, and daily routines of the people. What emerges is a picture of an admirable, tenacious people, not unlike the Nebraskan pioneers she celebrated in such early works as* O Pioneers! *and* My Ántonia.

In *Shadows on the Rock,* Willa Cather selected a historical situation and structured her story around it. The novel is a series of incidents set on the rock of Quebec in the late seventeenth century. It explores the qualities of the French civilization that grew up there through vignettes of simple people, their homes, labors, friendships, and desires. Willa Cather explained that the title of this novel was significant, for the people of Quebec have long "cast their shadows" on the city: the people have changed, but the culture has endured.

The story revolves primarily around the widowed apothecary, Euclide Auclair, and his young daughter, Cécile; much of what the reader sees in this settlement is seen through the eyes of young Cécile. The simplicity of her viewpoint is refreshing as well as colorful. She is presented as dutiful and responsive to others, while her father is affectionate and thoughtful. All of the characters are "types" that fit easily into the historical scenario; the sensitive and pitiful little Jacques, the strong and adventurous Pierre Charron, the noble but disillusioned old Count, and the flamboyant Bishop Laval. The characters lack great depth and dimension, but they fit carefully into their environment and contribute beautifully to the domestic picture of a French settlement. They are related to this rock, Quebec, to the world across the ocean in France, and to the challenge of the future. Cather draws a picture which emphasizes the hopes and expectations of the people in Quebec as her characters work to create order in a savage land.

One cannot look at this novel, however briefly, without noticing the innumerable descriptions of the religious traditions of the people. The colonists may be exiled from their homes in France, cut off from the families and friends, but they have brought their religious tradition and a great reverence for it with them. Cather spends the first three books emphasizing the religious foundations upon which the French colony was built. There are stories of saints and martyrs, such as the famous Montreal recluse, and involved explanations of the rivalry between the old Bishop and his successor. These narratives provide background and place the religious aspect in sharp contrast with the stories of adventure and bravery in the wilderness which follow in the last part of the book.

Through these vignettes, Willa Cather created a mood, a picture of life which illustrates the virtues in the lives of proud people and how those virtues are symbolized in the enduring rock of Quebec.

SHE

Type of work: Novel
Author: H. Rider Haggard (1856-1925)
Type of plot: Adventure romance
Time of plot: Late nineteenth century
Locale: Africa
First published: 1887

H. Rider Haggard invented, and was probably the greatest practitioner of, the jungle adventure-romance. She ranks with King Solomon's Mines *as one of his two finest achievements in the genre. The grotesque, exotic setting and, most of all, the unforgettable—if realistically unbelievable—character of Ayesha, "she-who-must-be-obeyed," the white jungle queen-goddess, give the novel the power of myth, despite all of its artistic shortcomings.*

England in the 1880's and 1890's saw a great upsurge of interest and popularity in the historical adventure romance and especially in the works of three vivid, skillful writers—Robert Louis Stevenson, Rudyard Kipling, and H. Rider Haggard. Although posterity has granted the greater artistic status to Stevenson and Kipling, the prolific Haggard was, in his own time, the most popular and immediately influential of the three. And, at his very best, as in *King Solomon's Mines* (1885) and *She,* Haggard's work is not unworthy of comparison with his two co-romancers. At the very least, in these two early works he established plot conventions and character types that have become central to the jungle romance from the Victorian age to the present.

Like *King Solomon's Mines,* and most adventure romances, *She* centers on a heroic quest, but this one is not for anything as mundane as hidden treasure, but for something much more mysterious and exotic—a white jungle queen who may or may not be a "goddess." This shift in emphasis almost turns *She* from an adventure narrative to a dark fantasy. The object of the quest, "She-who-must-be-obeyed," is found a little over halfway into the novel and, once "She"—or Ayesha—enters the story, the narrative question "What will happen to our heroes" changes to "Who or what is She?" "Where does She come from?" "What does She want?" "What will happen to her?"

Ayesha may never be completely believable, but her vivid, ambiguous presence dominates the book. She is, as American novelist Henry Miller once said, "*the* femme fatale." Haggard succeeds in conveying a sense of her incredible physical perfection and sensuality by judiciously presenting only a few details, leaving her essentially an abstract, idealized vision of feminine beauty. And yet she also comes through as very " human"—a woman deeply in love who is a bit of a coquette—even, for all of her two thousand years, somewhat girlish. At the same time, however, Ayesha is a determined, ruthless lover and ruler, a contradictory character who combines cynicism and innocence, weariness and eagerness, benign detachment and passionate involvement, generous good and vindictive evil in a single larger-than-life personality.

The scope and ferocity of her character further suggests powers far beyond the merely mortal, although it is difficult to say exactly *what* she is supposed to stand for. She identifies herself with nature and yet in many ways seems to be supremely unnatural. Having found Kallikrates, the lover she once jealously murdered, reincarnated in Leo Vincey, she plans a triumphant return to civilization and a use of her supernatural powers to create a magical paradise for mankind with herself and Leo as absolute monarchs. At this point she destroys herself by returning a second time to the Pillar of Fire. In short, Ayesha seems to embody the ultimate Paganism, even Satanism, which denies the limits set on man by a providential divinity—at least that is the final interpretation Holly attaches to her disintegration. But the ending of the book strongly hints that, in spite of what we have seen, she will somehow or other return to "finish" her story.

This bizarre, extreme character would be ridiculous, however, if Haggard had not surrounded her with a wealth of images and details that reinforce the mysterious, primordial atmosphere of the novel: the mysterious artifacts and documents that Leo's dying father gives Holly to establish Leo's ancestry, the savage Amahagger cannibals with their "hot-pot" ceremonies, the strange, extinct Kingdom of Kôr, with its peculiar architecture and legends from man's pre-history, and, most vivid of all, the incessant images of decay and death. The book is glutted with such scenes and details and they become more extreme and frequent as the novel develops: the killing and torturing of the natives, the tombs of Kôr where the characters sleep on burial slabs, the embalmed figures of long-dead Kôr aristocrats, including their greatest king, the great heap of bodies of the less favored, the wild native dance ritual where corpses are burned as torches and, finally, the image of Ayesha disintegrating before the eyes of her appalled comrades. Thus, the novel counterpoints and associates Ayesha's heroic sensuality with death and destruction—"Eros" and "Thanatos"—in a symbiotic relationship that gives the book much of its most disturbing emotional force.

Which is not to say that *She* is a great novel. The book is filled with serious flaws. The plot is crude and cumbersome. Its prose is overblown, falsely ornate, abstract, and very often dull. The secondary characters are weak; the natives are stereotypes, while the "whites" are bland, stiff, and trite. Holly's long rhetorical digressions, intended to expound the book's "philosophical and religious" themes, are at best pompous, at worst embarrassing. In short, the novel teeters on the edge of absurdity. Yet, if one approaches it openly and imaginatively, it leaves a more lasting and powerful impression than many a more "serious" book. Perhaps *She* is one of a handful of "great bad novels"—like Mary Shelley's *Frankenstein* and Herman Melville's *Pierre*

—that touch such vital centers and provoke such emotional responses in the reader that the flaws in their execution and the implausibility of their ideas seem relatively unimportant.

Keith Neilson

SHE STOOPS TO CONQUER

Type of work: Drama
Author: Oliver Goldsmith (1728-1774)
Type of plot: Comedy of situation
Time of plot: Eighteenth century
Locale: England
First presented: 1773

Oliver Goldsmith labeled She Stoops to Conquer *a "laughing comedy" to distinguish it from the "sentimental comedies" that dominated the theater in his day and which were, in his view, violations of the essential nature of the genre. In* She Stoops to Conquer *he succeeded brilliantly, both artistically and commercially, in writing a comedy that is funny as well as insightful.*

Oliver Goldsmith was a poverty-haunted, irritable, and envious man with a great wit and generosity and an essentially lovable nature; all of these contradictory characteristics are reflected in his writings. Hopelessly impractical, especially in money matters, in talk often foolish, he wrote with genius and Irish liveliness in many different forms and left a legacy of at least four masterpieces that will last as long as the English language endures. Goldsmith was forced, like Dr. Johnson before him, to plod away as a literary hack, trying to survive in London's Grub Street literary world. He did editorial work for booksellers, wrote essays and criticism, and gradually gained a modest reputation. *The Citizen of the World* essays appeared in 1760 and 1761, bringing him more recognition; when they were republished, the charm and grace of the satire in these letters, and their humor and good sense, caused a sensation. Although this success eased somewhat the pinch of poverty, Goldsmith continued to find it necesary to write pamphlets and miscellaneous journalism. A philosophic poem, *The Traveler,* brought high praise from Dr. Johnson, and *The Deserted Village* was a wide success. In 1766 *The Vicar of Wakefield,* written to pay his rent, brought Goldsmith fame as a novelist. His collected essays was a further triumph, although his money troubles continued. *She Stoops to Conquer,* Goldsmith's second comedy, received a flattering public response, but the financial returns paid off no more than a fraction of the author's huge debts. The drudgery of his efforts to raise money with his pen caused his health to fail, and he finally died in 1774, only forty-four year olds, a victim of his financial failure.

Goldsmith's writings reflected his whimsical, yet serious, nature. As he fluctuated from lighthearted foolishness to depths of depression, so his work demonstrates a somber, earthy thread running through the farce and sentiment. He belonged mainly to the neoclassical tradition, his style and vocabulary of the eighteenth century, but he avoided the ponderousness of his friend and mentor, Dr. Johnson. Even his sentimental streak was lightened with his Irish humor and wistfulness.

Of all of Goldsmith's varied writings, *She Stoops to Conquer* stands supreme, one of the most beloved comedies of all time. The humor and humanity of such characters as Kate Hardcastle and Tony Lumpkin had guaranteed the play's immortality. The sentimental drama, under the influence of such works as Steele's *The Conscious Lovers,* dominated the eighteenth century stage. The rising middle class craved this kind of drama, and it provided a conventional code of manners for these new prosperous theatergoers to emulate. In *She Stoops to Conquer,* Goldsmith tried to move toward real human motivation and escape the artificiality of the sentimental drama, which was in many respects a flight from reality. He satirized the posturings of the sentimental plays, but he did much more than that; his wit and style and shrewd eye for human foibles gave *She Stoops to Conquer* a vitality and sense of real life that has endured for more than two centuries.

With all of its polish, the eighteenth century was often crude and coarse and cruel; Goldsmith helped to humanize its imagination, to bring it around to his more gentle humor. At the conclusion of *She Stoops to Conquer,* the audience cannot help but be saner and more civilized, and to view its fellow mortals with a warmer sympathy. There is no viciousness in Goldsmith's comedy, as there might be found in the plays of Sheridan or Congreve and Molière. In *She Stoops to Conquer,* the emphasis is not on the outcome (which the audience never doubts) but on *how* the outcome will arrive. The basis of the plot is the sentimental conflict of the opposed lovematch and the subordinate trite plot complication (of the mistaken house as an inn, an incident which is said to have happened to Goldsmith in his youth). But Goldsmith takes these conventions and breathes new life into them, with a pace and humanity seldom approached in the drama. The characters are not cruel to each other; even Tony Lumpkin is essentially a goodhearted rogue. The conclusion is a happy one without anyone suffering or being left out in the cold. Unlike so many authors of comedies of manners, Goldsmith has no interest in punishing his characters.

Goldsmith was unlearned compared to his friends and compatriots Sheridan and Johnson, but he was a natural writer with a loathing for pretense and artificiality. If *She Stoops to Conquer* has any message, it is of the dangers of pretense and pretentiousness. Mr. Hardcastle's rule that Kate and her mother must dress plainly reflects this attitude of Goldsmith. The right of individuals to lead their own lives must be considered the second theme of the play, for both Kate and Marlow at last win their right to love and Tony wins his freedom from his mother.

Because of the failure of his previous play, *The Good Natur'd Man,* Goldsmith had difficulty getting *She Stoops to Conquer* produced. The great Garrick would have nothing to do with it, and general opinion was that it was too different from the prevailing mode to be a success. It was believed that only plays in the sentimental manner were wanted by audiences. After many difficulties, the comedy finally opened at Covent Garden and Dr. Johnson himself led a party to see his friend's play through its hour of judgment. "I know of no comedy for many years," Dr. Johnson said, after, "that has answered so much the great end of comedy—making an audience merry." As usual, the Doctor was right, for, while one or two comedies of the time might be considered superior, none of them is merrier. There is, in *She Stoops to Conquer,* something of the quality of the great Elizabethan comedies, a humanity and humor that might have revolutionized the eighteenth century theater. But Goldsmith wrote no more plays and he had no followers or imitators, and he produced almost no effect on the drama of the day. Perhaps technically the play is not as perfect as those of Sheridan and lacks the sharp wit of the Restoration comedies, but it reflects the author's own rich and genial personality and will continue to be produced and read and loved as one of the kindliest and funniest of all comedies.

Bruce D. Reeves

THE SHEEP WELL

Type of work: Drama
Author: Lope de Vega (Lope Félix de Vega Carpio, 1562-1635)
Type of plot: Social criticism
Time of plot: 1476
Locale: Spain
First presented: c. 1619

The Sheep Well, one of Lope de Vega's best plays, uses the entire peasant population of a Spanish village as heroes and heroines. For this reason, and because it reflects such sympathy for the poor classes on the part of the author, The Sheep Well *has been described as the first proletarian drama.*

Cervantes nicknamed him the "Monster" (or prodigy) "of nature" and a brief glance at his incredible career as a soldier, courtier, adventurer, lover, father (of at least 16, legitimate and otherwise), poet, novelist, and Inquisition priest makes one wonder how Lope de Vega found the time and energy to write any plays at all, much less the voluminous quantity—estimates range from 600 to 2000 with almost 500 still extant—that established him as the most prolific playwright of all time.

But Lope de Vega's enormous output was a mixed blessing. The bulk of his works, admittedly written solely for popular consumption, are trivial "formula" works—sensational melodramas, "cape and sword" comedies— with little present-day relevance. But in a few of his plays, especially those historical epics which reflect his own personal antecedents, his greatness as a dramatist is forcefully demonstrated. And, among those peasant dramas, the two plays most generally accepted as his masterpieces are *The King the Greatest Alcalde* (1620-1623) and *The Sheep Well (La fuente ovejuna).*

It is perhaps an exaggeration to call *The Sheep Well* a "proletarian" drama. The peasants do not rebel against the monarchal concept—they willingly seek succor from King Ferdinand and Queen Isabella and make no protest against the treatment, including the torturings, his legal representatives accord the villagers. Nor do they object to the feudal arrangement that gave Commander Guzmán power over them. They only seek to justify their one violent reaction against an obviously vicious and dishonorable tyrant. Indeed, it is Guzmán who really rebels against legitimate authority by supporting the Portuguese claims against King Ferdinand. In the end *The Sheep Well* is a play that demonstrates the validity of the monarchy. Ferdinand's kingly superiority is proven by the charity, mercy, and wisdom he shows not only in pardoning the citizens of Fuente Ovejuna, but also in forgiving Rodrigo Téllez Girón who had, on Guzman's evil advice, fought against his ruler.

The Sheep Well is, however, one of the very rare—and modern—plays with a believable collective hero. Lope probably succeeds here because, unlike so many of his less skillful successors, he creates his "mob" out of several vivid, credible individuals. To develop a convincing group protagonist, the playwright must identify the primary characters, provoke audience understanding and sympathy for them as separate personages, and at the same time create a sense of the group dynamic and momentum. Lope accomplishes this by dramatizing the vivid characteristics, strong passions, and intense relationships of his principals in a few brief, intimate scenes which he juxtaposes against colorful, animated scenes of group activity—Guzmán's "welcome," Laurencia's wedding, the town meeting, and the trial before King Ferdinand.

Thus, the real greatness of the play lies in the marvelous balance Lope maintains between the powerful individual portraits, notably the shy, persistent Frondoso, who becomes the first to defy Guzmán; the venerable, diplomatic Esteban, who combines wisdom with ferocity in guiding the rebellion; the passionate, volatile, articulate Laurencia, a most "modern" woman, whose fiery speech to the villagers rallies them to action; and the overriding sense of the group as a whole asserting its collective will and virtue to demand—and receive—justice.

THE SHELTERED LIFE

Type of work: Novel
Author: Ellen Glasgow (1874-1945)
Type of plot: Social criticism
Time of plot: Twentieth century
Locale: Virginia
First published: 1932

A traditionalist by inclination, both as a Southern lady and as a writer, Ellen Glasgow made that tradition the subject of her incisive, carefully controlled, ironical novels. The Sheltered Life *is one of her most penetrating dissections of upper-class deterioration in the early twentieth century. The characters form a microcosm of Glasgow's society. Especially notable is Eva Birdsong, the ideal Southern lady, who becomes the final victim of its false illusions.*

As a realist of the Southern regional school, Ellen Glasgow sought, in *The Sheltered Life,* to depict the genuine, day-to-day actualities of Southern life without sentimental overlays. Although an American author and thoroughly imbued with American—and especially Southern—values, Glasgow was more nearly attuned to anachronistic Victorian British novelists of manners than has generally been recognized. While she precisely portrayed manners and mores of a particular age and place, Glasgow nonetheless fell prey to the fascination of her subject matter. Despite her skepticism, she thus presented the Southern class conflict from an overly favorable point of view, although *The Sheltered Life* ends tragically. In this sense, Glasgow accurately and valuably reflected a current trend.

The Sheltered Life is a satire of the genteel South trying to cope with modern industrialism. As such, the novel represents a fundamental class conflict between a conventional way of life and the necessary demands of progress. How to resolve the dilemma between traditional commitments and the requirements of modern life constitutes the fulcrum of *The Sheltered Life,* and the resolution of the problem is the resolution of the novel.

Yet, in a related vein, the plot revolves around a very timely issue of feminism, for the women in the novel assume roles of decision-makers. With proper deference to the sly irony in the book's title, it is necessary to see the world as Glasgow would have us see it—through the eyes of affluent Virginia housewives in the early twentieth century. Such a point of view, radical for Glasgow's times and even radical for the present, nonetheless presents a refreshing perspective on such universal and ubiquitous problems as socioeconomic conflicts, racial strife, and regional differences in approaches to reconciliation of disparate interests. Glasgow's novel also provides solid and compelling entertainment aside from its social significance.

SHIRLEY

Type of work: Novel
Author: Charlotte Brontë (1816-1855)
Type of plot: Psychological romance
Time of plot: Nineteenth century
Locale: Yorkshire, England
First published: 1849

Shirley is a badly flawed but memorable novel. Its failure can probably be ascribed to Charlotte Brontë's choice of a subject matter—labor conflicts in the weaving industry—which was beyond her experience and unsuited to her use of the omniscient point of view. But, even though their stories are awkwardly linked, the two dominant females, Shirley Keeldar and Caroline Helstone, are potent characterizations that represent two new, distinct, vital kinds of women.

During 1848-1849 while Charlotte Brontë was writing *Shirley,* her sisters Emily and Anne and her brother Branwell all died. Since her two older sisters and her mother had died earlier, Charlotte, thirty-three and unmarried, was left to care for her father. Some evidence suggests that these sad experiences made her add a happy ending to *Shirley.* Her original plan called for Caroline to become an old maid.

In *Shirley* Brontë uses the omniscient point of view, an experiment which did not suit her artistic theory. Further, she tried to write about historical social movements outside her immediate experience, and although she researched the material carefully, she was unable to endow it with the intense living quality *Jane Eyre* possesses. She was no doubt influenced to use the omniscient narrator—who comments often and at length to the reader—by the contemporary writers she admired, Thackeray and George Henry Lewes (life-long companion of George Eliot). *Shirley* is in the Victorian tradition of a "public" novel, employing characters of various classes and much information about the society of the time. The novel is set in 1811-1812, during the Luddite riots, the latters years of the Napoleonic Wars when the Orders in Council had cut off most markets of the Yorkshire woolen trade. The Luddites were textile workers who banded together to destroy the new labor-saving machinery in protest against reduced wages and unemployment.

Such subject matter demands the omniscient narrator, and the Victorian novelists excelled in this manner of presentation. But *Shirley's* point of view lacks coherence. The omniscient narrator never seems to understand clearly her own voice: she is at various times ironic, amused, sympathetic, or analytic. There is none of the unity of tone that marks the first-person narrator in *Jane Eyre* or *Villette.*

Still, *Shirley* is interesting if only to present ideas with which Charlotte Brontë was much concerned, especially the problem of the unmarried woman in a society which accorded status only to the wife and mother.

THE SHOEMAKER'S HOLIDAY

Type of work: Drama
Author: Thomas Dekker (c. 1572-1632?)
Type of plot: Romantic comedy
Time of plot: Reign of Henry V of England
Locale: London and the nearby village of Old Ford
First presented: 1599

The Shoemaker's Holiday is Thomas Dekker's finest achievement. This rollicking success story of a shoemaker's rise to the office of Lord Mayor of London celebrates the middle classes with frolicsome kindliness and vigor. The humorous romantic entanglements—an earl disguises himself as a shoemaker in order to win a middle-class girl, and a shoemaker's assistant wins his wife back from a well-to-do tradesman—further reinforce the democratic sentiments of this Elizabethan masterwork.

The first performance of *The Shoemaker's Holiday* was given for Queen Elizabeth's court during the Chirstmas season of 1599. At that time the drama scene in London was experiencing a state of transition; the earlier romantic style of Greene and Lyly now seemed superficial and escapist, but the darkly realistic comedies of Jonson or the later Shakespeare had not yet been written. As comic drama, *The Shoemaker's Holiday* is an excellent example of the "transitional period" which produced it. Dekker possessed an uncanny talent for mingling realism and romanticism, and this, his first extant play, belongs to two strikingly contradictory literary currents. On the other hand, *The Shoemaker's Holiday* is probably the best illustration of romantic comedy that we have. Yet, at the same time, subtle, but frequent, "realistic" touches make the play an effective tool for discussing the transition in English comedy from romance to realism which can be pinpointed as occurring roughly at the turn of the seventeenth century.

The tone of exuberance—zest for life—which filters through *The Shoemaker's Holiday* may reflect the youthful Dekker who wrote the play. Though he lived for another generation, he never wrote anything better than this early comedy. A poet at heart, Dekker collaborated in writing more than thirty plays and was known as one of "Henslowe's hacks." He was in and out of debtor's prison much of his life.

The play's realistic undercoating—found in the street scenes and whenever the shoemakers are onstage—suggests that even at an early age Dekker was already aware of the dramatic possibilities of realism in comedy. Realism became increasingly evident in his later plays, especially *The Honest Whore* (1604-1605).

The romantic essence of *The Shoemaker's Holiday* may well lie in the absence of a palpable evil, of really dangerous villains in the play. In terms of the genre, it exhibits all the motifs and thematic conventions of romantic comedy. The standard theme of "rival wooers," for example, is carried out through Lacy and Rose and, in the subplot, by Ralph and Jane. Dekker carries the theme through its conventional turns as the true love between these couples is blocked by disapproving and uncomprehending guardians or by circumstances beyond their control, and finally, as they are each in turn separated and then joyfully reunited.

A second major convention is the "gentility theme," the idea that true nobility is inborn, not simply inherited. The gentility theme weaves its way through all romantic comedy plots, and it is best displayed in *The Shoemaker's Holiday* by the dignity and pride with which Simon Eyre approaches humble labor. The most succinct statement of the theme also belongs to Eyre: "Prince am I none, yet nobly born." In the fifth act King Henry, whose role is to rectify all the play's complications, makes the gentility theme rule supreme as he chides Lacy's uncle for thinking Rose not noble enough to marry Lacy:

> Lincoln, no more.
> Dost thou not know that love respects no blood,
> Cares not for difference of birth or state?
> The maid is young, well born, fair, virtuous,
> A worthy bride for any gentleman.

Other stock features of romantic comedy in this play are the disguises (Lacy becomes Hans the shoemaker), the song and dance of the Morris dancers, and the use of mythic machinery and folklore. And of course Eyre's blazingly quick rise to fortune and fame is perhaps the most romantic touch of all.

But Dekker's romantic plot is firmly wedded with realistic manners and scenes, a combination reminiscent of Chaucer. During the transition years 1598-1603, comedies began catering to a rising interest in actual city types, and Dekker's choice of Simon Eyre as the central character of his play reflects an innovative turn. Although Eyre is on stage during less than half the scenes, and although the action of his plot involves no conflict, it is his characterization which sets and to a large extent controls the mood of the play. His occupation as shoemaker is definitely a step away from the more aristocratic leanings of Lyly and Greene and reflects a growing bourgeois audience's increasing interest in itself.

More central to the success of Eyre's characterization is its break from the traditional and the stereotyped, for he seems to be a living character. Perhaps the most memorable thing about the play is its brisk, workaday-morning mood of healthy, goodhearted, and not overly sensitive people. Eyre's personality combines with that of his lively shoemakers, his shrewish wife, and Lacy and Rose, to present a copious picture of London life.

The extent of Dekker's "realistic" touches is indicated by the fact that the play refers specifically to thirty-five landmarks within a radius of three miles of the city. The references reveal that the playwright is mirroring the London of his own time, and not the real Simon Eyre's time a hundred and fifty years earlier. Dekker is not careful to avoid anachronisms; but, if comic realism is defined as the frequent interjection of material familiar to the audience—bits of current speech, little natural touches of everyday environment, or references to well-known but ordinary people, Dekker's treatment is clearly realistic.

There is also evidence that the Rose-Lacy story has a parallel to real people and real situations contemporary to Dekker. Sir John Spencer, actual Lord Mayor of London, had forbidden his daughter to marry her chosen lover. He gained notoriety by hiding his daughter so she could not run away and by mistreating her so badly that the law was finally invoked to place her in the custody of an uncle. All of this happened in the months directly preceding the first performance of Dekker's play. Although the stingy Spencer is more an antithesis of the generous Eyre, the comparison offers another intriguing parallel between the play and the time in which it was written.

Dekker's inveterate interest in dialect (Irish, Welsh, French, Spanish, thieves' Latin, and Dutch) may reflect a foreign background, and that may help explain the uncannily perceptive realistic touches imposed on the play. A partly foreign eye can sometimes pick out cultural characteristics which a native observer is engulfed by and therefore blind to. Dekker's best scenes— early morning in Tower Street, Eyre's election to the shrievalty, the party at Old Ford, Jane in the sempster's shop, Firk outwitting Otley and Lincoln, the "stir" outside St. Faith's, and the pancake feast at Leadenhall on Shrove Tuesday—demonstrate his ability to see continuity in London life throughout the ages, an ability by which he creates in *The Shoemaker's Holiday* an atmosphere of old and merry England at its jolliest.

Jean G. Marlowe

THE SIEGE OF RHODES

Type of work: Drama
Author: Sir William Davenant (1606-1668)
Type of plot: Historical romance
Time of plot: 1522
Locale: The fortress at Rhodes and the nearby coast of Caria
First presented: 1656

William Davenant is a transitional figure between Elizabethan and Restoration drama. His early plays were authored prior to the 1641 Puritan ban, and during the closing years of the interregnum he was the pivotal figure in the reawakening of the theater. Produced with an emphasis on its music and scenery to mitigate its dramatic qualities, The Siege of Rhodes *foreshadowed the heroic drama of the Restoration and signaled the beginning of a new, vital theatrical era.*

Although *The Siege of Rhodes* preceded the actual restoration of the monarchy by four years, historians of the drama agree that it anticipates all the major traits of Restoration Heroic Drama: the themes of love and honor, exotic settings and historical tone, intensely felt love between heroes and virtuous but passionate heroines, and characters larger than life, capable of lordly magnanimity. The glorification of honor and love, although derived from Corneille's neoclassic plays, is primarily a refutation of the Puritan insistence on yoking honor exclusively to religion and theocracy. The fondness for exalted and highly magnanimous characters can be interpreted as a rejection of the democratic and leveling characteristics of Cromwell's social order.

The principal conflicts arise from the tensions created between love and honor. Or, to put it another way—because love is an overwhelming emotion, it is the only force that can shake the centrality of honor in a noble mind. There is no braver soldier in the Christian ranks than Alphonso; even though his jealousy makes him fight all the harder, his honor is in serious jeopardy because his jealousy has weakened the strength of his love. It is only when he discards jealousy that he rediscovers the proper connection between love and honor: "For honour should no leader have but love," he says. The same insight moves Solyman to his great magnanimity at the end of the play.

The bombastic diction and operatic quality of heroic drama give it a slightly ludicrous air. And the monotony and stylized quality of the heroic couplets, together with the exaggerated characters are also hindrances to modern enjoyment. Many burlesques and farces of the eighteenth and nineteenth century theater were based on heroic conventions. However, if one interprets the play as a dramatic example of the Baroque spirit, its larger-than-life quality becomes more comprehensible. The play is constructed on assumptions similar to those behind a Rubens painting or a Bach oratorio.

THE SIGN OF FOUR

Type of work: Novel
Author: Arthur Conan Doyle (1859-1930)
Type of plot: Mystery romance
Time of plot: 1888
Locale: London
First published: 1889

In The Sign of the Four, *Sherlock Holmes uses his miraculous powers of observation, deduction, and induction to solve a mysterious locked room murder which leads to the revelation of an exotic Eastern plot, reminiscent of Wilkie Collins'* The Moonstone, *an exciting boat chase on the Thames, and a pair of bizarre villains, the one-legged Jonathan Small and his pygmy accomplice, Tonga.*

Although considerable dispute exists as to the relative merits of the fifty-six short stories, there is a general agreement among most critics and "Sherlockians" as to the rating of the four Sherlock Holmes novels. *The Sign of Four* is usually placed second to *The Hound of the Baskervilles* and solidly ahead of *A Study in Scarlet* and *The Valley of Fear. The Sign of Four* is praised for its picture of Holmes in action and the ingenuity of the initial puzzle, for its evocation of the atmosphere of London in the 1880's, for its sharp delineation of character, and for its dramatic effectiveness. It is sometimes faulted, however, for a plot too closely reminiscent of Wilkie Collins' *The Moonstone,* a solution that comes too early in the narrative (slightly over half-way), and for Jonathan Small's overly long confession. Critic Julian Symons is probably right in his opinion that "the prime defect of both books (*A Study in Scarlet* and *The Sign of Four*) . . . is that they could have been condensed into short stories."

But if *The Sign of Four* is too long, it still contains some of Conan Doyle's best writing as well as all of the elements that have made the Holmes stories so popular and entertaining. Indeed, the more leisurely structure of the novelette, if unnecessary for the substance of the events described, does allow for a fuller treatment of such "incidentals" as character development, general background, colorful digressions, and atmosphere—"peripheral" elements that are essential to the Holmes stories and that go a long way toward explaining their durability and universality.

One evident reason for this long-standing popularity lies in the character of the principals and their unique relationship. Perhaps Doyle's most important contribution to the detective story was his "humanizing" of the detective. Edgar Allan Poe's C. Auguste Dupin is little more than a disembodied intellect. Wilkie Collins' Sergeant Cuff is more personable, but considerably less skillful. Émile Gaboriau's two early examples, M. Lecoq and Père Tabaret, are ingenious detectives and amiable fellows, but have almost no distinguishing personal traits. Sherlock Holmes is the first fictional detective who is both an extraordinary investigator and a sharply delineated character, and his relationship with Dr. Watson is the first distinctive partnership in novelistic crime fighting.

The most obvious things about Holmes are his incredible powers of observation, deduction, and induction (in spite of what he says, most of Holmes's conclusions are arrived at by induction; that is, he draws answers from a mass of small details). This talent is demonstrated over and over in unraveling the most exotic and obscure crimes. Holmes's procedures are always the same: first, his close examination; next, the impossible set of conclusions; and, finally, the minute "elementary" explication. Usually, in the opening passages, Holmes "practices" on the client's superficial characteristics and then, as the substance of the story, he applies his extraordinary talents to the major problem of the narrative. In novels, such as *The Sign of Four,* there is usually a sequence of problems; as Holmes unscrambles one puzzle, the solution points to a new, more sinister one, and so on until the entire problem is finally solved and the malefactor brought to justice.

But there is more to the Sherlock Holmes stories than ingenious problem solving. If it was Wilkie Collins who originated the practice of "humanizing" his detective by giving him eccentric traits and hobbies (Sergeant Cuff raises roses), it was Doyle who perfected the technique. He supplies Holmes with a wide range of sidelines and interests: bee keeping, violin playing, opera, boxing, toxology, swordplay, food, theater, tobacco ash, and many others. But Holmes is no Renaissance Man. He prides himself on large areas of total ignorance: art, philosophy, literature, astronomy, and politics, to name a few. The unifying factor is that all of Holmes's diverse knowledge and talent goes into the solving of intricate problems. Holmes is, finally, a monomaniacal rationalist who feels lost without a challenging intellectual puzzle. That is why, he tells Watson near the beginning of *The Sign of Four,* when he is without a case, he must resort to drugs: "Hence the cocaine. I cannot live without brainwork. What else is there to live for? Stand at the window there. Was ever such a dreary, dismal, unprofitable world? . . . What is the use of having powers, Doctor, when one has no field upon which to exert them?"

Thus, although Holmes is infinitely more interesting, he is, like Poe's Dupin, an intellectual freak. "You are an automaton," Watson tells him, "a calculating machine. . . . There is something positively inhuman in you at times." All in all, Holmes is a genius, detached from common society, even a Nietzschean "Superman" who has chosen to use his extraordinary powers in the service of man, not so much from a sense of justice (although he has a strong one), but out of a need to use those abilities to fend off the triviality and meaninglessness of everyday existence. Much of Holmes's long-term popularity is due to the fact that, as an "Outsider," Holmes excites the popular imagination, but, as a defender of the *status quo,* he is ultimately reassuring.

But, given the detective's one-sidedness, if Holmes were presented alone, he would be grotesque. That which really humanizes Holmes is Dr. John Watson. If Holmes is the "Superman" and "Outsider," Watson is the ordinary professional man, astonished by his friend's capacities, but aware of his human imperfections. Watson is neither a slavish worshiper of genius, like Dupin's narrator, nor an amiable drunk, like Father Absinthe, who assists Gaboriau's M. Lecoq. If Watson has little talent for deduction, he is not the blustering boob of many Holmes movies.

When Holmes says "a client is to me a mere unit, a factor in a problem," Watson recoils. To Watson, clients are people to be helped and it is through the good doctor that we establish our own emotional connection to them. Doyle almost always centers his crime on a personal or family situation and the fate of the people involved is as important as the working out of the puzzle. Because of this, Watson is every bit as important as Holmes. Indeed, without Watson, it is doubtful that there could be a Sherlock Holmes.

This relationship is most evident in *The Sign of Four,* which is, in addition to a mystery, a love story in which Watson meets the client, Mary Morstan, falls in love, courts her, and, with the resolution of the problem, wins her. Doyle adroitly weaves this romance in and around the mystery story and deftly shows Watson's emotional reactions without distracting from the main line of detection. The fact that Watson pursues a bride while Holmes chases a criminal adds an extra dimension and flavor to *The Sign of Four,* as well as sharpening and deepening our picture of Watson as a man. Although his behavior, under the influence of his feelings for Mary, may occasionally be a bit foolish, his actions are admirable and resourceful. He never forgets the main problem and he assists Holmes in his solution with considerable skill and courage. And we must admire his resolute determination to rescue the fortune for Mary in spite of the fact that it will doom their romance. Thus, when Jonathan Small throws the jewelry into the Thames, we are glad, since it will enable Watson to realize his romantic ambition.

The Sign of Four has all of the ingredients of the best Holmes puzzles: a peculiar situation, a tentative revelation that leads to further enigmas, a vivid London environment that leads to an exotic setting, and, most important, a spectacular and bizarre crime which can be explained only through the most elaborate and imaginative deductions. Mary Morstan's initial problem is strange enough to seize immediately a reader's attention, but it does not become actually threatening until we are involved with the Sholto family and the sinister events that surround them.

The actual crime, the killing of Bartholomew Sholto, is a variation of the "locked room" murder situation so dear to the hearts of mystery story fans in general and "Sherlockians" in particular. The bizarre quality of the murder is further emphasized by the discovery of "a long dark thorn stuck in the skin just above the ear," the marks of a "wooden stump," and a set of footprints "half the size of an ordinary man."

As soon as these exotic clues are enumerated, however, they lead Holmes directly to Jonathan Small and Tonga, his dwarfish native accomplice. The novel is at this point, unfortunately, little over half finished: the rest is divided between Holmes's pursuit of the malefactors and a long statement by the villain, Jonathan Small, explaining the events leading up to the crime. The thwarted efforts of Holmes and Watson to track down Small and Tonga with a lumbering mixed breed dog named Toby are amusing, Holmes's skill in accurately predicting Small's escape route and his strategy in tracing him are impressive, and the final boat chase on the Thames is exciting. Added to all this is Small's confession, which gives us a fascinating villain who is both repulsive and sympathetic. But, with the major mystery already solved, all of this is anticlimactic. Once we have seen Holmes's brilliant mind cut through the tangle of clues and ambiguities that surround Sholto's murder to identify the killers, their methods, and their motives, the rest is superfluous.

Keith Neilson

SILAS MARNER

Type of work: Novel
Author: George Eliot (Mary Ann Evans, 1819-1880)
Type of plot: Domestic realism
Time of plot: Early nineteenth century
Locale: England
First published: 1861

This charming tale of a poor dissenting weaver who, betrayed and unjustly accused, becomes bitter and miserly until redeemed and transformed by a foundling, is virtually perfect in structure, tone, and execution. As several critics have pointed out, the novel combines the emotional and moral satisfactions of the fairy tale with the solid intellectual appeal of the realistic narrative.

In four remarkable years George Eliot published in succession *Scenes from Clerical Life* (1858), *Adam Bede* (1859), *The Mill on the Floss* (1860), and *Silas Marner* (1861). The last, a short novel or novella, is unlike the other works, for its narrative combines elements of myth—some critics have called it a fairy tale—with the otherwise realistic details of English country life centering around the rustic village of Raveloe. Certainly the novel can be understood as a moral tale. Its message, however sentimental to a modern reader, is unambiguous: true wealth is love, not gold. As a myth of loss and redemption, the novel concerns the miser Silas Marner, who loses his material riches only to reclaim a greater treasure of contentment. Silas comes to learn that happiness is possible only for the pure and self-sacrificing. Because of his love for Eppie, he is transformed, as if by magic, from a narrow, selfish, bitter recluse into a truly human, spiritually fulfilled man.

The novel, however, has a dimension other than the moralistic. George Eliot skillfully counterpoints the experiences of Silas with those of Godfrey Cass. Whereas Godfrey appears, when the reader first meets him, to be a fortunate man entirely the opposite of the sullen miser, his fortunes fail just as Silas' improve. The wealthy, genial Godfrey has a secret guilt—an unacknowledged marriage to a woman beneath him in social class and refinement. Silas, on the other hand, carries with him the smoldering resentment for a wrong which he had suffered (and suffered innocently) from his friend William Dane. Godfrey's sense of guilt festers, especially after he learns about the terrible circumstances of the woman's death. Nevertheless, he remains silent, fearful of exposing his past. Eppie, the child of his brief union with the woman, thus becomes the miser's treasure, to replace the sterile gold stolen by Dunstan. Thereafter for Godfrey, the happiness of the old man is his doom. His second wife, Nancy, is barren; and when he offers, too late, to adopt Eppie as his own child, she clings to her foster father. Silas' love has earned what Godfrey's power had failed to command.

By contrasting Silas' good fortune with Godfrey's disappointment, the author expands the mythic scope of her fiction. If some men—the pure and deserving—discover almost by accident the truths of happiness, others, maybe no less deserving, pass by their chances and endure misery. Silas is reformed not only spiritually but also psychologically. Once blasphemous, he returns to the Christian faith of his childhood. But his religious reaffirmation is not so important as the improvement of his psychological health. Freed of his neurotic resentment for past injustices, he becomes a friend to all, beloved of the village. For Godfrey, whose history is realistic rather than marvelous, quite the opposite fate happens. Without an heir, he shrinks within himself. He may endure his disgrace, even eventually make up to Eppie and her husband Aaron some of the material things he owes her; yet he cannot shake his sense of wrongdoing, appease his sorrow for betrayal, nor make restitution for the evils of the past. George Eliot, who once described her novel as "rather somber," thus balances her miraculous fable of rebirth for the favored Silas with another more common human story, that of the defeated Godfrey Cass.

THE SILENT WOMAN

Type of work: Drama
Author: Ben Jonson (1573?-1637)
Type of plot: Satirical comedy
Time of plot: Early seventeenth century
Locale: London
First presented: 1609

A superbly constructed comedy, The Silent Woman *was the first play that Jonson set in his native land. It is, therefore, the forerunner of the great play* The Alchemist, *of the second version of* Every Man in His Humour, *and of* Bartholomew Fair, *another magnificent prose comedy. The laughter in* The Silent Woman *is less savage than the laughter frequently characteristic of Jonson.*

The Silent Woman, a masterful comedy of humors that verges upon farce, gently satirizes the follies of women and women-haters. The principal butt of the satire is Morose, whose "humor"—that is, psychological unbalance—is an exaggerated fear of noise. This weakness, more a fretful hypersensitivity than a madness, betrays his judgment when he determines to court a suitable mate. Gullibly—and to the audience, comically—he accepts at face value the pretended virtues of the "silent woman," Epicœne, who speaks softly and with modest deference, much to his delight. Morose's foolish credulity must be punished, of course, and Jonson has the old man discover, all in good time, that Epicœne is neither silent nor a woman.

Beyond exposing Morose's folly, caused by his testy humor, *The Silent Woman* satirizes on a grander scale the vanity both of women and of their pursuers. In this connection it should be remembered that many seventeenth century clergymen and moralistic pamphleteers, most of them Puritans, inveighed against women. From Eve onward, the female sex was castigated for a multitude of weaknesses. By treating a subject popular in this anti-feminist tradition, Jonson could exploit with comic irony the absurd stereotypes concerning both sexes. At first Epicœne, the supposed "silent gentlewoman," is seen as "a woman of excellent assurance and an extraordinary happy wit and tongue," but is later revealed as a screaming—although counterfeit—virago. The real women of the play—Lady Haughty, Lady Centaure, and Mistress Doll Mavis—the "Ladies Collegiates," are idle gossips whose "actions are governed by crude opinion without reason or cause." Finally, Mistress Otter, the most aggressive of the harridans, is a terrible scold who vexes and even beats her pitiful henpecked husband, the captain. Taken as a group, the women are furies, whom men should wisely fly from rather than embrace.

Yet in fairness Jonson does not hand over to the gallants any unwarranted prize of superiority. In the comedy of the sexes—measured and sly enough to approach a comedy of manners—the author despises the male braggarts and liars just as he has rebuked the women. Tom Otter can curse his wife in private, but in her presence he is a coward. Sir Jack Daw and Sir Amorous La-Foole, also cowardly louts, boast of their prowess with women but cannot prove their mettle when it comes to a test. As for Morose, at one point he declares himself impotent, so that he might have grounds to divorce his disappointing "bride." Lucky for Morose, Epicœne is no more woman than he is a gentleman. For his sad experience the old codger simply loses his money to his heir, Sir Dauphine, rather than what remains of his sanity. For Jonson, most of whose comedies are more bitter, the punishment is mild indeed.

SIMPLICISSIMUS THE VAGABOND

Type of work: Novel
Author: H. J. C. von Grimmelshausen (c. 1625-1676)
Type of plot: Picaresque romance
Time of plot: The Thirty Years' War (1618-1648)
Locale: Germany
First published: 1669

Simplicissimus *is primarily a rambling, episodic, vivid account of the Thirty Years' War narrated by a footloose participant—from both sides. The book is of special interest to students of the modern drama since it was a primary source of, and inspiration for, Bertolt Brecht's great epic play* Mother Courage.

Simplicissimus is a picaresque romance in the Spanish picaresque tradition, but it is peculiarly German. It is in part autobiographical, and its constant meditation on the meaning and values of life reflects the earnestness of seventeenth century Germany, dominated by the trauma of the Thirty Years' War.

Grimmelshausen was himself a soldier in the war, alternately fighting on both sides. After the war, his career was varied and his writings, aside from his war novel, are unremarkable. In *Simplicissimus,* however, he captures the German experience of the war, which underlies all literature of the period. Life is seen as unpredictable, ruled by fate and fortune. Man is caught in a whirlpool of constant change and seen at his most bestial as well as his most sublime. The novel is filled with adventures, told in short chapters, often more like anecdotes. The composition is loose, and it was easy for Grimmelshausen to continue the novel in a sixth book after the publication of the original five. The unity of the work is thus not in its structure but in its attitude. Grimmelshausen begins with the destruction of the family and the innocent young boy's upbringing in religious isolation, a kind of Utopia. This early religious life provides a measure by which all the subsequent events can be evaluated. His life as a soldier is without foundation or direction, colorful, but without spiritual substance.

The reader continually is led to see behind the deceptive charms of the world and it is no surprise that Simplicius' path leads to disillusionment and despair, finally bringing him back to the hermit's life where he began. Thus, the ultimate sense of the novel is anti-picaresque and beneath the adventure one finds a serious commentary on the world and its values.

SIR CHARLES GRANDISON

Type of work: Novel
Author: Samuel Richardson (1689-1761)
Type of plot: Epistolary novel of manners
Time of plot: Eighteenth century
Locale: England
First published: 1753-1754

Sir Charles Grandison represents Samuel Richardson's ideal of manly virtue, the "just man made perfect." In his character the novelist deliberately and obviously attempts to offset the negative picture of the male he presented in Mr. B. (Pamela) and Lovelace (Clarissa). And perhaps he is intended as an idealized self-portrait. The artistic result, however, is dullness, the usual result of unalloyed virtue in literature.

"Pot-boiler," a pejorative, twentieth century appelation directed at popular works without literary merit, has been applied unjustly to *Sir Charles Grandison.* Although the novel was deliberately written for popular consumption, it nonetheless has intrinsic literary qualities and holds an important place in the history of literature.

As a young man, Samuel Richardson, because he was literate at a time when many people were not, was often asked by young ladies to compose love letters for them. He later used those letters and other personal correspondence as bases for his novels, which were composed in the epistolary form, cast in an essentially first-person narrative. His first novel, *Pamela,* was published in 1740; the second, *Clarissa,* was published in 1747-1748. Both dealt with stories of virtuous women and brought him great acclaim. Thus it was by popular request that he wrote *Sir Charles Grandison,* a story of the ideal, virtuous man. In all three novels, Richardson used the epistolary form, as a simple and very personal way of narrating his tales; he has, in fact, been called the "father" of the English novel for having developed this narrative technique and for developing the novel of sensibility.

Richardson's sentimental portrayal of Sir Charles is as contrived as that of Pamela or Clarissa, since that approach appealed to his readers, and above all, Richardson sought to satisfy his readers. As a consequence, Sir Charles is a popular ideal rather than a real figure struggling with real-life problems. In an age of enlightenment, when rationality was supposed to overcome superstition, Sir Charles was an unrealistic figure, for he represented not what was, but what some believed ought to be. His idealistic motives and pure approach to life may have made him a popular hero representing what readers wanted to believe, but his staunch virginity and fidelity —especially in his social context—make him fundamentally incredible. The modern reader is struck with disbelief: no one in that time was so naïve, nor is anyone now. Yet *Pamela* and *Clarissa* enjoyed great popular success, and

Sir Charles Grandison was only slightly less popular, because contradictions between ideal and real were not so fully recognized in the eighteenth century as they are in the twentieth.

In effect, *Sir Charles Grandison* contributed, like *Pamela* and *Clarissa,* to the development of the novel form, rather than to the body of enlightened thought. Still, the novel has compelling interest (who is immune to gossip?), and plot and characterization are paintstakingly nurtured to their melodramatic climax. Flaws notwithstanding, Richardson is, in the end, an effective novelist for capturing and holding our attention with a good story.

SIR GAWAIN AND THE GREEN KNIGHT

Type of work: Poem
Author: Unknown
Type of plot: Chivalric romance
Time of plot: Sixth century
Locale: England
First transcribed: Fourteenth-century manuscript

In this Arthurian romance the unknown poet combines two famous medieval motifs: the beheading story and the temptation story. In the climactic scene Sir Gawain not only reveals his courage, but also his human fallibility. The ideal of knightly conduct—of courtesy, courage, and loyalty—against which the poem's action must be measured, was a long-standing ideal, which was still taken seriously in theory, if frequently compromised in practice.

This beautiful and subtly wrought poem is the outstanding example of artistry from the Northern alliterative group of fourteenth century poets. Although its author is anonymous, he must have been thoroughly skilled in writing. References in the romance to such intricate details as armor, tapestries, expensive clothing, and castle architecture, suggest he may well have been a member of the nobility or closely associated with life in castles. And, since much of the poem concerns itself with religion and Christian symbols, many critics believe the author to have been a cleric, perhaps in some noble household.

Most place him in the Northwest Midland area because of the realistic references to forests of Cheshire, Anglesey, and North Wales. His dialect seems to be that of Lancashire or Yorkshire.

Whoever he was, he constructed a highly sophisticated romance remarkable for tightness of plot and analysis of character. For example, he cleverly links together Gawain's two adventures which make up the narrative: the beheading game and the temptation. In other romances these do not always appear together and are not so artistically interdependent.

Also, there are no other works of this period in which an author handles simultaneously different concepts of time. At the outset he binds his poem to the Trojan War so that it operates under historical time. The story's action all takes place within the span of a year (from Christmas to Christmas). There is also a psychological time within Gawain himself. These uses of time serve to order the poem; they also provide complex structure.

The poet's nature description stands out in its exactness and charm. And he proves equally skillful in handling dialogue. The conversations between the Green Knight's Lady and Sir Gawain in the bed chamber scenes play upon all the nuances of repartee and meaning of the courtly love code.

Nor is this author bound to one point of view as the usual omniscient, distant narrator; he can change to a participant in the action. Close study of the three temptation scenes and those of the three hunts show him to be a master of contrasts and parallels in meaning as well as situation.

Though he draws Gawain's exploits and other plot elements from various sources, this anonymous poet transforms them into something new that stands as one of the most intricate, entertaining, and well-crafted works of the Middle Ages.

SIR JOHN VAN OLDEN BARNAVELT

Type of work: Drama
Authors: John Fletcher (1579-1625) and Philip Massinger (1583-1640)
Type of plot: Historical tragedy
Time of plot: 1618-1619
Locale: The Netherlands
First presented: 1619

Sir John Van Olden Barnavelt *represents an attempt by the playwrights to dramatize a contemporary event. The title figure is intended as a nobleman of high station who was brought to ruin by ambition. This intention is never realized, because these virtues are never dramatized. Thus, Barnavelt impresses us as a proud and crotchety old man whose unreasonable machinations lead eventually to a well-deserved beheading.*

Sir John van Olden Barnavelt, though billed as a historical tragedy, really was not based on a historical event by Philip Massinger and John Fletcher, the authors; rather, it was based on an event contemporary with their own times. Sir John van Olden Barnavelt, the famous Advocate of Holland, as letters of his contemporaries prove, was executed in May of 1619. A little more than a year later in August of 1620, the play *Sir John van Olden Barnavelt* was being performed by the King's Men—but not until withstanding the tests of censorship in script and on stage. Sir George Buc, Master of Revels, censored the script in 1619; and, during one of the first performances —if not *the* first performance—given between August 14 and 27, 1619, the play was stopped by the Bishop of London. The actors, however, were soon allowed to perform the play again.

The attempt by Massinger and Fletcher to place the play in front of an audience that had the event still fresh in its mind, led to some dramatic weaknesses that can be assigned to their haste. With the exception of Barnavelt and Grave Maurice, the characters are not well developed; and, there may be, for the reader, a flaw in the character of Barnavelt with his repeated and lengthy demonstrations of constancy as he faces death. With good utilization of the stage, however, this flaw may have been eliminated. There is also a triple repetition of Leidenberch's suicide and far too many scenes with sorrow-laden children. Because of the problems of censorship, an undertone of disparity arises between what appears in the text and what apparently the playwrights would liked to have had appear in the text. The last-minute attempt in Act V to reverse the previous stand on Barnavelt and try valiantly to make him more sympathetic seems to be evidence of this.

There are also, on the other hand, some scenes of strong interest in *Sir John van Olden Barnavelt.* One is in Act III, scene iv, in which Barnavelt visits Leidenberch, his coconspirator, in jail and urges him to take his life. The Fletcherian versification makes Leidenberch's moment of indecision, as he gazes on his sleeping son, even more poignant. Another meritorious scene is Act V, ii, in which Harlem, Utrecht, and Leyden—the three executioners—throw dice to see who will be at the chopping block to cut off Barnavelt's head. This scene, with its grim humor, is reminiscent of the gravedigger's scene in Shakespeare's *Hamlet*.

Although writing in haste, Massinger and Fletcher are to be commended for attempting to adapt a contemporary political event to the stage in *Sir John van Olden Barnavelt*. Unfortunately, although the haste and the politics did contribute to some of its weaknesses, the play has the distinction—along with George Chapman's French tragedies and Thomas Middleton's *Game of Chess*—of being one of the few plays of that time that dealt with a contemporary event.

SISTER CARRIE

Type of work: Novel
Author: Theodore Dreiser (1871-1945)
Type of plot: Naturalism
Time of plot: 1889
Locale: Chicago and New York
First published: 1900

Critically controversial and commercially unnoticed when first published, Sister
Carrie *is now recognized as one of America's finest naturalistic novels. The book
demonstrates a survival of the fittest ethic, with the survival qualities being largely
accidental. Carrie Meeber not only survives, but even flourishes, despite any
exceptional physical, intellectual, or moral qualities, merely because she has the
right instincts and her luck is good. George Hurstwood is destroyed because his
instincts betray him and his luck turns bad.*

Sister Carrie, like most of Theodore Dreiser's novels, embodies his naturalistic belief that while men are controlled and conditioned by heredity, instinct,
and chance, a few extraordinary and usually unsophisticated human beings
refuse to accept their fate wordlessly and instead strive, unsuccessfully, to
find meaning and purpose for their existence. Carrie, the title character,
senses that she is merely a cipher in an uncaring world yet seeks to grasp
the mysteries of life and thereby satisfy her need to matter. In pointing out
"how curious are the vagaries of fortune," Dreiser suggests that even though
life may be cruel, its enigmatic quality makes it all the more fascinating.

Despite its title, the novel is not a study of a family but of Carrie's strangely
unemotional relationships with three men and of the resulting and unexpected
changes which occur in her outlook and status. A "half-equipped little
knight" with small talent, Carrie's instincts nevertheless raise her from a poor
maiden to a successful actress. Basically the novel traces the rise, through
Carrie's increasing reliance on instinct, in a three-stage development. Initially
Carrie is at least partially ruled by reason, but by the end of the first phase
of her rise—marked by her accidental second meeting with Drouet and her
submission to his promises—Carrie begins to abandon the reason which has
not served her well. During this second portion, her blossoming instinct pulls
her to the material advantages offered by Drouet, and her life with him is
evidence of her growing commitment to these instincts. Yet it is her almost
unconscious and unplanned switch to Hurstwood which reveals how totally
she is now following her instincts. Hurstwood offers finer material possessions
and more emotional rapport, and Carrie drifts easily into his orbit. Now
fully and irrevocably tied to her instincts, Carrie throughout the rest of the
novel considers it an obligation to self to let these impulses lead her where
they will. When a stage career and her association with Ames replace Hurstwood, she is merely proceeding further toward the end to which she is bound

once she leaves Drouet and all trace of reason. As a plant must turn toward the sun, Carrie must feed her unsatisfied urge for happiness.

Closely related to Dreiser's belief that instinct must prevail is his thesis that man lacks responsibility for his fate, a thesis suggested by all three main characters. Drouet leads Carrie to what some consider her moral downfall, but, Dreiser tells us, "There was nothing evil in the fellow." His glands, not he, are to blame. Neither is there any question of guilt in Hurstwood's case. Since he rarely makes a choice, he cannot be expected to answer for what happens to him. Chance, not conviction, makes him a thief. His wife, not Hurstwood, ends their marriage. And even his attraction to Carrie is a thing of chance, for "He was merely floating those gossamer threads of thought which, like the spider's, he hoped would lay hold somewhere." Although merely a sham without true power or greatness (a fact Dreiser, dazzled by his own creation, seems to forget), Hurstwood in his decline from semi-prominence to degradation reminds the reader that the forces which send Carrie to stardom can with equal ease reduce a man to nothing. Similarly, we must neither praise Carrie nor be shocked because she is not punished for her sins.

Dreiser presents his ideas through many symbolic images, but most important are the city, the sea, and the rocking chair. The city, in the book represented by both New York and Chicago, is a microcosm of Dreiser's universe. Nature is grim and unfeeling; so is the city. Unless a man is strong and productive and fortunate, he faces the world's indifference, a state magnified in the city where man is perhaps more isolated than elsewhere. When Hurstwood, for example, is dying, he does so alone despite Carrie's presence in a nearby apartment, Drouet's relative closeness in a hotel, and his wife's pending arrival on the train, for none know, nor care, about his tragedy. Dreiser's concept of an uncaring and ever-changing universe is equally conveyed by his use of the sea and the rocking chair. Again and again Carrie is described as a "lone figure in a tossing, thoughtless sea." Like its counterpart, the city, the sea symbol suggests that only the strong or the lucky survive. And the rocking chair hints at the futility of this constant flux, for a rocking chair is in continual motion but goes nowhere. Although Carrie's life would seem to improve, she is sitting miserably in the rocking chair not only at the novel's beginning but also at its end. While this circular development suggests that Carrie has small chance to become truly happy, the fact that she continues to rock provides evidence of her never-ceasing aspiration.

Part of the book reflects events from Dreiser's own turbulent life. In 1886, L. A. Hopkins, a clerk in a Chicago saloon, took $3,500 from his employers, and with Emma Dreiser, one of the author's many troubled siblings, fled to New York. Using this incident as the genesis for his novel, Dreiser modeled Carrie on his sister and used Hopkins for aspects of Hurstwood's personality. By the time Dreiser finished the novel in 1900, however, he had gone far beyond the cheap story of adultery and theft and had created a work which presented complex questions of innocence and guilt.

Surrounding the publication of Dreiser's first novel were the controversy and confusion which were to mark the career of this man from a poor and disturbed Indiana family in whose plight he saw reflected much of the irony of the world. Apparently the novel was accepted by Doubleday, Page during the absence of Frank Doubleday, the senior partner, who upon his return expressed doubt about its content and style. Refusing to release the firm from its unwritten commitment, however, Dreiser demanded that the book be published, and it appeared in 1900. Although it sold poorly (earning for Dreiser only $68.40) and was not aggressively promoted by the publishers, stories relating Mrs. Doubleday's violent objections to its moral view and the resulting suppression of the novel are unverified legend. In his own typical confusion of fact and half-fact, Dreiser added to the myths by telling conflicting accounts of what had happened.

Reaction to the book was surprisingly widespread, and many critics attacked its philosophical premises as immoral. Such charges and those that the novel was poorly written, wordy, and melodramatic would later greet each of Dreiser's productions. Yet as Dreiser wrote book after book exploring the yearning of the young for riches, position, and understanding, a yearning he personally experienced in an overwhelming form, readers were struck by the sincerity, powerful detail, and massive impact of his work. Especially known for *Jennie Gerhardt* (1911), and *An American Tragedy* (1925), Dreiser has a secure niche among top-ranking American naturalists.

Judith Bolch

SISTER PHILOMÈNE

Type of work: Novel
Authors: Edmond (1822-1896) and Jules (1830-1870) de Goncourt
Type of plot: Naturalism
Time of plot: Nineteenth century
Locale: Paris
First published: 1861

The Goncourt brothers were pioneers in the case-history school of naturalism, although their influence on other writers (notably Zola) is more important than their own works. Characterization and plot alike suffer in their novels as subtleties of motivation are lost in the inexorable grinding away of the chance events which cause or alleviate lower-class tragedy. However, in their best works, such as Sister Philomène, *the humanity in individual characters breaks through the mechanistic formulas to animate believable, moving narratives.*

An unusual and sensitive novel, *Sister Philomène* tells the story of a gentle, impoverished girl who suffers because the coarseness of real life is so different from the beauty she craves. Eventually, she comes to confuse romantic love with religious devotion. The first attraction of the girl for her young master, Monsieur Henri, is touchingly recounted, and the frustrated emotion foreshadows her tragic love for Dr. Barnier. Eventually, as a nun, the girl comes to find true joy and peace in serving the ill and bringing them comfort and help. Serenity feeds her gentleness. The plot is simple; it is the story of the development of true Christian piety and charity in a human soul, and the tragic torment of that soul when confronted with human passion.

The book is filled with brilliantly sketched characters who together suggest the variety of life in the Paris of a century and more ago. There is Céline, Philomène's girlhood friend, who learned to read from the *Lives of the Saints*; the hunchbacked Sister Marguerite; Barnier and Malivoire, the young doctors; the courtesan Romaine, and many others. But it is the growing relationship between Sister Philomène and young Dr. Barnier which forms the center of the novel. Tenderly, subtly, the shadings of the relationship are revealed; even the participants do not completely realize the depth of feeling that exists between them. Then, suddenly, the arrival in the hospital of Romaine exposes the truth, and it is too late for anything to be done to avoid the ultimate tragedy. The young nun, exhausted by her labors and her struggles against her initial repugnance for hospital work, and torn by her emotions, cannot cope with the abrupt turn of events. The doctor, amazed by the revelation of her love, and by the death of his former mistress, seeks escape in death. The tragic story is told simply and feelingly, with the careful craftsmanship of first class artists.

The stages of religious devotion (including the lapses) are accurately and precisely detailed in the book, as are the medical practices of the times, and the poverty and sickness of the mass of humanity. The authors skillfully paint pictures of hospital rooms, of operating theaters, and the meeting places of young surgeons and house physicians; the descriptions are obviously based on acute observation. At times, the action freezes for the reader to examine the scene in all of its details; then the story begins again, where it left off. However, the final chapters of the novel move swiftly, caught up in the powerful drama of the simple story. The sharp observation and the extraordinary and subtle delineation of the characters of Sister Philomène and Dr. Barnier raise this novel to a high level of artistic achievement.

SIX CHARACTERS IN SEARCH OF AN AUTHOR

Type of work: Drama
Author: Luigi Pirandello (1867-1936)
Type of plot: Intellectual comedy
Time of plot: Twentieth century
Locale: The stage of a theater
First presented: 1921

Both thematically and theatrically, Six Characters in Search of an Author *is a revolutionary play. Thematically Pirandello explores the ambiguous nature of reality, the fragmentation of personality, and the impossibility of capturing life in art. Theatrically he turns the well-made-play on end, and, refusing simply to tell a story, tries to create one on stage—thus destroying the hard line between stage and audience.*

The greatest Italian playwright of the twentieth century, Pirandello, is now generally recognized as a classic figure of world literature. His stature was recognized when he received the Nobel Prize in 1934, two years before his death. First a poet, then a novelist and writer of short stories, finally a dramatist, Pirandello evolved gradually toward the forms and themes on which his international reputation is based. If his early work is realistic and naturalistic, much of his later, major work may be characterized by his description of *Six Characters in Search of an Author* as "a mixture of tragic and comic, fantastic and realistic." The basic ideas of his major plays are somber, even bitter: the idea that no one can penetrate or understand anyone else's world; the idea that the picture we have of ourselves is different from the picture everyone else has of us; that none of our mental images—about ourselves or about others—can encompass the truth about life, which is always changing and always eluding us. There is, therefore, no such thing as The Truth: there is simply truth "A" that I believe, and truth "B" that you believe. But we are all wrong. To ourselves, however, we are always right. Or, to quote the title of one of his plays: *Right You Are—If You Think So.*

It is, of course, no wonder that these ideas should arise in the skeptical twentieth century. Pirandello was not alone among authors in feeling as he did, and a number of his attitudes may be traced to the French philosopher Henri Bergson (1859-1941). But Pirandello had a personal reason for his reaction, a reason that made the concept that men cannot possibly understand one another become an obsession with him. He was for many years tied to an insane wife who gave him no rest. Among other things, her insanity took the form of a violent, raging jealousy. Pirandello did everything he could to reassure his wife; he wouldn't go out, he turned from his friends, he even yielded up his entire salary to her. But his wife's image of him remained the same, so that alongside his own picture of himself as a patient, resigned, pitying family man, there always hovered the image in his wife's mind of a loathsome being who gave her nothing but pain. As far as Pirandello was concerned, such conflicting images underlay even the most normal of human relations, though in insanity the problem is multiplied, or at least seen more clearly.

Six Characters in Search of an Author deals with the problem of conflicting images and with the problem of reality in general, but it also deals with a special aspect of the same set of problems, for the playwright has a particularly difficult task. Not only must he struggle to pin down the very elusive, the ever-changing thing he calls reality, he must work with the knowledge that he can never deal directly with his audience. Between him and the audience stand the actors and the directors; they give life to the script but they can never give it quite the sort of life the author had in mind. Thus, we may get Tallulah Bankhead's version of a character, or Vivian Leigh's, or Mary Martin's. Even if Shakespeare were alive today, we would not know how he imagined that very mysterious character Hamlet. Instead we would know how Laurence Olivier presented him, or John Gielgud, or Maurice Evans: each with his own personality, his own background, his own voice. And they can never have quite the personality, background, voice, mannerisms that Shakespeare had in mind for Hamlet. No wonder, says one of Pirandello's characters, that a playwright may sometimes throw up his hands in despair and decide that the theater cannot present his situations and characters as he wants them presented.

That is just what has happened in *Six Characters in Search of an Author.* A playwright (Pirandello, of course) has given up. He has imagined six very tormented characters and a very sordid situation but has decided not to go on with his play. As one of his characters put it, "he abandoned us in a fit of depression, of disgust for the ordinary theater as the public knows it and likes it." But once the characters have been imagined they assume a life of their own. If the playwright refuses to look after them, they will look after themselves. Going to a theater where a play is in rehearsal, they insist that they have a play that must be produced. The story that the characters have to tell emerges in fits and starts. They are much too busy cursing or wrangling with one another to present a very coherent plot. For, as Pirandello insists, each character sees the central situation from his own point of view and each tries to justify himself loudly from that vantage point.

The Father is a great talker and a great explainer. He insists that he put the Mother and his clerk out of his house together because he assumed that they were attached to each other and pitied them; indeed, he asserts that he tried to help them afterward. But the Mother, uneducated and nonverbal, insists that the Father *threw* her and the clerk out of the house and forced her on the clerk. The Stepdaughter refuses to believe that her Mother did not love the clerk initially; after all, the clerk (now dead) was the only father she knew. The Son—the legitimate son of the Father and the Mother—who feels that he has been deserted by both father and mother, attempts to reject both. The Stepdaughter, consumed by a passionate hatred of the Son and the Father, passes up no opportunity to show her contempt and to remind the Father that, at a time when he did not recognize her, he almost had sexual relations with his own stepdaughter. Obviously, no one is completely right, and no one is completely wrong. But none is able to understand that.

Act II develops the theme of mutual misunderstanding but modulates it into a different key. For now the characters learn, to their consternation, that they will not be able to play their parts themselves (that is, as they were realized by their creator). The actors will do it for them. And, of course, the actors cannot possibly play the characters as the characters see themselves. As the Father explains: "It will be difficult to act me as I really am. The effect will be rather—apart from the make-up—according as to how he [the actor] supposes I am, as he senses me—if he does sense me—and not as I inside of myself feel myself to be." Later the act moves to a general attack on the conventions of the theater and the limits of the theater. As the Manager points out, "Acting is our business here. Truth up to a certain point, but no further."

In the last act, the Father gives still another twist to the problem of reality and the artistic presentation of it. In a sense, he insists, the characters are more real than the actors are. For people change from day to day. What a person seems to be one day no longer exists the next day (though his image of himself may persist). The characters, on the other hand, will always remain the same. Or—to turn the statement around—art, since it is static, can never deal with the fluid nature of reality. "All this present reality of yours," says the Father, "is fated to seem a mere illusion to you tomorrow . . . your reality is a mere transitory and fleeting illusion, taking this form today and that tomorrow. . . . " Pessimism can go no further.

Clearly Pirandello is a philosophical dramatist, the maker of a theater of ideas. Inevitably he has been attacked as an author who concerns himself more with concepts than with people and with action. He has also been stoutly defended as one who, immersed in certain basic, tragic facts of human existence, provides them with a hauntingly, overwhelmingly genuine dramatic substance.

Max Halperen

THE SKIN OF OUR TEETH

Type of work: Drama
Author: Thornton Wilder (1897-1975)
Type of plot: Fantastic parable
Time of plot: All human history
Locale: Excelsior, New Jersey, and the boardwalk at Atlantic City
First presented: 1942

The Skin of Our Teeth, influenced by Bertolt Brecht's epic theater as well as James Joyce's Finnegans Wake, *is a fantastic parable dealing with mankind's age-old struggle to civilize itself. The action covers three periods: an Ice Age, a great flood, and a devastating war. In each case man manages to survive in the face of overwhelming odds. Thus, Wilder expresses his underlying theme of faith in humanity and its ability to survive.*

To American audiences who saw the original production of *The Skin of Our Teeth,* the play seemed mad, incomprehensible, but highly entertaining. Their reaction was understandable, for few American playwrights have employed such bizarre forms to convey serious content. "Dream plays," German expressionism, the comic strip, musical comedy—Wilder once listed these as his sources of dramaturgical inspiration. The play is, however, basically a parody of old-fashioned American stock-company productions and vaudeville. European audiences, for whom the play was performed in bomb-scarred churches and beer halls, had less difficulty in grasping Wilder's message. As the dramatist himself observed, the play "mostly comes alive under conditions of crisis." Since depressions, Ice Ages, and wars have hardly vanished from the scene, *The Skin of Our Teeth* promises to remain a vital part of the world's theater experience.

Despite their range and complexity, Wilder's main ideas can be briefly summarized. Indeed, in Sabina's first direct address to the audience, Wilder does this very thing. The play is, she says, "all about the troubles the human race has gone through." Such troubles are of two kinds: those caused by nature and those caused by man himself. The Ice Age and the Flood are examples of the first type, though Wilder makes it plain that the real source of catastrophe in Act II is not the weather but man's disordered passions. Depression and war are clearly human creations. The "human race" is not for Wilder a disconnected assemblage of discrete cultures and generations. Rather, it is a being—a living person who experiences, remembers, and matures. The name "Antrobus" expresses this concept, being derived from the Greek word for man, *anthropos.*

As one learns from the closing philosophic quotations, man's best hope for "getting by" lies in his intellect. His first priority is to establish "order in himself" by means of disciplining reason. In doing so, man avails himself of a special energy which Aristotle considered divine. This holy energy is ultimately related to the force which created the heavens and the earth. The greatest threat to man's survival is not merely his unruly animal nature which brings disorder to his soul. More seriously, it is an inclination towards evil which infects even his rational faculties. To counter this threat, man can draw upon his capacity for love as well as on the accumulated wisdom which his history has given him.

This set of ideas shapes all aspects of the drama. Mr. and Mrs. Antrobus stand for Reason, which has masculine and feminine dimensions. Sabina, the maid, represents the passions, especially those which seek erotic pleasure and social power. Henry, their son, says Wilder, embodies "strong unreconciled evil." Like Sabina, he resists the rule of law in himself and society. But his murderous nature reveals a far graver sort of wickedness. Like Cain, he despises God and longs to overthrow His order. Wilder's characters are not merely allegorical types, however. Mr. Antrobus shows himself capable of homicidal intent, and because he loves his theories and machines too much, he is partly to blame for Henry's behavior. Sabina speaks for Wilder when she exclaims, "We're all just as wicked as we can be, and that's God's truth."

No single character symbolizes love in *The Skin of Our Teeth*. Rather this function is fulfilled by the Antrobus family as a whole. In Act I, they share their hearth with the refugees. In Act II, they refuse to enter the ship without Henry. In the final act they readmit Henry to their circle. But since the Antrobuses are a metaphor for mankind, their gestures have wider significance. The refugees are not strangers, but relatives. So are members of the audience, a fact which the invitation to "Pass up your chairs, everybody" conveys. Wilder symbolizes this condition by making the father of Gladys' beloved baby an anonymous someone, an Everyman. The final acceptance of Henry is the most powerful moment in the play. Despite Henry's evil, Mr. Antrobus grudgingly must acknowledge that "Oh, you're related, all right." Thus Henry may take his place in a family where all belong.

If the human race is actually one, there is finally only one experience and one memory. Wilder dramatizes this concept in a variety of ingenious ways, all of which involve seeing time as an eternal present. Dinosaurs, Biblical personages, and figures from Greek mythology crowd into the Antrobus' living room. Because each advance in technology requires a remembering of all previous discoveries, Wilder has the invention of the alphabet "occur" during the era of telegraphic communication. Sabina is, simultaneously, a figure from classical history, a "Napoleonic camp follower," and a contemporary American. The constant interruptions of the action force the audience to dwell in a single time dimension—the present, in which are contained both past and future as well as "real" and "imaginary time."

By these means Wilder also reinforces the notion that modern man is what he is because of the experiences of his forebearers. Or, more exactly, his nature has developed in certain ways because he has inherited certain principles of interpretation. These principles are found in clearest form in the great books of history. Insofar as such principles shape human thought, the thinkers who expressed them live on. But men can forget or ignore the education which history has afforded them and become animals again. Thus, books are instruments of humanization. In this sense, Mr. Antrobus is entirely correct when he says to the book-burning Henry, "You are my deadly enemy." And part of Wilder's optimism about mankind's future stems from the mere existence of books and libraries.

The full seriousness and profundity of Wilder's themes tend, unfortunately, to escape most audiences. Indeed, the play's rapid pace and dramaturgical gimmicks draw attention away from its key symbols. Invited to participate on a superficial level, the typical viewer feels puzzled and a bit resentful when, in the third act, the drama suddenly becomes very somber and too heavily philosophical.

Leslie E. Gerber

THE SLEEPWALKERS

Type of work: Novel
Author: Hermann Broch (1886-1951)
Type of plot: Philosophical and social chronicle
Time of plot: 1888-1918
Locale: Germany
First published: 1930-1932

When first published in 1932, Hermann Broch's The Sleepwalkers *was not only a powerfully incisive moral history of Germany, but also a prophetic exploration of the ethical and intellectual climate that would soon produce Adolf Hitler. The book consists of three short novels,* The Romantic, The Anarchist, *and* The Realist, *which delineate, from the perspective of the central character, three crucial points in this moral deterioration: 1888, 1903, and 1918.*

The Sleepwalkers is considered by many critics to be one of the major literary achievements of the twentieth century, ranking with *Ulysses, The Magic Mountain,* and *Remembrance of Things Past.* The three-volume novel bears as little resemblance to any of these works as they do to one another; it stands uniquely alone, an uncompromising experiment in the art of fiction writing. Using the technique sometimes referred to as essayism, Broch examines the intellectual, psychological, and moral forces in Germany culminating in World War I. The book presents an unsparing picture of the character traits and attitudes of the German people that resulted in the glorification of the militaristic personality. These traits are exemplified in the rigid, proud personalities of the Pasenow family.

This carefully constructed novel builds slowly, but with great skill, its power deriving from the cumulative effect of the parts; the narrative relies not on melodrama or romance, but on logical development to hold the reader's interest. Each incident in *The Sleepwalkers* serves to make an intellectual point, to symbolize an attitude, or to represent a psychological condition. Like somnambulists, the characters move rigidly and unavoidably to their fates, becoming symbols themselves, in a world reduced to dehumanized symbols. Intellectual conversations, discussing philosophical and moral attitudes, occupy much of the time of these characters, but often they repeat only platitudes and safe assumptions that will not disturb their world. More than anything else, *The Sleepwalkers* is an exploration of moral and ethical principles.

For these people correctness of conduct is all, no matter what hypocrisy and deceit lies beneath their stern, proper façade. They seek safety behind their elaborate manners and correct wardrobes and uniforms. Military uniforms assume symbolic proportions in the novel. When people cast off their uniforms, their true natures and animal instincts are freed, for good and for evil. Joachim's and Bertrand's thoughts about military uniforms become an essay on the nature of uniforms in general. Much space is given to the significance of clothing of all kinds—any human covering becomes, in effect, a uniform, labeling the wearer. Women prefer men in uniform, men feel more like men when in uniform; above all, men escape responsibility for being themselves when they are in uniform.

The military code has overtaken all aspects of these peoples' lives, including their ability to love or experience grief. When Joachim was a boy, even the pastor called him a "young warrior" and assumed that the boy would happily attend the cadet school and devote his life to military service. Hypocrisy, the narrator explains, is so ingrained in the attitudes of the people that they could not recognize it in any form, but particularly in regard to any aspect of the military code of honor. When Joachim's brother, Helmuth, is killed in a duel, their father states, "He died for honor." They have deceived themselves for so long that they are not capable of experiencing genuine grief. Yet, they still uphold the military code which makes duels not only possible but noble examples of correct conduct.

The novel moves slowly, like an underwater ballet, the characters forever circling around one another and striking dramatic but grotesque poses. The characters are presented in a stylized form. Little attempt is made to render them as physical human beings; they are representations of ideas, and as such clash in an almost dreamlike manner. Most of the characters sooner or later complain of being bored. Most people, Joachim and Bertrand agree, live in a state of vegetative indolence and inertia of feeling. Life, they repeat to one another, consists of compromises. But, above all, one's name must be protected. Traditions and customs, habits and routines, are the first and last defense of these mediocre individuals. Even murder is permissible, if handled with the proper decorum. Their lives are lived in an aura of unreality, but Bertrand proclaims early in the book that the artificial is always superior to the real, just as play is the true reality of life.

The form of *The Sleepwalkers* is absolutely wedded to the content. Particularly in the third volume, we find a dazzling range of technique, from the total objectivity of the abstract essay to the subjectivity of lyric poetry. The parallel plots of the novel and the interpolated essays serve to broaden the horizon of the narrative, to break out of the mold of the ordinary novel form, and to create new implications of meaning. Broch was striving in this novel to achieve an artistic detachment that would allow the work to stand separate and aloof, its many facets reflecting the reader's interpretation rather than that of the author. Perhaps only André Gide in *The Counterfeiters* and Hermann Hesse in *The Glass Bead Game* have attempted any similar experiment.

The progression of the three volumes is philosophic and aesthetic, rather than narrative. In the first two books, Broch describes the deterioration of outmoded values in the Prussian Pasenow and the Rhineland proletarian mystic Esch; the final volume, which takes place in 1918, shows at last the triumph of Huguenau, the symbol of the new valueless society of postwar Germany, over the forces of the past. It is society which is on trial in this book, and Broch is a merciless judge.

Through the first two parts of Broch's trilogy, and well into the third, the reader is kept purposefully under the illusion that he is reading a story written by an objective third-person narrator (to be identified with Hermann Broch). In the middle of part three, however, it becomes apparent that the narrator of all three parts is in reality the author of the essay, "The Disintegration of Values," that has been encapsulated into the fiction. Yet, at the close of the book, another shift has taken place: the author of the essay turns out to be identical with the first-person narrator of one of the framework stories. The whole novel thus lives in a timeless state of suspension, an aesthetic whole with its own self-contained author and its own laws. Broch has taken a common modern narrative device, the unreliable narrator, and turned the device back upon itself, rendering the entire novel as a symbol of the chaos of the modern world. In *The Sleepwalkers,* as is often the case with modern literature, the medium is, and must be, the message.

Bruce D. Reeves

THE SLIPKNOT

Type of work: Drama
Author: Titus Maccius Plautus (c. 255-184 B.C.)
Type of plot: New comedy
Time of plot: Late third century B.C.
Locale: Cyrene, in Libya
First presented: Late third or early second century B.C.

Despite a number of unresolved loose ends in the play, The Slipknot is one of Plautus' most amusing comedies. The situation is typical of Roman comedy: a good man, whose daughter was kidnaped in childhood and sold to a procurer, recovers her at last after a riotous sequence of fast-paced, improbable events, including an elaborate swindle, a shipwreck, lost and found tokens, and several romantic entanglements.

The Slipknot (the *Rudens,* also translated as *The Rope*) is a melodramatic comedy that some critics regard as one of Plautus' best plays. Based on a comedy by Diphilus which has not survived, *The Slipknot* has several earmarks of the Greek New Comedy; pious sentiment, a kidnaped child, a virtuous prostitute of good birth, young love thwarted, an arbitration scene for the recovery of birth tokens, a villain, a recognition scene, and the freeing of slaves. None of this was original with Plautus, who usually borrowed his plots and characters from Greek playwrights, and, remolding them to suit Roman tastes, included music and dance to produce a form remarkably like the American musical comedy.

This play is more romantic in treatment and subject than the usual Plautine comedy. It has an exotic setting on the African seacoast near Cyrene. In some respects the story bears a resemblance to Shakespeare's *The Tempest,* especially in the remote, poetic atmosphere, the supernatural intervention, the shipwreck, the gradual working out of justice, and the eventual triumph of young love. The interest of this play lies not so much in any formula of the plot, which has some striking loose ends, but in the revelation of character when the characters are confronted by difficulties that must be overcome.

Beneath the humor and melodrama serious assumptions are at work. One is that if a character is appealing and noble despite unfortunate circumstances, the legitimacy of their parentage must be established. Another is the superiority of unselfish virtue and youthful romance over mere self-seeking. The ingenious plot shows how these two principles work, overcoming all obstacles through coincidence upon coincidence.

THE SMALL HOUSE AT ALLINGTON

Type of work: Novel
Author: Anthony Trollope (1815-1882)
Type of plot: Domestic romance
Time of plot: Mid-nineteenth century
Locale: An unnamed county, "Barsetshire," London
First published: 1864

The Small House at Allington, fifth of the Barchester chronicles, was Trollope's own favorite of the series. In this novel the worldly-wise, conniving De Courcys are set in contrast to the honest, sturdy Dales of Allington. Lily Dale is the Victorian heroine, winning but also pathetic, and a perfect model of the type who was her counterpart in almost every novel of the period.

The dilemma central to so many nineteenth century novels—whether one should marry for love or for social position—is treated by Trollope without sentimentality in *The Small House at Allington.* In this novel the conventional solutions do not suffice. Lily Dale does not conveniently inherit a fortune, as does Mary in *Dr. Thorne* (1858); Adolphus Crosbie is not willing to give up marriage into a titled family and settle for love alone. Trollope took a bold step in denying his readers the usual happy ending, but the immense popularity of the novel testifies both to its quality and perhaps to the comfortable belief of many readers that Lily would eventually relent and marry the faithful John Eames. Yet when these characters reappear in *The Last Chronicle of Barset* (1867), Lily rejects both suitors and remains a spinster.

Trollope is not simply engaging in whimsical iconoclasm here; he is dealing with the crucial question of moderation versus excess. Crosbie is more weak than villainous, but he is ambitious in a world which rewards social connections above personal merit, and consequently, he snatches at the opportunity to marry the daughter of an earl. Lily's behavior is excessive when she cannot relinquish her love for Crosbie. When he first breaks the engagement, her grief is genuine and understandable, but while she remains a sympathetic character throughout the novel, Trollope ultimately shows that by clinging to her obsession she carries idealism to excess and brings misery to herself and those around her.

In Trollope's world, love takes precedence over worldly ambition, but moderation is the wiser course. Happiness most often comes to those who can adapt to society's standards without abandoning their moral principles. Bell rejects the squire's son and marries for love but it is her good fortune that love coincides with a moderately sufficient income. Crosbie, who rejects both love and moral principle, suffers total disenchantment.

SMALL SOULS

Type of work: Novel
Author: Louis Couperus (1863-1923)
Type of plot: Social criticism
Time of plot: Nineteenth century
Locale: The Hague
First published: 1901

Small Souls, *written by one of the foremost of modern Dutch novelists, is the first of a series of four novels known as* The Books of the Small Souls. *Constance, who divorced her prominent husband and married for love, is unable, even after twenty years, to escape the condemnation of a society which is composed of small souls who are very tender to criticism and are engaged in schemes of attaining status by the use of gossip, rumor, scandal, and fear.*

In *The Books of the Small Souls,* the romantic and the realistic are synthesized in family novels that trace the history of a bourgeois family over a period of generations. The Van Lowes are little people living out the life of a family whose innovative impulse has passed away. But through them the reader feels the essential things in Dutch life and culture not historically through the development of an epoch of political orientation, but statically, as befits a nation retired from business and living in the suburbs of the world, intent on well-being. Occasionally, there comes a whisper from across the seas, from the Indies, reminiscent of the days when Grand-papa Van Lowe was Governor General in his palaces at Batavia and Buitenzorg. But this only serves to emphasize by contrast the dull monotony of the world in which they live. The reader feels the ease and well-bred indolence, the triviality and mechanical precision of life, the lack of creative ambition, and the dull fatigue which takes possession of their consciousness.

Small Souls displays a close connection between the characters in the novel and their environment, and a mysterious oppressive force permeates the whole. As the human background of Dutch life and interests is understood, so without detailed description, the landscape is everywhere present. Its flatness and humility is in physical congruity with the beings who walk upon it. And the weather is a constant reminder of the melancholy of the Northland.

Couperus has written a family novel of small souls clinging pitifully together. He has written, at the same time, a national novel in which the condition of a country is mirrored in a gallery of family portraits. In doing this he has followed in the steps of the great sixteenth century Dutch painters who depicted man, nature, and society as existing in a sort of sympathetic relationship. This has resulted in an unusually successful portrayal of Dutch mores and of the Dutch landscape, which is for the foreign reader a valuable means for the understanding of the Dutch national character.

SMOKE

Type of work: Novel
Author: Ivan Turgenev (1818-1883)
Type of plot: Social criticism
Time of plot: 1862-1865
Locale: Germany and Russia
First published: 1867

A pleasant love story provides the thin plot line of Smoke, *but the primary focus of the novel is on the group of Russian reactionaries, liberals, Slavophiles, and Westerners gathered in Baden-Baden to exchange opinions on contemporary issues. While the various romantic relationships suggest some possible happiness on the personal level, the overall mood of the book is bitter in its tone and pessimistic in its conclusions regarding the future of Russia.*

One of the great novels of Russian literature, *Smoke* is a rich and complex novel with a deceptively simple surface. Although brief, the novel presents subtle and sensitive descriptions of nature and the human condition, and realistic and complex portraits of a variety of human beings. Turgenev penetrates the sensibilities of his characters, exploring the refinements of personality and intellect, the complex changes and adjustments that they must make in their lives. Both success and disappointment, Turgenev shows, can profoundly affect human beings in subtle, painful ways.

Litvínoff is a sensitive and intelligent man, Turgenev's ideal protagonist, a man who observes the world around him but cannot easily adjust himself to it or to the people who fill it. He is particularly vulnerable to the observations of Potúgin and to the fascination of the intelligent and headstrong Irína. The love story is a vehicle or Turgenev's picture of the upper-class Russian expatriots and the attitudes they represent. Turgenev does not use plot as much as suggestion and nuance to convey his message. He prefers the indirect approach to literature.

Structurally, *Smoke* is built upon a simple framework; all of the action occurs in or around Baden-Baden within a short period of time. Litvínoff is preoccupied with his relationship with Irína, which is seen as set against the bigger issues which form the underlying theme throughout the novel: the political situation in Russia at the time. Turgenev satirizes the left-wing "intelligentsia" represented by the so-called advanced thinkers Litvínoff meets in Baden, as well as the conservative "official set" of which Irína is so much a part. Potúgin voices Turgenev's own opinion regarding the necessity of Russia's looking to Europe for inspiration in building a strong country after the emancipation of the serfs.

The title of the book, *Smoke,* refers to Litvínoff's meditation as the train pulls away from Baden after he has lost his quest for Irína. He feels that everything real resembles smoke and is insubstantial. He muses that every-

thing that has been achieved in life vanishes. The tone is somber and pessimistic, but this tone does not follow Litvínoff to the end of the book, for in
the novel's last pages the reader sees Litvínoff rebuild his life, much as Turgenev hopes Russia will rebuild. Litvínoff is a practical man, the symbol of
the new generation of Russians who are ambitious, spirited, and willing to
work the land to reap its benefits. The note of futility is all but gone in the
last scenes when Litvínoff reconciles himself with his fiancée, Tánya. The
book is brought to a close with the narrator's last comments about Irína
and Potúgin, tying up all the loose ends and completing this vivid literary
portrait of Turgenev's Russia.

THE SNAKE PIT

Type of work: Novel
Author: Sigrid Undset (1882-1949)
Type of plot: Historical chronicle
Time of plot: Late thirteenth, early fourteenth centuries
Locale: Norway
First published: 1925

The Snake Pit *is the most hopeless and despairing of the four novels which make up* The Master of Hestviken. *Here Olav Audunsson and his wife Ingunn have passed the period of youthful passion, outlawry, and violence which gave* The Axe *its tragic poignancy. There is little warmth or color to brighten the years of Ingunn's illness and Olav's struggle with his conscience. Burdened by a sin which he cannot confess, Olav feels himself doomed.*

The lives of the characters in this epic novel are filled with barely contained emotions, with hatreds and cravings for revenge, and with unendurable remorse. Their family ties are as complicated as they are vital to their mode of existence. The tale is filled with portrayals of superstitions, inarticulate fears, and blind religious convictions. The religion of these people is inextricably united with ancient terrors and dark legends. The author makes clear that their lives are circumscribed by folk sayings and traditions which are ignored only at great risk, and that their hearts and minds bear a burden of ancient guilt. Undset's graceful yet solid prose perfectly conveys the tragedy of these trapped human lives. The work is both a historical picture of a grim age and a human testament of man's ability to survive.

The snake pit that gives this work its title is a symbol of considerable flexibility. Though it seems to Olav to illustrate his own predicament, to the reader it shows a further aspect of his situation, one which ultimately proves fatal to Olav's efforts toward his own salvation. When Olav first comes home to Hestviken, he remembers the doorpost carved with the legendary figure of Gunnar in the snake pit. He applies it in his mind to the Hestvik people's historical propensity to disaster through keeping faith with those unworthy of it, as was Olav Ribbung's case, or through deliberately transgressing God's law as Torhild Björnsdatter did. Later, seeing a parallel in his own situation, he congratulates himself miserably for upholding the Hestvik tradition of dogged endurance under misfortune. For the unconfessed murder of Teit seems to him to be a serpent at the heart of his life with Ingunn.

But, in reality, the serpent in his bosom is pride. In his pride, he takes to himself all the guilt and suffering occasioned by Ingunn's fall. His intention in bringing her to Hestviken is to protect and cherish her. At no time does he refer to Ingunn's sin as sin, or acknowledge her need for expiation, or show concern for the state of her soul. It is as though he does not reckon her female soul of any importance, compared to his. Thus, at the peak of his resolution to confess, he is thrown into confusion by the revelation that she too has suffered, and not for his sin but for her own. He realizes that in confessing his own guilt, he would set her suffering at naught; in the end, Ingunn herself is the adder at his breast. Through this story, Undset shows how blind human beings can be to the inner state of those nearest to them, and how selfish their apparent sacrifices really are. Although set in the thirteenth century, Undset's novel deals with the darker side of human passions of any age or era. The greatness of the novel lies in the breadth of its vision and the depth of its penetration into human nature.

SNOW-BOUND

Type of work: Poem
Author: John Greenleaf Whittier (1807-1892)
Type of plot: Pastoral idyl
Time of plot: Early nineteenth century
Locale: Haverhill, Massachusetts
First published: 1866

In Snow-Bound. *Whittier's popular idyl, the harshness of winter life on a New England farm is scarcely suggested, for the glow of the aging poet's memory gives the impression that in his youth life was serene, secure, and joyful. The title suggests a nature poem, but the poet's chief interest centers upon the people who were dear to him, picturing a family circle which represents an idealization of the American home.*

"Snow-bound" is a pastoral elegy in the classic mold of "Lycidas" and Gray's "Elegy," a lament for people and things that are past. In form and matter, it claims kinship with the European literary tradition, rejecting the naturalism and anti-formalism of the literature of the expanding West. It is in effect the swan song of the dynamic literary and philosophical movement that flowered in the Northeast before the Civil War. This movement celebrated the ideal of the Yankee farmer, whose independence, egalitarianism, and natural nobility of mind excited the admiration of that society of which he was the energizing element. But when "Snow-bound" was written, the cultural dominance of New England was at an end. The war had just ended, and the paradise of racial equality and national rectitude which Whittier had envisioned had not materialized. Instead, the agrarian economy was giving way to industrialism, and the adventurous impulses in art had moved West with the pioneers. The literary establishment, left in a backwater, could only react against the unrest of new times and ideas. Thus the poem commemorates rather than celebrates the agrarian ideal.

Whittier had more contact with the life of common men than his contemporaries Lowell, Longfellow, and Holmes; but like them, he believed that it was the life of the nation writ small. In "Snow-bound" he records such minute details of that life as the nightly round of chores and the precise construction of the fire, with loving fidelity. The language of the poem is "rich and picturesque and free," colloquial without being commonplace. The point of view is unabashedly nostalgic, seeking to distill from harsh reality warm visions of family and community life by which to judge, if not guide, the tumultuous present.

SO RED THE ROSE

Type of work: Novel
Author: Stark Young (1881-1963)
Type of plot: Historical romance
Time of plot: 1860-1865
Locale: Mississippi
First published: 1934

Stark Young unfolds character and scene gradually in So Red the Rose, *because the book is not so much a story of the political and military aspects of the Civil War as it is a study of the effects of the war, from a Southern perspective, upon those who stayed at home.*

This beautiful story is told tranquilly but deeply. It is tinged with yearning for life, for peace, for an unrecoverable past when peach trees bloomed in April and loved ones who were destined to march off and die in war were still happily alive. *So Red the Rose* is a muted cry against war's stupidity, a lament over the passing of an idyllic way of life. It is also a philosophy of life for the future. In his unhurried narration, moreover, Stark Young not only shows the rosy side of life in the antebellum South, the dreadful war years, and the malicious brutality of Reconstruction, but, almost with touches of the Spanish "Costumbrista" movement, he archives "pictures of customs," including details of dress, furniture, thought, imagery, psychology, and the way of life.

The novel's essence is in its final scene, where Agnes sits meditating at her son's grave in the Montrose family graveyard, with little Middleton at her side. Suddenly she can feel the hard gravel under her feet at Shiloh, where she had sought Edward's body three years earlier. Now she reflects, sitting by Edward's grave (while little Middleton sits, staring at the foliage over the cemetery wall, where the sun's rays are slanting), on how Edward had died at Shiloh, where ranks of half-trained men and boys had been cut down on each side, epitomizing war's insanity and "the childish urges of men." She now grasps the interrelationship of war to men, and men to war, as contrasted with the same relationship for women. She concludes that the glory and folly and pain of war must remain for men even as women dream, delight, and are afraid when confronting childbirth. And the rivers of red blood, soaked up by the earth on so many "Shilohs," must be born again in women.

Then again, trance-like, Agnes is back at Shiloh, listening to the wounded moan in the darkness ahead. She discerns their shapes scattered on the battle-ground. Edward must be lying somewhere among them, but she considers all of the dead as hers. Suddenly now, at her side, Middleton is no longer gazing ahead, but up at her, ecstatically, with pale face and rapt expression. She scarcely glances at him, but is stirred by his expression. Tugged by memory back to her thoughts, she spiritually returns to Shiloh, amid the eerie silence, hearing only her heartbeat. The novel ends as she gazes over the gloomy field and the sleeping dead.

But Agnes now knows that a hallowed memory, living through time, is the finest learning to live by:

> "I sometimes think that never blows so red
> The rose as where some buried Caesar bled;
> That every hyacinth the garden wears
> Dropt in her lap from some once lovely head."

SOHRAB AND RUSTUM

Type of work: Poem
Author: Matthew Arnold (1822-1888)
Type of plot: Heroic romance
Time of plot: Remote antiquity
Locale: Western Asia, on the banks of the Oxus River
First published: 1853

In the mournful verse tale Sohrab and Rustum. *Matthew Arnold fuses somberness and sentiment in just the right proportions to appeal to the taste of Victorian readers. Not only in its high seriousness—to use Arnold's own phrase— does* Sohrab and Rustum *accord with the popular taste of the author's own time, but also the Oriental theme serves to justify, perhaps to demand, an unusual extravagance of language and emotion.*

In his *Preface to Poems* (1853) Matthew Arnold set forth his theory of objective art. He argued that, to achieve the noblest poetic aims, it was necessary for the poet to leave his subjective self behind. The best way to ensure objectivity was to deal with the past, as the Greeks had done, to avoid introducing "what was accidental and passing." Moreover, Arnold contended, success overwhelmingly depended on the choice of subject matter, which must be human action. In the collection of verse which followed, *Sohrab and Rustum* is the first and most ambitious poem. We know from Arnold's letters that the poem was written as a demonstration piece for the theory. Although the poem was popular with the public, it and the poetic theory it exemplified did not receive critical acclaim.

Based on a familiar folktale, the poem is set in the distant past and does concentrate on the representation of significant human action, but it frequently suffers from an excessive burden of pathos. For example, the pathetic fallacy in which both heroes address Ruksh, Rutsum's concerned horse, nudges sentiment into sentimentality. Thus, the poem is perhaps more impressive as an object lesson in poetic theory than as a successive work of art.

Nevertheless, in manner and style the poem is admirable. An epyllion, or short heroic poem, it includes many of the standard epic features: a catalogue of warriors, a council of leaders, epic boasts, single combat, foreboding, and Homeric similes. Both the pathos, when under control, and the pervasive presence of an unrelenting fate are reminiscent of the more elegiac parts of the *Iliad.* In addition, the archaic diction helps to sustain a consistent high style. Indeed, the blank verse, the manipulation of syntax, and the control of lines are consciously, and often successfully, Miltonic.

THE SOLDIER'S FORTUNE

Type of work: Drama
Author: Thomas Otway (1652-1685)
Type of plot: Comedy of intrigue
Time of plot: c. 1680
Locale: London
First presented: 1681

Lacking the sophisticated comedic skills of his best Restoration contemporaries, Thomas Otway depends on simple farce in lieu of elegant wit. While some of the humor of The Soldier's Fortune *is that of the comedy of manners, much of it depends instead on bawdiness and slapstick.*

Otway is best known as the author of *Venice Preserved,* a steamy tragedy of romance and politics that, despite its defects, stands head-and-shoulders above the mediocre tragic output of the Restoration period (Dryden's work excepted). As a writer of comedy, however, Otway is considerably outclassed by such contemporaries as Etherege, Wycherley, and Congreve. Lacking their elegance, subtleties of tone, and rapier wit, Otway takes refuge in broad and often coarse effects. His talent is for low comedy, comedy of situation, not comedy of manners or of character. He focuses on the underside of life, rather than on its falsely glittering surface. Unfortunately, such comedy is difficult to appreciate on the printed page; the success of a farcical work like *The Soldier's Fortune* depends largely on the skill of the principal comic actors, those playing Sir Jolly Jumble and Sir Davy Dunce.

This is not to say that Otway's comedy is entirely lacking in wit: there is, for example, the long dialogue between Courtine and Sylvia who discuss their future marriage entirely in agricultural imagery with such statements as: "you shall promise to keep the estate well-fenced, and enclosed, lest sometime or other your neighbor's cattle break in and spoil the crop on the ground. . . ." But most of the time, the knaves and fools claim center stage. Even Courtine, suspended by a rope under his mistress' balcony, and then trussed up in a drunken stupor, can hardly be compared to the typical Restoration gentleman-rake.

Otway's play does convey a far more immediate sense of time and place than other contemporary comedies, whose closed-in world seems limited to the salon, the bedchamber, the coffeehouse, and St. James's Park. Seldom a scene goes by without some reference to the recent Commonwealth period, the pre-Commonwealth (Rump) Parliament, loyalty to the king, the unsettled state of the nation, foreign wars, and other concerns of the larger world outside. Occasionally, the action stops completely while Beaugard and Courtine discuss (as mouthpieces for Otway) such matters as the undeserved preferment of former rebels, the stings of genteel poverty, or the ungrateful attitude of the nation in peacetime to her savior in time of war, the military. And indeed, only a former soldier could have written Lady Dunce's vivid speech to Beaugard after the consummation of their love: "What think you now of a cold, wet march over the mountains, your men tired, your baggage not come up, but at night a dirty, watery plain to encamp upon, and nothing to shelter you but an old leaguer cloak as tattered as your colors?"

If Otway resembles any major Restoration comic dramatist, it is Wycherley, whose cynicism about human behavior and whose sense of degraded humanity is somewhat like his own. In viewing the spectacle of a "beastly, unsavory, old, groaning, grunting, wheezing wretch" who, through a systematic process of deceit and intimidation, is made to serve as whoremaster of his wife, we are forced to acknowledge that the playwright has demonstrated the truth of Courtine's opening observation that the world is "so thronged and crammed with knaves and fools, that an honest man can hardly get a living in it."

THE SON AVENGER

Type of work: Novel
Author: Sigrid Undset (1882-1949)
Type of plot: Historical chronicle
Time of plot: Fourteenth century
Locale: Norway
First published: 1927

The Son Avenger, the second novel in Sigrid Undset's series The Master of
Hestviken, *dealing with Norse life in the Middle Ages, gathers together the many
threads of Olav Audunsson's story in an inevitable and tragic close. Both this book
and Undset's other prose epic,* Kristin Lavransdatter, *are great works of the
historical imagination and of Christian morality.*

The Son Avenger deals with the effects of Olav's concealed sin on his
children's lives and on his own old age and death. Because of his old misfortunes in the uplands, he denies Cecilia a match with a man from that part
of the country, making way for her unhappy union for Jörund Rypa. By this
decision, every kind of evil springs—from Eirik's broken match with Gunhild
Beresdatter, to the murder of a cripple. The last and worst consequence is
that Olav believes Cecilia guilty of murder; his stroke comes on at the
realization of the monstrous wrong he had done her in thinking her capable
of his own sin—murder compounded by concealment.

In that moment of being struck down, and afterward as he lies, speechless
but conscious, awaiting death, the full consequence of his sin breaks upon
him. Olav has spent the better part of his life so absorbed in his secret that
self-pity and remorse have been a wall between his daughter and himself.
He realizes that he does not really know her, but has fabricated a personality
for her out of her mother's frailties and his own wishes, thus thinking her
likely either to forget her first love or murder her wedded husband. Worse,
Olav knows he has lost Eirik in the same way, realizing only at the end that
Eirik has loved him best. As he lies dying, Olav has a vision of Eirik gleaning
among the tare of his father's life for good deeds to lay on the scales of
divine judgment. He senses at last the depth of the love Eirik has always
offered him, its quality of absorbing slights and hurts, its constancy saintly.
Eirik has been the avenger, not of the slain Icelander as Olav had always
thought, but of God, whose rod is love. In a strange way he is Olav's avenger
as well. Eirik, who always had the most cause for complaint against his
father, by his words and demeanor in later life belies all the evil gossip
against which Olav, because of his guilty secret, had never been able to defend
himself.

SONEZAKI SHINJÛ

Type of work: Drama
Author: Chikamatsu Monzaemon (1653-1725)
Type of plot: Domestic romance
Time of plot: Eighteenth century
Locale: Osaka, Japan
First presented: 1703

A classic Japanese drama of the early Tokugawa Period (1600–1868), Sonezaki
Shinjû *was the first and remains one of the most popular of Chikamatsu's domestic
plays. Originally written for the puppet theater and staged in 1703, it was soon
presented also for the* Kabuki *theater, for which it continues to be performed in
contemporary Japan.*

Although Chikamatsu Monzaemon has been called the "most Western" of
the great Japanese dramatists, two obvious obstacles—one cultural, the other
artistic—confront the Western reader who attempts to understand and appreciate Chikamatsu's dramas. The cultural gulf that separates the contemporary
Western reader from the eighteenth century Japanese characters frequently
seems too great to bridge and, since the West has almost no tradition of adult
puppet theater, or even any highly stylized, ritualized drama comparable to
Kabuki Theatre, it is most difficult to visualize theatrically the plays on the
basis of translated texts. But, even so, moments of great feeling and dramatic
power come through to interest and move the Western reader. Perhaps Chikamatsu's most accessible play is his first "domestic tragedy" *Sonezaki Shinjû
(The Love Suicides at Sonezaki).*

The story of *Sonezaki Shinjû* established the basic plot line for all of Chikamatsu's domestic tragedies. A young tradesman and a prostitute fall in love.
He is unable to "ransom" her (purchase her "contract") and so, frustrated,
the lovers eventually commit suicide together. Although the persistent choice
of a prostitute for a heroine (an accurate reflection of social conditions) may
strike the modern Western reader as peculiar, Chikamatsu's "anti-heroic"
characterizations seem quite modern. It is through Chikamatsu's domestic
plays that realism can be said to have come to Japanese theater. Caught between intense human emotion (*ninjo*) and a rigid social morality (*giri*), the
characters are inevitably destroyed by circumstances which are essentially
beyond their control. Tokubei is weak, volatile, erratic, and foolishly trusting;
O Hatsu is, from the beginning, the more heroic—she determines on suicide
long before he does and urges him to it. He vacillates and postures; she offers
him her strength and example. Ultimately the only choice for them is suicide;
they carry it out with great courage and mutual devotion, thereby achieving
a tragic dignity. If the social context of their behavior is not completely clear
and their fatalistic attitudes seem psychologically obscure, the purity of their
love and the nobility of their suicides are convincing and touching. Both in

the reading and the presentation, the high point of the dramatic in *Sonezaki Shinjû,* as in all the *shinjû* plays, is the poetic "lovers' journey" (*michiyuki*) to their appointed end.

Although Chikamatsu used this love-suicide formula with greater flexibility, subtlety, and complexity in later plays, the poetic immediacy and dramatic impact of *Sonezaki Shinjû* have kept it a permanent favorite with the Japanese public. Not only did *Sonezaki Shinjû* begin a theatrical vogue (in addition to Chikamatsu, many other Japanese playwrights exploited the formula), but it also produced widespread public reaction. Originally stimulated by a real incident, it and its successors provoked so many real-life love-suicides that in 1722 the government felt it necessary to ban the production of any play which contained, in its title, the word *shinjû.*

THE SONG OF BERNADETTE

Type of work: Novel
Author: Franz Werfel (1890-1945)
Type of plot: Religious chronicle
Time of plot: 1858-1875
Locale: Lourdes, France
First published: 1941

Unlike the more conventional Saint's Life, which is often pietistic and narrowly sentimental, The Song of Bernadette *is a fully developed religious chronicle, rich in characterization, shrewd in its analysis of Church and provincial politics.*

Franz Werfel, lyric poet, dramatist, and novelist was probably best known for *The Song of Bernadette,* which became his greatest popular success. Werfel was a German Jew born in Prague. His background, his love of music, and his intense interest in the mystery of man and his relation to the divinity all found expression in his writings. *The Song of Bernadette* is no exception. In fact, it is representative of many common elements of Werfel's literary style, even though its subject matter is somewhat narrow and confined by important facts, dates, and details.

During the early stages of World War II, Werfel and his wife, in their flight from the German Nazis, found refuge in the town of Lourdes. While there, Werfel made the now-famous vow that if he ever got to America he would make it his first priority to "sing the song of Bernadette," as he eventually did in the form of a novel.

Werfel gathered extensive facts concerning the experiences of Bernadette Soubirous at the famous grotto of Massabielle. His careful detailed study of life at that time—the political passions of leaders and intricacies of the Church hierarchy in France—made his work like that of a reporter gathering facts. The "reporting" aspect of his account, however, is sublime. The reader is caught up in the emotions, physical and spiritual, of every character to cross the pages. In his preface to the work, Werfel tells the reader that even though he is a Jew and not a Catholic, he drew courage for undertaking a work of this type from a very early artistic commitment. His intention in all of his writings had been to examine and magnify the divine mystery and holiness of man. In *The Song of Bernadette,* he is able to guard the truth of the mystery of Lourdes while examining and experiencing through his characters an enormous variety of fears, longings, and hopes. While the particulars of Bernadette Soubirous' visions of the lady in the grotto are indeed singular, the author imparts a mystical yearning to his characters that makes Bernadette's experiences far more real and universal than one would expect. Werfel's language takes on an aspect of Catholicism so explicit and involved that it is difficult to believe that one not of the Catholic faith could become so intimately involved with a mystery of that religion.

Today's critics of German literature do not seem to be as preoccupied with Werfel as they are with the writings of Kafka and Rilke. Yet, the earnest student of Franz Werfel will find a beautiful style, rich in baroque feeling and melody, in his great variety of works.

THE SONG OF HIAWATHA

Type of work: Poem
Author: Henry Wadsworth Longfellow (1807-1882)
Type of plot: Legendary romance
Time of plot: Aboriginal period
Locale: Indian territory around Lake Superior
First published: 1855

The Song of Hiawatha *is the most famous long narrative poem written on the subject of the North American Indian. Although Longfellow intended the work to be a national epic, retelling in the Romantic manner a number of native American myths and examples of folklore, the sentimentality and monotonous metrics of the poem have limited its appeal among contemporary readers.*

As a renowned and widely respected professor of modern languages, Longfellow traveled and studied the languages and literatures of many European countries. His endeavors in cultural exchange promoted European literature in the United States and American folklore on the Continent. He was a prolific author in a variety of literary forms, including translation, but he is best known for his poetry. Personally, he held high ideals of a conventional sort, but was uninvolved in social issues except for the anti-slavery movement.

In general, Longfellow's literary style was influenced by the German Romantic Movement, although Longfellow himself was not an extreme Romantic. His poetry has been described as gentle, sweet, and pure.

When it came to writing *The Song of Hiawatha,* the background characteristics coalesced. In form, Longfellow drew on his knowledge of European literature. He modeled the poem after the Finnish epic *Kalevala,* using unrhymed trochaic tetrameter and demonstrating an adept skill at using that poetic meter. In content, he hewed the Romantic line, telling a simple, dispassionate, not-too-imaginative story, sometimes criticized for its preachiness and an over-reliance on symbolism. He presented a "proper," rather detached, and somewhat benignly negligent view of the American Indian experience. Hence, Longfellow's *The Song of Hiawatha* has come to be known as a "children's poem," which has little interest for so-called mature audiences. Consequently, both the cadenced meter and the simplistic content have become vulnerable victims to frequent parodies.

Hiawatha was, to be sure, a legendary figure with probable historical existence. But Longfellow did not recount the legendary traits or exploits of this Indian leader; he used only the name Hiawatha, in typical Romantic fashion, to lend legitimacy to his narrative. And, likewise, after the Romantic predilection, Longfellow incorporated in *The Song of Hiawatha* folkloric elements—the woodpecker story, the introduction of pictographs, the gift of corn, and the origin of the peace pipe—in much the same way that Rudyard Kipling used such elements in the *Jungle Books* and *Just So Stories*. Yet there are some qualities which *The Song of Hiawatha* shares with authentic epics, such as supernatural intervention, the long journey of quest, and the heroic sacrifice. Thus, the poem cannot be entirely relegated to the category of children's literature, for it has legitimate claim on serious literary criticism as well.

THE SONG OF ROLAND

Type of work: Tale
Author: Unknown
Type of plot: Chivalric romance
Time of plot: About 800
Locale: Western Europe
First transcribed: Medieval manuscript

Loosely based upon an eighth century military incident involving a part of Charlemagne's army, The Song of Roland, *one of the great medieval* chansons de geste, *is a composite of several hero legends interlaced with Christian moral sentiments.*

The Song of Roland (Chanson de Roland) is loosely associated with the "romance" literature—the adventure narratives—of medieval France. The romance is divided into three types on the basis of content. The first is the "Matter of Britain," dealing with Arthurian legend and Celtic lore. The second is the "Matter of Antiquity," taking its cue from the legends of Thebes, the legends of Troy (such as Chaucer's *Troilus and Criseyde*), and the legends about Alexander the Great. The third is the "Matter of France," focusing on stories of Charlemagne and his circle as well as stories of William of Orange, drawn from the *chansons de geste.* It is here that *The Song of Roland* becomes important, for it is, properly speaking, one of the *chansons de geste*—the "songs of great deeds."

The *chansons de geste* are epic in nature, although the precise origins of the form are unknown. A popular literary form between the eleventh and thirteenth centuries, they are written in French verse—as were early romances; late romances were written in prose—using first a ten-syllable then a twelve-syllable (Alexandrine) line and assonance. Rhyme was substituted for assonance in the late *chansons.* The lines are grouped in stanzas—called *laisses* or *tirades*—of varying lengths, and series of *chansons* developed into story cycles dealing with a particular person, such as Charlemagne, or a particular theme, such as the conflict between Christians and Saracens. Like the classical epics, the *chansons de geste* concentrate—as the name implies—on battles, heroic feats, and knightly ideals. Scant notice is paid to women or the theme of love. These tales furnish the material for the medieval romance; however, in the romance, the emphasis shifts from the heroic to the chivalric, from war to love, and from tragic seriousness to light hearted adventure. Thus, *The Song of Roland,* a *chanson de geste,* is a narrative of knights in battle, but Lodovico Ariosto's sixteenth century *Orlando Furioso* concerns itself with a smitten Roland (Orlando) gone mad over hopeless infatuation with the faithless Angelica, the Princess of Cathay.

Some verification for the events narrated in *The Song of Roland* is provided independently of the poem in the *Annales* of Einhard (or Eginhard), Charlemagne's biographer and chronicler. On this basis, it is possible to pinpoint the essential Roland story as a Basque ambush, in A.D. 778, of the rearguard of Charlemagne's army during a retreat through the Pyrenees. One unusual aspect of the story is that it tells of a defeat—not that defeat was a total stranger in the epic world of *chansons de geste,* but rather the heroic ambience which pervaded the *chansons* precluded much talk of defeat. Several hypotheses have been offered to explain the apparent anomaly. One scholar traces the place-names mentioned in the poem to the pilgrimage route to the shrine of St. James of Compostella, theorizing that clerics on pilgrimage knitted the stories of Roland's defeat into an intrinsically Christian epic—in effect, an adaptation of history to a Christian poem. Another construes the poem as a tribute to courage, loyalty, patriotism, and devotion in the face of overwhelming odds—in other words, a celebration of heroic ideals. A third more plausibly approaches the problem by way of the poem's purpose. If, so the reasoning goes, the poem were written to glorify Charlemagne and Christianity, then Roland dies a martyr's death and Charlemagne's vengeance redounds to his credit as a Defender of the Faith. Whatever their other merits, these theories suggest two recurring themes in any reading of *The Song of Roland*: the religious and the heroic, both of them major preoccupations of the High Middle Ages.

The religious theme pits Christians against Saracens, imbuing the story with a strong crusading spirit. On one hand, Charlemagne and his Peers display most, if not all, of the Seven Cardinal Virtues. Even the proud Roland dies humble and contrite, and Charlemagne's early indecision is resolved later in the poem when he becomes a courageous leader. The pagans, on the other hand, embody the Seven Deadly Sins. They are treacherous and greedy, fighting for personal glory or material gain rather than principle or faith. In this world of black-and-white morality, there are no good pagans, and the treasonous, deceitful Ganelon is severely punished for his perfidy. By contrast, the good Charlemagne is rewarded by the direct intervention of the Archangel Gabriel who deals the pagan Saracens a final defeat by slaying their leader, Baligant, while God makes the sun stand still. Divine intervention even affects the trial of Ganelon. The Christian cause is never questioned, nor is there any doubt about its justice. The forced baptism of the Saracen captives is described without qualm, just as is the battlefield bloodshed. If contradictions appear to the modern reader, they certainly did not occur to the medieval mind, for religious faith—by no means the least of the Cardinal Virtues—obliterated any inconsistencies between, for example, the virtue of temperance and the slaughter of pagans.

The heroic theme in *The Song of Roland* is closely linked to the religious, since most heroic deeds are done in the name of religious principle. The hero's role, however, requires dedication to ideals which have only peripheral, if any, relationship to religious precepts. Loyalty and bravery, for instance, are held in high esteem, but they are such basic heroic ideals that they are more implicit than explicit in the poem. Decision of major issues and even major battles by single combat is another heroic ideal which manifests itself many times over in the poem. In addition, the motifs of victory-defeat and treason-vengeance weigh heavily in the balance of heroic ideals. Still another factor, which the modern reader might call "team spirit," is the knightly obligation to subsume individual or personal honor and glory in furtherance of the cause. Thus, Roland's early pride, especially his insistence upon the use of force to subdue the Saracens and his subsequent refusal to blow his horn to summon Charlemagne's aid until all were dead or dying, was later brought low. Finally, Roland regretted his stubborn pride in a vivid demonstration of the need for that heroic ideal, teamwork. Of course, not all is a self-evident exercise in primitive democracy. Charlemagne's word was still law, although the most powerful peers insisted upon a voice in decision-making; nor is there much attention paid to morality (as distinct from ethics) or to social courtesies. In fact, a pristine system of social and political justice characterized Charlemagne's court as an essential ingredient in the heroic ideal, quite apart from religious considerations altogether. Thus, the unique features of the heroic ideal are distinguishable from religious precepts.

All in all, *The Song of Roland* is a remarkable panorama of medieval life and thought, imaginatively perceived. To those who would say that it is false history, one can answer only with the cliché that fiction is often truer than history, for in *The Song of Roland* such is the case. The poem affords so vivid a picture of medieval reality that its historical accuracy is irrelevant; it presents phychological, emotional, and sociological reality which transcends factual data to reach a new plateau of reality, one reflecting the spirit of the times rather than the substance. In this sense, *The Song of Roland* is, despite its ethical simplicities and its literary primitiveness, remarkably successful as a document of the medieval spirit, a characteristic which may explain its enduring popularity for nearly one thousand years.

Joanne G. Kashdan

THE SONG OF SONGS

Type of work: Novel
Author: Hermann Sudermann (1857-1928)
Type of plot: Naturalism
Time of plot: Early twentieth century
Locale: Germany
First published: 1909

The social message of this powerful, harshly naturalistic novel detailing a pure woman's fall from virtue is that the economic exploitation of the lower classes is attended by other evils as well, such as moral and sexual degeneration.

Hermann Sudermann belonged to the group of revolutionary young playwrights of the naturalist school who outraged traditionalists with their treatment of the most degraded and depraved aspects of human life in an absolutely uncompromising style. He was a rival of Gerhart Hauptmann in Berlin in the 1890's, and his skill at theatrical effect brought him great success. His plays were performed as far away as Japan.

The aims and style of his dramatic work gave form to his prose works, of which *The Song of Songs* is one of the most respected. Its themes of relentless sexual and economic exploitation, of class conflict, and of the despair of lower-class life are typical of naturalism, and represent a political protest as well as an artistic stance. Lilly experiences repeated assaults on her integrity, couched in various terms, but all turning upon her economic and sexual vulnerability. *The Song of Songs,* her father's composition, represents the ideal realm of love and personal fulfillment which is denied to everyone in the novel, the exploiters as well as the exploited.

Sudermann, likewise, transferred the technique of the stage to the composition of the novel, suppressing the narrator and allowing the characters to speak for themselves. His dialogue is rich in realistic touches: dialect, idiosyncratic speech patterns, and the coarseness of the street. He attempts to capture the manifold variety of life in its richness, as Lilly passes from sphere to sphere, rising and falling in her seeking after fulfillment. There is no explanation, judgment, or subjective evaluation by the author; his aim is to bring scenes to life in brevity and sharpness, and to leave the response to the reader. Like all naturalists, however, he was quite clear about the response he strove for: a recognition of the disillusion and desperation that darkens the lives of the masses, and of their source in the unjust structure of society and the self-seeking of those who have at their disposal any power.

THE SONG OF THE LARK

Type of work: Novel
Author: Willa Cather (1876-1947)
Type of plot: Impressionistic realism
Time of plot: Late nineteenth, early twentieth centuries
Locale: Colorado, Chicago, New York
First published: 1915

In this novel treating the subject of artistic development, Cather combines two of her most persistent themes, nostalgia for the past (particularly for an era of simple hardihood) and concern for the struggles of a sensitive, talented person in culturally blighted America.

Though it has never shared the success of some of Willa Cather's other works, *The Song of the Lark* is nonetheless a rewarding and significant part of the Cather canon. The novel has been criticized, and perhaps justly so, for its unselective use of detail and episode in developing Thea Kronborg's story; yet such thoroughness is also what has allowed Cather to convey so fully to the reader Thea's passionate spirit for living. Thea's growth as an artist is shown in the context of two themes which run throughout Cather's works: the invigorating, spiritual significance of the Southwest and its history, and the alienation of the artistic temperament from conventional life and values. *The Song of the Lark* is essentially a chronicle of the delicate awakening of the artistic sensibility and its consequent struggle to escape the limitations of a commonplace environment.

This theme is introduced in the novel through Thea's early opposition to the standards and values of Moonstone. The young girl's friends are those who, like Thea herself, display a quality of mind and spirit for life which Moonstone conventionality interprets as either wild and eccentric or blatantly selfish. The life styles of Dr. Archie, old Wunsch, Ray Kennedy, and Spanish Johnny are in marked contrast to the provincial conformity and petty materialism embodied in the likes of Mrs. "Livery" Johnson or the community's endorsement of Thea's less talented rival, Lily Fisher. Though Thea's talent and ardent nature set her apart from the rest of her community, she finds happiness and fulfillment in expanding her awareness of things. Visiting the countryside with Dr. Archie, learning German from Wunsch, or singing songs with Spanish Johnny, she is progressively introduced to a broader sense of values and culture than the narrow environment of Moonstone can supply. Her later experience with the ancient pottery at the cliff dwellings in Arizona only makes Thea more conscious of the immense aspirations and possibilities within her own spirit and the human spirit generally.

Seeking to develop her own aspirations to their fullest, Thea becomes more and more dedicated to the disciplines of her art. By the end of the novel her commitment has left almost no time in her life for other people, but she has fulfilled the artistic impulse that drove her beyond the limitations of a small town environment and into a world of intense, rapturous feeling for the quality of life. Her disciplined, self-imposed isolation from the conventional world is the price the serious artist must pay for an expansive spirit.

When *The Song of the Lark* was reissued in 1932, Cather revised the novel rather heavily in an attempt to reduce wordage and tighten its style. Most of the changes occurred in the last two books, where the author felt that, because Thea's struggle was now over, the dramatic pull of the story necessarily lagged into the anti-climatic. None of these changes, however, appreciably affected the novel's content or thematic statement.

SONG OF THE WORLD

Type of work: Novel
Author: Jean Giono (1895-1970)
Type of plot: Impressionistic romance
Time of plot: Early twentieth century
Locale: Basses-Alpes region, France
First published: 1934

Although Song of the World *superficially resembles other European fiction, such as that of Knut Hamsun, which treats with sympathy the sturdy peasant virtues and "growth of the soil," Giono's novel also has dimensions of myth and symbol concerning the maturation of society and the interrelatedness of man and nature.*

Jean Giono successfully combines his interests in the pastoral, simple life of the French peasant with the sociological issue of one's active response to human interaction and strife. *Song of the World,* perhaps because of its theme of the maturing of the individual through his social growth, is the best known of Giono's novels. His first two novels concentrated only on the individual without community; this, his third novel, expresses his love of the peasantry's commitment to preserving the family and its traditional ways, as well as his strong aversion to bloodshed and war. Giono became a pacifist after participating in the battle of Verdun during World War I.

Song of the World is an apt title for this work as it truly participates in the world myth patterns of the great epics. Giono, in fact, was a great lover of the Latin and Greek epic forms; his favorite was Homer's *Odyssey,* which greatly influenced his writing. The obvious structural correlation is the journey motif. Besides being the basic pattern of myth, it is also the form of the epic, and in this novel all of the elements of the journey theme are employed. There is first of all a call to the hero, Antonio, who is widely known as Goldenmouth, to help his friend, Sailor, find a lost son. Of course, the hero accepts the call and sets forth on a journey of physical as well as spiritual trials. He is risking his life to preserve life in the sacrificial pattern associated with heroic travels. Symbolically, one of the first encounters Antonio and Sailor have is with a woman giving birth to a son. They save the woman and thus the child. She is eventually the hero's prize; her love is his reward for the risk he took to find and save her; later, great risk is involved in saving his friend's son.

Another familiar element of the epic is the helper motif present in the guise of the barmaid and, more importantly, in Monsieur Toussaint. As is often the case with the "helper person" in an epic, Toussaint is a hunchback, a philosopher, and a magician doctor of sorts. Although seemingly unchanged by the events in his house, he is the catalyst for change for all those involved with him.

Antonio's goal is to rescue Sailor's red-haired son. The boy has married the daughter of wealthy and powerful Maudru, who controls the whole region. Besides marrying her secretly, in wooing and winning her he has slain her other suitor, the son of Maudru's sister. It is the hero's responsibility to free the boy and his bride from the domination of her father. The goal of the saga is to restore the boy to his homeland so that he may begin living as a man.

The son has experienced the initiation rite essential to his developing manhood. During the course of this process his father realizes he is dying. Giono employs Sailor's death symbolically as a commentary upon the growth of the son. It is at the death of the father that the son is finally freed to act on his own behalf (like a man freed in will and bursting with power) against the obstacle to his happiness, Maudru. The son boldly risks his life to right the wrong done to his father and thus to himself. He burns all that made Maudru wealthy and leaves the man so much the poorer for his jealousy and revenge.

The novel comes full circle when Maudru, on the hill overlooking the river, watches the entourage of his daughter, son-in-law, Antonio and his new bride drift down the river just as Maudru's man, when he was powerful, watched Antonio and Sailor come into the territory some time before. This river provides life to the foursome and a renewal or rebirth of spirit as well as a socialization through marriage. The hero, formerly one who lived in a hut in the woods, dreams of creating a home for his bride. The son, now a man, prepares to build a home for his young wife and to care for his now widowed mother.

The style of this novel certainly complements its epic content. The economy of language and vivid detail provide a fluidity and rhythmic tempo to *Song of the World*. Passages describing Antonio and his activities are mainly short, declarative sentences. They reflect the simple pastoral personality of the hero. Antonio's dialogue, however, reflects an eloquence and sensitivity more lofty than is characteristic of a simple peasant. From the first page, he is obviously a superior man.

The use of the three-part structural form divides the novel not only by seasons—spring, winter, and spring again—but by location—the setting forth, absence, and return to the homeland. Thus the title is meaningful, not only mythically but also seasonally. One is, of course, inextricably tied to the other as it is the seasons which evoke birth, death, and renewal.

Giono's novel urges the idea that action and risk are the price of freedom. Maudru, clinging to severity and power with an iron hand, loses the people and things he loves because he is unable to accept and respect his daughter's freedom. Obviously, Giono is searching for those modes of living in which man is both free to be himself and reunited harmoniously with nature and society.

Gayle Steck

SONS AND LOVERS

Type of work: Novel
Author: D. H. Lawrence (1885-1930)
Type of plot: Psychological realism
Time of plot: Late nineteenth century
Locale: England
First published: 1913

The basic theme of Sons and Lovers, *a partly autobiographical "education" novel, is that a young man's fixated Oedipal attachment to his mother destroys his chances for a successful romantic and sexual mating with a girl of his own age.*

Although Freud was the first to provide a systematic analysis of the Oedipal relationship and its function in man's fate, this instinct has been a part of man's unconscious from his earliest beginnings as a social animal. The establishment of the taboo against a son's murdering his father and having sexual relationships with his mother was man's initial step in the creation of civilization, because, according to Freud, this psychic drive lies deep in every man's subconscious or id as a reservoir of anarchistic energy. If man fails to acknowledge this biological compulsion and to incorporate its prohibition into his own ego, he invites annihilation, specifically in the form of castration by the father; generally, in the loss of freedom and power.

One of the earliest and best-known dramatizations of this drive is Sophocles' play, *Oedipus Rex.* Without foreknowledge and culpable guilt, Oedipus does murder his father and marry his mother. Yet, since he has transgressed, he must be punished; he blinds himself, a form of castration. Shakespeare's *Hamlet* has also been explored and explicated, most notably by Ernest Jones, as a reenactment of the Oedipal myth. *Sons and Lovers,* based directly on Lawrence's own childhood experiences, is the most significant post-Freudian novel dealing with a young man's murderous feelings towards his father and his erotic attraction to his mother.

Although it would be overly simplistic to explain *Sons and Lovers* as a mere gloss on a psychological concept, Freud's "complex" does offer a convenient way to begin understanding the character and cultural situation of Lawrence's hero, Paul Morel. He is the youngest and adored son of a mother who has married beneath herself. Of the failed middle class, she is educated to a degree, refined with pretensions toward the higher matters of life. Yet as a girl she is attracted to Walter Morel, a miner who possesses a passionate exuberance she missed on the frayed edges of the middle class. Their marriage, however, soon disintegrates under the pressures of poverty and unfulfilled expectations. As the father and mother grow apart and the older children leave home, Mrs. Morel turns toward her youngest, mapping out his life and intending to free him from the ignominy of the working class. Her ambitions for Paul are not untainted by her own frustrations, and it becomes clear that she wishes to live out her life through him.

Sensitive and frail, Paul finds his father's drunkenness and rough-edged masculinity repellent. Reared by his mother as if he were a fragile hot-house plant, he is alienated even further by his father's vulgar habits and degrading job. Without any sympathy or understanding of his father's suffering or his hard and abrupt love for him, Paul withdraws and joins his mother in the domestic battle. Enraged and disappointed by the loss of his son and wife, Morel withdraws into self-pity and alcohol.

Bereft of his father's influence, Paul's life becomes dominated by his mother. Smothered by her warm maternity, cut off from the real world, he returns her ardent affection and they form a relationship designed to hold off the horrors of reality. As he grows up, however, he discovers that he has traded his own "self" for security. His mother's protectiveness has cost him the power and freedom to relate to others. Every relationship he tries to create is inhibited by her jealousy and demands for his entire attention. Indeed, he comes to feel that every relationship he attempts is in some way a denial of her.

Paul's attraction to Miriam Leivers, which gradually develops into a love affair, is ironically both a rejection and a reaffirmation of his mother. Their immature love, which Mrs. Morel rightfully sees as a threat, is in some ways an acting out of the sexual implications of the mother-son relationship. In her passive dominance, Miriam unconsciously assumes for Paul the figure of his mother. Thus, if their love manages to remove him temporarily from his mother's sway, it also reinforces it. Both relationships are symbiotic; Paul draws sustenance from the women but loses the power of self-propulsion. That Paul does not completely acquiesce in the symbiosis is evident in both his brutal sexual treatment of Miriam and his sexual ambivalence toward his mother.

Paul's connection with Clara and Baxter Dawes is a much more interesting and complex one. Clara provides him with an adult sexual experience unlike that he had with Miriam. She is neither dominating nor submissive, but demands that he meet her as an equal. He must, therefore, remain emotionally on his own; he is expected to give affection as well as receive it. Unfortunately, Paul cannot maintain such an independence and this fact undermines their love. He cannot exist as a self-sufficient entity and Clara will not tolerate an invasion of her self. However, it is not until after Mrs. Morel's death that Paul understands this about their relationship. His subsequently successful attempt to reunite her with Baxter thus becomes his first sign of health; it is not only an admission that their romance is impossible, but is also a reparation for having alienated her from Baxter.

Paul's act of reparation is also symbolic. Having been released from his mother's dominance by her death, a death that he hastened, he must continue his growth toward freedom and power by making peace with his father. Unable to confront him directly, Paul admits by bringing together Clara and

Baxter the higher moral demands of marital love, a love he has helped to destroy—although innocently—between his father and mother. In this act, moreover, he negates the child in himself and salutes the reality of the father and husband.

David L. Kubal

THE SORROWS OF YOUNG WERTHER

Type of work: Novel
Author: Johann Wolfgang von Goethe (1749-1832)
Type of plot: Sentimental romance
Time of plot: Mid-eighteenth century
Locale: Germany
First published: 1774

A major novel of the German Romantic Movement of the late eighteenth century, The Sorrows of Young Werther *greatly influenced European literature for at least two generations. Goethe's theme of the tragic suffering and final suicide of a young man driven to despair by unrequited passion served as a model for many similar treatments of intense psychological self-analysis.*

Goethe wrote *The Sorrows of Young Werther* in the space of a few weeks in 1774, in a burst of creative energy that charged the whole work with a rare intensity. He drew upon his own experiences, and except for the suicide, much of the work is autobiographical. Perhaps because of this, it caught a mood of the times and it was greeted with great admiration and enthusiasm by the public. It was the work that made Goethe's reputation; to the end of his life, he was for many readers primarily "the author of *Werther*." At the same time, it was a turning point in his career, for it marked the end of his "Storm and Stress" period and this outburst of all-consuming emotion was followed by a quieter period leading to his classical style of the 1780's. Goethe himself later regarded the work as a kind of therapeutic expression of a dangerous side of his own personality, one which he overcame and controlled. He was appalled to find Werther become regarded as a model of behavior, influencing men's fashion (blue coat with yellow vest and trousers; long, unpowdered hair) and bringing a rash of suicides all over Europe.

The immediacy of the work is due in large part to its epistolary form. After a brief foreword by the fictional editor, the reader plunges straight into the world of Werther's mind, and his style, full of exclamations, broken sentences, and impassioned flights of imagination, expresses his personality better than could any description. Throughout the course of the novel, Werther moves from peak to peak of emotion—the letters pick out the high points of his life—and when he finally becomes too incoherent to write, the editor enters, creating a chilling effect, taking distance from the events, retarding the headlong rush of the story, and observing Werther with a sympathetic but dispassionate eye. The work possessed a further immediacy for its first readers in that it was set in their own contemporary world. The first letter is dated May 4, 1771, and we follow through the summer, fall, and winter into the next year with new hope coming in the spring and the final tragedy at the end of the year, in mid-winter. Werther shares the interests of his generation: he reads Homer, Klopstock, and Ossian, loves nature and the simple folk in the fashion of Rousseau, and chafes against the conventions and fashions of aristocratic eighteenth century society.

Aside from some secondary plot elements that mirror Werther's own predicament, especially the story of the peasant who commits murder out of frustrated love, the work is entirely developed around three characters: Werther, Lotte, and Albert. Lotte is in many ways the pivotal character since she is placed between the two men, who are almost opposites. She is attracted to each, perhaps more to Werther than to Albert since Werther appeals to her romantic side and she shares with him a capacity for passionate emotion that Albert lacks. But when we first met her, she is caring for her younger brothers and sisters, the very image of responsibility and self-sacrifice. Her mother is dead and she has taken over the duties of mother in the family. At the party in the storm, she takes over and organizes games to quiet the fears of her companions. However poetic she may be, she has a calm head and understands that Werther is hopelessly impractical in his emotion-centered life. Albert is a good husband and father, a bit dry perhaps and overly rational, but dependable, devoted, and clear headed. Lotte, who is a complex character, would like to have both men in her life and has been faulted by some for trying to carry on an impossible situation rather than discourage Werther from the beginning, or more emphatically, once the intensity of his feelings becomes obvious. While Werther is certainly the most directly autobiographical of the characters, Lotte is perhaps closer to Goethe's own personality, combining the practical, responsible traits that would find expression in his official activities in Weimar with the poetic imagination that constantly drew him back into the world of literature. This union of opposites is a common feature of Goethe's work, from *Faust* ("two souls dwell, alas, within my breast"), to Wilhelm Meister, who wants to be an actor but becomes a doctor instead.

From the very beginning, Goethe distinguished his own character from that of Werther, and *The Sorrows of Young Werther* is more a judgment upon the dangers of emotion than an incitement to emulation. The novel is, in fact, a tragedy of character, for the unhappy romance is not the cause of Werther's tragedy. From the very beginning, as Werther exclaims "what a thing is the heart of man!" his situation is clear. Werther is important as one of the first modern tragic figures for whom not events, but his own personality, is the tragedy. The conflict rests within him and the world merely provides the occasion for his inner conflict to express itself. He embodies a life-spirit that strives for the absolute, for the unconditional, which is carried forward by a stream of emotion which seizes upon life and constantly transforms it into an inner experience of great intensity. His life becomes centered around his own emotions and is drawn inward as in a whirlpool. There is no compensating outward flow in the form of activity or other-directedness, no objective pole which can counter the all-transforming subjectivity. It is the spirit of

Faust, or of Goethe's tragic poet-figure Torquato Tasso. It is the spirit that he saw as the inevitable consequence of the emotion-centered Storm and Stress writers, not a few of whom ended in madness or suicide. In writing the novel, Goethe created perhaps the most memorable representative of this tragic type, the embodiment of one extreme of the human personality. In his subsequent work, Goethe continued to keep this aspect of himself alive, to provide the motive force for a series of masterpieces. The novel itself became the inspiration for a host of Romantic writers in Germany, England, and France, and represents, thus, a landmark in European literature.

Steven C. Schaber

SOTILEZA

Type of work: Novel
Author: José María de Pereda (1833-1906)
Type of plot: Regional realism
Time of plot: 1880
Locale: Santander, Spain
First published: 1884

Sotileza, an early example of the Spanish regional novel, treats realistically but with ample affection the simple Santander folk living along the coastline of Northern Spain. Pereda's contempt for the middle class is as pronounced as his sympathy for the lower-class fishermen who struggle against the sea.

Pereda's literary career can best be described as that of an author in search of a style. He started writing when he was twenty-one, creating an unpretentious comedy which he rewrote and produced in Santander much later. After that, he continued to write regularly but was not much of a success. He thirsted for recognition, but it was not until 1881, with the publication of *El sabor de la tierruca* that he received public acclaim. What distinguished this work was its local flavor, its regional appeal. This was the key for Pereda, and he continued to write in this style. The publication of *Sotileza* established his reputation as an important writer of the period.

Pereda is credited with the creation of the Spanish regional novel. To be sure there are historical precedents, but he was the first to write novels that can thus be specifically labeled. Moreover, Pereda succeeded in integrating popular language with literary language. Again, there were many other writers who attempted this unification, and had some successes, but Pereda was the first novelist to do so consistently and with widespread appeal.

Pereda is a master of dialogue. In *Sotileza* the characters speak with the rhythms and color of everyday speech. In capturing, for instance, the local verbal flavor of the Santander fishermen, Pereda transposes to the written page the dynamics and movements of the spoken word.

Most of the characters in *Sotileza* spring from the author's memories and remembrances of people he knew as a child in Santander. Thus he presents us with a gallery of authentic local types whose lives, ideas, and goals are described with keen insight.

Sotileza, protagonist of the novel, is a product of Pereda's imagination, and perhaps for this reason she is the most enigmatic and mysterious character of the book. Pereda seems much more at ease when describing real people. His gift for depicting objective reality is manifest in his poignant and lyrical descriptions of the surrounding countryside.

Pereda's stated purpose in writing the novel was to pay homage to the brave, unknown heroes of his city, the fishermen. The book is his eulogy to the anonymous men who fascinated him as a child, and a tribute to their city.

The plot of the novel is no more than an excuse to do this, and is somewhat lacking in interest perhaps for this reason. But as a realistic portrayal of a region and the life of its inhabitants, *Sotileza* has achieved a permanent place in world literature.

THE SOUND AND THE FURY

Type of work: Novel
Author: William Faulkner (1897-1962)
Type of plot: Psychological realism
Time of plot: 1910-1928
Locale: Mississippi
First published: 1929

The Sound and the Fury, an extremely complex yet rewarding novel, traces from 1910 to 1928 the decline of a once-aristocratic but now degenerated Southern family. Faulkner's method of narration, involving the consciousness of different members and servants of the Compson family, provides four distinct points of view in depth psychology.

After early undistinguished efforts in verse (*The Marble Faun*, 1924) and fiction (*Soldier's Pay*, 1926; *Mosquitoes*, 1927), William Faulkner moved suddenly into the forefront of American literature in 1929 with the appearance of *Sartoris* and *The Sound and the Fury*, the first installments in the artistically complex and subtly satirical saga of Yoknapatawpha County that would be spun out further in *As I Lay Dying* (1930), *Light in August* (1932), *Absalom, Absalom!* (1936), *Go Down, Moses* (1942), *The Unvanquished* (1938), *Intruder in the Dust* (1948), The *Hamlet-Town-Mansion* trilogy (1940, 1957, 1959), and *Requiem for a Nun* (1951)—the last an extension of materials in *Sanctuary* (1931). Chiefly in recognition of the monumental literary importance of the Yoknapatawpha Saga, Faulkner was awarded the Nobel Prize in 1949.

The Sound and the Fury marked the beginning of the most fertile period of Faulkner's creativity, when he was in his early thirties. Yet both for its form and for its thematic significance this novel may well be considered Faulkner's masterpiece. Never again would his work demonstrate such tight, precise structure, combined with the complexities of syntax and punctuation that became his most characteristic stylistic trait. Furthermore, the themes recorded in his simple but elegant Nobel Prize speech—"love and honor and pity and pride and compassion and sacrifice"—are already present in this novel with a forcefulness of characterization that could hardly be improved upon. It was in this novel that Faulkner found a way of embodying his peculiar view of time in an appropriate style, a style much influenced by Joycean stream-of-consciousness, and by Faulkner's own stated desire ultimately to "put all of human experience between one Cap and one period." That concept of time, most emphatic in Quentin's section, can be summarized by Faulkner's statement that "there is no such thing as *was*; if *was* existed there would be no grief or sorrow." The continuation of the past into the present, as a shaping influence that cannot be avoided, is the larger theme of Faulkner's life work.

In this novel, that theme is embodied specifically in the history of the decline of the once-aristocratic Compson family. Nearly twenty years after the original publication of the novel, at the instigation of his publisher Malcolm Cowley, Faulkner wrote the background history of the Compsons as an "Appendix" that appears at the front of the book. The Appendix records the noble origins of the Compson landstead, once the possession of a Chickasaw king named Ikkemotubbe, or "the man." After then proceeding through the Compson succession—beginning with Quentin Maclachan Compson, who immigrated from Glasgow, and proceeding to Jason III, the "dipsomaniac" lawyer who could not tear himself away from the Roman classics long enough to preserve the vestiges of his family's good name, Faulkner presents terse but invaluable insight into the chief characters of *The Sound and the Fury*: Candace, who knew she was doomed, who regarded her virginity as no more than a "hangnail," and whose promiscuity represents the moral sterility of the family; Quentin III, who "identified family with his sister's membrane," convinced himself he had committed incest with her, but really loved only death—in his sublimation of emotions into a kind of latter-day courtly love mystique—and found his love in June, 1910, by committing the physical suicide which the destruction of his grandfather's watch symbolized; Benjy, the "idiot" whose "tale" forms the remarkable first section of the novel, and who "loved three things: the pasture . . . his sister Candace (who 'smelled like trees'), and firelight" and who symbolizes both the mental deterioration of the family and through his castration, its physical sterility; Jason IV, "the first sane Compson since before Culloden and (a childless bachelor) hence the last," who commits Benjy to an asylum, sells the house, and displays the pathetically mediocre intelligence that alone is able to cope with the incursions of the modern world symbolized by the Snopes family; and Quentin IV, the child of Candace, "already doomed to be unwed from the instant the dividing egg determined its sex," who is the last Compson and the final burden destined for Mrs. Compson, the personification, to Jason, of all the evil and insanity of his decaying, decadent family.

Benjy's section takes place on April 7, 1928, the day before Quentin IV steals her uncle's money. It is written with incredibly delicate perception, pronouncing the lucidity of a simple-minded innocence that can yet be accompanied by a terrible sharpness and consistency of memory. In its confusion of his father's funeral with Candace's wedding, in its constant painful reactivation by the sound of the golfers crying "caddie" to cause him to bellow out his hollow sense of his sister's loss, Benjy's mind becomes the focus of more cruelty, compassion, and love than anyone but Dilsey imagines. Quentin III's section, taking place eighteen years earlier on the day of his suicide at Harvard, is one of the most sustained lyrical passages of twentieth century prose. The concentration of Quentin's stream-of-consciousness around the broken, handless watch is one of Faulkner's greatest achievements. Just as the leitmotiv of Benjy's section was the smell of trees associated with Caddy's loss, the recurring refrain of Quentin's is the desperate rhetorical question, "Did you ever have a sister?" Jason's theme is hate, a hate as pitiful as is the diminution of Compson pride into pathetic vanity; and this third section of the novel may be the greatest for its evocation of deep, moving passions from even the most mediocre. The last section is focused on Dilsey, who "seed de first en de last" and who represents, to Faulkner, the only humanity that survives the fall of the house of Compson—the only humanity to endure.

Kenneth John Atchity

SOUTH WIND

Type of work: Novel
Author: Norman Douglas (1868-1952)
Type of plot: Social satire
Time of plot: Early twentieth century
Locale: Island of Nepenthe
First published: 1917

Witty, sophisticated, and sly, South Wind *is a satirical novel rich in character and setting but casual in plot. Through his humane, genially tolerant attitude toward the morals of the expatriates on Nepenthe, Douglas spoofs the stuffy hypocrisy of English Edwardian society.*

Often the country house novel, such as *South Wind,* is also a *roman à clef,* its characters transparently disguised contemporaries of the author. In a later preface, where Douglas said that he had used the benign and innocent Bishop of Bampopo to reflect the reactions of his readers to the bizarre events and fascinating but amoral discourse of his assembled eccentrics, he denied, however, that his characters had living originals; yet the incessant and brilliant chatter recalls the dialogues of Bernard Shaw and Oscar Wilde. Besides, the entire novel has a *fin de siècle* atmosphere calling up the wit and decadence of the Yellow 'Nineties. Yet, finally, Douglas celebrates the unconventionality of his characters, who are designed not merely to shock his readers but also to expose and ridicule their stuffy Georgian manners and hypocritical morality.

Douglas's serious intent—to satirize his own society—is slowly revealed through the "conversion" of Bishop Heard. Although a good Christian, he has been separated from the social morality of England because of his work in Africa. Thus he comes to Nepenthe without prejudice, used to the naturalness of his native flock. Miss Wilberforce's exhibitionism, consequently, which would have horrified a proper Englishman, does not disturb him.

Gradually the Bishop of Bampopo realizes that if people are allowed to do what they want with their lives, justice and humanity triumph. Therefore when he witnesses Mrs. Meadows' "murder" of Retlow, he takes the law into his own hands and judges it as an act of proper retribution for the villain's attempted blackmail. With Denis Phipps' newly discovered sense of self, all comes to a happy ending. If Douglas's morality, which asserts man's natural goodness, is preposterously naïve, it acts as an effective—and humorous—counterfoil to the remnants of Victorian morality which still shaped the proper Englishman's world.

THE SPANISH FRIAR

Type of work: Drama
Author: John Dryden (1631-1700)
Type of plot: Tragi-comedy
Time of plot: Fifteenth century
Locale: Aragon, Spain
First presented: 1681

The Spanish Friar, or, The Double Discovery *was popular in Dryden's day partly because of its anti-Catholic sentiments and partly because of its successful fusion of the love-honor theme of conventional heroic drama with the ribald comedy elements involving the antics of Dominic, the licentious friar.*

The Spanish Friar is a modified form of Dryden's earlier heroic drama. Features in this play common to the mode are a noble hero of great ability and renown, violently torn between his love for a lady and his honor, which impels him to give her up; an exaggerated, often bombastic style of language; an intricate (and often barely credible) plot, sometimes with a comic, dramatically parallel subplot; and a dramatic movement which threatens, even if it does not actually end in, tragedy. *The Spanish Friar* is a considerably more controlled example of the genre than Dryden's *The Conquest of Granada,* but the family resemblance is clear.

It is easy enough to ridicule the fantastic plot complications of heroic drama, and the often extravagant language in which the heroes and heroines express themselves: ("Despair, Death, Hell, have seized my tortured soul . . ."); but it must be remembered that these plays were designed primarily as entertainment (" 'tis my interest to please my audience," Dryden noted in his preface), not as historical dramas or studies of character. The modern reader is likely to groan in dismay at the final revelation that old King Sancho is really alive, saved by Bertran's better nature. True, this development tends to render academic, if not nonsensical, Torrismond's earlier anguish over whether or not he must turn against his still virginal wife Leonora, and the queen's own painful resolve to renounce her husband and retire to a convent. But the earlier dramatic action which leads to this crisis is, in reality, not much less fanciful than the conclusion.

If one passes over the unlikely plot twists and the larger-than-life characters, it becomes apparent how skillfully Dryden, largely through brilliant dialogue, has manipulated the intellectual and emotional sympathies of his audiences, to make them see the issues of the play from the same points of view as the participants. No one character is either fully unsympathetic or fully sympathetic. We condemn Leonora for her crime and her evasion of responsibility, while pitying her in her plight ("to lose a crown and a lover in a day"); we would like to see justice done, but not at the expense of her life or happiness. Similarly, we can admire General Torrismond for his love and devotion, but it is easy enough to see the "womanish" quality in him that makes Raymond's contempt for his love-lethargy eminently reasonable. The audience—not just the hero—is torn by conflicting sympathies; and Dryden's dramatic prowess in creating and modulating this audience involvement is never more apparent than in the exciting exchange between Torrismond and Raymond, at the end of Act IV, that crystallizes the love-honor conflict.

Dryden, author of the stinging lampoon *MacFlecknoe* (1682), had a sure hand for comedy, and the comic subplot that gives the play its title is a rollicking one. Friar Dominic is a splendid compendium of all the avaricious, hypocritical, debauched friars that populate English literature since the Middle Ages. Here again, however, Dryden's dramatic portrait is not purely vitriolic, but also sympathetic, even half-admiring; certainly it is difficult to take the part of the near-cuckold Gomez over that of the witty and exuberant "old gouty friar."

In addition to his anti-Catholicism, many other of the playwright's sentiments show through in *The Spanish Friar*. Possibly most objectionable is the strain of misogyny (another long-established literary tradition) that characterizes women as the weak, lustful, or seductive (depending on whether they are in the subplot or the main plot), and inferior sex: "that toy a woman," says Raymond, "made from the dross and refuse of a man." Finally, Dryden's essential political and religious conservatism, his deep-rooted mistrust of the popular will, and his dread of any kind of rebellion against legitimate power, are everywhere apparent here. Even in a work devoted primarily to thrills and laughter, Dryden's implication is clear: without the guides of established political and religious authority, morality becomes relative and behavior mechanical, as Leonora realizes when she allows Bertran to effect the murder of the lawful king.

THE SPANISH GIPSY

Type of work: Drama
Authors: Thomas Middleton (1580-1627) with William Rowley (1585?-1642?) and possibly John Ford (1586-c. 1640?)
Type of plot: Tragi-comedy
Time of plot: Early years of the seventeenth century
Locale: Madrid
First presented: 1623

An intricate tragic-comedy, The Spanish Gypsy *derives most of its action from portions of two novels by Cervantes. Interwoven with the main melodramatic plot involving the fates of Roderigo and Clara is the gipsy subplot, remarkable for its charming scenes of pastoral comedy.*

Swinburne, that avid lover and critic of Elizabethan and Jacobean playwrights, has described *The Spanish Gipsy* as "one of those half-baked or underdone dishes of various and confused ingredients, in which the cook's or the baker's hurry has impaired the excellent materials of wholesome bread and savoury meat." He meant that the play is uneven; it is both "tragic" and "romantic," and its structure could have been improved by rewriting. Be that as it may, *The Spanish Gipsy* flows smoothly and to a large extent lacks the bawdiness of other contemporary dramas, such as, for example, Middleton's own *A Chaste Maid in Cheapside.* This, however, does not reduce the comic aspect of the play. Much of the humor derives from the antics of Sancho, a gentleman and ward to Pedro, and Soto, Sancho's man. Sancho and Soto join the gipsies in disguise, as do so many characters in the play; the pair act the fools throughout.

The tone of the play is jocular and pleasant enough that we never really expect it to end tragically. It is filled with songs and festivity. The tragic aspect, such as it is, has parallels to the popular revenge genre; and this is one way the two plots are tied together. Louis wants revenge on Alvarez, who killed his father. Pedro and Maria want revenge on Roderigo, the friend of Louis, who raped their daughter. Further, Cardochia must revenge herself on John because he rejected her advances. As in *Hamlet,* the best revenge play, *The Spanish Gipsy* employs the play-within-a-play device. Roderigo must play a character not unlike himself, and Alvarez, his father in the play-within-a-play, speaks words that express exactly the sentiments of Roderigo's actual father: "the anger of a father; / Although it be as loud and quick as thunder, / Yet 'tis done instantly. . . ." Though the plot is at first a bit confusing, we are not surprised that all returns to the comic norm at the end.

THE SPANISH TRAGEDY

Type of work: Drama
Author: Thomas Kyd (1558?-1594)
Type of plot: Tragedy of revenge
Time of plot: Sixteenth century
Locale: The Spanish and Portuguese courts
First presented: c. 1586

Evidence for the popularity of The Spanish Tragedy *during the sixteenth century is the fact that the play is known to have gone through at least ten editions by 1634. Kyd's violent, often lurid play began the vogue for "revenge tragedies" that included among its imitations Shakespeare's* Hamlet.

The Spanish Tragedy, more so than *Hamlet,* with which it shares some striking similarities, is a nearly perfect example of Elizabethan blood-revenge tragedy. In fact Kyd's spectacular play—with its eight onstage murders and suicides, a public hanging, lunatic scenes, and the biting out of Hieronimo's tongue—initiated the genre's popularity at the beginning of the seventeenth century. Kyd upstages all his contemporaries in his ability to devise thrilling stage tricks, and the nine extant quarto editions of *The Spanish Tragedy* dated during the early seventeenth century testify to the play's ability to draw an audience.

The play itself neatly defines Elizabethan revenge tragedy. The major stock features are all to be found in it, including a revenge, directed either by the father or the son for the sake of the other; a ghost, outside the action of the play, who aids the revenger; hesitation of the hero or revenger (the hero often is contaminated by his passion and becomes, because of the delay, Machiavellian); real or pretended insanity; the presence of suicides, intrigues, scheming villains, and other various horrors.

Comparison between *The Spanish Tragedy* and Shakespeare's *Hamlet,* written about fifteen years later, is provocative. Both plays have an amiable Horatio, ghosts returning from the dead, father-son vengeance themes, justice retarded by the mental state of the avenger, a dumb show, a play within a play, and profound sensationalism. No doubt Kyd's play in some ways helped shape *Hamlet.* Kyd is in fact attributed as author of the *Ur-Hamlet* (translate "before Hamlet"), a lost play which is probably an earlier version of the Hamlet story.

But *The Spanish Tragedy* withstands the test of critical analysis on its own merits. Its three-ring-circus construction produces some interesting and sophisticated critical questions. Because of the liveliness of his play, Kyd is not always regarded as a careful playwright. But the revenge motif, for example, plays itself out through three characters, Don Andrea, Bel-Imperia, and Hieronimo. Furthermore, in addition to the audience of the play, there are two other onstage audiences, the ghost-Don Andrea team, and the onstage audience of the Spanish court which witnesses the dumb show.

The major critical issue of *The Spanish Tragedy* is the question of audience response to Hieronimo. Is he a hero or a villain? Ambiguously, he is both. Judged by Elizabethan ethical and legal standards of behavior, Hieronimo becomes a wholly despicable Italianate villain when he decides to effect his revenge by secret—private, rather than public—means. In terms of revenge tragedy, the development in Hieronimo's character from public avenger-hero to private avenger-villain is evidence that Kyd is deliberately turning his audience's sympathy against the revengeful father.

It is in the "Vindicta mihi" passage that Hieronimo concludes he will act out private vengeance for his son's death:

> And to conclude, I will revenge his death.
> But how? Not as the vulgar wits of men,
> With open, but inevitable ills,
> As by a secret, yet a certain mean,
> Which under kindship will be cloaked best.

Hieronimo chooses his secret plan over the publicly acceptable alternative of open duel, or, better yet, due process of law. Moreover, his final atrocity of killing the innocent Duke of Castile, brother to the king, marks him as total villain. By this deed he departs so far from the English sense of justice that all sympathy is withdrawn. Hieronimo's suicide is then forced by the audience's demand that the villain be properly punished. His death satisfies the stern Elizabethan doctrine that murder by private individuals, no matter what the motive, must not be tolerated.

But does Hieronimo have a choice? His reversal is forced by events in the play. He is the Chief Magistrate of Spain, and his life has been devoted to administering the law. He believes in public justice and wants compensation for wrongs by due process. Hieronimo, in fact, is the only character in the play who attempts to circumvent disaster by appeals to public law. But his appeal to the king is blocked. The king is busy when Hieronimo approaches him, and Hieronimo is hit by another fit of distraction at the moment when he most needs to be in complete control of his faculties. Believing that Horatio's murderer must not go unpunished, and believing that no recourse to public vengeance is left open, Hieronimo assumes that he, the next of kin, must be the appointed avenger and he becomes a scourge of God, attempting justice on his own terms. Only if the play is read as a treatise on the nature of divine justice operating on the human level, can Hieronimo's character be interpreted as heroic.

Structurally, Kyd manipulates his audience to feel both satisfaction and horror at the catastrophe of the play by using his two onstage audiences to guide the responses of the real audience. The ghost's promise of revenge to Don Andrea sets up a pattern of anticipation for the audience, which then expects certain conventions from a revenge tragedy. This response may be described as aesthetic, and the ghost Revenge becomes a spokesman for the playwright's intent. Revenge says in effect that he is making it all up, that the play is a work of art rather than a piece of reality.

But the audience of Hieronimo's dumb show sees, not a "fiction," but a story with clear ties to "nonartistic reality." And only at the end of his show does Hieronimo reveal that the actors in his play have not been feigning but, instead, have stabbed in earnest. The audience's response is, understandably, horror. The line between art and reality is momentarily erased. Rather than responding to a play, the Spanish court audience finds itself suddenly responding to a real and immediate experience. Kyd's audience picks up on this second level of response, so that we the spectators see the play through the eyes of the onstage audience, but still also "created" by Revenge.

The effect of such a double vision is a sense of immediacy, of the close relationship between art and life. The audience leaves the theater with a sense —conscious or not—of having witnessed a play with very real implications for their everyday lives. Audience response on this level is of course necessary for any good drama, or for that matter any good work of art. Kyd seems to have built in a sense of relevancy and meaning on a structural level in *The Spanish Tragedy* that makes the play more than the thrilling bloodbath it is often labeled.

Jean Marlowe

THE SPOILERS

Type of work: Novel
Author: Rex Beach (1877-1949)
Type of plot: Adventure romance
Time of plot: The Alaska gold rush
Locale: The Yukon
First published: 1906

More than a romantic novel of adventure set in the Yukon during the time of the Alaska gold rush, The Spoilers *explores primitive emotions, particularly those of brutality and violence, in stark, semi-naturalistic detail.*

Pure and simple, Beach is a master of physical violence. His novel abounds in terrifying fights, made doubly realistic by allusion in closest detail to crunching bones and tearing clothes. In the titanic duel that ends the novel—the final confrontation between Glenister and McNamara—both men turn into wild beasts. After the hero loses the use of his hand ("A sudden darting agony paralyzed Roy's hand, and he realized that he had broken the metacarpal bones. . . ."), boxing is discarded for brutal wrestling. Roy subdues the villain with a hammerlock and breaks his arm. The climax of the novel, this event gives the title to the penultimate chapter: "The Hammer-Lock."

Beach blends a vulgarized naturalism with adventure and romance. His hero's brutishness, though at first odious to Helen Chester, finally enthralls her because of its directness and honesty. "My pagan," she murmurs at the final embrace, somewhat cowed by the realization that all human beings have brutal instincts: "You told me once that the wilderness had made you a savage, and I laughed . . . when you said . . . that we're all alike, and that those motives are in us all. I see now that you were right and I was very simple."

It is Beach's context for this cardinal principle of naturalism—the primitive streak in all human existence—that is simple. Naturalists like Norris and Dreiser demonstrate in such powerful works as *McTeague* and *Sister Carrie* that brutality and corruption are very near the surface in all of us; what they do not do is suggest that the release of these forces can lead to adventure and romance. Quite the contrary. Naturalism often approaches tragedy by revealing the dark limitations of man, the obstacles that heredity and environment present to his happiness and moral health.

The Spoilers is primarily an entertainment, and its influence is still felt every time John Wayne, who played Glenister in the movie version of the novel, smashes someone against a table.

THE SPOILS OF POYNTON

Type of work: Novel
Author: Henry James (1843-1916)
Type of plot: Social morality
Time of plot: Late nineteenth century
Locale: England
First published: 1897

A finely perceived psychological novel written during the middle period of James's career, The Spoils of Poynton *turns upon the theme of conflicting values— material as opposed to moral—as they affect the acquisition both of property and love rights.*

According to Henry James in his "Preface" to *The Spoils of Poynton,* he perceived the "germ" of the short novel in a friend's casual mention of an acrimonious conflict between a mother and her son over the disposition of the family furniture following the death of the father. "There had been but ten words, yet I recognized in them, as in a flash, all the possibilities of the little drama of my 'Spoils.' " "On the face of it," he went on to say, "the 'things' themselves would form the very center of such a crisis; these grouped objects, all conscious of their eminence and their price, would enjoy, in any picture of a conflict, the heroic importance."

But the "things" alone must not have been enough to provoke James to immediate creation, since he left the idea unused for almost two years. In 1895, however, needing a story to fulfill an obligation to the *Atlantic,* James returned to the "spoils" idea and added the necessary missing ingredient, the central character. "For something like Fleda Vetch had surely been latent in one's first appreciation of the theme."

Thus James found the two lines of action that give the story its final shape: the conflict between Mrs. Gereth and her son, goaded on by Mona Brigstock, over the furnishings of Poynton and the romance between Owen Gereth and Fleda Vetch. The problem of who is to get the "spoils" dominates the first third of the book, but by chapter eight the center of interest has shifted to the question of who will marry Owen. The two issues are, of course, completely intertwined since Owen is actually one of the "spoils" himself and his marital decision also determines the disposition of the "things."

The dispute over the "spoils" is really a trial between two strong-willed, determined women, Mona Brigstock and Mrs. Gereth, who direct their strategies through Owen Gereth and Fleda Vetch. The contest becomes ambiguous and the outcome doubtful because the "agents" prove unreliable: Owen's emotional involvement with Fleda upsets Mona's calculations, and Fleda's ambivalent reactions threaten Mrs. Gereth's design.

It is unlikely that Mona cares much for the "things" of Poynton for themselves. After she finally wins Owen and Poynton, she flaunts her indifference

2146 The Spoils of Poynton/JAMES

to the house by not even living there. Her tenacity in seeking the "spoils" is a matter of willful pride: "Mona," wrote James, "is *all* will." She insists on the furniture because it "goes with the house"—and the house goes with Owen. In addition, it is probable that Mona sees the dispute as a "test" of Owen; or, rather, of her ability to control him. If she can force him to act against his mother's deepest wishes, then she can be confident of dominance in their marriage.

Even though Mrs. Gereth is no less strong-willed and ruthless in her passion to keep control of the artifacts of Poynton, she is a considerably more sympathetic figure. If her attitude toward Poynton reveals her to be a thorough materialist, she is at least a materialist with taste; Poynton, the fruit of her labors, is a fine art product and her devotion to it is passionate and complete. If she is a snob, judging people solely in terms of their taste and "cleverness," she seems accurate in her judgments: Mona is vulgar, Owen is stupid, and Fleda is superior. If Mrs. Gereth's actions are arrogant and extreme, they are mitigated by her situation; the English law that grants all inheritance rights directly to the son, regardless of the widow's needs, is an unjust one. And, if she "collected" Fleda to use as part of a scheme to regain Poynton, she does, in the end, show genuine feeling and concern toward the girl as a person, not just a "piece of furniture."

However, the most sympathetic and interesting person in the story is Fleda Vetch. In his "Preface" James identifies her as the only real "character" in the story; that is, the one figure of feeling and intelligence who is capable of development and change. It is through her perception and sensibility that the reader experiences the story and, in James's words, "the progress and march of my tale became and remained that of her understanding."

Not surprisingly, Fleda is the most complex and puzzling character in the book. Although her intelligence and moral superiority are evident throughout, her behavior frequently seems contradictory and self-defeating. Critics have disputed the motivations behind many of her actions and especially those during the crucial scenes that determine the outcome of her romance with Owen. The primary question is this: at the point where Owen says he loves her and wants to marry her, why does she send him straight back to Mona with "conditions" that virtually guarantee losing him? Or, to put it more generally, why does she throw away her one chance for happiness at the very time she seems to have it within her grasp?

In attempting to answer that question, three variables must be kept in mind: Fleda's relationship with Mrs. Gereth, her relationship with Owen, and her own aesthetic and moral values.

From the beginning Fleda is flattered and awed by Mrs. Gereth's attentions and compliments. The older woman sees in Fleda the perfect protégée, a girl gifted with intelligence and intuitive good taste, but with little background experience, who can be influenced, even molded, by an astute mentor. Thus,

Mrs. Gereth grooms a "replacement" for herself who can not only keep Poynton out of Mona's grasp, but can even minister to its treasures long after she, Mrs. Gereth, is gone. In matters of artistic taste Mrs. Gereth probably has her way with Fleda, but after Owen becomes a factor her control over the girl becomes doubtful. In addition, as the book progresses Fleda becomes increasingly aware of being manipulated by Mrs. Gereth and, while she may not personally object to being a "piece of furniture," she does feel quite guilty about being used as bait in a trap for Owen.

Fleda's relations with Owen are equally problematical. At first she rejects him on the grounds that he is "too stupid," but even from the beginning his amiable personality and physical desirability make a strong impression on her. As their relationship grows, Fleda's view of him becomes more and more clouded by self-deception. Her first impressions of him as "stupid" and "weak" are accurate, but, as she falls in love with him, she suppresses these obvious insights or rationalizes them into strengths. She insists that he act with "independence" and "maturity," yet, like Mona, she fully expects to dominate him after marriage ("It's because he's so weak that he needs me").

Fleda feels strongly attracted and obligated to both people, so she gives each of them the impression that she favors their cause. From these contending loyalties come such self-defeating acts as her persistent claim to Owen that she is winning his mother over and her lies to Mrs. Gereth regarding her emotions and, more importantly, Owen's feelings for her.

Thus, conflicting impulses probably determine her final self-defeating act. Because of her innate morality and her Victorian upbringing, Fleda is unable to accept the idea of winning a previously committed man away from his intended; she cannot act the part of the "designing woman"—especially in someone else's design. Given her tendency to self-deception, she probably convinces herself that Owen can, in fact, meet the conditions she imposes; unfortunately "her Owen" is largely imaginary and the real Owen cannot resist a fully aroused Mona Brigstock. And emotionally Fleda seems to lack the capacity, as Mrs. Gereth put it, to "let go."

But these speculations do not answer the central question about Fleda. Does her final act represent a failure of nerve, a running away from life and experience? Or does it represent the moral victory of a woman too proud to jeopardize her ethics in return for a chance at happiness? Both views, and most positions in between, have been argued by the critics with little consensus. Each reader must make up his or her own mind on the point.

However, if Fleda's actions cost her a life with Owen, her reaction to that loss demonstrates her strength of character and her mature appreciation of life. It is she who senses the "meaning" of Ricks and brings a measure of solace to the defeated Mrs. Gereth. It is here that we come really to understand Fleda's aesthetic sensibility; to her, objects have moral qualities and their beauty is a product of the human experience they reflect. If she can succeed in impressing that view on her companion, a mellowed Mrs. Gereth may find a measure of happiness at Ricks—even after that accidental fire which resolves forever the fate of the "spoils" of Poynton.

Keith Neilson

THE SPY

Type of work: Novel
Author: James Fenimore Cooper (1789-1851)
Type of plot: Historical romance
Time of plot: 1780; 1812
Locale: New York State
First published: 1821

The Spy: A Tale of the Neutral Ground is a historical novel that clearly advances the author's patriotic sentiments. Cooper's Peyton Dunwoodie is supposed to represent the ideal American soldier and officer; Frances Wharton, the ideal of American womanhood; and George Washington, the supreme father of his country.

The Spy is an important novel both in James Fenimore Cooper's career and in the history of American literature. For Cooper, *The Spy* represented a first success in a literary career which was to include thirty-three fictional works as well as a number of other writings over a period of thirty-one years. But *The Spy* also signifies the establishment of an independent American literature, a literature based on American life, American characters, and set in an American landscape. It is significant, then, that the novel which declared "independence" from European, and especially English, literature should take for its subject the American War for Independence.

In his Preface to *The Spy*, Cooper showed he was acutely conscious of being an American writer and of writing about American subjects. Still, there is no doubt he was influenced by the major currents in literature written abroad; and, though in his Preface he offers a tongue-in-cheek apology for not including castles and nobles, as Sir Walter Scott had done, it is certain that Scott influenced Cooper in *The Spy* and in his later career as well. Scott was a great pioneer in the art of the historical novel and *The Spy* shows that Cooper learned much from Scott.

An important aspect of the historical novel are the historical types, characters who live in a specific historical period and in a particular place. One of the key differences between an authentic historical novel and a contemporary novel in a historical setting is characterization. Though one may argue that people are, in a sense, the same everywhere and at all times, it is apparent that the differences cannot be merely overlooked if one is mainly interested in accurately portraying a specific era. Thus to capture a particular place at a particular time, the novelist must do more than merely dress his contemporaries in the clothing of days past. He must have a grasp of those human features and aspects which a historical period typically requires of men and women.

The Spy is full of historically typical men. The spy himself is a courageous and ingenious man able not only to affect the times in which he lives but permitted (and encouraged) by those times to display such qualities. Thus another difference between an ordinary novel in a historical setting and a historical novel as such is that the characters help fashion history as they are fashioned by it.

In the War for Independence, fought on political as well as military grounds, involving civilians to a great extent and always posing the problem of divided loyalties, Cooper's choice of a spy is especially effective. The spy is not only a soldier in a war, he must have a grasp of politics (and theater) as well.

Cooper discovered another advantage in the use of a spy as a central character. This advantage is connected to the subtitle of the novel, "A Tale of the Neutral Ground." Effective historical novels tend to focus on periods in which significant conflicts occur. Such conflicts as the War for Independence provide not only good dramatic material for the novelist but also offer later readers an insight into their own condition, since significant conflicts in the past have shaped their lives.

But there is an artistic problem in portraying such conflicts. To give a full picture of the clash of forces one must describe both sides in the fight (in Cooper's case both the British and the Americans). Describing only one side tends to rob the novel of drama—but how is the novelist to show both and, at the same time, focus these forces on a single, central character?

Scott solved this problem by using figures of secondary historical interest as his primary focus of dramatic action. These secondary figures are able to move from one side to another as negotiators, go-betweens, and messengers. This movement back and forth allows scope for the novelist to show in a specific, concrete fashion both sides of the conflict.

Cooper has done this in *The Spy*. Instead of choosing Washington himself as a central character, Cooper has chosen a spy, a man able (and required) to move from one side to the other and yet a man who remains in the thick of the dramatic action. The "Neutral Ground," the space between opposing forces that Birch must cross and recross in his missions, the seam between the opponents, also reflects the need for an effective historical novel to move from one side to the other.

Other aspects of the historical novel are also significant. Besides the presence of other, minor "type" characters (the doctor, the housekeeper, the servant), there are the details of the warfare, the names, dates, places, historical facts, that Cooper made a conscious effort to use; and *The Spy* reflects a degree of historical accuracy and fidelity to the facts which, despite moments of highly imaginative drama and humor, lend an air of reality to the action of the book as a whole.

Additionally, Cooper expends much print and dialogue on the arguments for and against the War for Independence. The revolutionaries argue with the counter-revolutionaries. Because he is able to show both sides dramatically, in real life, Cooper is able to describe the intellectual and political conflict of the era. In this way, Cooper avoids the trap of turning a historical novel into a mere adventure story; for in the course of history, and certainly in the course of the Revolutionary War, the battle of ideas deeply influences the physical battles. If Cooper is less successful in showing how arguments change individuals, he is still able to give a richer sense of the times and of the war than if he had concentrated entirely on physical action and adventure.

There are, of course, weaknesses in Cooper's work that are all too obvious. Cooper was, apart from being an opinionated man, one who shared many of the prejudices and preconceptions of his day. These views naturally affected the quality of his work.

One of his problems, for example, was that he seemed unable to characterize certain sorts of people in much depth. His attitude toward women and black people specifically is condescending. As a result, his portrayal of these figures is almost always superficial and unreal. Cooper's women in *The Spy* and elsewhere tend to be either precious darlings or selfish schemers.

Cooper also has a tendency to use an ironic tone rather heavy-handedly. In *The Spy* Cooper follows a long tradition in English literature by making his comic characters members of the lower class. One senses that the class characteristics of those below him were humorous to Cooper. Corresponding to this general characterization of the lower orders (not true in every case, to be sure) is a general deference to those of higher rank.

Thus, in finally evaluating *The Spy* as literature the reader is drawn to a central contradiction. On the one hand, Cooper clearly supports the American side and agrees with the arguments for independence, especially those arguments based on the God-given equality of men. In Cooper's mind, men *are* equal before God. At the same time, Cooper himself is a creature of his own time and upbringing. For him, though men may be equal under God they are by no means equal to one another.

The conflict between ideals and reality is an old one in the United States and it is no surprise that Cooper, declaring himself an authentic American novelist, should exhibit that conflict. Thus, *The Spy* is an informative historical novel both because it reflects a basic conflict in the history of a nation and because, as a work of art, it contains a basic conflict.

Howard Lee Hertz

THE STAR OF SEVILLE

Type of work: Drama
Author: Unknown, but sometimes attributed to Lope de Vega (1562-1635)
Type of plot: Cape-and-sword tragedy
Time of plot: Thirteenth century
Locale: Seville
First presented: c. 1617

Among the seventeenth century dramatists to whom the authorship of this classical play has been attributed are Pedro de Cárdenas y Angulo and Andrés de Claramonte, both somewhat obscure figures but more reasonable choices for the honor than the famous Lope de Vega. The Star of Seville, an elegant melodramatic tragedy, turns upon the traditional Spanish themes of loyalty and honor.

The Star of Seville is one of the great masterpieces written during the golden age of literature in Spain. It really is not important who wrote it. The important thing is that it was written and the modern reader can compare it with the Spanish literary traditions of that time.

Three giants of literature were writing then: Lope de Vega, Tirso de Molina, and Alarcón. Calderón started writing soon afterwards and Cervantes had just died. At the time Spain was the most powerful nation on earth, but shortly afterward its decline began. Fortunately the literature of the golden age survived.

At the time this play was first staged, the land was still under the influence of medieval superstitions and customs. The Spanish Inquisition had purged the land of heretics and infidels. Through their love of adventure the Spaniards had conquered the New World, and silver was pouring into the king's coffers. The war with the Moors was still fresh in the memory of the people. Duels were fought every day and sometimes several were fought in one day. In this setting the playwright wrote—more for money than for posterity—primarily for the lower classes rather than for the nobility. He wrote about the beliefs and cusoms prevalent at that particular time. The playwright wrote for the audience, paying particular attention to the ethical and moral values of the time. The Catholic Church was presumably the guardian watchman over the performances. But since, at one time, two theaters supported the hospitals of Madrid, the theologians often turned deaf ears and dimmed vision on the content of the plays.

The Spaniards, in their make-believe lives as in their wars and explorations, had no fear of the unknown. They were certain that God is supreme and the ultimate reality. God allows evil and mischance to enter one's life, but nothing is hopeless because God is the rewarder of the faithful. Miraculous and accidental events govern their lives and circumstances. It could be said that behavior in the lives of the people and in the lives played out before them on the stage were reactions rather than actions since they were helpless in the face of events which are caused by the intervention of forces outside themselves.

The Star of Seville dramatically portrays this belief in the intervention of the stars. Throughout the drama the stars are referred to many times. Estrella Tabera denies their influence in her life as long as it appears to be going in the direction which she desires. But as soon as her wishes are thwarted, by the execution of her brother by her lover, she gives vent to her grief and declares that her star is on the decline. Estrella Tabera, known as the Star of Seville, is so beautiful and bright that her influence is enough to change the lives of all the men who love or desire her—her brother, her lover, and even the king.

In his position as councilor Bustos Tabera's honor astonishes the king. For in a world where all is illusion, honor at times is illusory also. Bustos refuses the offer of a post which he does not deserve and inspires the king to exclaim that he has never known such honor before. Tabera's reply that "he desires only what is right and in accord with justice" inspires the king to say that his "good counsel puts him to shame." Bustos then gallantly says, "They are but mirrors of truth, and so in them you see yourself."

The king further portrays, with the help of Tabera, the inherent belief of the Spaniards that ultimately all things are in the hand of God. Monarchs are appointed by God and are accountable only to him. The duty and responsibility of any loyal subject is to obey the king. The plot thickens so that one of the king's men reminds him that the staves of his office point to God and signify his accountability to Him, but if the staves are bent, they point to man and his opinion. Herein lies the king's dilemma. He cannot be true to God and achieve his heart's desire.

In the character of Don Sancho Ortiz the audience sees portrayed the terrible consequences of loyalty and obedience to the king. He knows he must kill his friend or disobey his monarch. He struggles with his conscience until he finally rationalizes that the king is accountable to God alone and he, Don Sancho Ortiz, is accountable to the king. In this way he resolves the conflct within and does the king's bidding.

The beliefs of the men of Seville cause them to be like pawns in a giant chess game with outside forces moving them to and fro—without malice or forethought—wreaking havoc in their lives.

There are several scenes where a morbid humor is displayed, notably in the third act where the disguised king tries to break into the Taberas' house and is caught. Another humorous scene occurs when Don Sancho and Clarindo debate upon "the other world" where all professions are represented except lawyers. Don Sancho asks why and is told it is because they would bring lawsuits if they were there. He then says, "If there are no lawsuits . . . , hell's not so bad."

The action and speech does drag in the final act, but it is because of the king's dilemma. He cannot make up his mind to confess his part in the death of Bustos Tabera. Finally he decides he must confess, and honor, or the illusion of it, is thus upheld.

The modern reader and critic may well be amused at the machinations of the king and the struggles and heartbreak attendant upon the decisions of the other characters in *The Star of Seville,* but they are responses characteristic of the time.

Virginia Addington

STATE FAIR

Type of work: Novel
Author: Phil Stong (1899-1957)
Type of plot: Regional romance
Time of plot: Early 1930's
Locale: Iowa
First published: 1932

An unpretentious, entertaining novel set in the heartland of Iowa, State Fair *treats superficially but with quiet humor a piece of Americana, the Des Moines fair. Stong's attitude toward the Frake family is one of tolerant amusement rather than satire.*

Reviews of *State Fair* during the months following its publication in 1932 were unquestionably favorable. Critics agreed that Phil Stong drew an accurate picture of midwestern life, especially as it related to that much revered event, the state fair. Stong was praised for his vivid descriptions of characters, young and old, and his ability to produce a novel which was robust and entertaining. Slight mention was made of the fact that there is no great depth or moral to the story beyond the dime store bits of philosophy espoused by the storekeeper. Reviewers at the time seemed to agree that Stong brought a certain degree of "city-slicker's knowingness and humor" to his sound understanding of farming life in Iowa. The novel is saved from being purely sentimental and superficially structured by Stong's style, which is full of assurance, ease, and grace.

One cannot help but notice the tight symmetry of *State Fair*. The novel revolves around a week which includes a five day trip by car to Des Moines for the great "kermess." The Frake family is as closely knit as the novel itself. The four family members are constantly referring to what it means to be a Frake and how their strength, inner conviction, and endurance help them to achieve all their goals. Mama is painfully committed to her pickles, and father Abel to his fattened, prize-winning boar, Blue Boy. Each character is sketched briefly but carefully early in the novel, to be picked up a greater length later in the book as he or she relates his experiences at the fair. Both Wayne and Margy, the young teenagers, leave sweethearts at home on the farm the night before they depart for the fair and both have had an altercation of some sort with their sweethearts. The fair is a turning point for all the Frakes, and it transports the mother and father to glory which only prize-winning pickles and champion hogs can bring. The fair supplies Wayne and Margy with some exciting interludes, including a little behind-the-exhibits sex, and perhaps some maturity. Margy meets Pat, the man-about-town newspaper reporter who makes her head spin, and who wants to marry her at week's end. But Margy, true to Frake form, realizes her allegiance to the farm and the life it offers and knows that Pat would soon be discontented with that. On the other hand, Wayne is wooed and seduced by the red-headed Emily who shows him how to bet on horses, dine fashionably in Des Moines, and take in the theater with style. Wayne falls for Emily in much the same way that Pat falls for Margy, but to no avail here either, for Emily also realizes that farm life is not for her. She anticipates many more experiences before she plans to settle down. Wayne and Margy learn much about life in general, and their goals in particular during that short week. They both return home to their former sweethearts, having taken some risks, suffered a little, but grown a great deal.

The storekeeper's pessimism is apparent from the beginning of the novel when he says that all good is necessarily followed by some bad. In the end, one is found reflecting, momentarily at least, as to whether that is always true. For in the case of Wayne and Margy Frake, their salutary dip into pleasure brought them a week's worth of exhilarating happiness and fond memories which renewed their dedication to farm life.

STEPPENWOLF

Type of work: Novel
Author: Hermann Hesse (1877- 1962)
Type of plot: Psychological romance
Time of plot: The 1920's
Locale: Germany
First published: 1927

Steppenwolf. *a major work by the 1946 Nobel Prize-winning novelist, concerns Harry Haller's romantic search for identity in a world of shifting moral values. Hesse's vision of Germany during the 1920's is one of mad hedonism falling into degeneration.*

Hermann Hesse is one of the most influential German writers of the twentieth century. His father, who was a religious journalist and missionary, exerted a significant influence on Hesse's thinking and writing. Hesse traveled widely, living for a time in Italy and at another period in India. Following his journey to the Orient he settled in Switzerland, where he spent the remainder of his life. He began writing at the turn of the century and published short stories, essays, and poems as well as several novels. In 1946 he was awarded the Nobel Prize for literature. *Steppenwolf* comes in the middle of his literary career.

Hesse has called *Steppenwolf* his most misunderstood novel and for good reason. It is a complex and confusing novel because of its narrator—Harry Haller. The reader must first decide if he is reading the narrative of a schizophrenic or not. There is ample evidence to indicate that Haller is schizophrenic, but to dismiss the novel as the vision of a madman is to ignore the basic conflict of *Steppenwolf*. The safe, middle-class reaction sees Haller as mad; this is the type of reaction that Hesse and Haller find most despicable. As Hesse has said: "You cannot be a vagabond and an artist and at the same time a bourgeois and a respectable, healthy person. You want the ecstasy so you have to take the hangover." Hesse's attitude is basically Romantic and the novel is a Romantic statement that must be taken seriously. If it fails, it is not because Haller is mad.

The most dangerous way of misreading the novel is to see Harry Haller-Steppenwolf as a hero. He sees himself that way, but the reader must realize by the final scene that Haller is a qualified failure. Younger readers tend to see the character of the Steppenwolf—the intellectual outsider at war with the middle class—as admirable. This is a mistake. When he is put to the final test in the Magic Theatre, Haller is unable to divest himself totally of the middle-class values he so hates. Faced with the hallucination of Hermine in the arms of Pablo, Haller reacts as any bourgeois husband and stabs, or believes he stabs, Hermine. He has not learned how to laugh. He has not become one of the Immortals which was the purpose of his quest. He tells the reader: "One day I would be a better hand at the game. One day I would learn how to laugh." Haller realizes his failure, and the reader cannot ignore it.

Throughout the novel mirrors assume an important function. The doubling effect of a mirror is first indicative of the split that Haller sees in himself. This act of doubling abounds in *Steppenwolf*. Street lights reflect on wet pavement. Haller sees himself in Hermine's eyes. Hermine, herself, doubles at the Fasching ball: she first appears in male costume and then in female. As a male, she reminds Haller of a high school male friend. Mirrors appear everywhere in the novel from Hermine's pocket mirror to Pablo's magic Cabinet of Mirrors. One is reminded of the standard magician's reply: "It was done with mirrors." Pablo is the Magician who shows Haller that magic is the creative will of the imagination. Man is not singular or even double; one man is filled with infinite possibilities all of which can be realized if he will only open himself to the experience.

The novel is a definition of the moral and intellectual condition of modern times and, more particularly, Germany in the 1920's. It is set in a large, modern city filled with electric lights, signs, bars, movies, music, and impersonal streets. The culture depicted is essentially humorless, just as Harry Haller is without humor. Throughout the novel Haller and the reader are told that they must learn to laugh; that is, to laugh at themselves and their condition. They must achieve impersonal detachment. When we first see Haller, he is taking himself far too seriously. At the age of forty-eight, he had promised himself the luxury of suicide at fifty.

The structure of the novel divides into three general sections: The introduction of Harry Haller, the education of Harry Haller, the test of Harry Haller. The introduction itself is divided into three parts. First we have the burgher's view of Haller. Haller identifies himself as a split personality: middle class and Steppenwolf. And finally there is the Tract. The burgher's view is superficial; Haller's view is subjective; the Tract is the objective observation of a higher intelligence. It is the Tract that is most important. Haller sees only the conflict between his Steppenwolf character and the middle class. The Tract distinguishes three types of individuals: saints, middle class, and sinners. The burgher must resist the temptation to either extreme. It is with this burgher mentality that Haller is at odds. The Tract points out that this is the wrong battle. Haller is pulled in all three directions: he wants to be Burgher, yet he hates it; he enjoys the role of Steppenwolf, and at the same time loathes it; he desires to be an Immortal but does not have the Humor to achieve that level. Thus the introduction gives us an exposition, development, and a recapitulation. This structure is the same as the opening section of a musical sonata.

Music is central to much of Hesse's writing. He himself played the violin; his first wife was a gifted pianist. *Gertrude* (1910) is the story of a composer. *Journey to the East* (1932) concerns a violinist. In *Glass Bead Game* (1943) there is a pianist and musical theorist. In *Steppenwolf,* music plays an important role. Pablo is a jazz musician, and the music of Mozart epitomizes the achievement of the Immortal. Music becomes the synthesis of opposites—harmony within dissonance. Music, for Hesse, is the ideal abstract statement of harmony: it is written, heard, and felt. Moreover it is timeless or outside of time at a level language can never achieve.

During the middle section of the novel—the education of Harry Haller—the narrator, on the verge of mental collapse, discovers his initiator to self-understanding under the unlikely guise of a strange young girl named Hermine. Under her tutelage, Haller must first learn to dance; that is, to experience the sensual side of his nature without disgust. In the introduction, Haller characterized himself as two personalities—burgher and Steppenwolf. Following the direction of Hermine and her friends, Maria and Pablo, Haller is forced to realize that the self has infinite possibilities. By experiencing the sensual, Haller is following the downward path to wisdom and sainthood. The trip is essentially a mystical one, and Haller experiences what so many mystics before him have discovered. Many of the Christian saints were first profligates who rose from sinner to saint. Other mystics, such as Whitman, tell us that salvation is through indulgence of the flesh, not through denial of it. As T. S. Eliot was to discover in *The Four Quartets,* the way down and the way up are one and the same. In order to get where you want to be—sainthood, immortality—you must go by the way that does not lead there; that is, the flesh. In learning to dance, Haller learns to divest himself of his ego which is crucial in his quest. He experiences dance, drink, music, sex, and drugs, on his way to the intuitive mystic vision which all Romantics eventually achieve. Haller is, however, flawed. Like the quester in Eliot's *The Waste Land,* Haller, when put to the final test, fails.

In Pablo's Magic Theatre during the Fasching ball, Haller, on a hallucinatory drug trip, experiences the recapitulation of the first two sections of the novel and sees his personality in all its aspects. Pablo tells him: "I help you make your own world visible, that's all." From the Magic Mirror spring two versions of himself, one of which goes off with Pablo implying the latent homosexual side of Haller which Freud insisted exists in all men. During The Great Automobile Hunt, Haller, the pacifist, learns that he loves to kill. All things contain their opposites. In his third vision—The Marvels of Steppenwolf Training—Haller sees a surrealistic presentation of the main metaphor of the novel which reappears from the introduction. Finally Haller is faced with the vision of Hermine unfaithful to him—a vision with which he is unable to cope. He stabs her in the hallucination, but Pablo cannot take it seriously, just as Haller cannot laugh at it. Haller cannot let his ego dissolve; he cannot join the universal flow of things.

Michael S. Reynolds

THE STOIC

Type of work: Novel
Author: Theodore Dreiser (1871-1945)
Type of plot: Naturalism
Time of plot: Early twentieth century
Locale: Chicago, New York, London, Paris
First published: 1947

Dreiser never quite finished The Stoic; *his wife, following his notes, wrote the final chapter before the novel was published posthumously in 1947. The final book of the naturalistic trilogy that includes* The Financier *and* The Titan, The Stoic *completes on a note of failure the story of Frank Algernon Cowperwood, a man of great power and inner resources who is nevertheless a victim of social forces beyond his control.*

The Stoic, the final novel in Dreiser's *Trilogy of Desire,* relates Frank Algernon Cowperwood's attempt to take over the London underground transportation system. His maneuvers toward that end are of a morally questionable nature, in keeping with the tactics he has used throughout his career. Cowperwood's fortune crumbles rapidly in the last pages of the novel, and one sees that his whole life has led to nothing. Berenice's desperate quest for life's meaning and fulfillment is answered, ironically, in the message of the Indian guru who suggests that happiness can be realized only through concern for humanity and selflessness.

A study of Dreiser's notes for *The Stoic* makes it clear that in the beginning, Dreiser saw Cowperwood as glamorous, richly dressed, goodlooking, and in many ways enviable. Cowperwood triumphs, for Dreiser and for himself, when he faces a meeting of bankers who think he is short of funds as a result of a crisis in Chicago. He has foreseen their doubts and counters with a promise that he can repay every loan he has received, but that if they insist upon it he will "gut every bank from here to the river." Cowperwood is in control.

Dreiser has built an indomitable figure for whom one must feel admiration, just as later one can only pity him. Cowperwood's methods consist in skillful manipulation, the greater power conquering little men at every move. He does not know what it is to fail or be insecure. Even when Cowperwood faces his darkest hour and is sentenced to jail (*The Financier*), he remains self-confident and optimistic. He feels that greatness is "inherent in him." Cowperwood reflects Dreiser's belief that men are instruments of higher forces, no more and no less than their natures dictate. Dreiser took the life of an American financier and economic manipulator, Charles Tyson Yerkes, and through his genius transformed it into a complex and dazzling study of the natures of success and failure. Cowperwood's successes are not always what he expects them to be, and his failures are integrally connected to his apparent successes. Although Dreiser's craftsmanship is often faulty in this last volume of the trilogy, the very force of his vision and the intensity of his convictions sweep the reader along. *The Stoic* is a bad novel that also happens to be an engrossing and great book.

STONE DESERT

Type of work: Novel
Author: Hugo Wast (Gustavo Martínez Zuviría, 1883-1962)
Type of plot: Regional romance
Time of plot: Early twentieth century
Locale: The rocky tablelands of northern Argentina
First published: 1925

With its theme of the city-dweller's need to return to nature, Stone Desert *(in* Spanish, Desierta de Piedra) *is a representative regional novel by this important and prolific Argentinian writer. Wast emphasizes the important role that hard-working immigrants have played in revitalizing his nation's economy.*

Although not considered Hugo Wast's best novel, *Stone Desert* is remarkable for the number of themes that it handles well. One such theme has rarely been treated elsewhere in Latin American novels; namely, the alleged economic superiority of foreign immigrants to Latin America over the natives. This allegation is heard from Southern Brazil (where Italians, Portuguese, Japanese, Germans, Poles, and Lebanese have shown notable energy), to Venezuela (where Italians, Spaniards, and Portuguese have done the same), to Uruguay and Argentina, where immigrants have renovated entire areas. In *Stone Desert,* Wast portrays the hard work done by Peninsular Spaniards in a far-off and rocky corner of the Argentine Republic. *Stone Desert* is one of the few Latin American novels to treat the important subject of ethnic minorities in Latin America, and the contribution to their adopted lands.

Wast's novel is unusual in other ways. It is one of the relatively few Argentine novels set in the "lost" Northwest of the country, where Argentina fuses into Bolivia and Chile in the high, windy, cold, stony, and dun-brown Puna Atacama. *Stone Desert* also reflects the fact that Latin America's true vitality has sprung from the country and nourished the city. This has been notable in Argentine history, from the dictatorial days of Juan Manuel de Rosas to Juan Perón, and has been at times a dominant note in national literature, including Argentina's two masterworks, *Martín Fierro,* and Domingo Sarmiento's great *Facundo* (although the latter views rural Argentina as a vigorous, barbaric drawback to progress and civilization.)

It is noteworthy, then, that *Stone Desert* has also treated so many other themes, such as the nostalgic return home of Roque Carpio; the superstition of country folk (for example, the staking out of the toad in the patio to bring rain); the ruggedness of rural Argentines compared to city-dwelling "porteños," or inhabitants of Buenos Aires; and the return to nature as a cure for the decadence of urbanites.

THE STORY OF A BAD BOY

Type of work: Novel
Author: Thomas Bailey Aldrich (1836-1907)
Type of plot: Regional romance
Time of plot: Nineteenth century
Locale: New Hampshire
First published: 1869

The popularity of Aldrich's largely autobiographical novel influenced the production during the late nineteenth century of several more notable works using the same subject of a boy's life, among them Mark Twain's Tom Sawyer *and* Huckleberry Finn. *The fictional Rivermouth of* The Story of a Bad Boy *is Portsmouth, New Hampshire, the author's childhood home.*

He was, of course, not a very bad boy at all, and therein lies much of the story's charm. Boyhood, as any boy knows, looks best from the vantage point of maturity, and Thomas Bailey Aldrich tenderly and charmingly renders typical scenes of mischief and misdemeanor, friendship and puppy love.

The novel rises to no overall dramatic impact, but it is not without moments of heightened intensity. The tale of little Binny Wallace washing out to sea in a rowboat, never to be seen alive again, is narrated deftly enough to fetch a tear to the eye of the susceptible reader. There are memorable portraits of Tom's barnacle-ridden crony, Sailor Ben, and of that almost forgotten institution, The Oldest Inhabitant. Many of the adventures of Tom and his friends have that authentic ring of what nostalgia would like boyhood to have been.

The genteel sensibility which informs *The Story of a Bad Boy* helped insure Aldrich's literary prominence—he was editor of *Every Saturday* magazine while writing the novel, and was to take over the reins at the prestigious *Atlantic Monthly* when William Dean Howells resigned in 1881. Other characteristics of the novel—the coy archness of its accomplished yet uninspiring prose style, the romanticizing of its subject matter, its loose, semi-autobiographical structure, and lack of dramatic intensity and moral force—all help indicate why Aldrich gained prominence first as an editor and poet, second as a short-story writer, and only later as a novelist. Indeed, perhaps chief among the book's virtues is that it touched off among post-Civil War New England writers a whole series of "books about boys." Prominent among those which surpassed it in both popularity and literary merit are Howells' *A Boy's Town* (1890) and Samuel Clemens' *Tom Sawyer* (1876) and *Huckleberry Finn* (1884).

THE STORY OF A COUNTRY TOWN

Type of work: Novel
Author: Edgar Watson Howe (1853-1937)
Type of plot: Social criticism
Time of plot: Mid-nineteenth century
Locale: The Middle West
First published: 1883

Historically Howe's novel is important as an early satire on the meanness of spirit, shallowness, and petty materialism of small-town America. The theme of "revolt from the village" was to become a major subject of social criticism in American literature during the 1920's.

Howells and Twain praised Edgar W. Howe's novel, and one early reviewer believed that at last someone had created the "great American novel." For the modern reader, however, its interest is historical rather than literary. Howe's style is often cumbersome with frequent errors of spelling, word usage, and construction.

Many reviewers have noted the novel's Dickensian tones. The most obvious influence is in the characters' names—Jo Erring, Ned's tragic, misunderstood uncle; the Reverend Goode Shepherd; the worthless but wordy philosopher, Lytle Biggs; and the boastful villain, Clinton Bragg. There is also the sense of melancholy Dickens gives to his child heroes. Ned resembles Pip and David Copperfield in the dismal circumstances of his early life. Dominated by work, death, religion, and rejection, Ned comes to a fatalistic acceptance that life is a wretched experience.

Unfortunately, the adult Ned is less interesting. His story is submerged as the book sinks into trite melodrama, and Ned remains important only as narrator of the misfortunes of Jo and Mateel. Another departure from Dickens is that there is no humor to relieve the book's starkness. The gray, wooden church with its graveyard dominates Fairview, and the Indian graves of Twin Mounds oversee the meanness of small-town culture.

Howe implies that country living makes men cruel. Trying desperately to wring an existence from the dry soil, the characters find the work ethic to be all-encompassing. Their only relief is religion, which is grimly Calvinistic. Ned begins his narrative by observing that his father's religion would have been incomplete without a hell, for Mr. Westlock hoped that everyone who did not share his piety would be punished. It is ironic that through the church Mr. Westlock meets Mrs. Tremaine, a temperance fanatic, with whom he elopes. When last seen, he is a broken, guilt-ridden old man who returns to Twin Mounds on the snowy eve of his wife's funeral.

The melodrama and sketchy characterization weaken the novel, but the book is of definite value when seen as a precursor to *Winesburg, Ohio*; *Main Street*; and *Spoon River Anthology*.

THE STORY OF AN AFRICAN FARM

Type of work: Novel
Author: Olive Schreiner (1855-1920)
Type of plot: Social criticism
Time of plot: 1880's
Locale: South Africa
First published: 1883

A partly autobiographical "education" novel, The Story of an African Farm *is memorable for its early scenes that evoke memories both of a lyrical and frightening childhood, and for its later poignant revelations about a strong, fine-natured woman's disappointments in a male-dominated world mostly closed to her ambitions.*

Olive Schreiner, a white South African, first published under a male pseudonym, Ralph Iron; nevertheless, *The Story of an African Farm* was an influential work in the British feminist movement before and after World War I. Lyndall, clearly the strongest character, becomes an overt feminist who refuses to marry and lose her freedom. After four years at finishing school, she is aware of the realities of "the woman's place" and refuses to submit to that fate. The long chapter in which she expounds on the oppression of women comes at the center of the book and is the most important of the several essay-like sections.

Lyndall resists the idea that young women exist to embroider and snare good husbands. Tant' Sannie, who entraps one husband after another, represents everything Lyndall comes to despise. The humiliating Boer courtship and marriage customs are satirized, particularly that of "upsitting" (when a Boer man courting a woman sits up all night with her). Lyndall dreams of becoming an actress, but her illness following childbirth prevents her from accomplishing anything beyond refusing to marry, a refusal she adheres to even as she is dying. Schreiner's interest in feminist issues is also evident in her treatment of Gregory Rose. Lyndall's evaluation of him as "a woman" becomes ironic when Gregory impersonates a female nurse in ministering to Lyndall. Such an examination of transvestitism and changes in sexual identity was highly unusual in this period.

The book is also remarkable in its early parts for its handling of the point of view of the children—Waldo, Em, and Lyndall—which shows the way that children's consciousnesses function and, more importantly, the ways in which children are oppressed. Another sidelight of the book is its depiction of the rigid caste-like social structure of South Africa of a hundred years ago, where class lines are made even more stringent by the enforcement of race lines.

THE STORY OF BURNT NJAL

Type of work: Saga
Author: Unknown
Type of plot: Adventure romance
Time of plot: Tenth century
Locale: Iceland
First transcribed: Thirteenth-century manuscript

Probably the best known of the thirty-odd surviving Icelandic sagas, The Story of Burnt Njal *concerns the adventures of the lawman Njal and his neighbors, who are more than figures in a primitive tale of violence; they also stand for a people, a society, and an age.*

Icelanders defined sagas as the telling over and over of great ancestral feuds and battles; the sagas were often told during long winter nights. The distinction between fact and fiction was not made. Actually, the saga form had a more lofty purpose: to maintain pride in family history and to tell the stories of the ancestral heroic age and of the introduction of Christianity to Iceland. The king's sagas and the family sagas were the most popular. *The Story of Burnt Njal* is of the latter form. Some scholars argued up until the 1920's that the work was originally two distinct sagas, Gunnar's saga and Njal's saga. Presently it is considered to be the work of one author because of the cohesion of stylistic form and thematic structure. The saga is differentiated from the epic in that the former is prose. Otherwise there are great similarities with the Njal and Homer's epics. The use of battle scenes and festivals and games are prevalent in both and delight the reader in their pageantry.

The Story of Burnt Njal is of the late classical period in Icelandic literary history. The romanticism and chivalry are not evident in the more skeletal earlier sagas. Njal's role of hero is that of a more ordinary man than known to us in the Greek epics. His initial naïveté over the deteriorating social situation and the misunderstood peace offering to Flosi conspire to cause Njal's death. He is a victim of fate and of the old code of honor, exemplified throughout the saga in his wife Bergthora. Foreshadowings in this saga are effected by employing dreams and portents, a much different literary device than the modern technique of suspense. In *The Story of Burnt Njal* the reader is usually aware of the events to transpire as he is in the Homeric works. The purpose of the saga and epic forms was to retell and remind the listeners of history and myth, not, as with the moderns, to compose something completely new.

Although this Icelandic saga contains an elaborate plot and subplot structure, an abundance of characters often mentioned briefly then forgotten, and a recalling of events and names foreign and relatively unknown to our ears, the saga provides us with insight into the oral tradition and codes of a society at its height. It offers a comparison with our own sacred saga, the

Bible. The Bible's message is that the Lord is the final avenger of sin, but *The Story of Burnt Njal* names the Thing, the Icelandic assembly or parliament, as the supreme lawgiver. The Thing was established in A.D. 930 and served the Old Icelandic Commonwealth while it lasted until 1262. The problem of the system, and the crucial concern for the characters of the saga is that even after being judged as correct in an audience at the Thing, the individual had to carry out justice for himself.

One of the fundamental issues relating to the execution of justice was the interplay between the heathen code of killing and revenge and the Christian idea of forgiveness. Christianity was introduced into Iceland in A.D. 1000. In the saga it is recalled by Thangbrand's journey to Iceland which initiated that land's adoption of Christianity as the national religion. The intertwining of codes and religions again comes into play with the juxtaposition of pagan magic and Christian miracles. Ironically, often the miracles were performed not to provide healing but to carry out pagan vengeance. Kari and Flosi journey to Rome to obtain forgiveness for the bloodshed caused by their animosity, yet the reason this hostility began involved the heathen code of honor. Thus the saga involves not only the continuous decisions of the Thing and their often tragic aftermath, but also the inception of a new religion and code of order. The narrator of this saga maintained an objective eye. Very little moralizing or psychological probing of actions is evident. The characters, six hundred in all with twenty-five main actors, are developed through their actions, a behavioristic approach, rather than by their thoughts or reflections.

The Story of Burnt Njal follows a tripart structure: first, the downfall of Gunnar; second, the burning of Njal and his sons; and third, the exacting revenge required by Kari. The middle section for which the saga was named is the climax and turning point of the story. All events lead toward it and it involves all of the preceding arguments and attempted honorable reconciliations. Also it reflects the breakdown of the lawmaking by the Thing into jealousy and seeming dishonor; the battle is fought essentially because of the misunderstood intentions of Njal's gift. The saga then leads away from the burning and death of Njal toward atonement at the Thing as all parties meet to arrange a settlement. Finally the saga ends on a Christian note: forgiveness is sought from the Church and reconciliation is effected between the enemies.

Gayle Steck

THE STORY OF GÖSTA BERLING

Type of work: Novel
Author: Selma Lagerlöf (1858-1940)
Type of plot: Picaresque romance
Time of plot: Early nineteenth century
Locale: Sweden
First published: 1891

In her engaging tale of the scapegrace Gösta's moral redemption, Lagerlöf blends realism with fantasy. The Story of Gösta Berling was the first and remains the most popular novel of this Swedish Nobel Prize-winning writer.

Selma Lagerlöf was born into a once-prosperous Värmland family that had, like most other families in the district, fallen on bad times. Although circumstances were straitened and fear of poverty was a constant presence, memories of better times in the recent past were still vivid and carefully preserved as part of the family lore which Lagerlöf absorbed in anecdotes as she was growing up. In many ways, *The Story of Gösta Berling* reflects this background, with characters and scenes drawn from rural Swedish life, reminiscent of Anton Chekhov's treatment of similar material dealing with life in rural Russia. The loss of ancestral estates, for example, strongly affects the plot development in *The Story of Gösta Berling* as it does in Chekhov's *The Cherry Orchard* (1904), just as upper-middle-class decadence seems to direct the course of events both in Lagerlöf's novel and in Chekhov's *The Three Sisters* (1901). Other parallels can be drawn with Lagerlöf's depiction of the deterioration of a comfortable way of life and the generous hospitality which accompanied it. So, too, does the psychology of fear— suspicion of being exploited when the security of property is lost—find Chekhovian echoes. Moreover, these factors most particularly shape Lagerlöf's portrayal of the pensioners in her novel.

The Story of Gösta Berling was Lagerlöf's first and most famous novel, but it is not unique in her total artistic output, for which she won a Nobel Prize for Literature in 1909—the first woman and the first Swede to be so honored. Her later novels and tales—*The Miracles of Antichrist, Jerusalem,* and *The Wonderful Adventures of Nils,* especially—also show the same concerns with the failure of the social system, the plight of the peasant, the corruption of people in positions of authority, and the eternal verities of folk wisdom. The latter aspect of Lagerlöf's novels is one of her strongest and most unusual points, for the folkloric qualities—expressed through supernatural elements and a great sensitivity toward nature—combine romanticism with a shrewd socio-political insight, releasing Lagerlöf's powerful imagination in *The Story of Gösta Berling* to reveal a happily reckless amalgam of unlikely, even contradictory, attitudes.

Despite apparently disparate elements in the novel, Gösta himself is the unifying force. He is certainly not the perfect hero or protagonist. Nevertheless, Lagerlöf seems blind to his imperfections. To a certain extent, this blindness is understandable and excusable. Lagerlöf led a somewhat sheltered life, even for her times, and she was never married. Such factors, without a doubt, rendered her a poor judge of Gösta's obsessive sexual conquests, for example, although she tried valiantly to depict them authentically and demonstrated a genuine sympathy for the experiences which ultimately eluded her.

All things considered, however, Gösta is not a credible protagonist because of Lagerlöf's unawareness. Lagerlöf observed certain conventional taboos—mostly dealing with sex, religion, and politics—which obscured the realities of life around her and which blocked her creative mind in dealing with such matters in her novels. Consequently, Lagerlöf unconsciously passed over contradictions in the substantive development of her novel in favor of situations which she would like to see occur or situations which she was trained, by her background, to expect. The net result is not bad art but a novel which must be accepted on its own unconventional terms.

In Lagerlöf's time, conventional terms meant naturalism *à la* Zola and Strindberg. However, Lagerlöf brooked no patience with such dogmas. She followed the old ways, the ancient tales and archetypal myths, and the timeless truths. Yet she portrayed timely problems, without historical or chronological constraints. Such utter indifference to contemporaneity made Lagerlöf an anomaly, but the compelling power of her art elevated her to a position of respect in the literary world. Without bowing to literary fashion, she wrote a novel—a *first* novel—that has captured the attention of readers since the time it was first published. In this work Lagerlöf commanded a theme that is of enduring interest: Can one have fun and still be good? This question is as much of moment today as it was in the 1890's when *The Story of Gösta Berling* was first published.

Ultimately the question confronts the sanctions of social opinion. What is "fun," and what is "good"? To Gösta, "fun" was drinking and wenching. His modern-day counterpart would hardly dispute such a value system. Yet in Gösta's time as today, there are those who would strongly disapprove of such activities.

A nineteenth century preacher should not shock twentieth century readers, no matter what he does as a character in a novel. In 1836, Nathaniel Hawthorne published *The Minister's Black Veil*, exposing a heretofore unexplored aspect of clerical activity. Henrik Ibsen's *Brand*, in 1866, similarly revealed the contradictions of a clergyman caught between duty and inclination. Lagerlöf's *The Story of Gösta Berling* in 1894 was midstream of the exposés of religious crises which were later echoed in such works as Sinclair Lewis's *Elmer Gantry* (1927). These dilemmas are part of a theme in Western literature which comprises a serious exploration of ethical responsibility. Lagerlöf probes this problem with extraordinary sensitivity and insight, even though her perceptions are circumscribed by her biases and her experience.

Finally, *The Story of Gösta Berling* is a novel which uniquely combines elements of realism, to suit the fashion of the time when it was written (the characterization of Gösta Berling is here exemplary), and elements of fantasy which suited Lagerlöf's own predilections (deferences to ancient custom and observance of traditional ways). Lagerlöf herself was not aware of contradictions between these two ways of viewing reality. Rather, she saw a compatibility between the two. The fact that she created a viable novel out of her ambivalence is no less than a tribute to her artistic accomplishment and her psychological grasp of human interaction. The modern reader can hardly do less than pay her the tribute she is due for her essential gift of revelation about human relationships on the most elemental plane.

Joanne G. Kashdan

STORY OF THE GUITAR

Type of work: Drama
Author: Kao Tse-ch'eng (Kao Ming, c. 1305-c. 1368)
Type of plot: Tragi-comedy
Time of plot: c. 200
Locale: Honan Province, China
First presented: Fourteenth century

Sometimes staged under the title Lute Song. Story of the Guitar *(in Chinese, P'i P'a Chi) is a classic drama in which the main female character, the virtuous Chao Wu-niang, proves her worth through her sacrifice, endurance, and devotion to her husband.*

Best known in the United States as *Lute Song,* this old classic Chinese drama has been adapted for the stage many times by different authors, but always the simple, tender story of family devotion has retained its power. The original author, Kao Tse-ch'eng, certainly based the central incident concerning the Imperial Examination on his own experiences, for he left his post as a provincial schoolmaster and went to the capital of the "Flowery Kingdom" to take the examinations which for centuries were the only gateway to advancement and service under the Imperial Government. However, he failed the examinations and turned to his pen to make his fortune. Like many an author, he transformed his personal experiences into literature.

A gentle and graceful melancholy pervades the drama of the young scholar and his two wives. Most of the characters in the play attempt to live noble, honorable lives, but circumstances interfere, and they must compromise and hope that somehow they eventually will be able to get back onto the ideal course they once had envisioned. The play illustrates how inadvertently one individual may cause others to suffer. Ts'ai Jung is a good man, and it is through no fault of his own that his parents and wife are left uncared for, or that his wife is forced to sacrifice so much in order to care for her parents-in-law. The neighbor, Chang, suggests the ties of brotherhood which unite all honorable men. Willingly, he shares what he has with the unfortunate Chao Wu-niang; no decent man, he feels, would do less. Ts'ai's second wife is also a sympathetic person, well-intentioned, and determined to make the situation resolve itself in a manner that will bring contentment to all concerned. Only the messenger who disappears with the letter and gold meant for the young wife is thoroughly wicked.

This simple but profound drama is presented in a poetic, far from realistic, style in which the narrator steps in and out of the action and helps to make clear the meaning of the story. A stately manner and leisurely pace help to lend the drama a sense of timelessness, as if it could have happened in any time or age. The truths presented in the play, it is suggested, transcend the world of the characters. The virtuous wife is intended to be a noble example for the audience. Yet the sincerity of the emotions and the delicacy of the writing prevent the play from becoming a mere moral lesson.

STRANGE INTERLUDE

Type of work: Drama
Author: Eugene O'Neill (1888-1953)
Type of plot: Psychological realism
Time of plot: Early twentieth century
Locale: New England and New York
First presented: 1928

In Strange Interlude, *an experimental drama employing Freudian imagery and theory, O'Neill attempts to bring to the stage a style of expression similar to the stream-of-consciousness technique of the modern psychological novel. By means of devices such as the soliloquy and the aside, he allows his characters to reveal to the audience their inner thoughts and feelings.*

Enormously long, *Strange Interlude* was enormously successful. The curtain went up on its nine acts at 5:30. There was a supper break after the fifth act. The curtain fell after 11 o'clock. The play covers 26 years in the lives of Nina Leeds and her five men, embracing, by the use of soliloquies and asides, both the exterior and interior perceptions and drives of the characters. The American theatergoers of 1928 responded by making it O'Neill's biggest hit. There were two touring companies and a London production, a Pulitzer Prize (O'Neill's third), and, in book form, a bestseller. Later there was a motion picture (starring Norma Shearer), and, in the midst of posthumous revival of interest in the playwright, a restaging of the play in 1963.

While its psychology now seems dated, the play appeared to be fresh, experimental, and exciting to the Freudian 1920's. Its major dramatic departure, the soliloquies (in themselves, of course, scarcely new to the theater), are as long as the regular surface dialogue. The action freezes when they are delivered. The technique is a way of dramatizing the fact that below the surface of our lives there are fears, drives, obsessions that rarely see the light of day. The technique also enables O'Neill to present one of his favorite themes, that of identity conflict or division, a theme evident in play after play, including, for example, *The Emperor Jones, The Hairy Ape, All God's Chillun Got Wings, The Great God Brown, Days Without End,* and *A Touch of the Poet.* At times, as in *The Great God Brown,* O'Neill employed masks to suggest sharp conflict between our public and our private images. In *Days Without End,* he divides his hero literally in two, employing two actors to present the two sides of his hero. Sometimes, as in *Days Without End,* O'Neill sought to heal the divisions, but elsewhere, as in *A Touch of the Poet,* he presents them as tragic facts of life.

The technique also suggests another favorite theme of O'Neill—that of the past reaching into and controling the present. As the characters deliver their soliloquies, they seem to live, not only in the moment, but in their remembered pasts as well. Thus, thick heaps of time surround them and control them. Past and future are always present. We also see this theme in other O'Neill plays such as *The Emperor Jones, Mourning Becomes Electra,* and *Long Day's Journey into Night.* O'Neill occasionally suggests the possibility of redemption from the past, as in *Anna Christie* and *The Fountain,* but finds it increasingly difficult to do so, and, in the very last plays, his most pessimistic, he lapses into complete negation.

As a character Nina Leeds suggests a figure who appears in other plays: the woman who is at once wife, mother, and lover. We see her in Cybele of *The Great God Brown,* in Josie Hogan of *A Moon for the Misbegotten.* Nina is the archetypal woman; she is everywoman; she is daughter, adolescent hero worshiper, wife, mistress, possessive mother. Each part of her being seeks expression and, frequently, gets in the way of the others, leading to much of the play's bitter torment. But, while all the feminine drives are located in one person, Nina finds it necessary to satisfy these urges with different men, and this leads to conflict and bitternes. Nina summarizes the conflicting drives of the play when she speaks of "God the Mother," an image of the life force, as opposed to God the Father, who is hard, arbitrary, moral.

Conflict and ambivalence appear at the very beginning of the play. Nina's hero worship is vested in the aviator Gordon Shaw who, as a youthful ideal, appropriately does not appear. He is dead when the curtain rises. As daughter, Nina lives with the genteel, withdrawn history professor Henry Leeds. Nina's father and her hero have already been in conflict, the professor in his jealousy having seen to it that Gordon went off to war without marrying Nina. The result is further conflict. Feeling cheated and guilty, Nina retreats into nymphomania. Her father moves through a series of emotions: fear of what Nina will do, contempt for himself, resignation. A third character who appears in Act I, Charles Marsden, is the victim of a mother-fixation. He loathes sex, but feels alternately drawn and repelled by Nina; the result is inner torment for "good old Charlie." For O'Neill's purposes, he early establishes himself as Nina's father-substitute. Thus both hero and (in the guise of Charlie) father follow Nina through the play.

Having reacted from hero-worship to cynical depravity, Nina reacts again, exhibiting another necessary facet of woman's being: she seeks solace in conventional family life with still another man, Sam Evans. Pregnant, and briefly happy in her role as would-be mother, Nina reacts against her role as wife when she discovers that she cannot have her baby. Thus it is that she calls on Edmund Darrell, who supplies her with a son and makes her happy again, but discovers that his relations with Nina are interfering with his career. In fact each of the men in the play has his own problems and urges and needs, but each is drawn into Nina's orbit as she seeks to fulfill her different roles.

At the end of Part One of the play, Nina has her son, her husband, and her father-substitute, but loses her lover. Only at the beginning of Part Two, and then briefly, is Nina fully in control of all her men; thus there is a momentary sense of wholeness on her part. Quickly enough, the splintering, the fragmentation, the tension begins again. Ultimately, we are to understand, there is no escape except in the loss of Nina's drives, and these drives are her life. As she moves from stage to stage of her existence, nothing really changes for Nina, and nothing really changes in life—O'Neill insists—except those who play the roles. Thus Nina finally discovers herself in her father's position, playing the possessive mother for her son, appropriately named Gordon. After Sam dies, Edmund leaves, and Gordon flies off with his fiancée, Nina returns to her father in the guise of Charlie, who can provide her with a sexless, passionless haven.

Max Halperen

STREET SCENE

Type of work: Drama
Author: Elmer Rice (1892-1967)
Type of plot: Social realism
Time of plot: 1929
Locale: New York
First presented: 1929

Street Scene, *a forerunner of the social drama of the 1930's, is a pitilessly realistic play about ordinary lower-class people trapped in a tenement-crowded district of New York City.*

Among the important American dramatists of the 1920's and early 1930's, Elmer Rice was probably second only to Eugene O'Neill in the scope of his vision and the range of his theatrical experimentation. Although he had achieved some early recognition with his courtroom drama *On Trial* (1914), it was *The Adding Machine* (1923), a wildly "expressionistic" episodic fantasy about a harried average man, Mr. Zero, who is trapped in an eternity of meaningless, machine-like activities, that earned Rice recognition as one of America's most important dramatists. Then, having written one of the best nonrealistic plays of his time, Rice turned around and, in 1929, realized his greatest commercial and critical success with *Street Scene,* one of the most starkly realistic plays ever put on the American stage.

But in spite of their radically differing theatrical styles, the two plays are about the same thing: the dehumanizing effect of modern, urban, industrial society on the human spirit. And because Rice dramatizes his thesis by showing real human beings in situations of painful personal suffering, instead of abstract characters in symbolic settings, *Street Scene* is by far the more powerful play.

As soon as the curtain rises, before any "plot" is set in motion, the audience sees and feels the crowding, ugliness, noise, heat, and general agitation that constantly surrounds these urban dwellers. Such an environment is certain to bring out the worst in people; their necessary proximity guarantees conflict and violence. The situation is bad enough for the unimaginative person, who is unaware of the stifling quality of his condition, but for the more sensitive soul, who is conscious of being dehumanized, the life is doubly painful. *Street Scene* is a play about individuals who, rebelling in the most limited ways against their plight, unleash the fury that exists beneath the surface of the oppressive *status quo.*

The story begins with a scene of everyday life in front of the teeming tenement. This collage of the various racial and social types instantly establishes the general atmosphere of tension, bitterness, and petty viciousness. From this agitated surface, Rice skillfully and naturally draws out one major story and a number of minor ones. The primary plot line concerns Frank Maurrant's inevitable violent attack on his wife, Anna, and her lover, Sankey. Paralleled to this is the bittersweet "Romeo and Juliet" style love affair between Maurrant's daughter, Rose, and Sam Kaplan, a sensitive, young Jewish neighbor. The Maurrant family story is counterpointed against several other action lines and character studies such as the birth of the Buchanan baby, the eviction of the Hildebrands, Harry Easter's attempt to seduce Rose, old man Kaplan's Marxist rhetoric, and Mae Jones's open promiscuity. And it is all powerfully punctuated by the constant intrusions of the neighbors who, out of boredom and petty vindictiveness, meddle whenever they can.

However, although the tenement inhabitants are confined by their economic circumstances, they are even more thoroughly "imprisoned" by their own distorted social, racial, and religious beliefs and assumptions. All the characters retain their ethnic prejudices and cling to notions of social superiority. But the worst family in the building is the most "purely American," the Joneses, with their bullying taxi-driver son, Vincent, their whorish daughter, Mae, and their most vicious of gossips, Mrs. Jones.

Maurrant is driven to murder his wife from a combination of half understood frustration and residual Puritan moralism. It is clear that the Maurrants had once been happy together, but time, circumstance, and Frank's distorted concept of the "husband's role" have combined to destroy their closeness. Anna Maurrant takes Sankey as a lover because she feels lost and in need of a kind word. After the killings, Maurrant admits that he cannot understand what it was that drove him to murder.

Rose understands and, because she does, she is the pivotal figure in the play. The romance with Sam is never really serious, because he is a bright child and she is already a mature woman. Rose alone affirms life and sees the possibility of living it meaningfully as an autonomous human being. The only answer, Rice seems to say, is to insist on one's humanity in the face of all the pressures that modern civilization can bring against it.

STRIFE

Type of work: Drama
Author: John Galsworthy (1867-1933)
Type of plot: Social criticism
Time of plot: Early twentieth century
Locale: Industrial town near London
First presented: 1909

Strife, one of Galsworthy's most successful social dramas, criticizes with impartiality the selfish, obstinate motives of both sides to a labor dispute. The writer's argument is that only tolerance, compromise, and the exercise of common sense will prevent the suffering of innocent parties and achieve an equitable solution to the problem.

It was with the production of *Strife* in 1909 that John Galsworthy's reputation as one of Britain's foremost playwrights was established and, although one of his earliest stage works, it remains, in the opinion of most critics, his finest dramatic effort. Even today, when the issues of economic agitation and social change have become much more complex and ambiguous than they seemed in Galsworthy's time, *Strife* retains its power and relevance because it is not rooted in the problems of a particular situation, but in a clash of wills between sharply defined, forceful, believable characters.

The ostensible dispute in *Strife* is between the Directors of the Trenartha Tin Plate Works and their striking workers, but, as the play progresses, it becomes evident that the conflict is actually between John Anthony, the Chairman of the Directors, and David Roberts, the leader of the strikers. Thus, the play is not so much about Capital versus Labor as it is about the relationship between leaders and followers and the thin line that separates dedicated, courageous idealism from egocentric, self-destructive fanaticism.

Both leaders are adamantly opposed to compromise and have, at least for most of the play, the power to impose their views on the others. Each of them sees the conflict solely in terms of total victory or abject defeat. Both Anthony and Roberts believe that the future of the entire economic and social system is at stake in this particular strike.

Each man's intransigence, however, is also fed by motives that are purely personal, even petty. Hardened by advancing age and precarious health, Anthony has identified with the company to the point where he sees it as an extension of himself; he can accept no questioning of his motives or judgments by anybody. On the other hand, because of a profitable invention that he feels was "stolen" from him for a pittance, Roberts nurses a personal vendetta against the company. Thus, both men are deeply committed to their respective causes and to the social classes they represent; at the same time, both are obviously flawed and bring questionable personal motives into the struggle. It is this mixture of good and bad, strength and weakness, idealism and petty spite, that gives these characters their reality and stature and adds a tragic dimension to their clash.

However, in spite of his awareness of human fallibility, Galsworthy was essentially a believer in man's rationality and capacity to control his own fate. In fixing their rigid postures, Anthony and Roberts have both ignored the human element, but before the confrontation leads to ruin for the company and general starvation for the workers, the moderate elements on both sides rise up and shunt their fanatical leaders aside. However, it takes the death of Roberts' wife to provoke those followers to action.

Man's moderation and sensible self-interest, Galsworthy seems to say, will ultimately win out over fanaticism, but the process is slow, painful, and very imperfect. And, in the meantime, the innocent will suffer—for nothing.

A STUDY IN SCARLET

Type of work: Novel
Author: Arthur Conan Doyle (1859-1930)
Type of plot: Mystery romance
Time of plot: Nineteenth century
Locale: London
First published: 1887

The first and one of the most enduringly popular of the Sherlock Holmes mysteries, A Study in Scarlet *set the basic pattern for the major character-types and plot contrivances of the subsequent sixty-odd novels and short stories that Doyle was to create for his master detective from 1887 until the 1920's.*

A Study in Scarlet is composed on two levels: the detective story written by Holmes's affable foil, Dr. Watson, and the history of the crime, recounted by Jefferson Hope, the murderer, after his capture. This pattern enabled Conan Doyle to confront us with some of the mysteries which are most baffling to his critics—such as the nature of Watson's wounds and the exact location of 221B Baker Street—and to prepare us for subsequent problems in other stories, such as the exact chronology of the cases and Watson's shifting marital status. Yet much more interesting in this first adventure of Sherlock Holmes is the drama which underlies it as well as all of the Holmes stories. Even though Holmes is an enigmatic figure, given to unorthodox and unaccountable behavior, he is at heart a rationalist, enamoured like any enlightened nineteenth century scientist by the idea that there is no such thing as a mystery; there are only puzzles which anyone devoted to fact can solve. Hence, his famous exclamation: " 'It's elementary, my dear Watson!' " Opposing his conviction is the apparent mystery of human behavior and especially the nature of evil, not to mention Dr. Watson's superstitious nature and mental impenetrability.

Typical of this dramatic pattern is *The Study in Scarlet.* To Scotland Yard and Dr. Watson the murders of Drebber and Stangerson are inexplicable, made more enigmatic by the clues. Yet the same clues, examined by the completely methodical Holmes, reveal the murderer and his strange but perfectly logical story. Human evil and passion for Holmes are not without reason and motive and are, therefore, rational. The world is only mysterious and uncontrollable to those who will not see. Holmes always leaves us confident of ourselves because it is all so elementary.

THE SUN ALSO RISES

Type of work: Novel
Author: Ernest Hemingway (1899-1961)
Type of plot: Social criticism
Time of plot: 1920's
Locale: Paris and Pamplona, Spain
First published: 1926

The Sun Also Rises, a major novel of the 1920's, treats the aimlessness of a group of American and English expatriates who represent the so-called "lost generation" following the disillusionment of World War I. Unlike most of the other characters, who cynically acquiesce in their own moral disintegration, Jake Barnes searches for a personal, proto-existential code of values.

Upon its publication in 1926, *The Sun Also Rises* was instantly accepted as one of the important American novels of the post-World War I period. Part of this recognition was due to the superficial fact that sophisticated readers "identified" current expatriate "celebrities" among the book's characters, but, as most of these personages faded into obscurity, this *roman à clef* aspect of the novel soon lost its appeal. A more important reason for the book's immediate success is that it perfectly captured the mood and style of the American artistic and intellectual "exiles" who drank, loved, and searched for meaning on the Paris Left Bank in the aftermath of that first world struggle.

The overall theme of *A Sun Also Rises* is indicated by Hemingway's two epigraphs. Gertrude Stein's comment that "you are all a lost generation" suggests the ambiguous and pointless lives of Hemingway's exiles as they aimlessly wander about the Continent drinking, making love, and traveling from place to place and party to party. The quote from Ecclesiastes, which gives the novel its title, implies a larger frame of reference, a sense of permanence, order, and value. If the activities of the characters seem to justify the former quotation, their search for new meanings to replace the old ones—or at least to enable them to deal with that loss—demonstrates their desire to connect with the latter one.

Early in the novel the hero, Jake Barnes, declines to kiss Georgette, a prostitute, on the grounds that he is "sick." "Everybody's sick. I'm sick too," she responds. But this sickness motif is opposed in another early conversation Jake has, this one with Count Mippipopolous, a most vivid minor character, who tells him "that is the secret. You must get to know the values." The search for "values" and the willingness to pay the price, first to acquire them and then to live by them, are what separates Hemingway's exiles, at least some of them, from simple, pointless hedonism.

At the center of this search for values is the "Hemingway hero," Jake Barnes. As in all of Hemingway's important fictions, *The Sun Also Rises* is a novel of "education"—of learning to live with the conditions faced.

Jake's problem is, of course, complicated by his war injury. Having been emasculated in combat, Jake's "affair" with Lady Brett Ashley takes on a comical aspect—as he himself freely admits. But Hemingway has a very serious intention: Jake's wound is a metaphor for the condition of the entire expatriate group. They have all been damaged in some fundamental way by the war—physically, morally, psychologically, economically—and their aimless existence can be traced back to it. But the real symbolic importance of Jake's wound is that it has deprived him of the *capacity* to perform sexually, but it has not rid him of the *desire*. The people in *The Sun Also Rises* fervently want meaning and fulfillment, but they lack the ability and equipment to find it.

The heroes in Hemingway's major works learn the "values" in two ways: through their own actions and by contact with other characters who already know them. These "exemplars" understand the values either from long, hard experience, like Count Mippipopolous, or intuitively, automatically, like the bullfighter, Pedro Romero. But such heroes never articulate these values; they only embody them in action. Indeed, once talked about they become, in the Hemingway lexicon, "spoiled." Jake's education can be most clearly seen in his relationship to three characters: Robert Cohn, Pedro Romero, and Lady Brett Ashley.

Critics have speculated on why Hemingway begins the novel with a long discussion of Robert Cohn, a relatively minor character. The reason is simple: if it is hard to say exactly what the values *are,* it is easy to say what they *are not* and Robert Cohn embodies the old, false, "romantic" values that Hemingway is reacting against.

In the beginning Jake feels that Cohn is "nice and awful," but tolerates and pities him as a case of "arrested development." By the end of the book he thoroughly hates him. Cohn's flaws include a false sense of superiority— reinforced by his pugilistic skills—and a romantic attitude toward himself and his activities that distorts his relationship wth everyone around him. To reinforce this false romanticism, Cohn alters reality to suit his preconceptions. Falling "in love" with Brett, he refuses to see her realistically, but idealizes her. When she spends a weekend with him, because she thinks it would be "good for him," he treats it as a great affair and demands the "rights" of a serious lover, striking out at all the other men who approach her. In short, Cohn's false perception of reality and his self-romanticization underscore his chief fault, the cardinal sin in Hemingway's view: Cohn refuses to "pay his bill."

Cohn's romantic self-image is finally destroyed by the book's "exemplar," the bullfighter Pedro Romero. After being introduced to Brett by Jake, Romero becomes enamoured of her and they go off together. Affronted that Brett has been "taken" from him, Cohn reacts predictably and forces the young man into a prolonged fist fight. But, although totally outmanned as a boxer, Romero refuses to give in to Cohn. After absorbing considerable punishment, Romero, by sheer will, courage, and endurance, rallies to defeat and humiliate his opponent. His romantic bubble deflated, Cohn bursts into tears and fades from the novel.

It is appropriate that Cohn's false values be exposed by Pedro Romero, because his example is also central to the educations of both Jake and Brett. As an instinctively great bullfighter, Romero embodies the values in action and especially in the bullring. In a world bereft of religious certainties, Hemingway saw the bullfighter's performance as an aesthetic ceremony which substituted for obsolete religious ritual. Without transcendental meanings, man's dignity must come from the manner in which he faces his certain destiny; the bullfighter, who repeatedly does so by choice, was, for Hemingway, the supreme modern hero, providing he performs with skill, precision, style, and without "falsity" (that is, making it look harder or more dangerous than it really is). Shortly before the bullfight, Jake's group watches the local citizenry "run with the bulls" down the main street of the town. They see one man gored to death from behind. The following day that same bull is presented to Romero and he kills it perfectly by standing directly in front of it as he drives home his sword. This obvious symbolism states in a single image the most important of all the values, the need to confront reality directly and honestly.

But it is not only Pedro's example that helps to educate Jake, but also Jake's involvement in the Brett-Romero affair. His role as intermediary is the result of his "would-be" romance with her. They have long been in love and deeply frustrated by Jake's "funny-sad" war injury. Yet, despite the impossibility of a meaningful relationship, Jake can neither accept Brett as a "friend" nor cut himself off from her—although he knows that such a procedure would be the wisest course of action. She can, therefore, only be a "temptress" to him; she is quite accurate when she refers to herself as "Circe."

The only time in the book when Jake feels whole and happy is when he and Bill Gorton take a fishing trip at Bayonne. There, in a world without women, they fish with skill and precision, drink wine, naturally chilled in the stream, instead of whiskey, relate to the hearty exuberance of the Basque peasantry, and feel serene in the rhythms of nature. But once they return and Jake meets Brett at San Sebastian, his serenity is destroyed.

Jake puts his group up at a hotel owned by Montoya, an old friend and the most honored bullfighting patron. Montoya is an admirer and accepts Jake as a true *aficionado,* that is, one who truly understands and appreciates bullfighting not merely with his intellect, but with his whole being, his *passion.* Montoya even trusts Jake to the point of asking advice about the handling of this newest, potentially greatest young bullfighter, Pedro Romero. When Jake presents Brett to Pedro, fully understanding the implications of his act, he violates his trust with Montoya. His frustrated love for Brett exposes Pedro to her potentially corrupting influence. Jake's realization of his own weakness in betraying Romero, plus the fact that it has cost him his *aficionado* status, leaves him a sadder, wiser Hemingway hero.

But Pedro is not destroyed because Brett sends him away before she can do any damage. Of course more than simple altruism is involved in her decision. Life with Pedro held the possibility of wholeness for her—as it held the possibility of dissipation for him. So by sending him away she relinquishes her "last chance" for health and happiness rather than risk damaging her lover.

Whether or not Jake's insights and Brett's final "moral act" give meaning to the lives of these exiles is problematical. During their Bayonne fishing trip, Jake's friend Bill Gorton sings a song about "pity and irony" and that seems to be the overall tone of the book, and especially of the ending: pity for the personal anguish and aimless searching of these people, but ironic detachment toward characters whose lives and situations are, at best, at least as comical as they are tragic.

Keith Neilson

THE SUNKEN BELL

Type of work: Drama
Author: Gerhart Hauptmann (1862-1946)
Type of plot: Poetic fantasy
Time of plot: Indefinite, timeless
Locale: A mountain, a valley, and the paths between
First presented: 1897

In this poetical play, quite different in theme and style from his early naturalistic social drama, Hauptmann symbolically presents the problem of the artist struggling against the world, the creative spirit against reality.

Gerhart Hauptmann, one of the major German authors of the last century, achieved his first fame in 1889, working in the then-revolutionary naturalist style. Grimly realistic, naturalism portrayed a slice of life presenting the real problems facing everyday people. Hauptmann's prolific genius, however, soon ranged across the entire spectrum of dramatic styles: historical tragedy, fantasy, symbolism, and neoclassicism. His work is extremely uneven, at times brilliant, at times banal, but it is marked by an intensity of expression and a sympathy with his characters that created numerous works of genius.

The Sunken Bell, ninth of Hauptmann's major plays, harkens back to the Romantic style of the early nineteenth century, and is based in part on a number of folk motifs which may be traced widely in the works of Romantic writers, not only Germans, but also Ibsen (*Peer Gynt*) and Byron (*Manfred*). It may be seen simply as a fantasy piece woven out of timeless mythical elements; yet, like the Faust legend, it also clearly has symbolic overtones, and has been interpreted in an autobiographical sense as the problem of the artist torn between bondage to the real and striving for the ideal—in a wider sense, a metaphor for all man's striving. Heinrich lacks the titanic drives of a Faust, however, and his situation traps him in a conflict which is beyond resolution.

The world of nature and the world of man are seen here as divided from, and almost hostile to each other. Those who would cross the boundaries are doomed to failure, and rejected by their own. Thus, the tragedy extends beyond Heinrich himself, and touches both the spirit world and the world of man. Only in the eternal realm, for which Heinrich, through his art, has been striving in his earthly life, are the opposites reconciled.

THE SUPPLIANTS

Type of work: Drama
Author: Aeschylus (525-456 B. C.)
Type of plot: Classical tragedy
Time of plot: Age of myth
Locale: Argos
First presented: c. 490 B. C.

Although The Suppliants *is complete as an artistic work, the play is better appreciated as the first and only extant drama in a trilogy that presumably told the entire tragic story of Danaüs and Aegyptus, and their sons and daughters.*

This play (Latin title *Supplices,* Greek *Hiketides*) was until recently judged the first performed of Aeschylus' extant works by virtue of its primitive simplicity of plot and emphasis on the chorus. But a papyrus fragment has placed the performance of the *Danaïds,* presumably the last play of this trilogy, in the Sophoclean era, sometime after 468 B.C. Thus, scholars debate whether Aeschylus kept this play "in a drawer" for twenty years or decided to revert to an archaic form.

The role of the chorus of Danaïds is still much discussed for several reasons. First, it is unlikely that the fifty maids were represented by more than the usual twelve members of the chorus; second, although the lyrical choral passages are frequently enchanting, they would no doubt become tedious, were it not for the brevity of the play; third, the use of the chorus as protagonist is necessarily a challenge for any playwright since the spectator finds it more difficult to identify with a crowd. This might explain why critics accuse the chorus of dispassionate commentary in lieu of involvement: their speeches are as artificial and forced as their odes are majestic. Another point of intense debate is why the Danaïds refuse the Egyptians, but no reason has been advanced more compelling than that they and their father simply wish not to be forced into a marriage. Perhaps Aeschylus purposely makes their case weak to strengthen the conclusion of the trilogy.

The Danaïds' idealistic search for true love in marriage nearly upstages the drama's pivotal character, Pelasgus. He is caught in a grand dilemma: if he grants the women sanctuary, he jeopardizes Argos; if he turns them away, he incurs the wrath of Zeus. His allowing the citizens to decide the issue is not an abdication of his responsibility; rather, it is the playwright's statement that the will of the people bespeaks Greek respect for human rights and divine authority. Such a stand in the face of barbarous lust and violence is not only morally right, but invincible.

In the *Egyptians,* the missing second play of the trilogy, most likely the Egyptians force the surrender of the maidens who perhaps are led off to their "marriage" beds. The concluding *Danaïds* would have related how forty-nine of the maids murdered their husbands according to their father's command,

and it probably ended with the trial and acquittal of the disobedient Hypermnestra. For their crime her sisters traditionally are placed in Tartarus where they are obliged continually to try to carry water in sieves.

THE SUPPLIANTS

Type of work: Drama
Author: Euripides (c. 485-c. 406 B.C.)
Type of plot: Classical tragedy
Time of plot: Immediately after the War of the Seven against Thebes
Locale: Eleusis, not far from Athens
First presented: c. 424 B.C.

This drama has the same title as, but a subject altogether different from, that of the earlier play by Aeschylus. Morally urgent and didactic, Euripides' tragedy is intended to serve as a warning to his fellow Athenians against the follies of war.

Regardless of their particular themes, Euripides' dramas all reflect an underlying criticism of conventional religious attitudes and of the convenient modifications in mythical belief made by his contemporaries to accommodate their particular institutions and justify their actions. Because they feel that *The Suppliants* departs from this pattern, many critics have judged the play to be inconsistent with Euripides' value system as established in his other works. This idea is due to the fact that most critics have viewed the character of Theseus as a model of piety, and the war he wages on Thebes as a just one; and certainly this interpretation places the play in sharp contrast to Euripides' usual cynical stance regarding piety and the role of the gods in human affairs. This reading necessitates a somewhat negative evaluation of the play on both thematic and structural grounds, since it cannot account for many ironic statements of the characters and contradictory occurrences in the plot. Other critics—although in the minority—use these same ironies and seeming contradictions in the play as evidence that Euripides in *The Suppliants* was perfectly consistent in maintaining his unorthodox religious viewpoint.

Whether one reads the play as atypical of Euripides in its orthodoxy or or consistent in its rational skepticism, one must agree on certain points. One is that in *The Suppliants* Euripides has written an eloquent and impassioned indictment of the folly and wastefulness, the heartbreak and loss brought on by war. In this play he is concerned more with political and ethical considerations than with religious problems, and as always he takes a humanistic and rationalistic position on the issues under examination. Theseus is admirable both for his ability to reason calmly—as when he weighs the case for aiding Adrastus—and for his capacity for moderation and control—as when he refuses to sack Thebes after his victory over that city. Like Euripides, Theseus is an optimistic rationalist who believes in man's capacity to better his own conditions by using reason; much of the thematic concern in *The Suppliants,* therefore, is with arguing for international justice and Panhellenic peace. Athens is presented in ideal form to represent the greater possibilities for a rational government and humanistic society which the playwright believed were inherent in the democratic as opposed to the autocratic state.

Another point is that *The Suppliants* is structurally weak. There is a loss of unity following the account of the climactic victory of Athens over Thebes. Nevertheless, however artistically inadvisable the remaining scenes of lament by the Argive women over their slain sons might be, they are some of the most moving scenes in any of Euripides' dramas. They form almost a play in their own right, with their own particular beauty of language and unity of structure.

I SUPPOSITI

Type of work: Drama
Author: Ludovico Ariosto (1474-1533)
Type of plot: Farce
Time of plot: c. 1500
Locale: Ferrara, Italy
First presented: 1509

Ariosto wrote two versions of I Suppositi (The Substitutes), *the first in prose, the second in poetry; the action of the comedy, however, following to the letter the rules laid down by Landino, is essentially the same in each. Translated into English by George Gascoigne under the title* Supposes, *the work had a strong influence upon Elizabethan dramatists, including Shakespeare.*

Ludovico Ariosto's *I Suppositi* was one of the most popular comic dramas of the sixteenth century. Comedy was the major dramatic form of Italian letters at this time, and Ariosto was the king of Italian comedy. He, like his contemporaries in Italy and abroad, thrived on the Plautine comedy of the ancient Romans. His plots always included elements of Roman comedies; a sprinkling of stock characters along with slapstick situations and romantic farce. Always enjoyable to read, and even more delightful to watch, Ariosto's plays were able to combine successfully the traditional themes of slapstick comedy with a brilliance of verse and sensitive insights into the foibles of human nature.

Originally written in prose form, as were some of Ariosto's other works, *I Suppositi* was later reworked into a ten syllable blank verse line ending in two unstressed syllables. This gave the work a lively pace while at the same time bringing it close to the rhythm of ordinary Italian speech.

Satire is one of the primary elements of *I Suppositi* as it was with all comedies of the period. Ariosto had a keen eye for seeing the comic side of human nature. This trait enabled him to have a strong social comment in each one of his works which raised him above the level of the ordinary imitator of Roman comedy. The social criticism and truly humorous situations portrayed in Ariosto's plays make them as entertaining today as they were in the sixteenth century.

One handicap for the modern reader, however, is the fact that many of the puns which were amusing to Ariosto's audience have no contemporary meaning unless they are carefully explained. For this reason, anyone reading *I Suppositi* should pay careful attention to notes supplied in the text.

SURRY OF EAGLE'S-NEST

Type of work: Novel
Author: John Esten Cooke (1830-1886)
Type of plot: Historical romance
Time of plot: 1861-1863
Locale: Virginia
First published: 1866

Based in part upon the wartime experience of a captain in the Confederate army, Surry of Eagle's-Nest *blends a great deal of melodramatic fiction with some historical facts concerning the campaigns of General Stonewall Jackson and other prominent Confederate military figures.*

Surry of Eagle's-Nest remains of interest primarily as a romanticized version of Cooke's firsthand experiences as a Confederate officer during the Civil War—an ordeal that ranged from participation in the First Manassas to the final surrender at Appomattox Court House. While Cooke served primarily as a staff officer with J. E. B. Stuart's cavalry, he numbered Stonewall Jackson, Robert E. Lee, and other high-ranking Confederates among his personal acquaintances. Cooke published military biographies of Jackson (1863 and 1866) and of Lee (1871).

On the whole, *Surry of Eagle's-Nest,* a product of six weeks' work, is an uneven attempt to blend historical fact and fiction. The novel climaxes with a romanticized account of Stonewall Jackson's death in 1863, and, in its historical aspects, draws upon the author's earlier military biographies of Jackson (just as *Mohun* [1869], the sequel to *Surry of Eagle's-Nest,* parallels Cooke's later biography of Robert E. Lee). In *Surry of Eagle's-Nest,* Cooke merely combined the fictional trappings of conventional historical romance with real wartime events and experiences. The highly melodramatic aspects of the novel, particularly the purely Gothic subplot of the antagonists Mordaunt and Fenwick and the often confusing integration of historical and fictional characters, render the work less satisfactory than *The Virginia Comedians* (1854), Cooke's most successful historical romance. Cooke's idealization of antebellum Southern society and his acceptance of the myth of Cavalier origins of the Virginia aristocracy are also more prevalent in *Surry of Eagle's-Nest* than in his previous work. The novel was one of the earliest and most important contributions to the myth of the "Lost Cause" in the postwar South.

The novel, first published in 1866, found a receptive audience among celebrants of the "Lost Cause," and it has remained one of the most popular of Cooke's historical romances. Along with *Mohun, Surry of Eagle's-Nest* ranks as the best of Cooke's war novel, but neither possesses the unity or literary quality earlier achieved in *The Virginia Comedians.*

SWALLOW BARN

Type of work: Novel
Author: John P. Kennedy (1795-1870)
Type of plot: Comedy of manners
Time of plot: Early nineteenth century
Locale: Virginia
First published: 1832

Swallow Barn, *consisting of a series of amusing episodes loosely connected as a romance, presents sketches of plantation life and manners in Virginia during the early eighteenth century. Kennedy's popular fiction was to be the forerunner of a large number of novels dealing with the historic background of that state.*

Had John Pendleton Kennedy approached literature as a profession rather than an avocation, he might have become one of America's most important nineteenth century writers. But he felt his first obligation was to his career, initially as a lawyer in Baltimore, where his second marriage allied him firmly to the business community, and, subsequently, in the face of growing political and sectional unrest, as a man of public affairs, serving terms in the Maryland House of Delegates, United States House of Representatives, and as the Secretary of the Navy. In between legal, business, and political commitments, he managed to write three very different novels; *Swallow Barn; Horseshoe Robinson* (1835), a historical novel about the Revolutionary War in South Carolina; and *Rob of the Bowl* (1838), a "Cavalier Romance" of Colonial Maryland. In addition, he wrote numerous essays, satires, and miscellaneous writings.

For all his lightness of touch, Kennedy had very serious motives in the writing of all of his literary efforts, especially in *Swallow Barn*. Having become progressively alarmed by the growing national tension and disunity, Kennedy hoped that this realistic, yet sympathetic portrait of Southern society might foster harmony by stimulating understanding.

In its own time, *Swallow Barn* was highly praised for its "realism," but today Kennedy's vision of the Old Dominion seems quite romanticized; indeed, the book's primary interest for a modern reader lies in the fact that it was the novel in which the "myth" of the old plantation South was first fictionalized. This atmosphere of serenity and pastoral elegance, described with affection and gentle, humorous irony, is based on a fixed, secure society without major social or political problems. In *Swallow Barn* the most serious issue revolves around how to give away one hundred worthless acres in a manner that will not hurt the recipient's feelings. This uncomplicated vision of things was not, as Kennedy freely admitted, an unbiased one. The author carefully keeps the conflicts in the background—but he also makes sure they are there.

The primary conflict was, of course, the issue of slavery. The slaves at

Swallow Barn and The Brakes conform to the plantation myth stereotype; they are well-treated, contented, amusing, and affectionate. But at the same time Kennedy acknowledges the basic injustice of the system. Far from being a Southern apologist, he was a mild abolitionist, feeling slavery to be both immoral and inefficient, and he remained a Unionist throughout the Civil War. But as a Southerner living in the midst of the situation, he saw and felt the complexity of the issue, and probably expressed his own sentiments through Frank Meriwether, who stated that it is wrong to keep slaves, but:

> We should not be justified in taking the hazard of internal convulsions to get rid of them; nor have we a right, in the desire to free ourselves, to whelm them in greater evils than their present bondage. A violent removal of them, or a general emancipation, would assuredly produce one or the other of these calamities.

To his own personal sorrow, Kennedy lived to see the worst of his expectations realized.

THE SWISS FAMILY ROBINSON

Type of work: Novel
Author: Johann Rudolf Wyss (1781-1830)
Type of plot: Adventure romance
Time of plot: Late eighteenth century
Locale: An island near New Guinea
First published: 1813

A longtime favorite of children, The Swiss Family Robinson *is an adventure story with a strong moral message. In order for the castaways to survive, Wyss stresses their obedience to parental authority, and their interdependence.*

There have been nearly two hundred versions of *The Swiss Family Robinson* since the first English translation appeared in 1814. It is no wonder, then, that it is difficult to discuss the novel as Johann David Wyss, a Swiss army chaplain about whom very little has been recorded, originally related its story to his four young sons. One of the Wyss boys, Johann Rudolf, published it in 1813. An early French translator received permission from the younger Wyss to change the original ending and add some of her own episodes to the story. The novel was added to and altered repeatedly, but its authorship is, nonetheless, attributed to Johann Rudolf Wyss. His place in Swiss literature was gained by virtue of his work as a reviewer and popularizer of Swiss folk history and tradition.

The Swiss Family Robinson is not remembered and studied as a great work of literature, but children have enjoyed it for years simply for its story of adventure and the excitement that the theme of being stranded provokes. The style is basic and straightforward. The main character, Mr. Robinson, narrates the tale in the first person with numerous parenthetical bits of piety. Each of the sons represents a different type of juvenile personality that must be dealt with and nurtured carefully, and in the idyllic surroundings of the island, harmony is achieved easily.

The book is episodic and events are strung together through Mr. Robinson's narration. Many episodes have a mini-climax which holds the attention of young readers and provides a sustained feeling of excitement. The ingenuity of the family is remarkable—perhaps unbelievable—as is the account of the thousands of fruits and animals that they find at their disposal on the island.

THE TALE OF GENJI

Type of work: Novel
Author: Lady Murasaki Shikibu (978?-1031?)
Type of plot: Court romance
Time of plot: Early medieval period
Locale: Japan
First transcribed: 1001-1015

Undoubtedly the finest example of medieval Japanese storytelling, The Tale of
Genji *is the first and title volume of an extended court romance written by a
cultured lady-in-waiting to the Empress Akiko.*

The Tale of Genji comprises a long (more than eleven hundred pages),
elegant, wittily ironical court romance that some critics have also described
as a prototype of the novel. The whole book is in six parts, consisting of the
title section, followed by *The Sacred Tree, A Wreath of Cloud, Blue Trousers,
The Lady of the Boat,* and *The Bridge of Dreams.* Although Arthur Waley's
famous modern translation from the Japanese has made the work accessible
to a greater audience, few Western readers generally venture beyond the first
section, *The Tale of Genji,* to complete the massive volume. That is unfortunate, because Lady Murasaki Shikibu's style improves as she continues
her fiction (her first chapter crudely imitates the manner of old court romances); her characterizations become richer, more complex; and her full
design—to fashion a moral picture of the Emperor's court of her time—is
made apparent. For some readers *The Tale of Genji* is an incomparable
re-creation of life in eleventh century Japan, with the smallest details of the
customs, ceremonies, and manners of the aristocracy faithfully reproduced;
for others, the book is an enchanting collection of interwoven stories, some
slightly erotic, all vividly recounted; for still others the book is a psychologically honest examination of passion and pretense, of the hearts of men
and women.

The first section treats Genji, "the Shining One," as a child and as a young
man, idealistic but often unwise, learning the arts of courtship and love. It
also introduces Murasaki (who is certainly not the author, unless by ironic
contrast), first as Genji's child-concubine, then as his second wife. Her character, thus, is tentatively sketched. In the other parts of the book, she will
learn about the romantic and political intrigues of court life, become sophisticated in practicing her own wiles, and finally—in the section titled *Blue
Trousers*—die of a lingering, wasting disease. But the early *Tale of Genji*
treats the hero and heroine as youthful, hopeful, and inexperienced, before
they fully understand how to play the cynical games of love and dissembling.

In Chapter Two of *The Tale of Genji* the author advances the main theme
of her work, that of the romantic education of innocent lovers. The Equerry
of the palace, To no Chujo, regales several noblemen, including Genji, with

stories about the weakness of women. He has at last discovered that "there exists no woman of whom one can say: 'Here is perfection.' " Genji's youthful experiences tend to support this observation. Just twelve years old when he is married to the sixteen-year-old Princess Aoi, he is more amused by amorous adventures than by matrimonial responsibilities, and comes to care for his wife only at the point of her untimely death. Nevertheless, with Fujitsubo (whom later he makes pregnant) he enjoys his first dalliance; thereafter he sports with the easily yielding but jealous Utsusemi; with a complaisant lady who happens, conveniently, to be sleeping in Utsusemi's bed; with the lower-class but refined Yūgao, who dies tragically; finally with the child Murasaki. Except for the last, each woman disappoints him. Murasaki, the most innocent and childlike of his lovers, is the only one spirited, imaginative, and beautiful enough to hold his affections.

Yet Murasaki also undergoes a romantic education. She must learn how to thrive in a world controlled by men, without becoming submissive to their power. When Genji brings her to the palace, he warns her: "Little girls ought to be very gentle and obedient in their ways." At this speech the author wryly comments: "And thus her education was begun." Several years later, Genji takes sexual liberties with Murasaki, who is too innocent and confused either to oppose or enjoy his attentions. Indeed, her own innocence excites his desire. As the author explains, "It is in general the unexplored that attracts us, and Genji tended to fall most deeply in love with those who gave him least encouragement." When Genji decides to marry the girl, she has no choice in the matter; in fact, he criticizes her lack of enthusiasm for the arrangement, since she owes so much to his friendship. In the closed world of the Emperor's palace, where court ladies at best play submissive parts, Lady Murasaki Shikibu shows how women must develop resources of their own—both of mind and heart—to live with dignity. By the end of *The Tale of Genji,* her heroine is already beginning to learn that lesson.

A TALE OF TWO CITIES

Type of work: Novel
Author: Charles Dickens (1812-1870)
Type of plot: Historical romance
Time of plot: French Revolution
Locale: France and England
First published: 1859

Without attempting a rigorous analysis of the political, social, and economic causes or consequences of the French Revolution, Dickens uses this historical background as the panoramic setting for a complicated romantic novel culminating in Sidney Carton's famous personal drama of love and renunciation.

The central paradox of *A Tale of Two Cities* consists in the fact that its action involves the most important political event of modern European history—and perhaps of its entire history—the French Revolution, while the values of the novel are ultimately anti-political. Politics and history, neither of which Dickens renders with great faithfulness, loom as a necessity from which his characters must flee to save their souls. Throughout the novel Dickens reminds us that all of man's acts, whether magnanimous or petty, when viewed in a cosmic context, shrink to nil. Indeed, for him the goal of politics, the finding of a just community, is an absurd one in this world. To paraphrase Sydney Carton's famous last speech: it is a far better thing to die and join such a community in heaven—the existence of which Dickens cannot with certainty assert—than to engage with society. *A Tale of Two Cities* demonstrates that Dickens' political will, wan in his previous novels, has finally been exhausted.

In this regard and in one of the first substantial essays dealing with Dickens' art and thought, published a year before *A Tale of Two Cities* was completed, Walter Bagehot said: "Mr. Dickens has not unfrequently spoken, and what is worse, he has taught a great number of parrot-like imitators to speak, in what really is, if they knew it, a tone of objection to the necessary constitution of human society." Dickens' strength, Bagehot agreed, appeared in the quality of his moral cry, his protest against the injustices of society; yet, as he said, the novelist never indicated how these inequalities might be removed.

By the time of *A Tale of Two Cities,* distinguished by its outrage against both the tyranny of the governors and the governed, Dickens clearly indicates that society cannot be made to progress, or even be substantially ameliorated. For him the great grasp for freedom by the French people, for example, goes finally unsung, drowned out by the terrible cacophony of the guillotine. To Dickens' unwillingness to accept the "necessary constitution of human society," then, must be added his refusal to understand and accept the necessarily slow and painful processes of history.

In his early comic and satiric novels, such as *Pickwick Papers, Nicholas*

Nickleby and *Oliver Twist,* Dickens' simple stance of protest carried with it a zestful anger that was both invigorating and liberating. But as he grew more serious in his artistic intent, beginning with *Dombey and Son,* completed in 1848, and continuing through *David Copperfield, Bleak House, Hard Times* and *Little Dorrit,* for many readers his masterpiece, he lost his sense of the efficacy of the human will to deal with the complexities of a modern, industrial society. His gradual loss of faith was accompanied by a diminishing moral energy; his imagination seemed unable to create viable and pertinent responses to a civilization increasingly encroaching on individual freedom. Particularly in *Little Dorrit,* the novel published immediately before *A Tale of Two Cities,* we are stunned as well as enervated by the hopelessness of the conclusion.

There is a significant scene in *A Tale of Two Cities,* appearing at the conclusion of Book the First, relevant to Dickens' social despair. After Doctor Manette has been saved from the Bastille, and on the way from Paris to London, his rescuer, Mr. Jarvis Lorry, asks him, "I hope you care to be recalled to life?" Doctor Manette answers, "I can't say." In some ways, the question is never answered by the doctor, for at the novel's conclusion he is rendered an inarticulate vegetable by his sufferings during the Reign of Terror. But it does seem to be answered by the working out of the plot which culminates in Carton's self-sacrifice.

If to be "recalled to life" means to be called back into civilization and history, then the novel implies the answer: "No." For the quality of life in society is actually no better, Dickens tells us, than perpetual imprisonment in the Bastille: man is caught up in an undertow of events which leaves him helpless; his imagination, intelligence, and will are useless when pitted against politics.

Indeed the novelist goes further than this in his view of man's ineptitude: if he consents to join in the machinations of society, Dickens asserts, he must expect inevitable corruption. It is a tragic view unrelieved by any sense of man's dignity, a nobility obtained through a will to control time, even if that exertion is fated to be unrewarded. We are left with a vision of unmitigated pathos, unconsoled in our own existence, which is inextricably bound up with the demands of history and politics.

The consolation which Dickens offers—if indeed comfort can be forthcoming after the absoluteness of his negation—takes the form of a vague promise of supernatural communion and a picture of human fellowship and love. Composed of Doctor and Lucie Manette, Charles Darnay and Sydney Carton, together with the minor characters of Mr. Lorry, Miss Pross and Jerry Cruncher, the fellowship provides a sanctuary within the confines of history. There affection, trust, and sacrifice stand opposed to the hate, treachery, and tyranny of the world.

Yet even this consolation is finally unsatisfying. That sanctuary is populated by the good-hearted, naïve, sentimental, and feeble; it is a childlike fellowship in which passion and mind, those qualities we associate with a real, adult world, are absent. Not only does the merely innocent fail to attract us, but the refuge remains unconvincing and vulnerable when we realize the power that it is supposed to stand against. In short, one cannot imagine Charles and Lucie along with Doctor Manette and their faithful retainers surviving the *realpolitik* of civilization. Despite its great subject, *A Tale of Two Cities* is, at last, a simplistic novel; it is deficient in the complex human experience which we expect from great fiction.

David L. Kubal

THE TALISMAN

Type of work: Novel
Author: Sir Walter Scott (1771-1832)
Type of plot: Historical romance
Time of plot: Twelfth century
Locale: The Holy Land
First published: 1825

For youthful readers one of Scott's enduringly popular historical novels, The Talisman *is a well-constructed fiction that contains many ingredients for romantic adventure: faraway lands, love, mystery, chivalric courage, and magnanimity of spirit.*

The Talisman, while functioning very effectively as sheer entertainment, operates more importantly on another level of expression. This other level comprises the thematic bases underlying virtually all of Scott's art. Throughout his life, Scott committed himself to serving truth, both historical and moral; hence, he chose the historical novel, encompassing the facts of time as well as the truths of morality that endure the test of time, as the medium for his artistic expression. Furthermore, he was thoroughly an eighteenth century man, concerned with the triumph of reason over passion and with proper conduct in an orderly society. These are the elements that inform *The Talisman,* placing its importance beyond that of simple entertainment.

Using a particular historical period as the basic framework for each of his novels, Scott seeks to reveal an era or a way of life representative of that particular period and to demonstrate the relationship between past and present, pointing out attitudes, conflicts, and behavior common to all men in all ages of history. To create economically the historical setting, Scott introduces a character that embodies the period or manner of life with which the novel concerns itself, thus avoiding unnecessary clarifying detail. In *The Talisman,* therefore, King Richard represents the chivalric code and way of life as it was known in England during the Middle Ages. At the same time, Richard represents also the excess pride and the imprudence that can infect any man, showing that certain attitudes, weaknesses, and behavior patterns are common among men in all ages; similarly, Sir Kenneth represents the universal figure seeking the path to order and honor through right conduct, and Saladin, though a pagan, symbolizes the object of Sir Kenneth's quest. Clearly, Scott's approach to history does not rely on individual facts but on general historical context. As a writer of fiction, he realized that a reader required more than fact, that reality must be altered and improved upon to correspond with the reader's desire for unexpected developments. Hence, Scott did not abuse history, as some accuse him, but he used it accurately and correctly as narrative fiction demanded of him.

Scott's dual purpose in *The Talisman* is to reveal the decadence of the chivalric code and at the same time to determine if there is intrinsic value in it. To this end, King Richard the Lion-Hearted symbolizes chivalry, its ceremony and its power over individuals. This power has become tainted, however, as evidenced by Richard's continual impetuosity and prideful acts; he represents the fanaticism that blocks clear, rational thought. And honor, as we see it in Richard, has become an empty ritual, arising from rashness rather than judicious thought and conduct. Moreover, the presence of such evil forces as the Grand Master and the Marquis of Montserrat further demonstrates the degenerate state to which the chivalric order has fallen.

To illustrate most clearly this deterioration, an antithetical figure, Saladin, is presented as a basis for comparison. He represents the rationality, fidelity, and compassion that are missing in the Crusader's camp. Saladin does not symbolize a code, however, but the honor that evolves from the organic growth of right conduct nourished by the use of reason and common sense. Finally, to absorb and discriminate between the influences of the two polar forces, Sir Kenneth, Knight of the Couchant Leopard is introduced as the innocent who experiences the influences of both forces and must choose between them. Sir Kenneth, occupying the middle ground between the two opposing forces, is susceptible to the positive influence of Saladin from the beginning, as the young knight's structural role requires. Already schooled in the chivalric code and displaying the narrow vision that ensues—even before we meet the distortion of chivalry in Richard—Sir Kenneth meets Saladin, disguised as Sheerkohf, in a duel, and the young knight emerges victorious in might but not in honor. For afterwards, Kenneth doubts the Saracen's sincerity in offering peace between them. Saladin, however, makes clear the earnestness of his pledge, and the "confidence of the Moslem" makes Kenneth "ashamed of his own doubts." Saladin's wisdom, rationality, and sense of honor affect Kenneth's development throughout the novel.

Saladin's impact on Sir Kenneth succeeds largely through the Saracen's many disguises. Just as King Richard's irrational interpretation of the chivalric code holds sway, primarily because of rank, over the young knight, so too would Saladin's influence be an artificial imposition because of his sovereignty. It is Scott's purpose to show that reason, prudence, and the *via media* of right conduct must grow organically from within the individual rather than be imposed by external forces or rituals of behavior. Scott illustrates this truth in disguising Saladin as Adonbec El Hakim, the wise paynim healer. In this role, Saladin appears as a more common individual, like Kenneth, and one who has objectively witnessed the course of events leading to the young knight's conviction and impending execution. The Saracen tries to reason with Kenneth, pointing out that it is foolish to die for a crime of which he is not entirely guilty; we realize actually that the knight's guilt must be tempered with the realization that it was Richard's pride, along with the jealousy and treachery breeding in the Crusader's camp, that created the precariousness of the situation in the first place. Kenneth ignores the Saracen's advice, and it his irrational adherence to his code of honor, honor based on ritual not careful thought and action, that forces El Hakim to bargain with Richard and his rash pride for the young knight's life. The Saracen's wise and compassionate intervention enables him to convince Kenneth later that it is more practical to stay alive and redeem himself and his reputation by revealing the real culprit to King Richard and to the entire camp.

Shortly thereafter, when El Hakim spurs Kenneth and himself away from the attacking band of Templars in the desert, the Saracen demonstrates to Sir Kenneth that more good can be gained in living and accomplishing their positive goals than in dying foolishly at the hands of the traitorous Templars. Later, when El Hakim becomes identified with Sheerkohf, a character with whom Kenneth can relate more closely because of their previous relationship, Kenneth begins to recognize the value of Saladin's code of honor, based more positively on reason, common sense, and prudent action. Sheerkohf convinces Kenneth that he is free to choose whatever path he wishes to follow, either to wander off aimlessly or to move forward in seeking his redemption. As Sheerkohf unfolds his plan to disguise Sir Kenneth as a mute Ethiopian slave, enabling him to infiltrate secretly the Crusaders' camp and to reveal the real thief of England's banner, the young knight chooses this time to follow the Saracen's advice, beginning to absorb the value derived from reason and prudence and to appreciate the efficacy of judicious thought and self-restrained action. From this point on, the expected resolution of the conflict is inevitable.

Sir Kenneth carries through admirably with his disguise and his plan for redemption; moreover, he enjoys the opportunity to save King Richard's life, and his self-restraint overcomes even the temptation offered during his interview with Lady Edith, his beloved. Hence, the denouement proceeds: the Marquis' guilt is revealed; the treachery of the Grand Master is punished; Richard also seems to learn the lessons of prudence and self-restraint; and the victorious Sir Kenneth enjoys his rewards, the announcement of his real identity and sovereignty as David, Earl of Huntingdon, and the hand of Lady Edith Plantagenet in marriage. The positive influence of Saladin's character becomes clear as he is identified by all concerned with his various disguises and his valuable deeds; and his impact is apparent also in Kenneth's potential as a great leader, for the young knight succeeded in formulating and pledging himself to a code of honor based on rationality, prudence, and self-restraint, largely because of Saladin's influence upon him. As a final act in the story, the talisman—essentially the symbol of reason, order, and right conduct—is transferred from East to West, from pagan to Christian, to carry on the magic yet curative work that it had already begun. This somewhat ironic turn reaffirms Scott's belief that men, regardless of origin, share a common nature throughout history and that reason and order in society, by exposing the imprudence of outdated codes like chivalry, transcend the boundaries of race, creed, nationality, and time.

Larry K. Bright

TAMAR

Type of work: Poem
Author: Robinson Jeffers (1887-1962)
Type of plot: Psychological melodrama
Time of plot: World War I
Locale: Carmel Coast Range, California
First published: 1924

Tamar, one of the greatest of Jeffers' long narrative poems, is a violent and powerful story—raised to the level of myth—of the doomed Cauldwell family, set against the harshly magnificent background of the Carmel Coast Range.

Of modern poets perhaps none has been so maligned on the one hand as a cold mystic, capable of flashes of greatness, and praised on the other for his evocation of nature's power and his concern for men as has Robinson Jeffers. His life implied these contradictions as well. His solitary tower, Tor House, built on the rugged coast of California separated him from man and his institutions and kept him close to nature. Much of his poetry, however, is concerned with the dilemma of man trapped by his institutions and technology and thus separated from nature and his natural, spontaneous self, though often conscious of the loss.

It is this conflict which lies at the center of *Tamar*. In the largest sense this theme is reflected by World War I—one of the periodic convulsions of man's institutions in which he destroys himself through his technology. The events of the poem are played out against the background of this conflict. Man's institutions and technology find more detailed symbolic form in objects such as Lee Cauldwell's spurs, his dreams of war, the decaying house in which the Cauldwell family lives, the family itself—which is in decay, falling towards idiocy—and Will Andrews, the social man whom Tamar victimizes.

Opposed to these forces is that of the indifferent, eternal, and healing power of nature. It is most strongly embodied in the traditional symbols of the earth which finally swallows the house and all that have been burned in it: in the air, primarily the wind, which fans the flames that destroy the house; in fire, which destroys and thus purifies; and in water—the sea which is present throughout the story, the river by which Tamar seduces Will, and the pool in Mal Paso creek by which the act of incest is committed. Other natural elements in the poem include the spirits who, being divorced from man by death, see clearly the natural purity and inevitability of Tamar's incest, and its element of corruption in the light of human institutions.

The conflict cannot be resolved because man is a product of both elements, neither of which he escapes. It is, in the end, the conflict between these two levels of knowledge that drives all of the characters to their destruction.

TAMBURLAINE THE GREAT

Type of work: Drama
Author: Christopher Marlowe (1564-1593)
Type of plot: Romantic tragedy
Time of plot: Fourteenth century
Locale: Asia
First presented: 1587

A study of driving ambition glorified as a heroic virtue, Tamburlaine the Great is historically important for a number of reasons, chief among them Marlowe's effective use of blank verse, which served as a model for other great Elizabethan dramatists, including Shakespeare.

After a legendary life of irreverence, challenging convention, Marlowe's turbulent career ended tragically, and no doubt characteristically, in a barroom brawl with a man named Ingram Frizer. Even though he was only twenty-nine when he died, Marlowe managed to set a precedent for the development of English drama by leaving behind a Renaissance model of Senecan dramatic form. His first production, *Tamburlaine the Great,* more a dramatic masque than a proper play, was a milestone of early Elizabethan drama, equaled in impact only by Kyd's *The Spanish Tragedy.* Certainly Shakespeare must have been influenced, especially in *Julius Caesar,* by the conjunction of "Nature," "Fortune," and "stars" in the construction of Tamburlaine's character. More than anything else, Marlowe made blank verse the accepted mode of Elizabethan theatrical expression, both with his "mighty line"—for example, "Even as when windy exhalations/Fighting for passage, tilt within the earth"—and with the delicate grace he develops even in this early work. Tamburlaine is thus capable of a certain tenderness simply because of Marlowe's poetic versatility. As the hero says to Zenocrate,

> With milk-white harts upon an ivory sled
> Thou shalt be drawn amidst the frozen pools,
> And scale the icy mountains' lofty tops,
> Which with thy beauty will be soon resolv'd.

Basing his drama on the history of Timur the Lane (1336-1406), a Mongol conqueror and descendant of Genghis Khan, Marlowe constructed his first Herculean hero who, in his own bloodthirsty way, is a personification of the Renaissance spirit of boldness, defiance, and determination to test the limitations of human ability. Invulnerable to all attacks but that of death, Tamburlaine moves upward toward his lofty goals undaunted by considerations of destiny or accidental circumstances. He is the master of his own destiny simply because he decides to be and finds no one strong enough to deny him his ambitions. He says to Theridamas:

> Forsake thy king, and do but join with me
> And we will triumph over all the world:
> I hold the Fates bound fast in iron chains,
> And with my hand turn Fortune's wheel about.

Here is the hubris of classical Athenian tragedy, but with a difference: Tamburlaine is not struck down because of it; in fact, he succeeds in everything he has time to undertake. One of the most effective moments of Part Two, which is generally much less compelling than the first play, is in Act V when Tamburlaine says, "Give me a map; then let me see how much/Is left for me to conquer all the world." Only physical inevitabilities bring Marlowe's hero low, although it is clear that the gaining of loves and possessions and sons makes Tamburlaine at least vulnerable, even if he manages to resist the incursions of these responsibilities.

He is able to resist, and to succeed in attaining his goals in the first place, because he regards the world and everything and every person in it as an object. It is not surprising, then, that his mighty, rhetorical speeches are filled with references to crimson robes, meteors, jewels, vermilion tents, and gold crowns. There is, in fact, a close connection between Tamburlaine's rhetoric and his achievements. He is godlike in the sense that what he says he does; his words become deeds. Finally we are not surprised that he regards even Zenocrate's dead body as an object, "Embalm'd with cassia, ambergris, and myrrh/Not lapp'd in lead, but in a sheet of gold." It is but another splendid, colorful toy—under his control to preserve or destroy. In the same vein he uses his victims as horses to pull his chariots. Tamburlaine is the egotistic dream of the Renaissance epitomized: "Of stature tall, and straightly fashioned/Like his desire, lift upwards and divine." In the correspondence between his appearance and his character there is a prediction of Shakespeare's Hamlet. But the difference between the two heroes is much more striking than any similarities we might detect. Tamburlaine does not falter in his purpose for a moment.

From the very beginning, after Tamburlaine steps into the power vacuum created by Mycetes' insufficiency (because he uses no "great and thundering speech"), the play is a series of episodic atrocities—connected only by the unswerving ambition of the hero. The action of the play, that is, has nothing to recommend it by way of originality or structural genius. The hero is both the center and the continuity of the work. Cosroe calls him the model of humanity, as Shakespeare calls his Hamlet and his Brutus. As such, one of Tamburlaine's most sympathetic characteristics is his never-wanting enthusiasm —the *sprezzatura* of the Italian Renaissance:

> Tamb.:   What say my other friends? Will you be kings?
> Tech. :   Ay, if I could, with all my heart, my lord.
> Tamb.:   Why, that's well said, Techelles, so would I.

Combined with this essential enthusiasm is Tamburlaine's expression of a typically Renaissance longing for the infinite *something* (whether it be the infinite knowledge sought by Faustus, the infinite riches of the Jew of Malta, or Tamburlaine's insatiable thirst for power). The Prologue of the play promises that we shall hear the hero "threatening the world with high astounding terms," and all three last words have thematic significance. Tamburlaine's description of himself as "the chiefest lamp of all the earth" is only the most explicit indication that he desires to join the company of the stars; that is, to escape from earth and wander among realms unknown to ordinary man, a recognition of human potential characteristic of the Renaissance since Pico di Mirandola's oration on the *Dignity of Man*. The root of the word "astounding," secondly, is related to the intensely rhetorical nature of Tamburlaine's every speech. His approach to stellar glory, that is, is primarily through the flamboyant energy of his language—Marlowe's "mighty line." It is not by coincidence that we rarely see Tamburlaine in action, usually in speech.

Finally "terms" draws the thematic structure together, indicating the boundaries and limitations of human experience and behavior that Tamburlaine means to break through and cast aside through his speech. That is why his victims are always so startled. He has no respect for ordinary conventions and not only does the most outlandish things to kings and generals, but also slays them, compounding his iconoclastic character. Yet it is just as important to note that Tamburlaine has no *divine* aspirations. What he seeks to accomplish nevertheless remains human: "A god is not so glorious as a king:/I think the pleasures they enjoy in heaven/Cannot compare with kingly joys in earth." It is for his successful extension of the terms of human nature that Tamburlaine becomes a seminal character in the development of English Renaissance drama.

Kenneth John Atchity

THE TAMING OF THE SHREW

Type of work: Drama
Author: William Shakespeare (1564-1616)
Type of plot: Farce
Time of plot: Sixteenth century
Locale: Padua, Italy
First presented: c. 1593

A lusty, witty, well-crafted comedy, The Taming of the Shrew *abounds in vigorous, often ribald wordplay. Too farcical to be taken seriously as anti-feminist, the work is a romp on the hoary subject of the battle of the sexes.*

Discussions of Shakespeare's *The Taming of the Shrew* almost always devote some space to the problem of the play's sources and its connection to an earlier work, *The Taming of a Shrew* (1594), of unknown authorship. However, tireless scholarly research and endless debates have still not solved the riddles; opinion is so widely divided that some even attribute the early anonymous play to Shakespeare, or deny his authorship of the later one. However the debate is finally settled remains to be seen; meanwhile, certain facts are incontrovertible, such as the unmistakable connection between the main plot (the taming of Katharina by Petruchio) of *The Taming of the Shrew* and that of *The Taming of a Shrew*. Likewise, the subplot (the court-ship of Bianca by rival wooers) of Shakespeare's comedy is definitely trace-able to Gascoigne's *The Supposes* (1556), a translation of Ariosto's *I Suppositi* (1509). *The Taming of the Shrew* is uncharacteristic of Shakespeare's other comedies in many ways, one of the most noticeable being its often farcical action and always thoroughly unromantic tone; at least one critic has suggested as an explanation that Shakespeare wrote the play as an antidote for his overly romantic *Two Gentlemen of Verona*.

Both plot and theme in *The Taming of the Shrew* are built around the contrasting characters of the partners in the two parallel love stories. The two suitors, Petruchio and Lucentio, are different in every way. Lucentio is a stereotype of the dreamy, lovesick wooer, who moves about in a trance and must be looked after by his clever and down-to-earth servant (Tranio). Lucentio is completely traditional in his views; his expressions of love often seem learned from the romantic conventions in books, rather than springing spontaneously from his heart. Petruchio, on the other hand, is unorthodox on every count. He descends on the complacent and stolid town of Padua like a storm, shocking—and also probably secretly pleasing—its inhabitants by his complete disregard for all the forms of polite and mannered society. His speech, dress, and behavior evoke images of adventure in foreign lands and danger on the high seas. He is a rude, coarse, brawling bully; but his values as reflected in his blatant announcement, "I come to wive it wealthily in Padua; / If wealthily, then happily in Padua," or his claim "She is my goods, my chattels, she is my house," are values accepted by the townspeople as well. The only difference is that Petruchio trumpets his beliefs loudly and openly, while Padua's citizens hide theirs under a cloak of propriety.

Similarly, the two sisters, Bianca and Katharina, are opposites—on the surface at least. Bianca behaves in a totally conventional way playing the socially accepted roles and games with ease. Her exterior is deceptive, however, for she is actually subtly manipulating the men around her, as becomes apparent in the unusual post-wedding scene at the end of the play. Bianca plays for the highest stakes, and wins: she makes a match that is at once romantically, socially, and monetarily advantageous. Katharina, on the other hand, is unorthodox in her behavior; she insists on defying convention. This tactic earns more immediate results than her sister's, since the girl's father at least insists that any prospective husband for Katharina must love her, while Bianca's submissiveness allows him to attempt selling her to the highest bidder. Katharina meets her match, however, in Petruchio, but only because he is even more unorthodox than she; Petruchio understands this, and overcomes his wife's shrewishness by disrupting those conventions in her life which she has never questioned: good food, sufficient sleep, and nice clothing.

TAPS FOR PRIVATE TUSSIE

Type of work: Novel
Author: Jesse Stuart (1907-   )
Type of plot: Regional romance
Time of plot: Twentieth century
Locale: Kentucky
First published: 1943

Set in the Kentucky mountains, this novel treats with deep familiarity and affection the region and common people whom Jesse Stuart, also author of many regional works including a book of Kentucky poems entitled Man with a Bull-Tongue Plow, *regards with amusement mingled with pity.*

Though it may seem on the surface no more than the comic tale of the determination of the shiftless Tussie family to survive without work, *Taps for Private Tussie,* on subtler levels, encompasses serious literary and social dimensions which justify its reputation as Stuart's best novel. Like Mark Twain and William Faulkner, with whom he shares a number of qualities, Jesse Stuart writes in the tradition of the frontier humorists of the past century, employing the vernacular style and episodic form to record the unique characteristics and folk customs of a dying culture. Also, as in the works of Twain and Faulkner, death and violence are just below the comic surface in Stuart's novels, mitigating his comic vision with a sense of the tragic in life.

Shiftless and lazy though they are, the Tussies are more victims than victimizers, and on this fact our sympathy for them is based. On one level, their determination not to work parodies the traditional independence of the mountaineer who called no man master. Yet, the tragic cost of this false freedom has been their traditional integrity and heritage—the loss of which is implicit in the Tussies' support of the county Democrats in return for welfare groceries. As they become increasingly dependent upon a destructive welfare system (and increasingly shiftless), only Grandpa Tussie, the benign old patriarch who holds the clan together, keeps alive the mountaineer's traditional love of the land.

Ironically, when Grandpa Tussie finally achieves his dream of owning a farm, the clan is much worse off than before, as they lose their welfare benefits but can no longer resume the life of independence and dignity the farm once offered. As Twain saw romanticism destroying the South, and as Faulkner linked its fall to the "curse" of slavery, Stuart seems to have prophesied in 1943 the threat modern welfare systems would become to the traditional world of his Southern Appalachians.

TARAS BULBA

Type of work: Novel
Author: Nikolai V. Gogol (1809-1852)
Type of plot: Historical romance
Time of plot: Fifteenth century
Locale: Russia
First published: 1835

A vigorous romantic novel with only the slightest pretensions to historical accuracy, Taras Bulba *celebrates the violent, often cruel, but freedom-loving spirit of the Cossacks, who were in Gogol's day already losing their essential character.*

Taras Bulba, a tribute to the Cossack way of life and the Cossack code of honor, reveals a nostalgic longing for the verities of the past, outdated even in the author's own time. From such nostalgia the novel takes its romantic flavor, for Nikolai Gogol depicts the acts and beliefs of the Cossacks as heroic. Neither is cruelty condemned, nor prejudice decried. The twentieth century reader may thus find some aspects of *Taras Bulba* shocking: the way of life in the Setch, the pogrom, Taras' execution of Andrii and Taras' fiery crucifixion, to name only a few. However, Gogol made no pretense at historical authenticity. Indeed, the story is highly fanciful, and even contradictory at times. For example, on the one hand, Taras is described as a character who could have lived only in the fifteenth century. On the other hand, Taras' sons, at the very beginning of the story, are returning home from a Kiev college which was not founded until the early seventeenth century. Thus, however shocking the story might seem, the shock is mitigated by inconsistencies which remind the reader that the story is a product less of the conventional historical romance tradition than of Gogol's unfettered imagination.

In fact, Taras himself was a larger-than-life hero, an incarnation of the ideal Cossack. Unswervingly loyal to the Cossack cause, he accepted the rules and punishments of the Setch and the Cossack's code of honor without question. Indeed, he endorsed these standards verbally and enforced them physically. On the three-day trip with his sons, from Mirgorod to Zaporozhsky Setch, for instance, Taras allowed no drinking, although he both encouraged and joined in marathon drinking bouts at the Cossack encampment in the Setch and elsewhere. He strictly adhered to the rule of celibacy at the Setch and expected others to do likewise. As far as he was concerned, the rules and punishments of the Setch were absolute: a Cossack who stole from another Cossack was flogged to death; a Cossack who did not promptly pay his debt to another Cossack was chained to a cannon until a comrade paid his debt for him; and a Cossack who murdered another Cossack was buried alive with his victim.

To Taras the Cossack code of honor—loyalty, dedication, and bravery—was paramount. His notions of loyalty were clearly expressed in his speech about comradeship to his fellow Cossacks on the eve of renewing the seige of Dubno. His dedication to the Cossack cause was reflected in his killing of Andŕii for betraying the cause. His bravery was demonstrated in his disparagement of his very serious wound and in his unflagging courage when he was burned at the stake. Taras Bulba is certainly the perfect Cossack, and his pristine integrity nobly shoulders the dramatic burden of this bloody but compelling novel.

TARR

Type of work: Novel
Author: Wyndham Lewis (1886-1957)
Type of plot: Psychological realism
Time of plot: About 1910
Locale: Paris
First published: 1918

Tarr is a satirical novel of ideas that examines with psychological penetration a group of artists living in Paris before World War I. By turns grotesque, farcical, and tragic, the story reveals Lewis' bias against certain presumed defects of the German character, such as sentimentality and solemnity.

In *Tarr,* Wyndham Lewis drew heavily on his own experiences as a young Englishman trying to find out about Art and Life in Paris. The novel is often thought, and perhaps correctly, to be the story of Otto Kreisler, rather than of the title character. Kreisler, whose person and activities take up most of the book, is a more completely realized character than Tarr himself. Indeed, Lewis said later that it might have been more honest to entitle the book *Kreisler;* yet, he admitted, that his original intention was to explore the character of Tarr, who seems to serve as a pedantic mouthpiece for Lewis's own philosophy.

Essentially, Lewis' novel is a satire of *fin de siècle* decadence with Kreisler representing the romantic artist who explores all the sensations of life, living all the time on the bourgeois wealth of his father. Kreisler's antics and the unembarrassed display of his emotions are thrown into vivid contrast by Tarr's typical English reserve which is exposed as hypocritical at the end of the novel when sentimentally he takes pity on Bertha Lunken's condition. Kreisler romanticizes his poverty, his spontaneous loves, his defiance of convention as well as the comic duel, and even his pointless suicide. In reality, however, as Lewis reveals to us, his self-dramatization is childlike and arises from a moral shabbiness, a paucity of real feelings, and a corrupt aesthetic. Still his seeming opposite, Tarr, is no better off; for he has disengaged himself from life.

If Kreisler is mere fire, Tarr is mere ice; both are impotent. But Lewis does not dismiss either of them as inconsequential, for they represent two distinct cultural attitudes which he would have us believe were behind World War I. For Lewis such moral infancy can only lead to outrageous violence. *Tarr* is satire edged in black.

TARTARIN OF TARASCON

Type of work: Novel
Author: Alphonse Daudet (1840-1897)
Type of plot: Satiric romance
Time of plot: Nineteenth century
Locale: France and North Africa
First published: 1872

Daudet's satirical tale of the comic misadventures and occasional lucky triumphs of Tartarin the braggart looks backward to Cervantes and forward to the early Dickens. Yet the spirit of the romance, its special gaiety and fantasy, is typically French.

Tartarin of Tarascon is the first volume of what was to become a trilogy, but the two later volumes, *Tartarin on the Alps* (1885) and *Port Tarascon* (1890), have been found by critics to be inferior to the book which first made Tartarin a popular comic hero. Readers of *Sketches by Boz* and *The Pickwick Papers* who then come to *Tartarin of Tarascon* may easily see why Alphonse Daudet has been called a French Dickens. There is the same bubbling flow of high spirits in the writing, and the author clearly has an affection for the hero he is mocking in his burlesque. If one seeks, however, for a specific literary influence upon Daudet, it must be Cervantes, whose *Don Quixote* is repeatedly referred to in the story. Tartarin is part Sancho Panza, whom he resembles in physique, in his love of food and easy living, and in his practicality. He is kin to Don Quixote in his romantic dreaming, his love of reading books of adventure and heroism, and his inability to distinguish between reality and illusion. When Tartarin determines to hunt lions in the Atlas mountains, Daudet shows his two-sided hero in conflict. Sancho-Tartarin quarrels with Quixote-Tartarin, calling him "a cracked head, a visionary, imprudent, and thrice an idiot," but Quixote-Tartarin, who has told a friend, "I *am* going," is, like any romantic hero, a man of his word.

Most of *Tartarin of Tarascon* is narrated in a relaxed, playful tone with occasional remarks like "You are all witness, dear readers" or "On my word as a story-teller" to suggest an intention only to entertain and amuse. One bit of fantasy even mocks the writers of sentimental fiction when an exiled and bedraggled stagecoach in Algeria mournfully recalls for Tartarin the good old days of its youth and shining beauty in Tarascon. But near the end of the story several passages contain sharp satire upon the shabby French administration in colonial Algeria. Daudet's brief descriptions and comments may interest twentieth century readers who remember the long and bitter war which finally ended in Algeria's independence from France in 1959.

TARTUFFE

Type of work: Drama
Author: Molière (Jean Baptiste Poquelin, 1622-1673)
Type of plot: Comedy
Time of plot: Seventeenth century
Locale: Paris
First presented: 1664

When Tartuffe, or, the Hypocrite *was originally produced, Molière was attacked by critics for undermining the very basis of religion; instead, his comedy was meant to satirize false piety, not true devotion. The famous portrait of the hypocrite has been the ancestor of similar types, from Dickens' Mr. Pecksniff to Sinclair Lewis' Elmer Gantry.*

Tartuffe was first produced in 1664 but was immediately censured by fanatical religious groups who viewed the play as an attack on religion. Despite three petitions to the king, Molière was unable to have the ban on the play lifted until 1669. Were the attacks on the play valid? According to Molière and to generations of readers and viewers since the seventeenth century, they were not.

In the "Preface" to the 1669 edition of the play, Molière pointed out that he was not attacking religion, but took "every possible precaution to distinguish the hypocrite from the truly devout man." This is evident from Tartuffe's behavior throughout the play.

Tartuffe is not truly religious, but an extreme example of false piety. His hypocrisy (or "imposture," as the subtitle to the 1669 version of the play depicts him) is evident from his first appearance on stage when he asks his valet to hang up his hair shirt. His hypocrisy is further emphasized by his lusting after Elmire (Act III). Although Tartuffe's language is couched in religious terms, his earthly desires are plainly discernible. His hypocrisy is most clearly revealed at the end of the play when he betrays Orgon, exposing Orgon's political secrets, and utilizing Orgon's gifts to destroy the entire family.

Religious hypocrisy, however, is not the only source of comic criticism in the play. Lack of moderation in other areas of human behavior is also under attack. Both Orgon and his mother exhibit extreme behavior in their inability to see through Tartuffe's imposture. Their absurd devotion to Tartuffe is illustrated in two important scenes. The first (Act I) exposes Orgon's foolish devotion when he returns from a trip and is oblivious to Dorine's accounts of his wife's illness; his only concern is for the health and welfare of Tartuffe. When middle-aged Orgon, feeling jealous and resentful over the youth, passion, and high spirits of the other members of his family, establishes Tartuffe as the household's moral adviser, his admiration of that scoundrel reaches idolatrous proportions. Under Tartuffe's auspices, Orgon wildly distorts the spirit of Christianity to suit his own spiteful ends; as he so outrageously asserts to Cléante, "My mother, children, brother, and wife could die / And I'd not feel a single moment's pain." A comic reversal of this situation is presented in Act V. After Orgon's eyes have seen Tartuffe's hypocrisy (in a scene in which Tartuffe attempts to seduce Elmire), he attempts to open his mother's eyes, only to be countered by her persistent devotion to Tartuffe.

Against the extreme comic figures of Tartuffe, Orgon, and Mme. Pernelle, Molière opposes those who see through hypocrisy because they view the world through the eyes of reason. Dorine, Elmire, and, above all, Cléante represent Molière's examples of moderation triumphing over excess. It is Cléante who clearly points out in Act I the distinction between false religious posturing and truly devout religious people. He cautions Orgon to distinguish between "artifice and sincerity . . . appearance and reality . . . false and true." He offers examples of "gentle and humane" religious people, particularly those who refrain from censuring others. When Orgon finally sees through Tartuffe's false appearance and is ready to condemn all "godly men," Orgon again warns him to learn to distinguish between "genuinely good men" and scoundrels like Tartuffe.

Cléante's advice indicates that the seventeenth century zealots who attacked the play were in error. Molière is not condemning true religion, only false piety.

THE TEMPEST

Type of work: Drama
Author: William Shakespeare (1564-1616)
Type of plot: Romantic fantasy
Time of plot: Fifteenth century
Locale: An island in the sea
First presented: 1611

The Tempest, written toward the close of Shakespeare's career, is a work of romantic fantasy. With its moving theme of reconciliation, the play has been variously interpreted as allegory or as the author's personal reflection on life itself.

Earlier critics of *The Tempest* concerned themselves with meaning and attempted to establish symbolic representations for Prospero, Ariel, Caliban and Miranda, suggesting such qualities as imagination, fancy, brute nature innocence. Many considered the play in terms of its spectacle and music, comparing it to the masque or *commedia dell'arte.* A major group have read into Prospero's control and direction of all the characters, climaxed by the famous speech in which he gives up his magic wand, Shakespeare's own dramatic progress and final farewell to the stage.

Contemporary criticism seems to explore different levels of both action and meaning. Attention has been directed to various themes such as illusion-reality, freedom-slavery, revenge-forgiveness, time, and self-knowledge. Some Shakespearean scholars of the latter half of this century suggest the enchanted isle upon which the shipwreck occurs is a symbol of life itself: an enclosed arena wherein are enacted the passions, dreams, conflicts and self-discoveries of man. Such a wide-angled perspective satisfies both the casual reader who wishes to be entertained and the serious scholar who desires to examine different aspects of Shakespeare's art and philosophy.

This latter view is consonant with one of Shakespeare's major techniques in all his work: the microcosm-macrocosm analogy. This Elizabethan way of looking at things simply meant that the world of man mirrored the universe. In the major tragedies this correspondence is shown in the pattern of order-disorder, usually with man's violent acts (murder of Caesar, usurpation of the throne by Richard III, Claudius' murder of Hamlet's father, Macbeth's killing of Duncan) finding sympathetic disruption of order in the world of nature. Attendant upon such events are happenings such as unnatural earthquakes, appearance of strange beasts at midday, unaccountable storms, voices from the sky, witches, and other strange phenomena.

The idea that the world is but an extension of man's mind, and that the cosmic order in turn is reflected in man himself, gives validity to diverse interpretations of *The Tempest.* As a matter of fact, it encompasses many of them.

The initial storm or "tempest" invoked by Prospero and which wrecks the ship, finds analogy in Antonio's long-past usurpation of Prospero's dukedom and his setting Prospero and his small daughter, Miranda, adrift at sea in a storm in the hope they would perish.

Now, years later, the court party, including Alonso, Sebastian, Antonio, and Ferdinand, along with the drunken Stephano and Trinculo, are cast upon the island which will prove with its "meanderings," pitfalls, and enchantments, a place where everyone will go through a learning process and most will come to greater self-knowledge.

Illusions upon this island such as Ariel's disguises, the disappearing banquet, the line of glittering costumes deluding Stephano, Trinculo, and Caliban, find counterparts in the characters' illusions about themselves. Antonio has come to believe he is the rightful duke; Sebastian and Antonio, deluded by ambition, plan to kill Alonso and Gonzalo and make Sebastian tyrant of Naples. The drunken trio of court jester, butler, and Caliban falsely see themselves as future conquerors and rulers of the island. Ferdinand is tricked into believing his father is drowned and that Miranda is a goddess. Miranda, in turn, nurtured upon illusions by her father, knows little of human beings and their evil. Even Prospero must come to see he is not master of the universe, and that revenge is no answer after all. He must move to greater reality in which justice and mercy have more power.

It has been noted that the island is different things to different people. Here again is an illustration of the microcosm-macrocosm analogy. The characters of integrity see it as a beautiful place; for honest Gonzalo it is a possible Utopia. But Sebastian and Antonio, whose outlook is soured by their villainy, characterize the island's air as perfumed by a rotten swamp.

The sense of freedom or slavery each character feels is again conditioned by his view of the island and his own makeup as well as by Prospero's magic. The most lovely expressions of the island's beauty and enchantment come from Caliban, the half-human, who knew its offerings far better than any before his enslavement by Prospero.

Perhaps in few of his other plays has Shakespeare effected a closer relationship between the human and natural universe. Beauty and ugliness, good and evil, cruelty and gentleness are matched with the external environment. And fortunately, in *The Tempest,* everything works toward a positive reconciliation of the best in both man and nature. This harmony is expressed, for example, by the delightful pastoral masque Prospero stages for the young lovers, Ferdinand and Miranda. In this entertainment, reapers and nymphs join in dancing, indicating the union of natural and supernatural. The coming marriage of Ferdinand and Miranda also foreshadows such harmony, as well as do the general repentance and forgiveness among the major characters.

It may be true as Prospero states in Act V that upon the island "no man was his own," but he also confirms that understanding has come like a "swelling tide." And he promises calm seas for the homeward journey where presumably each man will take up the tasks and responsibilities of his station with improved perspective.

As Prospero renounces his magic, Ariel is freed to return to the elements, and Caliban, true child of nature, is left to regain harmony with his hopefully unspoiled world. Perhaps the satisfaction Shakespeare's audience feels results from the harmony between man and nature that illumines the close of the play.

Muriel B. Ingham

THE TEMPLE BEAU

Type of work: Drama
Author: Henry Fielding (1707-1754)
Type of plot: Comedy of manners
Time of plot: Eighteenth century
Locale: London
First presented: 1730

Very apparent in The Temple Beau, *a late, sprightly example of the comedy of manners, is Fielding's attitude that high life in the eighteenth century was mean and dull, and that the people who made up the highest circles were entirely without shame.*

The subjects of Fielding's burlesques and farces are quite often the contemporary political and literary scenes. His satire of the titled upper class is incidental to these themes. The same is true of his novels. But in *The Temple Beau,* Fielding is concerned with the superficiality of the contemporary English upper class. He takes the conventional view of the Restoration comedy of manners, that, as Lady Lucy Pedant says, it is an age "when 'tis as immodest to love before marriage, as 'tis unfashionable to love after it. . . ." But he is also concerned with the vices exemplified by the name of Lady Pedant's husband: Sir Avarice Pedant. The tragic themes of *The Revenger's Tragedy*, gold and women, are here treated comically, along with a third theme, pedantry.

It has long been disputed among critics as to whether Fielding's purpose as a writer of satire is primarily comic or moral. In *The Temple Beau,* the upper class is the object of Fielding's comic satire, but implicit in the comedy is the need for change. Fielding accepts the system of social stratification, where people are divided into low, middle, and upper classes with varying levels within each class; but he believes that the upper class has a responsibility to act as moral models. If he makes fun of them in *The Temple Beau* and his other plays and his novels, he means to show that they are falling far short of what they should be. As the prologue to *The Temple Beau* states, the author of the play wants to

> Convince that town, which boasts its better breeding,
> That riches - - - - - - are not all that you exceed in.

The rich not only fall short in virtue, they exceed in their vices.

THE TEMPTATION OF SAINT ANTHONY

Type of work: Novel
Author: Gustave Flaubert (1821-1880)
Type of plot: Historical romance
Time of plot: The fourth century
Locale: Egypt
First published: 1874

Flaubert's philosophical and historical reconstruction of the early Christian era in The Temptation of Saint Anthony *is less gorgeously detailed than that of antiquity in* Salammbô, *but is surely more earnest and personal, especially in the scenes that show the struggle for faith.*

Flaubert's writing was at its best when rooted in reality; his historical novels yielded too much to the romantic excesses which formed the other side of his creative personality. The composition of *The Temptation of Saint Anthony* provides an example of the tenacity in the pursuit of perfection which made Flaubert go back to working constantly on subjects without ever being satisfied with the results. He ultimately wrote four versions on the theme, which he originally intended to be the *Faust* of French literature. The final version was influenced by his own travels in Egypt, Palestine, and Turkey.

Flaubert was really a romantic who devoted his life to the elaboration of an impersonal, classical art. Whether his subject was romantic or one of modern life based on the doctrine of realism, his work was always constructed on microscopic research and observation. After this preparation, he subjected the novel he was writing to the exact formation of plot and the demands of an impersonal style. In the case of *The Temptation of Saint Anthony,* however, the weight of the erudition stifled the inner life of the novel, and the meticulous style at times approaches the precious.

An argument could be made that the book is not a novel at all, but a prose poem. It possesses brilliant images, individual scenes of splendor, and moments of power; but these do not add up to a fluid narrative. The book is strangely static, and the reader feels at times as if he is walking through a very elaborate waxworks museum. The mannered excesses of the book suggest a scenario for an opera, all spectacle, verbose emotion and grandiose postures. At the same time, *The Temptation of Saint Anthony* is amazingly modern, almost surreal in its bizarre shifting of scenes. Flaubert's technical experiments were revolutionary for the period when he was writing, but they were a dead end to his contemporaries. Fifty years later, they might have been better appreciated and more influential.

THE TENANT OF WILDFELL HALL

Type of work: Novel
Author: Anne Brontë (1820-1849)
Type of plot: Domestic romance
Time of plot: Early nineteenth century
Locale: England
First published: 1848

An epistolary novel of moderate psychological range, The Tenant of Wildfell Hall *is notable chiefly for the portrait of Arthur Huntingdon, the attractive but drunken profligate, who has been identified with Bramwell Brontë, brother of the writer.*

The Tenant of Wildfell Hall is really two narratives. One is that of Gilbert Markham, in two long letters to Mr. Halford; the other is that of Helen Huntingdon, in her journal. The stronger narrative is Helen's, which tells of her marriage to Arthur Huntingdon and her separation from him. The development and degeneration of the relationship between them can be followed step by step, and the reasons for Helen's early infatuation with Arthur and her subsequent contempt for him can be seen clearly. In Helen's relatively short narrative, there are four other characters—Arthur's three friends and his first mistress—each of whom plays a special role in breaking up the marriage of Arthur and Helen.

Gilbert's narrative opens the book. The first letter consists of one chapter; the second letter takes up the rest of the book, and quotes all of Helen's narrative. A mystery is developed before the opening of Helen's narrative, and her journal solves the mystery. Gilbert's narrative, like a frame-story, then continues, telling of his marriage to Helen, though in ambiguous terms. It is clear why Gilbert falls in love with the mysterious Helen, and how he first begins to defy his domineering mother; but it is not as clear how, or whether, he ever becomes mature enough to love the real Helen, as he had loved the mysterious tenant. The reader may reasonably ask whether Helen's second marriage is on any firmer ground than her first one.

The Tenant of Wildfell Hall is skillfully plotted, and has more than its share of well-defined characters. But its outstanding feature is its careful exposure of the functioning of a human relationship. It is a remarkable accomplishment, especially considering the fact that it was written before the advent of sophisticated psychological theory by an author of seemingly limited experience in the world.

TENDER IS THE NIGHT

Type of work: Novel
Author: F. Scott Fitzgerald (1896-1940)
Type of plot: Social criticism
Time of plot: The 1920's
Locale: Europe
First published: 1934

This important psychological novel is also a roman à clef *in which a number of characters have been identified with real people. Fitzgerald describes the disintegrating social world of mostly affluent Americans wandering from one diversion to another in Europe and the United States.*

In all his literary work, F. Scott Fitzgerald proves to be a retrospective oracle. He describes an age of individuals who came on the scene and burned themselves out even before they were able to conceptualize themselves. His first published novel, *This Side of Paradise* (1920) is autobiographical and describes the early "Jazz Age" with its vague values of money, beauty, and a distorted sense of social propriety. His masterpiece, *The Great Gatsby,* came in 1925, and *Tender Is the Night* (1934) fictionalizes the personal and social disintegration that followed the success which *The Great Gatsby* brought Fitzgerald.

In addition to the glamor, the excitement, the frenetic pursuit of the good life between two world wars described in *Tender Is the Night,* the novel also contains a masterful attempt at thematic telescoping. The character of Dick Diver functions in a triple capacity: he is, on the largest scale, a contemporary American equivalent of the tragic hero; also, he signifies the complex disintegration of the American during this precarious point in time; and, by the close of the novel, the reader's attention is ultimately focused on Diver as a fictional character.

In many ways, Diver's fall follows Aristotle's formula for classical tragedy: he is an isolated hero upon whom an entire community of individuals depends for necessary form to their lives; he has a tragic flaw, since he is told by a classmate, "That's going to be your trouble—judgment about yourself . . . ," that is, he lacks perspective and introspection; he is a representative individual in that he is a psychiatrist expected to understand human motivation; he is at the mercy of fate, since the precipitating element, Nicole's case, "drifted into his hands"; and, his fall is monumental, from an elevated position in life into failure and anonymity. But most significant of all, Diver has a true sense of his own tragic importance; he realizes that he is losing his grip on situations, and, even though he recognizes some of the possible consequences of his actions, he is not equipped psychologically to combat them.

However, Dick Diver is not the strictly tragic figure prescribed in *The Poetics.* Rather, he is at most the sort of tragic hero that America would allow in the 1920's, and it is in this capacity that Diver serves to describe the gradual disintegration of the American character. Dick is not simply symbolic of an American; his character is instead individualized to represent what an American with his exemplary vulnerabilities could become in a special set of circumstances. Diver and his companions create their own mystique to avoid the realities of a world thrown into, and later extracting itself from, war. Their frenetic rites and the aura in which the compatriots hide ultimately form the confusion that grows larger than Diver, unleashing itself and swallowing him. For, Diver and the American character at this time are incomplete; each is detrimentally eclectic and at the mercy of the props, such as music, money, and material possessions, upon which it depends for support. Incompleteness nourishes Diver's paternalistic assimilation of portions of the personalities that surround him and depend on him. But his need to be needed causes him to assimilate weaknesses more often than strengths; and the organic process is abortive. For the American character is a limited one, a possessive one, and there is a sense of something existing beyond Diver's intellectual and emotional reach that could have proved to be his salvation. Fitzgerald emphasizes the eclectic and incomplete nature of the American during this era by interweaving elements of the romantic, the realistic, and the didactic when describing actions and motivations of his characters. The result presents a severely realistic emotional conflict that sporadically explodes several characters, including Dick Diver, into psychological chaos.

Finally, Diver functions most specifically as the pivotal character of the plot itself. Given the demands of a novel of such scope, Fitzgerald relays Diver's decline quite convincingly. He succeeds by providing the reader subliminally with the correct formula for observing Diver's actions and their consequences. Within the first three chapters of the novel, the reader is taught, through Nicole's exemplary case, to appreciate the importance of psychological analysis and to isolate the "precipitating factor" in a character's development, and then to consider that factor's influence in subsequent actions. The reader is thereby equipped to transfer these premises to his observations of Diver. Throughout the duration of the novel the reader realizes that Dick Diver is driven by a need to be needed; and it is this aspect of his personality that leads him increasingly into circumstances that involve him directly, causing him almost voluntarily to allow his energy to be sapped from him.

Tender Is the Night is above all a psychological novel that is more successful than most novels of its type. The device upon which the success of the novel depends is Fitzgerald's handling of time. Here, time serves both a horizontal and a vertical purpose. Horizontally, time is chronological, for chronological observation is an advantage the reader has—that Diver does not have—throughout the duration of the novel (this fact was not so in earlier drafts of the novel). The reader knows that Diver grows older; knows that Rosemary matures and finds other interests; knows that Nicole eventually recovers from her illness. But these are circumstances of which Diver is ignorant. For him, time is merely a psychological abstraction; only major events determine whether or not one is in stasis. Yet time also functions vertically, making the notion of thematic telescoping possible. Diver is not cognizant of the passing of time until his plunge is in its advanced stages. So as Diver's gradual acknowledging of time and of the vast gap between his "heroic period" and his encroaching anonymity becomes increasingly important, one's awareness of Diver's thematic function passes from the purely tragic figure, through the import of the national character, and, toward the close of the novel, rests ultimately on the individual Dick Diver and his acceptance of his situation.

Bonnie Fraser

LA TESEIDE

Type of work: Poetry
Author: Giovanni Boccaccio (1313-1375)
Type of plot: Medieval romance
Time of plot: Ancient Greece
Locale: Athens
First transcribed: c. 1341

La Teseide, *a romance primarily modeled on Statius'* Thebaid, *though partly on* Vergil's Aeneid, *had a direct influence upon English literature, beginning with Chaucer's borrowings that appeared in "The Knight's Tale,"* Anelida and Arcite, The Parliament of Fowls, *and* Troilus and Criseyde.

Boccaccio's *La Teseida* (termed *The Book of Theseus* in its first English translation, 1974) furnishes the reader with the most characteristic and lavish features of medieval romance. Across the vast expanse of his twelve-book poem, Boccaccio sketches the brilliant pageantry of tournaments with all their color of pennons, armor, horse trappings and rich cloths; he gathers the greatest Greek warriors in battle; he understandingly tells the suffering of the two lovers who must for years endure an unrequited, unattainable passion; he glories in the glittering wealth of kings and palaces—in short, he sketches the noble life in richest display.

But *La Teseida* is more than spectacle. Drawing from Statius' *Thebaid* and Vergil's *Aeneid,* the poet creates a narrative of love and war at once plausible and highly readable. In Book I, line 3, he invokes both Venus, goddess of love, and Mars, god of war, to give strength to his hand and voice "to show your accomplishments of little worth and steeped in sorrow." Thus Boccaccio reveals his dual subject matter: love and war. Although this is indeed what his poem deals with, yet the psychological, mythological treatment allows the story of Palemone's and Arcita's love for Emilia to unfold on different levels, with Teseo, ideal knight and godlike ruler, uniting events and their meaning into an ordered reason which dominates passion.

Unlike many medieval romancers who delight in characteristic meandering of plot and subplot with unmotivated action, Boccaccio carefully foreshadows attitudes and events. His protagonists are believable. He achieves this by different means. Suddenly, in the midst of exaggerated episodes he injects realism. In Book II when Teseo reached Thebes and pitched camp, he "smelled the corruption in the air because there were corpses left unburied." In the middle of the deciding battle with one hundred knights fighting for each of the contending lovers, the poet allows Arcita to dry "the bloody sweat coursing down his face," and to take "what little breathing space he could."

Boccaccio also makes great use of rhetoric. Animal similes abound as he compares individual warriors to a Libyan lion, or a "furious and scaly wild boar," or the struggle between the two sides to that between the eagle and "serpent who seizes her newborn young." Occasionally he employs flower or sea imagery; he constantly reckons time of day and seasons astrologically as is customary with medieval writers, who saw man's points of time related to cosmic movement.

In his extensive glosses to each book, Boccaccio is a thorough mythographer, providing in great detail the stories of gods and goddesses, history of place-names, extensive lineage of all participants in the narrative, and a wealth of etymologies. These glosses at times develop into involved allegory, as when the poet explains the paintings on the temples of Venus and Mars.

Boccaccio's style is lucid and smooth-flowing, the work well structured in spite of its great length. Speeches alternate with battle scenes in evenly paced progression.

The *La Teseida* has been known as a rich source book for Chaucer, perhaps Shakespeare, and other seventeenth century writers. Now, in its first English translation, this colorful, finely crafted romance is available to a much greater audience.

TESS OF THE D'URBERVILLES

Type of work: Novel
Author: Thomas Hardy (1840-1928)
Type of plot: Philosophical realism
Time of plot: Late nineteenth century
Locale: England
First published: 1891

A powerful tragic novel that shows how crass circumstances influence the destinies of people, Tess of the D'Urbervilles *is also a moral indictment of the smug Victorian attitude toward sexual purity.*

English fiction assumed a new dimension in the hands of Thomas Hardy. From its beginnings it had been a middle-class genre; it was written for and about the bourgeois, with the working class and the aristocracy taking only minor roles. The British novelist explored the workings of society in the space between the upper-reaches of the gentry and the new urban shopkeepers. In the eighteenth century Daniel Defoe treated the rogue on his or her way to wealth; Henry Fielding was concerned with the manners of the gentry; and Samuel Richardson dramatized romantic, middle-class sentimentality. In the nineteenth century, Jane Austen's subject matter was the comedy of manners among a very closely knit segment of the rural gentry; the farm laboring classes were conspicuous by their absence. After Walter Scott and his historical romances, the great Victorian novelists—the Brontës, Thackeray, Dickens, Trollope, and George Eliot—were all concerned with the nuances of middle class feelings and morality, treating their themes either romantically or comically.

Although he certainly drew on the work and experience of his predecessors, Hardy opened and explored fresh areas: indeed, he was constantly hounded by critics and censors for his realistic treatment of sexuality and the problems of faith. After his last novel, *Jude the Obscure,* was attacked for its immorality, he was driven from the field. The final thirty years or so of his life were devoted entirely to poetry. Even more important than this new honesty and openness toward sex and religion, however, was Hardy's development of the tragic possibilities of the novel and his opening of it to the experience of the rural laborer and artisan. His rendering of nature, moreover, influenced by Greek thought and Darwin's *On the Origin of the Species,* radically departed from the nineteenth century view of nature as benevolent and purposeful. In retrospect, Hardy's novels, written between 1868 and 1895, have a unity of thought and feeling that challenges all the accepted truths of his time. He is part of and perhaps the most formidable spokesman for that group of artists—including the Rossettis, Swinburne, Wilde, Yeats, and Housman—which reacted against the materialism, pieties, and unexamined faith of the Victorian Age. As he said of the age in his poem, "The Darkling

Thrush": "The land's sharp features seemed to be / The Century's corpse outleant. . . ." And, finally, he can be viewed as not only the last Victorian, but also as the first modern who defined the themes which were to occupy such great successors as Joseph Conrad and D. H. Lawrence.

Tess of the D'Urbervilles ranks as one of Hardy's finest achievements, along with *Far from the Madding Crowd, The Return of the Native, The Mayor of Casterbridge,* and *Jude the Obscure.* Together with the last novel mentioned, it forms his most powerful indictment of Victorian notions of virtue and social justice. Its subtitle, "A Pure Woman Faithfully Presented," is itself a mockery of a moral sense that works in rigid categories. Mesmerized and seduced by Alec D'Urberville, the mother of a bastard child, the married mistress of Alec, a murderess who is eventually hanged, Tess is yet revealed as an innocent victim of nature, chance, and a social and religious system which denies human feeling. Her purity is not only a matter of ethics—for Hardy finds her without sin—but also one of soul. Tess maintains a kind of gentle attitude toward everyone, and even when she is treated with the grossest injustice, she responds with forgiveness. It is not until the conclusion of the novel, when she has been deprived once again of her beloved, Angel Clare (a love which the reader has great difficulty in accepting, since he lacks any recognizable human passion), that she is ultimately overcome by forces beyond her control and murders Alec. Like her sister in tragedy, Sophocles' Antigone, she is driven by a higher justice to assert herself. That she must make reparation according to a law that she cannot accept does not disturb her, and like Antigone's, her death is a triumph rather than a defeat.

It is precisely at this point that Hardy most effectively challenges Victorian metaphysics. In Tess we witness a woman disposed of by irrational and accidental forces. Such impulses which the Victorians tried to deny—not always easily to be sure—through a devotion to reason in matters of law, science, and religion, were anomalies that could not be admitted if their world view were to stand. To insist, moreover, as Tess does, that she is not to be judged by human law is a radical attack on a culture that rested uncertainly on a fragile social contract. To compound the enigma, Tess acquiesces in the judgment and gives her life—for society does not really take it—with a sense of peace and fulfillment.

Thus, Hardy exposed the primitive passions and laws of nature to his readers. He threw them back into a state which they believed, in their smugness over social and material progress, was safely behind them and their culture. Breaking past the manners of the drawing room and ignoring the conventions of the novel, he called up to the Victorian memory scenes of the most fundamental kind of human behavior. Not only did he call into question their idea of law but also their notion of human nature. Indeed, Hardy seems to suggest that no matter the success of politics in removing social abuses, there remains an element in man that cannot be legislated; that is of course his instinctual nature that drives him to demand justice for his being, no matter the consequences. For Victorian civilization to accept Tess, therefore, would be to admit its own myopia—which it was not yet prepared to do.

David L. Kubal

THADDEUS OF WARSAW

Type of work: Novel
Author: Jane Porter (1776-1850)
Type of plot: Historical romance
Time of plot: Late eighteenth century
Locale: Poland and England
First published: 1803

A romantic novel derived from certain political events, largely fictionized, from the troubled history of late eighteenth century Poland, Thaddeus of Warsaw *is marked by Porter's pity for the plight of the exile who must adapt himself to a different land and strange customs.*

Political refugees and their woes are a familiar literary subject, and Poland has had more than its share of exiles to contribute to fiction dealing with them. Eight years before writing *Thaddeus of Warsaw,* Jane Porter saw Polish refugees walking through London's Saint James Park. Struck by their tragic appearance, she met many of them and studied Polish history, and after having lived among the models of her tale, she sought to portray what she felt every Christian should know. She wrote her novel in admiration of King John Sobieski of Poland (1624-1696), and created noble characters who were impervious to narrow, personal ambitions: "characters that prosperity could not inflate nor disappointment depress." She later added that she had dipped her pen into their tears.

Poland's fight against combined aggression from Europe's three most powerful states is one theme of the novel. Another concerns Poland's effort to maintain her own laws and what Jane Porter claimed was a way of life so unique as to be previously unknown in world history, one representing a domestic vitality and sense of integral being comparable to Biblical Israel. She describes such places as the University of Vilna and the other provincial colleges built in Old Poland, and relates how King John Sobieski had torn down peasant hovels and built decent homes instead.

Jane Porter felt that what had flattered Alexander the Great into a madman and Julius Caesar into a usurper, had left her Christian heroes, the Sobieskis, intact in virtue. When ensconced at the pinnacle of Polish power, the Sobieskis had not been puffed with pride, and when their souls were later pierced by sorrow and defeat, they never murmured. Thaddeus Sobieski is an authentically drawn nobleman of his time, motivated by the same *noblesse oblige* as had been his grandfather. Such noblemen were once a cultural factor in Europe, but they have almost vanished from the pages of modern literature, wherein a more common figure is the degenerate nobleman and antihero.

In her 1843 revision of the work, referring to her fictional creation, Thaddeus, and his models in real life, Jane Porter wrote that virtue's sunbeam had never dimmed its full ray in their chivalric hearts. Honor is a moving force in Jane Porter's story of eighteenth century Poland; her novel's motto is "Fealty to honor."

THERE ARE CRIMES AND CRIMES

Type of work: Drama
Author: August Strindberg (1849-1912)
Type of plot: Symbolic realism
Time of plot: Late nineteenth century
Locale: Paris
First presented: 1899

The theme of Strindberg's complex play, partly naturalistic and partly symbolic or expressionistic, is that there are crimes punishable by law, but there are others—undetected by human eyes—that are punished by an inner psychological guilt-mechanism or externally by a higher power.

There Are Crimes and Crimes stands on a thin line between the naturalism of August Strindberg's early works and the expressionism of his later plays. Although it lacks either the dramatic intensity and psychological complexity of the former or the poetic imagination and intellectual density of the latter, *There Are Crimes and Crimes* shares many of the qualities of both in a most provocative manner.

The realistic side of the play resembles a typical French sexual intrigue and crime melodrama. In part stimulated by his Paris sojourn of a few years earlier, Strindberg called *There Are Crimes and Crimes* his "boulevard play" and loosely modeled it on a contemporary potboiler, Octave Feuillet's *Dalila* (1850). It contains all of the standard type characters: the honest artist (Maurice), the devoted woman (Jeanne), the *femme fatale* (Henriette), the faithful friend (Adolphe), the common-sense matron (Madame Catherine), and the good priest (The Abbé). The plot is also a melodramatic cliché: the innocent is lured away from his devoted lady by a designing woman; she involves him in a crime; he is charged, harassed, and finally exonerated; penitent, he returns to his first love for a happy reunion.

Thus, as an example of realism, *There Are Crimes and Crimes* is a very thin, trite drama; but Strindberg never intended it to be judged by that criterion. What gives the play its unique interest is not its realism as such, but the way Strindberg has used a realistic context to present what is essentially a symbolic action.

When Maurice and Henriette talk about their "evil dreams" near the end of the first act, they articulate the mood and atmosphere of the play: it is like a dream which turns into a nightmare where one's half-stated longings and subconscious desires become realities, with the dreamer instantly subjected to the practical consequences of his fantasies. The plot moves with the speed and fluidity of a dream. One moment Maurice vows fidelity to Jeanne, the next he is enamored of Henriette; one instant Adolphe loves Henriette, the next he relinquishes her to Maurice with little more than a shrug; Maurice expresses his intense devotion for his daughter, seconds later he wishes her dead. In a purely realistic drama such behavioral gyrations would be shallow and contrived, perhaps absurd, but in *There Are Crimes and Crimes* they simply reinforce the dreamlike atmosphere.

Marion's death is the climax of the action, and in keeping with the fantasy mood of the play, it happens offstage. At this point Strindberg's belief that "psychic crime" is real and demands concrete punishment takes over. Maurice and Henriette realize that they are both "unpunished criminals" and are oppressed by their sense of guilt. Immediately, their crime, in Henriette's words, sets them "outside, on the other side of life and society and my fellow beings." This isolation leads directly to paranoia; they suspect everyone and everything in their environment—strangers, friends, and especially each other.

And, in the nightmare atmosphere of the play, real punishment instantly intensifies these psychological torments. Maurice is charged with murder, his play is closed, and his fortune negated. Henriette is verbally abused, branded a prostitute, and harassed by the police. Their "crowd" turns them out in disgrace.

And yet, in spite of these punishments, Strindberg's final attitude toward guilt and responsibility remains ambiguous. Even while Maurice expresses his contrition, he defends himself: "But at the same time I am guiltless. What has tied this net out of which I can never escape? Guilty and guiltless, guiltless and guilty." Everyone has committed hidden crimes, Strindberg concludes, with the implication that, if everyone is guilty, then no one is guilty. Maurice is ultimately cleared, his play is rescheduled, his fortune returned, his reputation restored, and his virtuous mistress, Jeanne, reconciled. Even his final desire to do penance and expiate his sin via "confession" to the priest is ambivalent; he will go to church with the Abbé that night, but the next day he returns to the theater.

Strindberg labeled *There Are Crimes and Crimes* a "comedy," and given its relative lightness of touch and tone, coupled with its happy ending, the label is accurate. But it is certainly a "dark comedy" at best. It is this very combination of the comic and the nightmarish that gives the play its special appeal.

THÉRÈSE

Type of work: Novel
Author: François Mauriac (1885-1970)
Type of plot: Psychological realism
Time of plot: Twentieth century
Locale: France
First published: 1927

Thérèse, a series of four stories tied together by the mind of the major character rather than by incident, is a powerful and dramatic revelation of the human condition and its relation to sin, as seen through the eyes of one of the most influential of Catholic writers.

François Mauriac was born in Bordeaux in 1885 of an upper bourgeois Catholic family. He was raised by his widowed mother, an austere and devout woman of Jansenist tendencies. He attended Catholic schools and later the University of Bordeaux. His provincial bourgeois background greatly influenced the choice of settings, characters, and some themes in his novels, but he turns his most acute criticisms against the hypocrisy, the false piety, and conventional opinions of his social class. This critical attitude is evidenced in his always liberal political stands; for example, his support of the Loyalists in the Spanish Civil War and his active participation in the struggle against the Nazis in World War II.

Although Mauriac did in one period rebel against the religious practices of his family and ultimately rejected Jansenism, he never rejected the Catholic faith. Such is the primacy that he gives to his religious beliefs that he has asked to be thought of as a Catholic who writes novels, rather than a Catholic novelist. To understand Mauriac's writings one must always have the intensity of his religious feeling in mind.

His literary career was launched in 1909 when he submitted his first volume of poems, "Les Mains Jointes," to Maurice Barrès who was so impressed that he predicted for the young Mauriac a glorious future. It was, however, in the writing of novels that Mauriac's talents flourished. His first novels already dealt with those themes that would preoccupy him throughout his life: the conflict of the flesh versus the spirit, sin versus grace, godliness versus godlessness. In addition to his many novels, Mauriac also wrote philosophical essays, a few biographies, and some plays. In 1952, he received the Nobel Prize for literature. He died in 1970 at the age of eighty-five.

Most of Mauriac's novels take place in Bordeaux and its surrounding countryside, with Paris appearing only incidentally. The estate of his grandmother, for instance, becomes the home of Thérèse Desqueyroux, in the village he names Argelouse. Beyond the very important fact that Mauriac was deeply attached to his native region, there is another reason why the pastoral setting is featured so prominently in his novels. For Mauriac the contrast between the physical world and the world of the spirit is more intense in the country, where nature bombards people with sensual stimuli that draw them into a preoccupation with physical things, with pleasures of the eye and ear, and ultimately with pleasures of the flesh. Thus the temptation to succumb to the allure of physical things is much greater. In *Thérèse,* the descriptions of natural scenes are suffused with an almost erotic atmosphere.

Throughout the novel, Thérèse is strongly identified with elemental things. She thrives on the odors, colors, and shapes of nature. She yearns, in fact, to become one with nature. She says at one point that she has the pine trees in her blood. During her confrontation with Bernard she wants to ask him to let her disappear into the night, into the forest; she is not afraid of the trees, they know her, they know each other. The illusory character of this union with nature is exposed a few paragraphs later, when Bernard tells Thérèse that she will be confined in Argelouse for the rest of her life. Suddenly the beloved pine trees become the bars of Thérèse's prison. For Mauriac, man's tragedy is that while he is *of* this world, he can never be really united *with* it. It is no coincidence that the key generic symbols used by Mauriac are earth, fire, and water. Whatever their immediate significance might be, and they are used in a variety of ways, the underlying sense is this dichotomy between man and nature.

All the characters in *Thérèse,* as in most of Mauriac's novels, are identifiable types from the social milieu of traditional provincial life. Bernard Desqueyroux, Madame de la Trave, Monsier Larroque, Anne de la Trave, Aunt Clara, are all representative of the various shades of bourgeois aspirations, ideals, opinions, and standards. The servants also have the values of their bosses. When his use of friends and acquaintances as characters was criticized, Mauriac would retort that it is impossible to create something that does not already exist.

As a young man, Mauriac witnessed the trial of a woman accused of poisoning her husband. The image of that woman, "pale and biting her lip" (as Mauriac describes Thérèse in the prologue), was the source of inspiration for the novel. All the rest is, of course, Mauriac's invention. The real woman's motivation for murder was her desire to be with another man; Thérèse's motive is not nearly so simple. The probing analysis of motivation in the novel comes, according to Mauriac, from the uncovering of the potential for evil found in his own nature. He could say, as Flaubert did of Madame Bovary, "Thérèse Desqueyroux, c'est moi."

Influenced like most other writers of the twentieth century by Freud's incursions into the unconscious processes of humanity, Mauriac's great contribution to French letters is the integration of these psychological insights with the teachings of Christianity. As a novelist writing after Proust's great probing of the inner life, Mauriac felt that it was his duty to give these investigations a dimension lacking in Proust's works, in other words, as Michael Moloney put it, to "integrate grace into these new territories." Whether Mauriac gives new depths to the naturalistic novel by imbuing it with moral values and in turn adds a scientific basis to his religious beliefs, or whether this is in fact a contradiction in terms, is a question still being debated by critics.

Thérèse is the study of a tormented woman's soul. Endowed with great emotional depth and intellectual curiosity, the heroine is from the beginning set apart from others. For example, her great affection for Anne de la Trave is tempered by Thérèse's awareness of the incongruities between them. Anne's simplicity and naïveté form a contrast to Thérèse's intelligence and subtle sensitivity. Thérèse feels superior to Anne, but this superiority is part of the reason for her alienation, and at times she almost seems to regret it.

Thérèse's marriage represents an unconscious attempt by the heroine to overcome her differentness. To be sure the marriage is pre-arranged on the basis of all the proper bourgeois concerns: status, wealth, family name. Without ever questioning the marriage or examining her own feelings, she behaves according to what is expected of her and plays the role of the enamoured fiancée. In retrospect, however, she realizes that she married Bernard out of a desperate hope that he would save her from a vague danger that haunts her. Although this danger is never named, it is in fact alienation itself, which Thérèse had thought would be assuaged in marriage.

During her engagement, she feels for the first time in her life that she belongs, that she is integrated into her milieu, that she fits in. She hopes that by doing what all other girls do, she will become more like them. As it turns out, however, the marriage accomplishes the opposite of what she had hoped; her alienation is intensified to an unbearable degree. The marriage sets in motion a chain of events which will bring about her final downfall.

As Azévédo points out in one of his conversations with Thérèse, the penalty for differentness in her society is annihilation. One either behaves as does everyone else, or one is destroyed. As an apparent example of this rule, the traces of Thérèse's grandmother, Julie Bellade, have been totally obliterated by the family in reaction to an undisclosed scandal.

There is an implication that Thérèse may be cursed by this past. This theme —the possibility of inherited evil—recurs throughout the novel. Thérèse herself is preoccupied with the legacy of shame she will bequeath to her daughter. Mauriac's concern with the inheritance of evil can be interpreted as a hold-over from his Jansenist beliefs which emphasize predestination. Thérèse can never determine at which point her crime had its inception; it was always there. The narrator augments this impression; for example, he describes Thérèse's peace at the time of her engagement as the temporary "quietness of the serpent in her bosom."

Thérèse's differentness is not in itself sinful, but is apparently what causes her to sin. Mauriac sympathizes with her refusal to conform to the hypocrisy and mediocrity around her, but as a Christian, he can only denounce the final turn her refusal takes.

If Thérèse has a basic flaw, it is her lack of self-awareness. She never consciously decides to murder Bernard; circumstances suggest it, she slips into it. The narrator points out that Thérèse never thought anything out, never premeditated anything in her entire life. She has no positive goals, only a retrospective awareness of what she sought to escape from. She never knew what she wanted, only what she did not want. The crime with which she is charged seems totally alien to her. She cannot satisfactorily explain, to herself or Bernard, why she did it.

Once freed from her marriage she attempts to give meaning to her life by engaging in a series of love affairs. That she fails should not be surprising in view of Mauriac's concept of human love, that it is destined to failure, being physical and therefore prey to time, corruption, decay. The only way to transcend one's mortality and finitude is through union with God.

Thérèse herself is dimly aware that human love is not the thing upon which to base one's hope. In the farewell scene at the Café de la Paix, she considers for a moment going back to Argelouse, there to embark on the only meaningful quest, the search for God. A few moments later, however, she reaffirms her intention to look for fulfillment among men.

Thérèse's lack of awareness is compounded by, if not generated by, intense self-involvement and self-indulgence. Anne's pain never evokes any sympathy, only self-pity. Thérèse is indignant that Anne, unlike herself, has been given the joy of knowing love. She always absolves herself of any responsibility in shaping her own destiny. To be sure, this may be a flaw in Mauriac, not Thérèse; Sartre feels that Thérèse is doomed beforehand by a flaw in her character on the one hand, and by a divine malediction on the other. Many other critics have denounced what they consider the lack of free will in Mauriac's characters. The line separating free will from predestination is at best nebulous in Mauriac's vision of human behavior.

Whether or not the novel is flawed by Mauriac's predispositions, it is unquestionably a profound, moving study of a woman lost in the contradictions between her own psychology and the realities of her society.

Vera Lucia de Araujo Haugse

THE THESMOPHORIAZUSAE

Type of work: Drama
Author: Aristophanes (c. 448-c. 385 B.C.)
Type of plot: Satiric comedy
Time of plot: Fifth Century B.C.
Locale: Athens
First presented: 411 B.C.

Targets for Aristophanes' satire in this lively, witty comedy are twofold: the affectations of Euripides—portrayed as a misogynist—and the loose morals of the women of Athens. The Thesmophoria referred to in the title was a fertility festival, celebrated only by women, at which the seed corn was mixed with the putrid remains of dead pigs.

The Thesmophoriazusae, or "Women at the Festival of Demeter," is one of Aristophanes' liveliest extant comedies, full of ribaldry, burlesque, parody, and farce. The play is, in part, a lusty battle of the sexes where both sides suffer comic injuries. In art, if not in life, a writer can have his cake and eat it too.

The tragedian Euripides was a prime laughingstock for Aristophanes. He also appears as a ludicrous figure in *The Acharnians* and *The Frogs,* and in several other comedies he is the butt of various gibes. Aristophanes disliked Euripides' pessimism and pretentiousness, his wretched heroes and vixenish heroines, his encouragement of atheism, and his debasement of the tragic theater. The comic playwright was conservative in artistic matters as well as politics, and his distaste for Euripides merely gave a sharper edge to his satire and provided a basis for some of his funniest fantasies.

The Thesmophoria was a feminine fertility festival. But in this play the celebration becomes a trial, in which Euripides is accused of slandering women and turning their husbands against them. The idea is not amusing in itself, but Aristophanes uses it to erect a wildly bizarre series of situations that are highly comic.

And no matter how improbable the circumstances, they always have a barbed point. Thus Aristophanes mocks the all-male Athenian assembly through the orations and gestures of the women at the festival, or makes a comment on female drunkenness when Euripides' father-in-law tries to save himself by snatching up a baby and finds that it is really a wineskin. In the best scene of all the father-in-law must get Euripides to rescue him by acting out roles from his tragedies, which pokes fun at Euripides' plays and his egomania as well. After seeing *The Thesmophoriazusae* it would be hard to watch a Euripidean drama with a straight face. This, of course, was exactly what Aristophanes intended.

THE THIN MAN

Type of work: Novel
Author: Dashiell Hammett (1894- 1961)
Type of plot: Mystery romance
Time of plot: 1930's
Locale: New York
First published: 1934

Hammett's popular detective romance presents a sharp picture of the fashionable yet sleazy New York society set at the end of the prohibition era. Witty and sophisticated, the novel features a husband-and-wife team who add a dash of sexual spice to the usual ingredients served up in mysteries of this kind: the astute detectives, the somewhat obtuse and distrustful police, the questioning companion, the dropping of clues, and the final explanation by the master sleuths.

The Thin Man was the last and most popular of Hammett's novels. In Nick and Nora Charles he created probably the most distinctive detective couple in the entire genre. Not only did the book do very well commercially, but it also spawned a radio program, television series, and an extremely successful sequence of films with William Powell and Myrna Loy.

Reasons for the popularity of the novel and its offshoots are not hard to find. It is the most briskly paced of Hammett's books, with an intricate plot that is ingenious and deceptive, although logical and believable. The action takes place among the denizens of New York café society during the Prohibition era, and Hammett portrays this frenzied, colorful world of money, corruption, sex, booze, and violence with accuracy and energy.

In addition, his characters are unusually vivid—the most memorable being, of course, Nick and Nora Charles. They give the novel qualities seen only occasionally in Hammett's earlier works: verbal wit and situational humor. As an ex-detective of obvious skill and experience, Nick is adroit enough in dealing with crime solving, but he is no aggressive, hard-boiled Continental Op, Sam Spade, or Ned Beaumont. He has retired from the business to manage Nora's not inconsiderable lumber interests, and, at least until his curiosity is aroused, has no desire to get back to his former occupation. Nick reluctantly becomes involved because Nora coaxes and dares him. Nick is a witty, cocky, charming man who would rather party than fight. Nora is equally fun-loving. The mystery is, to her, an exciting game—until it gets dangerous. The best scenes in the novel are not those of action and violence, as in previous books, but those featuring witty banter and sexual byplay between Nick and Nora. Nick sums up this attitude at the end of the novel: "Let's stick around for a while. This excitement has put us behind in our drinking."

Yet, for all of its ingenuity and charm, *The Thin Man* is one of Hammett's weakest novels and shows clear decline in his powers. The picture of New

York in the 1920's is realistic and vivid, but superficial and cliché-ridden. The plot is clever and facile, but has no implications beyond that of an interesting puzzle. The character of Nick Charles, while witty and charming, is relatively shallow and frivolous—and somewhat questionable, morally. He is content to live off of Nora's money, indulge her whims, and drift from party to party and city to city. The intense personal morality of the earlier works gives way to a kind of lazy, benevolent hedonism in which nothing is more important than a 3 A.M. whiskey-and-soda. In short, the vital ethical and intellectual center seems replaced by slick, entertaining superficiality. In retrospect, it is not surprising that *The Thin Man* was Dashiell Hammett's last novel.

THE THIRTY-NINE STEPS

Type of work: Novel
Author: John Buchan (1875-1940)
Type of plot: Adventure romance
Time of plot: 1914
Locale: England and Scotland
First published: 1915

A well-crafted spy thriller, The Thirty-Nine Steps *created a formula for romances of intrigue, particularly involving an unadventurous hero galvanized by events into heroic action, that influenced Graham Greene and other significant twentieth century writers of espionage fiction.*

The Thirty-Nine Steps is generally recognized as the first authentic "Thriller." Although elements of the form are evident in earlier works—adventure tales, chase-and-capture narratives, detective stories, mysteries, Gothics—it was John Buchan who established the patterns that became basic to a genre which has, since *The Thirty-Nine Steps,* developed and flourished in the twentieth century. In an essay on Buchan, novelist Graham Greene singled out the first ingredient in his formula for the "shocker" (Buchan's own term)—a formula that Greene himself was to use with considerable success in his own intrigue novels: "John Buchan was the first to realize the enormous dramatic value of adventure in familiar surroundings happening to unadventurous men."

Buchan once stated that his own object was to write "romance where the ingredients defy the probabilities, and march just inside the borders of the possible," and *The Thirty-Nine Steps* follows that dictum quite well. The hero, Richard Hannay, is believable, and the settings are vivid and realistic, but the situations do "march" very close to the impossible.

Although not a deep characterization, Richard Hannay is colorful and convincing. He is bright, cultured, eager, and resourceful. His boredom and curiosity account for his willingness to participate in an intrigue. Once involved, his patriotism and optimism explain his willingness to commit himself totally to the cause and to believe steadfastly in final victory. And his experience as a mining engineer on the African veldt realistically accounts for his endurance and adroitness in evading capture as well as his skill in exploding his way out of danger.

The settings, too, are scrupulously accurate. Buchan used locations he knew personally and many of the sites, including the real "thirty-nine steps," were important to him. Not only is Hannay's escape route geographically possible, but, more importantly, Buchan creates a realistic atmosphere that adds considerable immediacy to the adventure.

But if the characters and settings in *The Thirty-Nine Steps* are realistic, the plot treads a thin line between the possible and the fantastic. The essence of the Thriller is the chase. The hero may or may not begin as the hunter, but he soon becomes the hunted, frequently both by the established authorities and the villains. Hannay is chased almost from the beginning, and in spite of several "close calls," avoids capture by utilizing several of the devices characteristic of the genre: disguise (a milkman, a political speaker, a rural "roadman"), physical concealment, and plain good luck (one does not look too closely at "coincidence" in the Thriller).

In *The Thirty-Nine Steps* Buchan also introduces the false rescue scene that is central to many intrigue novels: when the hero has apparently reached a sanctuary and is safe from his pursuers, he is suddenly thrust into his most dangerous situation—which leads to his most impressive escape. Hannay is rescued from the police by a kindly "Bald Archaeologist" who turns out to be his arch enemy. To get out of this perilous predicament, Hannay must demonstrate the most extreme physical courage and mental agility—which, of course, he does.

In Buchan's "shockers," the hero usually clears himself with the authorities and together they defeat the conspiracy. Other Thriller writers leave all of the responsibility up to their protagonist, but either way it is up to the hero to direct the villain's destruction. Hannay does so by finally deciphering Scudder's coded notebook (another common Thriller gimmick) and exposing the criminals personally. Thus, the central motif of the Thriller is that of the isolated individual who is, either by choice or by circumstance, outside of the established system, pitted against an implacable and immensely powerful criminal. Even civilization itself may be at stake.

Written during the first months of World War I, *The Thirty-Nine Steps* reflects a simpler, more logical world. The changes that have developed in the genre since Buchan—whether in "superman" intrigues like Ian Fleming's James Bond series or in the grimy realism of books produced by writers such as Eric Ambler and John LeCarre—have been the result of a more complex and ambiguous attitude toward the world and are not alterations in the basic formulas first established by John Buchan in *The Thirty-Nine Steps*.

THIS ABOVE ALL

Type of work: Novel
Author: Eric Knight (1897-1943)
Type of plot: Sentimental romance
Time of plot: Summer, 1940
Locale: England
First published: 1941

A wartime romance, This Above All *is a poignant story of emotional conflict between a well-bred girl who knew and loved the England of hunting, cricket, and afternoon tea, and a serviceman—survivor of the beaches of Dunkirk—who knew and hated the England of slums, mines, starvation, and disease.*

The title of *This Above All* is taken from Polonius' advice to Laertes: "This above all: to thine own self be true. . . ." This theme runs through the novel, and is the fundamental lesson which the principle characters must learn. The characters of *This Above All* and their problems are intended to represent the people and tribulations in any period of peril. The author made a conscious effort to achieve a universality with his picture of wartime England. The protagonist, Clive Briggs, doubts whether England is worth fighting for, but beneath his bitterness a deep loyalty remains firm. Eric Knight generally avoided sentimentality in his treatment of both love and war; he understood the dangers of romanticizing heroism and patriotism. The author questioned many assumptions of contemporary British life, but he always returned to a deeply rooted belief in the British people. *This Above All* is not a great novel, but it presents a vivid panorama of a violent and traumatic moment in British history.

The descriptions of the cities and countryside are well done, and the scenes of bombing raids are particularly effective. The dialogue is realistic, but too discursive. The book would have profited and been better art if the conversations had been condensed; dialogue in a novel should *seem* real, but cannot *be* authentic without risking boredom. Knight's greatest triumph is with his secondary characters, who seem to possess a vitality which escapes the principal characters. Old Hamish and Gertie, the elderly dancer who has lost her leg, are touching in their scenes together, and suggest a quality for endurance against all odds which is one of the great attributes of the British people.

Each person in the world, Clive insists, encompasses all the rest of the world within himself. People should admit, he tells Prue, that they are cowards as well as heroes, that they can be cold and yet friendly, moral and immoral, religious and indifferent to religion. The author represents all levels of society in this novel, and illustrates how peoples' fundamental natures are laid bare in time of crisis. Individuals, he seems to be saying, sometimes have more in common than they realize. If they are true to themselves, they cannot help but be true to one another.

THE THREE BLACK PENNYS

Type of work: Novel
Author: Joseph Hergesheimer (1880-1954)
Type of plot: Period chronicle
Time of plot: c. 1750-1910
Locale: Pennsylvania
First published: 1917

The Three Black Pennys, *a family chronicle, is also a selective history of American culture, the first of the Pennys representing the beginning of an enterprising culture, the second representing the essential crudeness of the early nineteenth century, and the last representing the effete qualities of a Victorian generation which passed away without ever understanding the modern society supplanting it.*

Hergesheimer's third novel, *The Three Black Pennys* was published two years after D. H. Lawrence's *The Rainbow.* Lawrence's novel, suppressed in England, was declared obscene by the Bow Street Magistrate, who ordered police to seize copies at the booksellers and at the press. Hergesheimer's novel, on the other hand, was widely popular; together with *Java Head* (1919) it established for the author a major reputation during the early 1920's. Apart from their different publication histories, the novels in many ways are similar. Both treat the theme of mating—successful or unsuccessful—of three generations of a family, the Brangwens for Lawrence and the Pennys for Hergesheimer; both examine, almost as a mystique, a special quality of "blood" that distinguishes members of the family; both begin with a marriage involving a "mixed" blood line from a Polish widow—Lydia Lensky in *The Rainbow* and Ludowika Winscombe in *The Three Black Pennys*—and show its effects upon the indigenous English or Welsh-American stock of the males of the family; both attempt, through symbolism concerning time, place, and character, to record the history of culture for their respective countries; both show, again through symbol and story, the diminishing vitality of the original family stock, from Ursula's failure in love (she marries in *Women in Love*) to the last Howat Penny's feeble bachelorhood that terminates his line; finally, both novels deal with the larger issues of vitality and degeneration, progress and decay.

Yet the novels, despite their remarkable similarities in theme, are markedly different in their effects. Lawrence's symbols, whether used on a conscious or subconscious Freudian-Jungian level, are worked integrally into the structure of his book; Hergesheimer's symbols—particularly those concerning the relationship between the men and the iron—are all quite obvious. They add substance to the narrative, but do not provide additional levels of significance, nor do they turn the story into myth. Furthermore, Lawrence's concept of "blood consciousness," both a psychological and moral argument, is carefully elaborated in the lives of the Brangwens; Hergesheimer's treatment of the "black" strain (that is, the Welsh ancestry) in the Penny family's blood-inheritance is superficial, a mere plot device without a psychological or moral frame of reference. Whether the "black" Welsh blood represents a behavioral atavism or is an odd coincidence of personality, its appearance over several generations is never fully explained. Finally, Lawrence's novel treats the partial or complete failures in sexuality as symbols for the disintegration of modern culture; Hergesheimer, however, treats the failures as isolated examples, without moving from the specific instance to the general malaise of American culture. Thus Lawrence's novel is clearly in the dominant tradition of modern psychological fiction. Hergesheimer's is a period piece, well crafted and entertaining, but not an innovative work of literature.

Nevertheless, critics in 1917 praised *The Three Black Pennys* for the author's accurate research into the history of the nation, for his mastery of prose style, and for his ability to create vigorous characters. As a chronicle, the novel contrasts with the popular sentimental romances of the time. In the reconstruction of three periods in America's past, the late Colonial period (concerning the first Howat Penny), the mid-nineteenth century (Jasper Penny), and the turn of the nineteenth century (the last Howat Penny), Hergesheimer is a realist with a scrupulous eye for details. Dividing the novel into "The Furnace," "The Forge," and "The Metal," the author shows how the lives of the "black" Pennys and their contemporaries relate to the growth of industrial America.

Before the Revolutionary War Gilbert Penny establishes in Pennsylvania the Myrtle Forge, a product of his own energy, persistence, and optimism. He and his rebellious son Howat are men of determination; their vision of America is one of struggle leading to power. Three generations later, Jasper Penny, Howat's great-grandson, inherits a mighty industrial complex built around the family's original forge. Like his ancestors, Jasper is concerned with power. A business magnate, he is accustomed to getting his way. But his own impetuosity nearly destroys his happiness. Entangled romantically with Essie Scofield, a worthless woman whom he had seduced and made pregnant while he was still a young man, he cannot in his mature years convince his true love, the idealistic Susan Brundon, to marry him. She insists that they wait until Essie's death. The child born of their middle age comes to represent the languishing vitality of the Penny family. By the time of the last "black" Penny, the effete second Howat, the family's failure to produce an heir corresponds with its decline from a position of industrial power. The foundry is silent, and Howat, merely the caretaker of the past, has memories of his energetic forebears to remind him of his own impotence.

To re-create a sense of the past, Hergesheimer unobtrusively works his research into the Penny chronicle. Without bogging down in the recital of historical facts, he allows the story to carry the reader forward. As a masterful stylist, he evokes setting with a few selective phrases, rather than a profusion of details. Compared to regional realists like his contemporaries Ellen Glasgow or Willa Cather, rarely is he able to describe a setting so fully that it comes alive in all its parts. Even the description of the Myrtle Forge lacks a sense of immediacy. However, Hergesheimer does create an impressionistic feeling for the scene—not from the close observation of particulars but the careful choice of meaningful details which linger in the memory.

To be sure, Hergesheimer's command of style is more impressive than his characterizations. Although his early critics admired the first two romantic Pennys, they appear, from a modern standpoint, deficient in psychological complexity. The first Howat Penny is described, at the beginning, as reclusive and tactless to the point of surliness—a kind of American Heathcliff mysteriously suffering from ambiguous passions. When he falls in love with Ludowika, he changes at once from a sullen misanthrope to an ardent, almost demonic lover. Jasper, also driven by contradictory passions, is the philandering cad with Essie, the practical-minded and affectionate father with Eunice, and the gentle, diffident lover of Susan. The greatest problem in psychology, however, is the last Howat, the American Victorian. If the strain of "black" Welsh blood is said to distinguish those Pennys "impatient of assuaging relationships and beliefs," how can the feeble aesthete belong to the same strain as the impetuous first Howat or the ruthless tycoon Jasper? Apart from his inability to relate to the younger generation, particularly to Mariana Jannan, Howat appears to lack the element of violent, contradictory passions that sets the other "black" Pennys at odds with their peers. A touching, pathetic figure, he represents a dying breed. Yet the reader does not understand whether the fault for his failure lies in Howat's times or in himself. Nevertheless, the portrait of the last Howat, though psychologically blurred, is interesting enough to arouse the reader's sympathies. More than his cardboard-romantic ancestors, he resembles a Henry James hero, morbidly introspective, sensitive but fastidious, capable of tender emotions but little direct action. With him the line of the "black" Pennys comes to an end.

Leslie B. Mittleman

THE THREE-CORNERED HAT

Type of work: Novel
Author: Pedro Antonio de Alarcón (1833-1891)
Type of plot: Comedy of intrigue
Time of plot: Early nineteenth century
Locale: Spain
First published: 1874

Based on a ribald folktale on the familiar theme of cuckolding, The Three-Cornered Hat *is a good-natured, simple, and amusing comedy that is remarkable for its inoffensive ending, rare in fabliaux-derived stories of this sort.*

The Three-Cornered Hat begins with leisurely descriptions of characters and setting, then abruptly picks up rhythm and moves into two climaxes. It is colorful, funny, and brisk. Most action occurs in the mill, but a dance air was noted in the story by Spain's greatest musician, Manuel de Falla (who later put the novel into a ballet). The story's archaic charm, wit, local flavor, and pleasant, almost vaudeville "Spanishism" are inimitable, as are its characterizations. Alarcónian characters are usually symbols of good or evil, and his action the struggle between the two forces, but this is less true of his masterpiece, *The Three-Cornered Hat.* This is also the only Alarcónian novel not soaked in melodrama. Its true significance is that it fuses simple, *costumbrista* descriptive techniques—once dominant in the Spanish novel—with techniques of the thesis novel. It also combines *picaresco* (romantic roguery) touches with Spanish realism, and is uniquely steeped in the flavor of a vanished past. The novel even inserts political meaning into the plot by reflecting a village's struggle against the Spanish national government and French ideas.

For *The Three-Cornered Hat,* Alarcón selected elements from stories of the so-called "blindman's ballad," or Spanish oral tradition, that he had heard as a child. His novel was also influenced by Boccaccio, and was originally intended as a humor story for a Cuban magazine. Remembering a childhood tale, however, Alarcón rewrote the work in six days as a novel. Professor Edwin Place strove to discover other of the novel's roots, and found some in a French tale of adultery that has notable similarities to *The Three-Cornered Hat.* Alarcón feared that adulterous themes from Boccaccio or French literature could be ruined through vulgarity, but believed that they could be beautified and made more Spanish by delicate, deep handling. One of Alarcón's associates once commented that if he were a knight, grandee, or banker, he would yield his sword, coat-of-arms, or money to become "the hat-maker of the hat that you have put so much into vogue."

THREE MEN IN A BOAT

Type of work: Novel
Author: Jerome K. Jerome (1859-1927)
Type of plot: Comic romance
Time of plot: Nineteenth century
Locale: England
First published: 1889

Most of the leisurely humor of Three Men in a Boat, *a slight tale with only a thin thread of plot, derives from its digressions, which make up the bulk of the book. With a light touch Jerome describes the characters' droll adventures or eccentric quirks.*

Three Men in a Boat, a period piece from a more leisurely and less sophisticated world than that of the twentieth century, is an uneven book, both funny and silly, at once well-observed and haphazardly artificial. The humor at times is labored, more journalistic than satirical, but some scenes of action are genuinely funny. Much of the humor is based on incongruities; when the reader can see these incongruities coming, they lose some of their effectiveness. One suspects that the humor of the novel was fresher in 1889.

At times, Jerome does make shrewd observations on human nature, such as his tale about the man who wallpapered his carved oak walls because the oak was so gloomy. Jerome is able to carry the particular observation into a general truth with a light and humorous touch. It is when he feels obliged to enliven a scene by dragging in something funny, whether it belongs there or not, that he becomes arch. Some scenes, such as Harris' leading the swelling crowd deeper and deeper into the maze of Hampton Court, are funny as far as they go, but might have been funnier if further developed. At this perspective in time, nearly a hundred years after the publication of the book, it is difficult to judge if the novel itself was dated or if ideas of humor have changed.

The novel's greatest strength is its wealth of detail about the life, times, and scenes the travelers encounter. The author's sharp eye picks out the idiosyncratic detail or startling touch in every landscape and scene, but always with a sense of authenticity. When Jerome focuses on the individuals the three men meet, he is equally precise. Only occasionally does he slip into excessive exaggeration, leaving behind reality in an attempt at humor. He is the funniest when straining the least to be funny. The trio of travelers are not unique personalities in themselves, but the character of the dog, Montmorency, is often original and humorous. A good-natured diversion, the book makes no pretense at possessing a message or being anything other than the comedy it is.

THE THREE MUSKETEERS

Type of work: Novel
Author: Alexandre Dumas, *père* (1802-1870)
Type of plot: Historical romance
Time of plot: 1626
Locale: France
First published: 1844

The most popular novel of Dumas' vast production, The Three Musketeers *is a swashbuckling adventure-romance that is full of exciting action, with enough suspenseful intrigue to sustain its melodramatic plot.*

The reputation of Alexandre Dumas père is based partly on the enormous quantity of novels, articles, and dramas which he and his collaborators produced over some forty years, and partly on his most famous novel, *The Three Musketeers.*

Like D'Artagnan, Dumas arrived in Paris with little more than a recommendation to a friend of his father. He had grown up in a small town and came to Paris desiring to participate in its literary and social life. Fortunately, he managed to land a job as a copyist for the Duke of Orleans. When he arrived in Paris a new literary movement, which had already taken hold of the leading imaginations of Germany and England, began to sweep through France. Literary Romanticism, in all its varieties, grew in reaction against the adherence to literary rules, and against the insistence on obsolete conventions that had hardened through the eighteenth century.

Against this inflexibility, Romanticism offered the excitement of literary freedom. A new, passionate hero—the Byronic hero—was born. Nature, liberated from the regularity of formal gardens, appeared in poetry and prose, exalted and full of wonder. Finally, Sir Walter Scott showed how themes from the past could be given new "romantic" meanings and how history, codified by the eighteenth century, could be humanized and made exciting. The young Dumas, who read Byron and Scott, felt himself awakening. He tried his hand at drama, and was successful. Though his work lacked the style and analytical power of Hugo, who was his friend, it did, nevertheless, have the power to move audiences deeply.

When Dumas was in his early forties, he made the acquaintance of Auguste Maquet through an intermediary. After Dumas had rewritten one of Maquet's plays, they became friends and collaborators.

Two other important factors helped give birth to *The Three Musketeers.* First, interest in the historical novel was rising. Dumas himself saw the potential in revealing the history of France to Frenchmen, and had done so in both his melodramas and comedies. Unfortunately, Dumas was vastly ignorant of the details of history. He needed someone to dig up the facts for him to construct a historical skeleton so to speak, which he could clothe in flesh, nerves, and skin, and into which he could breathe life and excitement.

Second, newspapers at the time had begun to popularize fiction in a mass way. Serials were run, and a vast new audience was being created. But these fictional serials required a certain type of popular writer, a writer able to maintain action and suspense in almost every episode. Thus many authors of high ability were not especially successful at this writing because they devoted long sections to description or characterization.

It seems that Maquet furnished Dumas with the idea for *The Three Musketeers*. But the idea was not original with him, either. In the early years of the eighteenth century a rather tedious book had been written by Gatien de Coutilz titled *Memoires of M. d'Artagnan, Captain-Lieutenant in the First Company of the King's Musketeers*. This book, rarely read and with little to recommend it, was turned into something of a narrative history by Maquet. Dumas, in turn, using Maquet's version as a rough draft, added details, characters, dialogue, and new action—all of which transformed the whole into a fast-paced, intriguing, and adventurous story.

It is possible, of course, to say that *The Three Musketeers* does not really belong to Dumas alone, and that Dumas should not receive sole credit as the author. In fact, Dumas himself was always ready to acknowledge his collaborators and the evidence suggests (as do reports of his character) that Dumas was generous in every respect. But the fact remains that Dumas reworked Maquet's version as much as (or more than) Maquet reworked the original. Thus, the finished popular version, or at least those qualities of *The Three Musketeers* which make it so popular, were indeed the work of Dumas.

The art of *The Three Musketeers* lies precisely in those techniques which give the novel its tremendous and lasting popularity. But at first glance, either those techniques are not obvious or Dumas is dismissed as a mere entertainer. It is true, certainly, that *The Three Musketeers* is entertaining, but all serious art need not be dull.

Dumas is not a great stylist if by that is meant one whose style is memorable or whose style draws attention to itself. Dumas does not have an interesting style—it is simply functional. On the other hand, he does not commit errors of stylistic taste in *The Three Musketeers*. Rather, the style helps carry forward the story.

The tone of *The Three Musketeers* is enjoyable, or pleasant, but not especially intense or agonized. Occasionally, there is mild irony; but for the most part the narrative voice directly suggests the author himself, generous, good natured, interested in life, adventure, and romance.

The characterizations are not profound or great, but they are adequate to the plot and to the connected adventures that Dumas relates. He is able to distinguish well enough between the characters (and he enables the reader to do the same), but Dumas' characters are not of the profound or agonized variety. On the contrary, they tend to be quite recognizable, motivated by interests which are everyday interests shared by his audience, or interests such as chivalric honor which are explained and for which sympathy can be generated. In short, character is subordinate to action. Dumas is mainly interested in characters for what they do, how they act, rather than for what they are or what they think they are.

The main ingredient in the success of *The Three Musketeers* is its action; and it is in action that Dumas excels as a novelist. Indeed, his sheer talent as a storyteller is enormous. First, he is quite expert in pacing the action and in varying it. He does not merely repeat the same adventure but builds from one action scene to the next. Related to this building is his use of force or violence. *The Three Musketeers* is full of violence, and men and women are bruised, wounded, and killed. What can be said is that the enterprise is carried off with such high spirits, the heroes have such good intentions and high motives, and their opposition is so malignant and full of duplicity that even the violence is subordinate to the action as a whole. In other words, there is no morbid invitation to mayhem for its own sake and no perverse lingering over the brutal aspects of human conduct.

Furthermore, the historical setting has a distancing effect. The weaponry and war cries were old-fashioned when the novel was published in the nineteenth century, and by the twentieth century they have become quaint. Actually, this setting lends much to the story and to the popularity of the story. Dumas is quite expert at weaving historical fact with purest fiction. One gives life and plausibility to the other. History is given drama and mobility, fiction is given that semblance of truth it demands.

In the end, the story of the musketeers is one of those romances, those quests, those wishful actions of daring adventure and excitement that requires the trappings of history. The musketeers, and especially D'Artagnan, win our attention and the historical set, containing political and sexual intrigues through which D'Artagnan and his friends pass, wins our acceptance.

Howard Lee Hertz

THE THREE SISTERS

Type of work: Drama
Author: Anton Chekhov (1860-1904)
Type of plot: Impressionistic realism
Time of plot: Nineteenth century
Locale: Russia
First presented: 1901

The Three Sisters, a poignant drama rich in perceptive character studies, treats the lassitude of the middle class with ironical scorn. Although Chekhov's male characters are weak-willed and, like Prozòrov or Tchebutykin, incapable of action, at least his women, among them the three sisters, have hopes of achieving happiness, if only because they live on dreams.

The Three Sisters is one of the high points of Anton Chekhov's dramatic art. It represents the mature work of his last years. In this play, Chekhov reflects his sensitivity to the themes of his epoch. For in the turn-of-the-century period of rapid social change, aristocratic leadership in politics as well as culture began to disintegrate, and the middle class, with aristocratic aspirations and pretensions, fell willy-nilly heir to the guidance of social and cultural affairs. Hence, we see in *The Three Sisters* the frustration and despair of directionless people trying to fulfill impossible goals.

The Prozòrovs are perfect examples of this middle-class dilemma. Not independently wealthy, they must work for their livings, but they consider the work that they do beneath their dignity. Irina and Olga, for instance, take menial jobs, and Andrey forsakes professorial ambitions out of sheer *ennui*. This theme of career dissatisfaction is counterbalanced by a strong suggestion throughout the play that hard physical labor (a basically peasant ethos) is rewarding. Nevertheless, Olga, Masha, and Irina long eternally for the sophistication of Moscow life, all the while deploring Natasha's common vulgarity. All of them are frustrated, their repressed energy and repressed sexuality ready to explode at any moment. Their thwarted ambitions put them in a self-devised psychological and geographical pressure-cooker of quite limited capacity.

The Prozòrovs are, in fact, intellectual neurotics. They are bored; they see their lives as futile; they are melancholy and moody. Their tragedy—the tragedy of the middle class—is that they totally lack the inner resources to overcome their circumstances. They wish; they hope; but they never take positive action. Their consequent apathy thus makes them early avatars of the Existential despair so popularly examined in the mid-twentieth century.

Chekhov's great accomplishment in *The Three Sisters* is the unmasking of the utter bankruptcy—intellectual, emotional, pragmatic, and political—of the middle class. To be sure, Chekhov was not a revolutionary in the Bolshevik sense; however, his merciless exposure of bourgeois ineffectuality insures his respectability even to present-day socialist critics. Still, Chekhov has Vershinin comment perceptively that life will be better in "two or three hundred years." Hence, Chekhov expresses his ambivalence about human and therefore social perfectability. Nonetheless, *The Three Sisters* constitutes an important play in Chekhov's corpus, for beyond its ideological implications, the play is a compelling theatrical experience.

THREE SOLDIERS

Type of work: Novel
Author: John Dos Passos (1896-1970)
Type of plot: Social criticism
Time of plot: 1917-1919
Locale: France
First published: 1921

More than a tough, realistic novel that exposes as a sham the myth of military heroics, Three Soldiers *advances early in Dos Passos' career his criticism of authority, whether that of the army command in World War I or that of the privileged social class with its institutionalized power.*

Three Soldiers is an early work by Dos Passos and does not incorporate many of the original stylistic devices of his later work. The language and organization of the novel are conventional and straightforward.

But the central idea of the work, elaborated in three variations, is highly unconventional. Dos Passos tries to show the immorality and brutality in the organization of society and especially in a society mechanized, armed, and functioning for purposes of war. When John Andrews deserts the army at the end of *Three Soldiers,* and indicts the army because it stifles the individual, a friend of his answers that an idea like that is "anarchistic."

Indeed it is. *Three Soldiers* is essentially an anarchistic novel, a dramatic polemic—using three exemplary lives—in which Dos Passos argues for a social-political vision. It is a classic anarchistic vision in which the supremacy of the individual over social organization is defended, even demanded.

In the case of Dan Fuselli, Dos Passos shows that the lure of advancement and rewards, a lure which uses arms to sustain discipline and therefore hierarchy, is both false and vicious. It is false because, in Fuselli's case, keeping his mouth shut and obeying orders achieved little for him. It is vicious because his superiors use that lure to take advantage of him; Fuselli's most tragic moment occurs when his girl friend is stolen by a man from whom he hopes to gain a promotion.

Chrisfield is a second type of soldier, and represents a second response to military life. He is a nervous, violent farm boy harassed by superior officers, one of whom takes inhuman advantage of Chrisfield's low rank. Finally Chrisfield is driven to murder and desertion.

Andrews, the third character, like Dos Passos, is an artist. Andrews felt that burying his individuality in the mass of the army would somehow bring him peace—and an escape from the pains of creativity. Andrews finds, however, that no matter how much he tries he cannot bury himself. Some elemental force asserts itself through him, and he realizes that above all he must remain a distinct individual. When Andrews deserts at the end of the novel, he is acting out of decency and integrity.

In each of these three cases, the individual comes into basic conflict with social organization. Despite Dos Passos' changing political beliefs, he kept this essential vision through his long, fruitful career as a novelist.

THROUGH THE LOOKING-GLASS

Type of work: Imaginative tale
Author: Lewis Carroll (Charles Lutwidge Dodgson, 1832-1898)
Type of plot: Fantasy
Time of plot: Nineteenth century
Locale: The dream world of an imaginative child
First published: 1871

Its plot structured around moves in a chess game, the story of this fantasy, which continues Alice's Adventures in Wonderland, *is set in a land peopled by live chessmen and talking insects, a land where everything happens backwards. Carroll's book may be read as a madcap children's fairy tale or interpreted as a complex, sophisticated adult fable laced with subtle ironies and inspired by inimitable humor.*

It is rare for the sequel to a highly creative literary work to surpass the original. Yet such is the case with *Through the Looking-Glass and What Alice Found There,* which in 1871 followed *Alice's Adventures in Wonderland,* published seven years earlier. For most readers the two books are so closely entwined that they are considered a unit, and many of Lewis Carroll's most famous Looking-Glass creations (Tweedledee, Tweedledum, and Humpty Dumpty, for example) are often mistakenly placed in *Alice's Adventures in Wonderland.* However, each, while joined by a common heroine and themes, is a distinct entity. And it is *Through the Looking-Glass* which most attracts adults, for it is in this second fantasy that Lewis Carroll (the pen name for Oxford mathematics lecturer and tutor the Rev. Charles Lutwidge Dodgson) presented an even more sophisticated puzzle about reality and logic than he did in the earlier story. It is in *Through the Looking-Glass* that one finds conscious suggestion of the cruel questions rather delicately presented in *Alice's Adventures in Wonderland.*

Sharing many characteristics, each book has twelve chapters, and both merge the fairy tale with science. Alice, seven years old in the first book, is seven and one-half on her second venture. A slight shift in scene turns the pleasant outdoor summer setting of *Alice's Adventures in Wonderland* into the more somber indoor winter stage of *Through the Looking-Glass.* Corresponding to the card game of the first book is chess in *Through the Looking-Glass,* another game which involves kings and queens. Within the chess-and-mirror framework of the Looking-Glass world, Carroll has, however, constructed an intricate symbolic plan unlike the seemingly spontaneous movement of Wonderland.

Although medieval and Renaissance sportsmen sometimes enjoyed chess which used human players on a giant field, Carroll is apparently the first to use the idea in literature. Science fiction has since, of course, often employed the technique. In the game plan, Alice is a white pawn on a giant chessboard of life in which the rows of the board are separated by brooks and the columns by hedges. Alice never speaks to any piece who is not in a square beside her, as appropriate for the pawn who never knows what is happening except at its spot on the board. Alice remains in the queen's field except for her last move by which time she has become a queen and captures the Red Queen (and shakes her into a kitten) and as a result checkmates the Red King who has slept throughout the game. Her behavior complements the personalities assigned to the other pieces, for each assumes the qualities of the figure it represents. As in chess, the queens are the most powerful and active beings and the kings are impotent. Erratic and stumbling, the White Knight recalls the movement of the chess knight which moves two squares in any direction, then again one square in a different direction, forming a sort of spastic "L."

Critics have noted inconsistencies in the chess game, charging that the White side makes nine consecutive moves; the White King is placed in an unnoticed check; the Queens castle; and the White Queen misses a chance to take the Red Knight. But Carroll, in a later explanatory note, said that the game is correct in relation to the moves even though the alternation of the sides is not strictly consistent, and that the "castling" of the Queens is merely his phrase to indicate that they have entered the palace. Not interested in the game as an example of chess strategy, Carroll conceived of it as a learning experience for a child who was to "be" a pawn warring against all the other pieces controlled by an adult, an idea apparently stimulated by the chess tales Carroll had fashioned for Alice Liddell, a young friend who was learning the game. Alice, daughter of the dean of Christ Church, Oxford, had also, of course, been the Alice whom he had placed in Wonderland.

Arising inevitably from Carroll's use of this structure has been the proposal that Alice is Everyman and that chess is Life. Like a human being who exists from birth to death only vaguely comprehending the forces directing his moves, Alice never understands her experience. Indeed none of the pieces really assimilates the total concept of the game. Even the mobile queens do not really grasp the idea that beyond the board there is a room and people who are determining the game. Our own reality thus becomes very unreal if we, like the chess pieces, have such a limited perception of the total environment.

Carroll pursues still another definition of reality when Alice confronts the Red King and is told that she exists merely as part of his dreams, not as an objective being. Upsetting to Alice is the sage advice of Tweedledum and Tweedledee to the effect that if the king were to wake, Alice would then vanish like the flame of a candle. The incident recalls Bishop Berkeley's empirical proposal that nothing exists except as it is perceived. Alice, like Samuel Johnson who refuted Berkeley by painfully kicking a stone, insists that she is "real" for she cries "real" tears. When she leaves the Looking-Glass world and supposedly awakens, Carroll mischievously permits her to ask herself: Which dreamed it? His final poem apparently provides the answer, for the last words in the book are: "Life, what is it but a dream?"

In examining the second structural device of the book, the mirror reversal theme (perfectly mated with chess since in that game the initial asymmetric arrangement of the pieces means that the opponents are mirror images of one another), we find that Carroll has achieved another *tour de force*. The left-right reversals—including, for example, the Tweedle brothers, Alice's attempt to reach the Red Queen by walking backwards, memory which occurs before the event, running to stay in the same place, and the like—are not merely mind-teasers. Scientists now seriously propose the existence of anti-matter which is, in effect, a mirror image of matter, just like Alice's Looking-Glass milk. And again we wonder: which is the real matter, the real milk?

Further developing this continuing paradox are Carroll's damaging attacks on our understanding of language. Humpty Dumpty (like the Tweedles, the Lion, the Unicorn, and Wonderland's Jack of Hearts, a nursery rhyme character) says a person's ideas are formulated in his mind and to express them he may use any word he pleases. Alice and the White Knight debate the difference between the name of the song and the song, between what the name is and what the name is called. The fawn becomes frightened of Alice only when it realizes she is a "child." In these and many more incidents, Carroll explores how our language works, directly and indirectly making fun of our misconceptions which, on the one hand, see language as part of a totally objective system of reality and, on the other, forget how language actually helps create that reality. His nonsense words and poems are his final jibe at our so-called logical language, for they are no more and no less disorderly than ordinary table talk.

A sparkling achievement, *Through the Looking-Glass* is, like *Alice's Adventures in Wonderland,* the incomparable vision of an alienated man who found in the world of fantasy all the delight and horror of the adult environment he was subconsciously attempting to escape.

Judith Bolch

THYESTES

Type of work: Drama
Author: Lucius Annaeus Seneca (c. 4 B.C.-A.D. 65)
Type of plot: Tragedy of revenge
Time of plot: The Heroic Age
Locale: Greece
First presented: c. A.D. 60

Thyestes, wooden on the stage, is nevertheless a closet drama of horrific intensity. Remarkable for its scenes of terror, such as the banquet at which the father partakes of his own children, the Senecan tragedy was a landmark in dramatic history, influencing in particular many Elizabethan and Jacobean revenge plays.

Seneca's *Thyestes* is undoubtedly the most lurid, gruesome, and undramatic tragedy to survive from antiquity. It is also the most fiendish revenge play in the literature. But it is spectacle rather than true drama. Whereas genuine tragedy arises from character conflicts or internal divisions within character, spectacle relies on sensational events carried out by *Dramatis personae* who exist merely for the sake of the events and who have no actual existence of their own. This is certainly the case with every character in *Thyestes.* Each exists simply to point up the horror of Atreus' revenge on his brother, Thyestes, where Thyestes is fed his own butchered sons at a hideous banquet.

Another important point of difference between true drama and spectacle is their use of language. The speech of authentic tragedy approximates, in a formal way, the devices of normal conversation to reveal passions. The language of spectacle, however, being florid and highly artificial, tends toward bombast. Spectacle operates by set pieces, rhetorical essays that develop simple ideas at great length, by tedious and lush descriptive passages, and by *sententiae,* which are moralizing epigrams. Seneca used all three, and the result is that his characters speak in a highly unnatural way. Instead of communicating they attitudinize, talking largely to the audience or soliloquizing.

This characteristic of Senecan drama has led many scholars to believe that Seneca wrote his plays for private recitation rather than public performance. But that is no reason for assuming they were not produced. Spectacle, rhetorical overindulgence, and horrors were a part of public entertainment under the Roman Emperors Caligula, Claudius, and Nero, who ruled during Seneca's maturity. We know for a fact that his tragedies were staged in the Elizabethan period, and that they had immense influence on the dramas of Kyd, Marlowe, Shakespeare, Webster, and others.

The subject of *Thyestes* derives from Greek legend, and is based upon an incident that occurred in the tragic family descended from Tantalus. Although Sophocles, Euripides, Ennius, Accius, and Varius had dramatized the story of Thyestes earlier, none of their plays has survived to provide a basis of comparison. Seneca's treatment of the myth has some interest in its own right, but it also serves to illuminate his own biography.

He handles the figure of Thyestes rather sympathetically, making him the victim of Atreus' lunatic lust for revenge. Seneca plays down the fact that Thyestes seduced Atreus' wife, stole his symbol of power, and caused a civil war. When Thyestes appears on stage, he assumes the role of the Stoic hero, determined to bear whatever fate he has in store for him, and he frankly prefers the hardships of exile to the pomp of power that Atreus has treacherously extended to him. Exile has tempered his character. And here we remember that Seneca himself underwent eight years of exile on Corsica, after being accused of an intrigue with Claudius' niece, Julia. The parallel is striking, but it extends even further. Like Thyestes, Seneca was recalled from exile with the promise of power. He was to tutor and guide Nero in the art of statesmanship. When Nero became Emperor in A.D. 54, Seneca was able to exercise some control over him for the first five years of his reign; but then Nero began acting on his own, and Seneca retired from public life. *Thyestes* is Seneca's personal testament on the instability of power, and the helplessness of those who incur the wrath of an absolute and maniacal ruler. The only solution Seneca finds in this play is the same one he found in life— to bear one's misfortune with Stoic dignity. Eventually Nero ordered Seneca to commit suicide for an alleged conspiracy. And Seneca met his death bravely.

Through the murky rhetoric of *Thyestes* three important themes emerge: cannibalism, the nature of kingship, and the necessity of maintaining a Stoic endurance in the face of a murderous disintegrating cosmos. The appearance of Tantalus and Megaera the Fury at the beginning is not accidental. Tantalus served his son, Pelops, as food for the gods, and as part of his eternal torment he must not only witness the kin murders of his descendants, he must abet them. Presumably he inspires the idea of the cannibalistic revenge in Atreus' mind, but Atreus carries it out with gloating satisfaction. Atreus is an unrelieved monster, raging with paranoid pride.

Against him Seneca sets the idea of kingship founded on morality and restraint. The aphoristic conversation between Atreus and the Attendant in Act Two, Scene One, is a debate on whether kings should serve the people or the people should be utterly subservient to the king. In the first case morality is the main law, and in the second the will of the tyrant. The point is made that morality creates a stable kingdom, but tyranny is supremely unstable. Later, the chorus says that true kingship lies in self-control, not in wealth, power, or pomp.

Unfortunately these observations make no impression whatever on Atreus, who is intent on proving his godlike power over human life, much like the Roman Emperors Seneca knew. In striving to become like a god in his pride,

Atreus becomes loathsomely bestial. Seneca constantly generalizes from the concrete situation of Atreus and Thyestes to the universe. When kings are corrupt, society is corrupted, and the rot extends throughout the cosmos. Nature mirrors human conditions in Seneca: the fire hesitates to boil the children; an unnatural night falls upon the banquet. The play is full of hyperbole about the disintegrating universe, rendered in very purple poetry. Against this profusion of rhetoric stand the pithy epigrams, like a Stoical element trying to bear up tightly against the frenetic declamations. The Stoic attitude can never prevail in a world full of crime, but it can enable a man to endure great stress with courage. Seneca, in *Thyestes,* embodied the shame of Rome and his own valor in a style eminently suited to his subject.

James Weigel, Jr.

THE TIME MACHINE

Type of work: Novel
Author: H. G. Wells (1866-1946)
Type of plot: Fantasy
Time of plot: Late nineteenth century
Locale: England
First published: 1895

Wells's first novel, despite its exuberant style, is a delineation of unfulfilled hope in which the Time Traveler's dreams for a future founded upon scientific technology and social organization are dashed by a vision of humankind reduced to a level of brutality or effeteness, then finally extinguished.

Wells's first novel, *The Time Machine,* enjoyed an instant popularity and rescued its author from obscurity and poverty. The book quickly established itself as a classic in the tradition of Swift and Defoe, and has since been praised by such readers as Winston Churchill and Arthur C. Clarke.

Wells rightly resented Oscar Wilde's description of him as "an English Jules Verne." For, as *The Time Machine* perfectly illustrates, his early works were much more than merely adventurous forecasts of coming technological feats. Besides employing the concept of machine-assisted movement through time, the novel works on the implications of three important theories: organisms evolve as they fight to adapt to hostile environments; history can best be viewed as an ever more violent struggle of social classes; the orderliness and energy in the universe will steadily decrease. By extending and dramatizing these theories, Wells produced an altogether shocking image of the future. The fascination of *The Time Machine* derives not only from the suspenseful exploits of the Professor, but also from the vividly depicted succession of doomsdays which he encounters.

If man is an animal which struggles to adapt, what will he become after nature is pacified? Since the environment will automatically sustain him, reasoned Wells, man will lose his intelligence, combativeness, and creativity which he formerly needed to survive. He will become, eventually, as dull and pitiful as the Eloi. Further, if the laboring classes were forced to adapt to a foul underground world of mines and machines, how would they look after a millenium or so? The Morlocks are Wells's answer. They are beings whose biological modifications condemn them to a subterranean existence, and whose superior intelligence permits them to use the Eloi as domestic animals. The Morlocks are not "cannibals" because "men" have effectively been superseded.

Finally, there is Wells's unforgettable picture of an almost dead universe: scenes of grotesque and enervated forms, a deoxygenated atmosphere, a huge, heatless red sun, and entropy. Many nineteenth century people believed more than anything else—with a depth of conviction now unimaginable—in Progress. Wells was himself a devotee of the idea. Ironically, one of the reasons for contemporary skepticism about Progress is the existence of *The Time Machine.*

THE TIME OF MAN

Type of work: Novel
Author: Elizabeth Madox Roberts (1886-1941)
Type of plot: Regional romance
Time of plot: Early twentieth century
Locale: Kentucky
First published: 1926

Although The Time of Man *is not, from the strictly Marxian sense of social class struggle, a protest novel, Roberts examines in powerful detail the grueling and often unrewarded toil of Kentucky migrant farmers. Yet she shows, in balance, their inner strength, love of the soil, and fierce independence.*

In *The Time of Man,* Elizabeth Madox Roberts draws on her own first-hand knowledge of poor rural whites in Kentucky—where she was born and reared—to present a stark portrait of impoverishment balancing between hope and despair. The tenant farmer's lot, of course, has never been an easy one, but the field workers and tenant farmers in Roberts' novel appear in especially dire straits. For them, it seems that each small advance is followed by a setback twice as large. In those days before government welfare programs, sheer endurance was their only defense against misfortune.

However, the wellsprings of their endurance derive from complex sources. For the easy assumption is that the poor work only because of need. Although necessity is indeed a compelling motivation, the characters in *The Time of Man* work for other reasons as well. The Chessers, Ellen and Henry, and the others, for example, are psychologically and spiritually compelled to work: they get satisfaction from farming the land, and they believe unquestioningly in the virtues of work. Despite occasional straying, they are nevertheless devoted to their families and have a strong sense of responsibility toward them. It may thus be said that they embody some of the most powerful tenets of the Protestant work ethic—a startling testimony, under the circumstances, to the ubiquity and the force of middle-class values even among the poor.

And the Chessers, the Kents, and their friends and neighbors are certainly poor, with a poverty that often extends to intellectual and emotional deprivation as well. For they are so preoccupied with the struggle for survival that they rarely, if ever, question or challenge the assumptions upon which the social system, or even their own lives, is based. Essentially unsophisticated people, they have no anxieties in the modern clinical sense, for their view of the present and their vision of the future are geared to the basic necessities for survival. Hence, they have worries and they have fears—of the most primitive sort. But identity crises and abstract intellectualizing do not concern them. In this sense, therefore, the novel's title, *The Time of Man,* must be construed as ironic, for the novel itself deals with people who have been denied access to the dignity of being "Man," part of mankind, and part of the human race.

TIMON OF ATHENS

Type of work: Drama
Author: William Shakespeare (1564-1616)
Type of plot: Tragedy of delusions
Time of plot: Fourth century B.C.
Locale: Athens and the nearby seacoast
First presented: c. 1605-1608

A tragedy rich in poetry and philosophical speculation but difficult to stage for the theater, Timon of Athens *treats with uncommon bitterness the theme of ingratitude. Shakespeare derived the plot from the life of Mark Antony in North's* Plutarch's Lives, *as well as from Lucian's dialogue* Timon, *which was available to him in Latin and French.*

The opening platonic discussion between the Poet and the Painter is the key to the philosophical theme of this rough and unfinished play. The two artists question the relationship between reality and art as imitation of reality. Ironically it is the Poet who thinks everyone loves Timon because they seem to love him; his artistic insight into character is radically inaccurate, mistaking seeming for being. But the Poet's vision of Fortune also hints accurately at another major theme—that of the "fall of illustrious men," a genre reaching back as far as Greek tragedy and coming to the Renaissance by way of Boethius (and to Shakespeare by way of Chaucer). *Timon of Athens,* like so many other plays by Shakespeare, belongs to this usually tragic drama, based on the capriciousness of Fortune that is consistent only in its inconsistency. Unlike most plays of this sort, however, Timon's fall is caused by a "fault" that is usually considered to be a "virtue." In a true Aristotelian vein the play demonstrates that a virtue carried to excess becomes a vice, as our sympathy for Timon, originally as strong as his generosity, quickly turns to impatience when his determined foolhardiness becomes evident.

The philosophical preoccupations are appropriate to a play set in fourth century Athens; Apemantus—impertinent, saucy, and truculent—resembles Aristophanes' portrait of Socrates. The idealism that brings Timon to his misanthropic end is less characteristic of the Renaissance and of Shakespeare's dramatic sensibilities. The play suffers from structural defects—such as the less than successful integration of Alcibiades into the plot and motivational pattern, the anticlimactical banquet scene, the awkward senatorial decision about the old soldier (3.5)—as well as stylistic mediocrity. Yet Flavius is a convincing character, whose speech about the excuses of Timon's fair-weather friends (2.1) is one of the most effective in Shakespeare. This "one honest man" is not enough to save the play from the neglect it richly deserves.

'TIS PITY SHE'S A WHORE

Type of work: Drama
Author: John Ford (1586-1640?)
Type of plot: Horror tragedy
Time of plot: Renaissance period
Locale: Parma, Italy
First presented: c. 1628

A revenge tragedy marked by Ford's customary interest in the psychology of intense suffering, 'Tis Pity She's a Whore *is a drama of underplayed violence and refined sensibility that treats with compassion the main theme of brother-sister incest.*

Although the first quarter of the seventeenth century saw the production of several plays dealing with incest—including Tourneur's *The Revenger's Tragedy* and Middleton's *Women Beware Women*—John Ford's *'Tis Pity She's a Whore* was the first drama to center on that theme exclusively. While Ford's work is usually categorized as a revenge play, it differs from other works in that group in its rational tone and objective approach; the author treats a sensational topic in a moderate, low-key fashion instead of descending into melodrama.

Perhaps because of the controversial nature of its subject, *'Tis Pity She's a Whore* has been open to a wide range of critical interpretations. The accusation has frequently been made, for instance, that incestuous love in the play is portrayed in too sympathetic a light; some modern critics have carried this view to the extreme, claiming that the playwright valued the power of love over social convention, and preferred even its perverse manifestations over traditional morality. Others have adopted the opposite stance, seeing Ford as a staunchly moral author out to illustrate the dire effects of sin. A sensible interpretation must fall somewhere between these two readings, which oversimplify a play of considerable complexity.

Ford's characterizations, for example, are drawn with sophistication and sensitivity. Giovanni is shown as an extremely intelligent young man whose overconfidence provokes a warning against intellectual pride from Friar Bonaventura. At first Giovanni suffers from the knowledge that his love is condemned by traditional morality, but soon his habit of independent thinking takes hold. He produces a variety of arguments to defend his incest, including the rationalization that it cannot be wrong to worship beauty, and that blood relationship creates an intimacy and bond which is stronger than other love bonds and should not be denied.

Giovanni, however, receives no strong counterarguments for his sophistic reasonings from the friar, and so persists in a self-willed destruction course. He begins to block out reality when it impinges on his conscience: since religion condemns him, he becomes an atheist; and when he receives Annabella's disturbing letter, he insists it is a forgery. Annabella is portrayed as a sensitive person who loves deeply, but refuses to rationalize her actions; who attempts to help her brother come to repentance once she has found it; and who remains faithfully affectionate even when he murders her. Probably the least admirable character in the play is the friar, who fails to offer convincing moral arguments when they are needed, and who encourages Annabella's marriage to Soranzo even though he knows she is pregnant.

THE TITAN

Type of work: Novel
Author: Theodore Dreiser (1871-1945)
Type of plot: Naturalism
Time of plot: 1890's
Locale: Chicago
First published: 1914

  The Titan, second novel of Dreiser's trilogy examining with naturalistic thoroughness the career of Frank Algernon Cowperwood, continues the story of the man's rise to greatness, and then his eventual collapse, as a result of deterministic forces begun in The Financier.

  The Titan is the second in Dreiser's trilogy of novels tracing the career of Frank Algernon Cowperwood. *The Financier* (1912) tells the story of Cowperwood's early successes in the financial world of Philadelphia, of the start of his extramarital affair with Aileen, and of his conviction and imprisonment for grand larceny. In *The Stoic* (1947) Cowperwood is again portrayed as shrewdly energetic and ambitious, now living abroad after his defeat in Chicago, and amassing a large but unneeded fortune in London. Estranged from Berenice, he dies a lonely death while his overextended empire finally comes to ruin.

  Cowperwood's character is based upon that of Charles Yerkes (1837-1905), a nineteenth century Chicago financier whose life and personality supplied the framework for *The Titan* and the other two novels which Dreiser had planned to call *A Trilogy of Desire.* Like Dreiser's Cowperwood, Yerkes was a shrewd schemer in business who made his fortune in Philadelphia public transportation, spent a short time in prison for illegal business manipulations, and then moved to Chicago and gained control of a gas trust. Yerkes later tried to monopolize the city's transportation system through long-term franchises, but finally failed and began new business interests in the London Tube. According to Richard Lehan's account in *Theodore Dreiser: His World and His Novels* (1969), several even more specific incidences in *The Titan* are taken directly from Dreiser's own exhaustive research into the life of Yerkes and the activities of the Chicago business world he came to dominate.

  The Titan, however, also demonstrates Dreiser's absorption of the ideas of Herbert Spencer, T. H. Huxley, and other nineteenth century social-Darwinists who viewed society as essentially controlled by the law of "the survival of the fittest." In Dreiser's view, it is the nature of the universe that "a balance is struck wherein the mass subdues the individual or the individual the mass." Cowperwood's struggle against Hand, Schryhart, and Arneel is one for survival in the financial jungle of Chicago big business.

  For Dreiser, such a struggle is wholly amoral; there is no right or wrong because it is man's nature as well as his condition to have to struggle for power and survival. Cowperwood's cause is neither more nor less just than that of his antagonists, nor are his means any less scrupulous than their own. He may be said to be more shrewd than they, or to possess more ruthlessness in certain circumstances; but for Dreiser his struggle is the elemental contest between the impulse-driven energies of the individual and those of others in his society.

The forces which motivate Cowperwood's ambitions, then, are actually larger than any mere individual desires on his part. Described in the novel as "impelled by some blazing internal force," Cowperwood is driven by instincts beyond his control. Caught up in a natural struggle for survival and for power over others, he is dominated by "the drug of a personality he could not gainsay." He can no more remain satisfied with the money and success he has already attained than he can stay content with one woman. Hence, the need to conquer, to dominate and control, characterizes both Cowperwood's financial and romantic interests in life. To both he brings the same shrewd scheming and forcefulness needed for his success.

These two major plots—Cowperwood's business life and his romantic life—alternately mirror each other throughout the novel and prove to be integrally related. Cowperwood is as direct in his dealings with women as he is in his confrontations with men of business. Compare the frankness with which he first approaches Rita Sohlberg and his blunt way of attempting to bribe Governor Swanson. Moreover, many of Cowperwood's mistresses are related to the very men who, mainly as a consequence of his amorous trespassings, will oppose him most bitterly in Chicago. His affairs with Butler's, Cochrane's, and Haguenin's daughters—like his interlude with Hand's wife—not only lessen his circle of friends, but also gain him a number of enemies who eventually group together to defeat him for business as well as personal reasons.

As the title of the novel suggests, Cowperwood is indeed a Titan among men, one striving after more and achieving greater victory because he is driven to do so by his very nature. As he had himself come to recognize, the "humdrum conventional world could not brook his daring, his insouciance, his constant desire to call a spade a spade. His genial sufficiency was a taunt and a mockery to many." Yet his is a lonely victory, a fact emphasized by his almost self-imposed alienation from the business community with which his life is so connected, and by his being socially ostracized in Chicago, despite his wealth, almost from the start.

In a sense, Cowperwood is as much a victim of his will to power as any of those he has defeated on the stock exchange. For such men as he, power is the very means of survival. And in the world of Chicago business, power generates money, which in turn generates more power. The cycle, as much as the struggle, is endless. If a balance is ever struck between the power of the individual and that of the group, it is, Dreiser suggests, only temporary: for "without variance, how should the balance be maintained?" For Dreiser, as for Cowperwood, this is the meaning of life, a continual rebalancing, a necessary searching after on the part of the individual to discover a means of maintaining or acquiring his own desires against those of his society. Man is but a tool of his own private nature, "forever suffering the goad of a restless heart."

For men like Cowperwood, then, defeat is no more final or settling than triumph. If he has won anything permanent by the novel's end, it is the love of Berenice. She is part, at least, of the whole Cowperwood has been driven to seek after and attain. More than that he will never achieve nor understand about life. "Thou hast lived," concludes Dreiser at the end of the novel, as if to say that the struggle and the searching after are themselves the whole and the balance men seek.

Robert Dees

TITUS ANDRONICUS

Type of work: Drama
Author: William Shakespeare (1564-1616)
Type of plot: Tragedy of revenge
Time of plot: Early Christian era
Locale: Rome and vicinity
First presented: 1594

For the plot of this early crude, lurid, but surprisingly theatrical tragedy of revenge, Shakespeare had recourse to two classical sources, the revenge of Atreus from Seneca's Thyestes *and the rape of Philomela from Ovid's* Metamorphoses.

Titus Andronicus appears to have been Shakespeare's first attempt at formal tragedy. Although it may seem un-Shakespearean in its excessive brutality, it is similar, in some important ways, to the tragedies of his "golden period." Shakespeare's use of sources here is certainly less imaginative than later, but the play is not mere sensationalism, as it has often been accused of being.

Through its exaggerated dramatic scenes, the play condemns its characters' many brutal crimes. This style of theater was more suggestive than realistic, so one must not imagine these mutilations with the vividness of the hand-chopping scene in Fellini's *Satyricon*. But, more importantly, it soon becomes apparent that the brutality is a kind of shorthand for a powerful sense of evil the poet later was able to translate into psychic and spiritual violence. The equivalence here is achieved, such as it is, by the manipulation of form. And, in this respect, there is an adumbration of the great tragedies.

Elements of the opening scene (Act I has only one scene), foreshadow the play's main action, much as the practically vestigial technique of the dumb-show in the same scene symbolically shows undeveloped action. The scene is at a tomb, and the hacking up of Tamora's son's body is a promise of further bloody retribution. This morally links the hero to the crimes that will be committed against him, similar to the great opening scene of *King Lear*. Other gestures of symbolic status are Saturninus' courting of Tamora while accepting Lavinia's pledge, the "rape" of Lavinia by Bassianus, and Titus' slaying of his own son, Mutius.

This play develops foreshadowing within the conventions of a revenge tragedy to a sophisticated technique. There is the dumb-show, which had traditionally been used to show the philosophical or spiritual "moral" of a scene, followed by the same notion, in an evolved form, in the fly-killing scene. The latter's emblematic function is now enhanced by greater complexity. All major themes of the play as a whole are all figured in this short, symbolic scene: the rapid shifts of alliance, Titus' satiety of slaughter, the evil of Aaron, the hatred in revenge, mutilation, and the ambiguity of interpretation.

The problem with this play is in its excesses. The reader or viewer may become, because of the dearth of motivation and reflective action, "cloyed," like Titus, with so much killing.

TO BE A PILGRIM

Type of work: Novel
Author: Joyce Cary (1888-1957)
Type of plot: Social realism
Time of plot: Late 1930's
Locale: Tolbrook, England
First published: 1942

The second novel in Cary's Sara Monday trilogy, To Be a Pilgrim *depicts events from the point of view of the dying Tom Wilcher, the last surviving member of his generation of an old West-Country liberal and religious family.*

To Be a Pilgrim is the second novel in a trilogy published in the early 1940's (the other titles are *Herself Surprised,* and *The Horse's Mouth*). Each novel may be read by itself with satisfaction, but is best read with its companions. In the trilogy each novel is given over to a single character who tells his or her story. The basic scheme of the trilogy involves the conflict between the conservative attitude represented by the lawyer and landholder Tom Wilcher (*To Be a Pilgrim*), and the liberal attitude represented by the painter Gulley Jimson (*The Horse's Mouth*). Cary also attempts to create a rich overlap of the three subjective worlds.

Tom Wilcher is an old man when he tells his story. Indeed, his novel is one of the supreme studies of old age. All his life he has obeyed the injunctions of duty. He has persevered as a lawyer while his brother Edward enters then abandons politics for art and an expatriate life. He has maintained the family estate of Tolbrook and has never married. His narrative is a moving reflection upon England's past traditions. It is also a superb depiction of history as lived experience. In his recounting of his life Tom Wilcher shows us vividly the virtues of a concern with the past and with tradition. For him the past is more alive than the present, and he manages to make it so for us. His concern with tradition is not mere stiff-legged conservatism but a vital need for a sense of continuity. Cary's sympathetic portrait of Wilcher is set against his equally sympathetic portrait of the artist and image-breaker Gulley Jimson in *The Horse's Mouth*.

TO THE LIGHTHOUSE

Type of work: Novel
Author: Virginia Woolf (1882-1941)
Type of plot: Psychological realism
Time of plot: c. 1910-1920
Locale: The Isle of Skye in the Hebrides
First published: 1927

This major psychological novel, based in part upon the author's own family background, is significant for its impressionistic evocation of setting and character; its effective use of stream-of-consciousness technique; its complex, unified structure; and its advancement of Woolf's theory of androgynous personality.

Because of its unity of theme and technique, *To the Lighthouse* is probably Virginia Woolf's most satisfying novel. In theme, it is her most direct fictional statement about the importance of an androgynous artistic vision: that ideal which is neither masculine nor feminine but partakes of both. The book was almost contemporaneous with her important essay on women and fiction, *A Room of One's Own,* and *Orlando,* her androgynous fictional biography. In *A Room of One's Own* she appeals for androgynous creation, arguing that it is fatal for a writer to emphasize gender. For her, the mind which blends female and male themes "is naturally creative, incandescent and undivided." Many of her protagonists and most of the artists in her novels have both traditional "masculine" and "feminine" characteristics: Bernard in *The Waves,* Eleanor in *The Years,* Miss La Trobe in *Between the Acts,* and Lily Briscoe in *To the Lighthouse.* They have androgynous *consciousness,* even as Orlando completes the *physical* change from male to female.

To the Lighthouse clearly shows the deficiencies of the purely masculine (Mr. Ramsay) and the purely feminine (Mrs. Ramsay) personalities, and, as well, holds up the androgynous vision as a means of unifying the two—in the person of Lily Briscoe, the artist. Mr. Ramsay, a philosopher, has those qualities associated with the empirico-theoretical view, while Mrs. Ramsay employs a mythopoetic vision. Mr. Ramsay is concerned with the discovery of Truth, and his mind functions in a logical, reasoned fashion, moving, as he says, from A to Z, step by step. He worries that he has only so far reached Q. Mrs. Ramsay cares about details, about people's feelings, about her relationship with her husband and children; and her mind jumps and skips with the association of ideas—she can move from A to Z in one leap.

Mr. Ramsay is deficient in the attention he gives to his children and his wife, in concern for important financial details, in awareness of social and international situations. His character is satirized by Lily who always pictures him as seeing the whole of reality in a phantom kitchen table (the table is a traditional object for philosophic speculation). Mrs. Ramsay too is lacking:

she attempts to direct and fashion people's lives (she engineers the engagement of Minta and Paul and tries to match Lily Briscoe and William Bankes); she does not want her children to grow up; she cannot understand mathematics or history; she too often relies on men and their "masculine intelligence." The dinner scene shows Mrs. Ramsay's main strengths and weaknesses. She orchestrates the whole, directs the conversation, worries about the *Boeuf en Daube,* thinks about the lateness of the hour, makes sure all the guests are involved. Yet she lets her mind wander, looking ahead to the next details. She is the unifier in the first part of the book, but she fails because her vision is too limited; the trip to the lighthouse is not made, and she dies before the Ramsays can return to the island.

Lily Briscoe and her art become the true unifier of the story's disparate elements. During the dinner party, as she remembers Charles Tansley's dictum that "Women can't write, women can't paint," she suddenly envisions the way to give her picture coherence, and she moves the salt cellar to remind herself. But her painting remains incomplete, and, like the trip to the lighthouse, is not accomplished until many years later. Lily, an unmarried professional, embodies both rational (masculine) and imaginative (feminine) characteristics. She analyzes art with William Bankes and still feels emotionally attuned with Mrs. Ramsay. Lily becomes the central figure in the final section; her visions of Mrs. Ramsay and of Mr. Ramsay and the children finally landing at the lighthouse enable her to complete her work, uniting the rational and the imaginative into the androgynous whole which the painting symbolizes.

The novel's structure is thematically as well as technically brilliant. The work has three parts; the first, entitled "The Window," takes place about 1910, the last, entitled "The Lighthouse," about 1920. The middle section is entitled "Time Passes" and narrates the intervening time period. The window in the first section functions as a symbol of the female principle, as the narrator returns again and again to Mrs. Ramsay in her place near the open window. Mrs. Ramsay is the center and unifier of the family, and even as different characters participate in various activities, their thoughts and glances return to Mrs. Ramsay. The reddish-brown stocking she is knitting is another emblem of her unifying power. But, like the trip to the lighthouse and Lily's painting, it is not completed in the first section. The thoughts of different characters are narrated by means of interior monologue, and Woolf makes skillful use of the theory of association of ideas. Mrs. Ramsay's mind is most often viewed, however, and she is the most real of the characters.

Early in the novel, the lighthouse, in its faraway light-giving aspects, functions as a female symbol. Mrs. Ramsay identifies herself with the lighthouse: "she was stern, she was searching, she was beautiful like that light." In the last section, however, the lighthouse becomes a masculine principle; when seen from nearby it is a "tower, stark and straight . . . barred with black and white." But the male and female aspects become joined in that section as well; James thinks, "For nothing was simply one thing. The other Lighthouse was true too." So James and Cam come to understand their father as well as their dead mother. The line that Lily Briscoe draws in the center of her picture—perhaps her image of the lighthouse—enables her to complete her painting, uniting both the masculine and the feminine.

The center section, "Time Passes," is narrated from the viewpoint of the house itself, as the wind over the years peels wallpaper; rusts pots; brings mildew, dust, spider webs, and rats. Important events in the lives of the Ramsays are inserted into this poetic interlude prosaically by means of square brackets.

To the Lighthouse is a difficult work, but each successive reading brings new insights into Woolf's techniques and themes.

Margaret McFadden-Gerber

TOBACCO ROAD

Type of work: Novel
Author: Erskine Caldwell (1903-   )
Type of plot: Social melodrama
Time of plot: 1920's
Locale: Georgia
First published: 1932

Although certain exaggerated, Rabelaisian episodes of Tobacco Road *make the novel appear to be merely a burlesque on backwoods Georgia life, Caldwell's serious purpose is to show with realism the social problems of his region.*

Tobacco Road, published in the midst of the Great Depression, reflects the social and economic concerns of the 1930's, as well as principles of literary naturalism. During the 1930's, a time of extreme economic hardship, novels such as *Tobacco Road* helped make Americans (and others) aware of the destructive poverty and alienation at the bottom of society.

Naturalism, a significant movement in American literature from before the beginning of the twentieth century through World War II, stresses the impersonal and powerful forces that shape human destinies. The characters of *Tobacco Road* are caught in the backwaters of industrialization, in the grip of irresistible forces. Unable to farm effectively, yet bound to the land, and so unable to migrate to the factories, they are trapped from one generation to the next. Jeeter, for instance, cannot farm his land, and yet instinct binds him (and, finally, his son) to it.

These characters are also prisoners of other forces, most notably the past and their sexuality. They find modern technology beyond their understanding, and they ruin a new car Bessie has managed to buy. Unable to use modern farming methods, Jeeter and Ada die trying to burn the fields to clear them for an imaginary cotton crop. Sexuality also operates powerfully on these characters. Bessie's marriage to Dude and Lov's attraction for Ellie May are based entirely on sex; and, in fact, the reader is left with the impression that the characters of *Tobacco Road* are as little able to cope with sexual forces as with economic forces.

The style of the novel, marked by simple, declarative sentences and catching the rhythms of the dialect used by poor white Southerners, is appropriate for the tragically self-destructive life Caldwell describes. This plain style, typical of naturalism, corresponds to the basic drives for food, sex, and survival, drives which are not hidden or disguised by the demands of civilization, but which Caldwell lays bare for all to see in the changeless lives of his characters.

THE TOILERS OF THE SEA

Type of work: Novel
Author: Victor Hugo (1802-1885)
Type of plot: Sentimental romance
Time of plot: The 1820's
Locale: The Isle of Guernsey
First published: 1866

A romantic, sometimes emotionally overwrought novel of the sea, Hugo's fiction is notable for its sense of the mysteries transcending ordinary life; its evocative descriptions, especially of wild, untamed nature; and its celebration of heroic endeavor.

The Toilers of the Sea represents, most dramatically, many of the chief characteristics of French literary romanticism. The setting, action, characterization and style of the novel extend and exaggerate certain tendencies inherent in the romantic world view.

Les Miserables, an earlier work by Hugo, is concerned with human progress, justice, and social improvement. *The Toilers of the Sea,* on the other hand, is as much concerned with the mystical "world beyond" as with the ordinary world of men. It is a novel that embodies Hugo's late flowering interest in religion and the occult. Written in exile on the British-ruled Channel Islands, Hugo's loneliness and isolation no doubt magnified this interest.

The scene of the novel is lonely and exotic, far from the ordinary experiences of men and women. Although Hugo goes to great lengths to describe the islands and surrounding ocean, picturing everything in the most particular detail—including insects, types of grasses, the everyday conditions of nature—the landscape nevertheless appears both melodramatic and "supernatural." Hugo's landscape, or seascape, is overwhelming.

But the action, or plot, combines typical romantic features with these extremes. There is, first of all, an intense love story. This story is combined with considerable intrigue and mystery. Nothing is merely what it seems, everything suggests something else. These mysterious elements in the action, emphasized by Hugo at every step, are reminiscent of the devices of Edgar Allan Poe.

But the scope of the action, especially Gilliatt's struggle for the engine and his fight against the octopus, far exceeds the ambition of Poe. The will to struggle that Hugo portrays in Gilliatt is particularly notable in the light of Hugo's overall purpose: to glorify toil and the struggle against the elements, and to show that this struggle is actually part of the immense human effort to master infinity. Thus Hugo's approach to human labor is decisively opposed to the realist tradition. In other words, Hugo does not record the details of work or its social meaning and function; instead, Hugo's "toil" is primarily metaphysical and transcendent. The character of Gilliatt, which dominates the novel, is Promethean; Gilliatt knows and understands more than other men about the sea and the crafts of the sea. His energy and skill are wild and superhuman; just as Prometheus brings fire to men, Gilliatt salvages the steam engine (modern technology) for them.

But the atmosphere of the novel, its density, and its dramatic force, are generated in Hugo's descriptions of the sea, the rocks, and the struggles of Gilliatt. Using hyperbole and antithesis, Hugo presents a powerful image of the sea in storm and at rest, and of man in agony and in surrender.

TOM BROWN'S SCHOOL DAYS

Type of work: Novel
Author: Thomas Hughes (1822-1896)
Type of plot: Didactic romance
Time of plot: Early nineteenth century
Locale: England
First published: 1857

More than a nostalgic portrait of Rubgy during the time of Dr. Arnold, its famous reforming headmaster, Hughes's novel is a warning to abolish the evil practices of hazing and peer-administered brutality from boys' schools throughout England.

Tom Brown's School Days can be read as a thinly disguised autobiography of Thomas Hughes, an indictment of the English public school system before the 1830's, especially in its encouragement of tyranny of older boys over the younger ones, and at last a panegyric to the influential and progressive Doctor Thomas Arnold, the father of the great poet and critic, Matthew Arnold. The novel springs out of the Victorian rejection of Regency England and the consequent demand for moral and social reform of all institutions from Parliament to the school system.

Although certainly without room for the lower classes, Dr. Arnold's Rugby discouraged the class system, stressing the equality of all boys, punishing those such as Flashman, who insists that it is his social prerogative to haze the younger boy like Brown and East. Before Dr. Arnold assumed the headmastership of Rugby, the great public schools did not emphasize the inculcation of useful knowledge or morals but were rather aimless in their methods and purpose and tended to preserve without question the social *status quo* with its tyranny of one class over the other. After Dr. Arnold's innovations, such as the introduction of history and modern foreign languages (as well as the game of rugby) and the stress on the importance of moral character, the British public schools began to take on a more progressive form in which they acknowledged their social responsibility.

The education of young Tom Brown entails, then, his becoming a student after Dr. Arnold's model. After putting down the tyranny of Flashman, he grows under the pious influence of George Arthur to become a true English gentleman, the fruit of Rugby, with a sense of moral and social responsibility to his nation. One must question his lack of solid intellectual achievement, but one cannot doubt his real virtue, earnestness, and devotion.

TOM BURKE OF OURS

Type of work: Novel
Author: Charles Lever (1806-1872)
Type of plot: Historical romance
Time of plot: Early nineteenth century
Locale: Ireland and France
First published: 1844

A vivid, episodic, somewhat theatrical novel by a popular Irish writer of the nineteenth century, Tom Burke of Ours *is notable for its colorful re-creations of battle scenes, particularly those of Austerlitz and Jena; for its gallery of Irish personalities; and for its sympathetic treatment of Napoleon's career.*

Tom Burke of Ours is an excellent example of the rough-and-ready style of fiction which made Charles Lever famous. The vivacity of the novel, the picture it presents of devil-may-care, hard-riding Irish gentry, and a certain down-to-earth comic realism, make it entertaining reading. The book presents a vivid picture of the life and sentiments prevalent in Ireland during the early nineteenth century.

Tom Burke of Ours is the story of a second son, a younger brother who must make his own way in the world: a common story in British fiction. The first person narration is not always plausible. and the style makes little effort at consistency, but the vitality of the writing sweeps the reader along. The characters are drawn with a bold brush, and often seem to possess a life of their own. Darby M'Keown is particularly fine; a dynamic and forceful personality, he is an example of the Irish patriots of nearly two centuries ago, a man who held up the ideals of independence, and of the French Revolution and Napoleon. Captain Bubbleton and his sister, Anna Maria, are quite different, although excellent characterizations; while they are genuinely humorous characters almost worthy of Dickens, the author pushes a little too hard in an effort to make them extraordinary. Lever does possess a tendency to overwrite, a danger that probably stems from his technique of rattling off a story in the manner of a raconteur.

Although Lever's later novels are more strongly plotted and written with more control, this early, picaresque novel of the life and adventures of Tom Burke is considered one of his best. The very extravagance of the tale and the writing give the book its chief virtues. The novel's greatness almost seems to arise from its defects. Although there are serious passages in the novel, such as a thoughtful discussion of the Irish attitude toward death, it is the humor of the book which most readers will remember. The original edition of *Tom Burke of Ours* was embellished with masterful humorous illustrations by Phiz, who already was illustrating the novels of Lever's younger contemporary, Dickens. The style of caricature for which Phiz was famous was particularly suited to the flamboyant writing of Charles Lever. *Tom Burke of Ours* and Lever's other novels have been overshadowed by the more famous works of Lever's great contemporaries, but they are worth reading and treasuring for their vitality and humor.

TOM CRINGLE'S LOG

Type of work: Novel
Author: Michael Scott (1789-1835)
Type of plot: Adventure romance
Time of plot: Nineteenth century
Locale: West Indies
First published: 1833

Almost plotless, Tom Cringle's Log *is a series of loosely connected episodes and character sketches that give the reader some firsthand accurate accounts of minor actions in the war with Napoleon and many sidelights on the War of 1812 with America, although Scott mainly describes merry bibulous exploits ashore rather than the business of fighting.*

Tom Cringle's Log by Michael Scott is a fast-paced and loosely joined series of romantic sea adventures set in the North Sea during the Napoleonic Wars, and in the Caribbean shortly thereafter. Scott, a Scottish merchant rather than a professional writer, spent much of his early life in Jamaica and drew heavily upon his experiences in writing sketches and short stories. Like many of his contemporaries in England, Scott's book was first serialized in *Blackwood Magazine* from 1829 to 1833; hence, Scott belongs to what became known as the *"Blackwood* Group" of authors, including Christopher North, John Galt, John G. Lockwood, and Susan Ferrier.

The first-person journalistic narrative is wholly concerned with adventure, literally racing from one episode to another with little, if any, character development. Names such as Mr. Bong, Wagtail, Barnaby Blueblazes and Mr. Tailtackle serve to identify characters; but since the various personages appear and vanish with such rapidity, it is of little consequence.

Perhaps this mode of narration can be attributed to the age of the narrator (thirteen in the beginning). It would be natural for a boy of his age to avoid detailed characterizations in favor of the great adventures encountered while fighting the pirates. The fact is, however, youthful narrators are also capable of providing useful insights; but Scott does not fully exploit these possibilities.

This lack of characterization is partly offset by rousingly humorous scenes, such as those of Aaron Bong the plantation owner, and of heroic struggles between great vessels of the sea. Scott also has an excellent command of numerous dialects, which he learned from being a merchant, and a thorough knowledge of nautical terms—all of which serve as realistic trappings for this most romantic, disorganized novel.

TOM JONES

Type of work: Novel
Author: Henry Fielding (1707-1754)
Type of plot: Comic epic
Time of plot: Early eighteenth century
Locale: England
First published: 1749

Tom Jones, a major contribution to the history of the English novel, has been admired by many readers as the most meticulously crafted book of its type. With neoclassic objectivity, humor, and fine psychological delicacy, Fielding dissects the motives of his characters to reveal universal truths about human nature.

In a relatively short life span, Henry Fielding was a poet and a playwright, a journalist and a jurist, as well as a pioneer in the formal development of the modern novel. The early poetry may be disregarded, but his dramatic works gave Fielding the training which later enabled him to handle adeptly the complex plots of his novels. Although he wrote perhaps half-a-dozen novels (some attributions are disputed) Fielding is best remembered for *The History of Tom Jones, a Foundling.* This novel contains a strong infusion of auto-biographical elements. The character Sophia, for example, was based on Fielding's wife Charlotte, who was his one great love. They eloped in 1734 and had ten years together before she died in 1744. Squire Allworthy combined traits of a former schoolmate from Eton named George Lyttelton (to whom the novel is dedicated), and a generous benefactor of the Fielding family named James Ralph. Moreover, Fielding's origins in a career army family and his rejection of that background shaped his portrayal of various incidental military personnel in this and his other novels; he had an anti-army bias. Fielding's own feelings of revulsion against urban living are reflected in the conclusion of *Tom Jones* (and in his other novels): the "happy ending" consists of a retreat to the country. Published a scant five years before Fielding's death, *Tom Jones* was a runaway bestseller, going through four editions within a twelve-month period.

The structure of the novel is carefully divided into eighteen books in a fashion similar to the epic form which Fielding explicitly praised. Of those eighteen books, the first six are set on the Somersetshire estate of Squire All-worthy. Books VII-XII deal with events on the road to London. And the culmination of the six books is laid in London. The very midpoint of the novel, Books IX and X, covers the hilarious hiatus at the inn in Upton. Apparent diversions and digressions are actually intentional exercises in character exposition. And all episodes are deliberately choreographed to advance the plot —sometimes in ways not evident until later. Everything contributes to the overall organic development of the novel.

This kind of coherence was intimately connected with Fielding's concern about the craft of fiction. It is no accident that *Tom Jones* is one of the most carefully and meticulously written novels in the history of English literature. It is, in fact, remarkably free of inconsistencies and casual errors. Fielding saw his task as a novelist to be a "historian" of human nature and human events. And he felt obligated to emphasize the moral aspect of his work. But more importantly, Fielding introduced each of his eighteen books with a chapter about the craft of prose fiction. Indeed, the entire novel is dotted with intercalary chapters on the craft of the novel and on literary criticism. And the remainder of the novel applies the principles enunciated in the chapters on proper construction of prose fiction—an amazing *tour de force*. The detailed analyses in themselves constitute a substantial work of literary criticism; however, Fielding amplified these theories with his own demonstration of their application by writing a novel, *Tom Jones,* according to his own principles. So compelling a union of theory and practice rendered Fielding's hypotheses virtually unassailable.

As Fielding made practical application of his theories of craftsmanship, their validity became readily apparent in his handling of characterization. He viewed human nature ambivalently, as a combination of good and bad. But whereas the bad person had almost no hope of redemption, the fundamentally good person could be (and would and should be) somewhat tinged with bad but nonetheless worthy for all that, according to Fielding. Thus the good person could occasionally be unwise (as Allworthy was) or indiscreet (as Jones often was) but still be an estimable human being, for such a person was more credible as a "good" person, Fielding thought, than one who was without defect. Consequently, the villain Blifil is unreconstructibly wicked, but the hero Tom Jones is essentially good, although morally flawed. In order to succeed, Jones had to improve morally—to cultivate "prudence" and "religion," as Squire Allworthy recommended. In this dichotomy between evil and good, villain and hero, a species of determinism—possibly not a factor consciously recognized by Fielding—creeps in. Both Blifil and Jones are born and reared in the same environment, but one is wicked and one is good. Only innate qualities could logically explain the difference. Of course, some minor characters are not so fully psychologized; they are essentially allegorical, representing ideas (Thwackum and Square, for example). Yet overall, Fielding's command of characterization in general comprised a series of excellent portraits. But these portraits are never allowed to dominate the novel, for all of them are designed to contribute to the development of the story. Such a system of priorities provides insight into Fielding's aesthetic and epistemological predispositions.

Fielding subscribed to a fundamentally Classical-Neo-Classical set of values, ethically and aesthetically. He saw the novel as a *mirror* of life, not an *illumination* of life. He valued literary craftsmanship; he assumed a position of detached objectivity; he esteemed wit; and he followed the Neo-Classical

Unity of Action: his plot brought Tom Jones full circle from a favored position to disgrace back to the good graces of Squire Allworthy and Sophia. In the course of the novel, Fielding demonstrated his objectivity by commenting critically on the form of the novel. He further revealed his Classical commitments by embellishing his novel with historical detail, creating a high degree of verisimilitude. His sense of humor and his sharp wit also testified to his reliance on Classical ratiocination. The easygoing development of the plot additionally reveals Fielding's detachment and objectivity. And the great variety in types of characters whom he presents is another indication of his Classical inclinations toward universality. But above all, Fielding's moral stance and his insistence on ethical principles unequivocally mark him as a Neo-Classicist.

Joanne G. Kashdan

TOM SAWYER

Type of work: Novel
Author: Mark Twain (Samuel L. Clemens, 1835-1910)
Type of plot: Adventure romance
Time of plot: Nineteenth century
Locale: St. Petersburg on the Mississippi River
First published: 1876

More than a book for boys, The Adventures of Tom Sawyer, *with its rich native humor and shrewd observations of human character, is an idyl of American village life, of that quieter age that had already vanished when Mark Twain re-created St. Petersburg from memories of his own boyhood.*

Beginning his writing career as a frontier humorist and ending it as a bitter satirist, Mark Twain drew from his circus of experiences, as a child in a small Missouri town (who had little formal schooling), as a printer's apprentice, a journalist, a roving correspondent, a world traveler, silver prospector, Mississippi steamboat pilot, and lecturer. He was influenced, in turn, by Artemus Ward, Bret Harte, Longstreet, and G. W. Harris. Beginning with the publication of his first short story, "The Celebrated Jumping Frog of Calaveras County," in 1865, and proceeding through his best novels—*Innocents Abroad* (1869); *Roughing It* (1872); *The Gilded Age* (1873), brilliant in concept but a failure in design and execution; *Tom Sawyer* (1876); *Life on the Mississippi* (1883); *Huckleberry Finn* (1885); *A Connecticut Yankee in King Arthur's Court* (1889); and *The American Claimant* (1892)—Twain developed a characteristic style which, though uneven in its productions, made him the most important and most representative nineteenth century American writer. His service as delightful entertainment to generations of American youngsters is equaled, literarily, by his influence on such twentieth century admirers as Gertrude Stein, William Faulkner, and Ernest Hemingway.

Twain's generally careful and conscientious style was both a development of the southwestern humor tradition of Longstreet and Harris and a departure from the conventions of nineteenth century literary gentility. It is characterized by the adroit use of exaggeration, stalwart irreverence, deadpan seriousness, droll cynicism, and pungent commentary on the human situation. All of this is masked in an uncomplicated, straightforward narrative distinguished for its wholehearted introduction of the colloquial and vernacular into American fiction that was to have a profound impact on the development of American writing and also shape the world's view of America. Twain, according to Frank Baldanza, had a talent for "paring away the inessential and presenting the bare core of experience with devastating authenticity." The combination of childish rascality and innocence in his earlier writing gave way, in his later and posthumous works, to an ever darkening vision of man that left Twain bitter and disillusioned. But this darker vision is hardly present in the three Tom Sawyer books (1876, 1894, 1896) and in his masterpiece, *Huckleberry Finn.*

Twain's lifelong fascination with boyhood play led to the creation of *Tom Sawyer,* a book of nostalgic recollections of his own lost youth that has been dismissed too lightly by some sober-sided academics as "amusing but thin stuff" and taken too analytically and seriously by others who seek in it the complexities—of carefully controlled viewpoint, multiple irony, and social satire—found in *Huckleberry Finn,* begun in the year *Tom Sawyer* was published. Beyond noting that *Tom Sawyer* is a delicate balance of the romantic with the realistic, of humor and pathos, of innocence and evil, one must admit that the book defies analysis. In fact, Twain's opening statement in *Huckleberry Finn* is, ironically, more applicable to *Tom Sawyer*: "Persons attempting to find a motive in this narrative will be prosecuted; persons attempting to find a moral in it will be banished; persons attempting to find a plot in it will be shot." *Tom Sawyer* is purely, simply, and happily "the history of a boy," or as Twain also called it, "simply a hymn, put into prose form to give it a worldly air." It should be read first and last for pleasure, first by children, then by adults.

For *Tom Sawyer* is also, as even Twain admitted paradoxically, a book for those who have long since passed from boyhood: "It is *not* a boy's book at all. It will be read only by adults. It is written only for adults." Kenneth S. Lynn explicates the author's preface when he says that *Tom Sawyer* "confirms the profoundest wishes of the heart"; as does Christopher Morley, who calls the book "a panorama of happy memory" and who made a special visit to Hannibal because he wanted to see the town and house where Tom lived. During that visit, Morley and friends actually white-washed Aunt Polly's fence. Certainly there can be no greater testimony to the effectiveness of a literary work than its readers' desire to reenact the exploits of its hero.

Tom is the archetypal all-American boy, defining in himself the very concept of American boyhood, as he passes with equal seriousness from one obsession to another: whistling, glory, spying, sympathy, flirtation, exploration, piracy, shame, fear—always displaying to the utmost the child's ability to concentrate his entire energies on one thing at a time (as when he puts the treasure hunt out of his mind in favor of Becky's picnic). Tom is contrasted to both Sid, the sanctimonious "good boy" informant who loses the reader's sympathies as immediately as Tom gains them, and to Huck. As opposed to Huck's self-reliant, unschooled, parentless existence, his love of profanity, his passive preference for being a follower, his abhorrence of civilization, Tom is shrewd in the ways of civilization, adventurous and a leader. He comes from the respectable world of Aunt Polly, with a literary mind, with a conscious romantic desire for experience and for the hero's part, an insatiable egotism which assists him in his ingenious schematizations of life to achieve his heroic aspirations—and a general love of fame, money, attention, and "glory." The relationship between the two boys may be compared to that between the romantic Don Quixote and the realist Sancho Panza. It was Twain's genius to understand that the games Quixote played out of "madness" were, in fact, those played by children with deadly seriousness. Lionel Trilling summarizes Twain's achievement in this book when he says that "*Tom Sawyer* has the truth of honesty—what it says about things and feelings is never false and always both adequate and beautiful." Twain's book is an American classic, but a classic that travels well as an ambassador of American nostalgic idealism.

Kenneth John Atchity

TOM THUMB THE GREAT

Type of work: Drama
Author: Henry Fielding (1707-1754)
Type of plot: Farce
Time of plot: Age of chivalry
Locale: King Arthur's court
First presented: 1730

The full title of this play is The Tragedy of Tragedies, or, The Life and Death of Tom Thumb the Great. *It is a literary burlesque, pretending to be a newly discovered Elizabethan work, that makes fun of the absurd heroic tragedies popular during the seventeenth and eighteenth centuries, as well as a satire on so-called courtly greatness.*

The most famous literary burlesque between George Villiers' *The Rehearsal* (1671) and Sheridan's *The Critic* (1779) is *The Tragedy of Tragedies, Or, The Life and Death of Tom Thumb the Great.* Although written sixty years after Villiers' attack on the affectations of heroic tragedy, Fielding's farce continues to expose the absurdities of the same kind of drama—which is proof of its persistence and strange popularity. Fielding was clearly influenced by the social satire of John Gay's *The Beggar's Opera* (1728) because Fielding combines the ridicule of heroic tragedy with a satire on courtly magnificence. Just as Gay ridiculed middle-class avarice by suggesting that middle-class manners went nicely with organized thievery, Fielding lays bare the absurdity of a lordly monarchy by equating aristocratic self-importance with the fustian of a dated theatricality.

Fielding is a master at exposing affectation. It is the theme of his first great novel, *Joseph Andrews* (1742), in which the protection of the hero's virginity is gently mocked by framing his story within the conventions of Homeric epic. In *Tom Thumb the Great,* the exaggerated sentiments and puffed-up emotions of all the characters are harshly mocked by setting them in the actions and language of heroic tragedy. For example, when the king announces that his daughter, the princess Huncamunca, will be given in marriage to Tom Thumb, the queen objects strongly because she herself is in love with Tom. She cannot speak of her passion freely in the presence of her husband, but this does not prevent her from ranting in the manner befitting a virago in heroic drama. Her indignation reeks of hypocrisy, her curse is absurd, and the responding comment of Foodle, the courtier, impales the queen's false feeling with the punishing comedy of understatement:

> Queen: Who, but a dog, who, but a dog
> Would use me as thou dost? Me, who have lain
> These twenty years so loving by thy side!
> But I will be revenged. I'll hang myself.
> Then tremble all who did this match persuade,

> For riding on a cat, from high I'll fall,
> And squirt down royal vengeance on you all.

Foodle: Her majesty the queen is in a passion.

At the end of the play, the endless succession of corpses is a burlesque of *Hamlet* and its heroic descendants, particularly the heroic tragedies of Dryden. The king's boast that he is the "last" to fall captures the ultimate nonsense of "heroic" action, and is also a veiled blow at the English monarchy's French wars.

TONO-BUNGAY

Type of work: Novel
Author: H. G. Wells (1866-1946)
Type of plot: Social criticism
Time of plot: Late nineteenth and early twentieth centuries
Locale: England, West Africa, Bordeaux
First published: 1908

A mixture of several forms—novel of ideas, "education" novel, scientific romance, and social satire—the partly autobiographical Tono-Bungay *is a spirited though finally pessimistic book that exposes the shoddy commercial foundations of Edwardian society.*

H. G. Wells utilizes novels, as well as other literary forms, as vehicles for his social analysis and criticism. Some of his early works, such as *The Time Machine* (1895), *The Invisible Man* (1897), and *The War of the Worlds* (1898), reflect an extreme *fin de siècle* pessimism. In those works Wells predicts nothing ahead but doom and destruction for mankind. In later writings, however, such as *A Modern Utopia* (1905), he presents at least the possibility of salvation through an elite leadership called "the Samurai." If society can produce such an elite out of the morass of democratic mediocrity, survival of the species might become possible. This elitist ideology affected Wells's writing down to the time of his death. In *Tono-Bungay* Wells seems to take a position somewhere between the two extremes, with the emphasis leaning in the direction of the pessimistic. Yet elements in the character and behavior of George Ponderevo and his Aunt Susan suggest real, if qualified, signs of hope.

Tono-Bungay represents Wells at his best, utilizing witty language and clever plotting to dramatize his dire predictions of man's fate. It is also his most autobiographical and intensely personal work. Although Wells denied any resemblance, his own experiences remarkably paralleled those of his hero, George Ponderevo. Like that of his protagonist in *Tono-Bungay,* Wells's father exerted little influence over his life, deferring to a domineering mother, the housekeeper of a large country estate. Both Wells and Ponderevo studied science at the Consolidated Technical Schools at South Kensington, but dropped out after mediocre academic careers. Both married dull, insipid women and became unfaithful husbands. In fact, the many similarities between Wells's life and Ponderevo's strongly imply that the author wrote *Tono-Bungay* as a statement of his personal beliefs.

As the children of servants, both Wells and Ponderevo had opportunities to view English society from the bottom up. The descriptions of life at Bladesover House, particularly the afternoon teas over which George's mother presides, reveal its pomposity and pretension. The incident with Archie Garvell exposes the treachery and deceit of the supposed "better sort." Ponderevo's Bladesover experiences introduce an important theme which runs through the whole novel: the sham, artificiality and superficiality of the world as Wells saw it.

The history of Tono-Bungay, the patent medicine which brought fame and fortune to Edward Ponderevo and his nephew George, serves as a metaphor for Wells's view of English society. The tonic is an instant success, rising meteorically in the commercial sky. The book contains several allusions to dramatic spurts and rapid rises. Yet nothing sustains them; Tono-Bungay itself is a fraud, and the financial empire which it spawned depends upon manipulation, chicanery, and, in the end, even forgery. Its spectacular rise is followed by an equally spectacular demise; like a rocket it bursts into the sky, only to disintegrate and fall back to earth. So too, the world in which he lived was, for Wells, in a state of degeneration and disintegration.

Pervasive decay provides Wells with another theme, one which follows logically from the sudden success of a venture built upon a sham. As Edward Ponderevo's business conglomerate crumbles under the weight of its own inadequacies, the man responsible for it began to rot away himself. Wells's account of Edward's terminal illness emphasizes its deteriorating impact. Even Beatrice Normandy is affected by the decay. Her involvement with the upper class and her role as mistress to an English nobleman have corrupted her. She finally rejects the relationship with George because she feels herself contaminated by the stench of the dying carcass of high society. The ultimate symbol of decay is the quap, the item which, still through manipulation and fraud, was to save Edward Ponderevo and his assorted schemes. He looks on quap as a quick and total remedy for his dying empire, but instead it destroys everything it touches. It kills all life in its vicinity in Africa; it provokes George Ponderevo into killing an innocent African native; it even rots the ship carrying it back to England, causing the ship to sink to the bottom of the ocean.

Wells's criticism and accusations of degeneracy are not confined to the upper classes. All elements of English society, in his view, are equally at fault. The Ramboat family, for instance, represents the proletariat, but does not come across as a radical socialist might have portrayed it. Instead, they are dull, vacuous, and inept, as decayed in their own way as the gentility of Beatrice Normandy and Archie Garvell. No group emerges from Wells's attack unscathed.

Social criticism, of course, was hardly new with Wells and *Tono-Bungay*. The uniqueness and superior quality of this novel rests not on the novelty of its format, but on the skill with which Wells presents his argument in the context of an amusing story. Despite the somberness of its message, the book remains pleasant and easy reading. An almost puckish humor runs through the dialogue of the characters, and even their names show Wells's wit at work. Strong character development is not, however, an element of *Tono-*

Bungay. The personages remain almost stereotypes of their respective classes, caricatures rather than real humans.

Only two exceptions provide relief from Wells's pessimism and criticism. One, Edward's wife Susan, lives through all her husband's escapades without the loss of her sensible good nature or affection for George. Another very positive element appears in Ponderevo's research first with gliders and then with destroyers. "Sometimes," he says, "I call this reality Science, sometimes I call it Truth." Yet Wells fails to explain why or how Susan manages to resist the forces of illusion and decay which surrounded her, nor does he consider Ponderevo one of the "Samurai" who might save civilization through scientific research. Thus, neither exception offers an answer to the question of what might be done to provide mankind salvation from degeneration and destruction. At best Wells, through his alter ego Ponderevo, engages in a search for a solution.

R. David Weber

THE TOWER OF LONDON

Type of work: Novel
Author: William Harrison Ainsworth (1805-1882)
Type of plot: Historical romance
Time of plot: Sixteenth century
Locale: England
First published: 1840

Set during the time of Queen Mary's troubled reign, Ainsworth's novel is a well-plotted historical romance that makes the Tower itself a protagonist and witness to the gripping events.

The Tower of London is a historical novel in the tradition of Sir Walter Scott, yet Ainsworth's unique approach to his historical material makes the book stand apart from other novels of the genre. Ainsworth makes the tower itself the protagonist of the story. The author is quite explicit about this point. His goal in *The Tower of London* was to write about incidents that would illuminate every corner of the edifice, or, in his words, "Naturally introduce every relic of the old pile." Unlike a story which deals with a period in the life of a human being or with the unfolding of character development, *The Tower of London* centers on a phase in the history of a complex of buildings. If the reader is willing to accept this premise, he must be content to see action and character subordinate to setting and to some of his pre conceived notions concerning plot.

The tower not only functions as the historical backdrop for the incidents in the novel and the stage upon which the action takes place, but as the major structural device of the book. Indeed, the tower is so thoroughly integrated with the other materials of the novel that it becomes a vital participant in the action, and as such provides the novel's unity by acting as a focal point around which all other elements are organized. The novel has a clearly defined beginning in Lady Jane Grey Dudley's arrival at the tower on July 10, 1553, and an equally definite end: her execution on Tower Green, February 10, 1559. In between the two events, much of the major action of the book takes place in the tower, chapels, halls, chambers, and gateways.

The novel can be viewed as two distinct parts joined together by the tower. During the first half of the book, Lady Jane, the queen for barely a month, is supported in her tenuous claim to the throne by her father-in-law, the Duke of Northumberland, and by her husband, Lord Dudley. She is plotted against, however, by those who wish to put Mary on the throne. In the second part, Mary is queen; but she too is the object of conspiracies by the champions of both Elizabeth and the deposed Jane. At the novel's conclusion with the beheading of Lady Jane, Elizabeth is in protective custody and Mary is committed to a Spanish marriage which pleases no one. All that survives unimpaired is the tower, having been the scene of one more series of events in its long history.

Though one might at first suspect that Lady Jane is the heroine of the novel since it chronicles her stay in the tower, this is not the case. Mary Tudor and her half-sister play larger roles. Yet it is obviously the tower itself which dominates this novel, and the book's best writing is found in the passages describing the structure. Ainsworth spaces his descriptions judiciously throughout the novel in such a way as to heighten the effect. The only apparent exception to this general descriptive practice occurs in Book II, Chapter LV, where Ainsworth digresses for more than a dozen pages to relate an account of the tower's history from the time of William the Conqueror down to the nineteenth century. Yet this interruption is not enirely indefensible because even the architectural history of the tower has a decided part in creating mood, establishing motivation, and advancing action.

In turning his descriptive powers toward the people of the novel, Ainsworth generally achieves the same effectiveness that goes into his descriptions of the tower. Yet his characterizations also exhibit major flaws in technique. He describes in almost minute detail not only the physical appearance of the characters but also their dress and every aspect of the ceremonial occasions in which they participate. Although the amount of social-historical research necessary for Ainsworth's descriptions of ceremonial pomp and costumery is noteworthy, the sheer detail of the descriptions tends to slow down the action of the novel in places, and becomes tedious for even the most patient reader. Most readers, however, would admit that they are never left with any uncertainty concerning the appearance of the principal participants in any scene of *The Tower of London*—even regarding such minute details as the texture of the Duke of Suffolk's cloak, "flowered with gold and ribanded with nets of silver."

Ainsworth's characters often tend to be mere types, such as the meritorious young man who has to make his way in the world against great odds. He is in love with a chaste maiden who is subjected to a series of threats ranging from the inconvenient to the unspeakable. These types can be seen in *The Tower of London* in the characters of Dudley's squire, Cuthbert, and his loved one, Cicely, who are the victims of imprisonment and conspiracy but escape unscathed to marry at last. A second stock character is the power-hungry schemer personified in this book by Simon Renard, the Spanish ambassador who lurks in the background attempting to manipulate the fortunes of the other characters. His skill in plotting is seen when he effects a rupture in the relationship between Lady Jane and Northumberland by convincing her to deny Dudley the kingship as a part of a larger scheme to weaken Lady Jane's claim to the throne. A final example of Ainsworth's stock characters is the "unmotivated villain," Nightgall the jailer, who seems to perpetrate evil deeds for their own sake, and who adds greatly to the misfortunes of Cuthbert and Cicely.

Ainsworth compounds his problems of characterization by use of the hackneyed device of mistaken identities. In *The Tower of London,* the details of Cicely's birth are unknown until the novel's conclusion, when Nightgall confirms that she is the daughter of Lady Grace. This is at best only a slight variation of plots employed by Ainsworth in at least six of his other works. Sometimes these false identities are deliberately assumed, or, as in this novel, they stem from mysteries of parentage of which the main characters are themselves unaware. In any case the device was overworked long before Ainsworth employed it in *The Tower of London.*

The author's treatment of the nonfictional characters is somewhat more effective because he is dealing with real people about which something is known, but he nevertheless weakens their portraits through his intrusive moral judgments of their actions. He tells the reader quite clearly what he is to think of the characters. The Duke of Northumberland, for example, is "haughty and disdainful," while Queen Mary's "worst fault as a woman and her sole fault as a sovereign was her bigotry." No writer of his age was less reticent than Ainsworth about intruding his own personal views into his writing. Yet in accepting the premise of the novel, which is to narrate the history of the tower, these problems of characterization will be overlooked by most readers.

It is true that *The Tower of London* is an unusual work and not without its flaws, but it is an effective novel in terms of its vivid and ordered chronicling of fascinating historical events. Ainsworth's appeal springs from his sense of structure and his ability to arouse in the reader a sense of being in a crowded, swarming, self-contained world where adventure and intrigue are staples of everyday life.

Stephen Hanson

THE TOWN

Type of work: Novel
Author: William Faulkner (1897-1962)
Type of plot: Psychological realism
Time of plot: 1909-1927
Locale: Jefferson, Yoknapatawpha County, Mississippi
First published: 1957

A continuation of The Hamlet, *this novel treats both with wild comedy and savage indignation the further adventures of the degenerate Snopes clan, especially Flem's rise from restaurant owner to bank president, symbolic of the disintegrating values of the Old South.*

It was in the 1920's that William Faulkner first conceived of the Snopes Saga: a clan of crude, avaricious, amoral, unfeeling, but energetic and hard-driving individuals who would move into the settled, essentially moral society of the Old South and gradually, but inevitably, usurp the old order. To Faulkner the Snopeses were not a special Mississippi phenomenon, but a characteristic evil of the mechanized, dehumanized twentieth century which filled the void left by the collapse of the agrarian pre-Civil War South. Flem Snopes is the supreme example of the type, and the Snopes Trilogy is primarily a chronicle of his career and its implications.

However, it was 1940 before Faulkner finished *The Hamlet,* the first book in the series (although several short stories appeared earlier), and not until the 1950's that he completed the trilogy with *The Town* and *The Mansion.* In the intervening time Faulkner's vision of human morality and society had become more complex and, although the original design remained intact, the quest of the Snopes Clan became more devious and complicated, and "Snopesism" took on increasingly ambiguous meanings.

At the beginning of *The Town,* Flem arrives in Jefferson fresh from his triumphs in Frenchman's Bend, but with only a wagon, a new wife, Eula Varner Snopes, and their baby daughter, Linda. The book traces his rise in short order from restaurant owner to hotel owner, to power plant supervisor, to bank vice-president, and finally to bank president, church deacon, and grieving widower. The book also describes the life of his wife, Eula, her lengthy affair with Manfred de Spain, her relations to the community, and her efforts for her daughter—all of which leads her, at last, to suicide.

If Flem is the embodiment of ruthless, aggressive inhumanity and devitalized conformity, Eula is the essence of warmth, emotional involvement, sexuality, and freedom. Although their direct confrontations are muted, *The Town* is basically about the struggle between these two characters and the contrasting approaches to life that they represent.

The story is told by three anti-Snopesean citizens: V. K. Ratliff, the sewing machine salesman who previously tangled with Flem in Frenchman's Bend;

Gavin Stevens, Heidelberg and Harvard educated County Attorney; and Charles Mallinson, Stevens' young nephew. Although they confirm the essential facts, each speaker has a separate interpretation of the events. Thus, the reader must sift through their different attitudes and conclusions to arrive at the "truth" of the book. Frequently it is the ironical distance between the events and the characters' interpretations of them that gives the book its bite and message—as well as its humor.

Mallinson, who saw the events as a child but recounts them as an adult, is probably the most detached of the narrators. Ratliff is sardonic and realistic, but his bitter experiences with the Snopeses somewhat color his accounts. Gavin Stevens is the primary narrator and chief enemy of Flem, but the reliability of his statements is jeopardized by his lengthy, emotional, somewhat confused involvements with both Eula and Linda.

Stevens is a well-educated, sophisticated modern man who understands the complexities and difficulties of human relationships; but, at the same time, he is an old-fashioned Southern Gentleman who clings to old attitudes and traditions. When Eula offers herself to him, it is not morality, but romanticism coupled with self-doubt that stimulates his refusal. He insists on viewing her through a romantic haze which prevents him from reacting realistically in the most critical situations. "What he was doing was simply defending forever with his blood the principle that chastity and virtue in women shall be defended whether they exist or not."

The same kinds of assumptions determine his relationship to Linda Snopes. Since he is nearly twice her age, he cannot imagine a sexual or marital arrangement between them in spite of the fact that he loves her and is encouraged by her mother. So, in the role of father protector and educator, Stevens reads poetry to Linda over sodas and feeds her dreams with college catalogs. Thus, because of his intense emotions, sense of morality, and traditional assumptions, Gavin Stevens is unable to deal either with Eula's simple sensuality or Flem Snopes' one-dimensional inhumanity.

In the final conflict between these two forces, Flem's ruthless rationality easily overcomes Eula's passionate free spirit. Being both physically and spiritually impotent, Flem can coldly and callously manipulate the sexual and emotional drives in others. Not only does he do so to thwart Stevens' anti-Snopes efforts, but more importantly to his plans, he also uses them to gain control over his primary Jefferson rival, Manfred de Spain.

Flem learns of his wife's affair with de Spain soon after his arrival in Jefferson, but he chooses to ignore it as long as it is profitable. It is even suggested that the two men work out a tacit agreement whereby Flem overlooks the affair in return for an appointment to the newly created job of power plant superintendent. De Spain's influence is later instrumental in securing Flem the vice-presidency of the Sartoris Bank. After eighteen years, however, when Flem decides to make his move for the bank presidency, he suddenly becomes the outraged husband. He uses the threat of scandal to provoke Will Varner to action, to drive de Spain from the bank, to push Eula to suicide, and to coerce Stevens into unwilling complicity. Neither integrity nor sensuality can stop Snopesism.

However, as Flem succeeds in his drive to monetary wealth another goal becomes predominant—"respectability." He learns from de Spain that in Jefferson one can become respectable without being moral—if one has the necessary money. So Flem systematically acquires all the requisite signs of success and they, in turn, provide him with access to respectability. Only one last obstacle remains between Flem and complete social acceptance—the other Snopeses.

Consequently, it is Flem, himself, who finally rids Jefferson of the Snopeses. Using the same callous attitude and devious strategy on his kin that he used on other victims, he eliminates all of the lesser Snopeses who might pose a threat to his new status: Mink, Byron, Montgomery Ward, I.O., and, finally, Byron's brood of wild, half-breed children, "The last and final end of Snopes out-and-out unvarnished behavior in Jefferson."

So Flem becomes respectable. Faulkner's final question to the reader is this: has Flem's drive to social acceptance weakened and narrowed him to the point where he is vulnerable, if not to the morality of the Ratliffs, Stevenses, and Mallinsons, then to the latent vengeances of Snopesism? Faulkner answers that question in *The Mansion*.

Keith Neilson

THE TOWN

Type of work: Novel
Author: Conrad Richter (1890-1968)
Type of plot: Regional romance
Time of plot: Mid-nineteenth century
Locale: Ohio
First published: 1950

Beginning with The Trees, *and continuing with* The Fields, *Richter's story of the growth of an Ohio pioneer settlement is completed in* The Town, *a romance that brings to maturity Sayward Wheeler's children—a younger generation having little sympathy for the pioneers' philosophy of working for happiness.*

As the third novel in a trilogy on early American life, *The Town* completes the story of Sayward Luckett Wheeler, her husband Portius, and their nine children. It depicts the settlement and growth of a town and describes the way of life experienced by the families who live and work in that period of American history when the frontier is closing down. In this historical novel, Richter gives sharp details about the everyday life and possessions of the early settlers. He uses authentic speech and describes their food, clothing, tableware, and furniture. Even accounts of medical practices and methods of printing are woven into the family experiences. Richter gives descriptions to fit each era of the trilogy and much of the interest and warmth of the story comes from these ordinary aspects of daily life.

In addition to its value as history, *The Town* is also a commentary on progress and civilization. It compares the past, as in the Luckett's early years on the Ohio frontier, with the present in the town of Americus, Ohio. As participants in and builders of the new town, Sayward and the other old timers wonder if the "easy life" they now have is really advancement or if it is the opposite—a demoralizing situation. The radical opinion, which Sayward's youngest son Chancey holds, is that pioneer times were brutal and wild and that true progress should continue. As times change, labor will not be necessary, and peace and happiness will flourish in a life of ease. Many of the discussions in the book concern the validity of each of these opposing ideas.

Conrad Michael Richter, the son of a minister, was born in 1890 in Pennsylvania. At age fifteen he finished high school and began a succession of jobs which included being a clerk, a farm laborer, and a county correspondent. He also reported on the Johnstown, Pennsylvania, *Journal,* and by age nineteen he was the editor of the weekly *Courier* at Patton, Pennsylvania. From there he went on to report for daily newspapers and then worked as a private secretary in Cleveland, where he sold his first fiction story.

In 1928 Richter moved to the West and began collecting materials on early American life. Not satisfied with his research into original sources, early rare books, newspapers, and manuscripts, he found and talked to early pioneers who were still alive. His lengthy visits with them provided much of the historical detail for his novels.

Richter published his first book in 1924, *Brothers of No Kin and Other Stories.* During his lifetime he wrote approximately twenty-five books and published his last, *The Aristocrat,* shortly before his death in 1968. In 1950 he published *The Town* and in 1951 received the Pulitzer Prize for Fiction for that book.

Like the earlier novels in the trilogy, *The Town* is written in the third person, and much of it is from Sayward's point of view. In this last novel, however, the reader is also given the viewpoint of Chancey, Sayward's son. Even in Chancey's early years, his thoughts, feelings, and dream world are known to the reader.

As *The Town* begins, Sayward is in her late forties but remains the strong, practical woman she was in her earlier years. She represents realism, the acceptance of events as they happen. In character and determination she is similar to the fictional characters of Scarlett O'Hara and Selina DeJong. She believes that physical work and hardship develop moral strength, healthy values, and happiness. Money and "society" mean nothing to her, although she is probably the richest and best-known person in town. She loves her simple cabin, built by her father when the Lucketts first moved to Ohio, and she moves to the mansion in town only when Portius insists on it. Sayward, who hated the trees when she first moved to Ohio and worked for years to clear away the growth and plant crops, now discovers she misses the huge old trees. She begins to see backbiting, pride, and greed for material things, attitudes she does not remember existing in frontier life. In Chancey and other town children, she discovers an aversion to work, and she considers this a weakness unheard of in her youth. It is these realizations that cause her to question the good of change and advancement.

It is also these observations that deepen the conflict between Sayward and Chancey. He is a dreamer, an idealist in a family of realists. Perhaps because he is weak and sickly, he has few friends and always feels misunderstood. Even Sayward, who has insight into her other children, lacks an understanding of Chancey's feelings and opinions. As a believer in progress, he stands against the brutal labor that opened the frontier. Although he ridicules her accomplishments and beliefs, she continues to support his newspaper work; this indicates her mother love and her attempt to understand him. On his part, he feels only hate and does not accept or even tolerate another's opinions. Only at Sayward's deathbed does he even reconsider his attitudes toward her. Sayward's and Chancey's relationship illustrates the not-so-modern generation gap. As a real character, Chancey is not very believable, but as a representative of an idealistic and radical theory, he is a credible part of the story. Age versus youth and realism versus idealism are strong

2304 *The Town*/RICHTER

Minor issues in *The Town* include a conflict between a belief in God and agnosticism, exemplified by Sayward and Portius, and the Indian-white relationships. This novel tells of the white man's fears, friendships, and attitudes toward the Indians. Another of Richter's novels, *Light in the Forest,* discusses the relationship from the Indians' point of view.

When the novel ends, Portius and most of the old timers are dead, and Sayward is dying. *The Town* has portrayed a family—its problems, joys, and adventures—but it has also told the story of a growing town and the changes in people, economics, and attitudes. It leaves the reader to draw his own conclusion about the advantages and disadvantages of progress.

Elaine Mathiasen

THE TRACK OF THE CAT

Type of work: Novel
Author: Walter Van Tilburg Clark (1909-1971)
Type of plot: Symbolic allegory
Time of plot: Early twentieth century
Locale: Sierra Nevada Mountains
First published: 1949

Like his earlier novel The Ox-Bow Incident. *Clark's* The Track of the Cat *is a tragedy laid in Nevada, his adopted state. A long psychological and symbolic study of the effect of evil on a ranch family, the novel offers vivid contrasts between dream and fact, white man and Indian, tragedy and hope.*

The Track of the Cat falls into four parts: one for the testing of each of the brothers, and a fourth to show the state of life at the novel's psychological center, the ranch house kitchen. The kitchen, too, becomes a proving ground for the love between Gwen and Harold, and, in a sense, a further test of Harold as a man.

The panther, the force against which each of the brothers is tried in turn, changes shape to meet the character of each antagonist. For Arthur, the mystic, it takes the form of malevolent reality, whose onslaught might easily have been parried by the most elementary precautions—reloading his gun, and "keeping his eyes peeled." But practicality is foreign to a man whose interior life is richer, more beautiful, and more hopeful than reality. For Curt, the cat assumes the mythic shape of the "black painter"; it means despair, a sense of the death of gods, or, as Arthur says, "the end of things." It means Curt's gods are his own strength and skill; when these fail him, he has no psychic resources to fall back on, and so falls into the grip of an egoistic mirage and dies. Harold, whose nature shows both mystical and practical elements, sees the panther complexly, both as wantonly destructive and harmful to the life of the ranch, but as beautiful in itself, a mysterious life force. He stalks it circumspectly and kills it reverently.

The novel seems to make the point that Arthur, identifying the cat as a brother-creature, is unable to kill it, while Curt in his self-absorption is unfit to kill it. Only Harold, whose compassion succors all the people of the ranch, and whose sense of human superiority and responsibility nurtures all the animals, is both fit and able to gain a victory over the wilderness of which the panther is a symbol. Fittingly, the cat's pelt will deck the marriage bed of Harold and Gwen, whose union is to renew the life of the ranch. The "end of everything" for Joe Sam, made all the more awful by being accomplished by the likes of Curt, is to some degree mitigated by this union of strong, earthy, yet sensitive natures.

THE TRAGIC MUSE

Type of work: Novel
Author: Henry James (1843-1916)
Type of plot: Social narrative
Time of plot: The 1880's
Locale: Paris and England
First published: 1890

The "tragic muse" of the title of this psychological novel represents a number of elements: it is the phrase attached to the actress Miriam Rooth; the title of a portrait of her; and an idea in the minds of the three central characters, each of whom represents some aspect of the conflict between ordinary life and the demands of art.

For Henry James, art was the supreme value to which a man might sacrifice himself, and, to some extent, James's own life was such a sacrifice. Few writers have been more fascinated by the artistic process and the artistic personality, and James dealt with these subjects again and again both as practicing critic and in his many stories of writers and artists. Though not his best writing on the topic, *The Tragic Muse* is nevertheless a significant example of James's concern with the relationship between the individual and his art.

Miriam Rooth—whose name may suggest the ruthlessness with which she is prepared to sacrifice everything for her career—is a symbol of the "tragic muse" as James perceives it. She is not tragic in the usual sense—her career is an uninterrupted rise to success—but her total dedication to the theater has its tragic aspect. For Miriam, art takes precedence over all else, and she willingly gives up for the stage any hope of happiness in the usual sense. In so doing, she dramatizes on one level the history of her own individual sacrifices and perhaps her alluring dehumanization as well. As the "tragic muse," she symbolizes the total dedication she demands of herself, and of anyone who would possess her.

Whereas Miriam never faced any real conflict in regard to her art, Nick Dormer is the dramatic center of the novel because he must choose between "art" and "life," between his career as a painter and the everyday world of political affairs. Unlike Peter Sherringham, who gives up pursuit of the "tragic muse" for his diplomatic career, Nick elects to make the personal, financial, and social sacrifices his art demands. For James, this is a right choice even if Nick never materially succeeds, because he will live at the higher level of consciousness characteristic of the artist.

THE TRAITOR

Type of work: Drama
Author: James Shirley (1596-1666)
Type of plot: Tragedy of blood
Time of plot: c. 1480
Locale: Florence, Italy
First presented: 1631

Shirley's The Traitor, *attributed falsely in the late seventeenth century to a Jesuit who died in Newgate Prison, is a smoothly crafted revenge tragedy that, although looking backward to an earlier and more powerful tradition, remained in theatrical repertoires for over 150 years.*

James Shirley was lauded by some as "the last of the Elizabethans" and by Charles Lamb as "the last of a great race." He edited the first collected edition of the plays of Francis Beaumont and John Fletcher in 1647, and he had the distinction of writing the last tragedy to be performed before the upheaval of the Civil War began: *The Cardinal* (1641). Indeed, he could probably be called the savior of the English drama—for it is his dramatic skill that provided some continuity between the Elizabethan and Restoration periods. His play *The Traitor* made its contributions to this end by perpetuating some of the qualities of the early Elizabethan revenge tragedy.

It had been the practice of earlier Elizabethan dramatists to introduce integral subplots that gave the play full, world-view importance. The plot of *The Traitor* incorporates the state, but there is no international involvement; and the involvement of the spiritual and allegorical worlds—represented by the presence of the Furies and Lust—is almost negligible. The reduction of involvement in a multiple number of spheres also brought about the appearance, in later Elizabethan plays, of fewer places of action. In the twelve scenes of *The Traitor,* for example, only two are exterior scenes—one in a street, one in a garden. The remaining scenes are restricted to rooms within the homes of different individuals and to one rather large hall.

Accompanying this scaling down of the world-view and places of action was a diminishing in the earlier Elizabethan traditions of the blood-revenge style. Rather than searching through the ethical problems and the psychological motivations of the character entangled by revenge, as the earlier writers of this style had done, the revenge was put to the baser task—to some extent even within *The Traitor*—of simply placing characters in opposition to one another and creating suspense and complications within the plot. Deemphasizing the psychological in the tragedy of blood gave rise to stock character types—particularly the Machiavellian villain of which Lorenzo is representative. Perhaps the closest that *The Traitor* brings the reader to pangs of conscience within a developing character is the concern evidenced by Sciarrha that his younger brother, Florio, not take part in the revenge. He realizes that his revenge has wounded his soul "almost to death" and that he has become "more spotted than the marble"; he fears the same for his brother.

It is also through Shirley's characterization of Sciarrha that he comes closest to the Kydian form of revenge tragedy. As in the earlier form, Sciarrha's feeling of overpowering duty to revenge arouses excessive emotional excitement; and, with each step in the revenge, he receives a feeling of relief—death being his welcomed final relief from what he recognizes has been a ruthless life. For this characterization, Shirley may owe some credit to Foreste in *Cruel Brother* (1627) by Sir William Davenant. He can, however, in his characterization of and plot development with Sciarrha in *The Traitor,* be credited with saving the revenge tragedy from total disintegration at the end of the Elizabethan period.

THE TRAVELS OF MARCO POLO

Type of work: Record of travel
Author: Marco Polo (1254-1324), as set down by the scribe, Rustigielo
Type of plot: Adventure romance
Time of plot: 1260-1295
Locale: Greater Asia
First transcribed: Fourteenth-century manuscript

An enchanting mixture of fact and fiction, the story of Marco Polo's Asiatic journey is a classic of travel literature. His book is the record of a merchant-gentleman who sets forth his own observations and at the same time reveals the medieval viewpoints and prejudices concerning the court of Kublai Khan.

The Travels of Marco Polo has come down to us in many manuscript versions, none of which is the original. Although it is nearly certain that the scribe Rustigielo transcribed the original manuscript in French, extant manuscripts are in almost all of the western European languages, the most important being those in French, Italian dialects, and Latin. None of the extant manuscripts is definitively complete; hence, much scholarly attention has been focused on speculation about what material was present in the original version and what material was interpolated by later scribes. At least an equal amount of attention has also been focused upon trying to distinguish Marco Polo's observations from the embellishments of Rustigielo. To some extent, Chinese historical records have been helpful in settling some of these questions. And a lesser, though nonetheless vexing, problem arises in attempting to correlate Marco Polo's citation of personal names and place names with their modern-day equivalents and counterparts—a problem stemming from irregular orthography and compounded by transliteration from one alphabet to another as well as by other changes which have occurred. (For example, Constantinople became Istanbul.) The aggregate of these textual difficulties makes analysis and evaluation of Marco Polo's narrative, at best, tentative.

One matter, however, is considerably less debatable than others: the place of *The Travels of Marco Polo* in literature, for Marco Polo's account is without doubt soundly within the mainstream of medieval and Renaissance historical-travel literature. Geoffrey of Monmouth's *History of the Kings of Britain,* Joinville's *History of St. Louis,* Froissart's *Chronicles,* Mandeville's *Travels,* and Hakluyt's *Voyages* join Marco Polo's *Travels* to form the superstructure of this literary tradition. All of these works, and other similar ones, have in common certain features, most of which reflect the attitudes of the age (as distinguished from modern attitudes): a mixture of fact and fantasy, a certain cultural ingenuousness, and a rather pervasive credulity about the supernatural. The modern reader is thus entitled to some legitimate skepticism about Marco Polo's report.

This report had the advantage of being designed for a Western readership largely ignorant about the East. Polo's overriding interest was thus to present the East as something interesting about which the West should learn. His motives were primarily commercial. However, Polo's access to information was limited by his exclusive contact with only overlords. And his judgments were based largely on mercantile and religious factors. He was apparently impervious to socio-political considerations, for his interest was in trade and merchandise, not in ideas. Consequently, the credibility of his eyewitness account was turned toward generating enthusiasm for finding a safe sea route to the East. Yet much of what Marco Polo had to say provides valuable insight not only into Western medieval attitudes but also into contemporary conditions in the East.

Several significant issues are connected with these insights and attitudes. Among them is the impact of Christianity on the East. Kublai Khan, for example, asked Nicolo and Maffeo Polo, on their earlier journey, to return with 100 learned Christians (priests and scholars) to discuss Christianity with the wise men of the East. Yet Marco Polo recorded but two priests who came only part of the way with the Polos on their second, more important journey. But Kublai Khan made other similar inquiries of Moslem scholars about Islam. One possible implication is that Kublai Khan—and thus the entire Chinese court—was not interested in evangelical Christianity and conversion to Christianity but was intellectually curious about foreign cultures and religions, Marco Polo's Christian biases notwithstanding.

Another issue revolves around Marco Polo's claim to have learned four of the languages of the Tartar nation. Probably he knew Mongol and Turkish—linguistically related languages. It is highly likely that he knew some Persian. The fourth language remains in doubt, but strong evidence suggests that he did not know Chinese. These language skills and limitations most certainly affected Polo's access to information, his perspective on his sources of information, and, as a result, his presentation of information.

Still another issue involves the spurious matter in Polo's account. He confused, for example, the locations of Alexander's barricade and the Great Wall of China with uncharacteristic geographical naïveté. He also insisted upon including the Prester John legend with no empirical evidence to support it. And the narrative further refers to several high administrative posts which Marco Polo held under the appointment of Kublai Khan, although meticulously kept records of Chinese administrators and bureaucrats reveal no such appointments at all. Yet it is likely that Polo did execute some brief missions for the Khan. In addition, while Polo noted the ubiquity of rice in the diet throughout the East, he did not refer to the equally imporant tea, nor did he mention the well developed art of Chinese printing—both of which could hardly have escaped his notice. Despite these inaccuracies and inconsistencies, Polo's narrative does present a generally correct picture of conditions in the East, as corroborated by other historical records.

Finally, the issue of cultural judgments reveals that Polo categorized people on the basis of religion rather than on the basis of ethnic origin or color. Polo distinguished among Jews, Christians, Moslems, and idolatrous heathens (Buddhists and Hindus, for the most part), but he had no patience for intra-faith disputes, even among Christians. His system for identifying human beings was therefore simplistically confined to professed theology. As a consequence, he proved a remarkably tolerant person, for he made no evaluations along racial or cultural lines. Even his judgment that certain African peoples were ugly was an aesthetic pronouncement rather than a racial slur, since he did not consider them inferior. He thought of people primarily as grouped according to their religious beliefs and only remotely gave thought to their appearance. Such an approach was reasonably typical for Marco Polo's day, for at that time, religious affiliation was the crux of all matters. Cultural, racial, and ethnic considerations did not emerge as controversial questions until modern times. In this sense, Polo, like his contemporaries, may be considered tolerant by modern standards.

These aspects of *The Travels of Marco Polo* barely scratch the surface of this remarkable literary document, an extraordinarily rewarding tale that has much to offer, not only for the historian and the student of literature but also for the thoughtful modern citizen.

Joanne G. Kashdan

TRAVELS WITH A DONKEY

Type of work: Record of travel
Author: Robert Louis Stevenson (1850-1894)
Type of plot: Sketches and impressions
Time of plot: 1878
Locale: The Cévennes, French Highlands
First published: 1879

Leisurely paced and narrated with exquisite skill, Travels with a Donkey in the Cévennes *is a book of travel sketches that records with precision and warm sympathy Stevenson's impressions of the French Highlands.*

Travels with a Donkey is one of the most perfect pieces of prose composition in the English language. With infinite grace and precision, Stevenson tells of his simple journey through the French countryside. The author's style is flawless and yet without pretension. *Travels with a Donkey* is a book easily underrated because it presents such a simple, unaffected appearance, but its charm and humor and the beauty of the writing make it a sheer delight to read.

The book illustrates Stevenson's continual strain to overcome his physical handicap and lead a natural and vigorous life in the out-of-doors. At the same time, Stevenson possessed the gift to turn everything into art, from his encounters with peasants to his battles with a stubborn donkey. Although a learned and sophisticated writer, he was able to view his experiences and the scenes of his travels with a fresh eye. The descriptions of the mountains and the farm lands are exquisite, the meetings with the peasants are earthy and humorous, and the donkey, Modestine, proves to have a distinctive and intractable personality.

Stevenson understood the fascination of apparently petty details. Much of the book is taken up with minute descriptions of his preparations, of his equipment, and of the plotting and planning of routes. The reader, because of these carefully presented details, comes to feel that he is sharing the experience with Stevenson. The freshness of mountain air, the shade of a cloud, the aromas of the cattle, are all described vividly and made real by Stevenson's immense skill. The discovery of the unknown little French villages tucked away in tiny mountain valleys results in some of the most charming passages in the book. The chapters dealing with the Trappist monastery of Our Lady of the Snows are handled with a sensitivity and beauty which make them the heart of the book. The distance of the trip is only a hundred and twenty miles, but it is a fascinating experience and shows that one need not cover vast distances if one is able to observe truly and interpret what one sees.

TREASURE ISLAND

Type of work: Novel
Author: Robert Louis Stevenson (1850-1894)
Type of plot: Adventure romance
Time of plot: 1740's
Locale: England and the Spanish Main
First published: 1883

A favorite boys' adventure story, Treasure Island *is also a kind of "education" novel concerning Jim Hawkins' rites of passage into the dangerous world of mature responsibilities. Stevenson's romance is noted for its swift, clearly depicted action; its memorable character types, especially Long John Silver; and its sustained atmosphere of menace.*

Although Robert Louis Stevenson produced a large number and variety of writings during his relatively short life and was considered a "serious adult" author in his own day, he is largely remembered now as the writer of one "horror story," *Dr. Jekyll and Mr. Hyde* (1886), and two "boys' books," *Treasure Island* and *Kidnapped* (1886). Such a view is undoubtedly unfair and slights many valuable literary accomplishments, but the fact that these three works have endured not only as citations in literary histories, but as readable, exciting, essentially contemporary books is a tribute to their author's genius. And, of the three, *Treasure Island* remains Stevenson's supreme achievement. Although critics may debate its "seriousness," few question its status as the purest and most perfect of adventure stories.

When Jim Hawkins begins by stating that he is telling the story in retrospect, at the request of "Squire Trelawney, Doctor Livesey, and the rest of these gentlemen," we are assured that all the principals survived the quest successfully, thus giving us that security necessary in a romantic adventure intended primarily for young people. Although many exciting scenes will ensue and the heroes will face great danger on a number of occasions, we know that they will overcome all such obstacles. Thus, the suspense centers on *how* they escape, not on their personal survival as such. At the same time, by denying us details of either the precise time of the adventure (sometime prior to "17--") or the exact location, Stevenson sets us imaginatively free to enjoy the story unencumbered by the specifics of when or where.

By introducing the mysterious, threatening Billy Bones into the serene atmosphere of the Admiral Benbow Inn, Stevenson immerses us directly into the story. The strange secret of Bones's background and nature creates the novel's initial excitement which is then intensified by his apparent fear and subsequent encounters with Black Dog and Blind Pew. In all, the sequence that begins with Billy's arrival and ends with Pew's death acts as an overture to the adventure and sets up most of the important elements in the story, especially Captain Flint's map, which directs the group to Treasure Island,

and the warnings to beware of "the seafaring man with one leg," which prepares us for the arch villain of the tale, Long John Silver.

Thus, in the classic adventure story pattern, an ordinary individual, Jim Hawkins, living a normal, routine life, is suddenly thrust into an extraordinary and dangerous situation, which soon gets beyond the control of the individual and his cohorts. But, although the hero is involuntarily pressed into danger, he can extricate himself and return the situation to normality only through his own efforts. The adventure story is, therefore, usually to some extent a "coming of age" novel, whether the hero be fourteen or sixty-four. And since *Treasure Island* is essentially a boys' book, it is appropriate that it center on the transition of its hero from a boy to a man.

The death of Jim's father near the beginning of the book frees Jim to seek his fortune and places the responsibility upon him to find it for the sake of his widowed mother. And without a father of his own, Jim can look to the other male father-figures as substitutes. He finds two: Doctor Livesey, who represents stability, maturity, and moral responsibility, and John Silver, who suggests imagination, daring, bravado, and energy. Between these two and, more importantly, through his own actions, Jim finds his own manhood along with the treasure.

His education begins with the act of searching the belongings of the dead Billy Bones in spite of the proximity of Pew's pirate band. To accomplish this feat, however, he needs his mother's support. Once the *Hispaniola* sets sail, though, he is on his own. The next stage in his growth occurs when, crouching in the apple barrel, he overhears Silver reveal his plans to his co-conspirators. Jim keeps calm, cooly informs his friends, and, with them, devises survival tactics. His initial positive, independent action takes place when they first reach the island and he goes off on his own, without a specific plan, but sure he can further the cause in some undetermined way. Wandering in the woods he meets Ben Gunn, rejoins his party at the stockade, and engages in his first combat.

Next, Jim makes a second solo trip, but this time with a definite course of action in mind; he plans to board the *Hispaniola* and cut it loose to drift inland with the tide, thus depriving the pirates of a refuge and an escape route. His final test in action comes on board the boat when he encounters the evil first mate, Israel Hands. When Hands tries to manipulate him, Jim sees through the deception and, acting with considerable courage and dexterity, manages to outmaneuver the experienced pirate. Finally, faced with an enraged adversary, Jim remains calm and, with a knife sticking in his own shoulder, still manages to shoot the villain.

His final test of manhood is not physical, however, but moral. Returning to the stockade, which he believes to be still occupied by his friends, Jim is captured by the pirates. Given the opportunity a short time later to talk privately with Dr. Livesey, Jim refuses to escape: "No . . . you know right well you wouldn't do the thing yourself, neither you, nor squire, nor captain, and no more will I. Silver trusted me, I passed my word, and back I go." Thus, Jim puts his word above his life, and with that he signals the transition not just from boy to man but, more important to Stevenson, from boy to Gentleman.

But, however important Jim's development is to the novel, the most vivid and memorable element in the book remains the character of Long John Silver. All critics have pointed out the obvious about him, that he is both bad and good, cruel and generous, despicable and admirable. Some have tried to fuse these elements into a single character "type," a "hero-villain," in which the good and bad are traced back to a common source. Such an effort is probably wrong: Silver is both good and bad, and his role in the novel demands both kinds of actions. Rather than try to "explain" Silver psychologically, it is probably more profitable to analyze the ways in which Stevenson manipulates the readers' feelings toward the character.

In any pirate story aimed at youth, the author faces a moral and artistic dilemma. On the one hand pirates can hardly be presented as moral exemplars or heroes; they must be criminals and cutthroats. On the other hand, they are the most romantically attractive and interesting characters to the young— or even adult—reader. Enhance their attractiveness and the book becomes morally distorted; mute it and the book becomes dull.

One solution for the dilemma is to mitigate their badness by introducing an element of moral ambiguity into the characterization and behavior of some of them without denying the evil effects of their actions and then to separate the "good-bad" villains from the "bad-bad" ones. That technique is the one Stevenson uses in *Treasure Island*. Silver is separated from his purely villainous cronies and set against the truly evil figures, Israel Hands and George Merry, with the other faceless pirates remaining in the background.

Stevenson mitigates Silver's evil side with two simple strategies: he presents the ruthless, cruel aspects of Silver's character early in the novel and lets his "better" side reveal itself late in the book, and he keeps the "evil" Silver at a distance and gives us an intimate view only of the relatively good Long John. Thus, although we never forget the viciousness of his early words and deeds, they recede into the background more and more as the adventure goes on.

We are prepared for the bad Long John Silver by the many early warnings to beware of the "one legged man." Then we see him manipulate Squire Trelawney and even Jim in their first encounters. Thus, we admire his role-playing while we fear the conspiratorial evil that obviously lies behind it. Silver's overt treachery is evident in the apple barrel scene, especially in his callous "vote" to kill all of the nonconspirators when given the chance. Long John reaches the peak of his villainy in the killing of a sailor who refuses to join the mutiny, first stunning the sailor with his crutch and then knifing him to death.

But even these two evidences of Silver's badness are seen at a distance, from inside an apple barrel and from behind a clump of trees. When Long John moves to the center of the novel and assumes an intimate relationship with Jim, his character is automatically softened. And by the time Silver and Jim become unwilling partners in survival, the pirate's image and status have considerably changed.

The early view we have of Silver is not only evil, but invincible. As he becomes less one-dimensionally evil, he also becomes progressively vulnerable, and vulnerability always stimulates sympathy in a reader, regardless of the character's moral status. As the tide begins to turn against the pirates, Silver begins to lose control not only of the treasure hunting expedition, but even of his own men. This erosion of power is signaled by an increasing emphasis on his physical disability. The John Silver who must crawl on his hands and knees out of the stockade, after the failure of his "embassy," is a far cry from the Silver who can knock down an opponent with a flying crutch and then pounce on him like an animal.

Silver's glibness and adroitness in manipulating the good men of the *Hispaniola* were components of his villainy in the first parts of the book, but when Silver is threatened by a mutiny of his own men and must utilize those same talents to save himself and Jim, they become positive virtues. And although he is obviously motivated by an instinct for self-preservation, Silver does protect Jim from the others and gives a feeling of honestly liking and wanting to help the lad.

Thus, the morally ambiguous ending of the novel is the only one artistically possible. John Silver has not been bad enough to hang, and it is hard to imagine his vitality stifled in prison. Yet if he has edged away from the villains, he hardly qualifies as a hero. So he is neither punished nor greatly rewarded for his machinations and heroics, but left to seek another fortune elsewhere.

Keith Neilson

A TREE GROWS IN BROOKLYN

Type of work: Novel
Author: Betty Smith (1904-1972)
Type of plot: Domestic romance
Time of plot: Early twentieth century
Locale: Brooklyn, New York
First published: 1943

Although A Tree Grows in Brooklyn is nostalgically sentimental in its depiction of the strong, goodhearted Nolan family, and especially of the ambitious Francie, Smith does not gloss over the suffering of the poor immigrants who struggled for a precarious survival in the East Side tenements of New York City during the early 1900's.

With scenes recalling the photographic zeal of a Jacob Riis, this book is more than a television melodrama. It is an effective blend of romance and social criticism. The author gives the reader an imaginative re-creation of pre-World War I Brooklyn tenement life, and some of its residents—the permanent members, and those who escaped from this monotonous, demanding existence through premature death, or by moving elsewhere. We are returned to the days when bread was the staff of life for the masses, to the ethnic cultural richness of the Lower East Side area.

During the summer of 1912, as the story begins, Brooklyn was swollen with unwanted recent arrivals from Europe. Both young and old roamed the streets and alleys picking up rags and valuable junk, a humble testimony to the wastefulness of the modern economy, and the maldistribution of wealth. Teeming with life, with Irish Catholics, Russian Jews, and refugees from Poland and China, Brooklyn was never serene.

Timeless observations about cultural differences, a fundamental element of ethnocentrism, formed the backdrop for this book. Realism was important to the author; a pregnant Jewess waits for the Messiah, but the Irish women knew their babies would never make a Jesus. Francie Nolan was born in this milieu. She embodied the fundamental aspiration of tenement dwellers—to escape.

Francie's parents were of recent European stock. Katie Rommely was Austrian, and her husband, Johnnie Nolan, shanty Irish. Katie, a petite yet strong woman, was fiercely devoted to her children. Of limited ability, good-looking Johnnie resorted to drinking away his inadequacies, his inability to give his family a better life. Francie's father was the type of man the temperance societies worried about, and there were many such men. When he died, Katie, for the sake of her children's future, begged to have the cause of death recorded as pneumonia, which was the immediate cause, and not alcoholism.

Even with her valiant efforts, and those of her mother, who had through her self-deprivation attempted to get her offspring out of the ghetto, Francie never leaves. Through the subtle use of metaphor, Francie becomes the "Tree of Heaven," the tree that liked poor people. Her innocence and beauty survive. The tree that grew in her yard was chopped down, but new life sprouted from the trunk, symbols of poverty and hope.

THE TREE OF THE FOLKUNGS

Type of work: Novel
Author: Verner von Heidenstam (1859-1940)
Type of plot: Historical romance
Time of plot: Eleventh and thirteenth centuries
Locale: Sweden
First published: 1905-1907

The first part of this romance by the Swedish Nobel Prize-winning novelist deals with the period at the end of the eleventh century, a barbaric, brutal age which in the North saw heathenism and Christianity in conflict; the second half concerns the Folkung family, proud descendants of an ancient peasant freebooter, who have pushed their way to the Swedish throne by the middle of the thirteenth century.

This novel by Verner von Heidenstam, the leader of the Romantic school of fiction in Sweden, is probably his best-known and finest work. Romantic with an undercore of realism, the book presents the saga of a great family that held sway in Sweden from the close of the Viking age to the end of the thirteenth century. Written in a style reminiscent of the style of ancient legends, this massive novel records the destiny of a race, the rise of a clan and a people, the stirrings of an infant nation. In deceptively simple, richly poetic prose, the author vividly brings to life those long ago times. The primitive religion and lingering superstitions of the people are woven into the narrative, and the close union between these beliefs and the constant struggle of the people with the land and the forces of nature is clearly and dramatically drawn. A deep tranquillity often pervades the exquisite descriptions of the locales; a stolid force suggests throughout the book that the land and the sea are the vital elements in existence, while men come and go, transitory visitors to the scene.

The life of these ancient people is meticulously detailed, their clothes, battle gear, and homes all described with the detail of an anthropological report, yet these details never intrude into the narrative; they give the story a verisimilitude necessary for a modern reader's enjoyment. Perhaps a certain ponderous, humorless quality that exists in the writing was unavoidable, for the people Heidenstam was writing about were tough, serious individuals struggling with a world that allowed little time for gracious living or humor. The characters strongly believe in the power of fate, and possess a great sense of their own destiny. This aspect of the book is both stirring and touching, and provides the true emotional impetus to the narrative.

For all of their toughness, these people are essentially innocent, almost childlike. Jealousies, rivalries, hatreds, and primitive passions motivate them. Pride above all rules their lives; loss of pride is more than they can bear. The great Folke Filbyter, the founder of the clan, is a memorable, almost superhuman man, who weds a dwarf's daughter and lives to see his family great. And over all of the family stands the lime tree and the spirit that dwells within it, watching over the family. The branches and spreading roots of the tree provide a rich symbolic framework for the novel equal to the great tree of generations begun by Folke Filbyter.

The Tree of the Folkungs is very different from the novels of today and requires a reader to make an effort to be drawn into the legendary past of the tale, but the effort is richly rewarded by a moving and often exciting narrative experience.

THE TREES

Type of work: Novel
Author: Conrad Richter (1890-1968)
Type of plot: Regional romance
Time of plot: Late eighteenth and early nineteenth centuries
Locale: Old Northwest Territory
First published: 1940

The first of a trilogy of novels that includes The Fields *and* The Town, *this romance of pioneer life narrates in a direct, lucid style the story of Sayward Luckett from the time she left Pennsylvania to enter the deep woods in the Ohio wilderness.*

As a lone novel, *The Trees* is an uncomplicated story of the life and feelings of an early pioneer family. When read with the other two novels of Richter's trilogy, *The Fields* and *The Town,* it becomes part of a commentary on progress in early America and its effects upon the land and its people.

Although written in the third person, much of the story involves Sayward's thoughts and feelings about her family and her home. Her attitudes and philosophy develop during three stages of her life: as a young, dutiful daughter, as a "big sister" in the role of mother, and as a wife to Portius Wheeler. Although illiterate, Sayward displays an understanding of people that even trained psychologists would find difficult. This perception enriches the portrayals of other characters, and leaves no doubt that this is Sayward's story.

Although with less depth than with Sayward, Richter also gives considerable insight into the behavior and thoughts of the family's other members. Each individual represents a different response to life on the new and diminishing frontier. Jary cannot face the realities of pioneer life and gives up, physically and mentally; Worth and Wyitt are not satisfied to stay in one place, remaining only from loyalty to family; Genny is the gentle lady who insists that civilities can exist in the wilderness; Achsa is as wild, irresponsible, and stubborn as the thick forest growth; Sulie is the lost child, not quite old or wise or strong enough to survive; and Sayward is the mainstay—dependable, hardworking, and accepting of her fate.

The trees, as representative of all nature, are the other leading characters in the story. To Worth and Wyitt, the forest is the home of animals to hunt and the only place of privacy for man. But to Sayward and the other homesteaders, trees are villains preventing the easy cultivation of fields.

The Trees traces Sayward's gradual victory over the stubborn growth around her. It is a story of a determined people and of their love, labor, and courage.

THE TRIAL

Type of work: Novel
Author: Franz Kafka (1883-1924)
Type of plot: Fantasy
Time of plot: Twentieth century
Locale: Germany
First published: 1925

Left unfinished at the time of his death, Kafka's disturbing and vastly influential novel has been interpreted on many levels of structure and symbol; but most commentators agree that the book treats the themes of guilt, anxiety, and moral impotency in the face of some ambiguous external force.

The Trial, one of the pillars upon which Kafka's reputation as a major twentieth century author rests, was one of the works he ordered destroyed in his will. It survives only because his friend Max Brod, who possessed a manuscript of the unfinished novel, disobeyed Kafka and preserved it, along with *The Castle, America,* and a host of fragments and shorter works. The salvaging of this novel from the manuscript was not an easy task, however, and controversy still exists as to the proper order of the chapters, as well as over the placement and interpretation of a number of unfinished segments which are not included in the usual editions. Fortunately, both the beginning and the end of the novel are extant, and because of the peculiar structure of the work, minor changes in the order of the sections do not really alter our understanding of it.

The novel is structured within an exact time frame: exactly one year elapses between the arrest of Joseph K. (the K. clearly refers to Kafka himself, though the work is hardly biographical in the usual sense), which takes place on his thirtieth birthday, and his execution, which takes place in the night before his thirty-first birthday. Moreover, the novel tells us almost nothing about Joseph K.'s past; there are no memories, no flashbacks, no expository passages explaining the background. As in so many of his works, Kafka begins *The Trial* with the incursion of a totally unexpected force into an otherwise uneventful life, and the situation never again returns to normal. Kafka felt that the moment of waking was the most dangerous moment of the day, a time when one was unprotected by the structures of one's life, and open to such an incursion. Joseph K., in his vulnerable state, responds to the messengers of the court; from this point, there is no turning back. Yet the court is invisible—a hierarchy in which even the lowest members are somehow beyond his grasp. There are no formal charges, no procedures, and little information to guide the defendant. Indeed, one of the most unsettling aspects of the novel is the constant uncertainty, the continual juxtaposition of alternative hypotheses, the multiple explanations for events, and the differing interpretations regarding cause and effect. The whole rational structure of our world is undermined, as perceived reality becomes the subject of detailed exegesis such as one might apply to sacred Scripture. Reality itself becomes a vague concept, since the reader is denied the guiding commentary of a narrator and sees everything from Joseph's point of view. The entire work is composed of Joseph's experiences; he is present in every scene. Secondary characters appear only as they relate to him, and the reader knows no more than he does. With Joseph, the reader receives information which may be misinformation, experiences bizarre, barely credible incidents, and moves from scene to scene as if in a trance. This narrowness of the point of view becomes oppressive, but it is highly effective as a technique: the reader, in effect, *becomes* Joseph K.

The body of the novel consists of Joseph's attempts to approach the court through a series of "helpers." These helpers, however, offer no encouragement to his possible defense or acquittal. Since there are no charges, a defense is virtually impossible. Their advice is simply to prolong the trial, to avoid a decision, to adjust to the idea of living on trial without seeking a judgment. It is for this reason that the order of the central chapters is not crucial: aside from Joseph's increasing exhaustion, there is no real development, merely a series of false starts, leading him no closer to a solution. Whether or not there is any development in Joseph's position before his death is open to debate, and critics have disagreed strongly. In the next to the last chapter, "In the Cathedral," Joseph is told the parable of the man who comes seeking entrance into the Law. His way is blocked by a doorkeeper, and the man's entire life is spent waiting. As he dies, he learns that this door, which he could never enter, was nevertheless meant for him alone. Typically, several possible interpretations are offered, but it is perhaps significant that the next chapter finds Joseph waiting for his executioners. Has he come to an acceptance? Does the paradox achieve meaning for him? However that may be, he does not have the strength to act, and dies, as he thinks at the end, "like a dog."

One is left with the question of what it all means. This is perhaps the wrong question to ask, because it implies that there is a meaning which can be defined, a key to understanding which generally involves assigning some allegorical value to the court: authoritarian society, man's alienation from a sense of wholeness and purpose in life, the search for God's grace. Yet it is the genius of Kafka's works that they are inexhaustible, and veiled in an ultimately impenetrable mystery. They admit of many interpretations, but the more specific the definition of the meaning of the work, the more inadequate it is to encompass the full amplitude of the novel. Kafka's works are less allegorical than symbolic; their symbolism lies in the construction of an image or an experience that is analogous to a human experience that lies far deeper than any of the specific problems offered as explanations for the work's meaning. In *The Trial,* Joseph K. is confronted with the need to justify his life,

and to justify it at a metaphysical level deeper than any *ex post facto* rationalization of his actions. It is a demand he cannot meet, and yet it is in-
escapable because it arises from within him. He is an Everyman, but stripped
of his religion, and on trial for his life. For Kafka, the trial becomes a metaphor for life itself, and every sentence is a sentence of death.

Steven C. Schaber

TRIAL BY JURY

Type of work: Comic opera
Author: W. S. Gilbert (1836-1911)
Type of plot: Humorous romance
Time of plot: Nineteenth century
Locale: England
First presented: 1875

> *Among the reasons for the success of* Trial by Jury, *a second effort at collaboration by Gilbert and Sullivan, are the play's verbal dexterity and brief though witty story that gently satirizes pomposity in the English judicial system.*

Trial by Jury was the first successful collaboration by the team of playwright W. S. Gilbert and composer Arthur Sullivan. An earlier collaboration, *Thespis,* had been a total failure. Gilbert wrote this text for another occasion, but was persuaded to offer it to Sullivan by Richard D'Oyly Carte, a theater manager who later became virtually the third member of the team, producing almost all their works. The D'Oyly Carte company today is still the foremost producer of Gilbert and Sullivan opera. Though Gilbert was an established writer, Sullivan was the more famous, and the work was first advertised as a "dramatic cantata" by Arthur Sullivan. In fact, it is Gilbert's most independent contribution among their team efforts, and it is a model of compact and economical literary structure. In performance it lasts only forty minutes.

The setting of the play was the contemporary world of the audience, and the ingredients of the plot are all realistic: judge, jury, plaintiff, and defendant. Gilbert had himself served as a barrister in his early years. Yet the play develops an utterly absurd world, with its own bizarre logic, a humorous situation only heightened by its juxtaposition to the normal setting. It is a comedy that ranges from puns and facetious exaggeration to serious satire, all of which is presented in a text that sparkles with wit, while retaining absolute clarity of expression, necessary if the text is to be understood when sung. The play is full of what later became typical Gilbert and Sullivan types: the judge who sings a patter-song describing his rise to high position in spite of utter incompetence, the maiden who lyrically laments her misfortune, and the chorus, which avidly follows the action, commenting and taking part in the madness. A good part of the fun is created by Sullivan's score, combining lovely ballads and spritely songs with grand parodies of the more serious musical styles of Italian opera then in vogue.

A TRICK TO CATCH THE OLD ONE

Type of work: Drama
Author: Thomas Middleton (1580-1627)
Type of plot: Comedy of intrigue
Time of plot: First years of seventeenth century
Locale: London
First presented: c. 1605

*Middleton's sharp, realistic, and inventive comedy, centered around the common
life of London rather than the fashionable court world, influenced Philip Massinger's* A New Way to Pay Old Debts.

"How should a man live now that has no living?" asks Witgood in the opening speech of the play. A solution to this perennial problem of the prodigal
young wit in comedy is, in comedy, the invention of a "trick." Snowballing in
its effects, this trick not only extricates Witgood from his financial problems,
but thwarts the greedy old fools who bar his happiness. He is even extricated
from the amorous demands of his cast-off mistress (to the satisfaction of
both), and this leaves the way clear for a marriage to his true love. The ingenious plotting of the intrigue, the robust lifelikeness of the characters and
the contemporary scene, and the brisk and racy dialogue help make this one
of Middleton's best comedies.

The success of Witgood's trick depends on the mutual hatred of Lucre and
Hoard (all the characters have significant names, of course) and on their
frantic efforts to outwit and be revenged upon each other, not realizing that
in working to further their own advantage, they are being exploited by Witgood and furthering *his* fortunes. As Hoard remarks ruefully at the end,
"who seem most crafty prove ofttimes most fools." But if the losers are the
crafty and the foolish, the winners—Witgood and his Courtesan—are hardly
paragons of virtue themselves. It seems that Middleton is tacitly endorsing
trickery; and indeed, the praise of many critics (including T. S. Eliot) for the
play has been counterbalanced by the concern of many others for the dubious
morality of the action. There seems here to be no ethical norm of behavior.
Certainly the earnest protestations of reform by the hero and heroine at the
end would satisfy only the most credulous spectators that morality has triumphed. On the other hand, Middleton draws all the characters with an irony
that is constantly working to undermine chicanery of all kinds more effectively
than a crudely appended moral could do; and the audience and readers are
left to draw their own conclusions.

Middleton's fecundity of invention results in a few loose ends. For instance,
he introduces the idea of a rivalry between Sam Freedom and Moneylove for
the affections of Joyce. Later there is a counterplot by Lucre's wife to get
Sam (her son by her first marriage) married to the widow, eliminating Witgood, the other suitor. Neither of these motifs comes to anything. And there is

an embryonic subplot involving the usurers Harry Dampit and Gulf which bears only the most tenuous relationship—a thematic one—to the main action. This side issue is enjoyable mainly for the vigor of Dampit's braggings, cursings, and ravings. But overabundance of material is always more excusable than poverty of invention; and Middleton's exuberant spectacle of two gullible old rogues gleefully digging their own pits to the tune of the likable young rogue makes for hearty and satisfying comic fare.

THE TRICKSTER

Type of work: Drama
Author: Titus Maccius Plautus (c. 255-184 B.C.)
Type of plot: Comedy of intrigue
Time of plot: Late third century B.C.
Locale: Athens
First presented: 191 B.C.

Although The Trickster (Pseudolus) *exhibits the unities of place and time—the whole of the action occurs before a single house in Athens in precisely the time it would have occupied in reality—the comedy violates the unity of action. The plot, ingenious although filled with stock situations, is crowded with irrelevant events introduced primarily to provide time for other more essential events to take place offstage.*

Plautus was a prolific playwright who borrowed much from the Greeks. Yet his comedies display a verve that was uniquely his, and which comes through even in synopsis. Presented with song and dance in a carnival-like atmosphere, his plays had to hold the attention of a restive Roman audience. This meant that Plautus had to use every trick in his repertoire to engage the spectators, and dramatic unity often suffered as a result. However, critics tend to be the only people who insist on dramatic unity in their public entertainment.

In *The Trickster* Plautus uses the stock comic figures of his day to create amusing situations. We have the amorous youth in romantic difficulties, his obstinate and stingy father, the dealer in white slaves, the innocuous love-object whose life is subject to her owner's whims, and, of course, the wily and impudent servant who solves everything. Throughout the play our attention is directed at Pseudolus, the virtuoso of cunning, as he juggles finances, deceptions, and love until every obstacle to Calidorus' romance is overcome.

What gives the plot piquancy is Pseudolus' amazing self-confidence. He makes sure his victims know that he intends to fleece them before attempting anything. The fact that Simo and Ballio are on their guard only makes Pseudolus' success the more delicious. He and his fellow rogue Simia are masters of psychological jujitsu, turning Ballio's own prudence and suspicion against him. If Pseudolus is the center of attraction, Plautus uses two wagers to engage and hold the audience in suspense. After all, there is nothing like a romance, a bet or two, and a likable rascal for creating a successful comedy. Plautus mastered the formula over two thousand years before comedy ever came to Broadway.

TRILBY

Type of work: Novel
Author: George du Maurier (1834-1896)
Type of plot: Sentimental romance
Time of plot: Nineteenth century
Locale: Paris and London
First published: 1894

A sentimental novel, Trilby *offers an idealized picture of Bohemian life in the Latin Quarter of Paris around the turn of the century. Memorable among the characters is the sinister Svengali.*

The common romantic conception of Paris' artistic "Bohemia" in the nineteenth century comes not so much from fact or from serious artistic productions of the era as from two highly successful, popular art works, Giacomo Puccini's opera *La Bohème* and George du Maurier's novel *Trilby.* Although hardly a serious literary classic, *Trilby* remains an entertaining book, and the elements that made it so successful are still clearly evident.

The first and most obvious quality of the book is the colorful, vigorous picture it paints of life in the Parisian Latin Quarter. It is glamorous, gay, free, and creative. The parties and activities are spontaneous and continuous. The company is loyal, energetic, and highly imaginative. And, although the excitement of the life is highly exaggerated, du Maurier gives the milieu an authentic flavor by his use of concrete details, names of real people and places, and intimate descriptions of the rituals, customs, and manners of his Bohemian world. It is all rendered in an ornate, highly charged, hyperbolic prose style that turns the most trivial incident into a major event.

At the same time, there is no real hint of struggle, poverty, or lack of talent among du Maurier's students. Taffy, Sandy, and Little Billee are well financed, live in considerable comfort, dine in fine restaurants, and pursue assured careers. All of their acquaintances, excepting Trilby, seem similarly situated. When poverty is hinted at, it is kept at a distance and idealized for its character-building capacities. There is no indolence in du Maurier's Bohemia; all the characters look forward to material success and respectable social positions for their efforts. Thus, one of the obvious elements in du Maurier's success with Victorian readers is that, for all of the free-spirited living practiced by his young artists, there is a solid basis of middle-class morality behind their actions.

The sexual morality expounded is likewise thoroughly proper by nineteenth century standards. Only two kinds of attraction are acknowledged: man-to-man comaraderie, which is the most prevalent, and pure, overwhelming man-to-woman love. The lightest taint on a lady's honor, whatever the extenuating circumstances, renders her unacceptable. Neither Trilby's beauty nor her essential goodness can overcome her social and moral "defects" enough to qualify her as Billee's bride. This moral judgment is loudly lamented in the novel, but it is never seriously challenged.

In keeping with popular Victorian novels, the emotions in *Trilby* are extravagantly expressed, especially between the central couple, Trilby and Little Billee. When their marriage is thwarted by Billee's mother, they both become ill. "Little Billee's attack appears to have been a kind of epileptic seizure. It ended in brain-fever and other complications—a long and tedious illness." At the end of the novel, when Trilby is taken from him a second time, Billee's brain-fever returns, this time fatally. For her part, Trilby's sacrificial renunciation of Billee starts her on a downward course that includes poverty, the death of her little brother, her alliance with Svengali, madness, and finally death.

However, although the novel concentrates on Little Billee's experiences, it was primarily the Trilby-Svengali relationship that made the book famous. Du Maurier exploits a number of Victorian tastes with that coupling. Although neither, *Trilby* combines aspects of both the "Gothic romance" and the sentimental "seduction novel." Svengali has many traits of the Gothic "hero-villain." He is mysterious, impressive, extremely intelligent, and talented. And, most important, he possesses strange powers that suggest the diabolical. "He seemed to her a dread, powerful demon, who . . . oppressed and weighed on her like an incubus." But, unlike the Gothic heroine, who usually escapes, Trilby is "possessed" by Svengali, and like the unfortunate ladies in seduction novels, must die in the end. A final Gothic touch can be seen in Svengali's return from the grave, via the mysterious photograph, to "claim" his victim.

Thus, *Trilby* is a very careful blend of the serious with the popular, the emancipated with the conservative, and the factual with the fantastic. Today the book remains enjoyable, if excessive, and its heroine and anti-hero, Trilby and Svengali, have, like Hamlet or Sherlock Holmes, left the confines of the particular work to become figures of popular mythology.

TRISTAN AND ISOLDE

Type of work: Poem
Author: Gottfried von Strassburg (fl. late twelfth and early thirteenth centuries)
Type of plot: Romantic tragedy
Time of plot: The Arthurian period
Locale: Northern Europe, Ireland, England
First transcribed: c.1210

Tristan and Isolde, the famous metrical romance attributed to the medieval German court poet Gottfried, belongs to the tradition of the Minnesang but differs from the line of chivalric tales in its emphasis upon ecstatic romantic love rather than knightly deeds of valor.

Gottfried von Strassburg's *Tristan and Isolde* is unique in many ways. Though its material is courtly in nature, the poem ends tragically, rather than in the usual redemptive resolution, and the sphere of reference is not specifically courtly. In his prologue, Gottfried defines his audience as those "noble hearts" who share the sufferings and joys of love, and who are willing to accept the power of love as the central value in life. All other courtly values —honor, religious faith, feudal fidelity—are subordinated to the one overriding force of passion conceived as an external objective force symbolized in the magic potion. Even Gottfried's conception of love departs from the courtly pattern, for rather than the usual unfulfilled longing and devoted service of the Minnesänger, love here is mutual and freely given, and cannot be contained within the conventions of courtly society. It is in fact a law unto itself and destructive of the social order.

The material of the legend, like that of the Arthurian sagas, may be traced back to Celtic origins, though no versions prior to the twelfth century are extant. In the late 1100's the story takes shape, and it is the French version by the Anglo-Norman poet Thomas of Brittany (or Britain) (c. 1160) that provided the direct source for Gottfried—and which enables us to guess as to the probable ending of Gottfried's unfinished work. In Thomas' version the approach is still distinctly courtly; Gottfried's departures from the norm may be attributed both to his own origin and to his time. Gottfried was most likely not a member of courtly society himself, but rather a member of the middle class of the important commercial city of Strassburg, wealthy and well-educated —as evidenced by his extensive knowledge of theology and law—and familiar with both French and German literature, as well as the Latin that was the universal language of higher education at the time. His work shows mastery of formal rhetorical devices and a knowledge of Latin literature remarkable for his time. His literary sophistication is evident in the extended discussion of German authors of his day that he inserts into the story at a point where Tristan's investiture would be discussed. It is in this literary excursus that he voices his praise of Hartmann von Aue and castigates Wolfram von Eschenbach for his excessively difficult and erratic style.

This critical attitude toward his courtly contemporaries is reflected in his whole approach to the conventions of courtly romance, and helps to explain the uniqueness of his work. He is not above mocking even the rituals of the Church, as when Isolde successfully passes a trial by fire through an elaborate ruse that enables her to avoid perjury on a technicality, but destroys the intent and integrity of the trial. "Christ," Gottfried says, "is as pliable as a wind-blown sleeve." One must in fairness point out that by 1210 such a mockery would not be terribly shocking to the educated classes, who would regard the whole idea of trial by fire as rather archaic and superstitious. What must have appeared virtually blasphemous to some, however, is the elevation of love—Minne—to a quasi-religious significance. There is considerable borrowing from the language of mystical writers in Gottfried's discussion of love, both in the prologue, where the elevating and ennobling qualities generally ascribed to courtly love take on religious significance through the use of specifically religious metaphor, and in the body of the work, where both in his imagery and in his presentation of a scale of values, Gottfried stresses the sacred and transfiguring power of love. St. Bernard of Clairvaux in particular has been pointed out as a source of much of Gottfried's religious love imagery. Scholars are divided on the degree to which one should view this cult of love as an attempt to create a surrogate religion; there is no question, however, but that Gottfried viewed love's claims as exerting a powerful counter-force against the social and religious conventions of the time.

The turning away from the public, external values of the courtly epics toward the inner, personal, emotional values of *Tristan and Isolde* is consistent with the wider cultural trends of the time: the new grace and sensitivity evident in the sculptures of the North Portal at Chartres, and the break with the conventions of courtly love in the later songs of Walther von der Vogelweide, in whose poems we also find the development of an ideal of love in which physical consummation replaces the state of prolonged yearning which is the subject of the poetry of the earlier phase of courtly love. The mystical qualities of this love are portrayed in the scene in the Cave of Love, which is an elaborate allegory expressing the ideal state towards which love strives. But the sequence of trials and traps surrounding Tristan and Isolde depicts the reality experienced by the "noble hearts" whom Gottfried is addressing in his poem when they must live in a world which does not accord to the power of love its due respect.

In this world, the lovers are in fact far from ideal. Isolde uses her servant Brangäne shamelessly, and even considers murdering her to prevent possible exposure, while Tristan, banished from the court at last, falls in love with Isolde of the White Hands, lacking the sustaining power of fidelity that Isolde demonstrates. How Gottfried might have resolved this dichotomy can only be guessed, but viewing the work from the stance of the prologue, it is clear that Gottfried saw the company of "noble hearts" as forever torn between love's joy and sorrow, and accepting both as equally valid. It is precisely this quality of bitterness that separates love's votaries from the mundane world of pleasure seekers, and it is in relation to this ambivalent state that Gottfried explains the purpose of his work: sad stories of love do indeed increase the pain of a heart that already feels love's sadness, yet the noble heart cannot help but be drawn again and again to the contemplation of love. Like the sacraments of the Church, Gottfried's work is mystical communion: "Their death is the bread of the living." In this insistence upon the centrality of love, Gottfried's romantic tragedy is both the culmination and turning point of the tradition of courtly love in Germany.

Steven C. Schaber

TRISTRAM

Type of work: Poem
Author: Edwin Arlington Robinson (1869-1935)
Type of plot: Chivalric romance
Time of plot: Arthurian period
Locale: England and Brittany
First published: 1927

In Robinson's long poetic narrative, a modern version of the old Breton lay of Tristram and Yseult, *the characters talk and think in a plausible, realistic manner; yet the poet largely maintains the romantic quality of the original source.*

Tristram is the third of Robinson's book-length Arthurian poems, following *Merlin* (1917) and *Lancelot* (1920). Whether the three poems form a trilogy is still debated; certainly each poem can be taken alone and on its own terms. In its time, *Tristram* was by far the most successful of the three: it won the Pulitzer Prize (Robinson's third) and, thanks partly to being selected by the Literary Guild, it sold over seventy-five thousand copies during the first year of its publication.

However, current critical opinion places *Merlin* and *Lancelot* ahead of *Tristram* on the grounds that Robinson's willful exclusion of magic from the ancient romance makes it, paradoxically, unconvincing. The problem arises from the great difficulty of modernizing the speech of well-known characters who still move against a background of Dark Ages pageantry.

This device of retelling a myth in unmythological terms was quite effective in *Merlin* and *Lancelot,* where modern poetic dialogue does indeed emphasize and clarify the themes which Robinson perceived in the old romances. Theoretically, at least, the modern reader will likely agree that the risks of misplaced passion are more believable if they are taken by people who act of their own will, rather than under the influence of magic potions. But while *Merlin* and *Lancelot* retain a certain amount of rendered action performed by interesting characters—especially strong and believable women—Tristram carries the absence of mythology too far. The characters spend so much time discussing past actions that there is too little time for them to be portrayed in the process of action.

True, the poem remains readable, and it places its characters more nearly within the grasp of the modern reader than the characters in Tennyson's Arthurian poems, for example. But *Tristram* is no longer considered the masterpiece that many people once believed it to be.

TRISTRAM SHANDY

Type of work: Novel
Author: Laurence Sterne (1713-1768)
Type of plot: Humorous sensibility
Time of plot: 1718-1766
Locale: Shandy Hall in England
First published: 1759-1767 (published in several books)

The Life and Opinions of Tristram Shandy, Gentleman *blends Rabelaisian prankishness, sound psychological insight, sensibility, neoclassic common sense, and much irreverent nonsense in a comic masterwork remarkable for its technical inventiveness.*

This masterpiece of eighteenth century narrative was written by a man who never reconciled his sentimental nature with his roguish tendencies, and who never tried to reconcile them. Sterne was educated at Jesus College, Cambridge, where he met John Hall-Stevenson, a young aristocrat who shared and encouraged his taste for erotic subjects and exaggeration. After taking holy orders, Sterne received, through family connections, an ecclesiastical appointment in Sutton; but he was temperamentally completely unsuited for the clerical, pastoral life. In fact, the only part of religion he mastered was sermonwriting and, at that, he excelled. Eventually he turned his pen to miscellaneous journalism in York periodicals. In 1759, *A Political Romance* appeared, including many elements that would characterize his Shandean masterpiece: allegory, levels of meaning, verbal fanfare, whimsical use of scholastic learning, profanity, and great stylistic versatility.

But it was the appearance of the first two volumes of *Tristram Shandy* that made Sterne an instant celebrity, despite the immediate denunciation of Johnson, Richardson, Walpole, Goldsmith, and other literary establishment figures who condemned Sterne's iconoclastic style and frankly mercenary attitude for both ethical and artistic reasons. Sterne characterized the first part of his life's work as "taking on, not only the weak part of the sciences in which the true part of Ridicule lies, but everything else which I find laugh-at-able." The reader soon discovers that Sterne finds *everything* laughable, his comic vision as universal, and as detailed, as that of Rabelais and Cervantes, whose works influenced Sterne's very strongly. Like Rabelais' *Gargantua* and *Pantagruel,* moreover, Sterne's is a work held together only by the unswerving and exuberant force of the author's own personality. " 'Tis a picture of myself," he admitted; indeed it is impossible to distinguish the profane minister from the "alleged" narrator, young Tristram—just as Rabelais makes his narrator Alcofibras tangible only when it suits his whim.

Tristram Shandy has also been called "a prolonged conversation" between Sterne and his reader, a conversation in which acquaintance becomes familiarity and, then, an enduring friendship. For this friendship to occur, however, the reader must accept certain ground rules and be willing to adopt a role he rarely embraces so willingly as he does here. In his endless comments to the reader (who is sometimes addressed in the plural, sometimes in the singular, sometimes as "your worship," sometimes as "Madam"), Sterne scolds us for wanting to know everything at once (Book 1, Chapter 4), asks us to help him sell his "dedication" (1:9), assures us that our company (of Sterne-readers) will swell to include all the world and all time, and dismisses our objections with a mad swirl of his pen. He tells us he is quite aware that some will understand and others will not; indeed the varying forms of address to the reader indicate his astute consciousness of the variety of his audience. He says the "cholerick" reader will toss the book away, the "mercurial will laugh most heartily at it," and the "saturnine" will condemn it as fanciful and extravagant. Like Cervantes he is not interested (or so he claims) in apologizing for his work, or for himself. We either take him, or leave him. So at the very beginning, as he begins one of his great digressions, he warns the strict reader that to continue may annoy him—only the curious need pass through the narrative line into this first of many excursions with him. "Shut the door," he directs the first kind of reader; if we pass through it with him, we realize the door is never opened again. Only the reader who is willing to let "anything go" will remain on speaking terms with this most quixotic, irrepressible author.

The work itself, alternately characterized by Tristram as "vile" and as "rhapsodic," defies structural analysis. Sterne makes his formal principles clear from the beginning: "not to be in a hurry," but to follow every new thought in whatever direction it may beckon until he loses track of his starting point and has to flip back the pages to find his place; "to spend two years discussing one," just as Tristram's mental and emotional autobiography reflects his father's *Tristrapaedia* (the gargantuan work of pedagogy which takes so long in the writing that Tristram grows up before he can start following its directives); and "in writing what I have set about, [to] shall confine myself neither to his [Horace's] rules, nor to any man's rules that ever lived." Sterne would have understood T. S. Eliot's dictum, "Immature poets borrow, mature poets steal." He not only steals—whether it is the actual music of Uncle Toby's "Lilliburlero" or a medieval French theological tract on baptism—but also openly admits and boasts of his theft. Yet the boast is itself misleading since, as Shakespeare did with North's Plutarch, Sterne subtlely but most effectively alters his thieveries to fit the chaotic image of his own work. At one point, in discussing the nature of digressions, Sterne characterizes that work as "digressive, and . . . progressive too—and at the same time." Digressions, he continues, are "the sunshine" of a writer's art, the very stuff of literary and fictional vitality. Life itself, in the ultimate reading, is nothing but a diverting digression for Sterne; the role of the author, as he embraces it, is to make that essential human digression as diverting, as complicated, as emotionally and intellectually rich, as possible.

The greatness of his comic wit lies in its indefatigable mastery of making one detail relevant to another, a detail from Tristram's unfortunate life immediately provoking in "my father" a pointed consideration of Saxo Grammaticus' Danish history or causing Uncle Toby to expound its relationship to the siege of Navarre. Reading *Tristram Shandy* is an education in the esoteric and picayune minutiae of forgotten scholarship at the same time that it is a parody of the irrelevance of scholarship (also following closely in the spirit of Rabelais). By the time we close even the first volume we are convinced of the validity of Sterne's point of departure: Epictetus' statement that, "Not actions but opinions of actions are the concern of men." In other words, it is not what happens to us that matters, but what we think of what happens to us. The relationship between the Shandean world and the real world is a very close, in fact a promiscuous, relationship; it is defined by Sterne's deliberate blurring of the line between fictional and real events, but also by his thematic insistence on the interdependence of thought, feeling, and action. Thought without emotion, he would say, is futile; but feeling without reason is equally sterile. All of the elements in human life, love, war, business, theology, religion, science, trade, medicine, are treated in an epic comprehensiveness and everything is shown to be related absolutely to everything else. The texture of the style, however, is not the reassuring predictability of epic; instead, it is a formal collage of typographical caprice, gestures, dramatic devices, soliloquies, offhand obscenity, serious and mock-serious treatises— all mixed together extemporaneously and punctuated orally. Sterne is like a magician juggling more balls than anyone can see, but who never loses control because his magic is as unflagging as it is electric. More than any other work of his century, Sterne's is a monument to the complexity, vitality, and *sprezzatura* of the mind.

Kenneth John Atchity

THE TRIUMPH OF DEATH

Type of work: Novel
Author: Gabriele D'Annunzio (1863-1938)
Type of plot: Psychological romance
Time of plot: Nineteenth century
Locale: Italy
First published: 1894

An extravagantly romantic novel marked by a florid prose style, The Triumph of Death *treats the psychologies of George Aurispa and his mistress Hippolyte, who represent both a triumph of egocentrism and a failure of humanity.*

Gabriele D'Annunzio was one of the greatest, yet strangest authors of the Risorgimento, the Italian neo-Renaissance of the late nineteenth and early twentieth centuries which followed the political reunification of Italy. His works were forerunners of the great works of the Italian cinema of the middle twentieth century. Not only his works, but also his life story would make a worthy addition to films of the Fellini and de Sica type. Like the main character of *The Triumph of Death,* D'Annunzio was an amoral pleasure seeker who was obsessed with the morbid. And although he did not commit suicide, several of his World War I adventures could be considered suicidal in nature.

Most of D'Annunzio's characters are almost Nietzschean. They are wealthy, aristocratic and intelligent, and feel that they are above society's laws because of their superior qualities. This is quite true of George in *The Triumph of Death*; his adulterous relationship with Hippolyte, and his longing for her death at his own hands represent this superman ideal combined with a deep morbidity.

The Nietzschean ideal fitted well into the philosophy of the Fascist regime of Benito Mussolini in the 1920's and 1930's. D'Annunzio had been in a self-imposed exile from his creditors after World War I, but was brought back to Italy in glory by the Fascists. Whereas his books were previously banned, they were now some of the most popular in Italy.

The Triumph of Death is not D'Annunzio's greatest work, but it is representative of his style and philosophy. It is a fascinating piece of literature, but it is not a novel to be recommended to those easily depressed.

TROILUS AND CRESSIDA

Type of work: Drama
Author: William Shakespeare (1564-1616)
Type of plot: Realistic comedy
Time of plot: Trojan War
Locale: Troy
First presented: 1601-1602; first published: 1609 Quarto

A bitter but fascinating problem play on the theme of the corruption of love,
Troilus and Cressida combines characteristics of comedy, tragedy, and history.
Shakespeare knew the story from Chaucer and Henryson; but where these sources
gave the story a medieval color, Shakespeare transferred his Troy in spirit to the
decadent days of the late Renaissance.

In the Folio of 1623 *Troilus and Cressida* is described as a tragedy; in the
Quarto it is called a history; in most structural respects it seems to be a
comedy, though a very grim and bitter one. Critics have frequently classified
it, with *Measure for Measure* and *All's Well That Ends Well,* as a "problem
play," perhaps as much because the play poses a problem in literary taxonomy
as because it sets out to examine some problematic thesis. Probably written
between *Hamlet* and *Othello,* during the period of the great tragedies, the
play is so full of gloom and venom, so lacking in the playfulness and idealism of the earlier comedies, that critics have attributed its tone and manner
either to a period of personal disillusionment in Shakespeare's life or to his
preoccupation at that time with tragic themes.

There is no external and little internal evidence for the biographical
conclusion. It may be, however, that in *Troilus and Cressida* Shakespeare
has been affected by the surrounding tragedies. It is as if he took the moral
ambiguities and potential chaos of the worlds of the tragedies, but ruled out
the possibility of redemption and transcendence through heroic suffering.
Instead he peoples this tenuous world with blowhards, cynics, and poltroons
and ruthlessly lets them muddle through for themselves. The world of *Lear,*
for example, is on the brink of chaos, but at least there is the sublimity of
Lear to salvage it. The world of *Troilus and Cressida* has no one to shore up
its structure and challenge disintegration.

Although there were many contemporary versions of the relevant Homeric
materials available to Shakespeare, it is clear that he was also familiar with
the story as told by Chaucer in *Troilus and Criseyde.* Chaucer's world, however, was full of innocence, brilliance, and hope. If the Medieval Criseyde
behaves shabbily, it is only the result of feminine weakness and long impor-
tuning. If Chaucer's Troilus is naïve and a victim of courtly idealism, at least
he can finally sort things out from an Olympian perspective. Shakespeare does
not give his lovers, or the rest of the Greek heroes, this sympathy or opportunity, but drags them through a drab and seamy degradation.

Shakespeare begins with characters traditionally honored for their nobility, but he does nothing to develop them even for a fall. He simply proceeds to betray them, to show them up, and thereby to represent the extreme precariousness of their world. The bloom of courtly love is gone as is the Christian optimism of the Middle Ages. Shakespeare seems to be reflecting not a personal situation but a late Renaissance malaise as he has his characters impotently preside at the dissolution of the revered old order.

In Chaucer, Troilus' love and woe had been instrumental in his maturation and, ultimately, in his salvation. Shakespeare's Troilus is more frankly sensual and his liaison is correspondingly sordid. He does not benefit from an ennobling passion, nor is he allowed to transcend his folly. He is not even accorded the dignity of a significant death. He fights on in pointless, imperceptive frenzy,

Cressida is also debased. She has fallen from courtly heroine to common whore. Perhaps Shakespeare borrowed her degradation from Henryson's highly moralistic *Testament of Cressid* in which the heroine sinks to prostitution. In any case, she does not have the initial austerity and later reserve which dignify the passion and fall of Chaucer's Criseyde. Her language, her every movement, suggests that she is more slut than courtly heroine. Even as she enters the Greek camp her promiscuous behavior betrays her, and her quick submission to Diomedes confirms what we have suspected all along. As if the lovers could not behave foully enough by themselves, Shakespeare provides them with Pandarus, as go-between and commentator, to further sully the relationship.

In Chaucer the Trojan war had provided a fatalistic backdrop which enhanced the progress of the tragic love. In Shakespeare, the circumambient Homeric heroes serve only to discredit themselves and amplify the chaos. Mark Van Doren has pointed out that, if Pandarus' role is to degrade the lovers, "the role of Thersites is to cheapen the heroes." But they do not need much help from their interlocutor. For example, when Ulysses gives his famous speech on order, we are more struck by the pointless bombast and strangulated rhetoric than by erudition. We are led to suspect that this world is out of touch with its ordering principles and that it is vainly trying to recapture them or preserve their appearance with tortured language. Similarly, when Achilles delivers his set speech in Act III, it has all of the bitterness but none of the grace of Lear's corresponding speech. This Achilles is a petulant sybarite and the world is in trouble if he is its hero. The bombast, the irritability, and the inconsequentiality are all-pervasive. Agememnon and Nestor are nothing more than windbags. When the Greeks meet to discuss plans, or the Trojans meet to discuss returning Helen, the conferences both quickly degenerate into pompous vacuity.

The moral and political disintegration is reflected in the shrill and strident language of the play. The diction, which is jawbreakingly full of inkhornisms, and the rhetorical excesses reinforce the notion that the characters are spinning out of control, no longer able to gain control of their language, no longer able to give even verbal orders to their frustrations. The result is a play that can easily seem tedious. Consequently, *Troilus and Cressida* is rarely performed. It has, however, fascinated the critics. What all of this suggests is that the play is more interesting than appealing, more intriguing than satisfying, as it chronicles the demise of a world in which no one is left with the moral stature to make a last stand.

Edward E. Foster

TROILUS AND CRISEYDE

Type of work: Poem
Author: Geoffrey Chaucer (1340?-1400)
Type of plot: Chivalric romance
Time of plot: Trojan War
Locale: Troy
First transcribed: c. 1382

In some 8,000 lines structured in stanzas of rime royal, Chaucer's longest complete poem tells with psychological acumen, humor, and sustained narrative power the tragic love story based upon the legend of the Trojan War. Chaucer's immediate source was Boccaccio's Il Filostrato.

Troilus and Criseyde is a paradox of artistic creation. At once both medieval and modern, it holds vast problems of interpretation for us, yet pleases with its wit, style, comedy, and humanity.

We cannot date the poem with complete certainty, but 1385 is close. By this point in his career, Chaucer—diplomat, man of letters, public official, and one-time prisoner of war—already had a reputation for his literary works, which the appearance of *Troilus and Criseyde* did nothing to diminish. Chaucer's contemporary reputation, in fact, probably rested with this poem at least as much as his later, much-loved, *Canterbury Tales.* It was certainly *Troilus and Criseyde* more than any of the other poems that later poets used as a source for their own works. The fifteenth century Scottish poet, Henryson, for example, wrote of Criseyde's ignoble end in *The Testament of Cressid,* and Shakespeare tried his hand at the story with *Troilus and Cressida.*

Chaucer himself found the story in Boccaccio's *Il Filostrato,* written several years before *Troilus and Criseyde.* It has recently been asserted that Chaucer was working from an intermediate source—*Le Roman de Troyle et de Creseida* by Beauvau—but the more traditional view of the direct influence of *Il Filostrato* is generally accepted. The story itself derives from the Troy legend, but Troilus and Criseyde are such minor figures in Homer's story (and never meet there) that it is apparent that Chaucer had more in mind than simply retelling a classical tale.

Exactly what Chaucer's purpose was in *Troilus and Criseyde* is still a topic of lively discussion among scholars and critics. Much of the discussion in the nineteenth and early twentieth centuries concerned Chaucer's intent in the palinode, that is, the concluding section of about one hundred lines, in which the narrator repudiates courtly love, which has governed the action of the lovers for more than eight thousand lines. More recent criticism has focused on Chaucer's attitude toward courtly love and love as we think of it today, on the poem as tragedy, and on the general matter of how best to read the poem.

Courtly love was a highly conventionalized, and un-Christian, tradition, dating back at least to Eleanor of Aquitane's court in twelfth century northern

France. The courtly love tradition held that love was sensual, illicit, adulterous, secret, and hard to obtain. The lady was the embodiment of virtue, yet cruel to her lover, granting him her favors only after his agony of frustration.

Troilus and Criseyde practice courtly love, until Criseyde violates one of its prime tenets, loyalty. By defecting from Troilus, she destroys the spell the courtly love tradition casts upon the minds of Chaucer's audience. At the very end of the poem all listeners are made to examine the priorities of courtly love, and on a deeper plane, devotion to human love, rather than love of God. The palinode at the end subjects our attention to the question of *how* one should live one's life, whether one should live in thrall to Fortune, that is, to desire and want, to things of this earth, which even if obtained in quantity, can still be stripped away. Troilus clearly was subject to Fortune—in this case to the love of a weak woman—and discovered that he was living in a tragedy. The narrator's statement at the end asks us to remove ourselves from Fortune's domain by devoting ourselves to God and God's love. Good studies on the matter of tragedy and moral intent are Sanford Meech's *Design in Chaucer's Troilus* and D. W. Robertson's *Preface to Chaucer*. For contrasting assessments of Chaucer's views on courtly love, see C. S. Lewis, *The Allegory of Love,* and A. J. Denomy's "The Two Moralities of Chaucer's *Troilus and Criseyde," Transactions of the Royal Society of Canada,* Ser. III, Sec. 2, XLIV (1950), 35-46.

One of the most important aspects of the poem is the elaborate psychological development of its characters. Before Chaucer, the most advanced way of representing psychological states in literature was to abstract feelings and emotions, as well as virtues and vices, embody each in a character, and have these characters contend for possession of the individual. Never before Chaucer had the whole human being as a feeling, growing person been adequately depicted. The tendency in earlier literature was to make the protagonist universal, as is Everyman in the morality play. The characters in Chaucer's poem are in no sense universal. They are not particularly admirable characters, which matters little. The point is that they are like us insofar as we have a shared psychology; that is, their weaknesses and strengths, while not universal, are fully human.

Criseyde's character, for example, depends upon her situation. In the opening of the poem she is in a dangerous position, afraid of the Trojans, afraid of love, afraid of human involvement, afraid, even, of herself. Her natural inclination suggests holding back when Pandarus approaches on Troilus' behalf, but Pandarus makes a union with Troilus seem desirable, even reasonable. Troilus can protect her socially and politically, so when Pandarus approaches her we begin to see complex reactions develop: fear, resistance, flattery, questioning, need, hope, accepting. The point is that while she is not a universal character, what happens to her is typical—it can happen to anyone. Troilus and Criseyde are characters who enter the real world of human flaws, vices, joys, hopes, and predicaments. Chaucer's achievement in perfecting psychological realism is of the first magnitude.

One problem we in the twentieth century have with the poem is the shifts in the narrator's stance. Today we expect a consistent point of view, and Chaucer does not give us such a view. For example, the narrator in the beginning of Book II is privy to Criseyde's thoughts. Through the first 800 lines of Book II he knows what she is thinking until the point she decides to accept Troilus as her lover. After that the narrator does not know what she is thinking, only what she says.

While Chaucer is modern in his psychological realism, he is medieval in his shifting points of view and other inconsistencies, such as seeming to praise courtly love for so long, and then suddenly rejecting it at the poem's end. In these inconsistencies, Chaucer is fully practicing the medieval aesthetic theory, which holds that art should convey truth. Since the only real truth, in this view, is the permanence of God's laws in God's realm (which is unknowable to man), man, who lives in his own separate, lower realm, cannot know absolute truth. What he sees in his own realm is changeable and impermanent. The artist, trying to depict truth as best he can, finds that his art becomes as changing and inconsistent as the world he observes. Yet, since he cannot share immediately in God's realm, he must be content to have inconsistencies in his art, just as Chaucer was (and just as the medieval cathedral-builders were, who happily could make two of a cathedral's towers in altogether different styles). When Chaucer, therefore, changes his narrator's point of view and his outlook, Chaucer is being a good medieval artist, and *Troilus and Criseyde,* while modern in its psychological aspects, is a perfect exemplar of medieval art at its best. For a clear and thorough explanation of Chaucer's medieval aesthetic theory, see Robert Jordan, *Chaucer and the Shape of Creation.*

Brian L. Mark

THE TROJAN WOMEN

Type of work: Drama
Author: Euripides (c. 485-c. 406 B.C.)
Type of plot: Classical tragedy
Time of plot: Age of the Trojan War
Locale: Before the ruined walls of Troy
First presented: 415 B.C.

The Trojan Women *(the* Troades) *is not, strictly speaking, an Aristotelian tragedy, for it has no central tragic hero; neither is it simply a tragic pageant. The Greek warriors collectively constitute the tragic hero in that they commit* hubris *by defiling the Trojan temples and brutally murdering the innocent. In this powerful indictment of war, Euripides protests the Athenian massacres in Melos in 415 B.C.*

The Trojan Women is a masterpiece of pathos, as well as a timeless and chilling indictment of the brutality of war. Yet the circumstances of its composition, and the raging moral indignation behind it, all refer to an incident in the Peloponnesian War that occurred a few months before the tragedy was presented in March, 415 B.C. The people of Melos had tried to remain neutral in the Athenian conflict with Sparta, and Athens responded by massacring the grown males and enslaving the women and children. In *The Trojan Women* Euripides shows Troy after the men had been slaughtered, with a handful of women waiting to be taken into bondage. The parallel is clear and painful. But Euripides does not stop with that. The women in their anguish have dignity, pride, and compassion, whereas their conquerors are vain, unscrupulous, empty. Further, the conquering Greeks are shown to be headed for disaster, since the gods have turned against them. When this play was produced, Athens was preparing a large fleet to take over Sicily, the expedition that ended in calamity. The prophecies of sea disasters in the play must have made the Athenian audience squirm. Indeed, the whole tragedy seems calculated to sting the consciences of the Athenians. That they allowed it to be produced is amazing. The fact that a nonentity named Xenocles won first prize that year, defeating Euripides, is scarcely surprising.

This play concluded a trilogy of tragedies on the legend of Troy. It was preceded by *Alexandros* (another name for Paris), which dealt with the refusal of Priam and Hecuba to murder their infant Paris, who would eventually bring about the destruction of Troy. This is important, because in *The Trojan Women* Hecuba sees the full consequences of her choice. *Alexandros* was followed by *Palamedes,* where Odysseus exacts a dire revenge on the clever Palamedes through treachery. *The Trojan Women* merges the Trojan and Greek lines of tragedy, showing them to be complementary aspects of a central agony. Since *Alexandros* and *Palamedes,* along with the satyr play, *Sisyphus,* have not survived, we must rely on the *Troades* for Euripides' depiction of the Trojan War. It is as bleak and agonizing a portrait of war as has ever been shown on the stage.

However, Euripides merely dramatizes a brief portion of the aftermath, about an hour or two the morning after Troy has been looted and burned and the Trojan men put to death. But in that time we see enough to realize that war is the most devastating, unheroic activity that man has ever devised. No one wins. The Greeks in their swollen vanity have committed atrocities against both the gods and human decency, and they are about to receive their just punishment, as Poseidon, Athena, and Cassandra point out. The action of the play consists of the revelation of those atrocities, one after the other, as they overwhelm the helpless old queen, Hecuba. It is primarily through Hecuba that we experience the enormity of Troy's fall. The chorus of captive women, Cassandra, Andromache, and Helen serve to balance and counter-point Hecuba's anguish, as well as contribute to it.

A brief time before, Hecuba was the proud queen of a great, wealthy city, and within the space of a night she has been reduced to a slave. Hecuba has witnessed her husband Priam's murder, and knows almost all of her children have been butchered. And, longing for death, she experiences one dreadful thing after another. She learns that she is Odysseus' prize, the vilest Greek of all, and that her few daughters will be handed out as concubines. She sees her daughter Cassandra madly singing a marriage hymn, and she finally grasps that Cassandra, through prescience, is really singing a death song for herself and the commander of the Greeks, Agamemnon. Believing her daughter Polyxena to be alive, Hecuba learns from Andromache that the girl had her throat slit. Hecuba, trying to comfort Andromache with the prospect of Astyanax's growing to manhood, sees the little boy taken from Andromache to be smashed to death. Menelaus arrives to drag Helen off, and Helen, who caused the whole war, calmly faces him down, oblivious of Hecuba's accusations. So Hecuba loses the satisfaction of seeing her worst enemy killed. We know that shallow, worthless Helen will go unpunished. In her final anguish Hecuba must look upon her poor, mangled grandchild lying on the shield of her dead son, Hector. The last ounce of torment is wrung from her, and she makes an abortive suicide attempt. Hecuba's stark pathos has been drawn out to an excruciating degree.

Yet the play is not a mere shapeless depiction of human pain. Hecuba's suffering is cumulative. And there is a pattern to the appearances of the chorus, Cassandra, Andromache, and Helen. The chorus of captive women serves to generalize Hecuba's grief. If Poseidon will create future misery for the Greeks, the chorus shows the past and present pain of the Trojans on a large canvas. It places Hecuba's agony in perspective as one calamity among many. Moreover, Cassandra, Andromache, and Helen extend the portrayal of women as the spoils of war: Cassandra, the raped virgin and crazed bride of death; Andromache, the exemplary wife and mother turned into a childless widow and handed over to the son of the man who killed her husband; and brazen Helen, the faithless wife who has the knack of getting her own way in every circumstance. The contrast among these three could not be more striking.

Euripides takes pains in *The Trojan Women* to show that the only justice in war is punitive and nihilistic. War arises from numerous individual choices and leads to disaster for everyone, the conquered and the victors alike. With Thucydides the historian, Euripides shares the view that power corrupts, promoting arrogance and criminality. His vision of the suffering caused by the war is as valid today as it was when he wrote the play, and as it must have been when Troy presumably fell.

James Weigel, Jr.

THE TRUE HISTORY

Type of work: Prose romance
Author: Lucian (c. 120-c. 200)
Type of plot: Satiric fantasy
Time of plot: Second century
Locale: The universe
First transcribed: Second century

Ridiculing the exaggerated travel books of his age, like Antonius Diogenes' The Marvels of Ultima Thule *and others now lost, Lucian's* The True History *is a two-part parody that greatly influenced Rabelais and Swift.*

The very title of this, the best-known Lucianic narrative, betrays its satirical purpose. *Historia* originally meant "investigation" and was the title of Herodotus' monumental work—the first deliberate objective inquiry into causes and effects of past human events. Lucian's investigation is a patent sham made even more outrageous by its emphasized claim to veracity. Even its structure is a ridiculous parody, since it is pretentiously divided into two *logoi* or books, to be followed by others—so he assures us in his closing sentence; but of course they never come. (Herodotus' *History* is in nine books.) It must, however, be noted that Lucian is not satirizing the works of the greats but those of poets and prevaricators from Homer on who have entertained and deceived their audiences with accounts of fantastic voyages. Indeed, Herodotus is paid the highest compliment in this work by being placed among those punished for lying: Lucian has warned us that he would tell the biggest lies we have ever heard, and certainly that would be the truest statement in the work.

A companion piece to *The True History* is *How to Write History*—that is, how *not* to write it! Both works, in addition to other essays and dialogues, demonstrate Lucian's intense critical interest in maintaining literary and rhetorical standards. He is the forerunner of writers such as Swift and Voltaire, but his work is less contrived, more transparently constructed according to free association and familiar literary allusion, which results in a very relaxed narrative style. Even so, to a modern reader Lucian's devout illogicality and predictable antitheses tend toward boredom. Although this may well have been intended, Lucian nevertheless was writing for an audience more familiar with such "literature," and so the constant comparisons would have been more humorous. The closest we might approach this appreciation would perhaps come from reading parodies of today's abundant science fiction.

TRUTH SUSPECTED

Type of work: Drama
Author: Juan Ruiz de Alarcón (c. 1581-1639)
Type of plot: Thesis comedy
Time of plot: Seventeenth century
Locale: Madrid
First published: 1628

Mexican-born Juan Ruiz de Alarcón became one of the leading dramatists of the Golden Age in Spain. His Truth Suspected, *a moralistic comedy which later inspired Corneille's* Le Menteur *(1643), presents an excellent character study of a congenital liar.*

While lying, as such, is not listed among the seven deadly sins of the Middle Ages, it comes close to becoming so in the Renaissance. Medieval moralists had tended to externalize evil, visualizing it in the forms of assorted evil spirits and human actions, whereas Renaissance moralists were more eager to search for evil in the innermost part of man, in his emotions and thoughts. Medieval thinkers habitually cited Nero as representative of the worst form of man, while Iago is quite possibly the most evil man created by a Renaissance mind; Nero had been guilty of such overt crimes as adultery, incest, and wanton slaughter, while Iago's most destructive acts were his lies.

It is not surprising then that Alarcón should construct one of his best plays with this one vice as its cornerstone. This play deals solely and entirely with that disjunction of reality and human relationships called lying.

Don García not only cannot tell the truth, but he also cannot hear it. That is to say, he does not believe the truth when he hears it, even though everyone around him does tell the truth. Lucrecia makes a vain attempt to set straight his identification of the two women, and Don Beltrán forcefully informs him of the disastrous circumstances inevitably resulting from lying, but still the young man persists almost mindlessly in distorting the truth.

Jacinta obviously was meant to be Don García's wife, for not only did he love her at first sight, with her evident approval, but she is also the one young lady of the entire city of Madrid who is chosen by Don Beltrán to become his son's bride. These two events, independent as they are, indicate by their coincidence a kind of providence at work which is subverted by Don García's affliction. In the final analysis, Don García's pathological lying is a disease which results in sterility and death.

This is a departure from the mainstream of sixteenth and seventeenth century comedy, in which societal sterility is threatened by the *senex,* always an old man, usually the father of the boy or girl whose love serves as a focal point for the plot. In this play, by contrast, the deadly hand of the *senex* is that of no one's father; it is Don García's debilitating habit. Don Beltrán, far from hindering the love match, exerts himself to aid it. In *Truth Suspected,* lying is the *senex*.

This play departs from most comedies of the period in yet another way. Don García would seem, at first glance, to bear the full brunt of the consequences which result from his lying: he loses the young lady he loves and is forced to marry another whom he does not love. Were these the only results, it could be said that the catastrophe befalls one individual, not a society. But Don Beltrán shares heavily in the disaster. When his first and more virtuous son died, unbeknown to him at the time his hopes for retention of honor in his family's future also died. Don Beltrán is left with one heir who carries a disease fatal to honor. The young lover loses his love; the honorable older man loses his honor. The older man evidently does nothing to deserve his loss of honor. The question remains, does Don García deserve his downfall?

If this question turns, as often it does, on the motivation for his destructive lying, the question is unanswerable. Other liars lie for pleasure or for profit, but we see no such rationale behind Don García's lying. He lies when the truth would have served his purposes as well or better than his lies, as when he lies about having given the banquet and then lies again in order to extricate himself from the duel. There is no indication here that he is too cowardly to fight the duel. There is only the sense that he is driven to lie somewhat as a kleptomaniac steals or as a hyperactive child runs himself to exhaustion.

Similarly, he lies when the truth is sure to be discovered in a matter of days. When, for example, he tells Jacinta of his Peruvian wealth, it seems to matter not at all that his true background is quite adequate to attract her attention.

It is tempting to the modern reader, but probably an error, to psychoanalyze Don García. If his father rejected him or his mother dropped him, or if the trauma of birth inflicted irreparable damage to a delicate psyche, Ruiz de Alarcón does not mention it in the play. Don García, like any other literary creation, exists only to the extent that his author gives him existence. There can be no doubt that his lack of motivation was a part of Ruiz de Alarcón's design, but this part of the design most probably was meant to isolate the central thesis of the play—the evils of lying—so as to present the phenomenon in something very near to its pure form. Certainly Ruiz de Alarcón's method serves to depict the fault as being even more ludicrous and damaging than it usually is in real life, thereby holding it up to ridicule and scorn.

There are minor, but telling, similarities between Don García and that other, more famous *hidalgo* of Spanish literature, Don Quixote. While García has little of Quixote's more engaging qualities, such as his eagerness to aid other people and his curious quixotic brand of wisdom, nevertheless Don García obviously shares Quixote's addiction to the beautiful lie. While García is not in love with the heroic motions of ridding the earth of giants and malevolent knights, he definitely is enamoured of casting himself in the roles of traveler from a mystical land (as Peru was at this time), as silent and adoring lover-from-afar, and as giver of lavish feasts.

With both characters, the beautiful lie blinds the liar to the real world. The essential differences between the two lies is that Quixote's has a form and an ethos of its own (outmoded though it may have been) whereas García's lies are piecemeal and extemporaneous. Quixote's lies led to insights and revelations; García's lead only to chaos and disappointment.

John J. Brugaletta

TURCARET

Type of work: Drama
Author: Alain René Le Sage (1668-1747)
Type of plot: Social comedy
Time of plot: Seventeenth century
Locale: Paris
First presented: 1709

In Turcaret, or, The Financier—*an action-packed, zesty satirical comedy centering around the character of the parvenu profiteer—Le Sage presents a clear picture of the social disintegration which began in the last years of Louis XIV, a period of gross fiscal mismanagement.*

In *Turcaret,* plot is subordinated to the depiction of character, much in the manner of Molière. The rich financier is revealed in all his diversity: gallant lover, jealous lover, rapacious businessman. The portrait of Turcaret reaches completion with the satirical touches in his character that render him not only obnoxious and ridiculous, but menacing. As a type, Turcaret represents everything that the people had come to detest in those difficult times: bad taste, execrable manners, alleged immorality, and especially easy success and influence. He worships money and uses any means to obtain it, including speculation, usury, and crooked deals.

The world in which Turcaret operates is depicted with exceptional acuity. It is a sort of no-man's-land between the middle class and the common people, whose denizens are of the most doubtful stripe; at the center is the Baroness, an adventurous coquette, around whom flutter suspicious businessmen, worldly young fops, a go-between, and dishonest valets. The Baroness, busily occupied with her plans to extract as much money as possible from Turcaret, herself appears ridiculous when the Knight easily fleeces her.

Le Sage's *Turcaret,* although without the power of Molière's psychological analysis, does offer a vivid picture of the manners of the time. The satire in the play is not very ferocious, but its low ethical tone does provide a unique style of humor; the characters all possess such loose moral codes that they cannot avoid preying upon one another, until they seem to be involved in a grotesque kind of dance. Although the play is episodic, the plot possesses a certain briskness, bringing Turcaret to an effective end. The greatest character in the play may be Frontin, a lively and unscrupulous rogue with quick wits and amoral ambitions; he suggests both Molière's Scapin and Beaumarchais' Figaro. Despite whatever faults the play possesses, *Turcaret* is genuinely amusing, filled with acute observation, a rapid pace, and witty speeches. *Turcaret* shows life as Le Sage saw it about him, without too much comment; he is content to let the story make its own point, without philosophizing, and to make it with that happiest of mediums, laughter.

THE TURN OF THE SCREW

Type of work: Novelette
Author: Henry James (1843-1916)
Type of plot: Moral allegory
Time of plot: Mid-nineteenth century
Locale: England
First published: 1898

More than a horrific ghost story, The Turn of the Screw *is an enigmatic and disturbing psychological novel that probes the sources of terror in neurosis and moral degradation.*

One of the world's most famous ghost stories, *The Turn of the Screw* was first published serially in *Collier's Weekly* (Jan. 27, 1898-Apr. 16, 1898) and in book form, along with a second story, *Covering End,* late in 1898. In 1908 James discussed at some length the origin and nature of the tale in the Preface to Volume XII of *The Novels and Tales of Henry James.* Considerable critical discussion and controversy have been devoted to the story, especially since Edmund Wilson's 1934 essay on "The Ambiguity of Henry James," in which Wilson argues that "the governess who is made to tell the story is a neurotic case of sex repression, and that the ghosts are not real ghosts but hallucinations of the governess." Since many critics have taken issue with Wilson and since Wilson later modified his interpretation, it is important to note briefly what James himself says about his story, his characters, and his theme in the Preface. He calls *The Turn of the Screw* "a piece of ingenuity pure and simple, of cold artistic calculation, an *amusette* to catch those not easily caught . . . the jaded, the disillusioned, the fastidious." He terms the governess' account "her record of so many anomalies and obscurities." He comments that he purposely limited his revelation of the governess' character: "We have surely as much of her nature as we can swallow in watching it reflect her anxieties and inductions." He says he presented the ghosts as "real" ones and he describes them as "my hovering prowling blighting presences, my pair of abnormal agents . . . [who] would be agents in fact; there would be laid on them the dire duty of causing the situation to reek with the air of Evil. Their desire and their ability to do so, visibly measuring meanwhile their effect, together with their observed and described success—this was exactly my central idea." Concluding his discussion of "my fable," James explains that he purposely did not specify the evils in which the ghosts either attempt to or actually involve Miles and Flora: "Only make the reader's general vision of evil intense enough, I said to myself . . . and his own experience, his own imagination, his own sympathy (with the children) and horror (of their false friends) will supply him quite sufficiently with all the particulars."

Thus, we see that James conceived of the tale as one in which the governess, a young woman with limited experience and education but high moral principles, attempts to protect two seemingly innocent children from corruption by the malign ghosts of two former servants who in life were evil persons. His capitalizing of "Evil" and his use of the term "fable" to describe the story suggest a moral as well as an aesthetic intent in writing it. To interpret *The Turn of the Screw* in terms of Freudian sex psychology, as Wilson and some other critics have done, is to go beyond James and to find what he did not put there—consciously anyway. Admittedly, some of the "anomalies and obscurities" which puzzle and trouble the governess do lead the reader in the direction of a Freudian interpretation. The account is the governess' alone and there is no proof that anyone else actually saw the ghosts though she believes that the children saw them and lied to her or tried otherwise to hide the truth from her. Before his reading of the governess' journal, Douglas admits that she was in love with her employer, the children's handsome uncle who showed no personal interest in her. Within the account itself the reader who hunts may find apparent Freudian sex symbolism. For example, the male ghost, Peter Quint, first appears standing on a *tower* when the governess has been deeply longing for her employer to appear and approve her care of the children. The female ghost, Miss Jessel, first appears by a *lake* and watches as little Flora, also watched absorbedly by the governess, plays a childish game:

> She had picked up a small flat piece of wood, which happened to have in it a little hole that had evidently suggested to her the idea of sticking in another fragment that might figure as a mast and make the thing a boat. This second morsel . . . she was very markedly and intently attempting to tighten in its place.

Ten-year-old Miles's repeated use of the word "dear" in speaking to the governess may suggest a precocious boy's sexual interest in his pretty governess.

One can go on, but it is important to remember that James's story was published in 1898 and that Freud's first significant work explaining his sexual theory did not appear until 1905. Perhaps it is best to regard such details in the story as those cited as no more than coincidental, though they may seem suggestive to the post-Freudian reader of *The Turn of the Screw*.

Among the most difficult facts to explain away in developing the theory that the ghosts are mere hallucinations of a sexually frustrated young woman, is the governess' detailed description of a man she has never seen or heard of:

> "He has no hat. . . . He has red hair, very red, close-curling, and a pale face, long in shape, with straight, good features and little, rather queer whiskers that are as red as his hair. His eyebrows are, somehow, darker;

they look particularly arched. . . . His eyes are sharp—awfully. . . . His mouth's wide, and his lips are thin, and except for his whiskers he's quite clean-shaven."

Mrs. Grose easily identifies him as the dead Peter Quint. She just as easily identifies Miss Jessel when the governess describes the person she later saw: " . . . a figure of quite an unmistakable horror and evil: a woman in black, pale and dreadful—with such an air also, and such a face!—on the other side of the lake." It is difficult to argue convincingly that Peter Quint and Miss Jessel are not "real" ghosts.

The Turn of the Screw will continue to fascinate and to intrigue because James's "cold artistic calculation" has so filled it with suggestiveness and intentional ambiguity that it may be read at different levels and with new revelations at each successive reading. As Leon Edel has said, "The reader's mind is forced to hold to two levels of awareness: *the story as told,* and *the story to be deduced.*"

Henderson Kincheloe

TWELFTH NIGHT

Type of work: Drama
Author: William Shakespeare (1564-1616)
Type of plot: Romantic comedy
Time of plot: Sixteenth century
Locale: Ilyria
First presented: 1600

The principal charm of Twelfth Night, Or, What You Will, *one of Shakespeare's most delightful comedies, lies in its gallery of characters: the dour Puritan Malvolio; the clownish Sir Toby Belch and Sir Andrew Aguecheek; and the witty Maria. The original source of the plot was a novella by Bandello, based on an earlier work by Cinthio, but the story was translated into various secondary sources which Shakespeare probably used.*

Twelfth Night, Or, What You Will, was apparently composed to be performed on that feast day, the joyous climax of the Renaissance Christmas season, for the feast has nothing intrinsic to do with the substance of the play. The subtitle perhaps suggests that it is a festive bagatelle to be lightly, but artfully, tossed off. Indeed, the play may have been written earlier and revised for the occasion; surely there are many signs of revision, as in the assignment of some songs to Feste which must originally have been intended for Viola. The tone of the play is consistenly appropriate to the high merriment of the season. This is Shakespeare at the height of his comic powers, with nine comedies behind him, in an exalted mood to which he never returned, for this play immediately precedes the great tragedies and the problem plays. In *Twelfth Night,* he recombines many elements and devices from earlier plays, particularly *Two Gentlemen of Verona* and *The Comedy of Errors,* into a new triumph, unsurpassed in its deft execution.

It is a brilliant irony that this most joyous play should be compounded out of the sadnesses of the principal characters. Yet the sadnesses are, for the most part, the mannered sadnesses which the Elizabethans so much savored. Orsino particularly revels in a sweet melancholy which is reminiscent of that which afflicted Antonio at the beginning of *The Merchant of Venice.* His opening speech, which has often been taken too seriously, is not a grief-stricken condemnation of love. It owes much more to Petrarch. Orsino revels in love-longing and the bittersweet satiety of his romantic self-indulgence. He is in love with love and he is loving every minute of it.

Set up at the other end of town, in balance with Orsino and his establishment, is the household of Olivia. Although her sadness for her brother's death initially seems more substantial than Orsino's airy fantasies, the fact is that she too is a Renaissance melancholic who is wringing the last ounce of enjoyment out of her grief. Her plan to isolate herself for seven years of mourning is an excess, which is wittily pointed out by Feste among others, but it does provide an excellent counterbalance to Orsino's fancy and sets the plot in motion, since Orsino's love-longing is frustrated, or should we say gratified, by Olivia's being a recluse.

The point of contact, ferrying back and forth between the two, is Viola—as Cesario. She too is sad, but her sadness, like the rest of her behavior, is more direct and human. The sweet beauty which shines through her disguise is elevated beyond a vulgar joke by the immediate, though circumstantially ridiculous, response of Olivia to her human appeal. Viola's grief is not stylized and her love is for human beings rather than abstractions. She seems destined to unite the two melancholy dreamers, but what the play in fact accomplishes is the infusion of Viola, in her own person and in her *alter ego,* her brother, into both households. The outcome is a glorious resolution. It is, of course, immaterial to the dreamy Orsino that he gets Viola instead of Olivia—the emotion is more important than the person. And Olivia, already drawn out of her study by the disguised Viola, gets the next best thing—Sebastian.

The glittering plot is reinforced by some of Shakespeare's best, most delicate dramatic poetry. Moreover, the drama is suffused with bittersweet music. The idyllic setting in Illyria cooperates with language and imagery to create a most delightful atmosphere wholly appropriate to the celebration of love and the enjoyment of this world.

There is one notable briar in the rose garden, Malvolio, but he is perhaps the most interesting character in the play. Malvolio is called a puritan and, though he is not a type, he does betray characteristics contemporarily associated with that sect. He is the sort of self-important, serious-minded person with high ideals, who cannot bear the happiness of others. As Sir Toby puts it, "Dost thou think because thou art virtuous, there shall be no more cakes and ale?" Malvolio is in a tough spot in this joyous world and, against his will, he becomes part of the fun when he is duped and made to appear ridiculous. He is, however, the representative of a group, growing in power, whose earnestness threatened to take the joy out of life (and, incidentally, close the theaters). Yet, Shakespeare does not indulge in a satire on puritanism. As Dover Wilson has noted, he does not, characteristically, avail himself of the critical powers of comedy except in a most indirect way.

Malvolio is ridiculous, but so are the cavaliers who surround him. The absurd Aguecheek and the usually drunken Sir Toby Belch are the representatives, on the political level, of the old order which Malvolio's confreres in the real world were soon to topple. Yet, if these characters are flawed, they are certainly more engaging than the inflated Malvolio. Shakespeare does not set up the contrast as a political allegory, with right on one side and wrong on the other. Nevertheless, Malvolio is an intrusion on the idyllic world of the play. He cannot love; his desire for the hand of Olivia is grounded in an earnest will to get ahead. He cannot celebrate; he is too pious and self-involved. What is left for him but to be the butt of the joke? That is his role in the celebration. Some critics have suggested that he has been treated too harshly. However, a Renaissance audience would have understood how ludicrous and indecorous it was for a man of his class to think for a moment of courting Olivia. His pompous and blustery language are the key to how alien he is to this festive context. When he has done his bit, Olivia casually mentions that perhaps he has been put upon, but this is the only gesture he deserves. He is the force that can ruin the celebration of all that is good and refined and joyful in Elizabethan society.

Edward E. Foster

TWENTY THOUSAND LEAGUES UNDER THE SEA

Type of work: Novel
Author: Jules Verne (1828-1905)
Type of plot: Adventure romance
Time of plot: 1866-1867
Locale: The Seven Seas
First published: 1870

An imaginative romance prophetic of modern scientific inventions, most notably the submarine, Twenty Thousand Leagues Under the Sea *is an exciting adventure story that features the exploits of Captain Nemo of the* Nautilus.

Jules Verne was a fascinating and gifted man about whom most readers of his works know relatively little. Americans usually base their opinions of Verne solely upon inaccurate and shoddy translations of his works. Unfortunately, many of Verne's books were published and translated hurriedly in the last quarter of the nineteenth century, and they lost much of the detail and concern for accuracy which Verne had put into the French originals. Consequently, Jules Verne is regarded as a great storyteller, even the father of science fiction by many; but in no way do most people respect him as a scientist. A study of Verne in his original French offers a much more impressive look at the author's expertise in his field. The plots of his books are structured around pages and pages of scientific notes, observations, and investigations made into his subject matter. *Twenty Thousand Leagues Under the Sea* is no exception. Before writing the book, Verne interviewed marine engineering specialists, scientists, fishermen, sailors—in short, everyone who could add new dimensions to the plans he had for a novel about the fascinating depths of the ocean floor and travel in that realm in an enclosed vessel. After much thought, Verne developed a plot around these many facts and used his fictional characters to bring it to life.

The basic outline of *Twenty Thousand Leagues Under the Sea* is a simple one. The greatest creation is Captain Nemo, whose name means "no one." He has rejected all that society stands for and has taken refuge in his underwater realm. As Captain of the *Nautilus,* he is the supreme commander who holds the fate of his three prisoners in his hands. He is, on the one hand, kind, patient, and cultured, while on the other, he is vengeful and mysterious. His tragic flaw seems to be that the hate he has for society, a hate never fully explained, is returned with pure hate. The senseless and unjust destruction of the warship in the last pages of the book makes Professor Aronnax all too eager to escape the *Nautilus* and the clutches of Captain Nemo.

Professor Aronnax is the most real character in the book. He is the teacher, observer, and appreciator of all that goes on around him. The professor narrates this story and answers the questions of his comrades while dispensing great amounts of information regarding things he has studied about marine life and the underwater world. The professor provides Jules Verne with an outlet for some of the innumerable details he has collected for his story.

Conseil, the professor's servant whose devotion to his master is unquestioned, is a simple character. His chief eccentricity seems to be his habit of addressing the professor exclusively in the third person. Ned, the harpooner, represents the more physical, temperamental, and self-reliant personality. He is the common man whose makeup reflects extremes of good and bad. Ned's passions and his anger at being made a prisoner of Captain Nemo make him seem a little more normal than the rest.

Throughout the book, Verne combines science fiction with humor, and fascinating characterization with vivid detail and description. Jules Verne was not an especially great literary stylist, but he was, without doubt, a great researcher. In his enthusiasm for the discoveries of science and his communication of such findings through his writings, he foresaw the future's shape, and he built a valuable stepping stone for writers of science fiction in the decades that followed.

TWENTY YEARS AFTER

Type of work: Novel
Author: Alexandre Dumas, *père* (1802-1870)
Type of plot: Historical romance
Time of plot: Mid-seventeenth century
Locale: France and England
First published: 1845

Intricate in plot, though not so complicated as The Count of Monte-Cristo, *this sequel to* The Three Musketeers *is in some ways a less original work than its predecessor. Dumas was repeating himself in his infallibly clever D'Artagnan and his persistently saintly Athos. But the action of the romance, set against the background of a fictionalized history of the times of Cardinal Mazarin, is rapid enough to satisfy most readers.*

Twenty Years After was published in 1845 at the beginning of Alexandre Dumas, *père's* most productive decade, when he had turned his back on successful playwriting to exploit the rich, romantic possibilities of the French historical novel. The book, which appeared first as a serial in *Le Siécle,* was the first sequel to the immensely successful *The Three Musketeers,* published the year before.

The novel deals with the Fronde, a name given to two revolts against the absolutism of the monarchy, as well as the downfall and execution of Charles I, King of England. In terms of this book, the four musketeers are close to the leading actors in the history of their time, and are involved even more importantly in more major events than they were in the original story. Increasingly sophisticated, this time they are makers of history as well as witnesses.

It is hardly necessary to tell readers that Dumas played fast and loose with history. Often basing his stories on unreliable memoirs, he compounded unreliability. Working hastily and carelessly, he frequently failed to keep historical chronology straight. There are prime examples of his various kinds of faults in *Twenty Years After.* Charles I, for example, writes to his wife that he is preparing to fight a battle that actually took place three years before the date of the letter. Anne of Austria says that Louis will reach his majority "next year," at a time when he is only ten. The portrait of Mazarin, apparently based on the memoirs of one of his enemies, is entirely one-sided.

Dumas also took liberties with fiction. Never was the long arm of coincidence longer or more nearly omnipresent than it is in this novel. He embraced improbabilities with outstretched arms and consorted openly with impossibility. But these faults and inconsistencies, in a sense, do not matter. What remains important is the special magic of the author's storytelling, which has enthralled generations of readers, and will most certainly enchant generations to come. Dumas is an absolute master in the craft of storytelling, and his talent is showcased nearly as well in this novel as in his classic novel, *The Three Musketeers.*

TWO GENTLEMEN OF VERONA

Type of work: Drama
Author: William Shakespeare (1564-1616)
Type of plot: Romantic comedy
Time of plot: Sixteenth century
Locale: Italy
First presented: 1594

An early and comparatively immature romantic comedy, Two Gentlemen of Verona *is charming and witty; but the characters seem superficial, and the hero's quick and sympathetic forgiveness of the friend who had betrayed him strikes a false note.*

In Joyce's *Ulysses* Stephan Daedalus asserts (referring to Shakespeare), that "a great man makes no mistakes; his errors are volitional and are the portals of discovery." This sentiment, as well as changes in Shakespearean interpretation over the years, have made many commentators hesitant to name faults in the plays, when all too often "faults" have been later judged to be the strengths of Shakespeare. In *Two Gentlemen of Verona,* however, the fault is a real one, and lies in the forgiving of Proteus by Valentine.

Proteus was a demigod in Greek mythology who could constantly change form; Shakespeare's Proteus is the principle of inconstancy. His betrayal of his friend Valentine and of his fiancée, Julia, is rather too serious to be reconciled in a simple pardon. The moral hierarchy is disrupted.

But there is a discrepancy earlier than the pardon, in the very characterization of Proteus. He seems to be a good man because he is loved by two very positive characters, Valentine and Julia; indeed, he seems universally esteemed by those who know him. Also, in expressing his love for Silvia, Proteus uses the same rhetoric (even in soliloquies) as Valentine, the traditional sincere lover. He justifies his falseness with similarly "sincere" emotion in his arguments.

Although this discrepancy in character is a flaw in *Two Gentlemen of Verona,* however, Shakespeare later evolved such a moral contradiction into a rich ambiguity of rather ominous aspect; the "problem" or "dark" comedies (*Measure for Measure, All's Well That Ends Well*) are based on the same failure to explore and interpret the full moral dimensions of an action. If the ambiguity remains flat in *Two Gentlemen of Verona* (a simple contradiction), it is not simply that, in spite of Julia's awareness of all of Proteus' wrongs, she tolerates him more than she might (this would be typical of the problem comedies); it is that there is nothing in the play that dramatizes the implied compromise of moral order. The tone of this play is too sunny for its content.

THE TWO NOBLE KINSMEN

Type of work: Drama
Authors: William Shakespeare (1564-1616) and John Fletcher (1579-1625)
Type of plot: Chivalric romance
Time of plot: Age of legend
Locale: Athens and Thebes
First presented: c. 1613

The Two Noble Kinsmen *was a joint production of the aging Shakespeare and his protégé, John Fletcher. Specific scenes of this sentimental tragicomedy have been attributed, on the basis of stylistic traits, to each dramatist. The main plot was taken from Chaucer's "The Knight's Tale," which derived from Boccaccio's* Teseide *and finally from Statius'* Thebais.

The Two Noble Kinsmen more closely resembles the tragic-comedies of Beaumont and Fletcher than it does the manner of Shakespeare's later plays imitative of the type: *Pericles* (1608), *Cymbeline* (1609), *The Winter's Tale* (1610-1611), and *The Tempest* (1611). Even though the "frame" subplot of Theseus and Hippolyta recalls the same characters in *A Midsummer Night's Dream,* the mirthful, exuberant tone of Shakespeare's youthful comedy is replaced with one more serious, heroic, and formally stylized. For both authors, the main source of the play, as the Prologue mentions, is Chaucer's *The Knight's Tale* from *The Canterbury Tales.* Act I derives also from Sir Thomas North's translation of Plutarch's "Life of Theseus." The underlying basis of both the play and Chaucer's narrative is the *Thebais* of Statius, with which both Shakespeare and Fletcher were probably familiar.

The major theme of the play, the tragic conflict between loyal friendship on the one hand and romantic passion on the other, is clearly but too rigidly drawn. Palamon and Arcite, bound by noble comradeship and affection, turn at once into rivals and deadly enemies when they fall in love, nearly simultaneously and at first sight, with Emilia. Since their code is heroic, neither one compromises his claims for sole possession of the beloved. Instead of courting and winning the romantic prize, the kinsmen prepare to fight for her. Arcite, who calls upon Mars for assistance, wins the contest but loses his bride. Palamon, whose claim to Emilia is slightly more persuasive because he saw her first, wisely calls upon Venus to champion him. Thus, although he loses the contest he succeeds in love—which is quite the point of the play. When Sir William Davenant adapted *The Two Noble Kinsmen* in 1664 as *The Rivals,* he emphasized even more than did Shakespeare and Fletcher the code of heroic passion by which Palamon and Arcite live, a convention that would become exaggeratedly idealistic during the period of Cavalier drama.

In spite of the artificial conventions governing its mode, *The Two Noble Kinsmen* is not without merit, particularly Shakespeare's limited part of the play. In Act I he introduces two themes which Fletcher fails to develop later: that of the intimate friendships between Theseus and Pirithous and between Emilia and Flavinia. Had the theme of these parallel friendships been advanced with greater complexity and psychological insight, the play would have surely engaged the modern reader's attention as something more than a curiosity in the history of seventeenth century drama.

THE TWO TOWERS

Type of work: Novel
Author: J. R. R. Tolkien (1892-1973)
Type of plot: Epic romance
Time of plot: The Third Age in a remote legendary past
Locale: The Middle-Earth, chiefly Rohan, Fangorn, Gondor, and Ithilien
First published: 1954

The Two Towers *is the second volume of* The Lord of the Rings, *a mythological and legendary narrative laid in an imaginary past of great antiquity. Like its predecessor,* The Fellowship of the Ring, *and its successor,* The Return of the King, *this book treats in symbolic fashion the theme of choice, or free will.*

The Lord of the Rings abounds in patterns of symbols that are both internally consistent and interrelated. Of these, the color code is most readily apparent. The colors of the Hobbits are yellow and green, the Rohan green and white, and the Elves white, gray, and silver. Elven cloaks are gray-green, those of the Rangers dark green. These are the colors of growing things, or of water, or of starlight. The banner of King Elessar is black with a white device, indicating the victory of the White Tree over Mordor. Saruman's device is a white hand, showing that he was once among The Wise. But the colors of Mordor are black and red, its blazon The Red Eye, and its elements fire and darkness.

Since the industrial revolution, tree-cutting, slag-piling, and general spoliation of the countryside appear regularly in English and American literature as symbols of a loss of innocence, and harbingers of a new and grimmer age. In this tradition, *The Lord of the Rings* depicts a moral hierarchy in which trees represent the greatest good. Trees and all the folk that live among them signify a benevolent force that strives toward the light. This color symbolism holds from the Party Tree, through the trees of The Old Forest whose hostility results from tree-cutting and burning (and whose presiding daemon, Tom Bombadil, denotes natural order and generation) to the mallorns that shelter the Elves in Lothlórien and the Wildmen of Druadan Forest, to the Ents, and even to the White Tree itself. Mordor, on the other hand, is treeless, a place of ashes. What life there is looks downward and loves nothing. The smoke that issues from Mordor to hide the sun is a sign of that imprisoning lust which, in desiring to possess everything and to destroy what it cannot possess, is itself more wretched than the most miserable of its victims. Contrarily, as Frodo points out, the willingness of some beings to give up the world so that their fellow creatures may enjoy it exalts both giver and receiver; and the romance suggests, elliptically, that sacrifice makes things grow.

TWO YEARS BEFORE THE MAST

Type of work: Record of travel
Author: Richard Henry Dana, Jr. (1815-1882)
Type of plot: Adventure romance
Time of plot: 1834-1836
Locale: California and the high seas
First published: 1840

Intended to make the public aware of the hardships and injustices to which American sailors were subjected, Dana's realistic narrative—chiefly in the form of a journal—is noted for its careful observation of life at sea and its accurate report on Spanish California during the early nineteenth century.

If an attack of measles had not threatened Richard Henry Dana, Jr.'s, eyesight and forced his withdrawal from Harvard, America would have lost one of the most popular travel adventure books ever written, *Two Years Before the Mast*. But this physical condition could not have been the only reason for Dana's desire to ship out as a common sailor; surely less arduous and unpredictable forms of convalescence were available to a well-born young Bostonian. His decision must have, to some extent, represented important psychological and emotional needs—to have an "adventure," to "test" himself and his "manhood," to separate himself, at least temporarily, from the narrow, stifling environment and the conservative religious atmosphere of his Brahmin social class and his illustrious, formal family.

Immediately after returning from his voyage, Dana began to record his experiences, largely from memory (his brother Frank having lost the "log" he had kept of the voyage), while he finished his studies at Harvard and then pursued a law degree. The book was published in 1840 and, to everyone's surprise, became an instant commercial success. Ten years later, following the discovery of gold in California, it enjoyed a second burst of popularity, since it was almost the only book available which dealt with the early California environment. Ironically, Dana profited little from the book in a material way since, discouraged in his attempts to find a publisher, he had sold all rights to the work to Harper's for $250.

The great and perennial popularity of *Two Years Before the Mast* probably is due to the fact that it combines two of the most popular genres in a very skillful, vivid manner—the "travel-adventure romance" and the "coming-of-age" narrative.

The travel-adventure romance, which has attracted not only commercial writers, but also some of our best literary talents—James Fenimore Cooper, Herman Melville, Henry David Thoreau, Mark Twain, and Ernest Hemingway among others—has long been a favorite American genre and was especially so in the mid-nineteenth century. It vicariously fulfills at least two emotional needs in the reader: the glorification of physical hardship and an identification with the overcoming of rugged obstacles, especially nature itself; and an escape from the confines of a narrow, dull, middle-class environment to a world of sensuous experience. *Two Years Before the Mast* combines a great deal of the former and generous hints of the latter, especially in the quaint customs and free life style of the Californians. The secret to the depiction of such an "escape" vision is, of course, to make the exotic, unknown world as real to the reader as his own bland, sedate one, and this is where Dana succeeds brilliantly.

Although *Two Years Before the Mast* is autobiographical, many readers accepted it as fiction—which is a tribute to Dana's storytelling abilities. His prose style is direct, concrete, and muted, lacking the rhetorical embellishment so characteristic of most mid-nineteenth century writing, but frequently laced with colloquial shipboard phraseology. On the whole the book does not depend on exciting adventures or bizarre situations, but rather on careful, restrained descriptions of the seamen's everyday routines and activities, punctuated by periodic crises that Dana renders in vivid, dramatic scenes. The book capitalizes on what has always been one of the primary appeals of realistic writing, the intimate description of a profession or activity that seems exotic to the reader.

Moreover, *Two Years Before the Mast* is almost the only nineteenth century narrative of life at sea—Herman Melville not excepted—that does not romanticize the common sailor. Dana clearly likes his mates, but he presents them as very flawed, distinctive human beings, who may not be heroic, but who labor at a very dangerous, difficult job with courage, endurance, and tenacity. This realism, occasionally ironic but never sentimental, is quite modern in tone and attitude, a characteristic which largely accounts for the fact that the book is as entertaining and informative today as it was in 1840.

The "coming-of-age" theme in *Two Years Before the Mast* is given a special twist by the fact that Dana, the initiate, is a young, relatively naïve, religiously conservative Boston aristocrat who thrusts himself into a trial among crude, uneducated, generally amoral sailors. Therefore, he must not only move from youth to manhood, and from innocence to experience, but also from outsider to member of this seafaring subculture. Throughout the book there is, on his side, a constant tension between his aristocratic inclinations and sensibilities and his democratic convictions and the desire to identify with his cohorts; and, on the part of the crew, there is a resentment of Dana for his social background and intellectual pretensions coupled with an admiration for his growth and development as an efficient, hardworking seaman.

In the beginning of the book Dana is an obvious novice and the crew isolates him to the steerage. But he learns quickly and gives a good account of himself in the first bad storm. He also establishes the pattern of volunteering for every difficult and dangerous job that comes up, a trait that brings him admiration from the crew, but also a reputation for foolhardiness. Then, when a young sailor is washed overboard, Dana confronts sudden death at sea and comes to learn the "joking" attitude the men have toward danger and mortality. His view of the basic futility of their lives is also crystalized: "a sailor's life is at best but a mixture of little good with much evil, and a little pleasure with much pain. The beautiful is linked with the revolting, the sublime with the commonplace, and the solemn with the ludicrous."

His initiation into the institutional side of sailing and the "justice" of the high seas comes when Captain Thompson flogs two men for trivial reasons. Young Dana had known of the Captain's absolute power, but, not until he watched this almost demented, hysterical captain dancing about on deck ranting and swearing as he viciously flogged the men, did he realize the full meaning of the custom. It was at this point that Dana committed himself to fighting for a reform of the maritime laws that allowed such flagrant and arbitrary injustice—a commitment he pursued all his life.

The flogging scene also intensifies his desire not to spend his life as a seaman, and this leads directly to his most serious moral dilemma. Throughout the book Dana tries to identify with the sailors, but, when threatened with a possible disruption of his own career plans, Dana invokes the family name and his place is taken by a less well situated substitute. He tries to mitigate the use of family influence by giving the substitute a handsome share of his pay, but the moral onus remains.

Dana's final initiation comes on the return voyage as the *Alert* rounds the Horn through a field of dangerous icebergs. During the perilous navigation he is confined below with a toothache that almost kills him. Thus, a parallel is suggested between this disruption of nature and his own personal condition. The *Alert* survives the crisis and Dana recovers his health. Having come through this double ordeal, he has become fully initiated and is a man and a sailor.

Some critics have gone so far as to suggest that his overall "coming-of-age" development is the classical mythic quest of a hero; that is, Dana as a nineteenth century Jason or Ulysses. Such a view seems forced. If *Two Years Before the Mast* is more than a "boys' book," it is less than an epic. To claim so much for it simply obscures its very real merits.

Two Years Before the Mast is an intelligent, exciting, sensitive story of a young man's transition to maturity, a vivid, convincing description of man's struggle with the elements and with himself, an accurate account of life at sea, a colorful portrait of life in California in the early nineteenth century, and a series of colorful, dramatic vignettes. But it remains the first work of a talented beginner. Had Dana decided to devote his life to letters, his writings might very well be compared today to those of his contemporary and friend, Herman Melville. But he chose law, lecturing, and public service, where he had a moderately successful, if unspectacular, career. Although he was proud of its wide appeal, in time Dana came to consider *Two Years Before the*

Mast as a "boys' book" and to recall his maritime adventures as almost a youthful fling. Little did Richard Henry Dana, Jr., realize, as he stood on the bow of the *Alert* in 1836 pondering what to do with the rest of his life, that he had already lived the most important part of it.

Keith Neilson

TYPEE

Type of work: Novel
Author: Herman Melville (1819-1891)
Type of plot: Adventure romance
Time of plot: Mid-nineteenth century
Locale: Marquesas Islands
First published: 1846

The first significant romance of the South Seas, Typee *is a fictionalized narrative of the actual adventures of young Herman Melville. More than a fascinating travel book, the novel foreshadows the development of many qualities later to appear in the writer's major productions.*

Melville's assertion in *Moby Dick* that a whale ship was his Yale and Harvard reminds us of how central to his development the sea adventures of his youth were, and how strongly they would shape his writing. It was from the whaler *Acushnet* that Melville jumped ship in the Marquesas to spend a few weeks among the Nukuheva natives. The episode ended, sooner and less dramatically than in *Typee,* when he departed the island on another whaler, eventually to join the American warship, *United States,* for a voyage back to Boston. But, though the adventure had ended in actuality, it only began imaginatively for Melville when he sought to discover its meaning in the fictionalized account of his sojourn among the cannibals which he called *Typee.* Though actually a novel based upon experience, *Typee* was regarded generally as simply a travel narrative when it appeared, and the work's reputation since has had to fight against that classification. In fact, *Typee* contains more of the basic elements of Melville's later fiction than its detractors have realized, and it deserves a primary place among such other early works as *Redburn* and *White-Jacket*, which give meaning to the idea of Melville's education on board the ships he sailed as a young man.

The essential facts of *Typee,* except for the time, which Melville considerably exaggerates, are true: he did jump ship in company of a friend named Toby Greene and spend a few weeks among the natives of the Typee valley where he enjoyed a somewhat ambiguous status as a prisoner-guest; Melville did injure his leg escaping the *Acushnet* and allowed Toby to go for medical supplies; Toby failed to return, having been shanghaied by another whaler; and, after a few weeks, Melville was taken off the island by a whaler in search of crewmen. The novel, however, is more than the sum of these few facts, and it cannot be done justice by a reading which regards it as no more than a slightly fictionalized autobiographical narrative. Far from simply recounting his adventures, Melville is, in *Typee,* discovering the fundamental ambiguities in man and nature which would characterize his best work as the basis for the unanswerable questions his novels propose.

From its very beginning, the boys' journey into Typee valley promises to be more than it seems. Running not only from the ship and its cruelly authoritarian master, but from the world of the coast natives which has been hopelessly corrupted by sailors, administrators, and missionaries, these adventurers make their way down a precipitous route which carries them metaphorically backward in time as it takes them beyond the reach of civilization. Eventually reaching the valley floor, the boys initially encounter Typee (which they still believe to be Happar) as a new paradise. Not only the fecundity and lushness of the rich valley but also the young lovers who are the first inhabitants encountered, point to the discovery of a South Sea Eden. This vision of innocence and beauty in the South Sea islands was, to some extent, typical of nineteenth century Romanticism with its recurrent theme of the Noble Savage, but Melville, even this early in his career, was no typical Romantic writer.

From the time Tom (now renamed Tommo) settles, albeit unwillingly, into life with the Typees, Melville begins to develop around him a series of symbols which point to the fundamental ambiguity which lies at the heart of the island "paradise." On the one hand, the simplicity, loyalty, and unselfconscious devotion offered by Kory-Kory, and, more particularly, the innocent love and natural sexuality of Fayaway, keep alive the vision of an Edenic garden. On the other hand, Tommo's discovery that he is in the land of the dread Typees rather than among the peaceful Happars leads to his fear of cannibalism, the most dread of all man's aberrations. Tommo's injured leg, which mysteriously grows worse as his suspicions of cannibalism near confirmation, becomes an objective correlative for his sick spirit which, cut off from the civilization it sought to escape, languishes. Tatooing also develops a symbolic value, since it would complete the initiation into the Typean world begun with the ritual name-change. Once tatooed, Tommo would never again be able to return to his own world.

The essential ambiguity in *Typee* centers around the prospect of a paradise corrupted at its heart by the horror of cannibalism. In later years, Melville would assert that he could look upon a horror and be familiar with it, but this is not so of Tommo, who cannot reconcile himself to this discovery. More generally, the implications of the innate evil of *Typee* seriously challenge the view of optimistic philosophers of Melville's period who argued that the universe, and man, were essentially good, evil being only an appearance rather than a reality. Tommo might like to think that he, as a civilized human being, somehow transcends the essentially savage nature of man, but Melville will not have it so. In the escape scene, Tommo repays the hospitality of his hosts by driving the boat hook into the throat of one of his recent friends. Even as Tommo feels the horror of his violent act, we feel the horror of Melville's world in which the savage impulse dwells even in the most civilized breast.

Though perhaps less orderly than this reading suggests, Melville's symbols are clearly present, and they serve to put his vision in a direct line of descent from that of his Calvinist forebears, who endorsed the doctrine of the essential depravity of man. It is only because the symbols are tentative and nascent, rather than fully developed into Melville's mature symbolism, that *Typee* must be seen more as an anticipation of later Melville than as a fully realized work of art in itself. *Typee* does reveal, however, how early Melville began to develop the symbolic mode which would become the hallmark of his greatest romances, and how soon he began to discover those unsolvable questions of the nature of good and evil which would preoccupy him throughout his career.

William E. Grant

THE UGLY DUCHESS

Type of work: Novel
Author: Lion Feuchtwanger (1884-1959)
Type of plot: Historical chronicle
Time of plot: Fourteenth century
Locale: Central Europe
First published: 1926

A panoramic historical novel of fourteenth century Europe centering around the life of Margarete of Luxemburg, The Ugly Duchess *describes with vividness the corrupt political intrigues of royalty.*

Because of the vast pageant of the story, it is easy to overestimate Feuchtwanger's achievement in *The Ugly Duchess;* it is also easy to underestimate the novel. The author is not a mere showman. *The Ugly Duchess* is a good romantic historical melodrama which pulls the reader into the orbit and times of the characters with irresistible force. Margarete's efforts to spend herself in services which would give sublimated expression to her instincts of love and maternity are sensitively pictured. The subsequent degeneration of her spirit is portrayed convincingly. The life of the robber barons and ruthless kings in their high castles is portrayed with mordant, devastating gusto on a canvas of blood-hues and dark browns and burnished golds. But of all the many characters, only the anti-heroine, Margarete, engrosses the reader's interest.

Feuchtwanger, a student of philosophy and history, was born in 1884. During World War I, while abroad, he was kidnaped and forced to join the German army. He wrote numerous anti-war plays and was best known in pre-Nazi Germany as a playwright. His novel *Jud Süss* could find no publisher until after he had written *The Ugly Duchess*. In 1933, the Nazis confiscated his house and fortune; he escaped to Moscow, then by way of France and Spain to the United States. His international reputation was as a historical novelist.

Feuchtwanger possessed gifts of sharp historical observation and often brought the past to life with vivid immediacy, as in *The Ugly Duchess*. He used the same careful mastery of detail in his novels of contemporary life. His later works became excessively long and the style ponderous, but his historical romances remained popular for many years. *The Ugly Duchess* stands as one of his best-crafted, most engrossing books, principally because he had the insight to see what a fascinating and complex person the notorious Duchess Margarete actually was. But the novel would have been better if he had been able to use his insight to penetrate to the hearts and souls of his other characters. As a result of this lack, *The Ugly Duchess* misses being a great novel.

ULYSSES

Type of work: Novel
Author: James Joyce (1882-1941)
Type of plot: Psychological realism
Time of plot: June 16, 1904
Locale: Dublin
First published: 1922

A continuation of the story of Stephen Dedalus told in A Portrait of the Artist as a Young Man, *this major psychological novel is structured around Homeric parallels, so that the incidents, characters, and scenes of a single day in Dublin in 1904 correspond to those of the Odyssean myth.*

Approaching *Ulysses* for the first time should be done somewhat aggressively. If comprehension lapses—even for pages at a time—it is better to push on. For one thing, it is notoriously a novel to reread. Many elements early in the story make sense only after having read much further along. Bloom's potato talisman, for example, is mentioned in the fourth episode, but remains unexplained until the fifteenth. There are so many such difficulties, and of such variety, that readers sometimes feel lost in random flux. The persistent reader, however, will find that the novel is intensely structured. Joyce later speculated that he had made it perhaps too structured.

Too much or too little, structured it surely is. Although he said he did not want them published, Joyce let out two (very similar) "schemas." These charts indicate for each of the eighteen episodes a title corresponding to an episode in the *Odyssey*; the time of day; a dominant color; a "technic" (the style of the episode: for example, "narrative, young," "catechism, personal," "monologue, male"); a dominant "art" (history, literature, philology); an organ of the body (adding up to a more or less complete person); a dominant symbol (in the first episode: "Hamlet, Ireland, Stephan"); and correspondences between Homeric and Joycean characters. These schemes can be found, in their most complete form, in Richard Ellmann's *Ulysses on the Liffey.*

The schemas have not been an unalloyed blessing to Joycean criticism, for they are sometimes ambiguous or cryptic. However, it is difficult to think of another major author whose critics have been so influenced, indeed dominated, by a single piece of external evidence. The schemas are at least suggestive with regard to three of the more salient (and problematic) aspects of the book. These three, which will be discussed here, are the Homeric parallels, Stephen's theory about Shakespeare and Art, and the episodic structure and use of style.

Shortly after the publication of *Ulysses* the Homeric parallel was lauded by T. S. Eliot as having "the importance of a scientific discovery" and denigrated by Ezra Pound as a more or less gratuitous double-exposure "which any block-head could trace." The schemas and Joyce's notes make clear that he took the parallels very seriously, although "seriousness," for Joyce, is best understood in his word "jocoserious." The elaborate Homeric analogy is, however, surely not, as Eliot thought, merely a backdrop to heighten "the immense panorama of futility that is the modern world."

Ulysses had been Joyce's favorite hero even from his childhood. The quality he was to isolate as unique to the Greek hero was *completeness*. He observed that Ulysses had been a father, a son, a husband, a lover, a soldier who was at first a draft dodger and then a "hawk." Although this is a rather curious ideal, it suggests what may have been Joyce's purpose. The story of Ulysses constitutes such a full representation of a given complex of attitudes and values that Joyce was able to use it as a paradigm for the structure of a modern story. The *Odyssey* itself no doubt had been determined by the structure of Homer's intuitions about the nature of life. These intuitions, we would say, correspond, in the abstract, to Joyce's own. The at times rather wide digressions from Homer's story in Joyce's suggest this kind of substratum "beneath" the Homeric substratum, which determines both in a manner similar to the combinatory processes of mathematical probability.

This ideal "complete" hero "beyond" even Ulysses would be the abstract person, possessor of the "organs of the body" of the schema. The schema supports this general contention in that the distribution of correspondences to Homer is not consistent. Bloom and Stephen are, in fact, only "in general" Ulysses and Telemachus. Correspondences listed on the schema indicate that in the first episode, for example, Stephen is Telemachus, but also Hamlet. In the ninth episode Ulysses is "Jesus, Socrates, Shakespeare"; they are each important there. Furthermore, as has been remarked, Stephen is more like a youthful aspect of Ulysses than like Telemachus, who is almost a minor character in Homer. There is, then, no one-to-one impersonation of Homeric characters. Rather, there is a play of functions pointing to an essential human, the abstract "Ulysses" who belongs not exclusively to Homer, but to the entire tradition of the Ulysses theme.

The ninth episode, *Scylla and Charybdis,* contains Stephen's aesthetic theory. The action is presented as a parable of artistic creation based on Shakespeare's biography. The way the "Ulysses" of the schema functions is rather complex. The schema says that Scylla is "The Rock—Aristotle, Dogma" and Charybdis "The Whirlpool—Plato, Mysticism." "Ulysses," who must sail between these perils, is given as "Socrates, Jesus, Shakespeare." This aspect of "Ulysses" is manifested in Stephen's discourse; Bloom is not even immediately present. The course is the one the artist must take. It includes going between extremes of the inner and outer worlds of his personal experience. There is a struggle between the flux of everyday life and a permanent, repeated structure in the artist's Self. This structure is compared to the mole which remains on Stephen's breast although all the molecules of his body have changed, and, in the parable, to a supposed psychological trauma in Shakespeare's youth which determined the structure of his plays and their themes of usurpation, humiliation, and, later, reconciliation. The theory recapitulates, at the level of the individual artistic psyche, the determinism treated by the novel as historical and sociological.

As to the individual episodes, the schema names a variety of elements of style which make each unique. Joyce told friends that he intended each to be able to stand on its own. Various episodes are sometimes anthologized and read like short stories. *Circe,* episode fifteen, has been produced as a play many times. There is narrational point of view in each episode, but it is clearly never the same. There is abundant exegetical literature for each episode, treating in detail the unity derived of its tone, style, and themes. For this overview, however, it is more important to note that the various episodic styles are part of a second structural principle in the novel.

Total autonomy *and* interdependence combine in the episodic structure; Stephen and Bloom, component elements of the "Ulysses" composite, partake of this combination and therefore avoid becoming mere allegorical types. They are, in fact, complete individuals. This pattern suggests the paradoxical doctrine of the Trinity, where three complete and equal Persons have one Essence. Of the Trinity, Joyce once said that when contemplating one Person, the others slip from view. So it is with Stephen and Bloom; for that matter, any individual episode in *Ulysses* seems capable of absorbing our whole attention. It is, therefore, the overview which leads us best through the myriad captivations of Joyce's odyssey.

James Marc Hovde

THE UNBEARABLE BASSINGTON

Type of work: Novel
Author: Saki (Hector Hugh Munro, 1870-1916)
Type of plot: Social satire
Time of plot: Early 1900's
Locale: London
First published: 1912

The Unbearable Bassington *represents the essence of Saki: his amusing dialogue, his skillful use of poetic figures, his sharp wit, his tart ending. This short satirical novel examines the shallow materialism of the English upper class.*

The Unbearable Bassington synthesizes the attitudes, ideas, techniques, stylistic mannerisms, and narrative quirks that had made "Saki" (Hector Hugh Munro) one of the most entertaining and provocative writers in Edwardian England. It was also his first novel and represents his most serious attempt to gain recognition as an important literary artist. *The Unbearable Bassington* suggests that, had he not been killed in World War I, Saki might well have ranked with Aldous Huxley as a satirical chronicler of the disillusioned, disintegrating British upper class in the years following the war.

The Unbearable Bassington immediately impresses the reader as a vivid, brilliant, amusing, ironical portrait of prewar upper-class English society. As a member of that Establishment, Saki knew it intimately and, although he never seriously questioned the social and political institutions which supported it—the rigid class system, economic and social injustice, Imperialism —he saw its brittleness, shallowness, frivolity, and materialism, and he described it with a deft and bitter wit that is as provoking as it is amusing. If most of the personages are more caricature than character, they are a colorful crew, in constant motion and conflict. The dialogue is made up of a steady stream of acute observations, sharp, witty exchanges, and brilliant epigrams. The social rituals, subtle class distinctions, and special mannerisms of the group are sketched with careful precision and ironical understatement.

But there is more to *The Unbearable Bassington* than a witty description of a superficial social strata. The real importance of the novel depends on the seriousness of the action and the fates of the primary characters because it is here that Saki reveals his true feelings about not only his own social grouping, but also life itself. At the center of *The Unbearable Bassington* is the tragi-comic mother-son relationship of the two "unbearable" Bassingtons, Comus and Francesca.

Comus' "unbearableness" is mitigated by his wit, his liveliness, and his honest awareness of, and ironical attitude toward, the self-destructive streak that guarantees he will do precisely the wrong thing at exactly the right time to destroy any chance he may have for "success" or "happiness." He is both frustrated by his Edwardian society and alienated from it. He desperately wants to belong to it, yet he systematically botches every opportunity he has to consolidate his position in it, first in driving off Emmeline Chetrof and then, more importantly, in alienating himself from Elaine de Frey. It is impossible to say whether these impulsive, apparently subconscious, self-defeating actions are the result of a curious integrity or a weak perversity.

The love-hate relationship Comus feels toward his social milieu is most importantly focused in his feelings toward his mother. When Comus systematically ruins his chances for "good" marriages, does he do it to upset his mother's plans? If so, is it hostility? Or perhaps resentment at being "used" to assure her financial security? Or love—an attempt to force her to come out of her materialistic shell and behave toward him as a real mother?

The climax of the relationship comes when, after Comus has lost Elaine to Courtney Youghal, they discuss his future. He suggests they "sell something"—meaning the "Van der Meulen" painting—in order to give him the capital to go into business. She refuses and so, discouraged, Comus agrees to try West Africa, where he withers and pointlessly dies.

In view of the close identification of Comus' fate with the picture, it is difficult to understand the critical objections to the final revelation that the "Van der Meulen" is, in fact, a fake. The pathos and bitterness that emerge from *The Unbearable Bassington* are due to the fact that, at the end, having chosen her material objects over her son, Francesca discovers, too late, how much she really loved and needed him and how little her possessions really matter. Thus, Henry Greech's final revelation that the picture is phoney, told to Francesca as she sits clutching the cablegram informing her of Comus' death, brings together all of the book's thematic and emotional elements into a bitterly ironic and dramatically potent conclusion. Without it, the book's ending would be merely sad; with it, the finale touches the fringes of tragedy.

But only the fringes. Neither Comus nor his mother are the stuff of which real tragedy can be made. Their lives are too artificial, their preoccupations too trivial, their values too frivolous, and their flaws too menial to be taken too seriously. However, the anti-heroic view of life that has developed and flourished since Saki's time makes the poignancy and absurdity of their final situation most vivid and acceptable to the modern reader. If Saki was the chronicler of a society and world that vanished with World War I, his attitude toward that world seems especially valid for the complex, ambiguous world that succeeded it.

UNCLE SILAS

Type of work: Novel
Author: Joseph Sheridan Le Fanu (1814-1873)
Type of plot: Mystery romance
Time of plot: Nineteenth century
Locale: England
First published: 1864

A well-constructed romance, leisurely in the Victorian fashion but highly effective in the mechanics of atmosphere and suspense, Uncle Silas *is the gripping story of a designing uncle, guardian of a lovely heiress driven almost insane by terror.*

Uncle Silas may well represent the supreme achievement in the development of the Gothic novel of terror. In the leisurely pace of its early chapters, the careful, thorough delineation of the setting and atmosphere, the ornate, sensuous prose style, the utilization of traditional Gothic devices, and the creation of a sinister larger-than-life villain, *Uncle Silas* resembles the earlier masterpieces of "Monk" Lewis, Mrs. Radcliffe, and Charles Maturin. However, the directness and simplicity of the action, the sharpness, subtlety, and psychological accuracy of the characterizations, and the carefully controlled first-person point of view all point to the sophisticated, economical modern suspense or crime novel.

The heroine of the book, Maud Ruthyn, is not particularly sympathetic as a person; she is intellectually unimpressive, emotionally erratic, frequently snobbish, and occasionally haughty. As a narrator, however, she is excellent. We see everything through her eyes and therefore her fears become our fears, but, since her judgments are frequently inaccurate or incorrect, we often see her danger and understand her mistakes long before she does. Like many Gothic heroines, Maud realizes her precarious situation only after she has missed the opportunity to escape from it. It is primarily through her growing sense of desperation and panic, accompanied by a gradual, belated understanding of her plight, that our own sense of impending doom is developed.

As is often the case with Gothic novels, the "bad" characters are more impressive than the "good" ones. As a group, the conspirators are perfectly contrasted and complement one another's particular villainies. Individually, even the scoundrels, Dudley Ruthyn and "Pegtop" Hawkes, are sharply defined, while the major villains, Madame de la Rougierre and Uncle Silas, are two of the most memorable characters in the genre.

From our first glance of the governess, she is a dominating presence—huge, grotesque, and foreboding. While Silas remains in the background, Madame de la Rougierre hovers over Maud, "gobbling and cackling shrilly," with her exaggerated French manners, her crude physical gestures, her effusive expressions of concern, all performed in such an overwrought and clearly hypocritical fashion that even Maud detects the conspiracy behind her actions. Her sudden reappearance in the secret room at Bartram-Haugh is one of the novel's real shocks.

But it is the image of Silas Ruthyn that remains most vividly in the mind. Even before he is introduced, our expectations are aroused by numerous sinister hints: Austin Ruthyn's mysterious references to him, Monica Knollys' revelation of his suspected crime, rumors about his peculiar habits and religious fanaticism. When Silas appears, he is frightening and puzzling. Above all, he is associated with death. His health is precarious, and the atmosphere he projects, the objects he surrounds himself with, the habits he indulges in—his narcotics, his religious extremism—all give off suggestions of mortality and impending doom. In him the lines between reality and illusion and between life and death are blurred.

But the conspirators are not simply evil incarnate. While they have all the trappings of typical Gothic villains, looked at from another perspective they are pathetic and even comic; their villainy is more the result of frustration and desperation than of evil as such. Dudley is a wastrel, possessing good looks, but neither the intellectual capacity nor the emotional stability necessary to make anything of himself. For all her sinister behavior and grotesque looks, Madame de la Rougierre is revealed, in the end, to be weak and pitiable. She is, as Monica Knollys suggests early in the book, nothing more than a crude, petty thief, mixed up in a conspiracy she only half understands, and suffering from a weakness for alcohol that finally costs her her life.

And even Silas is almost as much to be pitied as condemned. A man of obvious talent and intellect, he has become dissipated and perverted by weakness of character. All his life he has made the wrong decisions, bet on the wrong horses, and seen all of his efforts turn out badly. And, to a man as firmly committed to the idea of hereditary aristocracy as Silas, the spectacle of his son Dudley is the final disillusionment. Pressed by creditors, weakened by drug addiction, unsatisfied by frantic religious speculations, and painfully aware of his own worthlessness, Silas persecutes Maud as a last desperate attempt to salvage something out of his wasted life.

UNCLE TOM'S CABIN

Type of work: Novel
Author: Harriet Beecher Stowe (1811-1896)
Type of plot: Sentimental romance
Time of plot: Mid-nineteenth century
Locale: Kentucky and Mississippi
First published: 1852

A sentimental but powerful document in the controversy over slavery, Uncle Tom's Cabin, or, Life Among the Lowly *is a novel whose political and humanitarian pleading greatly influenced the cause for abolitionism.*

It has been suggested that Mark Twain wrote the first book in the American idiom, but surely Mrs. Stowe's powerful novel introduces the reader to an in-depth use of a regional dialect from an earlier period. The author intentionally created the characters of Tom, Legree, Eva, and Sambo, all of whom subsequently became the stereotypes of white southern womanhood, the brutal slave owner, and various slave personalities, because these features were a part of the conventional wisdom of ante-bellum America. These characters were convenient, effective agencies to warn the Christians of the nation of an impending doom: "every nation that carries in its bosom great and unredressed injustice has in it the elements of this last convulsion." God would certainly punish such a nation.

First published in book form in 1852, this book attracted millions of readers then, and is now often required reading in high schools and colleges. This work will always provide an added dimension to our understanding of the spiritual crisis of pre-Civil War America. The human tragedy in the story symbolizes the moral decay of the country. Simon Legree becomes the manhood of white America that supported slavery, feared hell, yet was more concerned with the material world. Tom lost his wife, children, and life to the ravages of the "peculiar institution." The collective guilt of the nation could only be cleansed by the abolition of slavery.

The fate of the nation and the role of Christian churches in perpetuating slavery were topics of great concern to the author: "And yet, O my country, these things are done under the Shadow of thy laws! O Christ! Thy Church sees them, almost in silence." The author observed and wrote about the crisis that divided Protestantism into sectional churches, a spiritual antecedent of the war. Clearly, the moral regeneration of the individual would lead to the abolition of slavery. Seeking support for her cause, the author admonished the reader to pity "those mothers that are constantly made childless by the American slave trade."

The author was a colonizationist, but she believed deeply that white America must first pay reparations to the nation's enslaved blacks. Once freed, the author points out, blacks needed and desired education and skills.

She hoped that her testimony might bring an end to man's inhumanity to man. Little wonder, then, that President Lincoln, upon meeting the author, remarked, "So you're the little lady who started the war."

UNCLE VANYA

Type of work: Drama
Author: Anton Chekhov (1860-1904)
Type of plot: Impressionistic realism
Time of plot: Nineteenth century
Locale: Russia
First presented: 1899

A play subtle in its evocation of moods and somber emotions, Uncle Vanya *depicts with psychological penetration people nearly overwhelmed by misery but capable nevertheless of heroic endurance.*

Originally planned as *The Forest Spirit* (possibly as early as 1888), *Uncle Vanya* in its final form takes a much more serious view of its characters than the first title suggested. Uncle Vanya is not portrayed frivolously as the forest spirit who has tended the professor's groves as well as his other needs for twenty-five years; rather, Uncle Vanya has evolved into a complex, profoundly troubled but still admirable person. To a certain extent, the onus implied in the original title is shifted to Yelena, whom Vanya characterizes in Act III as a mermaid, the fickle nature of such "sea spirits" being as familiar as that of "forest spirits." Nevertheless, Chekhov treats all of his characters in the final *Uncle Vanya* with great respect, for he places high value on human life—an attitude perhaps related to his professional training as a physician.

Thus, whereas Chekhov sets his play in a simple situation and peoples it with quite ordinary human beings, he explores those people deeply, showing the intensity of their emotions. In his extraordinarily honest portrayal of human feelings, Chekhov emphasizes people and their feelings over action. He has consequently been unjustly berated by insensitive critics who demand the priority of action over emotion in drama. But Chekhov must properly be taken on his own terms, since the emotional candor of his characterization set the standard for realistic theater so definitively that it persists to the present.

Chekhov's view of the human condition, as revealed in *Uncle Vanya,* thus becomes the key to his influence on modern drama. In this play, we find people alienated from one another, despite temporary "truces." Everyone feels isolated in his or her role—except possibly Marina—and unable to communicate meaningfully with others. In fact, genuine communication between or among any of the characters in the play seems hopeless and they therefore view themselves as helpless to control their own destinies.

If ever there were a depiction of Existential despair, *Uncle Vanya* would appear to be it. But such is not Chekhov's view. His faith in human endurance is reflected in his characters' seemingly indestructible hope for something better in the as-yet-uncharted future. It is with this hope that the professor and Yelena depart; that Marya resumes her pamphleteering; that Marina knits and Astrov continues to treat the sick; and that Sonya reassures Uncle Vanya in the last line of the play, "We shall rest!" after their herculean labors to maintain the estate. Against all odds and all reason, Chekhov's characters are not emotionally destroyed. Therein lies their strength; therein lies the strength of the play.

UNDER FIRE

Type of work: Novel
Author: Henri Barbusse (1874-1935)
Type of plot: Social criticism
Time of plot: 1914-1915
Locale: France
First published: 1917

A novel deglorifying World War I, Under Fire *presents a series of incidents rather than a connected plot, each with vivid pictures of the horrors in the trenches—a saga of mud, lice, and death.*

Under Fire is a brilliant description of war and, at the same time, an important marker in the literary and political career of an extraordinary individual. Henri Barbusse was both a writer of international reputation and a political revolutionary. *Under Fire* stands midway in his career. It reflects the growing influence of socialist, if not revolutionary, ideas upon him, and it indicates the extent to which Zola's naturalism has affected him. The novel stops short, however, of advocating revoltuion itself as the answer to international war.

Under Fire is full of the details that only experience in the trenches could provide. Barbusse, despite his pacifism, had volunteered for duty, and even after being wounded, made great efforts to help his fellow soldiers. There is the mud, the tedium, the profound impact of the weather, the insects, the filth, the sudden horrors of bombardments, woundings, blood, and hoarse cries for help. Unlike his naturalist predecessors, however, Barbusse does not give independent life to abstract forces embodied in the earth or the weather or the opposing armies. Rather, all these things are rendered in the most detailed, conventional manner. They are only what they are—not abstract principles over which men have no control.

The ending of the novel can support a variety of interpretations. On the one hand, it appears as if the men can do nothing to stop war; on the other, many of them perceive the officers—not the men—of the German army (and the French) as their enemies. There is sympathy for the ordinary men of the other side, and Barbusse writes kindly of fraternization. *Under Fire* has thus been understandably interpreted as a pacifist novel; but there is a puzzling line at the end which indicates that, if the war yielded any progress at all for mankind, it was worth the effort.

In short, there do not seem to be clearly defined, unambiguous conclusions to be drawn from *Under Fire.* But at the stage in his political career at which Barbusse wrote *Under Fire,* he himself had not yet drawn them.

UNDER THE GREENWOOD TREE

Type of work: Novel
Author: Thomas Hardy (1840-1928)
Type of plot: Regional romance
Time of plot: Nineteenth century
Locale: Rural England
First published: 1872

In this early romance, a gentle story full of whimsical, simple humor, Hardy characterizes his Wessex folk with lyrical but somewhat ingenuous sympathy. Once Dick Dewy wins for a bride his flighty Fancy Day, the author draws a curtain on the action.

Hardy's original title for his second novel was *The Mellstock Quire* (Choir), and it is true that the plot, slight as it may be, deals mainly with the rustic choir members and their replacement by an organ and the new schoolteacher organist. However, Hardy may have chosen the final title from Shakespeare's *As You Like It* to call attention to the work as a pastoral or woodland idyl. The setting of the story has definite similarities to the Forest of Arden in Shakespeare's play; the wedding of Dick Dewy and Fancy Day, for example, takes place at the end of the novel in Yalbury Wood under a real greenwood tree.

Appropriately, the book is divided into four sections: Winter, Spring, Summer, and Autumn. And the characters' actions are tied in with rural activities: nutting, honey gathering, apple picking, country dances, and cider making. Even the names of the major participants in this delightful romance are evocative of nature and its varied manifestations: Dick Dewy, Fancy Day, Mr. Maybold, Farmer Shiner, Thomas Wood and even poor-witted Thomas Leaf.

Throughout the novel Hardy painstakingly draws his background of summer mornings when "fuchsias and dahlias were laden till eleven o'clock with small drops and dashes of water," and of winter in Mellstock-Lane where the breeze makes "fir-trees sob and moan no less distinctly than they rock" and "holly whistles as it battles with itself." The Mellstock choir en route to its Christmas Eve caroling is an intrinsic part of the interlaced branches of the copse, above which stars shine frostily. Dick Dewy's passion for the new schoolteacher, Fancy Day, blooms with the delicate woodland flowers and warm sun upon the grass. Hardy constantly blends the triangular love plot and story of the choir members with seasonal activities, so the reader sees all in terms of a benevolent nature, enveloping, urging, shaping the story's outcome.

Hardy gives special emphasis to the role of music in the tale, which, again, stems from Dorset's environment. The novel opens with the choir and their caroling, and the plot centers around the new organist who is to supplant the choir. Dick and Farmer Shiner sing snatches of ballads about lasses and lads "a-sheep-shearing," the choir sings an entire hymn, the music and dancing at the tranter's Christmas party form almost two chapters, and at the wedding, "five country dances, two reels and three fragments of horn-pipes" carry the guests to supper time. Harmony or music, like nature, not only sketches background and informs the action, but defines the characters themselves.

Here, as in his other novels, Hardy shows an affectionate knowledge of the Dorset (Wessex) countryside, rural customs, rustic speech, peculiar humor of country dialect, and delights of the woodland. Nature has not yet become the dire, ineluctable force it proves to be in his later novels like *Tess of the D'Urbervilles* and *Return of the Native*. Unease and complications, which are certainly present even at the end of *Under the Greenwood Tree,* have not become tragedy; and the reader is left with a pleasant sense of a natural succession of generations consonant with seasonal change.

UNDER THE YOKE

Type of work: Novel
Author: Ivan Vazov (1850-1921)
Type of plot: Romantic tragedy
Time of plot: 1875-1876
Locale: Bulgaria
First published: 1889

Although the story of this political novel is tragic, Vazov's treatment of the theme is romantic in the manner of Scott. Through the author's sharp selection of realistic details, he faithfully communicates a sense of the suffering of the Bulgarians in their struggle against Turkish rule.

Under the Yoke is a competently written political novel which glorifies Bulgarian independence through the story of a young revolutionary and his struggles. Although melodramatic and unrealistic in parts, the novel is very effective in presenting a picture of life in Bulgaria in the years of Turkish domination. *Under the Yoke* reflects Ivan Vazov's keen interest in the details of the Bulgarian nationalist movement's activities. He himself had participated in the independence movement, and many of the novel's memorable scenes owe their vividness to the fact that when he wrote them Vazov was relying heavily on deeply felt personal experiences. His home town of Sopot is the model for Bela Cherkva in the novel, and was the town where he had been involved in preparations for what turned out to be an unsuccessful uprising much like that led by Kralich in Klissoura. Unlike Bela Chervka, however, which in the novel escapes harm by backing out of the planned rebellion, Sopot was attacked by the Turks; when Vazov returned there in 1878 after independence had been won, he found the town destroyed and his father among those murdered.

Vazov is at his best in the political scenes at the school where Kralich teaches or at the theater, and in his scenes of domestic life. The opening scene in the book, for example, in which we see the Marko family at dinner and get a vivid description of their table manners and conversation, immediately provides a realistic setting for the story. Likewise, Vazov handles the scenes at the school, with his portrayals of Rada and Kralich and their students, very skillfully. He shows how many of the underlying political and social problems in Bulgaria's history are crucially related to the education of the young. At the same time, on a more personal level, he weaves in the love story of Kralich and Rada. There are also weaknesses in the plot, however, such as Vazov's tendency to use action scenes such as police searches and murders, to fill in between the much more central political scenes. These episodes occur so frequently and are over so quickly that they become almost mechanical; they seem to be tools used to hurry the narrative forward to the next key event.

The ending of *Under the Yoke* is at once melodramatic and bitter, and reflects the author's romantic conception of revolution and his depression over the failure of the movement. It also dramatizes his basic distrust of the masses and his feeling that the common people are in some way responsible for their own oppression. It is clear, too, that the author believes that small-group terrorist acts are the only truly effective revolutionary device. In Rada's and Kralich's death scene we can see simultaneously the author's romanticism, reminiscent of Scott, and his cynicism about human nature.

UNDER TWO FLAGS

Type of work: Novel
Author: Ouida (Marie Louise de la Ramée, 1839-1908)
Type of plot: Sentimental romance
Time of plot: Early nineteenth century
Locale: London and environs, the continent, Algeria
First published: 1867

The most popular of Ouida's many successful novels, Under Two Flags, *set in Algeria during the early nineteenth century, is a sentimental adventure story that treats in melodramatic fashion the exploits of the Foreign Legion. A memorable character is Cigarette, the patriotic French heroine.*

The sentimental novel or melodrama flourished during the latter half of the nineteenth century. Americans had become harder and more cynical as increased prosperity interested them in the sophistication of European continental life. This fascination led them to read many foreign writings, particularly those set in exotic places with complicated plots and princely characters. These sensational novels were usually focused on the strange and mysterious. They did not aspire to be good literature; instead, they were written solely to produce a thrill for the reader and money for the author. Presumably the more exotic the setting and the more complicated the circumstances, the greater the thrill. The most popular of these authors was Ouida. Her work is characterized by the representation of the "high life," of guardsmen and their mistresses, and of the everyday problems and pleasures of noble families—intrigue, debt, gambling, murder, adultery, bigamy, mistaken identity, and incest.

Under Two Flags was Ouida's most popular novel, perhaps because of the Algerian setting and the appearance of the French Foreign Legion; but to the modern reader the "hero," Bertie, is not nearly as interesting as Cigarette, the violently patriotic French girl "with the heart of a girl and of a soldier."

Although she loves Bertie, he ignores her for the rich and beautiful Princess Corona. Even then Cigarette is "proud of her immunity from the weaknesses of her sex; she had neither meanness nor selfishness," and demonstrates the nobleness of her character and her love for Bertie when she throws herself in front of the bullets intended for him.

Her self-sacrifice underscores her virtues, as well as her essential simplicity, which stand in marked contrast to the mannered and class-conscious world of Bertie and the others—aristocrats in transparent disguises. Ouida flattered the moral superiority of her mass readers at the same time she allowed them to share the thoughts and feelings of the upper classes.

UNDER WESTERN EYES

Type of work: Novel
Author: Joseph Conrad (Józef Teodor Konrad Korzeniowski, 1857-1924)
Type of plot: Psychological realism
Time of plot: Early twentieth century
Locale: St. Petersburg, Russia, and Geneva, Switzerland
First published: 1911

Under Western Eyes, a major novel of political psychology, is both a perceptive study of the revolutionary character, as exemplified by the student Razumov, and an exposition of the Russian temperament. Once comparatively neglected, the novel is now acknowledged as one of Conrad's great productions.

Under Western Eyes is Conrad's third and last major treatment of the subject of political revolution (the first two are *Nostromo* and *The Secret Agent*). The novel is a study of the isolating and corrupting effects of revolutionary behavior.

Razumov, the central character, is not, however, a willing participant in politics. He is forced out of his carefully arranged isolation by the police. Razumov is very like a prototype of certain of today's graduate students in his intellectual pride and his delicately arranged system of principles ("Evolution not Revolution, Direction not Destruction") which he has concocted in nearly total isolation from the world. When he betrays Haldin, who assumes by his silences that he sympathizes with the revolutionary cause, the police make use of him as a spy among the revolutionaries. He falls in love with Haldin's sister and thus is placed by Conrad in a doubly intolerable situation.

Conrad's portrayal of revolutionary types has the same satiric bite as in *The Secret Agent* with the important exception of Sophia Antonovna, a largely sympathetic figure. But even in his long dialogue with her, Razumov cannot say what is on his mind. He has to survive by double talk and evasion —until he can stand it no longer and he gladly submits to punishment. Razumov's position through most of the novel is an accurate reflection of the compromised and uneasy condition of revolutionary politics with its necessary emphasis upon secrecy, violence, and betrayal.

The novel is profoundly influenced by Dostoevski's *Crime and Punishment* but it is no mere echo of that great book. The first part of *Under Western Eyes* is as good as anything Conrad ever wrote, which is very good indeed. The old teacher of languages who pops in and out as narrator is not entirely successful, but he does not really detract from this somber and magnificent treatment of politics.

THE UNDERDOGS

Type of work: Novel
Author: Mariano Azuela (1873-1952)
Type of plot: Social and historical chronicle
Time of plot: 1914-1915
Locale: Zacatecas, northern Mexico
First published: 1915

Best known of Azuela's sixteen novels, The Underdogs *is an influential and powerful political chronicle based upon the author's vivid experiences of revolutionary Mexico. Pessimism marks this story of those coming up from below—*Los de abajo—*at the beginning of conflict.*

This old favorite of the 1910-1917 Mexican Revolution still merits its international fame. Vivid and deep, it has literary and sociological worth. Azuela's honesty glitters in it, since he does not overly caricature his Porfirista enemy even while lampooning him, but bares the hypocrisies of his own side with the skill of a surgeon's scalpel. His characterization is true to life, his action scenes are fast and clear. Violence, pathos, beauty, and tragedy are etched against Jalisco's night-blackened hills, so that the reader receives an indelible image of revolutionary pageantry with its women soldaderas, bandoleered rebels, uniformed federales, and greedy *nouveau riche* who muddy the pond of revolutionary ideals. Thus, while painting only local vignettes of a nation-wide holocaust, *The Underdogs* presents the seedy as well as inspiring aspects of the entire contortion well enough to be a historical document.

The genuine worth of this novel was not recognized until almost a decade after its publication. But by the mid-1920's it had been translated into various languages and was considered a Latin-American as well as a Mexican classic. It was written almost literally amidst powder smoke, when Azuela was in black despair because he saw that the revolution was drowning some injustices in blood only to spawn others as bad and as self-perpetuating. The virtue of the novel thus lies in its taut swiftness, in its throbbing heart beat, and its eye-witness impressions of intense, futile events. Azuela captured the excitement of times when bandoleered peons rode and marched off to war to the strains of the "Zacatecas March" or "La Cucaracha," when the Victorian, Bourbonic, ordered age of Don Porfirio Diaz was dying. Lamentably, it was being supplanted by a violently conceived but stillborn new order that was not even to attempt many of its reforms until many dismal years later.

Noted for its "Mexicanness," and still ranked internationally as the best novel of the Mexican Revolution, *The Underdogs* helped transform the Latin-American novel (which before 1910 had inspired few translations or fame beyond the local region that had produced each novel) into the most important literary genre of Latin America. *The Underdogs* is also possibly the

first Latin American novel whose singular literary style was deliberately engendered by the subject matter. For example, time is telescoped to reflect
the rapidity of events, while linguistic nuances tinge different aspects of the
novel, including characters, scenes, and episodes. Individual members of
Demetrio's command symbolize certain features of Mexican society—one
soldier is a former barber, others are peons, both poor and prosperous, and
there are also prostitutes, virtuous country women, an ex-waiter, and many
other types. Each such individual also has a personality representative of those
to be found frequently in Mexico. Although venal characters are city dwellers,
never country folk, the latter are sometimes ignorant.

An elliptical style selects and spotlights a few specific characteristics of a
person, a scene, or a situation so as to describe it deftly. Disjointed scenes
are thus used, rather than systematic chapters, so as to strengthen the over-
tone of violent eruption. Selfishness wins, idealism is crucified, and the novel's
true protagonist—Mexico's poor—does *not* march out of misery into a
sunny horizon.

Although fragmented into many swift scenes, the novel is divided into
three basic sections. The first section has twenty-one chapters and reflects
hope; the last two sections have a total of twenty-one chapters and reflect
failure. It is in the latter two portions of the novel that the filth, nastiness,
lewdness, and garbage of war are best painted, when personalities such as
Cervantes realize that the revolutionary issues will not be decided by logic
or delicacy but by brute power as symbolized by self-made, upstart generals
who care little for ideals.

Azuela used colors and details well. The natural dialogue is regionalistic
but not difficult and, even though each personality uses special shades of
language that subtly characterize him, there is a high percentage of standard
Spanish.

It is sometimes felt of Mariano Azuela that he saw the Revolution coming
like a silver cloud of hope, next as a black tornado; but then he watched it
hit destructively, unleashing the contorted features of primeval chaos. It finally
disappeared without having helped but having further flagellated the common
people who needed help. Azuela's sympathy in *The Underdogs* is thus always
with the poor, whom he neither idealizes nor attacks. For the opportunists
who betrayed the revolutionary ideals he reserves a special spleen, a sour
sarcasm.

Azuela's masterpiece became the standard-bearer of the novel of the Revolution of 1910-1917, the first significant socio-economic upheaval in Latin
America. Most other revolutionary movements of the preceding years had not
sought to aid the submerged masses, the mestizo, the Indian, the laborer,
"the underdog" in general. Following Azuela's example, many Mexican and
other Latin American novelists took up the fight for reform, denouncing
tyranny and championing the cause of the "forgotten man." Since 1916,

hence, numerous starkly realistic novels have been published in Mexico and throughout Latin America, defending the underdog, whether he lives in the pampa, the llanos, sierra, jungle, city slum, or desert areas of this hemisphere.

William Freitas

UNDINE

Type of work: Novel
Author: Friedrich de La Motte-Fouqué (1777-1843)
Type of plot: Symbolic allegory
Time of plot: The Middle Ages
Locale: Austria
First published: 1811

Essentially a fairy tale, Undine *is a highly imaginative and romantic narrative derived from an old German ballad. The novel, simple but well-told, treats as an allegory the theme of man's need to form a harmonious relationship with nature.*

The German Romantic movement came in reaction to the Enlightenment philosophy which put its faith in the ability of man to solve all his problems by reason alone. The Romantic movement was inspired by a rather complex philosophy. Part of it was the concept of man's essential belonging to nature, to generations and traditions of the past as well as to the future, and of his necessity to live in harmony with nature, rather than merely exploiting it. Romantic poets often used folk themes and themes from the Middle Ages to create fairy tales expressing these ideas.

The German-born French baron Friedrich de La Motte-Fouqué was interested in bringing the heroic epic back to life in the form of drama and novels. However, he also produced a number of other works using themes from old French and German ballads. A stylized picture of the Middle Ages forms the background for *Undine,* a romantic story of living nature seeking harmony with man, based on an old German ballad about knight Stauffenberg. According to romantic philosophy, in order to acquire a soul, Undine, a nature spirit, must marry a loving human being. As long as man remains true to nature, there exists a harmonious relationship beneficial to both. The dark and threatening side of nature becomes apparent when man exploits and rejects nature. Man cannot be permanently happy and at peace living inharmoniously with nature—nature then becomes dangerous to man and eventually destroys him. *Undine* portrays this duality of nature: loving and serving, but also potentially destructive. An interesting literary device, "romantic irony," is used in *Undine* (as well as in many other romantic works) to dispel the fairy-tale atmosphere: the author speaks as narrator and comments on the course of events.

Undine was received with great enthusiasm and translated into many languages. It also served as an inspiration for three operas. The first one, by E. T. A. Hoffmann, had the libretto written by Fouqué himself, and premiered in 1816. Unfortunately its score was destroyed in a fire. The second opera, written by A. Lortzing, came out in 1845 and the third, by Jean Giraudoux, appeared in 1939.

THE UNFORTUNATE TRAVELLER

Type of work: Novel
Author: Thomas Nash (1567-1601)
Type of plot: Picaresque romance
Time of plot: Reign of King Henry VIII
Locale: England and Europe
First published: 1594

The Unfortunate Traveller. Or, The Life of Jack Wilton, an episodic tale, is an important forerunner of the English novel as it was to develop in the eighteenth century. Nash's work abounds in realistic details, but the author catered also to the Elizabethan taste for the romantic and far-fetched, especially in the Italian scenes.

Following the example of Robert Greene, one of his predecessors at St. John's College, Cambridge, Nash overcame whatever religious scruples might have been bred into him as a preacher's son and set out with profane determination to become one of the first "professional writers" in England, and one of the most controversial. As a member of the University Wits, he distinguished himself by the diversity of his authorial talents, unashamedly plying the writer's trade as polemical pamphleteer, poet, dramatist, and reporter. He said of himself, "I have written in all sorts of humours more than any young man of my age in England." And when he died, still a young man in his thirties, Nash left behind a veritable explosion of miscellaneous literary pieces. Picking up the pieces since then, critics have often concluded that Nash's explosive productivity was more comparable to that of a scatter-gun than to the big cannons of his contemporaries Shakespeare, Jonson, and Marlowe. Nash has been accused of superficiality, both of thought and style; and he richly merits the accusation. Nonetheless all would agree that at least two of his works deserve the continued attention of all those interested in the development of English literary style—*The Unfortunate Traveller, Or, The Life of Jack Wilton* and *Pierce Penniless His Supplication to the Devil* (the latter receiving three editions in the year of its first publication alone, 1592). *Pierce Penniless,* Nash's most popular and widest-ranging satirical pamphlet, is a graphic indictment of the follies and vices of contemporary England seen from the harshly realistic perspective of one of the first indisputable forerunners of yellow journalism. Nash's ready talent for immediately distilling the fruits of his observation and experience into gripping first-hand reports served him as well in his perplexing narrative of Jack Wilton.

Rambling narrative, travelogue, earthy memoirs, diary, tavern yarn, picaresque adventure, political, nationalistic, and religious diatribe, *The Unfortunate Traveller,* though impossible to classify generically, is nonetheless clearly one seminal starting-point in the development of the English novel. The critics are in general agreement with Wells, who declares that the work "has no organic principle; it is not a unified work of art." Though Nash's narrative is certainly not "a unified work of art" by the severest standards of unity, it definitely has an organic wholeness. But that wholeness is as much external as internal, provided more by the pen of Nash than by the ephemeral character of Jack. Therefore the lack of unity is still a true *imitation* because it reflects accurately the mind of the author—a mind as chaotically diverse as the narrative it has produced. The structure of the book is absolutely arbitrary, simply a loosely organized recounting of Jack's travels through Great Britain, the Low Countries, Germany, France, and Italy—a structure comfortably suited to Nash's always changeable purpose and varying (not alternating) interests. The reader will look in vain for a balance between one part of Jack's travels and another; there is none, since Nash sees contemporary life as completely unbalanced. Like Jack, the author stays where he likes as long as he likes, and especially as long as he senses the reader can still be interested. Nash's sense of his audience is one of his most charming assets, and it is highly appropriate that this tale is set up in the guise of a barroom brag on the part of Jack, lately returned from Bologna. Nash's structural nonchalance almost certainly influenced Sterne's *Tristram Shandy*.

Sterne must also have been intrigued by the ambiguity of viewpoint found in *The Unfortunate Traveller*. There are times when it is almost certain that the author forgets about Jack entirely, setting off on his own to denounce, castigate, ridicule, expound on one thing or another. At other times Nash can be most subtle in his handling of the complicated relationship between narrator and fictive reader—as when Jack constantly quotes a Latin phrase to justify his actions, mistranslating it for his ignorant victims while we are left to wonder whether the mistranslation is also intended to poke fun at us (for example, *Tendit ad sydera virtus,* which Jack renders as, "there's great virtue belongs, I can tell you, to a cup of cider"). If *Tristram Shandy* overlooks the neat narrative distinctions, drawn by Dante between his naïve pilgrim and his narrator-pilgrim or by Chaucer in *The Booke of the Duchesse,* it does so with the comfortable knowledge that Nash did it first and succeeded brilliantly.

Nash's style reaches its finest and most characteristic expression in this book: the vivacity of an undiminishing *sprezzatura*—brilliantly uneven, uncontrolled and disorganized. *The Unfortunate Traveller* walks a precarious line between realistic and romantic perspective and frequently, as Nash did in his own mind and life, gains its appeal from its inability to prevent one side of the line from flowing over into the other. The journalistic nature of Nash's prose is marked both positively and negatively; positively, for its unprecedented precision of detail, proving the author's considerable powers of observation (equalled only by his lack of discipline); negatively, for his inability to separate objective narration from personal viewpoint—indeed, his unwillingness to see the value of such a separation. The result is a work as prodigious for its literary "faults" as it is for its "virtues," a work that constantly raises the question of why it is still being read and taught.

The beginning of the answer lies in the character of Jack Wilton, the semi-fictional counterpart of Nash's own personality. In his ambivalence between ambition and cowardice, the desire for adventure and the need for security, aggressiveness and passivity; in his switch from awestruck observer to cantankerous prankster, innocent victim to devious culprit; in his love of acting and enjoyment of performance, passionate enthusiasms and vicious hatred; in all these things Jack is an earthy, everyday kind of Everyman with whom every new reader may associate. But he is just as truly typical of the Renaissance English spirit as he is universal. In him Nash has depicted brilliantly that rare mixture of the devout and the debauched, the sacred and the profane, the scholarly and the vulgar, the delicate and the hideously brutal, the aristocratic and the common (a mixture emphasized when Jack and Surrey exchange identities, like the beasts in Spenser's *Mother Hubberd's Tale,* and discover that each delights in living in the other's shoes), the explorer and the patriot that made Elizabethan and Tudor England an era quite different from any other before or after. The singularity of an age, after all, can be found only in its tensions, in the peculiar coupling of opposing forces; all forces can be found at all times and only special magnetic attraction that brings them into new configurations at one period or another really makes uniqueness possible. *The Unfortunate Traveller,* in the unforgettable crudity and refinement of its humor, in its instantaneous leaps from highly serious didacticism to profoundly trivial farce, is a kind of templet shaped by and reproducing the shape of its times.

Kenneth John Atchity

U. S. A.

Type of work: Novel
Author: John Dos Passos (1896-1970)
Type of plot: Social chronicle
Time of plot: 1900-1935
Locale: The United States
First published: 1930, 1932, 1936

The separate titles of Dos Passos' major trilogy are The 42nd Parallel. Nineteen
Nineteen, *and* The Big Money. *A sprawling, powerful collective novel written from
the point of view of Marxist determinism,* U. S. A. *attempts to offer a complete
cross-section of American life covering the political, social, and economic history
of the people from the beginning of the century to the depression-ridden 1930's.*

John Dos Passos' statement at the beginning of *U.S.A.* that America is,
more than anything else, the sounds of its many voices, offers several insights into the style and content of the trilogy. The style, for example, reflects
the author's attempt to capture some sense of characteristically American
"voices," not just in the idiomatic narration of the chronicles (or novel sections), but in "Newsreels," "Biographies," and "The Camera Eye" as
well. While these sections reflect, respectively, the public voice of the media
and popular culture, the oratorical and eulogistic voice of the biographies, and
the personal and private voice of the artist, the most important voices in the
trilogy are those of the chronicles in which Dos Passos introduces a cross-
section of American voices ranging from the blue collar worker to the professional and managerial classes, and representing a variety of regional and
ethnic backgrounds. Like Walt Whitman, who profoundly influenced him,
Dos Passos takes all America as his subject matter as he tries to capture
through the sounds of the many voices which characterize its people and
institutions the meaning of *U.S.A.*

Many people have associated the social, political, and economic views expressed in *U.S.A.* with Marxism—as leftists in the 1930's liked to believe this
important author made common cause with them—but it is really the American economist Thornstein Veblen, rather than Marx, who seems to have
shaped Dos Passos' thinking about the economic and political situation in the
United States during the first quarter of this century. Dos Passos had read
Veblen's *The Theory of the Leisure Class, The Theory of Business Enterprise,*
and other writings, and it was from these sources that his attack on the American business economy stems. In *The Big Money,* Dos Passos offers a "Biography" of Veblen in which he summarizes this economist's theories of the
domination of society by monopoly capitalism and the sabotage of the workers' human rights by business interests dominated by the profit motive. According to Dos Passos, the alternatives Veblen saw were either a society
strangled and its workers destroyed by the capitalists' insatiable greed for

profit or a society in which the needs of those who do the work would be the prime consideration. Veblen, writing just at the turn of the century, still held out hope that the workers might yet take control of the means of production before monopoly capitalism could plunge the world into a new dark age. Dos Passos goes on to develop the idea that any such hope died with World War I, and that the American dream of democracy was dead from that time forward.

Against the background of Veblen's ideas, *U.S.A.* can be seen as a documentary chronicling the growing exploitation of the American worker by the capitalist system, and a lamentation for the lost hope of Veblen's dream of a society which would make the producer the prime beneficiary of his own labor. The best characterization of the blue collar worker is Mac McCreary— a rootless laborer constantly searching for some outlet for his idealistic hope of restoring power to the worker. Certainly one of the most sympathetic characters in *U.S.A.*, Mac dramatizes the isolation and frustration of the modern worker, who is only a human cog in the industrial machine, unable either to take pride in his work or finally to profit significantly by it. Other characters as well fit within the pattern of the capitalist system as Veblen described it, or else, like Mac, revolt against the injustice of the system. There are the exploiters and the exploited, and there are some few, like Mary French and Ben Compton, who make opposition to the system a way of life. Equally prevalent are those characters who dramatize Veblen's theory of conspicuous consumption by serving as playthings (Margo Dowling), lackeys (Dick Savage), or promoters (J. Ward Moorehouse) for those who control the wealth and power.

Throughout the trilogy, the essential conflict is that between the business interests who control the wealth, and the workers who produce it. But Dos Passos is almost equally concerned with the way in which the system of monopoly capitalism exploits and destroys even those of the managerial class who seem to profit most immediately from it. Dick Savage, for example, starts out as a talented young writer only to be corrupted by the system. And Charlie Anderson, who early could be seen as typifying the American dream of success through ingenuity and imagination, dies as much a victim of the system as any of its workers. J. Ward Moorehouse, on the other hand, makes nothing and produces nothing, but his is the talent that can parlay nothing into a fortune, and the mentality that can survive in the world of *U.S.A.*

The two national historical events to which Dos Passos gives most attention are World War I, and the execution of the anarchists Sacco and Vanzetti. The war, as Dos Passos saw it, under the pretense of making the world safe for democracy, gave the capitalists the opportunity they needed to solidify their power by actually crushing the democratic spirit. For Dos Passos, democracy was dead in America from World War I, and the Sacco and Vanzetti case proved it. The death of these two immigrant Italian radicals on a trumped-up charge of murder was, in Dos Passos' eyes, the ultimate demonstration of the fact that our traditional freedoms were lost and that monopoly capitalism had usurped power in America. When, in his later and more conservative years, John Dos Passos was accused of having deserted the liberal positions of his youth, he maintained that his views had not shifted from those he argued in *U.S.A.* The evidence of the novel would seem to bear him out. The *U.S.A.* trilogy is a more nostalgic than revolutionary work, and it looks back to that point in American history before the options were lost rather than forward to a socialist revolution. His finest work shows Dos Passos as a democratic idealist rather than as a socialist revolutionary.

William E. Grant

VANESSA

Type of work: Novel
Author: Hugh Walpole (1884-1941)
Type of plot: Historical chronicle
Time of plot: Late nineteenth and early twentieth centuries
Locale: England
First published: 1933

The last novel in the Herries chronicle, Vanessa *brings the family to the 1930's. Like its three predecessors, the novel—crowded with characters—attempts to show that the strength of the Herries family is the strength of England and that its weakness is a clue to the national defect.*

Vanessa is one of those British novels that seems to lack a certain quality of emotional involvement. The characters are carefully drawn and are placed against a detailed background, and their actions are elaborately choreographed, but the resulting production lacks the spark of life. One must admire the mind which so painstakingly created the huge chronicle of which *Vanessa* is a part, but effort and size alone do not make a book a notable literary work. Perhaps the problem is that Walpole overexplains; he announces a scene in advance and then presents it, or he interprets a scene immediately after, although only on a superficial level. There is no mystery to the characters; the reader does not feel compelled to ask "And then what?" about them. They are what they seem, no more and no less. And the prose lacks a compactness and tension which would make the reader want to read on; Walpole seems to have forgotten that his book is first composed of words, and these must be chosen with care. A novel should be a perfect blend of subject matter *and* technique.

But, there are other reasons for reading *Vanessa,* despite its defects. It presents a broad and detailed panorama of the last years of Queen Victoria's reign. And the book makes clear the importance of the family in Victorian society. No individual can be completely alone in such a world. As one character states, the consequences of acts occurring now can affect the next generation. The book is the working out of such consequences for the latest members of the vast Herries clan. Walpole is sometimes perceptive in his picture of human relationships, all of which, according to one of the characters, carry potential dangers. This idea seems to be especially true with the impetuous Herries family. But they never lose sight, whatever their personal involvements, of the fact that they are part of British history. They are proud of their place in society's passing parade, and guard it jealously. Early in the novel, they predict with both fear and scorn that another fifty years will bring about the end of social history—at least as they know it. And, a world war and world-wide depression do greatly transform the world in which the Herries had fought their way to the top.

As a sidelight, Vanessa's plea for independence and equality for women is a vivid illustration of the continuing struggle for women's rights which began in the nineteenth century. Although the reader finds it hard to believe in her fabulous beauty and charm, Vanessa is an intriguing character. As a precursor of modern woman, she is the most interesting and sympathetic person in the book, and, even after she dies, her presence continues to dominate the novel.

VANITY FAIR

Type of work: Novel
Author: William Makepeace Thackeray (1811-1863)
Type of plot: Social satire
Time of plot: Early nineteenth century
Locale: England and Europe
First published: 1847-1848

Thackeray's most famous novel, Vanity Fair *is intended to expose social hypocrisy and sham. Moralistic and sentimental, the work also has redeeming strengths: its panoramic sweep—especially the scenes of the battle of Waterloo— and its creations of lifelike characters, chief among them Becky Sharp.*

When we call Thackeray's characters in *Vanity Fair* "life-like," we are milking that term for a subtler meaning than it usually conveys. His people are not true to life in the sense of being fully rounded or drawn with psychological depth. On the contrary, we sometimes find their actions too farcical to be human: Jos Sedley's ignominious flight from Brussels after the battle of Waterloo; or too sinister to be credible: the implication that Becky poisons Jos to collect his insurance is totally out of keeping with what we have learned about her in the previous sixty-six chapters. She may be a selfish opportunist, but she is no murderess. Thackeray's characters *are* "life-like" if we think of "life" as a typological phenomenon; when we shrug our shoulders and say "that's life," we are indulging in a kind of judgment on the human race which is based on types, not individuals; on the common failings of all men and women, not on the unique goodness or evil of some. Insofar as we share one another's weaknesses we are all represented in *Vanity Fair.* Our banality levels us all. That is the satirical revelation that *Vanity Fair* provides; that is the way in which its characters are "life-like."

Thackeray's general approach is comic satire; his method is that of the theatrical producer, specifically, the puppeteer. In his prologue he calls himself the "Manager of the Performance" and refers to Becky, Amelia, and Dobbin as puppets of varying "flexibility . . . and liveliness." Critics usually interpret this offhanded way of referring to his principal characters as a vindication of his own intrusions and asides; as a reminder to the reader that he, the author, is as much involved in the action as any of his characters. But we should probably take a harder look at his metaphor: he is a puppeteer because he must be one; *because* his people are puppets, someone must pull the strings. The dehumanized state of Regency and early Victorian society comes to accurate life through the cynical vehicle of Thackeray's puppeteering. Sentimentality and hypocrisy, closely related social vices, seem interchangeable at the end of the novel when Thackeray gathers all the remaining puppets: Amelia and Dobbin, a "tender little parasite" clinging to her "rugged old oak," and Becky, acting out her new-found saintliness by burying herself "in works of piety" and "having stalls at Fancy Fairs" for the benefit of the poor. "Let us shut up," concludes Thackeray, "the box and the puppets, for our play is played out."

Despite the predictability of all the characters' puppet-like behavior, they often exhibit just enough humanity to make their dehumanization painful. Thackeray wants us to feel uncomfortable over the waste of human potential in the vulgar concerns of *Vanity Fair*. George Osborne lives like a cad, is arrogant about his spendthrift ways, unfaithful to his wife, and dies a hero, leading a charge against the retreating French at Waterloo. We are left with the impression that the heroism of his death is rendered irrelevant by the example of his life. Such satire is demanding in its moral vision precisely because it underscores the price of corruption: honor becomes absurd.

Rawdon Crawley's love for his little son slowly endows the father with a touch of decency, but he is exiled by the "Manager of the Performance" to Coventry Island where he dies of yellow fever "most deeply beloved and deplored." Presumably the wastrel, separated from his son, dies in a position of duty. Or are we to pity him for having been forced, by his financial situation, to accept the position at Coventry as a bribe from Lord Steyne? Thackeray is elusive; again, the suggestions of pathos are touched on so lightly they hardly matter. The indifference itself is *Vanity Fair's* reward. For all his jocularity and beef-eating familiarity, the "Manager of the Performance" sets a dark stage. *Vanity Fair* is colorful enough: the excitement at Brussels over Waterloo, the gardens at Vauxhall, the Rhine journey; but it is a panoply of meritricious and wasteful human endeavor. And we really do not need Thackeray's moralizing to convince us of the shabbiness of it all.

Astonishing is the fact that despite the novel's cynicism, it also has immense vitality. We sense the very essence of worldliness in its pages, and who can deny the attractiveness of *Vanity Fair?* Bunyan made that perfectly clear in *Pilgrim's Progress,* and Thackeray simply updates the vision. What was allegory in Bunyan becomes realism in Thackeray; the modern writer's objectivity in no way detracts from the alluring effect achieved by Bunyan's imaginary Vanity Fair. Bunyan still operates in the Renaissance tradition of Spenserian façade; evil traps man through illusion, as exemplified in the trials of the Knight of the Red Crosse. Thackeray drops the metaphor of illusion, and shows us corruption bared—and still it is attractive.

Becky Sharp is described as "worldliness incarnate" by Louis Kronenberger, but the reader cannot deny her charms. Thackeray calls his book "A Novel Without a Hero," but we and Thackeray know better. Becky's pluck and ambition are extraordinary; her triumph is all the more impressive because of the formidable barriers of class and poverty she has to scale. When she throws the Johnson dictionary out of the coach window on leaving Miss Pinkerton's academy, we cannot help but thrill to her refusal to be patronized; her destructive and cruel manipulations of the Crawleys have all the implications of a revolutionary act. Thackeray actually emphasizes Becky's spirit and power by making virtuous Amelia so weak and sentimental. Although we are tempted to see this as a contradiction of Thackeray's moral intention, we must remember that he understood very clearly that true goodness must be built on strength: "clumsy Dobbin" is Thackeray's somewhat sentimental example. The human tragedy is that most men and women cannot reconcile their energies with their ideals; that in a fallen world of social injustices, we must all sin in order to survive. It is ironic that precisely because Becky Sharp is such an energetic opportunist, we almost believe her when she says "I think I could have been a good woman if I had 5000 a year."

Peter A. Brier

VATHEK

Type of work: Novel
Author: William Beckford (1759-1844)
Type of plot: Romantic allegory
Time of plot: The past
Locale: Arabia
First published: 1786

A pre-Romantic Oriental tale, Vathek *has many characteristics of the gothic novel, most notably the author's morbid curiosity about evil. Originally written in French, the novel is the most successful piece of exotic fiction of the eighteenth century.*

The intriguing and sometimes notorious lifestyle of William Beckford is reflected in *Vathek,* his most famous work. One of the earliest pre-Romantics, Beckford was an enormously wealthy man who loved nature, and dabbled in such fields as architecture, gardening, interior decorating, music, poetry, the occult, and collecting rare manuscripts. His Gothic country estate was also the scene of scandalous parties and bizarre escapades, one of which ended with Beckford's arraignment on a charge of sodomy.

Exotic landscapes, characters, and adventures permeate *Vathek.* Clearly the Arabian sultan hero is not meant to be realistic, but the embodiment of evil on a grand scale. Faust-like, Vathek's pilgrimage is to discover experiences; but unlike Faust, Vathek searches only for the depths of evil through his own madness and in exploiting the corruption of others. Vathek seeks power—over women, particularly the luckless Nouronihar, over other kingdoms, and finally even over the forces of blackness. Beckford so obviously relishes creating picturesque debaucheries, and so opulently describes the illicit pleasures of his palace, that his "moral" ending of right restored seems more contrived than the plot. Exciting, not instructing, the audience is Beckford's intention, as the colorful, spectacular, and brutal demise of Vathek and Nouronihar clearly demonstrates.

Despite the contrived "Oriental" atmosphere and pseudo-Gothic devices, a surprisingly modern, surrealistic quality can be found in *Vathek.* For all his bowing to gratuitous sensationalism and topical conventions, Beckford makes some serious explorations of evil. In this novel's violent world the sun is grotesque, the moon pure and good; white is black and black is white. Vathek expresses his alienation as a creative madness, exploring with sophistication the far reaches of *ennui,* melancholia, and sadism. His evil actions are a form of revenge, a vileness created out of the knowledge that Gulchenrouz's world of childhood innocence is beyond him forever. Thus the novel may be read as a parable on the theme of recognizing evil, with Vathek achieving a perverse maturity in so thoroughly exploring the nature of evil.

THE VENETIAN GLASS NEPHEW

Type of work: Novel
Author: Elinor Wylie (1885-1928)
Type of plot: Fantasy
Time of plot: 1782
Locale: Italy and France
First published: 1925

The Venetian Glass Nephew *is the most completely realized of Wylie's four fantastic and ironic novels. Stylized, witty, and artificial, the book is a subtle fable of life and art. M. de Chastelneuf—idealist, cynic, and charlatan—is the famous Casanova under thin disguise.*

Elinor Wylie came to fiction-writing late in her career. In her poetry, her famous intensity had been controlled though spectacular, but in her novels it took on a feverish and artificial quality. She did not have to strain to write well, for her feeling for style was instinctive, but she was obsessed with the need to create ornate pictures out of words. She became part of the group of "Exquisites" of the 1920's which included Joseph Hergesheimer, James Branch Cabell and Carl Van Vechten. The shadow behind *The Venetian Glass Nephew*, however, is the Oscar Wilde of *The Picture of Dorian Gray*. Both novels deal with artificially created beauty and both convey, beneath their baroque surfaces, a moral lesson.

A decadent eroticism (especially in the character of Chastelneuf) pervades the book. The question raised by Gozzi stands at the center of the novel: can this artificial youth be "better than human?" But Chastelneuf, who stage-manages the entire drama, cannot be concerned with ordinary moral questions. He is insistent upon carrying human passion and curiosity to the limits of possibility. Yet, it appears, at last his heart is touched by the plight of Virginio, composed of magic and glass, and Rosalba, that "burning and spiritual child of love."

Elinor Wylie's novels seem to invert Hemingway's aphorism: "Prose is architecture, not interior decoration," but there are in *The Venetian Glass Nephew* a gaiety and erudition that give the book a lovely, amused formality which the reader cannot easily resist. The tale poses a contest between Christian art and pagan nature and in this conflict there can be only one result: nature must yield. Venice is the appropriately artificial setting for the story, and the eighteenth century, the age of "reason," the inevitable setting for this moral romance of "exquisite monsters" and alchemists and brittle lovers.

VENICE PRESERVED

Type of work: Drama
Author: Thomas Otway (1652-1685)
Type of plot: Tragedy of intrigue
Time of plot: The Renaissance
Locale: Venice
First presented: 1682

Very popular when first staged because of the numerous plots and counterplots that were rife in the 1680's, Venice Preserved. Or, A Plot Discovered *is reputed also to have been revived more often than any other non-Shakespearean tragedy, largely because of the powerful emotional appeal of its story, which is reminiscent of* Othello.

First presented two years after the debut of *The Orphan, Venice Preserved* strengthened Otway's reputation as a new kind of dramatist, a playwright who could arouse strong feelings of pity and compassion in his audience. Whereas *The Orphan* is an explicitly domestic tragedy in which family suffering and misunderstanding made a direct appeal to the actual emotional experience of the audience, *Venice Preserved* is more impressive in its emotional power because it departs from the familiar feelings of family life to include political and social principles. Restoration audiences were familiar with plays of historical and political consequence in the formal dress of heroic drama. But it was a revelation to experience epical and political themes in a drama written by a poet who, as Edmund Gosse put it, "dipped his pen into his own heart."

The farcical treatment of the old senator Antonio is a satirical thrust at Anthony Ashley Cooper, Earl of Shaftesbury. The Earl was a Whig agitator who suffered temporary imprisonment in the year before Otway's play was produced. Otway was an outrageous Tory, and the irresponsible manner in which he indulged his political preference only added to his play's subjective and emotional appeal.

Aside from this example of political caricature, which is essentially irrelevant to the play, Otway's drama has a relentless pace and admirable dramatic unity. That unity comes largely from the way in which the play centers on Jaffeir's gradually growing desperation. He moves from financial insecurity to the overwhelming despair of a man who has jeopardized his beloved wife's life and betrayed his friends. His personal agony provides the tragedy with its driving force; the political and ethical issues of conspiracy, friendship, and love are intensified because of the context they provide for Jaffeir's personal turmoil.

Although the play is full of obvious borrowings from Shakespeare, specifically *Othello* and *Julius Caesar,* the influence of Jacobean drama is also preeminent. All "deeds are done in the dark," and Jaffeir's role as a mirror to all the play's principal characters and themes recalls Ben Jonson's manner of putting one character on the stage and confronting him in succession with all the other characters, as well as the central themes of the play. In the opening act of *Venice Preserved,* Jaffeir confronts Priuli and the questions of honor and duty, Pierre and the demands of friendship, and finally Belvidera, who embodies the redemption of love.

VENUS AND ADONIS

Type of work: Poem
Author: William Shakespeare (1564-1616)
Type of plot: Mythological romance
Time of plot: Remote antiquity
Locale: Ancient Greece
First published: 1593

An erotic verse-narrative, Venus and Adonis *is noted for its subtly comic and ironic retelling of the Ovid story. Among Shakespeare's additions to the original source are the incident of the stallion and the jennet, the discussion of hunting, and the scenes of the fox and the hare.*

Venus and Adonis and *The Rape of Lucrece,* two of Shakespeare's most famous nondramatic works, were probably composed during the period between June, 1592, and May, 1594, while the theaters were temporarily closed because of the plague. *Venus and Adonis,* the earlier of the two poems, was entered at the Stationers' Register on April 18, 1593, and was printed shortly thereafter by Richard Field, who, incidentally, had come originally from Stratford-on-Avon. Indeed, *Venus and Adonis* was the first work of Shakespeare ever to be printed.

It should not be supposed from the date of composition that *Venus and Adonis* was merely a way of passing time while the theaters were closed. All indications are that Shakespeare thought of this poem as the public commencement of his serious literary work as distinct from his quotidian employment as a dramatist. Indeed, Shakespeare never bothered to see his plays into print, a fact which has been the bane of editors ever since. However, *Venus and Adonis* was handsomely printed with an ornate dedication to the Earl of Southampton in which Shakespeare speaks of the poem as his first serious literary effort. It is a kind of poetry, in subject and style, which occupied most of Shakespeare's serious contemporaries.

Although the poem has been transmitted in only a few manuscripts, there is ample evidence that it was extremely popular in its own day. By 1600 it had become one of the most frequently quoted poems of the period. Many contemporaries referred to it with admiration. Even Gabriel Harvey, fellow of Cambridge and stern arbiter of critical taste, noted the great fame that the poem enjoyed among undergraduates, although he did add reservations about the erotic character of the poem. Yet, in its eroticism, the *Venus and Adonis* also shared in a vogue for such poetry, which appeared in profusion in the 1590's. These narrative or reflective poems, like Shakespeare's, generally drew on classical or pseudo-classical sources.

The story of *Venus and Adonis* is basically derived from Ovid's Metamorphoses (X, 11.503-579). The main difference is that in Shakespeare's poem Adonis becomes a coy and reluctant lover. This variation may be the result of accidental or intentional conflation of the tale with the story of Hermaphroditus and Salmacis (*Metamorphoses,* IV) or the story of Narcissus (*Metamorphoses,* III). It could also be the result of the influence of stories in Book III of the *Faerie Queene,* in Lodge's *Scylla's Metamorphoses,* or in Marlowe's *Hero and Leander.* In any case, the change brings it in line with other late sixteenth century poems which stress male beauty. Regardless of the source, the substance of the poem is almost entirely conventional.

The few original additions which Shakespeare seems to have made—the digressive episode of the jennet and the stallion and the descriptions of the hunting of the fox and the hare, for example—are notable more for the conventional beauty of their style than for their narrative power. The whole of the poem is, in fact, an excellent example of stylistic decoration, an ornate poem for a sophisticated audience more interested in execution than originality. All of the poetry is on the surface, in the ingenious handling of commonplaces and in brilliant flourishes of image and phrase.

Virtually nothing happens in the poem. The bulk of it is taken up with the amorous arguments of Venus interspersed with demurrers by Adonis. There is no forward movement, merely a debate which results in no conclusion. The characters do not develop; they simply are what they are and speak in accord with their stylized roles. The plot does not move from event to event by means of internal causality. Indeed, the only movement, that from the debate to the final scene in which Venus comes upon Adonis' body, is occasioned more by the emotional necessities of the poem than by an demands of plot.

It is tempting to see the poem, especially in the debate, as a moral allegory in which Venus represents not only passion but also the enduring love which triumphs over mutability and Adonis represents a rational control over sensual excess. It is hard, however, to support this interpretation very far. Neither view prevails and the interdeterminacy suggests that the allegory is merely another ornament, not the heart of the poem. Moreover, the tone of the speeches and the tone of the narrator's commentary do not support moral earnestness. The many puns and erotic innuendos provide a suave distance, true to Ovid and to Elizabethan taste.

The poem is a compendium of the themes which recurred in the amatory poems and sonnet sequences of the age. The arguments proposed by Venus, for example, are familiar appeals to the desire for immortality. *Carpe diem* is prominent as is the appeal to survival through procreation, and both are themes which Shakespeare thoroughly exploited in his own sonnets. Similarly, Adonis' rationalistic view of sex is reminiscent of Shakespeare's Sonnet 129 and many poems by Sidney.

The poem is also a storehouse of the rhetorical figures and imagistic techniques of Elizabethan lyric style. Balance and antithesis, alliteration and assonance produce a pleasing aural effect not so much to underline the sense as to call attention to their own beauty. The imagery is sharply and brilliantly visual with bright red and white as the dominant, and highly conventional, colors. The comparisons of eyes to sun or moon are a poet's stock in trade, but always splendidly done. Images are to embellish, not to explain, and even Adonis' fatal wound is gorgeous. The six-line stanza, with the rhyme scheme ababcc, provides a supple medium for the gentle rhythms and sound patterns. The whole is an elegantly decorated blend of common themes into a pathetic-ironic showpiece.

Edward E. Foster

THE VICAR OF BULLHAMPTON

Type of work: Novel
Author: Anthony Trollope (1815-1882)
Type of plot: Domestic realism
Time of plot: Nineteenth century
Locale: England
First published: 1870

The theme of this novel, as in so much of Trollope's fiction, centers about the difficulty of acquiring money and making a successful marriage. The Vicar of Bullhampton *is noteworthy for the introduction of a prostitute, Carry Brattle, as a sympathetic character.*

Anthony Trollope, because of his rapid rate of composition, has often been viewed suspiciously by critics. Could a man who produced forty-seven major novels in his late-starting career be a genuinely first-rate talent? Trollope's reputation has fluctuated and although he is still not considered one of the greatest English novelists, he is judged to be a highly gifted, professional, and sometimes even brilliant writer.

The Vicar of Bullhampton embodies some of the characteristic strengths and weaknesses of his work. The plot of the novel is, unfortunately, a patchwork affair; there are two strands of action, and the one concerning the relationships between Mary Lowther, Harry Gilmore, and Walter Marrable, has little to do with the core of the novel: the figure of Carry Brattle. Trollope himself was aware of this deficiency. In fact, he remarks in his *Autobiography* that his purpose in writing the novel was to explore the situation of a "fallen woman" and to expose and remedy some of the terrible attitudes to which such a woman is exposed. He did not expect his readers, so he said, to look very carefully at his nominal heroine.

It should also be noted that Trollope was not interested in the process of Carry's "fall," or in the feelings which led to it. Instead, through the opposing attitudes of the Vicar and Carry's father, the reader is led to an understanding of another moral dilemma: how should others react to Carry's "crime"? The unbending, destructive, unforgiving prejudice of Carry's father is clearly not good, and Trollope takes pains to reject it. The Vicar, who is absolutely willing to forgive, and even to excuse, represents an opposite but not necessarily superior position in Trollope's eyes; for the logic of the Vicar leads him to deny that Carry is responsible for her actions at all, a patronizing and perhaps dehumanizing viewpoint.

Apart from the treatment of his theme, which is the main interest of *The Vicar of Bullhampton,* Trollope displays ingenuity and perception in his portrayal of characters. His description of Walter Marrable's father, for example, is a small masterpiece. However, the atmosphere of the novel, despite its outcome, is not a happy one; there are too many unpleasant characters who give a depressing tone to the work as a whole. If Carry has been brought to "decency," as Trollope intended her to be, the reader is still left to wonder whether the rest of Bullhampton has been.

THE VICAR OF WAKEFIELD

Type of work: Novel
Author: Oliver Goldsmith (1728-1774)
Type of plot: Sentimental romance
Time of plot: Eighteenth century
Locale: Rural England
First published: 1766

A sentimental novel that presents a simple, lovable character in his struggle to maintain his ideals, The Vicar of Wakefield *is marked by Goldsmith's gentle good humor as well as his sense of the dignity of ordinary, decent people.*

The Vicar of Wakefield is difficult for many modern readers to take seriously. Burdened with the weight of experience and the harsh realities of life, they cannot easily share the novel's naïve insistence on the nobleness and goodness of men. Such readers find that other famous eighteenth century fable, *Candide,* much more representative of the true human condition. Both works, however, exaggerate their respective claims for the truth: *The Vicar of Wakefield* indulges in sentiment and religiosity; *Candide,* in cynicism and cruelty. Both are outrageously coincidental and purposely project their narratives into fantastic realms of improbability.

It may not be the "best of all possible worlds," as Dr. Pangloss insists, despite all his suffering, but neither is this a world totally without some redeeming qualities. Voltaire's work is a harsh Juvenalian satire, peppered with Aristophanic crudity and malice; Goldsmith's is only gently satirical and realized in domestic visions of order characteristic of the Classical New Comedy; despite some very threatening turns in the second half of the novel, all the right marriages eventually take place and the rightful master of the house, in this case the vicar himself, is restored to his dignity and rights. In other words, both works succeed in their exaggerations because they are artfully comedic. Goldsmith's book asserts that good is stronger than evil with a comic deftness that makes us accept the idea despite our skepticism.

Not only Goldsmith's humor but also his imaginative range ventilate this sentimental tale with an ingenious variety of literary forms. There are ballads and tales within tales, all of which orchestrate tones and ideas in such a manner as to give Goldsmith's gentle fable of the good vicar a strangely cosmopolitan and philosophical depth. It is precisely because Goldsmith makes us reflect in depth at the same time he entertains that we are at last willing to accept the artless simplicity of his theme. A writer who can please with sophisticated wit has the right to ask us to deem his belief in human goodness credible.

THE VICOMTE DE BRAGELONNE

Type of work: Novel
Author: Alexandre Dumas, *père* (1802-1870)
Type of plot: Historical romance
Time of plot: Seventeenth century
Locale: France and England
First published: 1848-1850

The Vicomte de Bragelonne, *last of the D'Artagnan romances, contains four different but related plots—the restoration of Charles II, the story of Louis XIV's infatuation for Louise de la Vallière, the intrigues and downfall of the ambitious Fouquet, and the perennially popular tale of the mysterious prisoner in the iron mask.*

The figure of Alexandre Dumas offers a unique paradox in the history of French and world literature. Since the days of his earliest acclaim, and through the years of his greatest literary triumphs, he was frequently dismissed as a mere entertainer. Yet his works have, for the most part, lasted far longer than those of other, supposedly greater, talents and longer than those of a mere entertainer.

Dumas had an enormous capacity for work; the French edition of his collected works fills 277 volumes. He collaborated with dozens of other writers in the course of his career as dramatist and novelist. One would suppose, in fact, that he was willing to sign his name to anything. Yet Dumas was a genuine artist of undeniable talent and succeeded in giving life to facts and bare outlines conceived by others. Indeed, though he collaborated time and again he was most successful when he could impress himself, his own personality, on a drama or romance.

There have been numerous attempts to explain the great and lasting popularity of Dumas' novels, such as *The Vicomte de Bragelonne,* the brilliant sequel to *The Three Musketeers.* The novels are said to have mass appeal on the basis of adventure, setting, action, and other strictly literary features. Of course these features must be noted. But what is most fetching in all Dumas' best work is Dumas himself. The great man, his generosity, strength, and good will, shine through his pages.

For this reason, the most valuable background for *The Vicomte de Bragelonne,* and Dumas' other popular novels, is knowledge of Dumas himself. It was his own humanity, after all, which he was able to impart to his fiction.

The novelist's grandfather, the Marquis de la Pailleterie, left France for the Caribbean in the eighteenth century to seek a new fortune and, probably, to escape old obligations. There he had a son by a black woman, a slave. This son was to be the father of Alexandre Dumas père. At the age of eighteen the son went to Paris with his father. He grew into an enormous man, tall, muscular, and fearless. He joined the army, using his mother's name of

Dumas. His exploits and heroism in the service of France, and of Napoleon, became legendary. Finally, however, he was imprisoned in Italy and lost his health and great strength; and, because he had a disagreement with Napoleon, he was denied a pension.

It was, then, in an atmosphere saturated with tales of adventure, physical heroism, and action that Alexandre Dumas père grew to manhood. Unwilling to remain in the provinces where he was raised, Dumas was attracted to the life of Paris. He was looking for adventure and for success, and he found both.

Dumas broke into the literary world as a dramatist, and his best work reflects this early training. His melodrama *Henri III et sa cour* (1829) played over one hundred performances in Paris alone.

Dumas made (and spent) fortunes. He gave huge, successful banquets, accumulated medallions and honorary ribbons, bragged endlessly, and enjoyed dozens of mistresses. He was a large, cream colored, attractive man with curly black hair who loved to tell stories, was capable of endless hours of work, had a famous, telling wit, and was incapable of holding on to his money.

D'Artagnan, Athos, Porthos, and Aramis reflect this liveliness and movement. It is undoubtedly Dumas' sense of life and the joyful, romantic possibilities of life that account for the popularity of all the D'Artagnan romances, and the stories which comprise *The Vicomte de Bragelonne*.

At the same time, it is also useful to describe the techniques and subjects chosen by Dumas which helped him communicate his sense of life. First, there is incessant action, from beginning to end, in the four volumes of *The Vicomte de Bragelonne*. This action occurs on a number of levels. There is physical movement from country to country and within France by horse, carriage, and boat. This physical motion literally sustains the pace of the narrative.

Combined with the geographical movement are scenes of action. There is swordplay, shooting, knife play, wrestling, and virtually every form of human conflict. This violent action is, furthermore, placed in every kind of setting from stables, to dusty roads, to the palace of the king.

Dumas was also a master of the trappings of such action. *The Vicomte de Bragelonne* is filled with disguises, trap doors, secret messages, codes, and ambushes. All this external action is, moreover, united with political intrigues, actual historical facts, romances (royal and otherwise), and the ideological and historical conflicts of the times, including those between Church and state and between factions in the court itself.

Dumas does not employ lengthy passages of description either for establishing character or landscape. Instead, he gives barely enough physical description of place so that the reader can visualize the action. Character is not pictured through analysis, but through action. Again, there is enough given to help the reader understand the action, and to become partial toward a character, but not enough to develop the full human potential of any single character.

The presence that seems most impressive and interesting in *The Vicomte de Bragelonne* is the author himself. He communicates himself not through a single one of the musketeers but through all of them at once. He is good-natured, generous, sly, lazy, and adventurous all at once. In *The Vicomte de Bragelonne* there is no room for another complete character. Yet at the same time one may sympathize with D'Artagnan, and certainly one supports him (applauding his successes, grateful for his good luck). However, one never fully comprehends him. When he dies at the end of the final volume, in a patriotic pose, there is a feeling that he has lived an exciting, interesting life. Somehow, though, he is never quite so alive as to be thoroughly gone.

In addition to his influence on characterization, Dumas' strong presence manipulates history itself in *The Vicomte de Bragelonne*. Because historical processes are transformed into complicated adventures, the audience experiences the sensation of the unveiling of history although the historical outcome of those events has long been determined. Dumas then molds this process, shaping it through his humor and his abundant dialogue. Thus, what Dumas had accomplished (as critics have noted) is little short of the annexation of French history.

Indeed, Dumas himself becomes—through *The Vicomte de Bragelonne*—that historical process. More than any mere entertainer, he lends himself and his life to his work. The reader participates in history not only through the manipulation of events but also through the living substance of Alexandre Dumas. That is why the ending of *The Vicomte de Bragelonne,* wherein the joyful D'Artagnan dies after receiving the baton of Marshal, leaves the reader less sad than wistful. A visit has been paid to a certain time, an era of delight, romance, and action in the company of a most agreeable friend. The visit is over but it is possible to return. There is death, but no darkness.

Howard Lee Hertz

VICTORY

Type of work: Novel
Author: Joseph Conrad (Józef Teodor Konrad Korzeniowski, 1857-1924)
Type of plot: Psychological romance
Time of plot: Early twentieth century
Locale: East Indies
First published: 1915

Although the plot of Victory *is sentimental and melodramatic, the novel operates on complex levels of symbol and allegory to demonstrate Conrad's warning about the psychological perils of moral isolation.*

Victory was regarded as a great success when it first appeared. The story is stark in its symbolic confrontations: Heyst, the hermit, is won back to life by the love of an uneducated girl who finds spiritual deliverance as his savior. In the darkness of World War I, Conrad's romance had the impact of a religious allegory. It asserted the redemptive powers of love and self-sacrifice at a time when millions of men were sacrificing their lives in war.

But the disillusionment that followed World War I caused many critics to take a closer look. Critical enthusiasm cooled considerably, and after World War II it turned openly hostile. Albert J. Guerard, in his definitive study *Conrad the Novelist* (1958) called *Victory* "one of the worst novels for which high claims have ever been made by critics of standing."

Victory presumes to the sublime, but its essentially melodramatic plot and adolescent fantasies of withdrawal on a tropical island weigh it down with embarrassingly superficial ballast. Lena is vaguely erotic but her transformation into a Magdalen to Heyst's Christ is largely unconvincing. Heyst's motivations for withdrawal are never sufficiently clarified, and his moral radiance, though constantly asserted, never clearly established. Davidson and Lena are, supposedly, charmed by his soul, but Heyst is never given enough to do or think to make us believe in his spiritual power. As a result, Lena's self-sacrifice is strangely ambiguous. Is her gesture one of faith or desperation? The flames of their funeral pyre make up in Wagnerian splendor for the dim glow of their characters in life. Perhaps the pasteboard quality of this novel is best illustrated in the villains: Mr. Jones is too oily, Ricardo too brutal, and Pedro too grotesque to believe. And since they are supposed to embody evil, the force Lena's goodness defeats, the victory of *Victory* is finally a hollow one.

VILE BODIES

Type of work: Novel
Author: Evelyn Waugh (1903-1966)
Type of plot: Social satire
Time of plot: A twentieth-century interval between wars
Locale: England
First published: 1930

Vile Bodies, *a witty but caustic satire on English life during the period between World War I and World War II, is Waugh's grotesque valediction to the Bright Young People, a generation running to waste in a manner that is personally corrupt as well as socially sterile.*

In another work by Waugh, an aged classicist remarks that it would be wrong to try to prepare a boy for the modern world, an utterance which effectively sums up the author's feelings about the state of things in England during the decade before World War I. What he thought was wrong was, simply, everything; all those features of the old order that elevated and sustained the soul and placed men in ennobling and comforting relations to one another had been supplanted by thoughtless vulgarity. Gone or debased were those institutions and ideas which made life a gracious and priestly procession, leaving in their place a sense of goalless speed and the reek of petrol fumes. The characters in *Vile Bodies,* as in certain other of Waugh's works, fall into two categories: those who are fitted for the modern world by their cunning, lack of scruple, or outright insanity, and those who are not fitted for it and are doomed to be victimized by it. Mrs. Ape, Colonel Blount, and the drunken major are examples of the former class; Adam Fenwick-Symes is a specimen of the latter.

Adam is also one of the Bright Young People, Waugh's name for the prewar generation of the old stock, whose excesses and affectations he records to such humorous effect. The humor is "black," though, and the laughter hollow because the antics of the Bright Young People are their salute to a mad world. When Adam, referring to their planned marriage, tells Nina not to get intense about it, he is simply following the rules of the new game. For by the terms of the work, if one truly loved or grieved, if one truly cared—one would be lost.

Vile Bodies is essentially a young man's book; only the detachment and conscious superiority of youth could carry off Agatha Runcible's death without bathos, or make Adam dreadful but not despicable. In later works Waugh sometimes lost this creative distance and the works correspondingly suffered. But *Vile Bodies* is a grand, gallant guffaw at the expense of everybody, the author included.

THE VILLAGE

Type of work: Novel
Author: Ivan Alexeyevich Bunin (1870-1953)
Type of plot: Social criticism
Time of plot: Early twentieth century
Locale: Russia
First published: 1910

A grimly realistic yet pitying account of Russian village life before the revolution, Bunin's novel shows the peasants as vicious, egocentric, and petty-souled people whose tragic lives are barren of hope.

Born of a noble though impoverished family in 1870, Ivan Bunin was raised on his father's country estate and educated by tutors. After a time at the University of Moscow, he traveled as a journalist and began writing poetry. By 1901, his poetry received some acclaim, and in 1903 his translations of Byron and Longfellow brought him the Pushkin Prize. His stories also brought him wide attention. *The Village,* in 1910, made him internationally famous.

In the years preceding World War I, Bunin traveled widely, especially in the Mideast. At the time of the Russian Revolution, Bunin sided with reactionary groups. He left Moscow in May, 1918, and the following February fled the country. He spent most of the rest of his life in France. His literary output, never large, maintained a high quality. In 1941, seventy-year-old Bunin and his ailing wife fled Paris after the Nazi conquest and lived destitute in unoccupied France. The Tolstoy Foundation solicited funds for the relief of the 1933 Nobel Prize winner. Later, it was revealed that he sheltered a Jewish journalist for the length of the occupation. In 1951, he published a brief autobiography which included his memories of such friends as Turgenev and Tolstoy. He died in semi-obscurity at eighty-three, at his home in Paris.

Bunin's novel *The Village* presents a grim picture of life in pre-Soviet Russia. It is a world in which people are known by nicknames or crude labels: the Bride, the Goat, Duckhead, the Fool. The villagers do not know even how to acknowledge one another's humanity. These country folk, uneducated and brutalized by hard lives, are stimulated only by disasters; they revel in wife-beatings and the thrashing of small children, and they gather around to watch fights or fires. Violence provides their only entertainment, their only break in the monotony of living. The Russia of this novel is a violent, primitive land, where poor men lash their beasts and women equally.

Bunin wrote with the care of a historian or a sociologist describing a kind of life doomed to extinction because of its rottenness. Dirt, filth, and manure seem to cling to everything and everyone in the village. At times, it is difficult to distinguish the human beings from the animals. Bunin does not romanticize the old ways or the country life. His precise, elegant prose pictures with vivid images and skillful, merciless irony the truth as he saw it.

The superstition-ridden peasants led wretched lives, struggling merely to subsist. People who had to struggle to exist got into the habit, so that even after the need ceased, they continued struggling. Their lives became bounded by possessions and prices. Tikhon Ilitch (known as Stiff-Leg) tried vainly to find salvation in "business," but neither busy-ness nor business could bring him happiness. After decades of labor, Tikhon Ilitch could only reflect: how brief, how devoid of meaning, is life! Deniska, with his short legs, mouse-colored hair, and earth-hued skin, was one character who might have offered hope for the future. He was bright and self-educated, and was known as an agitator. But it was Kuzma Krasoff, Tikhon's younger brother, who represented the aspirations of the self-educated poor man. His life, despite his efforts, had come to nothing, and he was reduced to working for his brother and to vague desires for writing about how he came to be a failure. True, he was born in a country with more than a hundred million illiterates, but he had hoped to make something of himself. He read, he wrote, he studied, but all to no avail. He despaired of both himself and his country. What kind of nation, his friend Balashkin cried, would seek to destroy all of its best writers? They killed Pushkin and Lermontov, imprisoned Shevtchenko for ten years, dragged Dostoevski out to be shot. Gogol went mad. Balashkin recounted the destruction of many other writers. But Kuzma clung to the belief that Russia was a great nation—that it must be great. And so must he. Kuzma was the kind of man who rushed from enthusiasm to enthusiasm, embracing the philosophy of Tolstoy, then patriotism, then something else. Perhaps, Bunin seems to suggest, his shallow idealism and lack of tenacity were characteristic of the Russia of that day. "All Russia is nothing but village," remarks one of the characters. And Kuzma quotes Gogol: "Russia! Russia! Wither art thou dashing?" And: "Vain Babblers, you stick at nothing!"

Like most of the greater Russian novelists who preceded him, Ivan Bunin was a craftsman who set forth the incidents in his narrative with an ease that added to the lifelike quality of his characters. And, also like most Russian writers, he threaded a somber symbolism through this novel. At times, Bunin's prose possesses the sadness and poetic enchantment of Chekhov's stories; his realism is tempered with an aristocratic dedication to art and style. Using simple methods, Bunin sketched an epoch in this almost plotless novel. There are moments when Russian village life seems almost too terrible to bear, yet it all rings true. Beneath the hues of gray and the careful objectivity, a deep understanding seems to radiate through, almost like a touch of sympathy.

Bunin's art was rooted in Turgenev, Chekhov, and Tolstoy. He always felt an aversion to Dostoevski's work. But Bunin did not attempt the psychological novel which dominated nineteenth century Russian fiction. Some readers might even hesitate to call *The Village* a novel. It is, rather, a picture of a place and a time, an invective against the cruelty and stupidity of Russian peasant life. When the book first appeared in Russia, many critics condemned its bleak vision, even while admiring its art and the blending of realism with poetry. Most readers even now prefer Bunin's short stories, especially the famous long tale, *The Gentleman from San Francisco,* certainly the writer's masterpiece.

Bruce D. Reeves

VILLETTE

Type of work: Novel
Author: Charlotte Brontë (1816-1855)
Type of plot: Psychological romance
Time of plot: Nineteenth century
Locale: Belgium
First published: 1853

Published six years after the author's famous Jane Eyre. Villette *is a flawed psychological novel that is nevertheless interesting for its autobiographical material. The author's passion for Constantin Héger is believed to find an echo in this fiction.*

In *Villette,* Charlotte Brontë returns to the first-person narration used so successfully in *Jane Eyre* and continues exploring the problems and consciousness of a lonely, plain heroine. Although Brontë knew well the scene and subject matter here—she had in Brussels experienced a *pensionnat* similar to that in which Lucy Snowe studies and teaches—she reworks autobiographical details to fit the exigencies of her plot and characters.

But *Villette's* first-person point of view differs from that used in *Jane Eyre,* in accordance with the nature of Lucy Snowe's character. One finds much more character analysis, description, and indirect dialogue as well as more use of reflections, and introspections. There are even short "essays" on diverse subjects. Thus, Brontë uses a first-person narrator who employs several omniscient-narrator techniques. There is little of the immediacy of *Jane Eyre,* as the aged Lucy Snowe relates her early adventures. *Villette* always incorporates that double focus on past and present, which the traditional "novels of education" exhibit. In such *Bildüngsromans,* a matured and now-wiser protagonist narrates his growth, education, and—usually—excesses, now able to look back with sympathy and irony. *Villette,* then, belongs to that illustrious sub-genre which includes Dickens' *Great Expectations,* Joyce's *A Portrait of the Artist as a Young Man,* and Austen's *Emma.* While Lucy Snowe's irony is often over-subtle, it does gradually appear as her personality develops, so that we smile at her earlier retiring, self-effacing attitudes.

Lucy as narrator is never so candid and naïve as Jane Eyre, and when she withholds key information from us—that Dr. John is the Graham of her childhood—we learn to doubt her judgment about other matters as well. We distrust her assessment of Ginevra, who clearly has more life than Lucy, and we do not accept her immoderate anti-Catholicism or her reliance on physiognomy in judging character. We also wish to question Lucy's relativism and timidity. Why does she not confront Madame Beck when she discovers the mistress searching her personal effects? Lucy's justification, that she did not want to make trouble, is not satisfactory. Lucy therefore is a forerunner of the modern unreliable narrator found in works such as Sartre's

Nausea and Moravia's *The Lie.* All of her judgments must be evaluated instead of being taken at face value.

Brontë had difficulty in making her heroine sympathetic and understandable, for Lucy Snowe has little of the fiery passion of Jane Eyre—at least for most of the novel. The reader may ask, with Ginevra, "Who *are* you, Miss Snowe?" and remain puzzled by Lucy's answer, "Perhaps a personage in disguise." Different characters see Lucy as possessing contradictory qualities: Madame Beck thinks her "learned and blue"; Ginevra regards her as "caustic, ironic, and cynical"; Mr. Home discovers a "sedate and discreet" person. Graham, says Lucy, misreads her character entirely, calling her his "inoffensive shadow"; Monsieur Paul alone persists in seeing her as "adventurous, indocile, and audacious." If in fact Monsieur Paul's estimation is correct, the reader cannot be faulted for agreeing with Graham's earlier view. For Lucy is so self-effacing at the beginning that we nearly forget it is *her* story and not little Polly's. Lucy Snowe's identity remains a theme of vital importance. Her birth and family situation are never made clear; though similar mysteries were solved in *Jane Eyre* and *Shirley,* in *Villette* Lucy is left alone to make her own destiny, to become the person she chooses.

One could say that *Villette* is less a story of Lucy Snowe's education than it is of her achieving an identity. Her inner conflict is always that of Reason and Imagination, Intellect and Passion. Her position, fortune, and upbringing most often favor Reason. She has trained herself to view her own prospects and emotions rationally, rejecting risks and avoiding disappointments, but her inner life is full of passion and turmoil. Imagination urges her to involve herself in life, but she reveals this side of herself only when illness, drugs, or an unreal situation suppress rationality. During a thunderstorm while the rest of the students offer frightened prayers, she creeps out on the roof to enjoy the spectacle; afterward she longs for a change in her existence. Instead of rebelling, however, Lucy figuratively "knocks her longing on the head." At a school play she is pressed into service as the foppish lover and is surprised and then frightened by the exhilaration of acting. Monsieur Paul is the only character who has correctly read the passionate part of her personality, and it is only as his affection for her grows that she gradually accepts and nourishes this part of her being. She expands her knowledge under his tutelage—he all the while mocking her in order to break down her reserve. She becomes less shy, more vocal, and harbors fewer feelings of inferiority.

The municipal fête visited by a drugged Lucy suggests how far she has come in her search for identity. The celebration commemorates an occasion in which the city successfully defended its freedom. Lucy's new free personality is at this time being threatened by Madame Beck. She sees various people she has depended on in the past, but now the active side of her being makes them unnecessary. Lucy is able to confront Madame Beck with honesty: "Oh, Madame! In *your* hand is both chill and poison." Finally, Lucy's new school, begun with Monsieur Paul's generosity, enables her to cultivate her precious new identity, conquering self-consciousness and timidity. That she does not submerge her personality into Monsieur Paul's is shown clearly in her maintenance of her Protestant faith. Her personality is disguised no more, and even Monsieur Paul's hinted death cannot change that.

A word about the fact that more than a little of the novel's conversation is carried on in French: without an annotated edition, a modern reader will have some difficulty if he cannot read French. The French conversation, though, helps to convey the sense of isolation Lucy feels until she is competent in the foreign tongue. Soon, however, she is making distinctions in the subtleties of the two languages, such as refusing to call Monsieur Paul "*mon ami*" while not quailing at "my friend."

Margaret McFadden-Gerber

THE VIOLENT LAND

Type of work: Novel
Author: Jorge Amado (1913-)
Type of plot: Historical romance
Time of plot: Late nineteenth century
Locale: State of Bahia, Brazil
First published: 1942

Amado's novel, skillfully plotted and impressive in its evocation of the Bahia Panhandle region of Brazil, is a romance of hardihood and the pioneer struggle for existence whose theme is well conveyed by its English title, The Violent Land.

Jorge Amado's novel is titled *Terras do Sem Fin (The Endless Lands)* in Portuguese. This story is the standard-bearer of the cacao cycle in Brazilian literature, a series of novels exposing exploitation of cacao workers. Brazilian novelists have for long been making a huge mosaic of Brazil with their novels, each novel being a tiny stone in the literary mosaic of that subcontinent, and Amado's work is a worthy one and his masterpiece.

The Violent Land is the story of Bahia's Panhandle, where a balmy climate, fertile soil, and lack of high winds make it one of the few areas on earth well-suited for chocolate trees, whose weak stems and heavy pods need heat but cannot stand strong winds. Amado's characterization is particularly representative of the raw frontier that the Panhandle of Bahia (a narrow strip stretching southward toward the mountains of Espirito Santo) has been for so long. The reader thus sees not only an area where "the Colonels" and their heavily-armed cohorts oppress the weak, but also the Bahian *sertão* (backlands) in general, brimming with blood, old feuds, religious messianism, and fanaticism. Even today, the Colonels, cowboys, professionals, and workers that sprinkle the novel's pages can be seen around the old town of Ilhéus and elsewhere in the Panhandle. Amado's characters are thus not larger-than-life but authentic, flesh-and-blood realities from rural Bahia. His principal characterization flaw is an error of omission, for the warmly human types so common everywhere in Brazil, including Bahia, are lacking in the violent pages of *The Violent Land.*

This novel refreshingly explodes the oft-heard myth that Brazil, unlike Spanish America, is a bland and frivolous land not given to violence. Amado's novel bristles with the violence and mystery endemic to the *sertão,* and it is for this reason that Amado's true title of *The Endless Lands* has been changed for the book's English translation into *The Violent Land.* Amado paints a land fertile with blood, as his preface indicates. Set about the turn of the twentieth century, when cacao was power, wealth, and life, the novel's action portrays the enslavement of everything and everyone to the cacao pod. The shadow of cacao darkens every heart. It smothers finer instincts, and levels all characters from aristocratic Colonel Horacio da Silveira to the more common Badarós. Nothing washes away the cacao stain. Workers in the orchards have a thick crust of cacao slime on their boots, while everyone from Colonels to lawyers, merchants, and *jagunços* (hired killers) have cacao slime in their hearts.

The Violent Land reflects progress, however, for the Colonels are drawn as a crude but civilizing force in Brazil's historic "march to the west" that, even today, is opening up the once trackless *sertão*. Amado himself was born on a cacao plantation in 1912 and admired the *fazendeiros* (ranchers), such as his own father, who settled the raw Panhandle, crossed *sertões,* built roads, and founded towns, all this through heroic strength and what Amado terms "the poetry of their lives." The novel's first scene, symbolically enough, is aboard a ship drawing away from the black-tile roofs of the baroque city of São Salvador de Bahia. The passengers aboard are immigrants to the rich but violent lands of the Panhandle, and are discussing lands, money, cacao, and death. They sing a sad song that presages disaster, but that night, in their staterooms and steerage quarters, they dream of laden cacao trees.

Landscape is an important factor in *The Violent Land* and reflects Brazil's intrinsic beauty. Amado paints the golden mornings dawning over green palms, the red soil under the cacao trees, the blue-green waves of the sea, and indigo skies. One also sees stormy nights, wild Brahma cattle, birds, and snakes. Trees are almost idolized, especially the cacao. Above all, Amado lyrically paints the forest in the uninterrupted sleep that it enjoyed before the Colonels came. Days and nights pass over the virginal expanses of trees, along with winter rains and summer suns. The waiting forest is like an unexplored sea, locked in its own mystery, virginal, lovely, and radiant. Amado also presents the varied Bahian racial types from Scandinavian-like blondes to Latin brunettes and Hamitic blacks. One also sees the Colonels in khaki trousers, white hats, and gun belts, as well as the leather-clad *jagunços,* legendarily ferocious *onças* (wild cats), ranch tools, and folklore.

Fear is an additional element in the story. The forest's mysteries incite fear—Ester hysterically fears snakes, and is haunted by the phobia that they will one night invade her house en masse. The backlanders tell many snake stories, while dogs howl at night, rain clouds are dark, and nights are jet black. But the violent Badaró family and the *jagunços* do not know what fear is. The Badarós even read the Bible daily for they, like the endless lands that they are so ruthlessly penetrating, are many-sided.

Lamentably, the storied and colorful old city of São Salvador de Bahia does not loom in *The Violent Land* as Atlanta does in *Gone with the Wind*. But little, pastel São Jorge dos Ilhéus, "a city of palms in the wind," is well-depicted. Its streets are lined by palms, but it is dominated by the cacao tree, for the scent of chocolate is in every conversation and each Colonel's fortune can be measured by the size of his mansion. And, inland from the pastel town, on every red-dirt road leading into the cacao lands, are crosses without names.

Brazilian novelists complained for decades that the harsh, nasal, Germanic-sounding Portuguese language in which they wrote was "the Graveyard of Literature," a literary cul-de-sac. But *The Violent Land* was translated into twenty-four languages, and translations of other novels into foreign languages have since been opening Brazilian literature to the world. Amado's masterwork also helps reveal that the key to Brazilian literature is not chronology, nor style, nor study of influences, but geography. Brazil is a literary archipelago with six literary "islands," and *The Violent Land* is to be read and regarded as a work of the "island" of Bahia.

William Freitas

VIRGIN SOIL

Type of work: Novel
Author: Ivan Turgenev (1818-1883)
Type of plot: Social criticism
Time of plot: 1868
Locale: Russia
First published: 1872

Virgin Soil, *an important novel of political psychology, offers a realistic but sensitive and sympathetic portrayal of the beginning of Russian liberalism following the emancipation of the serfs. Turgenev shows the essential humanitarianism of the socialists and the frivolity of the aristocracy as both sides struggle for dominance in the developing industrialization.*

Turgenev had lived in voluntary exile from his native land for a number of years by the time he wrote *Virgin Soil* and many critics said that the book showed how much he had lost touch with Russia; yet, with the hindsight of of a century, it seems astonishing that he was able to foretell so accurately the events which were to sweep over Russia in the fifty years after the novel's publication. The novel deals with revolutionaries, many of whom are ineffectual or half-hearted, but at the end of the novel it is clear that some of these people will continue to work for radical change and that others will succeed them. As Solómin tells Marianna, they will not live to see the revolution triumph, and perhaps several generations will not see it, but eventually it must succeed. And, as he foretold, it did, for better or for worse, alter the world.

Virgin Soil analyzes with shrewdness and great psychological penetration a broad spectrum of the individuals who are attracted to the revolutionary cause. Radical students, frustrated artists, unhappy young women, lonely young men, many different types, all fall together for a variety of reasons, not all of them idealistic. Because these people have so little in common, it is not surprising that they often fail to work together and frequently fall out among themselves. Yet, for the most part, Turgenev pictures them sympathetically. Even those who are not admirable are understandable; Turgenev never condemns people out of hand, but seeks to explain how and why individuals become what they are.

The novel is carefully structured, beginning and ending with Páhklin and Mashúrin discussing Nezhdánoff and the Cause. Between these two scenes, the story of the little band of radicals and the people its members come in contact with develops skillfully, the many threads uniting to create a frustrating picture of Russia in a ferment of change. The plot is both suspenseful and subtle, relying more on psychological motivations than on melodramatic action. As in all of Turgenev's novels, the story is told in exquisitely controlled prose, at once poetic and strong; the settings are brilliantly rendered, but never allowed to intrude between the reader and the characters. Above all, Turgenev is an artist perfectly in control of his material.

The weakness of Nezhdánoff's temperament is first suggested when he begins to compare himself to Hamlet, a comparison which then continues through the novel. Nezhdánoff is not certain that he believes enough in the radical cause to devote his life to it; he feels that he ought to believe, and he wants to believe, but he cannot make up his mind. Marianna later stirs him again, after his conviction has cooled, but eventually he again realizes that he has been deceiving himself: he never was a revolutionary at heart. Because of his inability to take a straightforward stand, he destroys himself and nearly takes several others with him. As in most of Turgenev's novels (only *Fathers and Sons* is an exception), the male protagonist is weak while the female is strong and sure of herself.

Nezhdánoff is from the start an ineffectual propagandist. He soon discovers that everybody is discontented, but no one cares to find out a remedy for the discontent. It is more difficult for a student and poet such as himself to confront real life than he had supposed. He calls himself a democrat and a lover of the people, yet even the smell of their vodka makes him sick. If people do take his pamphlets, they turn out to be the undesirable sort. Mashúrin, are sure of themselves. The two young women are very different from each other, but both are completely dedicated, and have the strength of character not to be sidetracked by personalities or temporary setbacks.

A far more effective liberal mover than Nezhdánoff is Solómin, the factory superintendent. It is no coincidence that his name suggests the wise king of the Bible, for he is the most completely admirable character in the book. Nearly everybody who comes in contact with him admires his intelligence, his integrity, his sense of honor, and his ability to get things done. Even the working people under him respect him and Valentína Mihailovna, although certain that she is superior to him, finds herself strangely attracted to this simple, direct man. He realizes that the Russian people are sleeping and will not awaken in his time, but he is willing to make his effort and let the future take care of the rest. Above all, he is a realist. Turgenev clearly admires this sensible man and implies that Russia could use more men like him, men more willing to be straightforward and hardworking and less concerned with saving face.

The most striking scenes in the novel are between women. Turgenev's genius emerges at its most powerful when he allows two women to confront each other, as when Marianna and Valentína Mihailovna finally tell each other their true feelings. Equally effective is the scene between Marianna and Mashúrina at the factory. In quite a different way, the scene in which the peasant woman, Tatiana, and the aristocratic radical Marianna become friends is very well done. An earthy and far from stupid woman, Tatiana is able to educate Marianna about the ways of the working class. She sees the humor of Marianna's seeking to lower herself, but is neither condescending nor resentful. The two women agree that education is the key to any radical movement. Turgenev showed a particularly powerful insight into the changes about to overtake Russia and the world when he described the revolutionary roles that women were to play in the battle for the new order. It is the women who break the silence of the "anonymous Russia," not the sensitive poet-revolutionary or even the narrow-minded professional radical.

The novel is filled with brilliantly sketched-in characters, many of them strikingly humorous. Fomishka and Fimishka Subotchev, two refugees from the eighteenth century, provide both comic relief and a touching contrast in the grotesque vignette in which they appear. Kallomyeitzev, a stupid and vain property owner, insecure in his position and therefore more conservative than any of the older landed gentry, is as absurd as he is repulsive; Turgenev perfectly understands him and portrays him in all of his pettiness and hypocritical gallantry. But perhaps the cool and beautiful Valentína Mihailovna is Turgenev's outstanding creation; complicated, subtle, vain, and vengeful, she also is honest and proud, a woman who understands her own faults and shortcomings as well as she does her gifts. She is not an admirable person, but she is a superb character, and Turgenev has made the most of her.

Virgin Soil, although written when Turgenev was no longer young, deals mostly with young people. With remarkable insight and skill, Turgenev entered into the psychology of his youthful characters, exploring their strengths and weaknesses, analyzing their ideals and dreams. The novel stands, after a century, as both a historical record of the beginnings of the radical movement in Russia and as a perceptive and subtle novel of human conviction and idealism.

Bruce D. Reeves

THE VIRGINIA COMEDIANS

Type of work: Novel
Author: John Esten Cooke (1830-1886)
Type of plot: Sentimental romance
Time of plot: 1763-1765
Locale: Colonial Virginia
First published: 1854

In this mostly sentimental romance which idealizes the Cavalier myth of the pre-Civil War South, Cooke nevertheless treats with vivid realism certain social attitudes as well as places and events in the early history of Virginia, especially that of the James River section.

By his own account, John Esten Cooke conceived and wrote *The Virginia Comedians* in a few weeks during the winter of 1853-1854. Its publication by D. Appleton and Company in two volumes in 1854 brought immediate recognition to the twenty-four-year-old author. In the opinion of John O. Beaty, his biographer, the novel was "by far the finest" of his more than thirty published volumes.

The enduring value of the novel lies beyond its maze of intricate subplots, melodramatic intrigues, multiple love affairs, and diffusive colloquies—the conventional trappings of popular nineteenth century historical romances. Cooke's avowed intention was to present "some view, however slight, of the various classes of individuals who formed that Virginia of 1765. . . . " Critics agree that the novel remains important for its realistic portrayal of the various elements in Virginia society on the eve of the American Revolution. The life style, and the manners and morals of the aristocratic Effinghams, the middle-class Waters, and the itinerant Hallams are particularly well delineated. Less satisfactory are Cooke's descriptions of the characters on the lower rungs of society, and, to a degree, he perpetuates the myth of the Cavalier origins of Southern aristocracy. But this fault is more pronounced in his post-Civil War works.

By choosing a transitional period for the novel's setting, Cooke, through the character of the revolution-fomenting Charles Waters, also injects an element of historical drama, and a foreboding sense of coming change into the work. The novel climaxes with Waters whipping a crowd of disgruntled citizens into a frenzy with his denunciation of the recent Stamp Act. Watching approvingly is Waters' mentor, the mysterious "man in the red cloak," whose identity is finally revealed as Patrick Henry.

Cooke never again matched the overall quality attained in *The Virginia Comedians,* although he attempted to exploit its successful formula in several additional novels before his death in 1886. The novel remains credible social history, and for this, and his subsequent work, Cooke became one of the most popular Southern novelists in the nineteenth century.

THE VIRGINIAN

Type of work: Novel
Author: Owen Wister (1860-1938)
Type of plot: Regional romance
Time of plot: Late nineteenth century
Locale: Wyoming
First published: 1902

The Virginian, one of the classic novels of the American West, fashions a romantic myth of the cowboy hero. More than conventionally brave, the Virginian is idealized by Wister as the perfect specimen—a natural American whose moral superiority is seen as innate.

This book appeared in 1902, some ten years after the closing of the frontier and shortly after Frederick Jackson Turner explained in his famous "safety-valve" thesis the function that the frontier had performed in American history. Perhaps *The Virginian* is an expression of the need, once the frontier was gone, to experience a frontier that never was. This book is one of the first serious novelistic treatments of the American cowboy, if one excludes the dime novels that had dismayed parents for almost the previous fifty years. When the open range was gone, the cowboy came into his own as a literary figure, and there seems to be more than coincidence in the two facts. The end of the frontier era and the beginning of the cowboy novel meld too closely for there to be much accident about it.

This book is not set in the American West so much as in a country called Cattle Land, where men are men and possess all the virtues and characteristics popularly associated with Horatio Alger. Wister associates one more element to this mythical character he is writing about—primal man. Wister very often describes the Virginian as "wild" or "natural" and the two words are seemingly interchangeable. The East is decadent and the American virtues have their last home in the West.

Tied up with this idea of primal innocence is the concept of an Americanism that is itself primal, free of the decadence of Europe. But decadence has swept westward, as Wister sees it, and has pushed Americanism in front of it. The only Vermonter, back in Molly's home state, to approve of her new husband is the great-aunt who sees in the Virginian the spirit of her own husband, a general in the Revolutionary War. This theme of Americanism being a primal, Adamic innocence and being found only in the West is brought out most forcefully when Judge Henry tries to explain to Molly why the Virginian and others had to lynch a cattle rustler. Molly objects that they took the law into their own hands. The Judge's reply is that the law came originally from people who delegated this responsibility to their representatives; in turn, they established in the Constitution machinery for administering the law. But in Wyoming the hands of the law were weak, and could not do the job that had been delegated them. So the Virginian had only been taking back what had been his own. The delegates to the Constitutional convention, then, were in spirit to be found in the far West, ironically at a Wyoming lynching party.

This is Wister's world and it is, as he said in his foreword to the novel, one that no longer exists. He was wrong when he said this in 1902, for men like the Virginian, although less romantic when seen in the flesh, are still spread over this country. They seem to be part of a dying breed. Many in America today would agree with much that the Virginian says and represents, and in that respect the cowboy has not vanished from the land any more than our belief in the primal innocence of America has lessened. He may have changed, perhaps become urbanized, but many contemporary Americans continue to live with the Virginian's values.

THE VIRGINIANS

Type of work: Novel
Author: William Makepeace Thackeray (1811-1863)
Type of plot: Historical romance
Time of plot: Late eighteenth century
Locale: England and the Colony of Virginia
First published: 1857-1859

A historical romance flawed in plot but memorable for the portrait of the Baroness Bernstein, the former Beatrix Esmond in her old age, The Virginians *is Thackeray's attempt to contrast the vitality of the New World with the corruption of the Old.*

Thackeray is popularly believed to have conceived the idea for *The Virginians* after seeing two swords, mementoes of the Battle of Bunker Hill, mounted in the manner described in the opening of the novel in the library of a contemporary historian named Prescott. While such anecdotes are often false, Thackeray did visit Prescott and later outlined to American novelist John Esten Cooke a plan for the novel which is, indeed, strongly suggested by the opening of the work. The story was to take place during the Revolution and was to include two brothers as the predominant characters who would take different sides in the conflict and who would be in love with the same girl. The war itself was to be given major emphasis. Obviously, Thackeray failed to adhere very closely to this plan, and the significant shortcomings of the work are probably chargeable to that regrettable fact.

Thackeray faced two problems in the writing of *The Virginians* which well may have been mutually responsible for his seemingly pointless deviation from a sound, organized plan. One of the problems is inherent in the writing of a sequel novel—the author is faced with the twin constraints of fidelity to previous characterizations and compatibility with an established history. Such constraints, as other authors have proved to us, are almost invariably detrimental to artistic achievement. The second problem arose from Thackeray's commitment to write the novel in serial form, which placed him under a compulsion to provide regular monthly installments that could wait neither for adequate historical research nor for proper artistic attention. Whether these problems were, in fact, the cause of Thackeray's abandoning many of the details of his original plan is, of course, mere speculation and is deserving of no more consideration than speculation warrants. What is clear, however, is that the compelling opening of the work suggests a promising study in comparative values and conflicting loyalties in a novel of epic scope that is in no wise delivered. What we are given instead is a largely shapeless work that begins promisingly enough but dawdles through stretches of irresolute composition and culminates in a series of major events that are crammed into a hasty lump of a denouement.

In *The Virginians,* as in most of Thackeray's works, we must bestow what critical acclaim we might feel inclined to give it principally on the artful characterizations it contains and on the value of its social commentary. Thackeray's settings somehow never quite emerge as definitive places, in marked contrast to later Victorians Hardy and Conrad, whose settings are so powerfully conceived that they become virtual characters in their own right and often influence events rather directly. Thackeray's descriptions of physical environment seem somehow deficient, as if he painted with temperas too much mixed with water. He succeeds in rendering for us only a faint impression of some sort of vague precincts in which his characters move, the nature and mood of which might well be appropriate to those characters and to their activities if only the setting could be clearly discerned. Nor can the scantiness of the settings be well defended by the argument that the environment in which Thackeray's characters pursue their thoughts and actions is of significantly less importance to his purpose than are the motivations and social interfaces of those characters, for in *The Virginians* they ought to have been inextricably bound. The central theme of the work—insofar as one can be said to exist—is the contrast between the innocence and simplicity of the New World and the corruption and sophistication of the Old. This contrast was, ultimately, the cause of the revolt in the colonies and no small contributor to the success of that revolt. Furthermore, it is the very hub about which the central conflict was surely intended to revolve. It does not, and included among the reasons why must be the lack of delineation of a physical as well as a societal identity, for the New Eden engendered the altered values that finally made the separation of England and the colonies a matter of more than mere distance.

The Virginians does contain a relatively effective contrast of social life in England and Virginia. The predominance given to English society, however, is excessive and at the expense of a complete treatment of plantation life in America. Furthermore, the effectiveness of the contrast is frustrated by Thackeray's failure to provide a parallel contrast between the twins. An attempt is apparent, but it is ineffectual because of the lack of structure of the work. The novel becomes not so much a story of conflict between brothers who respond to the sound of different drums, but separate stories of characters who only incidentally are twins. The motivations are not fully developed; the brothers seem to move independently rather than in opposition to each other, and, as a consequence, the conflict that should have been the very core of the novel is essentially nonexistent.

If there are major failures in the work, there are major triumphs as well. Numbered among the foremost of these must be the singular and fascinating portrait of the Baroness Bernstein, the former Beatrix of *Henry Esmond,* now an old woman. The Baroness is a minor masterpiece of characterization in a period of literature when authors did not yet consciously employ the subtlety of psychological motivation. Sapped by satiety of all interest and emotion except a single passion for cards, the Baroness' capacity for humanity appears to be as shriveled as her body. Yet, under the stimulus of Harry and George Warrington and the memories of their grandfather that they invoke in her, the Baroness briefly regains the capacity for human feeling with which she was endowed before a life of decadence and wealth displaced it with selfishness and callous indifference. The Baroness' final scene, in which she falls asleep over her cards during a visit of George and rouses to a lost contact with reality, possesses a vivid reality and dramatic impact that is impressive.

The secret of Thackeray's most successful characterizations seems to lie in the deft and subtle touches of inner conflict with which he invests them, and this is true of the better members of the cast of *The Virginians*. Beatrix displays a strength of character that is less incipient than it is suppressed by the society in which she moves. Parson Sampson's betting, cardplaying, dicing, drinking, and telling of "lively" jokes despite his moral convictions "humanizes" the unreverend Reverend and serves to suggest that all men are susceptible to corruption, regardless of calling.

Mrs. Esmond Warrington, if less captivating than the Baroness and less skillfully drawn than either she or Parson Sampson, nevertheless stands out as a notable characterization as well. What makes her role in the novel significant, however, is the careful juxtaposition of her and the Baroness, her half-sister. The very effectiveness of the contrast points to the obviously intended but unachieved parallel effect with George and Harry. Unhappily, the central protagonists are emphatic failures. Harry's weaknesses do not fit him either for sympathy or the interest a villain would generate, and George's benevolent nature is of the smug, self-satisfied kind that alienates rather than endears. The twins are neither disparate enough to present a conflict of interest nor interesting enough to make us care.

None of these things, however, constitutes the greatest flaw in the work. The novel, while containing much that is interesting, much that is delightful, and some social comment worthy of the making, must be judged less than successful. But its lack of success is more than a problem of desultory writing and excessive wandering by the author and more than a problem of adumbrated locales and major characters with essential features missing. The ultimate flaw is not even that the central conflict is resolved in a disappointing climax, but that the promised conflict does not, in fact, really occur at all.

Terrence R. Doyle

VIVIAN GREY

Type of work: Novel
Author: Benjamin Disraeli (1804-1881)
Type of plot: Political romance
Time of plot: Early nineteenth century
Locale: England and Germany
First published: 1826-1827

A romantic novel treating the political ambitions of a dandified young man,
Vivian Grey *owes much to the heroic postures of Lord Byron. The melodramatic*
scenes of terror strain credulity today, but the work was successful when it first
appeared.

Vivian Grey is one of those interesting, unsuccessful novels that appears
at the juncture of divergent literary movements, and which, at the same time,
is filled with intense personal and biographical energy.

In 1826-1827, when the two volumes of *Vivian Grey* were published, the
novel in England was divided between those of the romantics and those of
the "fashionable" set. The former stream is, of course, best represented by
Sir Walter Scott's followers and the prose descendants of Byron. The latter,
or "fashionable" novel, concerned itself with the habits, mannerisms, and
intrigues of the British upper class. This class, with its tightly developed
social rituals and elaborate, superficial manners provided the social setting
for what were nicknamed the "silver fork" novels. *Vivian Grey,* using this
class for its social setting, also incorporates much of the philosophical discourse and melodrama of the romantic tradition.

Disraeli, an offspring of a Spanish-Jewish family that had lived in England
for eighty years, the son of a minor literary figure and antiquarian, was a
fiercely ambitious and determined youth (as his later career in government
attests). He modeled *Vivian Grey* on *Tremaine,* a "silver fork" novel, but
changed the tone and gave it a romantic flair. *Vivian Grey* was written before
Disraeli had reached the age of twenty-one, and the novel displays all the
excesses to which young novelists are prone. The hero is an idealized version
of the author. His political manipulations, his romantic escapades, his various
adventures in Germany (disconnected and difficult to follow) and, above all,
his intense egotism are sometimes interesting, but frequently offensive. The
other characterizations, which suffer from the self-centered interest of Vivian
Grey himself, are most often wooden and without much life. They resemble,
in the tradition of fashionable novels, various important personages in upper-
class Britain; and they are stereotyped characters lacking humanity and
depth.

This weakness in characterization naturally affects the novel's action.
Because of his self-education, Vivian Grey shows little or no real development
through the two volumes. Hence, his political activities and romantic interests,

which provide the motivational force of the plot, are not always interesting in themselves. Further, the action resulting from conflicts between characters is usually as mechanical as the characters themselves.

What is interesting in the novel is the story of Vivian Grey's coming to age, and the spectacle of the author, through Vivian Grey, coming to grips with important ideas of the age. Finally, the novel does communicate a sense of restlessness and a youthful, searching energy—qualities which have an undeniable attraction.

VOLPONE

Type of work: Drama
Author: Ben Jonson (1573?-1637)
Type of plot: Social satire
Time of plot: Sixteenth century
Locale: Venice
First presented: 1605

One of Ben Jonson's most effective "humours" comedies, Volpone. or. The Fox. is intricately plotted, and vigorous and savage in its satire of hypocrisy, mendacity, and greed. In this play the characters resemble predatory beasts.

Written during a period in which Jonson had turned his hand largely to the making of entertaining masques and satirical anti-masques, *Volpone's* success did something to make up for the failure of his tragedy, *Sejanus. Volpone* was performed by the King's Men in London, and at the two universities, to which he later dedicated the play in his Prologue. The play also led to Jonson's most fertile dramatic period, that of the five great comedies (including *Epicoene* (1609), *The Alchemist* (1610), *Bartholomew Fair* (1614), and *The Devil Is an Ass* (1616). Jonson was preëminent among the Elizabethans and Jacobeans as that rare combination of the academic and creative genius. He was a serious classicist who criticized Shakespeare's "little Latin and less Greek," modeling his own plays on the Romans. As a humanist he brought classical control and purity to English forms, further strengthening those forms with Italian imports (his comedies were influenced strongly by Machiavelli). More than anyone else at the time, Jonson followed the prescriptions of Sidney's *Apologie for Poetrie* (1595). Like Sidney, he believed that the poet had a moral function in society; he viewed drama as a means of social education, paving the way for the great English satirists of the eighteenth century. His diverse artistic character makes Jonson both representative of his own age and a predecessor of the more rigorous classicism of the Augustans.

Jonson's style, as might be expected, is disciplined, formal, balanced, and classically simple and unembellished—a style that foreshadows the Cavalier School (who called themselves "the sons of Ben"). Though his dramatic verse is highly stylized it is nevertheless vibrant and fast-moving; we hardly feel we are reading poetry. Rarely does Jonson allow himself the lyrical excursions of Shakespeare or the rhetorical complexity of Marlowe, though he was capable of both. There is a solidity, firmness, and straightforward clarity in his comedies only equalled by the classical French comic theater of Molière. In *Volpone* Jonson follows the "Aristotelian" unities, as proclaimed to the Renaissance by Castelvetro. The action of the play takes in only one day (the unity of time); it occurs entirely in Venice (place); and, with the exception of some of the exchanges between Peregrine and Sir

Politic Would-Be, the action is unified structurally, all centered around the machinations of Volpone and his parasite, and their greedy suitors.

The satirical theme of the play is greed, the vice that dominates the actions of all the characters. Family bonds, marriage, legal justice are not merely disregarded by Corbaccio, Corvino, and Voltore; they are even made the means by which the characters' inhuman avarice destroys them. Actually, Jonson would insist that their greed is all too human, recalling what Spenser's Sir Calidore had exclaimed: "No greater crime to man/Than inhumanitie." It is ironic that the Politic Would-Be's, though they, too, want Volpone's money, seem less offensive and morally corrupt simply because they do not sell their souls for a hope of lucre. The passages in which they appear are a kind of relief. For though *Volpone* is a comedy it is so serious that it is almost equally tragic, predicting Byron's Don Juan who said, "And if I laugh at any mortal thing, 'tis that I may not weep." *Volpone* may be a comedy insofar as it deals with particular figures in a particular situation; but its social application is in deadly earnest. Jonson has succeeded brilliantly in combining the stereotyped *dramatis personae* of Latin comedy, the Renaissance characters based on *humours* (which he himself used in his first comedy, *Every Man in His Humour*), the popular tradition of beast-fables (from which he derived the names of his characters), with astute psychological insight that makes them all come alive before our eyes. Although the plot of *Volpone* is original, it is based on the common Roman *captatores* theme dealt with by Horace, Juvenal, Pliny, Lucian, and Petronius. Jonson turns his fortune hunters loose in contemporary Venice—chosen, no doubt, because the English of the time regarded Italy as a country of crime and rampant passions (cf. Nash's *The Unfortunate Traveller*)—and the audience understands that this kind of man is eternal. That is the point Jonson himself makes in defining the high moral purpose of comic satire in his Preface to the two universities.

Another important theme is that of imitation, as a distortion of normal reality. Sir Politic Would-Be seeks to imitate Volpone, an imitation of an imitation in the sense that led Plato to expel the poets from his republic; the tragedy is that though Volpone can be imitated, he is not imitable. And no one in the play has a firm moral standard that prevents them all from degrading their humanity. Lady Would-Be attempts to cover her mental deformities with physical cosmetics, and the dressing scene remains one of the most familiar and most pathetic in the play. Carrying imitation even further, Volpone pretends to be a mounteback in a complicated and convincing scene that leads to the question of how can we distinguish between a real imitator and an imitation imitator? Indeed Volpone and Mosca are actors throughout. They are also directors, leading the fortune-hunters, one by one, to give their best performances; in the process, they reveal how near beneath the surface lies the actor's instinct in all men. Any strong emotion can activate it: love of power in the case of Bolingbroke in *Richard the Second,* sheer ambition in *Macbeth,* jealousy in *Othello,* and greed in *Volpone. Volpone* creates chaos, associated with comedy from the time of Aristophanes, by confusing the identifying features of species, class, sex, and morals. Animals imitate men; men imitate animals.

Volpone is, of course, the guiding spirit who, like Marlowe's Jew of Malta, takes constant pleasure in his own mental agility and showmanship. Mosca is equally forceful; his only motive seems to be a delight in perpetrating perversities, and he accepts his inheritance only because it allows him to continue to be perverse. The three birds of prey, Corbaccio, Corvino, and Voltore, stumble over one another in their haste to devour the supposed carcass. If they are hideous caricatures, they are, in fact, caricatures of themselves—as the development of the play from the first scene demonstrates. Mosca and Volpone simply bring out the worst in them; they do not plant it—it is there. The sham trial in Act IV is the dramatic triumph of Jonson's career. When Corvino calls Voltore "mad" at the very point when the old man has become sane again, we see that we, too, have been beguiled by the terrible logic of greed.

Kenneth John Atchity

VOLUPTÉ

Type of work: Novel
Author: Charles Augustin Sainte-Beuve (1804-1869)
Type of plot: Psychological romance
Time of plot: Early nineteenth century
Locale: France
First published: 1832

Exaggerated in its emotionalism, Volupté *is nevertheless interesting for the psychological introspection of Amaury, the narrator, whose attitudes and neurotic griefs resemble those of the author at this time of his life.*

Fanciful, romantic, extreme, *Volupté* nevertheless is an effective work of fiction. It evokes a strangely powerful response, principally because of the intense emotions experienced by the protagonist. The often naïve and impetuous hero of this novel hurls himself from one intense experience to another, always seeking the elusive fulfillment which he fears can never be his. It is easy for the reader to see in Amaury the romanticism of the early nineteenth century. Although he is portrayed in an exaggerated fashion, he avoids appearing ridiculous; the obvious sincerity of the author and the intensity of the narrative save the book from its excesses. Both the lushness of the prose and the melodramatic moments in the plot can be viewed as reflections of a literary attitude and a historical period. In addition, the sweep of the novel suggests the broad range of interests which were to occupy Sainte-Beuve's career as critic and essayist.

Volupté is very much a young writer's book, but it nevertheless possesses riches for the reader willing to overlook its overly passionate stance. Many of the characterizations are sharply drawn, particularly of the minor characters, and the psychological analysis is often shrewd and insightful. The frustrated love affair which composes much of the narrative is recounted with sensitivity and delicacy, and the fact that it was based on a true and painful incident in the author's own life adds to its poignancy. To a more brittle, less romantic age, the emotions evoked might tax credulity, but if the reader is willing to suspend disbelief he will find himself strangely moved.

Like the novels of Thomas Wolfe, *Volupté* is an experience which readers of a certain age or attitude can find extremely powerful. It also possesses historical significance, both for its picture of the time and for its reflection of the life of the author who, as a critic, was to revolutionize the methods of literary analysis.

THE VOYAGE OF THE BEAGLE

Type of work: Journal
Author: Charles Darwin (1809-1882)
Type of plot: Travel and Natural History
Time of plot: 1831-1836
Locale: South America and the South Seas
First published: 1839

The title of this great work of natural history is somewhat misleading, for the author has little to say about the voyage. What interests him—and what he records with a fine sense of exactness—are the geological and biological data of the lands at which the Beagle *stops.*

Not only is *The Voyage of the Beagle* an important book in the history of modern thought, it is also a highly significant one in the life of Charles Darwin. Before he signed on as a naturalist on H.M.S. *Beagle,* Darwin had little sense of his own vocation or direction. When he was sixteen, he had begun a career of medicine at Edinburgh University. Discovering, however, that he was unfit for the profession, he entered Christ College, Cambridge, three years later in 1828 to prepare himself as a clergyman. Failing to take honors, or to distinguish himself at all, he sailed on the *Beagle.* During the five years of the voyage, he not only discovered himself and his career but also made his first observations, which would later develop into the theory of evolution revealed in *On the Origin of Species* (1859), which together with the work of Marx and Freud, form the most powerful influence on modern scientific thought as well as on modern values.

During the voyage it was in particular his observations on the relationships between animals segregated geographically, that is, those living on islands and those on the mainland, and on the relationship between species separated by time, that is, those living forms and those recently extinct ones, which forced him to reconsider the standard, scientific view of the fixity of the species. Further, he was also impressed by "the manner in which closely allied animals replace one another in proceeding southwards" in South America. Almost a year after he returned from the voyage he wrote in his journals, "In July opened first notebook on Transmutation of Species. Had been greatly struck from about the month of previous March on character of South American fossils, and species on Galápagos Archipelago. These facts (especially latter) origin of all my views."

Yet as important as *The Voyage of the Beagle* is to the understanding of the genesis of Darwin's theory of evolution and of an appreciation of his own struggle for self-discovery, the book's most significant aspect is the insight it provides into the Victorian mind. A part of the generation of the 1830's, which includes other Victorian sages such as Thomas Carlyle, John Stuart Mill, John Henry Newman, and Alfred, Lord Tennyson, Darwin shares many of their characteristics. Principally, we discover in this generation a sense of their own destiny, that they are in at the beginning of a new era in which the old ways of viewing matters would no longer apply. With the exception of Newman, they all came to embrace an idea of progress both in the spiritual and social areas of man's life. Darwin, of course, found in nature a reason to assert that there was biological progress. Indeed, he provided Tennyson, for example, with metaphoric proof, in his theory of natural selection, of the poet's own concept of ethical evolution. Finally in *The Voyage of the Beagle* we see Darwin's avid sense of adventure combined with a sense of mission, which identifies him most clearly with that new age and generation.

Always in these same Victorians, their zest for adventure with a mission is punctuated by an immense appetite for experience. Perhaps more than any other quality of Charles Darwin, the naturalist aboard the *Beagle,* we are impressed by his wide capacity for experiences of all kinds, whether those were connected with his official function or indeed any other. From his stay at Botofogo Bay and at the mouth of the River Plata where he began his observations and collections, Darwin reveals an immense energy and thoroughness. His commitment to the fundamental principles of the scientific method permits him to overlook no detail. (It is pertinent to remind ourselves at this point that Darwin's grand theory was based on the broadest possible observed evidence and was not the product of guess or intuition.) Yet despite his obsession with naturalistic data, he is always responsive to the mores of the inhabitants and watches the gauchos' manipulation of the lasso and bola with fascination.

We note that same kind of openness in him when he arrives in Buenos Aires. There he is surprised by the size of what he supposed was a primitive village. His openness and methods of observation are not, however, untouched by sentiment and indeed at times outrage. For example, his description of the sheep dogs that grew up with a unique attachment to their flocks could have only been written by an animal lover. His outrage and disgust are expressed when he visits Lima where the state of anarchy and poverty offended the uninitiated Darwin. In short, he was a highly impressionable man whose civilized character did not blind him to the nuances and ramifications of nature or man.

One of the most salient aspects of nature, which Darwin faced with unceasing honesty, particularly in the Galápagos islands, was that of cruelty. Some twenty years after the return of the *Beagle,* he wrote, "What a book a devil's chaplain might write on the clumsy, wasteful, blundering, low, and horribly cruel works of nature." To be sure this is an insight that developed only after he finished writing *The Voyage of the Beagle.* In a sense it is the other side of the coin of natural selection. If Darwin's theory of evolution points to a general progress of a species, it also reveals the indifference of nature to individuals within the type. Any total evaluation of Darwin must recognize both sides of his discovery. It is precisely his own openness to nature which allowed him to perceive this duality, and his scientific honesty—which necessitated his acceptance of his observation—that lay behind the final development of his thought. Both of these attributes we find in the young Darwin and in his first book, *The Voyage of the Beagle*.

David L. Kubal

WAITING FOR GODOT

Type of work: Drama
Author: Samuel Beckett (1906-   )
Type of plot: Tragi-comedy
Time of plot: The present
Locale: A country road
First presented: 1952

In this comedy of the absurd, antic yet philosophically troubling, Beckett views the human condition through symbolism that has its roots in Freudian psychology, the Christian myth, and Existentialism. The two tramps vacillate between hope and despair; they are obsessed by uncertainty and dominated by the absurd.

Waiting for Godot (En Attendant Godot) is a landmark in modern drama. When it premiered in Paris, its originality stunned audiences: no one had seen or heard anything like it before. Initially, some were disgusted; some were puzzled; and some were wildly enthusiastic. But within a short time, audiences came to the theater prepared for a wholly new dramatic experience and went away with praises for Samuel Beckett, then a playwright manqué. The play ran for more than three hundred performances in Paris, other productions were mounted in London and major cities on the Continent, and it was widely translated and performed around the world. After a disastrous United States premiere in Miami, *Waiting for Godot* went on to a successful New York run, suggesting that the play was best received by an audience of sophisticated intellectuals.

Nevertheless, audience enthusiasm has not been matched by unalloyed critical acclaim. To be sure, many critics as well as eminent playwrights have paid high tribute to the play. But several other critics, like some members of the first-night audience in Paris, have been repelled or baffled by *Waiting for Godot,* their reactions most often stemming from a misunderstanding of the play. In order to avert such misunderstanding, it is necessary to examine two crucial aspects of the play: its language and its philosophical orientation.

First of all, the language of the play is intimately connected to Beckett's own background in language studies and literary influences. Beckett was born in Dublin, Ireland, and took his A.B. degree in French and Italian at Trinity College. After teaching English in Paris for two years, he returned to Trinity to teach and complete his M.A. in French. Next, he traveled in England and on the Continent, and he wrote poems, short stories, and novels—in English. He at last settled permanently in Paris, except for a brief hiatus during World War II, and began writing in French in the late 1940's. (*Waiting for Godot* was thus originally written in French but translated into English by Beckett himself.)

Of equal importance, during Beckett's first sojourn in Paris (1928-1930),

Waiting for Godot/BECKETT

was his meeting with James Joyce, a meeting which launched a long and mutually satisfying friendship between the two Irish expatriates and language experts. The influence of Joyce on Beckett's work is evident in the language play in *Waiting for Godot,* for puns, allusions, and linguistic "tricks" abound.

Great effort has been expended, for instance, in trying to decipher the word "Godot," both as character and as concept. Beckett himself has declined to explain, but critics, undeterred, continue to speculate. The most common view sees Godot as God with the "-ot" as a diminutive suffix. The French title *En Attendant Godot* seems to lend support to this interpretation. Another suggestion is the analogy between Godot and Charlot (both utilizing the diminutive suffix), the latter an affectionate nickname for the Charlie Chaplin character in a derby hat, the kind of hat which plays a significant part in the stage business of *Waiting for Godot.* Some readings inevitably deteriorate into the preposterous—that Godot represents De Gaulle, for example. But the most likely explanation involves an allusion to a highly obscure source: Honore de Balzac's comedy, *Le Faisseur* (also known as *Mercadet*). Balzac's play revolves around a character—named Godeau—who strongly influences the action of the play but who never appears on stage. The parallels between the Balzac work and *Waiting for Godot* are too close to attribute to mere coincidence, for Beckett, like Joyce, has a marked fondness for the esoteric literary allusion. It is possible, of course, to circumvent these literary contortions and simply view Godot as the objectification of a state of being: the *waiting,* bracketed by birth and death, which we call life.

In addition, Beckett plays other word games in *Waiting for Godot.* Estragon, for instance, begins a sentence which Vladimir then finishes. Yet the overwhelming monotony of the dialogue, reflecting the monotony in the characters' lives, is reminiscent of the exercise drills in old language texts of the "La plume de ma tante est sur la table" variety, further suggesting the debasement of language and the consequent breakdown of communication. (This point is a major preoccupation of another modern playwright, Eugene Ionesco.) And the *non sequiturs* which emerge from rapid-fire exchanges in the dialogue echo the music-hall comedians in the heyday of vaudeville. Thus Beckett's penchant for word play reveals the influence of his language training, of his friend James Joyce, and of his conviction that language in the modern world is both necessary and impotent.

The philosophical orientation of *Waiting for Godot* is another matter, however, for the years of Beckett's residence in France coincided with a period of great ferment in Existential philosophy, most of it centered in Paris. Beckett is not a formal or doctrinaire Existentialist, but he could hardly avoid being affected by Existentialism, for such ideas were part of his cultural milieu. There is no systematically Existential point of view in *Waiting for Godot*—as there is in, say, the plays of Jean-Paul Sartre and the novels of Albert Camus. Yet a generally Existential view of the human condition comes through very clearly in the play. Vladimir and Estragon, Lucky and Pozzo are psychically isolated from one another; despite physical proximity, they are alienated and lonely, as indicated by their failure to communicate meaningfully. And in that state of mind, each despairs, feeling helpless in the face of an immutable destiny. But, unlike the formal Existentialists, Estragon and Vladimir hope, and it is that hope which sustains them through their monotonous and immobile existence. Thus, they wait. They wait for Godot, who will surely bring them words of comfort and advice, and who will intervene to alter their destinies. By maintaining this hope, by waiting for Godot to come, Vladimir and Estragon elude the inevitable Existential logic which postulates hopelessness followed by a sense of futility, reducing humankind to absurdity. In this way, Vladimir and Estragon attain truly heroic proportions; they endure.

Beckett's play has been criticized, even by Estragon, because, as the tramp puts it, "Nothing happens." But in fact, a great deal does happen: there is a lot of action, much coming and going. However, action in this sense is quite superficial, for all of it is meaningless. Yet that very action assumes a rhythm and a pattern which constitute the structure of the play. The repetitious movements and dialogue reinforce the quasi-Existential theme of the play: that life is a meaningless and monotonous performance of endlessly repeated routine. The pattern established in the first act is recapitulated in the second act, with only slight variation. Obviously the action in *Waiting for Godot* is not the action of conventional drama, but it is this unique fusion of theme and structure which accounts for the startling originality of the play and which rightly earns Beckett a place as one of the few genuine innovators in modern drama.

Joanne G. Kashdan

WALDEN

Type of work: Essays
Author: Henry David Thoreau (1817-1862)
Type of treatise: Autobiography and nature notes
Time of treatise: 1845-1847
Locale: Walden Pond, near Concord, Massachusetts
First published: 1854

More than a naturalist's record of finely observed phenomena, Walden. Or. Life in the Woods *is a major philosophical statement on the American character, the uses of a life of simple toil, and the values of rugged independence.*

Few contemporaries of Henry David Thoreau would have predicted the enormous popularity his small volume, *Walden,* would win in our century. Author and work were virtually neglected during Thoreau's lifetime. Locally, he was considered the village eccentric; even his great friend and mentor Ralph Waldo Emerson was disappointed because his young disciple seemingly frittered away his talent instead of "engineering for all America." After Thoreau's death in 1862, his works attracted serious critical attention, but unfavorable reviews by James Russell Lowell and Robert Louis Stevenson severely damaged his reputation. Towards the turn of the century he began to win favorable attention again, mainly in Britain. During the Depression of the 1930's, when most people were forced to cut the frills from their lives, *Walden,* whose author admonished readers voluntarily to "Simplify, simplify, simplify!" became something of a fad. In the 1960's, with new awareness of environment and emphasis on nonconformity, Thoreau was exalted as a prophet and *Walden* as the individualist's bible.

Walden can be approached in several different ways. Obviously it is an excellent nature book. During the Romantic era, many writers—Wordsworth, Byron, Shelley, Emerson, Whitman, to name a few—paid tribute to nature. But Thoreau went beyond simply rhapsodizing natural wonders. He was a serious student of the natural world, one who would spend hours observing a woodchuck or tribes of battling ants; who meticulously sounded and mapped Walden Pond; who enjoyed a hilarious game of tag with a loon. Like Emerson, he saw nature as a master teacher. In his observations of nature, Thoreau was a scientist; in his descriptions, a poet; in his interpretations, a philosopher and psychologist; and certainly he was an ecologist in his insistence on man's place *in* (not *over*) the natural universe, and on man's need for daily contact with the earth.

Walden may also be considered as a handbook for the simplification of life. As such, it becomes a commentary upon the sophistication, "refinement," frequently distorted values, and devotion to things of civilized society. Thoreau admits the necessities of food, shelter, clothing, and fuel; "for not till we have secured these are we prepared to entertain the true problems of life with freedom and a prospect of success." He then illustrates how we may strip these necessities to essentials for survival and health, ignoring the dictates of fashion or the yearning for luxury. "Most of the luxuries, and many of the so called comforts of life," he asserts, "are not only not indispensable, but positive hindrances to the elevation of mankind." With relentless logic he points out how making a living has come to take precedence over living itself; how a man mortgages himself to pay for more land and fancier clothing and food than he really requires; how he refuses to walk to a neighboring city because it will take too long—but then must work longer than the walk would take in order to pay for a train ticket. He questions our dedication to "progress," noting that it is technological, not spiritual: "We are in great haste to construct a magnetic telegraph from Maine to Texas; but Maine and Texas, it may be, have nothing important to communicate."

Perhaps the most serious purpose of *Walden* and its most powerful message is to call men to freedom as individuals. One looks at nature in order to learn about oneself; one simplifies one's life in order to have time to develop that self fully; and one must honor one's uniqueness if one is to know full self-realization. It is this emphasis on nonconformity that has so endeared Thoreau to the young, who have adopted as their call to life these words from the final chapter of *Walden*: "If a man does not keep pace with his companions, perhaps it is because he hears a different drummer. Let him step to the music which he hears, however measured or far away."

There is an ease, a clarity, a concreteness to Thoreau's prose that separates it from the more abstract, eloquent, and frequently involuted styles of his contemporaries. The ease and seeming spontaneity are deceptive. Thoreau revised the book meticulously during the five years it took to find a publisher; there are five complete drafts which demonstrate how consciously he organized not only the general outline, but every chapter and paragraph. For an overall pattern, he condensed the two years of his actual Walden experience into one fictional year, beginning and concluding with spring—the time of rebirth.

Pace and tone are also carefully controlled. Thoreau's sentences and paragraphs flow smoothly. The reader is frequently surprised to discover that sentences occasionally run to more than half a page, paragraphs to a page or more; syntax is so skillfully handled that one never feels tangled in verbiage. Tone varies from matter-of-fact to poetic to inspirational, and is spiced with humor—usually some well-placed satire—at all levels. Even the most abstract topics are handled in concrete terms; Thoreau's ready use of images and figurative language prepares us for twentieth century Imagist poetry.

Taken as a whole, *Walden* is a first-rate example of organic writing, with organization, style, and content fused to form a work that today, over one hundred years after its publication, is as readable and perhaps even more timely than when it was written. In *Walden,* Thoreau reaches across the years to continue to "brag as lustily as Chanticleer . . . to wake my neighbors up."

Sally Buckner

WALLENSTEIN

Type of work: Drama
Author: Johann Christoph Friedrich von Schiller (1759-1805)
Type of plot: Historical romance
Time of plot: The Thirty Years' War
Locale: Germany
First presented: 1799

Wallenstein, a romantic tragedy that often strays from historical facts, is actually a dramatic series composed of a one-act prelude, Wallenstein's Camp, *and two full-length plays,* The Piccolomini *and* The Death of Wallenstein. *Among other nineteenth century writers, Samuel Taylor Coleridge admired the work and compared it to Shakespeare's historical drama.*

On February 25, 1634, Albrecht Wallenstein, Duke of Friedland, was murdered in Eger. His career had been an astonishing one. He rose to power first as the savior of the Holy Roman Emperor, who after initial success in putting down a Protestant uprising, found himself facing an army led by King Christian IV of Denmark, and financed by England and the Netherlands. This was the second stage in the Thirty Years' War, which would sap the strength of the Empire against a series of opponents from 1618 to 1648. Wallenstein offered the Emperor nothing less than an army—twenty thousand men, raised at his own expense. His success was stupendous: he pursued the enemy across Europe and finally defeated Christian IV in his own kingdom. But the forces of his jealous rivals succeeded in persuading the Emperor, who was in fact alarmed by Wallenstein's success, to dismiss Wallenstein, who quietly retired, knowing that he would again be needed. In 1630, Sweden entered the war, and the Imperial forces were decisively defeated. At that point Wallenstein was recalled and he accepted, but on his own terms, leading an army of some forty thousand, with virtual autonomy. After initial victories, his thoughts turned to a negotiated peace, and again the Emperor began to fear, perhaps even anticipating a *coup d'état.* Schiller's great trilogy is the record of the downfall of the general, the overwhelming of a man who, it had seemed, was a creator of history, above the level of petty intrigue, perhaps even the harbinger of a new era of peace.

Schiller knew well that the historical Wallenstein was not really a suitable figure for tragedy. As professor of history at Jena, Schiller had written a history of the Thirty Years' War in the early 1790's, and his observations at that time pointed out that the General was in fact an unsympathetic character. It was less his personal magnetism than his money that held the army together, along with the prospect of the spoils to come with success. His fall was in reality a product of his own miscalculations; also, he lacked nobility of character. But as dramatist, Schiller saw in the subject the possibility of creating a tragedy that would rival Shakespeare and the Greeks. He developed both the character of Wallenstein and those of his principal associates, even inventing the idealized figures of Max and Thekla, shaping the events to create a coherent vision of conflicting loyalties, duty, guilt, and tragic expiation, while yet remaining remarkably faithful to the historic events.

In the first section of the trilogy, *Wallenstein's Camp,* Schiller creates the milieu of the time and presents both the visible sign of the General's greatness and an intimation of the divisions within his army, divisions which reflect those tensions which will destroy Wallenstein himself. In a prologue, Schiller explains that this portrait of the camp is an essential part of the work: it is Wallenstein's power that misleads his heart; his camp alone explains his crime. This symbolic representation, then, is meant to place the individual Wallenstein in the nexus of his time: the diverse interests, the expectations of his men, his power, the potential for its misuse, and also its limits. The army is his creation, but it also has its own independent existence now. Wallenstein may be the creator of historical forces, but he is also carried by those forces and becomes their victim.

The second section of the trilogy, *The Piccolomini,* presents the political intrigue which precipitates the tragedy. When Wallenstein first appears, the movement against him has already begun, and the forces which will lead to his destruction have been set in motion. He is unaware of this, however, and imagines himself still to be a free agent. Indeed, one of his main characteristics is that of keeping his options open, putting off decisions, as though he were the sole factor involved in directing the course of history. He has breadth of vision, and ranks far above his less imaginative subordinates, and yet he is guilty of a kind of hubris, expressed primarily in his readiness to betray his loyalty to the Emperor. Octavio Piccolomini, whom Schiller elevates to a major role in the plot, is unswervingly loyal to the Emperor—but betrays his commander. Thus Schiller has established a field of tension in which each figure in the plot experiences divided loyalty, and is forced to make a choice. The agony of decision has been intensified through the addition of the character of Max—Octavio was actually childless—who, in the midst of mutual betrayals, insists upon honesty, upon the authority of the heart over any pragmatic course of action. His father argues necessity, but he argues simple right and wrong. He is one of the most radiant of Schiller's creations, an idealist who cannot accept a breach of honor, and who is torn in his loyalty to his father and to Wallenstein, whom he regards as a second father. Schiller realized that this figure might well become the central focus of the play, and in fact for some readers this interpretation seems natural. Yet Schiller passes, in the last section, *Wallenstein's Death,* from emphasis on the conflict of those around Wallenstein and from the progress of the plot, to focus upon Wallenstein himself. Goethe observed that in this last section the purely human aspects are dominant. Wallenstein becomes more and more a tragic figure, as the plot against him moves inexorably while he is unaware of the net closing over him.

Yet the tragedy is more than that of Wallenstein alone; all the figures are caught in a movement of history, in part the creation of Wallenstein, and yet also independent, moving by its own laws. Insofar as he is a creator, Wallenstein is responsible for his own destruction; yet one also is aware that every character is forced by history to make a choice which compromises his integrity. All are stricken; even Max, the only pure soul, is destroyed by the intolerable conflict in which the net of betrayals has placed him, and for Octavio, the bereaved victor, it can only be a hollow triumph when he is elevated to the rank of prince.

Steven C. Schaber

THE WANDERER

Type of work: Novel
Author: Alain-Fournier (Henri Alain Fournier, 1886-1914)
Type of plot: Psychological romance
Time of plot: Nineteenth century
Locale: France
First published: 1913

A touchingly lyrical impressionistic novel, The Wanderer *explores with psychological insight the dreamlike world of a youth halfway between fantasy and reality, adolescence and maturity.*

"The novel that I have carried in my head for three years," Henri Alain-Fournier wrote in 1905, "was at first only me, me, and me, but it has gradually been depersonalized and enlarged and is no longer the novel which everybody plans at eighteen." That novel, *The Wanderer (Le Grand Meaulnes)*, written and revised over a period of six more years, is the major production of its author, who died in battle at Saint-Rémy in 1914. Although *The Wanderer* is surely more than a romantic autobiography, parts of the author appear in the three important male characters: the meditative, passive François Seurel; the adventurer Augustin Meaulnes; and the despairing lover Frantz de Galais. Like each of them, Alain-Fournier was a romantic idealist, a dreamer, a child-man not entirely able to come to terms with the demands of adult responsibilities. Precisely for this reason, his childlike vision of reality gives the story a psychological dimension beyond its trappings of sentimental fantasy.

Of the three heroes Seurel, the narrator, is the most timorous; he experiences life vicariously, through the intenser activities of others. Yet when he must act, to assist his beloved friend Meaulnes, he does so decisively. "Admiral" Meaulnes, on the other hand, is bold in dreams, indecisive when he needs most certainly to act. His will is paralyzed by guilt. Earlier, when he had lived in Paris, he betrayed Valentine Blondeau (as in real life Alain-Fournier deceived "Jeanne B.") and consequently cannot accept the pure love of Yvonne de Galais. Moreover, Meaulnes had betrayed her brother, his dear friend Frantz de Galais, who had truly loved Valentine. Toward the end of the novel, by reconciling Frantz with Valentine, Meaulnes partly eases his own guilt feelings and becomes free to accept the love of his young daughter. Yet is any happiness possible for Frantz? The most idealistic, most shadowy of the three hero-wanderers, he is driven wild by a child's dream of perfection that he cannot possibly realize. For Seurel, the passive sympathizer, love is a dream that only other, stronger souls can hope to attain; for Meaulnes, the adventurer, love is a quest, never a conquest; for Frantz, the hopeless searcher, love may be the final tragic deception.

As for the women characters of the novel, Yvonne and Valentine, they are merely projections of the idealized dreams (or guilty passions) of the child-heroes. Apart from their lovers, they have no lives of their own. Indeed, it is the heroes' peculiar childlike fantasy concerning women and love that unifies the novel and provides its psychological insights. The three male heroes are drawn to one another in a friendship so devoted that it resembles a ritual of brotherhood: protective, empathetic, nearly mystical. At the same time, they are half-maddened by love for "pure" women. This love is over-poweringly sudden, threatening (even when the object is as frail and delicate as Yvonne), and absolute. Once they have fallen in love, the child-heroes are victims of their fate: their bond of brotherhood is shattered, their lives fragmented.

To express this story of a child's fascination with (and fear of) love and sexuality, Alain-Fournier effectively uses a symbolistic-impressionistic style. Like Maeterlinck, he is a master of pauses—sudden breaks in the narrative—that underscore the sense of tension or menace. He subtly alternates scenes of realistic detail presented with perfect clarity (the wedding feast) with other scenes of haunting, ambiguous, hallucinatory mystery (Meaulnes' meeting with Yvonne). At his best, he writes passages touching in their simplicity. At other times, he loses artistic restraint and allows his characters to declaim speeches of romantic bombast. Some of his symbolic passages become too murky, the prose childish instead of childlike. Yet these lapses are rare. And of his one great novel Alain-Fournier is justified in writing: "If I have been childish and weak and foolish, at least I have, at moments, had the strength in this infamous city to create *my* life, like a marvelous fairy-tale."

THE WANDERING JEW

Type of work: Novel
Author: Eugène Sue (1804-1857)
Type of plot: Mystery melodrama
Time of plot: 1831-1832
Locale: France
First published: 1844-1845

The Wandering Jew *is a sprawling narrative written in a pedestrian style and dealing with one-dimensional characters; yet the romance has always attracted readers because of its imaginative sweep of history, its sense of mystery, and above all its retelling of the fascinating legend of Samuel, the Romantic hero as* Wandering Jew.

The Wandering Jew is an enormous novel. It touches several continents, the worlds of religion, economics, the supernatural, politics, medicine, and social protest. There are hundreds of characters on this vast stage, and dozens of plots, subplots, and plots within subplots.

The novel is in that tradition of French literary romanticism which mixes the supernatural with politics and social commentary. Yet its vast scale, reminiscent of *Les Misérables* (1862), also is remindful of the large social tapestry of eighteenth century novels. Further, Eugène Sue loves melodrama. He attempts, at every juncture, to induce the extremes of horror, anticipation, and suspense in his readers through a variety of well-tested literary techniques.

Mainly, however, it must be said that *The Wandering Jew* is not a successful novel. In terms of theme, action, character, and style it must be classified as one of those magnificent, towering failures. Central to the novel's difficulties is Sue's inability to connect and unify the vast and complicated action of the work. The intrigues and schemes of the Jesuits and the problem of the legacy, though convenient, simply cannot sustain the ambitious weight of this novel.

The Wandering Jew does not have the tight discipline or the moral stability of a large novel such as *Tom Jones* (1749). In that novel, Fielding is able to center his action in the movement of a few interesting and believable characters who operate within a strictly defined world. But the world of *The Wandering Jew* is overflowing without sufficient discipline imposed on the material. Indeed, Sue's romanticism carries him quite far in the opposite direction.

In *War and Peace,* another very large novel, the world is also enormous and the characters and motives are extremely various. But Tolstoy has a firm grasp of his war and peace theme and the processes of history. At the same time, he is able to offer the most vivid and accurate psychological and moral descriptions. But the thematic content of *The Wandering Jew* is clouded by romanticism and idealization; and, in addition to superficial and melodramatic characterizations, Sue offers large doses of the supernatural and mysticism.

Weaknesses of character, action, and theme are, naturally, reinforced and magnified as the scope of the work increases. As the novel lengthens, these weaknesses become qualitatively more striking and irritating. At the same time, however, Sue's attempt itself is impressive and there are frequent valid and touching individual scenes.

THE WANDERING SCHOLAR FROM PARADISE

Type of work: Drama
Author: Hans Sachs (1494-1576)
Type of plot: Farce
Time of plot: Sixteenth century
Locale: Nuremberg, Germany
First presented: 1550

This bucolic farce written in rhyming couplets is a Fastnachtspiel, *a type of short play performed in the German countryside on the night-before-fasting, or the night before Ash Wednesday. Presented in one act with scene changes indicated only by momentary closing and opening of the curtain, the play features broad humor and characterizations of burgher life, infidelity, and peasant stupidity.*

Hans Sachs was the most important of the sixteenth century Mastersingers of the prosperous city of Nuremberg, by profession a shoemaker, but devoted to literature and leader of the Guild of Mastersingers. Among his almost 7,000 works are a large number of dramas, mostly comic skits for Shrovetide, or the Mardi Gras season. At this time of pre-Lent festivity, amateur players performed such sketches in taverns and private homes, and Sachs even arranged to produce his own plays in public halls.

Following in the tradition of Hans Folz and Hans Rosenplüt, Sachs developed the traditional *Fastnachtsspiel* with an ingenious theatrical sense and a gift for manipulating the traditional stock characters of the form to create new situations. He carefully avoided the obscenity of earlier writers; his plays point to a moral, and in spite of the broad humor, Sachs reveals a basically conservative world view. He had become quite a spokesman for the Reformation in his earlier years, celebrating Luther as the "Wittenberg nightingale." In 1527, however, the Nuremberg town council had forbidden him to publish further inflammatory work, and by 1550 his work, aside from caricatures of priests and nuns, is nonpolemical.

His plays show advancement of technique, abandoning the earlier form in which a series of characters address the audience, for a self-contained play in which the characters speak to each other. His figures, though based on standard types—the shrewish wife, the dumb peasant, the con-man student— have all the touch of the common man about them and go beyond simple types to achieve a certain individuality. In spite of his seemingly naïve point of view, Sachs was widely read, and drew upon classical literature, the Bible, Italian literature, and German epics for material. While he was scorned by sophisticated readers of the Enlightenment, no less a figure than Goethe revived his work, and recognized in him an unassuming, down-to-earth, rustic talent close to genius.

WAR AND PEACE

Type of work: Novel
Author: Count Leo Tolstoy (1828-1910)
Type of plot: Historical romance
Time of plot: 1805-1813
Locale: Russia
First published: 1865-1869

This novel, often acclaimed as the greatest of its genre, is a panorama of Russian life in the Napoleonic era. War and Peace *is a moving record of historical progress, and the dual themes of this vast work—Age and Youth, War and Peace—are shown as simultaneous developments of history.*

War and Peace and *Anna Karenina,* two of the greatest works of fiction in Russian literature—or any literature—were both written when Tolstoy was at the height of his powers as a writer. He was in the longed-for state of a happy marriage and he was busy managing his country estate as well as writing. His life had a healthy, even exuberant, balance between physical and intellectual activities. *War and Peace,* in particular, reflects the passionate and wide-ranging tastes and energies of this period of his life—before domestic strife and profound spiritual conversion brought about a turning away from the world as well as from art. The novel is huge in size and scope; it presents a long list of characters and covers a splendid variety of scenes and settings. It is, however, a carefully organized and controlled work—not at all the vast, unshaped "monster" many readers and some writers have supposed.

The basic controlling device involves movement between clusters of characters surrounding the major characters: Natasha, Kutuzov, Andrey, Pierre. The second ordering device is thematic and involves Tolstoy's life-long investigation of the question: what is natural? This theme is offered in the first chapter at Anna Scherer's party where we encounter the artificiality of St. Petersburg society and meet both Andrey and Pierre, the two chief seekers of the natural. Both Andrey and Pierre love Natasha, who is an instinctive embodiment of the natural in particularly Russian terms. Kutuzov is also an embodiment of Russian naturalness; only he can lead the Russian soldiers in a successful war against the French. The Russian character of Tolstoy's investigation of the natural or the essential is the main reason one speaks of *War and Peace* as a national epic. Yet, Tolstoy's characters also represent all men.

Natasha's group of characters centers in the Rostov family (the novel is, among many things, a searching study of family life). Count Ilya Rostov, a landowning nobleman, is a sympathetic portrait of a carefree, warm-hearted rich man. His wife is somewhat anxious and less generous in spirit but they are happily married and the family as a whole is harmonious. Natasha's brothers and sisters are rendered with great vividness: the passionate, energetic Nikolay; the cold, formal Vera; the youthful Petya; the sweet, compliant Sonya, cousin to Natasha and used by Tolstoy as a foil to her. Natasha herself is bursting with life. She is willful, passionate, proud, humorous, capable of great growth and change. Like all the major characters she too seeks the natural. She *is* the natural; her instincts are right and true. All of Book VII, particularly Chapter 7 when she sings and dances, dramatizes the essential Russianness of her nature. Her nearly consummated love affair with Anatole Kuragin, her loss of Andrey, and her final happy marriage to Pierre show how intensely life-giving she is. One of the great experiences of reading *War and Peace* is to witness her slow transition from slim, exuberant youth to thick-waisted motherhood. For Tolstoy, Natasha can do nothing which is not natural and right.

Kutuzov stands above the generals who cluster about him. Forgotten at the start of the war, he is called into action when all else seems to have failed. Unlike the other generals, many of them German, Kutuzov knows that battles are not won in the staff room, by virtue of elaborate planning, but by the spirit of the soldiers who actually do the fighting. Kutuzov alone knows that one must wait for that moment when the soldiers' spirit is totally committed to the battle. He knows that the forces of war are greater than any one man can control and that one must wait upon events and know when not to act as well as when to act. His naturalness is opposed to Napoleon's artificiality. A brilliant strategist and planner, Napoleon believes that he controls events. His pride and vanity are self-blinding; he cannot see that if he invades Russia, he is doomed. Kutuzov's victory over Napoleon is a victory of the natural and the humble, for he is, after all, a man of the people. Furthermore, the figure of Kutuzov is very closely related to Tolstoy's philosophy of historical change and necessity.

The characters of Andrey and Pierre probably represent two sides of Tolstoy: the rational-spiritual versus the passionate-mystical, though these labels are far too simple. Andrey's group of characters centers in the Bolkonski family: the merciless, autocratic, but brilliant General Bolkonski, Andrey's father, and his sister Princess Marya, who is obedient, pious, and loving and who blossoms when she marries Nikolay Rostov. When we first see Andrey, he is bored and even appears cynical, yet he is, like Pierre, searching for an answer to life and, like Pierre, he undergoes a series of awakenings which bring him closer to the natural. The first awakening occurs when he is wounded at Austerlitz and glimpses infinity beyond the blue sky; the second occurs at his wife's death; the third occurs when he falls in love with Natasha, and the last when he dies. In all of these instances, Andrey moves closer to what he conceives of as the essential. This state of mind involves a repudiation of the world and its petty concerns and passions. In all but one of these instances, death is involved. Indeed, Andrey's perception of the natural is closely related to his acceptance of death. He comes to see death as the doorway to infinity and glory and not as a fearful black hole. Death becomes part of the natural rhythm, a cycle which promises spiritual rebirth.

Pierre's group is composed of St. Petersburg socialites and decadents: the Kuragin family, composed of the smooth, devious Prince Vasili; his son, the rake Anatole, and daughter, the beautiful, corrupt Hélène, Pierre's first wife; the rake Dolokhov; and finally, in Pierre's third or fourth transformation, the peasant Platon Karataev. Unlike Andrey, Pierre's approach to life seems almost strategically disordered and open—he embraces all forms of life passionately and hungrily. Compared to Andrey's rigorous and discriminating mind, Pierre seems hopelessly naïve and chaotic.

However, Pierre, even more than Natasha, is capable of vital and creative change. As Andrey seems fitted to perceive intimations of essences beyond the world, Pierre seems fitted to find his essences in the world. He shucks off his mistaken connection with Hélène and her family and experiences the first of his own awakenings in the conversion to Freemasonry (one of several interesting "false" conversions in the novel, one other being Natasha's after she is rejected by Andrey). He, too, learns from death, both in his duel with Dolokhov and in his observations of the battle of Borodino. But his two most important awakenings occur in his love for Natasha and in his experience as a prisoner of the French. In the latter instance, he encounters the harmonious, perfectly round (whole) peasant Karataev who teaches him to accept all things—even death—in good grace and composure of spirit. When Natasha encounters Pierre after this experience, she rightly sees that he has been transformed. All the superficial and nonessential are gone from him. Their marriage is a union of two vital human beings tempered by suffering. At the end, there is more than a hint that Pierre is involved in efforts on the part of the aristocracy to modify the ossified system of government under the tsars. Life and change go on.

War and Peace, perhaps beyond any other work, shows the advantages of the long novel. After reading the book, the reader feels a sense of space and a sense of change through the passage of time which are impossible to transmit so vividly in shorter fiction. This great novel reveals to us the beauty and injustice, the size and complexity, of life itself.

Benjamin Nyce

THE WAR OF THE WORLDS

Type of work: Novel
Author: H. G. Wells (1866-1946)
Type of plot: Pseudo-scientific romance
Time of plot: Late nineteenth century
Locale: London and environs
First published: 1898

A famous novel of science fiction, The War of the Worlds *is both a thriller and a prophecy of disaster for complacent Western society. Fast-moving and menacing, the romance ends with a satisfactory explanation for the Martian defeat.*

This novel's unique fame may tempt readers to overlook its most crucial dimensions.So concrete was Wells's vision that he wrote a virtual documentary history of the Martian invasion, a "history" so vivid that Orson Welles's legendary 1938 radio adaptation caused panic among American listeners. The popularity of the film version offers further inducement to focus only on the work's sensational aspects. But *The War of the Worlds* is much more than a classic thriller; it develops a disturbing theory about evolution, attacks the complacency of bourgeois civilization, and raises a serious question about the effects of prolonged world peace.

Shocking as are the appearance and immorality of the Martians, more shocking still is Wells's suggestion that these invaders are the very image of the human future; their hideous physical structure is the end product of an evolutionary path which mankind is also clearly following. The terms of survival on Mars are the same as on earth: intelligence, not physical strength, is increasingly the deciding factor. And the Martians' ruthlessness is merely the result of their upbringing in a severe environment; men would develop the same traits if placed in the same environment.

The War of the Worlds attacks the narrow complacency and intellectual smugness of modern man. Wells satirizes the inability of Englishmen to grasp the enormity of the disaster. He points to the numbing, softening effects of industrial routine, bureaucracy, and separation from nature. The scientific community is censured for its intolerance of mystery and paradox.

Related to this attack is Wells's skepticism about the benefits of peace, whose fruits are gentleness, moderation, and civilized rationality. But, distressingly, these qualities make man less fit for survival. Further, Wells intimates that combat may be man's natural state, and his narrator welcomes the onset of "the war-fever." The proto-Fascist artilleryman articulates these ideas most clearly: he sees the Martian attack as the chance for a flabby human race to redeem itself in violent struggle.

THE WARDEN

Type of work: Novel
Author: Anthony Trollope (1815-1882)
Type of plot: Domestic realism
Time of plot: Mid-nineteenth century
Locale: London and "Barchester," England
First published: 1855

The Warden, *the first of the Barchester novels, which concern British ecclesiastical life in the time of Queen Victoria, is a pleasant story, gently realistic in details, told in a leisurely manner. The plot is continued in* Barchester Towers.

The first in Trollope's series of novels about the provincial English clergy, *The Warden* enjoys the unique role of a pace setter; it is an indication of all that is to follow in plot, characterization, and theme. With Trollope we are always close to the simplicity and quiddity of actual life. The stories never tax our credulity; indeed they shower us with what Trollope designedly intended to be the *familiar.* His stories and people are within the possible experience of most of his readers, but his themes often challenge—with humor and subtlety—the moral and political assumptions of his time.

Behind Trollope's gossipy incursions into the domestic lives of the clergy lies a tough-minded purpose. In *The Warden,* for example, he is not only eavesdropping on the Grantlys but also relating a universal theme of great consequence, what Henry James described as "simply the history of an old man's conscience."

As the Reverend Septimus Harding grows steadily more uneasy at the idea of continuing to draw his high salary as warden at Hiram's Hospital, this "sweet and serious little old man" becomes an ethical giant who puts into the shadow the opportunistic Archdeacon, Dr. Grantly, and the legal establishment and parliament as well. He alone seems to grasp the significance of a moral principle; once he is determined to abide by it, he is invincible, for all his gentleness. Ironically, John Bold, whose "passion is the reform of all abuses," compromises his principles and withdraws his suit for love of Mr. Harding's daughter.

The cumulative effect of Mr. Harding's stand is to make him a far greater "Warden" than he was in the first place. Trollope has him lose Hiram's Hospital only to become a symbolic guardian of the English conscience.

WASHINGTON SQUARE

Type of work: Novel
Author: Henry James (1843-1916)
Type of plot: Psychological realism
Time of plot: About 1850
Locale: New York City
First published: 1881

The publication of Washington Square, *a psychological novella of great poignancy, marks the end of the first period of Henry James's work. Set in New York City about the middle of the nineteenth century, this lucid book explores the theme of a father's harshly authoritarian control of his daughter.*

Though one of Henry James's least complex and ambiguous novels, *Washington Square* is scarcely below the more complicated works in artistic quality. With characteristic skill, James explores the complex relationship between Dr. Sloper, disappointed because his plain and somewhat dull daughter cannot replace either his deceased wife or his lost son, and Catherine Sloper, whose essential goodness makes her one of James's most appealing heroines. Catherine, surviving and growing through the callous treatment by her father and her great disappointment in Morris Townsend, gradually develops a stoic strength and dignity which give her a tragic quality.

When we first encounter Catherine, she is torn between the extremes of her aunt's foolish romanticism and her father's hardheaded realism. In the course of the novel, she will move from one extreme to the other, but James does not present her growth as necessarily a victory of knowledge over naïveté. From the start, Dr. Sloper recognizes Morris' motives, but his handling of the situation borders on the sadistic. He neither tries to understand Catherine nor to consider her feelings or happiness. Rather, he devotes his attention to causing Morris finally to reveal his mercenary plans, thus making marriage impossible for his daughter. One wonders if marriage to Morris could have been worse than the lonely spinsterhood to which Catherine finally comes.

Catherine reveals her strength and pride in defying her father's demand that she renounce Townsend. Though, purged of her girlish romanticism, she undoubtedly knows already that she will never marry Morris, she nevertheless retains her autonomy by refusing on principle to submit to Dr. Sloper's demands. Unfortunately, however, neither the loss of romantic dreams of happiness nor the development of real inner strength has offered Catherine a fuller or richer life. At the end of the novel, we find her alone, facing an empty future.

THE WASPS

Type of work: Drama
Author: Aristophanes (c. 448-c. 385 B.C.)
Type of plot: Social satire
Time of plot: Fifth century B.C.
Locale: Athens
First presented: 422 B.C.

The Wasps *satirizes the abuses of the jury courts of Athens which, through the charging of admissions, provided the chief means of support for a large number of citizens. Racine imitated Aristophanes' play in* Les Plaideurs.

No doubt because the Athenians were by nature and cultivation a litigious and contentious people, they warmly received *The Wasps* at its Lenaean performance in 422. The Heliaea (civil court of Athens) required six thousand jurors chosen by lot, and four years before the production of this play, Aristophanes himself had been attacked in a lawsuit by the conservative demagogue Cleon, who the following year raised the daily salary for Heliasts. These facts might, then, help to explain the topical popularity of *The Wasps.* The Athenians would have agreed that Philocleon was well-suited to his name: like Cleon he is uncouth, belligerent, and vindictive; whereas his son Bdelycleon ("Disgust-for-Cleon") is urbane and civil, eager to distract his father from the waspish ways of the idle old men who sit on committees of the Heliaea.

The father-son conflict recalls that in *The Clouds,* although here the father and not the son has been seduced. The *agon* ("contest") is a special characteristic of Attic Old Comedy not only as a formal debate (see lines 526-724) but also as an underlying dynamic which tightens the intellectual tension of the drama. The father-son confrontation is a favorite topic especially in New Comedy and its close relative Roman Comedy. In this play Aristophanes creates in Philocleon one of the best comic figures in literature, for he is a marvelous complex of incongruity. Despite his age he is confoundingly agile, both in mind and body, constantly one step ahead of his son and Xanthias. He is boastful and boorish, but these are his manners, not his morals. A common man, he has been used by Cleon for mean purposes, and when he discovers this, he is genuinely shocked. On the other hand, Bdelycleon, despite his good sense, is for the most part merely the foil of the old man. Similarly, except for their ridiculous age and their wasp costumes there is comparatively little humor in the chorus of jurors. They lack the verve of Philocleon; they are truly bitter and hateful; they more than "love Cleon," they *are* Cleon.

WAVERLEY

Type of work: Novel
Author: Sir Walter Scott (1771-1832)
Type of plot: Historical romance
Time of plot: 1745
Locale: England and Scotland
First published 1814

In this historical romance treating Prince Charlie and the Scottish national cause, Scott attempted to pay tribute to his people by demonstrating their high degree of civilization. In the person of Fergus Mac Ivor we find not only intellect and sentiment, but also formal, courtly manners.

When *Waverley* appeared in 1814, it was immediately popular. One reason, of course, was the widespread conjecture about the mystery of the author, since Scott had published this first novel anonymously. Both in Scotland and in England literary individuals and laymen alike speculated as to its authorship.

Another reason for its extreme popularity was the fact that in *Waverley* Scott had literally created a new genre: the historical novel. Until its publication, Gothic novels were the vogue with all their paraphernalia of trap doors, vampires, ruined castles, and the like. Though their locales were often medieval, these novels were not accurate in historical setting or detail. *Waverley,* based on Scott's extensive reading of pamphlets, letters, diaries, personal interviews with survivors, and other material bearing on the Jacobite Rebellion of 1745, was a new literary form. This was fairly recent and valid history; the reading public felt close to the events, and so the recorded details of Edward Waverley's participation in the uprising were exciting and vivid. Scott sacrificed accuracy for picturesque effects, but he thought this justified because history for him was a dramatic process, the very evolution of a culture. He usually concentrated on history of the relatively recent past, particularly Scottish history.

One might think the regional dialects of Scotland would have proved a serious barrier to the English reading public, but quite the opposite was true. They loved the colorful Highland characters about whom they knew little and whose language was strange. If some remarked a glossary should have been included with *Waverley* for English readers, nevertheless they persevered and were so caught up with the romance and newness of the thing, it continued a sensation.

A third reason for its wide, enthusiastic reception was the fact that it was extravagantly romantic: escape literature at its best. The wild adventures of Waverley; the rugged glens of the Highlands with their inaccessible caves, foaming cataracts, somber forests; primitive bardic songs of the Northern tribes, as well as their striking dress; the beautiful if improbable heroines

Flora Mac Ivor and Rose Bradwardine; melodrama of battle and testing of gentlemen's honor; and, of course, "Bonnie Prince Charlie" the Pretender, who drew out the heroic in stout Highland hearts—all the uncritical, avid reader could wish for.

The fact that Scott wrote the novel "with almost unbelievable speed"— the last two volumes in a mere three weeks, prevented him from developing his characters or constructing a tightly knit or well-developed plot. He was a careless writer, and in spite of the merits of his style and dramatic presentation, one finds much that is faulty.

The hero, Edward Waverley, is passive and colorless. He is projected into the Jacobite cause with Fergus Mac Ivor's clan, not by conscious choice or intense sympathy for it, but by outside forces that thrust him forward. He extricates himself from the embroilment by contrived means. He is attracted to Fergus' sister Flora, mainly because of her beauty and the romantic setting in which she moves; but without soul-searching or much great passion, he settles, after several rebuffs from Flora, upon Rose Bradwardine, whom he had not seriously considered. Edward does not grow inwardly but changes according to external circumstances. Although Fergus is decisive, logical, and far more real, his actions are predictable; no one is surprised that his single-minded purpose leads to his death.

It is the Scots villagers, Mac Ivor's retainers and other humble people like Callum Beg, Widow Flockhart, and Farmer Williams, who come to life dramatically. Scott is at his best with these minor characters; their speech, their actions ring true. The reader wonders why he could not bring this validity to his upper-class heroes and heroines, who often conduct themselves woodenly and speak in stilted Latinate diction—even in moments of great passion.

The novel generally lacks descriptive detail, especially color words. Scott had great opportunity for this: for example, the Highland feast at Ian nan Chaistel's hall, the ball at Holyrood Castle, the battle at Preston. But of what must have been brilliant plaids, dirks and daggers in their ornamental sheaths, and gaily dressed bagpipers Scott says nothing. Prince Edward's court at Holyrood was an occasion for a glittering display of color in dress and setting, but the author merely speaks vaguely of its "liveliness and elegance" and states "the general effect was striking." And as for the military spectacle of Preston, Scott, intrigued with the action and emotion, cannot bring it to life before the reader's eyes. After Fergus cries "Forward, sons of Ivor or the Camerons will draw the first blood!" and they rush "on with a tremendous yell," Scott states laconically, "The rest is well known." Most of the battle action from this point on deals only with Colonel Gardiner's death. But considering the speed at which Scott dashed off his novels, he had no time to spend on small details of picturesque language and setting. Still this would have greatly enriched their texture.

The manner in which Waverley clears himself of charges of treason and desertion, inherits great wealth, and marries Rose is narrated by the author in long passages which reveal subterfuges, motives, and transactions that were not part of the novel's organic unity and about which the reader was not apprised. This type of *deus ex machina* procedure prohibits thematic coherence and is distracting to the intelligent reader.

It is easy today to see the novel's structural faults. But there was enough conflict between romance and reality to satisfy Scott's contemporary audience, sufficient history to render the work real to them. And his portrayal of Highland manners and customs was thorough. Herein lies *Waverley's* importance. It was the first of Scott's whole series drawn from these materials and so heralded a new genre for the eighteenth and nineteenth centuries.

Muriel B. Ingham

THE WAVES

Type of work: Novel
Author: Virginia Woolf (1882-1941)
Type of plot: Psychological realism
Time of plot: The present
Locale: England
First published: 1931

A major psychological novel, The Waves *presents a series of interlocking dramatic monologues in which six characters, all of them more or less androgynous types, reveal the hidden essence of being at successive stages of their lives. The action is a record of time passing as the six characters trace the course of their memories and sensations from childhood to old age and death.*

Virginia Woolf's *The Waves* is composed of soliloquies spoken by six different characters at different periods in their lives from childhood to old age. This series of soliloquies is not literally spoken aloud, however; in most cases the characters are verbalizing their thoughts and inner feelings. Often the narration is in the present tense, as a character explains what he is doing at that moment. Characters do not usually speak to one another, although at times they almost seem to communicate telepathically; each person is set apart, alone, although each knows and thinks about the others. The soliloquies are too well-ordered for random thought patterns and too sophisticated and artificial for actual speech; it is the atmosphere of a dreamworld. Each soliloquy is paralleled by the passing of a day from sunrise to sunset; descriptions of nature—of the sun, the sea, birds, and plants—precede each section, and serve to make implicit comparisons with the characters' speeches. The most dominant and highly metaphorical of these images of nature is that of the waves.

The characters have different qualities: Bernard is the leader and unifier; Jinny is an extrovert, Rhoda an introvert; Louis wants desperately to succeed; Neville is a poet; Susan loves the country life. But the quality of their speech is not differentiated, and it is perhaps more correct to say that the six characters are all parts of one being; or the six may all be aspects of the personality of Virginia Woolf herself, or of the human personality. In addition to these main characters, there is Percival, a schoolfellow of the other six who dies in India in his mid-twenties, and who never speaks directly in the novel, but appears as the others speak of him. He is a unifying element for the group, all of whom care deeply about him. He seems to have almost mythical powers over them as well, and his name is related to Parzival, the keeper of the Grail. They all look to him as their ideal and goal.

Woolf often uses Bernard to express ideas about the ambiguity of language, which is one of the book's major themes. A phrase-maker, Bernard comes to distrust words and believes in the experience which is inexpressible.

Words have always enabled Bernard to create order from chaos. But he comes to understand that words may not capture the reality of the experience at all, but only an image of it; thus he worries about the very process of telling the story. Actually, the "story" in *The Waves* is practically nonexistent. The crucial event is Bernard's renewal, as the wave of life's desires again rises in him; this reuniting with the cycle of life, death, and rebirth has been foreshadowed throughout the novel by the symbol of the waves. Thus, the shining ring that Bernard envisioned as a boy becomes an appropriate symbol for the oneness of art and life that Woolf has established by the end of the book.

THE WAY OF ALL FLESH

Type of work: Novel
Author: Samuel Butler (1835-1902)
Type of plot: Social criticism
Time of plot: Nineteeenth century
Locale: England
First published: 1903

Aimed at a type of parent-children relationship during the Victorian era that bred maladjusted, introverted children, this influential "education" novel depicts one son who broke the parental ties, thereby freeing himself to make his own way in life. Butler's partly autobiographical work is witty and cruelly satiric.

Samuel Butler wrote numerous essays and articles, and fifteen books, among them several travel books and five on science. Butler was frequently absorbed in theories of evolution for about twenty-five years after he read Darwin's *On the Origin of Species* in 1861-1862, an absorption strongly influencing the substance and style of *The Way of All Flesh*. That influence is not shown directly, however, and appears gradually in the philosophizing of Overton and Ernest. Butler began the novel in 1873, but interrupted its composition several times to do scientific writing and finally completed it in 1885. Butler used letters in the book actually written by his own mother and father to him (see Chapters VIII and XXV) as letters from Theobald and Christina to their son Ernest. The author refused to publish the novel so long as family members caustically satirized in it were living. His literary executor therefore arranged publication in 1903, although Butler's two sisters were still alive.

The letters mentioned above are among the countless bits of evidence in *The Way of All Flesh* which Butler wittily but relentlessly amasses through the narration of Edward Overton, friend of the Pontifex family, to persuade the reader that the "hero," Ernest, was indeed fortunate to survive, much less surmount his loving parents' Mid-Victorian Christian tutelage and his formal schooling. Ernest slowly and unevenly surmounts the narrow, stupid, and often cruel values imposed upon him. At last he dimly perceives what Butler thought man would instinctively remember had Victorianism not "educated" it out of him. Ernest learns mostly by hindsight in the wake of disastrous involvements such as those with Pryer and Ellen. But he also learns by a naïve and torturous sifting through the issues of fashionable intellectual controversy on religion and science. Butler gently satirizes Ernest's pursuit of "first causes" or other abstractions, and his fortunes take a decided change for the better when he gives up "abstractions" for the most part, sheds his alcoholic wife, and realizes that because he is a child of his own father and mother, he cannot be a good father himself. He therefore places his children with good, simple people who can love them and make them happy adults. Like Butler, Ernest then settles into bachelor quarters in London at about age thirty, where until his death he contentedly writes, paints, enjoys Handel's music, and reflects upon the folly of much that transpires in the world.

The circumstances of Ernest's life closely parallel those of Butler's life through the Cambridge period, and to a lesser extent following that period. Butler did not go to prison; instead he went to New Zealand where he raised sheep profitably from 1858-1864. Much critical discussion of the novel, however, centers on the author's personal life: Butler's fabled capacity for cruel parody of his well-meaning family, for instance. Walter Allen in *The English Novel* (1954) thinks Butler tips the scales unfairly against Theobald and Christina, thereby alienating the reader. Other critics have said of Butler, as Overton says of Ernest in contrasting him to Othello: "he hates not wisely but too well."

More productive critical comment might be made concerning the "coincidence" of Ernest's encountering John, the old family coachman, and learning that John and Ellen are legal man and wife, a fact which most happily frees Ernest from a dreadful marriage. Or, the wonderful ability of Overton to invest Ernest's inheritance from his Aunt Alethea and to increase it five times over so that Ernest may live his comfortable life.

Many critics interpret the autobiographical dimension in *The Way of All Flesh* as a literary precedent for "parent-son" and self-discovery novels such as *Of Human Bondage, Sons and Lovers,* or *A Portrait of the Artist as a Young Man.* Other perspectives are possible, however, particularly for readers long familiar with Freudian and post-Freudian psychological approaches to the novel. Readers of Norman Mailer's autobiographical works or Roth's *Portnoy's Complaint* may view Butler's work as more than either personal diatribe or over-reaction to the excesses of Victorianism. Novelists now thread through mazes of neuroses, attempt to expose the origins of neurotic and self-destructive behavior such as that practiced by Ernest, and often they propose therapeutic solutions to the protagonists' problems. However imperfectly Butler integrated the autobiographical or personal and the theories which underlie his novel, he was doubtless trying to show the causes of Ernest's stunted personality and his path to relative self-respect and happiness.

The narrative of the novel, slow and tedious perhaps to a reader of the 1970's, moves as it does because only through thirty years of painful experience could Ernest achieve some intellectual objectivity and self-knowledge. He learned that he must totally reject his self-centered parents' pious domination to become his own person. He learns (expressed by Overton) that virtue springs from man's experience concerning his own well-being—this is the "least fallible thing we have." When meditating in prison Ernest decides that a true Christian is he who takes the "highest and most self-respecting view of his own welfare which is in his power to conceive, and adheres to it in spite of conventionality. . . . " But circumstances change, as Overton informs the reader, and the self is always changing: life is nothing but the "process of accommodation," and a life will be successful or not according to the individual's power of accommodation. As narrator, Overton is doubtless Butler's alter ego, and his detached view of Ernest reveals that "smug hedonism" is more accurately seen as less than a perfect resolution: Ernest is somewhat withdrawn, lonely, bearing ineradicable marks of his heredity and environment.

Butler explores the themes of heredity and environment plurally through telling the histories of four generations of Pontifexes: only Ernest's greatgrandparents led happy, instinctive lives. The title of the novel gives a tagsummary of Butler's judgment: this is the way of all flesh—to learn if at all, by rejecting convention and dogma, and to live by self-direction.

Mary H. Hayden

THE WAY OF THE WORLD

Type of work: Drama
Author: William Congreve (1670-1729)
Type of plot: Comedy of manners
Time of plot: Seventeenth century
Locale: London
First presented: 1700

A true Restoration comedy of manners, The Way of the World *is elegant, sly, and witty. In this classic battle of the sexes, Congreve's Mirabell and Millamant are superbly matched.*

Although born in England, William Congreve was reared and educated in Ireland, thus joining the procession of great Irish comic writers which includes Sheridan and Goldsmith, Swift, and Wilde and Shaw. Returning to England as a young man, Congreve studied at law briefly, wrote a novel, and joined with Dryden in a translation of Juvenal. His literary rise was rapid, and his first comedies, *The Old Bachelor* and *Love for Love* were highly successful. His sole tragedy, *The Mourning Bride,* acclaimed by Dr. Johnson a generation later, was widely applauded. But *The Way of the World,* now considered the masterpiece of all Restoration comedies, was coolly received. Congreve became involved in a notorious controversy over the morality of the stage, being specifically attacked in Jeremy Collier's famous publication, *A Short View of the Immorality and Profaneness of the English Stage.* He defended strenuously his plays from what he felt was misrepresentation. Congreve held honorary posts under King William and Queen Anne, and was associated with Vanbrugh in the direction of the Queen's Theatre in Haymarket. He was one of the most admired literary figures of the Age of Anne; the Duchess of Marlborough was his patron, and Pope, Gay, Swift, Steele, and Voltaire were his friends. When Congreve died in 1729, he was buried with much pomp and ceremony in Westminster Abbey.

Restoration comedy was critical comedy, bringing "the sword of common sense" to bear upon the extravagances of the period. Congreve is perhaps as close to Molière as the English theater has ever come; his plays brought an ironic scrutiny to the affectations of his age, with a style and perfection of phrase that still dazzles audiences. He has been called the wittiest man who ever wrote the English language in the theater; certainly, his characters speak some of the wittiest dialogue. Without question, *The Way of the World* introduced a new standard of wit and polish to the theater. In Millamant, Congreve created one of the great characters of English drama, a comic heroine at once lovable and laughable. The poetry of the courtly life of the Restoration is summed up in the duet between those two brilliant lovers, Mirabell and Millamant.

The interest of *The Way of the World* is carried forward by the witty speeches of the characters rather than by dramatic reversals. The play is all of one piece, a world of wit and pleasure inhabited only by persons of quality and "deformed neither by realism nor by farce." The plot is confusing, but almost irrelevant, and the situations exist really only for the conversation. Although Congreve seemed almost above such concerns as careful plotting, he was surprisingly artful in some of his stage effects. By delaying the entrance of Millamant until the second act, he arouses intense anticipation in the audience. And the fifth act, crowded as it is with activity, flows with continual surprises.

Some critics have held that *The Way of the World* is marred by the artificial contrivances of the plot, but most audiences pay no attention to the complications, relishing instead the characters and dialogue. The design of the play was to ridicule affected, or false, wit. Possibly, the play's original lukewarm reception was because it came too close to the faults of the courtly audience to be wholly agreeable to them. The dialogue is, also, closely woven, and the repartee demands such close attention that it might have exhausted its listeners. *The Way of the World* now is the most frequently revived and enjoyed of all of the Restoration comedies.

Apart from the presentation of incidental wit, Restoration comedy had two main interests: the behavior of polite society and of pretenders to polite society, and some aspects of sexual relationships. The wit varied from a hard, metallic kind that seemed to exist for its own sake, without any relation to anything, to subtle satire. Occasionally, even Congreve falls into a pattern of too easy antitheses, monotonously repeated until the sting of surprise is lost. But there is feeling in *The Way of the World*, particularly in the battle of the sexes. Congreve could not view love merely as a gratification of lust, as some of the Restoration playwrights seemed to think of it. His wit is never as blunt or as ruthless as that of Wycherley. The twentieth century does not consider Restoration comedy as outspoken as previous generations did; rather, the comedy seems primarily to consist of titillation, to suggest more than it delivers. The best of the Restoration playwrights, such as Congreve, did not rely entirely on titillation to get their laughs.

The characters in *The Way of the World* are the best drawn in any Restoration comedy—or perhaps *any* play of the period, comic or tragic. Besides Mirabell and Millamant, the two most perfect lovers in any comedy, not excepting Shakespeare's Beatrice and Benedick, the play boasts a parade of such personalities as Foible, Witwoud, and Petulant, and particularly Lady Wishfort, who approaches the tragic in her desperate attempt to preserve her youth. No character in the play, not even Fainall, fails to surprise the audience with witty observations. In *The Way of the World*, Congreve penetrated deeper than any of his contemporaries into the mysteries of human nature; he possessed more feeling for the individual, and was subtler in his treatment of human idiosyncracies.

Although sexual roles are changing in the second half of the twentieth century, *The Way of the World* reflects attitudes that prevailed for centuries: above all, the play suggests, the most fascinating aspect of sexual relations is that of the chase. The pursuit, usually of the male for the female, although sometimes reversed, dominates Restoration comedy, and is both glorified and satirized in *The Way of the World*. The lovely and intelligent Millamant herself expresses her belief in the necessity for a period devoted to such pursuit if a woman is to attract and keep her lover. By playing hard to get, a woman proves her eventual worth. Congreve took these conventional attitudes and fabricated his comedy from them, weaving a complicated and fascinating satire that continues to delight after two centuries.

Bruce D. Reeves

THE WEAVERS

Type of work: Drama
Author: Gerhart Hauptmann (1862-1946)
Type of plot: Social criticism
Time of plot: The 1840's
Locale: Germany
First presented: 1892

Hauptmann's most admired play, The Weavers *is a naturalistic study of type-characters caught in irresistible forces of the social and industrial system under which they live. The author gives no answer to the problems of industrialization; rather, he shows us people who react in the only way they can when misery becomes too oppressive.*

Gerhart Hauptmann was the son of a prosperous innkeeper in Silesia where the weaver riots took place eighteen years before his birth. The Silesian dialect he uses in *The Weavers* and some of his other works is the language of his childhood. Following his parents' wishes, he attempted the study of science and agriculture. He then studied art and sculpture with little success, finally finding his medium in writing poetry and fiction. His association with politically active, idealistic circles served as an inspiration for his writing of *The Weavers,* whose story was familiar to him from his grandfather's tales. The work was soon acclaimed as the first German socialist drama. The controversy that immediately surrounded the work contributed a great deal to its becoming widely known. On the grounds that the nature and language of the drama were inflammatory, public performances were repeatedly banned by the police. The ban was eventually removed by court order, the controversy finally reaching the German Parliament.

The style of the drama is naturalistic, presenting starkly realistic scenes from the lives of destitute Silesian weavers. Since the work introduces new characters in every scene, and lacks a definite unity of plot, its very form as drama was questioned. The structure is in fact epic, rather than dramatic. While appearing objective, the author obviously selected aspects that created sympathy for the plight of the weavers, and, by extension, the plight of all poor and exploited people.

This was the era of Social Darwinism, and the treatment of subjects repugnant to society was in literary vogue, as was also the naturalistic style through the influence of Tolstoy, Dostoevski, Ibsen, Zola, and Flaubert. With *The Weavers,* based on a true incident, Hauptmann pioneered naturalistic drama in Germany. While his later subjects ranged from satire on society through middle-class personal conflicts to reworking themes of Greek tragedy, he is still best known for his naturalistic works, particularly for *The Weavers.*

THE WEB AND THE ROCK

Type of work: Novel
Author: Thomas Wolfe (1900-1938)
Type of plot: Impressionistic realism
Time of plot: 1900-1928
Locale: North Carolina, New York, Europe
First published: 1939

This partly autobiographical "education" novel, structurally uneven but with scenes of great emotional intensity, is marked by contrasts of innocence with sophistication, the mountain folk of North Carolina with the cosmopolitan smart set of Manhattan, the freedoms of America with the insidious beginnings of National Socialism in Germany. Wolfe's story is continued in You Can't Go Home Again.

In *The Story of a Novel* (1936), Wolfe responded to critics' complaints that he could write only about his own life and that his Scribners editor, Maxwell Perkins, was responsible for organizing the material of his first two novels, *Look Homeward, Angel* (1929) and *Of Time and the River* (1935). He promised to write in a more "objective," disciplined style; and to prove that he could, without assistance, structure his sprawling fiction, he severed his professional association with Perkins. In July 1938, two months before he died following a brain operation, Wolfe submitted to his new editor, Edward C. Ashwell, the manuscript from which his last two novels, *The Web and the Rock* and *You Can't Go Home Again,* were assembled. Although somewhat more objective, more finely controlled, than his earlier fiction, the novels continue the supreme subject of all his work: the story of his own life reshaped into myth.

George Webber, described as monkeylike with long arms and an awkward, ambling gait, scarcely resembles the tall, hawklike Eugene Gant of *Look Homeward, Angel.* Yet he is surely another psychological portrait of Wolfe, the tormented artist among Philistines. In the first part of *The Web and the Rock,* the author attempts to provide for his hero a new family and social background. But the Joyners, despite their vitality, are mere copies of the Pentlands; Lybia Hill resembles Altamont; and the moody, romantic Webber recalls the young Eugene. Some of the minor characters, notably the baseball hero Nebraska Crane and Aunt Maw, are brilliantly drawn. And the chapter "The Child by Tiger," originally published as a short story, reveals Wolfe's great power to create tragic myth. Above all, the strength of the first part of the book rests upon the author's heroic vision of the townspeople and the mountain folk of North Carolina—a stock of enterprising, stubborn, passionately independent souls. They represent the mysterious "web" of the earth. Like Webber, a child of the mountain folk, they are tied by threads of destiny not only to the land but also to the seasons, the workings of time.

As an artist, Webber understands intuitively the heart of things, the patterns of life and dreams.

In roughly the second half of the novel, Wolfe contrasts the "web" of the earth with the "rock" of the city of New York. At this point in his writing, he abandons, for the most part, his scheme of objectivity and deals with the experiences of his own life. Webber meets and falls in love with Esther Jack (the same Esther who first appears to Eugene Gant in the "Faust and Helen" chapter of *Of Time and the River*)—in real life the stage designer and artist Aline Bernstein. With remarkable frankness Wolfe describes the tragic course of the affair between these markedly different personalities: the egotistic, brilliant, despotic provincial genius and his mistress, a sophisticated, sensitive, upper-middle class Jewish wife and mother. As a realist Wolfe is at his best detailing scenes of lovemaking and eating, of tempestuous quarrels and passionate reconciliations. Throughout the extended part of the book dealing with the love affair—for all its excesses and absurdities—Wolfe is able to touch the reader: George and Esther truly care about each other. They try desperately to make their fragile relationship endure.

Yet the theme of the novel is the fragility of all dreams. The "rock" of New York, which George once loved as well as feared, begins to crumble in this novel; it will betray its fullest stresses in *You Can't Go Home Again*. The city, founded upon greed and selfish power, has no soul. To escape from his own sense of ruin, George visits pre-Nazi Germany, already ripe for the advent of a Hitler. George hopes to recapture, among the drunken revelers at a Munich Oktoberfest, the sense of joy of his own manhood. But he becomes violent, a savage fighting the beer hall swaggerers, and is terribly beaten. By the end of the novel, he wishes to return to America so that he might establish his dreams once again upon a foundation that will endure: upon the "web" of his failing sense of the earth, and upon the "rock" of an already insecure civilization. In the last chapter, "The Looking Glass," Webber comes to understand the futility of these dreams.

WESTWARD HO!

Type of work: Novel
Author: Charles Kingsley (1819-1875)
Type of plot: Historical romance
Time of plot: Sixteenth century
Locale: England and South America
First published: 1855

Westward Ho! *includes among its large number of characters the redoubtable names Sir Francis Drake, Sir Walter Raleigh, and Sir Richard Grenvile in a romantic story of great sea battles, duels of honor, romantic rescues, and deeds of horror in the Spanish Inquisition.*

The son of an Anglican clergyman, Charles Kingsley himself became a clergyman in 1842 upon completion of his studies at Cambridge. He early became involved in the Christian Socialism movement and for many years was considered an extreme radical. His early novels reflect his keen interest in reform, but in his later years this interest waned. His controversy with John Henry Newman resulted in the latter's famous *Apologia pro vita sua* (1864). A controversial figure in his day, it is primarily for his novels that Kingsley is now remembered.

Westward Ho! is a novel told at many levels. On the surface it is an adventure story. It is set in the great Age of Exploration and of Elizabeth following the voyages of Columbus. The novel's characters are thus contemporaries of such romantic figures as Sir Francis Drake and Sir Walter Raleigh, who both appear occasionally. The story has a fully conceived plot —which takes place largely in the exotic Caribbean—involving two highly romantic motifs—a lady in the hands of the enemy and a search for gold. Yet *Westward Ho!* is not merely an ordinary adventure story. It is also a naturalistic moral fable dramatizing the corrupting influences of bigotry, nationalism, and greed.

By the standards of an ecumenical age, Kingsley was decidedly unfair to Spain and to the Roman Catholic Church. *Westward Ho!* takes as fact the Black Legend of unmitigated Spanish cruelty toward the Indians. The many Jesuits mentioned in the book are depicted as scheming plotters and their heroism both in England and in the New World is entirely overlooked. The corrupt, ambitious Catholic bishop captured at New Granada is more typical of the Italian Renaissance than of the Spanish Counter-Reformation. (Considering, however, that Kingsley was himself an Anglican minister, he was not especially kind to the English clergy. The sincere, but bumbling, John Brimblecombe is inspiring only by comparison with his Catholic counterparts.)

Still Kingsley's image of the Spaniards and Jesuits reflected what Englishmen in general—even scholars—thought about them in 1855. Few English scholars were critical of the Black Legend, and few Protestants anywhere had any generous words for the Jesuits. *Westward Ho!* is not, in the context of its time and place, an anti-Spanish or anti-Catholic tract. Kingsley's Spaniards are cruel and the Jesuits scheming because nineteenth century English readers expected them to be. The balancing aspect of the novel can be seen in the lack of any real moral superiority of the English adventurers to the Spanish. The English, from whose viewpoint the story is told and with whom the readers can be expected to identify, share many of the enemy's faults. The English are blinded by greed in their search for gold, and act inhumanly in executing the Spanish dignitaries at New Granada. Fittingly, the English and the Spanish see one another as serving the Devil.

The moral dimension of the novel is delineated by an ironic twist in the motif to the lady-in-the-hands-of-the-enemy. The lady, Rose Salterne, is held by the Spanish, yet there is real love between her and the Spanish governor, Don Guzman, and, therefore, she does not appreciate the efforts of the English adventurers to rescue her. The possibility of genuine love between Rose and Don Guzman is entirely overlooked by the adventurers, who are themselves enamored of her.

The final illustration of Kingsley's moral is in the fate of the principal character, Amyas Leigh. Back from the Caribbean, having lost both his brother and the lady he sought to rescue, he joins the battle against the Spanish Armada in order to revenge himself on Spain and Don Guzman. But Don Guzman is killed and Amyas is blinded by the same storm. At first angry at being denied his vengeance, Amyas comes to realize that he never had any right to it, and that Don Guzman had really loved Rose. But his spite still burns and he recoils from his mother's suggestion that he marry Ayacanora. The girl who has shared his adventure and whose father had been his friend cannot be forgiven for having a Spanish mother. Ironically, in his blindness, his eyes are opened to the folly of his hatred for an entire nation.

The naturalistic level of *Westward Ho!* is manifested in its illustrations of a danger as serious as that posed by the Spanish enemy but far more prosaic. This danger is malnutrition, often ignored by adventure writers, but a grave concern to the actual explorers of the age. The dread disease, scurvy, caused by a lack of fresh fruit, plays a significant role in the novel.

Also aptly realistic are the portraits of the adventurers themselves. Three men, especially, stand out. Amyas Leigh, the principal character, is a giant who needs an outlet for his energy. Frank Leigh, a quiet scholar, is ill-suited for the Western adventure but drawn to it by his misdirected love for Rose. Salvation Yeo is a man with an explorer's love for the unknown, able to live anywhere, but without firm principles. Moved by love for God, country, adventure, women, gold, and blood, these three and their crewmen challenge the entrenched Spanish power in the New World, and the diseases that go with such a challenge. Conflicts of motives often lead to collisions between men, as when Amyas upbraids two of his officers for wanting to settle among the Indians and forego the religious and patriotic goals that were supposed to be their principal motivation. The search for gold ends, as so many such searches actually did, with bitter disappointment.

The composition of *Westward Ho!* is uneven in many respects and the nationalistic and religious biases of its author, as noted above, will limit its appeal to twentieth century readers. Yet when understood in the context of its own time, the novel is an appealing and powerful story.

Charles Johnson Taggart

WHAT EVERY WOMAN KNOWS

Type of work: Drama
Author: James M. Barrie (1860-1937)
Type of plot: Social satire
Time of plot: Early twentieth century
Locale: Scotland and England
First presented: 1908

In one of his most realistic plays, Barrie develops the familiar theme that behind every man there is a woman who makes him either a success or a failure. What Every Woman Knows *is marked by the writer's customary sly humor and irony.*

Early in James Barrie's play *What Every Woman Knows,* just after the "agreement" has been signed whereby John Shand will get £300 from the Wylie family for his education providing he is willing to marry their spinster sister Maggie in five years, the Scotsmen discuss their potential brother-and-son-in-law. They agree that he is canny, though no match for Maggie—a fact best kept from him at this time.

This idea forms the basis of the play and can be phrased as a dramatic question: can an intelligent, but plain woman manipulate her husband into both a successful political career and a satisfying marriage—without letting him know he is being so manipulated? Maggie Shand is convinced that her husband is by nature incapable of succeeding at anything on his own. She is also convinced that his over-serious pride and exaggerated sense of manhood cannot tolerate the idea that he needs help—least of all from his wife.

For most of the play Maggie's machinations succeed beautifully and the primary irony of the play comes from the continuing contrast between John Shand's vision of himself and the audience's awareness of the real basis for his success. But Maggie knows that their marriage is, to John, essentially a business arrangement between two people who admire and respect each other, but who are not in love. Because she thinks herself "plain" and lacking "charm," she fears that John, in spite of his passionless nature, will become infatuated with another woman and leave her, ruining both of them. When Lady Sybil Tenterden, a lovely, charming aristocrat, enters the picture, Maggie's talents are put to their supreme test.

Although John Shand's blindness and insensitivity toward Maggie show him unworthy of such devotion, he is, nevertheless, probably worth saving. John is a decent man with energy, drive, and intelligence; all he lacks is imagination and a sense of humor. The intensity of his ambition is proven by the lengths to which he will go for an education, but his methods are honest and he is never ruthless; he keeps his bargain with Maggie, even after she offers him freedom, although he does not love her and considers her a political liability. His career is at least partly motivated by a desire to serve the public, although the particulars of his political beliefs are unclear (except for his "liberal" views on the "Women Problem"). In his dealings with Maggie, John is always honest, never feigns unfelt affection, and feels extremely guilty about the affair with Sybil. And, finally, he is sincerely willing to forego his political ambitions in the name of love, although he would rather not do so.

But, however intelligent John may be, he is no match for Maggie. She is one of the most vital and fascinating females of the modern stage and is, perhaps, Barrie's finest characterization. Each act of the play ends with a victory for her, even the third when she seems to be magnanimously giving John up to Sybil. Her intelligence and energy are obvious from the beginning of the play; her complexity and subtle deviousness take a bit longer to appreciate. She is disarming in her honesty, but hedges when strategy requires —such as shaving a year from her age when talking to John.

Perhaps the most interesting aspect of her personality is the contrast between her "real" self and the role she assumes in public. In part this role is based on her notions about the proper—no, *necessary*—role of the wife in Edwardian society as well as her reading of John's emotional needs. But, for all of her confidence regarding her own abilities, she feels deeply insecure about herself; her plain face and figure, her absence of formal education, and her lack of experience in mannered society have made her feel socially inadequate; it is her only misperception. Consequently, she demeans herself at every available opportunity. Thus, the play is not only about the education of a single, unimaginative male, but also about that of a sensitive, dedicated but self-depreciating female.

On the level of simple strategy, even the threat of Sybil Tenterden is fairly easily disposed of. Maggie simply leaves John and Sybil alone together long enough for them to grow tired of each other. That tactic succeeds, but her second design, to keep John ignorant of her intrigues, fails because of the intervention of the play's other "knowing" female, the Comtesse de la Brière. The Comtesse, seeing Maggie's role in John's career, is determined to make it known to the insensitive husband. She sneaks Maggie's rewritten version of John's oration to Charles Venables, thus making public Mrs. Shand's contribution to the speech making and then, to complete the revelation, the Comtesse reads Maggie's confessional letter aloud to the group.

It is fortunate that she does so, because otherwise John would have gone on heedlessly until he met the next Sybil. But, when Shand finds out the truth, Maggie is surprised to learn he can bear it—with a little help from his wife.

Maggie: Every man who is high up loves to think that he has done it all himself; and the wife smiles, and lets it go at that. It's our only joke. Every woman knows that. . . . Oh John, if only you could laugh at me.

John: I can't laugh, Maggie.

But, after a few moments, he manages to and, in Barrie's words, "he is saved." And so is their marriage, his career, and Maggie's self-respect.

Abandoning his usual whimsy and fantasy, Barrie has written a social comedy that deftly and provocatively explores the relationships between men and women in the modern world with a depth and seriousness that goes much beyond the bulk of his always entertaining, usually successful, but not infrequently trivial plays. In a later time a Maggie Shand might turn her energies directly into politics and so realize her own potential for herself, but in Edwardian England the only possibility was to be the woman behind the man. That was the role that she understood, accepted, and played to perfection.

Keith Neilson

WHAT MAISIE KNEW

Type of work: Novel
Author: Henry James (1843-1916)
Type of plot: Social morality
Time of plot: 1890's
Locale: London, Folkestone, Boulogne
First published: 1897

This novel, one of the greatest of James's middle period, is the story of the growing moral and intellectual perception of the neglected daughter of divorced and irresponsible parents. The moral core of What Maisie Knew *is the child's incorruptible innocence.*

Henry James is credited with freeing fiction from a "moral" purpose. His influential theories on point of view and scenic power educated succeeding generations of writers to the formal capacities of the novel. However, the ultimate purpose of his dismissal of a simple-minded didacticism from fiction was not the eradication of moral vision as such. On the contrary, as his "technique" grew more subtle, the result was an increasingly profound exploration of human values and motives. He was reluctant to judge, which was probably the outstanding naturalist trait in his fiction, but he nevertheless served an ethical muse by demonstrating and revealing the moral realities of life.

What Maisie Knew has often been singled out as a neglected masterpiece; neither "early" nor "late" James, it is credited with combining the "story-telling virtues" of the earlier novels with the "psychological complexity" of the later. The truth is that its central position in James's canon invests it with almost more weight than it can bear. As the psychological intensity grows, the plot is contorted to keep up. Maisie's parents divorce, remarry, and *their* new spouses become lovers and finally surrogate parents to Maisie. It is diabolically neat, but almost farcical. And farce is not what James wants as a background for his moral and psychological development of Maisie.

The point is that Maisie herself is not always a convincing protagonist, especially as a vehicle for the novel's intricate, and often tortured, shifts in point of view: " . . . if he (Sir Claude) had an idea at the back of his head she had also one in a recess as deep, and for a time, while they sat together, there was an extraordinary mute passage between her vision of this vision of his, his vision of her vision, and her vision of his vision of her vision." Unlike Mrs. Wix, who never loses her "wonder" over what Maisie knew, the reader sometimes doubts that James was sure what she knew. He could, of course, experiment very freely with her capacity to know: she is only a child and therefore has an openended mind. But her child's identity is never adequately established. It is revealing that we never have a clear idea of her exact age. Lewis Carroll's Alice is a real child in an imaginary world; James's Maisie is an imaginary child in a moral jungle.

WHEN THE MOUNTAIN FELL

Type of work: Novel
Author: Charles-Ferdinand Ramuz (1878-1947)
Type of plot: Regional romance
Time of plot: Eighteenth century
Locale: Switzerland
First published: 1935

In When the Mountain Fell (*French title,* Derborence). *Ramuz takes as his subject a real force of nature and sets it against the smallness and inadequacy of men in a setting that is majestic and awe-inspiring enough to show how intensely the people of Aire felt dread at the time of the great avalanche.*

After an early attempt to learn the writer's craft in Paris, C. F. Ramuz returned to his native Swiss village in the canton of Vaud, near Lausanne. He spent the rest of his life among his own people, developing a provincial style that sets him apart as one of the very few Swiss writers with an international reputation.

While still a student, Ramuz had visions of being a painter. There is a preponderance of visual appeal in his work, emanating from a deep-seated love of nature and the artistic ability to represent it in words. His many novels and stories are all about the harsh life of the peasants. He is constantly concerned with the most elementary problems that confront man: What is man? What are his essential needs? Where is there room for love in the modern world? Where is there room for God? Inherently religious, he subscribed to no faith. His work often makes use of legendary material, and sometimes assumes the proportions of myth.

When the Mountain Fell displays all of these qualities; it is a dramatic, essentially poetic story that is a classic of man's endurance and courage. Ramuz is able to make us participate in the delight of a man reborn to life, able once again to see, to smell, to breathe, to feel himself alive. Antoine and his devoted wife Thérèse are, in Ramuz's mythology, archetypal peasants living in harmony with nature. In spite of the apparent harshness of nature, Ramuz's peasants triumph by learning to survive within the limits of the life that nature offers them. In this respect, they attain qualities of permanence and universality that permit them to transcend the geographical confines of the story. They could be any peasants, anywhere, any time.

Nature is accurately observed, providing the material from which Ramuz's characteristic effects are achieved. But it is the atmosphere that counts most, the infusion of feeling, the symbolic weight. Nature provides a setting of lyric beauty, of homely charm, of sinister brooding force, a backdrop for the human action; but nature is, at the same time, more than a backdrop. There is an interrelation between man and nature similar to the Wordsworthian communion.

WHEN WE DEAD AWAKEN

Type of work: Drama
Author: Henrik Ibsen (1828-1906)
Type of plot: Psychological symbolism
Time of plot: Nineteenth century
Locale: A coastal town of Norway
First presented: 1900; published 1899

Ibsen's last production, When We Dead Awaken *is a play rich in symbolic meaning in which the dramatist expresses a deeply felt message which could be clothed only in poetically suggestive language.*

When Arnold Rubek, the aged sculptor hero of Ibsen's last work, *When We Dead Awaken,* describes the three stages of his masterpiece "Resurrection Day," he is actually presenting a thinly disguised outline of Ibsen's mature playwrighting career. After the early apprentice works came the idealized, poetic plays (*Brand,* 1866; *Peer Gynt,* 1867), then the great social and psychological plays of his middle period, from *The Pillars of Society* (1877) through *Hedda Gabler* (1890), and finally the late symbolic and highly personal —even autobiographical—dramas, beginning with *The Master Builder* (1892) and ending with *When We Dead Awaken.*

Two kinds of characters dominate the plays of this final phase: the aging but powerful artist, who, having been driven by his obsessive ambition to the top of his profession, finds that he has paid too high a spiritual price, and the mysterious female out of his past who, acting as a kind of Nemesis figure, forces the hero to recognize and come to terms with his past "sin," even though it destroys him. And, although it may lack some of the dramatic intensity of *The Master Builder* or *John Gabriel Borkman* (1896), *When We Dead Awaken* is the most complete and final exploration of this process, and so it stands as Ibsen's final statement on the artist's relation to society and, more importantly, to his own soul.

Having achieved great personal success with his "masterpiece," yet feeling unaccountably uneasy about it, Rubek attempts to satisfy his needs by taking a young wife and living in moderately luxurious indolence, satisfying his artistic and financial needs by turning out satirical portrait busts. But he grows tired of Maia, and the ironical pleasure of making fun of his clients while taking their money wears off. So he "goes home" to try and find out what it is that bothers him.

When he meets Irene, she reminds him of their life together many years before when, as an innocent young girl, she had modelled for the first version of "Resurrection Day." On the realistic level, Irene simply wants revenge on the man who cast her off and thereby turned her to a life of promiscuity, prostitution, and, finally, insanity. But this is not a realistic play and Irene's function is to probe Rubek's soul, not end his life. As he tells her about the evolution of the statue, Irene toys with her knife, but she declines to use it when Rubek confesses his own anguish and sense of failure. "I suddenly realized you are already dead," she tells him, " . . . dead for years."

Rubek's crime in rejecting Irene's love in order to "create the one great work of my life" was the major reason for his failure, not only as a human being, but also as an artist. By withholding his emotions from her, he stifled them, and, ironically, dissipated his own talent in the process. Without the knowledge and experience of love, Rubek was unable to respond to man's nobler aspects, and so his works could, at best, be inhuman, merely satirical portraits. When Irene understands the reason for his depression and sense of failure, her desire for revenge changes to a feeling of pity and rekindled love. And, although Rubek cannot fully understand what is happening to him, his feelings for her are awakened; he senses that his own vindication—salvation, perhaps—lies in her.

The Irene-Rubek affair is juxtaposed against that of Rubek's wife, Maia, and the bear hunter, Ulfheim. The young couple represents youth, vigor, and sensual experience of all kinds—eating, drinking, sex, physicality, and a joyous relationship to the immediate, natural environment. Rubek and Irene, on the other hand, stand for age, wisdom, and spiritual realization.

When We Dead Awaken ends on a note of reconciliation. Although he spurned her love in his youth, Rubek is ready to accept it in age. He and Irene go to seek a higher reality in the frozen mountains than Maia and Ulfheim will find in the lush valley. The living "dead" can "awaken" only into a spiritual reality beyond death, and that, Ibsen suggests at the play's conclusion, is exactly what happens to Irene and Rubek as they are swept up in an avalanche. With Maia's voice echoing "I am free as a bird" in the background, the nun in black, apparently a symbol for Irene's tainted past, emerges and blesses the couple with the sign of the cross and a "pax vobiscum!"

WHERE ANGELS FEAR TO TREAD

Type of work: Novel
Author: E. M. Forster (1879-1970)
Type of plot: Social criticism
Time of plot: Early twentieth century
Locale: England and Italy
First published: 1905

In this novel, wryly amusing but serious in its satire of moral conventions, Forster is concerned with the gulf that is normally found between the Northern temperament of an overcivilized Englishwoman and the natural impulses of the South, which are personified in the Italian whom she marries.

Who are the "angels" and where do they "fear to tread" in Forster's novel? The "angels" are the English connected with Sawston, who with their Victorian ideas assume the world to be a rational, predictable, and controllable place. They are "angels," then, not in the sense that they are sinless, but rather in that they are arrogantly innocent about the nature of reality; therefore, they fear to step into a world of chance and passion, represented in the novel by Italy. Yet ironically and unfortunately for them, they must enter into that actuality in order to defend their assumptions, on which Forster implies England rests. The ensuing drama forms the dialectic center of the novel.

The Sawston world loses the argument to Italy, a foregone conclusion once it agrees to hold the debate in Monteriano. Chance, never a part of the British master plan, is dominant there, so that Lilia Herriton's death in childbirth and that of her son in a carriage accident, major turning points in the plot, undercut English confidence and expose English incompleteness. The unpredictability of nature together with the unknown experience of passion, found in Gino Carella, finally force the invaders from the field.

Still, if they leave confounded by Italy, they—Philip Herriton and Caroline Abbott at any rate—also depart with a new sense of tentativeness so necessary to any mature idea of reality. The narrator says of Philip, "Life was greater than he had supposed, but was even less complete. He had seen the need for strenuous work and righteousness. And now he saw what a very little way those things would go." If Harriet Herriton remains unconverted, two of the "angels," at least, have fallen into the actual world, where if they are less secure, they are also more alive.

THE WHITE COMPANY

Type of work: Novel
Author: Arthur Conan Doyle (1859-1930)
Type of plot: Historical romance
Time of plot: Fourteenth century
Locale: England, France, Spain
First published: 1891

The White Company, for many years a favorite with young readers, is a romance of exciting adventures near the end of the age of chivalry. From its pages we can get accurate pictures of the age of Edward III as well as some insight into the interminable and fruitless wars with France.

Sir Arthur Conan Doyle called *The White Company* "the most complete, satisfying and ambitious thing I have ever done." These are strange words from an author famous for the creation of Sherlock Holmes, one of the most popular figures in the annals of English literature. Written in the period before Doyle began work on his famous detective stories, *The White Company* is now largely forgotten. But the novel was highly popular in its time and established the author's reputation as a serious writer. It appealed to Doyle's audience because it recalled the invigorating age of chivalry to a people who longed to escape the dullness and stuffiness of the industrial age. Doyle expressed the aspirations of his age more thoroughly than any writer of his time—an age that was thirsting for action and mystery or anything exciting that would temporarily release it from the stifling air of respectability. And no one, except perhaps Dumas, could write more stirring scenes of action.

The charm of *The White Company* lies in its romantic plot. The English nobles are all valiant men but none so valiant as Sir Nigel. Hordle John is the strongest Englishman ever seen, as Aylward is the lustiest bowman. About the full-flowering of chivalry, in the age of Edward III, Doyle had no illusions. He saw its brutality, its grime, its pain. But, stripped of the brutality, the code remained. Its root was honor; and each of its laws became an article of faith which might strengthen and sustain it as powerfully as any religion.

Doyle had a high regard for his historical novels, which were based on meticulous research; he had read well over a hundred volumes on the period of Edward III and considered it the greatest epoch in English history. But as a consequence he underestimated the contemporary stories he wrote with ease. From our perspective we can see that the saga of Sherlock Holmes is more valuable as a period piece and has captured the imagination of a wider audience in the long run than the romance of Edward III; nevertheless, *The White Company* remains an exciting and robust tale, well worth the reading.

THE WHITE DEVIL

Type of work: Drama
Author: John Webster (?-Before 1635)
Type of plot: Revenge tragedy
Time of plot: Sixteenth century
Locale: Rome and Padua, Italy
First presented: c. 1612

Based on actual events which took place in sixteenth century Italy, The White
Devil; or, Vittoria Corombona *is a powerful, violent revenge tragedy memorable
for Webster's poetic intensity and his psychologically complex portrait of Vittoria.*

The White Devil is one of the two plays on which the literary reputation
of John Webster is based. The world he portrays in the play is a dark one
indeed, one of the darkest visions of human nature, in fact, ever to reach the
stage. In this amoral world, his characters are consumed by the folly of
political intrigues and the vanity of amorous complications. Within the corrupt society only the ruthless and powerful have any chance for survival;
the few good characters—Isabella, Cornelia, Marcello—are powerless to
change things and are soon destroyed. Through his imagery of violence and
disaster, Webster portrays the basic qualities of diseased and fallen human
nature.

In order to present such a world, Webster effectively used all the devices of
the "tragedy of blood"; his use of physical horror was rarely surpassed on the
Jacobean stage. Through the ghosts, villains, murders, and suicides he bared
the inner mysteries of crime, remorse, and pain. Although the basic story line
of the play is quite simple, Webster has often been criticized for his carelessness in allowing extraneous and irrelevant material to interrupt the plot.
Yet it is not in overall plot construction but in individual scenes and characters that we see Webster's best skills.

His portrayal of Vittoria is particularly fascinating; it is one which both
attracts and repels. Vittoria is a two-sided figure, beautiful and brave as well
as wicked. Despite the darker actions of which she is capable, including
murder, she holds our sympathy on one level because of her courage against
a hostile world. Although Webster's vivid characterization and his ability
to create tense dramatic scenes is often masterful, and his unconventional
verse sometimes reaches a rarely matched beauty, the play is marred by the
insertion of didactic statements often unsuited to the speaker and extraneous
to the progress of the play.

WHITE-JACKET

Type of work: Novel
Author: Herman Melville (1819-1891)
Type of plot: Adventure romance
Time of plot: The 1840's
Locale: A vessel of the U.S. Navy
First published: 1850

Based in part upon the author's experiences on board the U.S. frigate United States *in 1843-1844,* White-Jacket *is a loosely knit narrative that exposes a number of vicious practices of the day: flogging, the tyranny of commanders, issuance of liquor to sailors, and poor messing facilities of the naval vessels.*

Though ostensibly an autobiographical exposé of the abuses against crewmen aboard American naval vessels in the 1840's, *White-Jacket* nevertheless contains essential elements of a novel of initiation into a complex world of good and evil. White-Jacket's bizarre garment develops into a symbol of the naïve innocence of its wearer, who, through his adventures on the *Neversink,* comes to a knowledge of the real world as represented by the man-of-war. The boy's final plunge into the sea as a result of having become entangled in his white coat represents his baptism into the world of adult knowledge and the shedding of his childhood innocence.

Though not clearly developed in novelistic form, a number of themes in *White-Jacket* tie this novel to Melville's more mature works. The evil resulting from insecure authority and arbitrary laws underlies much of the abuse of power aboard ship, for example. In fact, Melville seems to suggest a distinction along class lines of the problems resulting from an abuse of power by the officers, and the "sins" of the sailors, both seen as resulting from the inhumane conditions aboard ship. But while these forms of physical abuse account for one type of evil aboard ship, and the behavior of the sailors at their worst represents another, a typically Melvillian suggestion of innate evil can be seen in certain characters. The inhumanity of Cadwallader Cuticle, M.D., who murders a sailor in the name of science, and the master-at-arms, Bland, said to be "without a soul," are manifestations of such innate evil.

Melville's world, however, is always ambiguous. Thus, in *White-Jacket* the evil represented by Bland and the doctor is balanced by Jack Chase, who epitomizes all that is best in man.

WICKFORD POINT

Type of work: Novel
Author: John P. Marquand (1893-1960)
Type of plot: Social satire
Time of plot: Twentieth century
Locale: New York and Wickford Point
First published: 1939

A satire on social pretensions, Marquand's novel treats the impact of the outside world upon the small, smugly complacent community of Wickford Point. Through the technique of flashbacks, the author makes the present meaningful and explains the motives of his characters.

Marquand has said that he started *Wickford Point* from memories of his childhood and adolescence that centered around a country home once owned by his great-grandmother. He then added to these memories patterns of relationships observable in any family. This family chronicle of the old Brill homestead at Wickford Point, north of Boston, is told by a cousin, Jim Calder. Jim is loyal to this self-satisfied and inefficient family, but he struggles to keep clear of their strangling affection and dependence. The novel's social implications are true and unpretentious. It is written with a brilliant manipulation of scenes and incidents. Marquand's literary workmanship and intelligence are unobtrusively evident everywhere. The prose seems informal, but is actually artful in the best sense. The satire and irony are never heavy handed, but are blended slyly with wit and a nice touch of sentiment. Somewhat repetitious, the novel nevertheless maintains the reader's interest.

The nuances of life in and around Boston are intricately detailed and often are as amusing as scenes from Jane Austen or Anthony Trollope. Nobody ever does anything about anything at Wickford Point. Jim Calder understands the chaotic Brill clan, but he still loves one of its members, the wicked and delightful Bella. This conflict between mind and emotion provides a humorous and touching struggle within the hero-narrator. The narration usually avoids the archness which often distorts satire. This is because Marquand *cares* about the people he chooses to portray.

Wickford Point does not have the unity of *The Late George Apley* (1937), but its portrayal of clan snobbishness is even more pointed than in the earlier novel. The true worth of *Wickford Point* lies below its satiric surface. It is a novel of importance because its underlying emphasis is upon the motivations of human behavior.

WIELAND

Type of work: Novel
Author: Charles Brockden Brown (1771-1810)
Type of plot: Mystery romance
Time of plot: Eighteenth century
Locale: Pennsylvania
First published: 1798

Wieland, the best of Brown's works, is a romantic tragedy in the genre of horror and remorse which Poe was to cultivate later on. In spite of many flaws of carelessness, the book features macabre effects that can still stir readers partial to gothic stories of grotesque terror.

Though badly flawed in plot and characterization, *Wieland* deserves a higher place in American literature than that accorded a historical curiosity. In this novel, Brown initiates the characteristically American use of the fantastic and grotesque Gothic tale to explore the moral and psychological dimensions of experience. Poe, Hawthorne, and Melville would refine the Gothic mode into the American romance, but it was Brown and *Wieland* that first introduced the genre into our literature and demonstrated its possibilities.

Like most romancers, Brown had little interest in such concrete details as time and place. His locales are generalized, and he offers little in the way of observation about manners in Pennsylvania society of the eighteenth century. Rather, his characters occupy a landscape of the mind, more symbolic than real, in which their actions dramatize basic human hopes, fears, and passions rather than realistic situations. But the Gothic horrors which abound in *Wieland* are not introduced for the sake of sensationalism. They represent symbolic dramatizations of aspects of the human condition and the American experience.

The two most memorable characters to emerge in *Wieland* are the religious fanatic, Wieland, and the mysterious Carwin. The latter character is only partly responsible for Wieland's dimentia. Driven by the madness of a monomaniacal religious obsession to commit unspeakable crimes upon his loved one, Wieland anticipates the obsessed characters of Poe, Hawthorne, and Melville. Carwin, on the other hand, represents the man whose cold, scientific curiosity impairs his humanity, so he experiments with human subjects without regard to the consequences. Frequently in later writers, these two figures merge into one to create such monomaniacal seekers after knowledge as Hawthorne's Ethan Brand or Melville's Ahab.

Others would take the American romance to greater heights than Brown could achieve, but they would do so within the tradition he established on American soil.

THE WILD ASS'S SKIN

Type of work: Novel
Author: Honoré de Balzac (1799-1850)
Type of plot: Philosophical allegory
Time of plot: Early nineteenth century
Locale: Paris
First published: 1830

The Wild Ass's Skin *(in French,* La Peau de Chagrin*) is a philosophical allegory that points up a sharp moral: whatever we receive, we must pay for. Moreover, Balzac shows that the payment is a kind of nemesis; try as we will we cannot escape a final reckoning.*

The Wild Ass's Skin is a brilliantly conceived philosophical novel; it presents a complex argument, supported by a wealth of detail, which addresses fundamental human concerns.

The argument might be briefly summarized as "You pay for what you get." The magic skin, the vehicle through which Raphael is able to gain his desires, is also the vehicle which diminishes and finally kills him. The assumption of this argument, which is an argument about ethical conduct, is that human life operates according to well-defined, almost Newtonian principles: for every action, (or excess in Raphael's case) there is an equal or corresponding reaction. Thus, Balzac argues that a principle of rough justice holds in human affairs, or at least in affairs of human passions.

This interest in excesses of emotion or passion concerns Balzac in *The Wild Ass's Skin,* as well as in other studies of *The Human Comedy.* It is through passion, or many passions, that Balzac's characters (and Raphael in particular) dehumanize themselves. The society in which they live may reflect and embody this dehumanization, in the vices of gambling, gluttony, sensuality, and other forms of degradation; but it is always the characters themselves, like Raphael, who must bear the consequences.

The Wild Ass's Skin, a relatively early novel in Balzac's career, is marked by his initial encounters with the Gothic. The device of the skin, though fictionally supported, remains superficial and weak in comparison with those social and personal mechanisms which bring later Balzacian characters to account. Nonetheless, Balzac is brilliant in his depiction of society and its institutions, and in his delineation of individual characters. In *The Wild Ass's Skin,* he shows himself a master both of the grotesque and of the everyday, detailing life in the most degraded of gambling halls and salons, as well as in the plainest and most honest rooming houses. In short, Balzac in this novel— as in *The Human Comedy* as a whole—displays his enormous epic range and understanding of both society and human nature; and if in *The Wild Ass's Skin* that range is somewhat limited by the philosophical intent, the novel still exhibits that vivid, lifelike texture so characteristic of Balzac's finest work.

THE WILD DUCK

Type of work: Drama
Author: Henrik Ibsen (1828-1906)
Type of plot: Social criticism
Time of plot: Nineteenth century
Locale: Norway
First presented: 1884

Ibsen's complex psychological and symbolic play represents the wild duck wounded by old Werle and retrieved by his dog as an image of the Ekdal family, hurt by the world, diving to the depths of self-deception and finally rescued, only to be hurt the more.

The Wild Duck by Henrik Ibsen is one of the playwright's major problem plays. First published in 1884 and produced in 1885, the play, set in a small town in Norway, has continued to capture audiences and readers with its vitality and universality. Ibsen is credited as the "father of modern drama," a recognition achieved over tremendous obstacles, not the least of which is that he wrote in a little-known language. Born into a provincial milieu in Norway, plunged into early poverty, poorly educated, apprenticed to a pharmacist, it is typical of Ibsen's determination, imagination, and integrity that he was able to become not only a national figure, but also an international one. In 1851 he became assistant manager of the Bergen Theater, studied stage production abroad, and in the next six years gained invaluable practical theatrical experience by putting into production 145 plays. When he started writing his own plays, he had a knowledge of the theater and its literature matched by very few playwrights.

In *A Doll's House* (1879), *Ghosts* (1881), *An Enemy of the People* (1882), *The Wild Duck* (1884), and *Hedda Gabler* (1890), Ibsen introduced realism to the modern stage and established its conventions so powerfully that it is still the dominant stage technique. He substituted middle-class protagonists for kings and queens and wrote prose dialogue rather than poetry, stating that "My plays . . . are not tragedies in the old meaning of the word; what I have wanted to portray is human beings and that is just why I did not want them to speak the language of the gods." He introduced detailed stage directions to authenticate the background scene. Ibsen also approached his characterizations with a desire to study them more scientifically than before, incorporating his age's new discoveries of the importance of instincts, biology, heredity, and environment. In plot innovation, he dispensed with the suspense-intrigue and trickery of the currently popular "well-made plays," while maintaining a skillful manipulation of plot, ending each act with strong, theatrical curtain scenes. Often Ibsen's innovations reveal his study of Greek tragedy: his extensive use of light-dark imagery; his pervasive irony; his elimination of all events antecedent to the critical situation;

his use of the unities of time, place, and action. *The Wild Duck* marked a turning away from Ibsen's realistic problem plays. From that time on his plays would be complex, enigmatic studies of the human condition employing expressionistic and symbolic techniques.

The Wild Duck is typical of Ibsen's dominant themes: the presentness of the past; man's search for his true identity and place in life; the effects of idealism as a social force; the conflict of reality and illusion; and the problem of man's ultimate freedom. Ibsen himself said that the critics would "find plenty to quarrel about, plenty to interpret" in this play.

The key to the universality of the play lies in the complexity of the strong, well-rounded characters. A lesser playwright would have settled, for example, for making old Werle the villain of a melodrama. Ibsen, instead, presents his human complexity. Gregers, the son, sees the elder Werle as an unredeemable villain who has ruined old Ekdal, made his housemaid pregnant, and then foisted her off on the unsuspecting son of Ekdal. Hjalmar Ekdal, however, describing what old Werle has done for him and his family, sees him as a fairy godfather. The truth in Ibsen, as in life, lies somewhere in between —perhaps in old Werle's espousal of "the attainable ideal." Gina Ekdal, too, moves far beyond the stereotype of the "fallen woman redeemed by marriage." It is Gina's work on the photographs and her sewing, her concern for practicalities and the welfare of Hedvig and her husband, that keep the family going and enable Hjalmar to indulge in his dreams.

The two major characters—Gregers Werle and Hjalmar Ekdal—are even more complex. Both men see themselves as intellectually and morally superior to all around them; both are judged by the audience as self-indulgent, egocentric men with no true sympathy or love for others, not even their own family. Both wish to attain Truth, but both live in worlds of illusion regarding the nobility and goodness of their actions. Gregers admired Hjalmar as the most gifted and intelligent of his schoolmates; yet we learn that his intelligence is only that of a photographer and a speech writer, not of an artistic creator. As for Gregers, how intelligent is a man who sees Hjalmar as a misused genius and cannot analyze the possible consequences of his acts even when they are pointed out to him? Gregers lacks the moral strength to stop his father from trapping Ekdal; Hjalmar lacks the courage to commit suicide as he claims to wish; both men fail to face their responsibility in the death of Hedvig. Yet can we reject the quest for truth entirely, as Dr. Relling suggests? The ambiguity and complexity of this thematic question exceeds that of O'Neill's powerful treatment of the same theme in *The Iceman Cometh*.

Dramatic irony is a strong device running throughout the play. Gregers, who will almost destroy a happy home and contribute to the suicide of Hedvig, accuses his father of leaving things like "a battlefield strewn with broken lives." Hjalmar remarks that happiness is home, just as Gregers knocks on his door to bring the information that will help destroy home and happiness. Many of the ironic reverberations follow the pattern of blindness and sight established in Sophocles' *Oedipus Rex*. Those really blind—old Werle and Hedvig—often see more clearly than those who have physically good vision. Like Oedipus, Gregers and Hjalmar are metaphorically blind to the real truth of their human condition. Unlike Oedipus, however, they never face the truth, and they thus remain in darkness at the end of the play. Ibsen also employs light and dark imagery in the set and dialogue: Act I begins, ironically, in brightness and candle glow, but the other acts grow darker until Act V ends cold and gray.

The title of the play carries a complexity of meanings for the different characters. The duck, wounded by old Werle, is saved and trapped. Relling sees it as a symbol of all the world's people who are wounded while attempting to live in this world. Hedvig associates the duck with herself, wounded and unable to fly yet happy to stay at home in a created world. Old Werle connects the duck with old Ekdal, who is unable to live in reality. Gregers at one time sees himself as the dog who rescues the duck from drowning in the sea of lies and illusions; later he identifies himself with the duck; still later, he suggests the identification of Hedvig with the duck. The duck's world is a surrogate for the real forest in which it could no longer live with its clipped wings. The family questions if the duck can adapt; they decide that as long as it cannot see the *real* sky, it can survive unconscious of its trapped condition. The sky, associated with light and freedom and the natural state of bird and man, is juxtaposed with the darkness of Ekdal's attic, the unnatural state that man has created for himself. The Ekdal father and son are capable only of hunting tamed or disabled animals in their artificial "forest" and are as unable as the duck to survive in the real world.

Ann E. Reynolds

WILHELM MEISTER'S APPRENTICESHIP

Type of work: Novel
Author: Johann Wolfgang von Goethe (1749-1832)
Type of plot: Philosophical romance
Time of plot: Eighteenth century
Locale: Germany
First published: 1795-1796

A germinal "education" novel, Wilhelm Meister's Apprenticeship *is a long, often rambling, but colorful novel that treats the contrasting themes of freedom and responsibility, of romantic rebelliousness and reason.*

The *Wilhelm Meister* theme, like that of Faust, occupied Goethe throughout his long life, and this novel is actually a revision and expansion of an earlier work, *Wilhelm Meister's Theatrical Mission,* which Goethe had sketched out in the 1770's. It is followed by a rambling sequel, *Wilhelm Meister's Travels,* or *Journeyman Years.* The theatrical career of Wilhelm occupies the first four books of *Wilhelm Meister's Apprenticeship;* the last books are a product of Goethe's mature years and represent his changed attitude to life. As the history of the novel mirrors Goethe's development, so the main theme of the novel is the development—education and character formation—of its hero, whose name implies eventual mastery after a long apprenticeship. *Wilhelm Meister's Apprenticeship* is looked upon as the first great *Bildüngsroman,* or novel of development, a genre that is perhaps Germany's most important contribution to world literature.

Wilhelm Meister's Apprenticeship combines an elaborate and realistically treated plot with a symbolic structure that elevates Wilhelm's often erring quest for self-fulfillment into a metaphor for the process of life itself. The early scenes have a colorfully romantic air, and Wilhelm's hopes for a theatrical career lead him through a series of adventures that only gradually begin to elevate his awareness, especially in his contact with Shakespeare, climaxing in the *Hamlet* discussions in the fifth book. From that point, however, Wilhelm turns from his free actor's life to acknowledge responsibility, in the form of his son, and to accept the guidance of the Society of the Tower, a secret society that represents the element of reason in human life, as opposed to the romantic mystery of Mignon and the Harpist. Lothario and Natalia, two highly idealized figures, become his guides, and his marriage cements his commitment to work henceforth in a socially responsible role, merging his own development with that of his fellow man.

WILHELM MEISTER'S TRAVELS

Type of work: Novel
Author: Johann Wolfgang von Goethe (1749-1832)
Type of plot: Philosophical romance
Time of plot: Early nineteenth century
Locale: Germany
First published: 1821-1829

A continuation of Wilhelm Meister's Apprenticeship, Wilhelm Meister's Travels *shows the further "education" of its romantic hero. Many characters from the earlier book reappear briefly, and some attempt is made to bring to a close the adventures of a large number of people. The novel is also notable for Goethe's exposition of his views on geology, art, and labor, as well as for lyric interpolations.*

The translation of "Travels" for *Wanderjahre* is misleading. The title actually refers to the journeyman stage of the process from apprentice to master of a craft. The craft here is life, and Goethe stretched the novel form to its utmost—not always successfully--to include the full panorama of life. But in doing so, he anticipated many techniques of the modern novel, creating a montage of narrative, poems, critical reflections, theoretical discussions, and self-contained short stories. Wilhelm is not the "hero" of this novel; nor is there a straightforward story line. Rather, the work becomes a kind of mosaic in which directness and action are replaced by intimation and thought. Whereas the personal development of Wilhelm was the theme of the *Apprenticeship,* here man and society are emphasized. The strivings of the young artist are turned to activity as a doctor, a functioning and serving member of the human community.

Goethe subtitled the novel "The Renunciants," centering it around a key idea of his old age, that of renunciation, or voluntary sacrifice of individual desires for a higher goal. The novel was written in the years after 1807, a period of great political upheaval under Napoleon and the subsequent restoration of monarchy. As his friends died and the world changed, Goethe became increasingly philosophical and less concerned with his own personal fortunes and those of his heroes. In this novel he expressed, as he did in Part II of *Faust,* his vision of the great course of human life, seen from society's point of view. His descriptions are still realistic, but the events become charged with symbolic value as each man's life recapitulates the course of universal human experience. Thus Wilhelm's son, Felix, grows and begins to follow the path of emotional striving that marked Wilhelm's own youth, while Wilhelm, now a mature man, is able to use his productive skills to save his son's life. We see in *Wilhelm Meister's Travels* the eternal cycle of life, weaving countless individuals, striving, and learning, into one great whole.

WILLIAM TELL

Type of work: Drama
Author: Johann Christoph Friedrich von Schiller (1759-1805)
Type of plot: Historical romance
Time of plot: Fifteenth century
Locale: Switzerland
First presented: 1804

In Schiller's version of William Tell, based on a popular legend which in time became localized in Switzerland, the author shows his respect for the dignity and worth of the common man, yet attempts to demonstrate that each man must acknowledge and serve his rightful master.

Schiller reports of his *William Tell* that he never planned to write it until he read rumors that he was working on a Tell-drama and decided to look into the Swiss chronicles. There he found material that, he said, brought him to desperation: many plot threads, no cohesion of time or location, masses of characters, and nothing, aside from the apple shooting, that lent itself to dramatic presentation. Yet he found in the story something classical, almost Homeric. His imagination was seized by the popular movement of the Swiss cantons, but also by the paradoxical relationship between the group and the individual.

In his play he wove together two separate events: the Rütli Oath, a community decision to act against their tyrant, and the Tell sequence, a personal act of an individual. Schiller purposely kept Tell out of the Rütli scene, allowing him no part in the plans of the community which are in any case quite conservative in spite of all the talk about freedom. The uprising they seek is to be strictly regulated, coordinated, and free of personal, private acts. Tell, on the other hand, is a loner, a hunter, and a basically unpolitical man, though he has a deep sense of humanity, as exhibited in the first episode. While he keeps distant from community action, he is drawn into the fight against tyranny by Gessler's own provocation. His subsequent murder of Gessler is a private action, retribution for the insult and outrage he suffered. That his act becomes the high point of the liberation of the Swiss cantons is ironic, and Tell's discomfort is evident. He renounces his crossbow, the means of his livelihood but also now a murder weapon; in the enigmatic scene with Duke John, who has just murdered the Emperor, Tell is at first horrified, but then, in a recognition of their common humanity and sinfulness, he aids John on his way to Rome to seek absolution from the Pope. Tell remains behind, a hero to his people, but silent amid the jubilation.

THE WIND IN THE WILLOWS

Type of work: Novel
Author: Kenneth Grahame (1859-1932)
Type of plot: Fantasy and allegory
Time of plot: Early twentieth century
Locale: England
First published: 1908

A famous children's story that adults also love, The Wind in the Willows *is a fantasy—marked by gentle satire—in which the humanized animals live in a self-contained world with its share both of pettiness and folly, loyalty and kindness.*

Grahame wrote his fantasy-allegories, including *The Wind in the Willows,* while employed as Secretary of the Bank of England. His animal characters belong to the same world in which human beings live; the same foibles and excesses, the same motives and loyalties possess them. But it is an optimist's world too, where hope exists, and where the visionary experience reveals "The Friend and the Helper."

Whether or not *The Wind in the Willows* is a children's book is a moot question. Mole's discoveries parallel a child's explorations in the world in which he lives. But the story has wider appeal, for Mole learns, as we all must, to live in the larger world outside his home. When he returns to the familiar scents and the simple welcome of his home, Mole realizes that, although it is an important part of his life, home is no longer his *entire* life. So he returns to the world of sunlight and further discoveries. Together with his friends, Rat, Badger, and Toad, he learns to live in the world they call the "Wild Wood."

The theme of escape, then, is quite important in *The Wind in the Willows*: Mole desires to escape from the boredom of maintaining his home and everyday existence; Badger's escape is from Society. Although he does not succumb, Water Rat is strongly intrigued by the stories of the Wide World told by Seafaring Rat, and Toad desires to elude every trace of responsibility to the rest of the world. Children's story or not, Grahame's book contains a certain amount of didacticism. Animals in the story, especially Water Rat, live according to a codified standard of existence. In this standard, the reader finds an implied, but not explicit, correspondence between the codes of conduct in the story and those normally taught to children. The reader is encouraged to reach up to his potential, but not to exceed it—a difficult concept to explain to adults, let alone children. Yet here, maturity emerges as the ability to recognize oneself realistically.

Grahame combines gentle satire with a keen understanding of the psychological realities which lie behind his characters' actions. Rat is the cautious, judgmental teacher; Badger, the philosopher who hates society but likes people; and Toad, the incorrigible playboy: conceited, careless, and always in trouble. Along with Mole, the four represent an example of true friendship. By banding together, they retake Toad Hall from the weasels and restore the place to order with clean bed linens and fresh bars of soap.

The meaning of the song of the wind in the willows is revealed only to Rat and Mole. Badger survives through his philosophical stance, Toad with his indomitable will to have fun. But Rat and Mole need a vision. Like modern-day Everymen, Rat and Mole are allowed to see the pantheistic "The Friend and the Helper," the horned, hook-nosed creature who plays pan-pipes at dawn and smiles benevolently through his beard. The vision is a moment when Rat and Mole fear neither death nor life, and, as they drop into the sleep of forgetfulness, their faces keep a blissful smile of peace.

WINDSOR CASTLE

Type of work: Novel
Author: William Harrison Ainsworth (1805-1882)
Type of plot: Historical romance
Time of plot: Sixteenth century
Locale: England
First published: 1843

Set in the reign of King Henry VIII, Windsor Castle *combines qualities of the historical romance and the gothic romance of mystery and terror. Most readers remember the chilling figure of Herne the Hunter, an apparition out of the imagination of medieval England, who serves on the level of psychology as the conscience of the castle.*

Windsor Castle illustrates various ways in which serious organizational problems can arise despite the author's careful adherence to what looks like neat structural division. The book shares with the body of William Harrison Ainsworth's fiction a variety of significant features; a complicated series of more or less interwoven actions and intrigues interlaced with historical matter, introducing a complex dimension all its own, as well as important architectural and scientific backgrounds and supernatural events, or what appear to be fated occurrences. The book is also well-researched, and descriptions and action scenes are as superbly drawn as in Ainsworth's other novels. But a feature which is disturbing and requires some consideration is the author's use of subplots.

It must not be assumed that Ainsworth's subplots are always mere padding. Frequently, such subplots significantly enlarge the scope of the principal action of the novel, but in *Windsor Castle,* Ainsworth repeatedly introduces motifs which he fails to develop fully. For example, the unhappy romance of Surrey and the fair Geraldine, though it serves to illustrate the power of Henry VIII, is too sketchily treated to sustain interest.

There are other loose ends in the book, but they do not really impair the structure. Book Six, for instance, takes place seven years after the first five parts, but, showing as it does the downfall of Anne Boleyn, it is a logical consequence if not an integral part of the main action. Nor is it disturbing to have the supernatural dimension involving Herne the Hunter and his repeated incursions because they consistently affect the king and have a definite place in advancing action and creating atmosphere.

Although Ainsworth allows himself to stray too often from the main track of his narrative, the average reader will not be disturbed by this lack of unity since the novel contains all of the exciting action, colorful descriptions, and living history for which the author is justly famous.

WINESBURG, OHIO

Type of work: Short stories
Author: Sherwood Anderson (1876-1941)
Type of plot: Psychological realism
Time of plot: Late nineteenth century
Locale: Winesburg, Ohio
First published: 1919

A collection of interrelated short stories that form the emotional pattern of a novel, Winesburg, Ohio *treats the theme of "revolt from the village," an important subject of American fiction in the 1920's. Anderson's extensive use of Freudian and Jungian psychology furnishes insights into the obsessions and aspirations of the characters in this small, morally confining town.*

Using young George Willard both as protagonist and observer, Sherwood Anderson creates in *Winesburg, Ohio* a probing psychological portrait of small-town America. Though his characters outwardly seem dull and commonplace, Anderson is acutely tuned to the tensions between their psychological and emotional needs and the restrictions placed upon their lives by the small-town atmosphere of Winesburg. Though not scientifically psychoanalytical, Anderson's work probes deeply into the psychic lives of these "grotesques" to discover the emotional wounds which have been inflicted by the Puritan attitudes of the midwestern village. Though Anderson may not have been directly influenced by Freud or Jung, his interests clearly parallel those of the depth psychology which became popular with American intellectuals during the first quarter of the century. In this respect, Anderson can legitimately be called our first psychological novelist.

Anderson believed the traditional forms of the novel were too restrictive and formal to adapt well to his American subject matter, so *Winesburg, Ohio* represents in part an experiment in form. Rather than unifying his work through a plot in the usual sense, Anderson uses patterns of imagery, tone, character, and theme to achieve a sense of wholeness. It is, however, George Willard's narrative voice and presence as either observer or protagonist in the stories which ultimately unifies them. As a small-town reporter, Willard can credibly serve as a confidant for his townspeople. Also, he is a kind of professional observer recording the surface lives of his people for the newspaper. At the same time, we must see him as the budding artist who is interested in discovering the deeper and more meaningful truths of peoples' lives than those seen at the surface. Eventually, George must make his own choice as to which of these roles he will elect, but meantime his function as the central consciousness of the book is vital to its aesthetic success.

Winesburg, Ohio also follows the classic pattern of the *Bildüngsroman* or "portrait of the artist as a young man" as it traces George Willard's growth from adolescence to maturity. Central to this aspect of the novel is George's relationship with his mother whose death eventually frees him to escape from Winesburg. Mrs. Willard is the first person to see, in George's ambition to write, a potential release for her own inarticulate suffering, so she encourages his ambition partly to fill her own needs. As George comes into contact with other characters in the novel, they too see in him a way to make their voices heard, so they tell him their stories so he might write them down.

Part of George's growing maturity results from the understanding he finds as a result of his willingness to listen, but this passive development is paralleled by more overt experience. In particular, sexual initiation is an essential part of George's learning and growth, as is his coming to understand something of the nature of love in its various aspects. Through this combination of active and passive experiences, George eventually comes to the realization that isolation is an essential part of the human condition. People, George realizes in the sketch called "Sophistication," must learn to live with the limited relationships possible in a world which must isolate them, and they must develop the strength not to be destroyed by loneliness. This knowledge gives George the maturity he needs to break with Winesburg and face the future as an adult and an artist. In "Departure," the final sketch, he goes toward that responsibility.

Anderson's introduction to *Winesburg, Ohio,* called "The Book of the Grotesque," suggests yet another way in which this work is unified. Conceived as a whole within which the sketches and stories are pulled together by the idea of the grotesques, the work can be seen as a group of stories connected by a central thematic concern. Anderson defined his grotesques as people who had seized upon some aspect of the truth which so dominates their lives as to distort their entire beings. This definition, however, only loosely fits the characters we actually encounter in the novel. Rather, the failure in some way of emotional life seems to account for the twists of character which lead Winesburg's citizens to their universal sense of failure and isolation. In spite of apparent differences, virtually all of Anderson's figures suffer from a deep sense of failure—frequently of material failure as well as emotional—and from a frustrating inability to express their pain and rage in a meaningful way. Essentially, they are emotional cripples who must turn to George Willard in search of a voice to articulate their suffering.

Paralleling that level of *Winesburg, Ohio* which is concerned with individual psychology is a general reaction against the American small town and its atmosphere of Puritanical repression. Though Anderson is not without some nostalgia for the village life which was already passing from the American scene when *Winesburg, Ohio* was published in 1919, he does not allow his sentiment to stand in the way of a powerful condemnation of the cultural and spiritual sterility characteristic of the American village scene. While other writers were mourning the passing of the nation's innocent youth by sentimentalizing the small agrarian community, Anderson reveals its dark underside of destroyed lives, thwarted ambitions, and crippled souls—all of which resulted in part from the repressive atmosphere of towns like Winesburg. Thus, even while *Winesburg, Ohio* marks the end of an era of agrarian order in America, it raises the very real possibility that our innocent past had been less of a paradise than the sentimentalist would have us believe.

Studies of the modern American novel tradition often begin with *Winesburg, Ohio* which, by its pioneering of new techniques, introduction of new subject matter, and development of new attitudes and ideas as well as a new frankness, changed the course of American literary history. In addition, Anderson's generous help to such younger writers as Hemingway and Faulkner, who would continue to shape the course of the American novel, justifies his position as the father of the modern American novel.

William E. Grant

THE WINGS OF THE DOVE

Type of work: Novel
Author: Henry James (1843-1916)
Type of plot: Psychological realism
Time of plot: c. 1900
Locale: London and Venice
First published: 1902

One of the major psychological novels of James's final period, The Wings of the Dove *concerns a young, fine-spirited woman afflicted by an incurable malady who attempts to live a lifetime in a few precious months. The admirable character of "the dove," Milly Theale, was modeled avowedly on the author's own cousin, Mary Temple.*

Henry James came of a family whose members considered themselves viewers of, rather than participators in, society. Their wealth enabled them to remove themselves from the common rout, and Henry and his father both suffered from physical disabilities which to some degree enforced this detachment, which was emotional as well as physical. The family traveled continually during the author's youth; as an adult he lived chiefly in Europe, though maintaining nonetheless close relations with his parents and siblings. The ties of blood, for him, took the place of national feeling. He considered himself a citizen of the world, and took of the life of his countrymen the same objective, albeit curious and sympathetic, view as of society in general. Coming as he did of parents whose chief business in life was the cultivation of their own and their children's sensibilities, and sharing the family's strong if eccentric religious bent, he took it as his artistic mission to examine the condition of human society at large as that condition manifested itself in the most subdued and civilized of human milieus.

The specifics of the plot of *The Wings of the Dove* were suggested to the author by the premature death of his cousin Mary Temple, called Minny. The girl had charm, beauty, money, and love. She had, as it is said, everything to live for, and grimly resisted her fate to the end. After her death of tuberculosis in 1870, James was, as he later wrote, "haunted" by the tragedy of her situation. Two of his most appealing heroines take their essential lines from her: Isabel Archer of *The Portrait of a Lady,* and Milly Theale.

James wrote three of his best novels in quick succession shortly after 1900. As the new century began, he produced *The Ambassadors* (1902), *The Wings of the Dove* (1903), and *The Golden Bowl* (1904). These three novels represent the highest expression of those ideas of art and life gleaned over nearly six decades of observation and analysis of European and American mores. The three themes that impel these novels, as well as most of his previous works, are: "the contrast of American sincerity and crudity with European deceit and culture, the conflicting realities of life and art, and the substitution of psychological for ethical measurements of good and evil " (Robert E. Spiller, *The Cycle of American Literature*). *The Wings of the Dove* treats all three.

The first is most neatly illustrated by the counterpoise of Mrs. Maud Lowder and Mrs. Stringham. Aunt Maud's wardship of Kate has a monetary quality made explicit in her remark to Merton Densher: " 'I've been saving (Kate's presence) up and letting it, as you say of investments, appreciate, and you may judge whether, now it has begun to pay so, I'm likely to consent to treat for it with any but a high bidder.' " Mrs. Stringham's attachment to Milly, on the other hand, takes for her the shape of a holy mission to shepherd through the hazards of the world a being so exalted that the heroines of literature pale beside her. Her view of Milly is essentially romantic; she calls her "an angel," "a princess in a palace," and ironically "the real thing"; ironically, because *real* is exactly what Milly is not for her companion, any more than Kate is at bottom anything more than a marketable commodity to Mrs. Lowder. The difference in the characters of Kate and Milly enlarges on this theme; Kate accepts that definition of herself, using it to her own purpose, but succumbs at the last to its corrupting influence in using Densher as just such another counter, thus losing both love and honor. Milly, resisting the dehumanizing effects of both hero worship and pity, works her own salvation as well as Densher's.

The life that Milly makes for herself, knowing her days are numbered and knowing, almost, their number, comprehends abysses both sublime and terrible. For she recognizes from the first the effects of her money on the company into which she is betrayed by her shepherd, so graphically if unintentionally particularized for her by kind, corrupt Lord Mark, who brings her before the Bronzino portrait; so like her but, most poignantly to Milly's sense, "dead, dead, dead." She has, even before she hears her sentence pronounced by Sir Luke Strett, a trick of deferring judgment, of not permitting the baseness of others to circumscribe or debase her experience. Afterward, this tendency flowers into a kind of divine duplicity, a double reverse which consists of her keeping from everyone but Mrs. Stringham the fact that she is dying. We are to keep in mind that after a certain point in the story she must inevitably see everyone else as acting in the light of this knowledge of her limited future. Yet she makes no move to defend herself; she simply, profoundly, trusts. In short, she offers herself as a dove for sacrifice, a gesture that parallels the willingness of others to sacrifice her to their own designs. All her putative friends deceive themselves in regard to her, acting for their own good but in the name of her happiness. But Milly does not deceive herself. Her surrender is deliberate. In this she is a supreme artist; she makes of her life an instrument for Mrs. Stringham's gratification, for Kate's enlightenment, and for Densher's redemption, a creative act of the highest kind.

And all this great work, as well as diverse strokes of wickedness, is done in a few murmured words, a nod or a look, an invitation accepted or declined, gestures always within the bounds of propriety. Such an exposition of the instincts of the jungle expressed in the manners of the salon generates, in the end, more force than many a less subdued narrative. For we are treated not only to the powerful spectacle of Kate Croy prowling her situation with the disciplined rage of a caged tigress, but also to the glorious vision of Milly Theale, triumphant over betrayal and death, fulfilling her extraordinary nature to its highest potential.

Jan Kennedy Foster

THE WINTER'S TALE

Type of work: Drama
Author: William Shakespeare (1564-1616)
Type of plot: Tragi-comedy
Time of plot: The legendary past
Locale: Sicilia and Bohemia
First presented: 1611

The motivating passion of this late Shakespearean play, a tragicomedy suffused by gentle melancholy, is unreasonable and cruel jealousy, the effects of which are moderated by the charming romance of the young lovers, Perdita and Florizel.

Written after *Cymbeline* and before *The Tempest, The Winter's Tale* is as hard to classify generically as is the fully mature dramatic genius of its author. Partaking of the elements of tragedy, the play yet ends in sheer comedy, just as it mingles elements of realism and romance. Shakespeare took his usual free hand with his source, Robert Greene's euphuistic romance *Pandosto: The Triumph of Time* (1588). Yet time remains the most crucial element in the play's structure, its clearest break with the pseudo-Aristotelian "unities." The effect of time on Hermione, moreover, when the "statue" is revealed to be wrinkled and aged, heightens the pathos and credibility of the triumphant discovery and recognition scene. In order to allow that final scene full effect, Shakespeare wisely has Perdita's discovery and recognition reported to the audience second-hand in Act 5, scene 2. In keeping with the maturity of Shakespeare's dramatic talent, the poetic style of this play is clear, rarely rhetorical, sparse in its imagery, but metaphorically sharp. Verse alternates with prose as court characters alternate with country personages.

Mamillius tells his mother, who asks him for a story, that "a sad tale's best for winter." Ironically the little boy's story is never told; the entrance of Leontes interrupts it, and Hermione's son, his role as story-teller once defined, strangely disappears. In his place the play itself takes over, invigorated by Mamillius' uncanny innocent wisdom that reflects a Platonic view of childhood. The story that unfolds winds within its skeins a multitude of themes, without losing sight of any of them. It presents two views of honor, a wholesome one represented by Hermione, and a demented view represented by Leontes. Like many of Shakespeare's plays, it treats of the unholy power of kings, kings who can be mistaken, but whose power, however mistaken, is final. Yet the finality, here, is spared, the tragic ending avoided. For the absolute goodness of Hermione, Paulina, Cammilo, the shepherd, and Florizel proves to be enough to overcome the evil of Leontes. Moving from the older generation's inability to love to the reflowering of love in the younger, the play spins out into a truly comic ending, with the reëstablishment of community, royal authority, and general happiness in a triple *gamos*. The balance of tension between youth and age, guilt and innocence, death and rebirth, is decided in favor of life and the play escapes the clutches of remorseless tragedy in a kind of ultimate mystical vision of human life made ideal through suffering.

Leontes is a most puzzling character. His antifeminism, as expressed in his cynical speech on cuckoldry (1.2), seems more fashionable than felt. He resembles, in his determined jealousy, Othello, and in his self-inflicted insanity, Lear. In fact, the words of Lear to Cordelia resound in Leontes' great speech, beginning, "Is whispering nothing?" and concluding, "My wife is nothing; nor nothing have these nothings, / If this be nothing" (1.2). It is almost impossible to sympathize with him further when he condemns even his helpless child in the face of Paulina's gentle pleas (2.3); and we are not surprised that he at first denies the oracle itself (3.2). Yet his sudden recognition of culpability is no more convincing than the un-motivated jealousy with which he begins the play. It is as if he changes too quickly for belief; and perhaps this is the reason for Hermione's decision to test his penitence with time, until it ripens into sincerity. Certainly his reaction to his wife's faint shows only a superficial emotion. Leontes is still self-centered, still regally assured that all can be put right with the proper words. Only after the years have passed in his loneliness does he realize it takes more than orderly words to undo the damage wrought by disorderly royal commands. His admission to Pauline that his words killed Hermione, in 5.1, paves the way for the happy ending.

Even the minor characters are drawn well and vividly. Camillo is the ideal courtier who chooses virtue in favor of favor. Paulina, like the nurse Anna in Euripides' *Hippolytus,* is the staunch helpmate of her mistress, especially in adversity, aided by magical powers that seem to spring from her own determined character. Her philosophy is also that of the classical Greeks: "What's gone and what's past help/Should be past grief." But this play does not have the tragic Greek ending, because Paulina preserves her mistress rather than assisting her to destroy herself. Even the rogue Autolycus is beguiling, with his verbal witticisms, his frank pursuit of self-betterment, and his lusty and delightful songs. His sign is Mercury, the thief of the gods, and he follows his sign like the best rascals in Renaissance tradition, Boccaccio's Friar Onion, Rabelais' Panurge, and Shakespeare's own Falstaff.

In Hermione and Perdita, Shakespeare achieves two of his greatest portraits of women. Hermione's speech reflects her personality, straightforward, without embroidery, as pure as virtue itself. Her reaction to Leontes' suspicion and condemnation is brief, but telling. "Adieu, my lord," she says, "I never wish'd to see you sorry; now/I trust I shall." She combines the hardness of Portia with the gentleness of Desdemona—and Antigonus' oath in her defense recalls the character of Othello's wife. Like Chaucer's patient Griselda, Hermione loses all; but she strikes back with the most devastating weapon of all: time. Yet in the final scene of the play it is clear that her punishment of Leontes has made Hermione suffer no less than him. Perdita personifies, though never in a stereotyped way, gentle innocence: "Nothing she does or seems/But smacks of something greater than herself/Too noble for this place." Indeed, when Polixenes' wrath, paralleling Leontes' previous folly, threatens Perdita's life for a second time, the audience holds its breath because she is too good to be safe. When Shakespeare saves her, we rejoice, and the play, sensing our joy, abruptly ends on its highest note.

In its theme and structure, *The Winter's Tale* bears a striking resemblance to Euripides' *Alcestis*. In both plays, the "death" of the queen threatens the stability and happiness of society and, in both, her restoration, which is miraculous and ambiguous, restores order to the world of the court. Shakespeare, however, widens the comic theme by adding the love of the younger generation. So *The Winter's Tale* defies the forces of death and hatred both romantically and realistically. The sad tale becomes happy, as winter becomes spring.

Kenneth John Atchity

WINTERSET

Type of work: Drama
Author: Maxwell Anderson (1888-1959)
Type of plot: Romantic tragedy
Time of plot: Twentieth century
Locale: New York
First presented: 1935

In Anderson's verse drama based upon the famous murder trial of Sacco and Vanzetti, Mio is a classical tragic character in the sense that his weakness lies in his desire to avenge his father's death, yet his love for Miriamne will not allow him to consummate his desire.

When it was written, *Winterset* reflected the emotions stirred by the Sacco-Vanzetti case. It is the story of a son, such as either of the condemned men might have had, and tells of his search for justice in the name of the wronged father. Very much a play of the Great Depression, *Winterset* combined the hatred of a young Hamlet with the frustrated love of a Romeo and Juliet, and tied it all together with a social consciousness message. The hero's quest, although successful, is frustrated by his love for the sister of one of his father's betrayers, but the tragedy seems less one of personal destiny than of the weight of social pressures.

Winterset is the only major verse-drama by Anderson to have a contemporary setting. His most successful plays written in verse, such as *Elizabeth the Queen* (1930), and *Mary of Scotland* (1933) adhere to the rule that poetic tragedy works better when dealing with distant places and times. His experiment of combining poetic tragedy with contemporary themes and characters, while widely acclaimed when first produced, now seems less plausible than it did then. But the sincerity of the author and the intensity with which the play is composed carry it along, despite occasional lapses into pretensiousness. The worst fault of the play is the tendency for the message of the author to intrude into the dramatic flow.

While it is difficult for the audience or reader to believe in the "ancient evil of the earth" which Esdras blames for the tragedy, the skill of the dramatic structure and the moving characterizations give the play a definite power. If Anderson's verse sometimes strains too hard to make an effect, more often it finds in colloquial phrases a haunting new kind of poetry. Uneven and dated, the play stands, however, as a valuable historical testament to the emotions and convictions of the period in which it was written.

WITH FIRE AND SWORD

Type of work: Novel
Author: Henryk Sienkiewicz (1846-1916)
Type of plot: Historical romance
Time of plot: Seventeenth century
Locale: Poland and the Ukraine
First published: 1883

> *The first and most successful novel of a trilogy that dramatizes Polish military history,* With Fire and Sword *describes the revolt of the Cossacks and the heroic defense of Zbaraż by the Poles in the days of the Commonwealth. The exploits of Prince Yeremi Vishnyevetski, Polish national hero, and his captains overshadow a rather conventional love story.*

Henryk Sienkiewicz, winner of the Nobel Prize for literature in 1905, is Poland's best-known author. His works include accounts of his travels in Africa and the United States as well as novels. In America his most widely read work was the historical novel *Quo Vadis?,* a story which undertook to bring to life the Rome of the years after the crucifixion, when the apostles were planting Christianity in pagan lands. His best work is undoubtedly the trilogy: *With Fire and Sword; The Deluge,* an account of a war in which Sweden invaded Poland; and *Pan Michael Volodyovski* (also translated as *The Little Soldier*), a novel based on the third successive attack on Poland, this time by Tartars and Turks. As Sienkiewicz makes clear, the three wars, all of which ended in Polish victories, established a strong and enduring pride in the Polish nation, but they drained Poland of her manpower so completely that she was unable to maintain her political independence.

In the trilogy, Sienkiewicz endows his heroes with courage and loyalty very close to absolute perfection, and his heroines are models of beauty and faithfulness. In the cold light of reason they may be hard to believe, yet the extreme demands of bitter war and the inhuman cruelty of the enemy point up the moral that people do sometimes have loyalties which they consider worth dying for in times when quarter is neither given nor expected. Also there are different kinds of bravery. Skshetuski has a courage born of love, nationalism, and daring. There is nothing he will not try, and little that he cannot endure or do. Prince Yeremi is faced with the most difficult of decisions: whether to abide by the democratic principles that have made Poland great, and, because he accepts the general will, see his country perish, or to seize power in order to save Poland. His decision is the climax of *With Fire and Sword.* The narrative moves quickly and smoothly, and has great emotional power; Sienkiewicz combines the best narrative qualities of Sir Walter Scott and Alexandre Dumas, père, both of whom probably influenced him.

WITHIN THE GATES

Type of work: Drama
Author: Sean O'Casey (1884-1964)
Type of plot: Morality play
Time of plot: Twentieth century
Locale: In a London park
First presented: 1933

This expressionistic morality play—in four parts or seasons—is a kind of war cry against the modern, impoverished spirit of man, weighed down by mass conformity, though protested against by the poet-dreamer.

In the period beginning with the Great Depression and ending with World War II, Sean O'Casey wrote four "morality plays," *Within the Gates, The Star Turns Red* (1940), *Red Roses for Me* (1942), and *Oak Leaves and Lavender* (1946), through which he hoped to show the chaos and crisis—economic, political, moral, and spiritual—of the modern world. And, following his split with the Abbey Theatre over its refusal to produce *The Silver Tassie* (1929), he continued to reject the realism of his earlier triumphs, especially *Juno and the Paycock* and *The Plough and the Stars,* in favor of experimentation with symbolic, poetic, and expressionistic theatrical styles. As he was quoted in *The Sunday Times* in 1934: "To hell with so-called realism for it leads nowhere."

But exactly where the nonrealism of *Within the Gates* "leads" is also difficult to determine. Such "plot" as there is concerns the efforts of The Young Woman, a prostitute gradually dying from a heart ailment, to find sympathy, security, and "meaning" from those she meets in a public park. In the fashion of a true morality play, it is her soul that becomes the object of contention. An illegitimate child raised by nuns in a charity orphanage, she is mentally tormented by images of hell and damnation. Her foster father, The Atheist, offers her sympathy, but cannot satisfy her emotional needs because his humanity is entirely theoretical and impersonal. Because of her profession, she is socially ostracized and harassed by the guardians of public morality, The Bishop's Sister and The Policewoman. Because of her health, she is rejected as a wife by The Gardener.

She accosts The Bishop, but is cast off as a "sinner" in need of purification. To gain acceptance she must first join The Down-and-Outs, those poor who agree that their fate is just, beg hopelessly for scraps, and offer no resistance or criticism toward the society which has pushed them to the bottom. Rather than demean herself, The Young Woman defiantly challenges The Bishop, claiming that "his Christ" is an opulent dandy totally unconcerned with the poor and the unfortunate. The Salvation Army evangelist is less formal than The Bishop, but his appeal, which offers emotion without compassion, is of no use to her either, especially after she realizes that the evangelist is more interested in her body than in her soul.

It remains for The Dreamer, a poet and songwriter who challenges all of the life-denying characters in the park, to "save" her and to proclaim her victory. The Dreamer and The Young Woman dance together in defiance of the chanting Down-and-Outs and, in dying, she supports O'Casey's belief that affirmation, joy, and compassion can survive even the most stifling of attitudes and institutions.

This summary, however, probably makes the play sound more coherent than it actually is. Although a line of action exists beneath the surface of the play, it is frequently obscured by extra characters, inappropriate speeches, gratuitous satire, and confusing digressions. The whole of *Within the Gates* is less than many of its parts; nevertheless, it has moments of power, rich comedy, and provocative thought. If it fails, it fails on a scale that few twentieth century playwrights have been able to match.

WOLF SOLENT

Type of work: Novel
Author: John Cowper Powys (1872-1963)
Type of plot: Psychological realism
Time of plot: Twentieth century
Locale: Devon, England
First published: 1929

In this novel Powys presents against a contemporary setting some of his ideas on the mystical agent that shapes all men's actions. The powerful spirits of Dorset, Solent's community, are reflections of the animal nature of human beings, forces springing from man that defy his best efforts to impose a rational order on himself and his world.

All three of them important writers, the Powys brothers are often confused with one another. John Cowper Powys, the eldest, outlived T. F. and Llewelyn by some years. Perhaps predictably, his distinctive quality was that of presenting twentieth century ideas and dilemmas in what is essentially a nineteenth century mode of expression. A follower of Dostoevski and Hardy, John Cowper Powys employed the idioms of English romanticism in exploring the nature of psychological compulsion and metaphysical isolation.

A novel of introspection, *Wolf Solent* is filled with long soliloquies and ruminations, which many critics have found to be over-written. But these excursions into Wolf's consciousness do succeed in establishing the dimensions of his struggle. Revealed are the dualistic tensions: his father's passive receptivity and his mother's assertiveness; Christie's spirituality and Gerda's sensuality; his need to live a life of moral responsibility and "objectivity" and his equally pressing desire to escape from and aestheticize that life. These tensions are presented against the more fundamental dualism of nature and civilization. Powys, like his protagonist, is an animist and nature mystic. Wolf yearns for absorption into natural processes; he feels the natural world's unfathomable workings in his unconscious, and he longs to relate these to his moral experience.

Solent's original philosophy changes as he develops the power of his will "to forget and enjoy." This power of will, which includes his power of contemplation, enables him to cease struggling against the dualism of good and evil, since he can now "will" himself to be good. The external action of the novel ends on a tragic note, but the psychological processes which these actions have engendered in Wolf clearly leave him more whole and more human than he was at first, when the pathetic sight of "the man on the Waterloo steps" plunged him into morbidness and confusion.

THE WOMAN HATER

Type of work: Drama
Author: Francis Beaumont (1585?-1616)
Type of plot: Romantic comedy
Time of plot: Early seventeenth century
Locale: Milan
First presented: c. 1606

In this play Beaumont, possibly with some assistance from Fletcher, creates two "humours" characters in the Jonson mold: Gondarino, who is motivated solely by a pathological hatred of women; and Lazarillo, a compulsive glutton. From a modern point of view the main subject of the play is offensive to women, but individual scenes are redeemed by brisk comedy.

The usual thrust of romantic comedy—the boy meets girl theme—is in *The Woman Hater* subordinated to the humours of the two main characters: the misogyny of Gondarino and the gluttony of Lazarillo. Their characters, however, are not sufficiently developed. Gondarino has no motivation for his extreme hatred of women (he calls Oriana, who is a stranger to him, a "filthy impudent whore," simply because she is a woman) beyond a mere hint that his dead wife had cuckolded him. Lazarillo, on the other hand, is less a glutton than a hyperbolic lover of rare and delicious foods; he is the most humorous of all the characters in the play. His anticipation of eating the umbrana's head leads him to personify it as a pure virgin—but he ends up marrying a prostitute in order to have his delicacy.

The Woman Hater touches on the issue of the subjugation of the lower classes by the upper classes; Julia, the prostitute who marries Lazarillo in order to better herself, bitterly complains that she and her kind are but "apes" to the upper class. The main issue in the play, however, is men's subjugation of women.

Although the play may be considered pro-feminist, it contains a subtle anti-feminism which is even more sinister than the blatant misogyny of Gondarino. The Duke, who is a woman lover, believes it is her "nature / To wish to taste that which is most forbidden," a bias based on the Edenic myth. And Valore, also an ostensible woman lover, feels that his sister has risen "above" her sex in remaining chaste. Although Oriana insists that she has "shew'd my sexe the better," it is the Duke who has the last word, celebrating the triumph of "True love," to end the play harmoniously, in true comic fashion.

THE WOMAN IN WHITE

Type of work: Novel
Author: Wilkie Collins (1824-1889)
Type of plot: Mystery romance
Time of plot: 1850's
Locale: England
First published: 1860

The story of The Woman in White, *a suspenseful romance based in part upon the case history of an actual crime, is told by a collection of papers by different hands. This method gives Collins a chance to show the versatility of his style and to lend variety to his narrative.*

Throughout his career, Wilkie Collins, like many other modern writers, was torn between a need to satisfy the demands of the popular reading public and a personal desire to create works of lasting artistic merit. He achieved the desired synthesis only twice, initially with *The Woman in White* and, six years later, with *The Moonstone.* The first of the two was both his most popular work and his most important serious book.

As fantastic as the plot of *The Woman in White* is, it was based, as were many of Collins' crime stories, on an actual case history he discovered in Maurice Méjan's *Recueil des Causes Célèbres.* In 1787 one Mme. de Douhault was cheated out of a portion of her father's estate by a brother. En route to Paris to launch proceedings against her brother, she stopped at a relative's home where she was drugged, confined to a mental hospital, and declared dead, the unscrupulous relatives collecting all that remained of the father's estate. Like her fictional counterpart, Mme. de Douhault finally escaped— wearing a white dress—but, unlike Laura Fairlie, she was never able to legally reestablish her identity, in spite of positive identifications from friends and associates. She died a pauper in 1817.

The crime becomes more elaborate and complicated in Collins' hands. Not only is the heroine drugged and secreted in an asylum, but a deceased double is buried in her place. "The first part of the story," Collins commented in a newspaper interview, "will deal with the destruction of the victim's identity. The second with its recovery." To this basic plot movement Collins added a number of secondary lines: the question of Laura Fairlie's marriage to Percival Glyde, the identity and story of the mysterious "woman in white," Anne Catherick, the love affair between Laura and Walter Hartright, Laura's "death" and the events surrounding it, Percival Glyde's relationship with Anne's mother, Mrs. Catherick, and his mysterious "secret," and, finally, Count Fosco's background and his "secret."

But, complex as this outline may look, Collins handles the threads of the narrative in such a way that they support and complement one another without ever obscuring the central thrust of the book. As Collins answers one question for his reader, he uses that answer to introduce new, more provocative ones. As the puzzles are gradually unraveled, the pressures on the hero and heroines become more and more extreme. For most of the book the victims seem nearly helpless before the villains' power. The reversal does not come until late in the novel and, when it does occur, the shift is sudden. And even in the last important scene, Hartright's confrontation with Fosco, when the initiative is clearly the hero's, the sense of danger remains intense. Nowhere does Collins demonstrate his mastery of intricate plotting more effectively than in *The Woman in White* and it remains, with the possible exception of *The Moonstone,* the most perfectly structured example of the "sensation novel."

The gradual revelation of the intricate conspiracy is made doubly effective by Collins' narrative method. The story is told in bits and pieces by a number of characters who reveal only as much as they know. Some of the narrators are major participants, such as Walter Hartright, Marian Halcombe, and Count Fosco, who explain and interpret the events as they occur or after the fact. Others are minor personages, such as Laura's uncle, Frederick Fairlie, Glyde's housekeeper, Eliza Michelson, and Laura's "tombstone," who can only provide fragments of information that reflect their brief connection to the story. This technique gives Collins a maximum of flexibility, allows him to control the mystery and suspense by revealing only as much information at any one time as convenient, insures variety in the narrative style, mood, and tone, and sharpens the characterizations. As the speakers offer their information, they characterize themselves through their diction, prose style, habits, and attitudes. And, most importantly, Collins' multiple narrative method offers the reader a gigantic prose jigsaw puzzle and leaves it to him to sift through the conflicting versions for the truth. A few years later Collins was to use this same method in writing what many have called the first English detective novel, *The Moonstone.*

The object of the conspiracy, Laura Fairlie, is a passive creature with little color or character. The real conflict is between Marian Halcombe and Walter Hartright on the one one side and Percival Glyde and Count Fosco on the other. In the first half of the book, the events leading up to Laura's falsified "death," it is Marian who acts as a foil to the villains. After Laura's escape, Walter Hartright becomes the primary hero. On the other side, Glyde enters the novel before Fosco, but quickly retreats in the reader's mind to a subordinate position. Of all the characters, it is Fosco who dominates the novel and most impresses the reader.

As Walter Hartright describes her, Marian Halcombe is a physically unattractive woman: "the lady's complexion was almost swarthy, and the dark down on her upper lip was almost a mustache. She had a large, firm, masculine mouth and jaw; prominent piercing resolute brown eyes and thick coal-black hair, growing unusually low on her forehead." But morally and intellectually she is a very strong character. Her qualities, when summed up—loyalty, steadfastness, courage, propriety, intelligence, sensitivity—sound like a list of stock Victorian virtues, but, as Collins presents her, she is most real.

It is Marian who first senses a conspiracy, but it has gone too far to stop. She manages, however, to hamper the villains for a time. The irony of her situation is that when, having courageously risked her life and gained the information she needs to expose the plot, she catches pneumonia in the act—thus exposing herself and becoming helpless when most needed. In addition, her illness gives Fosco an opportunity to read her journal and learn everything about her counter-strategy. But one final irony remains. Having read Marian's comments, Fosco is so impressed by her character and resourcefulness that, for the first time, he allows sentiment to mitigate his treatment of an adversary. This modest moral hesitation is ultimately one of the primary factors in his downfall.

Fosco is one of the most memorable literary criminals of all time. By contrast, Glyde is, in Collins own words, "a weak shabby villain." Glyde is clearly dominated by Fosco and, when he operates alone, does very badly. He reacts emotionally and physically to situations with little planning and crude execution, the most obvious example being the vicarage fire that costs him his life. Because Collins thought "the crime too ingenious for an English villain," he felt it necessary to create Isidor Ottavio Baldassare Fosco.

Collins wisely never introduces or describes Fosco directly to the reader, but allows his presence to grow by means of the reactions and impressions experienced by the other characters. The Count's most obvious physical feature is his size; he is the first of the great fat criminals, a common type in later crime fiction, but unorthodox in Collins' time. "I had begun my story when it struck me that my villain would be commonplace, and I made him fat in opposition to the recognized type of villain." Fosco's physical size is matched by his appetites for food, culture, money, and intrigue: he is, in short, a daemonic Falstaff.

Fosco's intellectual powers are, likewise, impressive; his conspiracy has style as well as intelligence; he is quite witty, extremely articulate, and suavely ironical. And he is no ordinary criminal; he justifies his amoral actions philosophically: "Crime," he tells Marian, "is a good friend to man and to those about him as often as it is an enemy."

For all of his evil, Fosco is an attractive man. In addition to his intelligence, style, courage, and strong, if distorted, sense of honor, he also possesses a number of vivid humanizing traits: his fondness for animals, especially his birds and mice, his feelings for his wife, and his honest admiration, even devotion, toward Marian Halcombe. Perhaps Collins assigned Fosco's punishment to a mysterious Italian political group, rather than to Walter Hartright, because he realized that his readers' ambiguous feelings about Fosco would place some onus on the man who brought him to justice.

But, while critics have long lauded the characterizations of Marian and Fosco, they have tended to ignore Walter Hartright. But he is too important to the novel to be so easily dismissed. If he lacks some of the color and sympathy of Marian, he is, nevertheless, her equal in courage and intelligence. More importantly, looking at the novel from the standpoint of a nineteenth century reader, it is Hartright that one would most likely identify with and it is he who upholds the English national character and middle-class morality in the face of Fosco's threat.

Hartright is the hardworking son of a thrifty drawing master set up against a nobleman and baronet and frustrated by a decadent member of the gentry (Fairlie)—all vestiges of aristocracy. Walter takes his work seriously, is industrious, loyal, rational, courageous, and tenacious—in short, he possesses all of the Puritan middle-class virtues. In contrast to the amoral Fosco, Hartright believes that virtue, truth, and justice must ultimately triumph, and he is given the job of demonstrating that assumption in the action. Because he does it so efficiently, the novel answers the intellectual and moral expectations of the Victorian reading public. And, even to a twentieth century reader, despite Fosco's style and charm, Hartright's final victory seems inevitable and satisfying.

Keith Neilson

A WOMAN KILLED WITH KINDNESS

Type of work: Drama
Author: Thomas Heywood (c. 1573-1641)
Type of plot: Domestic tragedy
Time of plot: Early seventeenth century
Locale: Yorkshire, England
First presented: 1603

A Woman Killed with Kindness, a major domestic drama in the seventeenth century, is marked by genuine theatrical force and considerable depth of feeling. The source of the play is William Painter's The Palace of Pleasure.

"Look for no glorious state, our Muse is bent / Upon a barren subject, a bare scene." So begins the prologue to *A Woman Killed with Kindness,* alerting the audience that this play differs from traditional Renaissance tragedy. Heywood treats typical private citizens in a rural setting, rather than heads of states and courtly scenes; he focuses on familiar and domestic actions instead of great and terrible ones; he utilizes a colloquial, direct style, even in the verse sections, instead of rhetorical, highly elevated speech. Anne's gaining of self-awareness takes the form of a repentance scene rather than a violent action, and therefore much more pathos—instead of terror—pervades the work than in the conventional tragedy of the period.

A Woman Killed with Kindness, like other seventeenth century domestic tragedies in prose or verse, is unmistakably Christian in its pattern of sin, repentance, atonement, and forgiveness; Biblical and theological allusions abound. Sin in this kind of play is always clear, never ambiguous as in some of Shakespeare's works. Thus, characters are portrayed as inherently sinful, a fact which explains their sudden seizure by passions and their rapid shifts of emotion—conventional in Jacobean times, but bothersome for modern audiences. Such abrupt and seemingly conflict-free actions as Anne's submission to Wendoll, her quick remorse, the violent argument between Mountford and Acton, and Acton's sudden love for Susan all illustrate this belief. Since drama developed out of the medieval homiletic tradition, these plays would be expected to emphasize the sinful tendency of mankind.

Anne, it must be noted in this regard, does not die of a broken heart—as Frankford incorrectly believes—but from a conscious decision to fast. She has a clear sense of having wronged her husband, her children, and the institution of marriage. Her crime against a sacrament can only be atoned for in death; so she deliberately refuses to eat or drink. At her deathbed Frankford visits and forgives her.

Heywood carefully unifies his double plot by means of a repetition of key words ("honor," "surcharged with kindness," for example), and a series of contrasts (Susan's chastity versus Anne's adultery, Acton's revenge versus Frankford's forgiveness, and Wendoll's sinful reaction to female beauty versus

Acton's virtuous action). A final test of Heywood's skill as a dramatic artist is the play's conclusion, in which he avoids a maudlin climax, creating in his audience a sense of true sympathy with the characters.

THE WOMAN OF ROME

Type of work: Novel
Author: Alberto Moravia (Alberto Pincherle, 1907-   )
Type of plot: Naturalism
Time of plot: Twentieth century
Locale: Rome
First published: 1947

A keen study of several years in a prostitute's life, The Woman of Rome *is a naturalistic novel totally unsentimental but compelling in its honesty and its accumulation of carefully observed details. Moravia probes the social depths of the post-World War II generation.*

The Woman of Rome examines the apparently different situations of a girl selling herself in marriage to one man, or selling herself as a prostitute to many men; in either case, Moravia makes clear, she is merely trying to survive. Adriana does not think of herself as a victim, although she is pushed by her poverty, by her mother, and by her friends, into a life of prostitution. She has no education, no training, no skills; as her mother shrewdly says, all Adriana has to trade on is her beauty and her body. It is a fact, and as such must be accepted. Moravia does not sentimentalize this girl's condition any more than he sensationalizes it. His approach is objective almost to the point of being clinical; he is simply revealing to the reader people in a particular social milieu. These people have learned, as Adriana learns, to take what they can. As her friend Gisella says: "Those who ask too little of life get nothing."

But Adriana does not know how to be totally grasping. She is too good-natured and too emotional to claw her way to the top of the heap, as her mother would like. She is a modern cousin of Dreiser's Carrie, and Jennie Gerhardt, aware that she must make her own way in a hostile world but basically too trusting of the men she encounters. She is a simple and likeable girl who never willingly hurts other people. Her mother seems to be a much harsher person, but again Moravia shows how the woman came to be what she is. He does not place the entire responsibility on the environment, as a naturalist would, but he does show how difficult it is for people to escape their backgrounds. At the end of the book, Adriana is hoping for better things for her child, just as her mother did for her. The cycle never ends.

A WOMAN'S LIFE

Type of work: Novel
Author: Guy de Maupassant (1850-1893)
Type of plot: Naturalism
Time of plot: Early nineteenth century
Locale: Normandy and the island of Corsica
First published: 1883

A Woman's Life *is a short, poignant novel that chronicles with objective detachment some thirty-five years of Jeanne de Lamare's existence, from the time of her sheltered youth, through her turbulent marriage, and culminating in her disappointed yet courageous old age.*

The first of Guy de Maupassant's six novels, *A Woman's Life (Une Vie)* was published in 1883, three years after the death of his master, Gustave Flaubert. Maupassant had tried and mostly failed to please Flaubert by aspiring to the highest distinction as an artist in poetry and the theater. With the publication of "Madame Tellier's Excursion" in 1881, he found a ready market for short stories that were admirably crafted but—judged by Flaubert's exacting standards—needlessly cynical, inelegant, often mechanically contrived. Nevertheless, their pungency, realism, and shrewd observation of character attracted a sizable audience that had ignored *Des Vers,* Maupassant's only volume of poetry. Many of the qualities of the stories appear also in *A Woman's Life,* a sustained, psychologically honest study of Jeanne de Lamare from the time she completes her idealistic education at a Rouen convent in 1819, full of childish hope, until her middle age about 1855, disillusioned and worn by many sorrows.

Maupassant's novel has frequently been compared, usually to its disadvantage, with two greater fictions that examine the fate of disappointed women, Flaubert's *Madame Bovary* (1857) and Arnold Bennett's *The Old Wives' Tale* (1908). For subtlety, richness of characterization, and harmonious prose style, *Madame Bovary* is assuredly a more profound, beautifully wrought work of art. And Bennett's novel, which was inspired by *A Woman's Life,* is vastly more detailed than the model, with a surer grasp of social history and specific place, a deeper sense of the poignancy of time passing. Yet Maupassant's short novel—half as long as *Madame Bovary* and less than a third the length of *The Old Wives' Tale*—is remarkable for its own sturdy virtues. Compact, unsentimental, and stark, *A Woman's Life* is a disturbing but affectionate study taken from human experience. The portrayal of Jeanne may have been drawn, emotionally if not exactly, from Maupassant's memories of his mother. Surely his description of The Poplars recalls the setting of the Château de Miromesnil in Normandy, where the author spent the early years of his childhood. And the book, which was Maupassant's favorite among his novels, taken as a whole, is memorable for its tender appreciation for the sufferings of women dominated by insensitive men.

Indeed, although Jeanne's story is central to the narrative, she is not the only woman whose life is one of disillusionment and quiet despair. Her mother, the Baroness Adélaïde, lives a protected yet narrow life, dissembling her knowledge of her husband's philandering with house servants, and secretly revenging herself on the Baron through her own infidelity. Rosalie, Jeanne's foster sister, is seduced and betrayed by her brother-in-law. And Aunt Lison, neglected and pathetic, voices the lonely agony of a woman who has never been attractive to men. When Julien, courting his pretty Jeanne early in the novel, solicitously asks whether her "darling little feet" are cold, Lison exclaims that "No one has ever asked me a question like that . . . never . . . never." Even when women, through passion, give themselves to their lovers, Maupassant sees them as frail, not equal partners in romance. Thus Rosalie confesses to Jeanne that she had submitted to Julien's lust, in spite of the consequences and her delicate position in the household, because he pleased her sexually. And the Countess de Fourville imprudently hazards a liaison with Julien out of her weakness. Similarly, Paul's mistress submits to her lover, excusing his spendthrift ways and casual neglect of her, because she is his victim, without resources of her own. While *A Woman's Life* focuses upon the history of Jeanne, her experiences are clearly shown to represent— for the time and place of the novel—those of her sex.

It is important to note that the story begins during the spring of 1819 and concludes some thirty-five years later. Hence the book is retrospective, looking backward to a time of relative calm, to a settled, conservative society. Most of Maupassant's short stories, on the other hand, concern his own time, the Third Republic, from 1870 to 1890. By reviewing the sources of his turbulent age, Maupassant shows that the calm of Jeanne's provincial society is illusionary, fixed in complacency rather than real tranquility. It is founded upon hypocrisy and outworn traditions. The Abbé Picot, Jeanne's casuistic parish priest, is a diplomat instead of a religious man, who smooths over problems of moral turpitude for the sake of expediency. His successor, the Abbé Tolbiac, is a fanatic, inflexible in his doctrine of sin. In the narrow society in which she moves, Jeanne has not the freedom to change, to reconstruct her life, guided as she is by the dead hand of tradition.

In spite of her limited opportunities, Jeanne does not surrender to self-pity. Instead, she develops strength of character. Although she does not master her fate, at least she endures its vicissitudes. Brutally mistreated (if not, indeed, raped) on her bridal night; denied the affection and even attention of her husband; humiliated, almost maddened, by his infidelities; neglected by her wastrel son Paul, she still maintains a sense of personal dignity, of courage in the face of defeat. Like Rosalie, who has also suffered much and matured in worldly competence, she sustains life. At the end of the book, Jeanne accepts the infant daughter of Paul and his dead wife, probably only to repeat with this child the pattern of indulgence that began with her worthless son. Although she is life's victim, she is willing to take further risks for the sake of advancing life. From the vantage of her experience, such an action is either heroic or insane. Rosalie's final words, which express Maupassant's stoic philosophy as well, allow the reader to understand the ambiguities of her choice: "You see, life is never as good or as bad as one thinks."

Leslie B. Mittleman

THE WOMAN'S PRIZE

Type of work: Drama
Author: John Fletcher (1579-1625)
Type of plot: Farce
Time of plot: Sixteenth century
Locale: Italy
First presented: c. 1604

A sequel to Shakespeare's The Taming of the Shrew. *Fletcher's farce turns the tables on Petruchio by having a new wife bring him to heel.* The Woman's Prize, or, The Tamer Tamed *is broader and more extravagant in its humor than the Shakespeare play; it enjoyed a successful stage run and was revived after the Restoration.*

The author of *The Woman's Prize,* John Fletcher, was born in 1579 into a well-placed family. He was the son of Richard Fletcher, the Bishop of London, and the cousin of the poets Giles and Phineas Fletcher. Little is known of his early life, but his father's death left debts and a large family, and the young Fletcher must have needed to provide for himself.

By the early years of the seventeenth century, Fletcher had become connected with the King's Men, one of London's leading dramatic companies. He remained their most productive playwright until his death of the plague in 1625. His output was enormous by any standard: in 1679, a folio of fifty-two plays was published, of which fifteen were written by Fletcher alone, and at least thirty others were the result of his collaboration with other authors.

Fletcher is chiefly remembered in conjunction with Francis Beaumont with whom he wrote at least eight plays, but he also co-authored *Henry the Eighth* and *The Two Noble Kinsmen* with William Shakespeare, and collaborated with Philip Massinger (among others) after Beaumont's retirement. To form an idea of his productivity, one should note that he worked on more than four plays a year for the last twelve years of his life.

The Woman's Prize shows Fletcher's unaided work at its best. As the subtitle suggests, the play is a sequel of sorts to Shakespeare's *The Taming of the Shrew.* The continuation of the story of the woman-taming Petruchio, it is recorded that Fletcher's play was better liked than Shakespeare's when both were played at court in 1633, and after the Restoration, *The Woman's Prize* was revived.

But Fletcher's play is more an extension of Shakespeare's main idea than a simple continuation of the story. Only three of Shakespeare's characters remain—Petruchio, Tranio, and Bianca—and the scene has been shifted from Padua to London. There are occasional references to the action of the earlier play, mainly concerning Petruchio's reputation as a master at bending spirited women to his will, but Fletcher succeeds entirely in giving a different direction to his story.

Fletcher conceived of the idea of furnishing Petruchio with a wife who could tame him as effectively as he had tamed Katharina, Shakespeare's "shrew." We are told, as the play opens, that Kate has died, and Petruchio has remarried a gentle girl named Maria. Through the main action of Maria's subjugation of Petruchio is skillfully woven a wholly new subplot, the successful resistance of Livia to an arranged marriage to an old man.

The plot of *The Woman's Prize* immediately invites comparison with Aristophanes' *Lysistrata,* where women likewise overrule their husbands by withholding their favors. But the full-scale engagement in Fletcher's battle of the sexes, the siege of Maria's chamber, ends with the second act, leaving the stage free for the single combat of Maria and Petruchio. In their struggle, Maria wins every skirmish, and is completely victorious in the end.

The play sounds exceptionally modern in this time of Women's Liberation, since Maria demands complete equality in her relationship with her husband and settles for nothing less. When Petruchio insists on obedience as his right in justice, she answers:

> That bare word
> Shall cost you many a pound more, build upon't;
> Tell me of due obedience? What's a husband?
> What are we married for, to carry sumpters?
> Are we not one piece with you, and as worthy
> Our own intentions, as you yours?
>
> .   .   .
>
> Take two small drops of water, equal weighed,
> Tell me which is the heaviest, and which ought
> First to descend in duty?
>
> (Act III, Scene iii, lines 95-103)

Maria successfully counters all of Petruchio's devices: shouts, the orders of her father, the pretended illness of Petruchio, his threats of violence, even his feigned death, a piece of fakery that is concealed from the audience until it fails.

Fletcher's comedy derives from two sources: first, there is the comedy of incident. Several scenes are exceptionally good theater: the women barricaded in their stronghold, appearing at the window of an upper floor to bargain with the men below is a comic situation seldom equalled; and the scene in which Petruchio, locked in his room and abandoned by friends fleeing his "sickness," breaks through the door with pistol in hand is a masterpiece.

The second source of humor is Fletcher's language. Ironically, the language may have kept the play from frequent performance. The speeches are often bawdy, and what is more surprising, the language of the women is as frank as that of the men. Fletcher seems to have felt that such speech from gentlewomen might be thought excessive, since he attempts to explain it. After an explicitly sexual statement by Maria, he has Livia ask, "Dear sister, / Where have you been you talk thus?" Maria answers, "Why at Church, wench; / Where I am tied to talk thus: I am a wife now." (Act I, Scene ii, lines 83-86).

Despite Fletcher's claim of greater license in speech for wives than maidens, there is a deeper justification for the often open sexuality we find. Fletcher's play concerns how a man and woman live together in marriage. In the society of the time of the play (and for centuries afterward), a wife's body was not just her main weapon, but often her only one. Hence the characters discuss their anatomy as a soldier might talk about his armament.

When the play was revived in 1633, it attracted the attention of the Master of the Revels, the official censor for the government. He demanded a copy of the play to be presented to him, and he then purged it of what he considered blasphemy, profanity, and obscenity. The play was much more drastically cut for an eighteenth century performance. In fact, the editors of the eighteenth and nineteenth centuries often seem to show an embarrassment at the franker language of the play. In our own time, T. M. Parrott and R. H. Ball have claimed that "the jesting is rather broad for modern taste" (*A Short View of Elizabethan Drama,* New York: 1943). So rapidly though has that taste changed that no one who sees today's motion pictures would be offended by *The Woman's Prize.*

All things considered, Fletcher's comedy is a play rich in wit and humor, with well-developed characters, a fast-moving plot, and a theme relevant to our time. Unlike many comedies of its day, it fully repays its readers in enjoyment.

Walter E. Meyers

WOMEN BEWARE WOMEN

Type of work: Drama
Author: Thomas Middleton (1580-1627)
Type of plot: Tragedy of revenge
Time of plot: Early seventeenth century
Locale: Florence, Italy
First presented: c. 1621

The dramatic structure of Women Beware Women *involves the movement of characters from deliberate scheming to uncontrollable violence and destruction. Middleton's tragedy is memorable not so much for its moral ending as for the nightmare quality of human passions revealed by the force of richly dramatic verse.*

As she dies from drinking a poisoned cup, Bianca exclaims: "Oh the deadly snares / That women set for women . . . . / Like our own sex, we have no enemy, no enemy!" Yet her judgment, like that expressed in the title of the tragedy, is patently false. The action of Middleton's play proves quite the opposite: that women should "beware" men, who set the snares of money and power to destroy them. Livia schemes in behalf of her brothers Fabricio and Hippolito; her motives have nothing to do with selfish exploitation. But when she takes a lover of her own choosing, Leantio, she is abused as sinful, and her lover is murdered so that the family "honor" may be restored. Set in the corrupt and libertine atmosphere of Renaissance Florence, with cool detachment the play shows the terrible effects of passions mingled with greed.

Middleton skillfully combines two separate stories that conclude with the same explosive catastrophe. The Bianca plot was based upon the notorious real-life history of Bianco Capello, born in 1548(?) of a family of Venetian nobility. In 1563 she eloped with a Florentine, Pietro Buonaventuri, who was not of the noble class; later she married him and bore him a daughter. But the powerful Francesco de' Medici soon favored her; she became his mistress, and her husband—doubtless on Francesco's orders—was assassinated in 1569. Both Francesco and Bianca died suddenly of a fever in 1587, under circumstances that, in the popular imagination, appeared suspicious; and Francesco's brother, the Cardinal, succeeded him as Grand Duke of Tuscany. This story of lust and betrayal is combined with the Isabella-Hippolito plot, derived probably from the *Histoire Veritable des Infortunees et Tragiques Amours d'Hypolite et d'Isabella, Neapolitains* (1597). In its theme of adultery and deceit the second plot corresponds to the first, emphasizing the moral object of the drama: to expose the ruinous effects of amorous plots and counterplots conceived through guile or greed.

In his moral vision Middleton is different from the other great Jacobean tragedians. Unlike Webster and Tourneur, in whose poetic drama horror is heaped upon horror, Middleton avoids melodramatic scenes of sheer terror until the final moments of the play, when the complications of the plot are resolved in a compressed action of mass slaughter. Unlike Ford, who is masterful in pathetic scenes of sexual aberration, Middleton is a realist who avoids abnormal psycho-sexual behavior. Although Isabella willingly submits to the embraces of Hippolito—and thus commits incest—she is deceived by Livia into believing that her uncle's blood-line is different from hers. As soon as she learns the truth about the relationship, she plots revenge on her betrayers. Yet her passion for Hippolito, so long as she could deny to herself the incest-inhibition, was as fierce as the man's.

As a psychologist Middleton is interested in the ruthless power of men as dominating, even sadistic, lovers; and in women as their victims, who often masochistically acquiesce in their own destruction. Bianca, like Beatrice-Joanna in Middleton and Rowley's *The Changling,* is a sensual girl who fixes her love on one man and then, driven by sexual urges, on another. Just as Beatrice-Joanna comes to love—or at least lust for—her seducer, the abhorrent De Flores, so Bianca comes to champion the Duke over her love-matched husband Leantio. It is not riches alone that has tempted her to cancel her marriage vows; it is lust for the more powerful man. Because of her sexual weakness, the woman is without moral resources; and the man, through his sexual power, uses women as property—as mere physical possessions to be bought and sold. Middleton objectively records the actions, without sentimentality or preaching, and allows the audience a chance to judge whether women should indeed "beware" women.

THE WOMEN OF TRACHIS

Type of work: Drama
Author: Sophocles (c. 496-406 or 405 B.C.)
Type of plot: Classical tragedy
Time of plot: Remote antiquity
Locale: Trachis
First presented: Before 408 B.C.

The Women of Trachis (Trachiniae), *recounting the last crisis in the life of Herakles, is the only surviving tragedy of Sophocles which ends in death for both of the chief characters. The tragedy is of universal interest because it emphasizes the devotion and love inherent in womanhood, while in the awful agonies of Herakles are embodied the heroic endurance and strength representative of ideal masculinity.*

The Women of Trachis has as its tragic protagonist not one person but a family of three. For this reason critics sometimes claim that the play lacks unity, since half is devoted to Deianira and half to Herakles, with neither appearing on stage at the same time. Yet to see this drama properly one must regard the tragedies of Deianira, Herakles, and Hyllus as one large event instigated by the gods, carried out by human will, and transcended in the end by strength of character. Even though this play lacks the smoothness and facility of *Oedipus Tyrannus,* it is still interesting and significant, and it treats the major problem of Sophocles' dramatic career, that of human freedom.

Briefly, the problem is this: when events are determined by the will of the gods, as revealed in oracles and prophecies, and by the passionate compulsions of the human animal, freedom lies in learning the truth and accepting it —not passively, but with all the force of one's being. For a person to be free he must knowingly seek to accomplish his destiny in harmony with divine law. In Sophocles that destiny is always hard and terrible, which makes the acceptance of it truly ennobling. This preoccupation is at the heart of *The Women of Trachis,* which was probably written when the dramatist was in his sixties, an age when he had looked at life fully and accurately. The play is a mature statement of Sophocles' deepest convictions.

The action moves from ignorance to truth, and from misconceptions to a revelation of the total pattern imposed by divine will. Each of the three tragic characters acts from a lack of understanding and then must confront the awful truth. We see this first in Deianira. Her greatest apprehension in the beginning is that her husband, Herakles, will not live much longer. Then she learns that he is both alive and returning home in triumph. She sympathizes with the most miserable of the captive women, Iole, only to learn that Herakles has taken that girl as his concubine to share Deianira's bed. Deianira does not find fault with either Iole or Herakles, but determines to win her husband's love by black magic. The potion is made from Nessus' poisoned gore, the centaur that Herakles killed, and the most lustful of beasts. After sending the deadly robe to Herakles, she realizes how dangerous it is. When her son Hyllus reviles and curses her for murdering Herakles by slow agony, she knows that she herself has accomplished her worst fear. Her knowledge is subject to reversal upon reversal until the original prophecy and dread have been fulfilled.

However, Deianira's character is as much a part of this sequence as fate. She is a fearful, devoted, and rather gullible wife. Her only reason for resorting to magic is to regain Herakles' love, and it wins for her his undying hatred, not to mention Hyllus' condemnation. She does not excuse herself but accepts full responsibility for the deed she committed in ignorance, and she atones for it by suicide, choosing the noble method of stabbing herself. In that acceptance of her guilt and in that atonement, she achieves true freedom. Deianira's tragic courage lifts her above fate.

Then Herakles himself, the greatest hero of Greece, is brought upon the stage in a litter. He is dying not from a foe but at the hands of a rather pathetic woman, which humiliates him tremendously. He bawls and rages in pain, wishing to murder his wife. As he cites his triumphs in killing beasts and monsters, we realize that the beasts have taken their revenge through Nessus' poisoned blood. We also know that it was Herakles' own bestial lust for Iole that precipitated his doom. Ironically, the beast-slayer is possessed of the same violence and lechery as the beasts he killed, and his body is mortally infected with the centaur's gore.

Once again the process of revelation begins. As Herakles learns that his death is being caused by Nessus' cunning, it dawns on him that the prophecy of his death is being completed and that Deianira was an innocent agent of the gods. When this is driven home by Hyllus' penitent and intrepid honesty, Herakles addresses himself to the fact of his death in earnest. He chooses the manner of his death freely, just as his wife had done. He determines to be burned alive rather than suffer death by poison passively. In that resolve he shows the same tragic courage as Deianira. He seizes the terrible will of Zeus and makes it his own. The audience is aware that Herakles will be transfigured as a god on his funeral pyre, but the important thing for Sophocles was the heroic determination of Herakles to make his death his own, in which he, too, transcends fate.

The third tragic figure is Hyllus, the son of Herakles and Deianira. Like his parents, he acts in ignorance, must suffer the truth, and make an atonement. Hyllus lays a dreadful curse on his mother, thinking she murdered Herakles out of jealousy and spite. By the time he learns what actually happened, Deianira has killed herself and he bears some of the guilt for her death. He loves both of his parents. Thus, he finds himself in an unbearable situation. He atones in part by braving Herakles' rage to justify his mother's intentions, which in turn leads to Herakles' recognition of the truth. But then his father makes two very hard demands on him and binds him to them by oath. The first is that he build the funeral pyre on which Herakles is to perish, thus taking a hand in the death of his father as well as his mother. And the second is that Hyllus marry the woman he loathes—Iole, the cause of all the trouble. It seems likely that this forthcoming marriage will put an end to the blood-and-lust syndrome which destroyed his parents. Hyllus shows his manliness in the fortitude with which he accepts both conditions.

The final statement of the play, "there is nothing here which is not Zeus," expresses Sophocles' faith that while the gods lay down the tragic circumstances of our lives and we fulfill them through inner compulsion, we can triumph over necessity by sheer strength of character. The divine pattern imposes hopeless suffering on men, which gives men the opportunity to show their nobility. This is a stern faith, but a stern faith is essential in a hard world.

James Weigel, Jr.

THE WOODLANDERS

Type of work: Novel
Author: Thomas Hardy (1840-1928)
Type of plot: Tragic romance
Time of plot: Nineteenth century
Locale: Rural England
First published: 1887

The Woodlanders, a romance that includes both scenes of rustic humor and of tragedy, is memorable for its mythic quality—in which characters are related symbolically to plants—and for the touching figure of Marty South, one of Hardy's noblest women.

Written between *The Mayor of Casterbridge* and *Tess of the D'Urbervilles,* this novel with its plot full of melodramatic excesses, is neither tragedy nor comedy. And it does not have the depth or majesty of Hardy's later works. Rather in its efforts to combine realism and sensationalism, it exhibits affinities with earlier novels like *Desperate Remedies.*

The oppressively enclosed society of Hintock, where the "woodlanders" dwell, is one of contrasting sets of individuals, rural and urban. Giles Winterborne, Marty South, George Melbury and the workers are opposed to exotic Felice Charmond of Hintock Manor and Edgar Fitzpiers, the new doctor. Grace Melbury vacillates between the two groups, finally committing herself, after the death of Giles, presumably to life with Fitzpiers in another area; Hardy leaves the end of the novel rather ambiguous.

The story revolves not only upon Grace's decisions and indecisions, but also upon those of Fitzpiers, who is simultaneously trapped in marriage with Grace and in an affair with Felice; of Mr. Melbury, who cannot make up his mind to marry his daughter to the apple grower or the doctor; and of Felice, who cannot settle on one lover.

Most events in the novel take place in dense woods, on forest paths, or in remote huts almost hidden by foliage. Trees and undergrowth are so omnipresent as to be stifling. Hintock dwellers plant trees, trim or tend them, fell them at maturity, and strip the bark to sell. The woods have utilitarian as well as symbolic significance. They are real and so are Giles and Marty, accepting with stolid, earth-like quality, their fate of endless hard work. The woodland here lacks the gentleness and beauty of that in *Under the Greenwood Tree*; it demands its price from those who make it their living.

The characters are even compared implicitly to trees and plants: Giles and Marty are the indigenous trees, Felice and Fitzpiers the imported plants that finally uproot themselves and seek climates more favorable to their growth.

After an almost unbelievable network of promises made and broken, infidelities, romantic seductions, and accidental deaths, Grace and the re-

pentant Fitzpiers are left to repair their ill-starred marriage. But the last
chapter points to no satisfactory or simple solution. Hardy does not extol
their renewed love; instead, he focuses on Marty South's devoted soliloquy
as she places flowers on Giles' grave. She, too, loved him but faithfully. In
contrast to other women in the novel, she is the epitome of self-sacrifice, and
it is Marty whom Hardy leaves with the reader, perhaps embodying in her the
residual human values when he comments, "she touched sublimity at points,
and looked almost like a being who had rejected . . . the attribute of sex
for the loftier quality of abstract humanism." Marty is more a figure of stoic
resignation, however, than of sublimity; and even Giles, for all his loyalty
and sacrifice for Grace, does not attain, like the Mayor of Casterbridge or
the later Jude, tragic stature.

WOODSTOCK

Type of work: Novel
Author: Sir Walter Scott (1771-1832)
Type of plot: Historical romance
Time of plot: 1651
Locale: England
First published: 1826

Originally titled The Cavalier, *this novel is primarily the story of gallant old Sir Henry Lee and of his efforts in behalf of his fugitive king, Charles II of England. There are enough historical facts to make the romance plausible, but Scott colors the story with his inventions of a monarch in disguise, thwarted lovers, and a hateful villain.*

Woodstock covers a pivotal period in English history, the Great Rebellion, and ends with the Restoration. The opposing forces are represented by Markham Everard, a Puritan Colonel, and the fugitive king Charles II, disguised as a page. Everard, who combines idealism and pragmatism, must struggle for freedom and fight against absolutism. Charles II, who is also a paradoxical blend of different traits, signifies the Restoration, but is finally obliged to come to terms with many of the demands and accomplishments of the rebels.

However, despite these interesting portrayals of historical figures, there are serious flaws in the work. Scott himself remarked that he wrote *Woodstock* so quickly that he was not sure how the tale would be ended when he was halfway through its composition; many of the novel's weaknesses arise from this hastiness. Some critics have pointed to the prominent role of Charles II in the novel as another weakness. Scott was accustomed to mediate between the great figures of history and his audience with relatively minor personages, observers, and go-betweens; but the melodrama in *Woodstock* is not softened by any of these intermediaries of humbler social standing. There is less historical and social realism, less description of various social groups, than in previous novels.

Other critics have questioned the use of language in *Woodstock*. A lengthy discussion in *Westminster Review* of April, 1826, makes the point that Scott has his characters use highly figurative, poetic language no matter how appropriate that language may be. For example, men of all social ranks, from high to low, speak in elaborate and ingenious poetical devices. The result is that characters are not adequately distinguished from one another, and the dialogue, which comprises such a large portion of the novel, is artificial and even distracting. Nevertheless, in spite of these defects *Woodstock* contains some memorable characterizations—such as that of old Sir Henry Lee—and has an intriguing plot; if not one of Scott's best works, the book is still a delight to read.

WORLD ENOUGH AND TIME

Type of work: Novel
Author: Robert Penn Warren (1905-   )
Type of plot: Philosophical romance
Time of plot: 1801-1826
Locale: Kentucky
First published: 1950

Based upon an actual nineteenth century historical event popularly called the "Kentucky Tragedy," Warren's novel centers around a theme of community guilt and expiation, illustrating the complex moral issues of the present age.

Given his lifelong preoccupation with Southern history, it is not surprising that Robert Penn Warren was attracted to the "Kentucky Tragedy" as a vehicle for expression of his ideas and feelings about idealism, fanaticism, politics, love, sex, and violence. In adapting this historical event—almost a folk legend—Warren begins with a story of innocence violated, villainy rewarded, revenge, political corruption, and backwoods violence. The raw material is, therefore, highly dramatic—almost too much so. Warren's first problem is: how can the story be told without descending to sentimental romance or lurid melodrama?

In the first place he mutes the obvious sensationalism of the events through his handling of point of view. An unnamed historian, having pieced together the story from Jeremiah Beaumont's "confession" and other data, narrates the events with scholarly objectivity and frequent moralizing in an ornate prose style. This elaborate, indirect approach, in combination with highly charged dramatic scenes, gives the book both historical distance and dramatic intensity.

Second, Warren shifts the usual focus of the tale from the sentimental, revenge-seeking woman, Rachael Jordan, to her idealistic but confused lover, Jeremiah. Thus, the novel takes on a shape not unlike Warren's earlier masterpiece, *All the King's Men.* As in the previous book, the novel centers around the relationship between a young man (Jeremiah), a powerful "father figure" (Cassius Fort), who combines idealistic good with pragmatic evil and who inspires worship as well as revulsion, and the woman (Rachael) who is the victim both of the older man's attractiveness and his ruthlessness. Again the "father figure" is murdered by the young man to avenge the "honor" of the woman.

Warren's analysis of the political context of the act further differentiates his handling of the "Kentucky Tragedy" from previous ones. The results of Jeremiah's act demonstrate the potential dangers of fanatical idealism in conflict with corrupt pragmatic politics. He is finally convicted not because he committed the crime, but because his guilt serves the selfish needs of those in power.

Warren's biggest deviation from the original events, however, lies in the novel's resolution. The historical couple attempted mutual suicide; the woman died, the man was hanged. In Warren's version an escape is arranged. In the course of their flight, Jeremiah and Rachael learn the truth of their situation, which drives Rachael to suicide and Jeremiah to an attempt at public confession. The important thing to Warren is not Jeremiah's legal punishment, but the growth of his personal awareness. Jeremiah, like other Warren protagonists, must finally accept responsibility not only for his own deed, but also for the sequence of turbulent events provoked by that first act of violence.

THE WORLD OF THE THIBAULTS

Type of work: Novel
Author: Roger Martin du Gard (1881- 1958)
Type of plot: Social chronicle
Time of plot: Early twentieth century
Locale: France
First published: 1922-1940

This eight-part novel—reprinted in the United States in two volumes, The
Thibaults *and* Summer 1914—*is a vast examination of French social history on a
Tolstoyan scale but without the Russian author's more philosophical treatment.*

The eight-part novel cycle, *Les Thibault,* was inspired by a desire on the
part of the author to emulate for his own time the scale of Tolstoy's *War and
Peace.* In fact, however, the style and pessimism is closer to Martin du Gard's
countryman, Flaubert, than to the Russian author. Although the historical
background of the action in the novel is of interest, for most readers the
powerful depiction of human relationships constitutes the book's chief merit.

In many respects, the most influential character in the vast novel is old
M. Thibault, the patriarch of the Thibault family. A complete hypocrite, he
announces to the world that his conscience is clear, yet he is concerned only
with his own convenience and peace. Cloaking his craving for power and
authority under a guise of fervent religiosity and philanthropy, he actually
has no sense of either religion or generosity. He possesses no love for his
sons, demanding only that they be completely docile. Any contradiction or
sign of individuality throws him into a rage. For all of his big gestures, he
is a petty man. Everyone automatically hides feelings from him, for one
never can tell what his reaction might be. He forces his family into hypocrisy
in order for them to live with him. By avoiding all introspection, M. Thibault
unknowingly condemns himself to a life of petty pride and cruelty, a life so
alone that he must find his only consolation in public honors and the
"knowledge" that he is a "good man." But, as he grows older, the fact of
approaching death terrifies him increasingly, and he desperately seeks some
kind of immortality, as if he realizes, in his unconscious mind, how futile
his busy life actually has been.

The volumes of the series are crowded with fascinating, well-drawn secondary characters, such as M. Chasle, the middle-aged secretary of M. Thibault,
who is suddenly revealed to have his own life, his own preoccupations, fears,
and miseries. The reader becomes aware of many other lives lurking in the
background, and beyond them still others. In the volume called *The Spring-
time of Life,* the adult Daniel and Jacques experience the bohemian life of
Paris, encountering "characters" such as Mother JuJu, the retired prostitute,
and many colorful girls of the streets, as well as the rich Jew, Ludwigson,
who sells Daniel's pictures. Earlier, the reader encounters the amazing pastor

Gregory, with his Rasputin personality, in a powerful scene at young Jenny's sickbed, when he chants and prays and condemns with equal fury, and somehow saves the girl's life.

The growth of the relationship between Jacques Thibault and Daniel de Fontanin is shown in many different ways, as the author explores the various paths the boys take in their lives as they mature. At first, the homely little redhaired Jacques dominates the older, more restrained, Daniel, when they run away together at the beginning of the book. But, after his first sexual experience, Daniel becomes less easily ruled by his friend. When Jacques is sent to the reformatory, their relationship nearly dies, but later it is restored on a quite different level. Martin du Gard skillfully captures the changing attitudes and emotions of young men in the process of maturing.

The strained relationship between Jacques and Antoine is portrayed with particular subtlety. The family reticence, the legacy of the tyrannical father, prevents an early comradeship between the brothers, but gradually, after Jacques returns from the reformatory, the brothers build a new and solid relationship.

A subplot of complexity and great interest is woven into the tale of the young men: it is the story of Madame de Fontanin and her unfaithful husband. She is an almost unique character in fiction, a good person who is neither boring nor cloying. Although not perfect, she is admirable in most of her thoughts and acts. She possesses no malice, although she suffers and occasionally reacts with anger. The touching scenes of her reunion in Holland with her husband and his dying mistress, whose daughter Mme. de Fontanin has cared for, are unforgettable. The complex relationships reveal the subtle and ever-changing realities of human emotions. It is as difficult to hate, Martin du Gard seems to be implying, as it is to love.

The death that waits for everyone, and for the two brothers in the war, is foreshadowed when Jacques and Jenny see Daniel and Jenny's dog crushed by an old car. The accident prompts Jacques and Jenny to discuss death, but neither realizes how soon World War I will cause the deaths of millions of young people such as themselves, including Jacques and his brother. The irony is appalling, yet not overdone.

Rachel, another of the fascinating secondary characters, tells Antoine that she is afraid of being lonely; this is a fear shared by most of the characters in the book. There is a gripping horror in Rachel's monologue as she shows Antoine her photographs and tells him about her past life and her lover, the infamous Hirsch. The Africa described by Rachel becomes a mythological place of fulfilled desires and strange passions, and Hirsch a fabulous manmonster. Nevertheless, the reader is hardly surprised when Mademoiselle Rachel leaves Antoine and returns to Hirsch. Rachel and Antoine Thibault never could find permanent happiness together.

The graphic realism of the sickbed and death scenes, and, in the seventh volume, *Summer, 1914,* the dramatic buildup of the war, as the European nations are swept relentlessly to destruction, are all impressive achievements. But, as the focus of the novel expands, the author never loses sight of the individuals who make up the world. For this vast, panoramic survey of society and the meaning of life, as well as for his earlier novel of the Dreyfus affair and atheism, *Jean Barois,* Roger Martin du Gard was awarded the Nobel Prize for literature in 1937.

Martin du Gard, a dramatist as well as novelist, was born into a professional middle-class family in 1881. He studied to be an archivist and paleographer, served with a motor-transport unit during World War I, and, for a brief period, worked in the theater. But most of his life was spent in seclusion, wholly dedicated to his writing. Literature was truly Martin du Gard's entire life. His closest friend was André Gide, about whom he eventually wrote a book. His last novel, which was to be his masterpiece, was never finished, and remains unpublished. But Martin du Gard's achievement was formidable, and his influence on French fiction was impressive.

Bruce D. Reeves

THE WORLD'S ILLUSION

Type of work: Novel
Author: Jacob Wassermann (1873-1934)
Type of plot: Social criticism
Time of plot: Prior to World War I
Locale: Europe
First published: 1919

Written in two parts, the first book of The World's Illusion *deals with brilliant, upper-class life in European society, of which the protagonist is an example. The second book deals with the same protagonist, who leaves the vanity and culture of his world for the horrors of life among the proletariat in the worst of European slums.*

The World's Illusion (in German titled *Christian Wahnschaffe* and published in two volumes) is a powerful philosophical novel that explores the decadence of the upper-middle-class European society prior to World War I. Completed in the last year of the war, the novel is a declaration of the author's faith that mankind, through suffering and the atonement of guilt, may be redeemed from its wickedness. At the same time, the book is a jeremiad on the old order of the privileged classes, exhausting themselves through frivolous pleasures, greed, and stupidity. Indeed, like an Old Testament prophet, Wassermann excoriates the evils of a corrupt society, even as he laments its waste; from this perspective of social criticism, his novel can be appreciated in the light of the German postwar Expressionist movement in art. But from a literary perspective, the book is clearly in the moral tradition of Dostoevski and Tolstoy. Sustained, eloquent, and at times hortatory, *The World's Illusion* attempts, on a grand scale, to summarize the passions, ideas, and ethics of an effete civilization.

Wassermann's hero is Christian Wahnschaffe, a wealthy, intelligent but spiritually restless searcher after self-knowledge. His search for perfect love is frustrated. Eva Sorel, who inspires in him the deepest passion, ultimately proves to be—in her own words—a sorceress who would enslave him. But Christian frees himself from the sorcery of submissive love; he will not serve any soul weaker than his own. Similarly, his search for perfect friendship, even with the "stainless knight" Bernard Crammon, is unfulfilling. He is bored with luxury, wearies of senseless pleasure, and rejects the feverish activities of political idealism. By the end of the novel, he has divested himself of wealth and station; through service in behalf of miserable, suffering humanity, he has attempted to live purely and simply; through abnegation of his own selfish desires, he has attempted to follow the paths of righteousness.

From Christian's moral pilgrimage Wassermann (as a twentieth century John Bunyan) points a clear message: that by following the evil gods of

Baal, the children of light have fallen into the darkness of "the world's illusion." This illusion is the worship of false gods—hedonistic delights, sterile vanity, sensuality—that conceals the real purpose of existence. In two important scenes of the novel Amadeus Voss alerts his friend Christian to this purpose. In the final chapter of "The Silver Cord," he reads to Christian two passages from Ecclesiastes, 11:9 and 12:1, to remind him that God's judgment will follow after those who pride themselves on their youthful vigor. And at an even more significant turning point in the novel, the section titled "Karen Engelschall," Amadeus reads to Christian from Isaiah 3:15. The passage beginning "What mean ye that ye crush my people" concludes with a terrible threat of doom to the "daughters of Zion" for their vanity. At once, Christian understands that his life has been one of fatuity, and leaves Berlin. Thus, like a Tolstoyan hero, he learns that social glory is a mere bauble. In the second volume of the book, he learns—like a Dostoevskian hero—that he must undergo suffering and renunciation to purge himself of guilt.

Yet as a novel of ideas, *The World's Illusion* perhaps resembles the fiction of Mann and Hesse, Wassermann's contemporaries, more closely than that of the Russians. Like Mann's *Buddenbrooks* (1901), *The World's Illusion* analyzes the decadence of a social class committed to vulgar materialism; and like Hesse's *Siddhartha* (1922) or *Steppenwolf* (1927), the book concerns the discovery of self through the visionary or intuitive stages of an interior journey. To make these stages clear to the reader, Wassermann's method is one of sharp contrasts: the ideal with the real; the life of power with the life of service; sincere affection (Letitia) with egoistic passion (Eva); the luxury of German aristocrats with the poverty of Polish peasants and Russian Jews; morality with sensuality; man's judgments with those of God. At times Wassermann's dialectic method lacks subtlety. But at his best, he writes with intensity, lyric beauty, and fervent moral conviction.

WOYZECK

Type of work: Drama
Author: Georg Büchner (1813-1837)
Type of plot: Psychological realism
Time of plot: Early nineteenth century
Locale: Germany
First presented: 1913; first published: 1879

> *This play, surprisingly modern in its blending of naturalism and expressionism, was based upon an actual event: Johann Christian Woyzeck, a conscript convicted of the murder of his common-law wife, was publicly executed at Leipzig on August 27, 1824. Büchner's drama provided the story for Alban Berg's experimental modern opera,* Wozzeck.

Woyzeck, though written early in the nineteenth century, achieved its fame almost a hundred years later, and it exerted great influence on writers of our own century. Like so much of Büchner's work, it was astonishingly ahead of of its time in language, in form, and in idea. The classical doctrine of tragedy stressed "catharsis," the elevating effect achieved when a character accepts his fate stoically, comes to terms with it, and triumphs inwardly in the face of destruction. The classical heroes were men of stature, usually kings or princes, and the common people appeared only as types, often caricatured as in Shakespeare. Büchner reverses this tradition: his "hero" is from the lowest, poorest class, a conscripted soldier, hopelessly ignorant, forced to serve as a medical guinea pig to earn a bit of money. He cannot possibly cope with his fate, the more so as his mind is deranged by the experiments. Here it is the upper class that is caricatured, in the mindless inhumanity of the doctor, and in the vapid metaphysics of the captain.

There is no elevation in Woyzeck's fate, only animal suffering and almost instinctive existence. Thus, the old rhetorical style of speech becomes irrelevant, and the structure of sentences breaks down with the structure of thought. The speech is affective: ideas give way to unstructured fragments, pauses, sounds, a kind of stream of consciousness that expresses a state of mind rather than a content. The scenes, too, shrink; exposition, no longer possible, is replaced by brief crystallizations of experience, again expressive rather than rhetorical. The chronology is unclear and there is little real development.

Woyzeck, despised and exploited, betrayed by Marie, the victim of her own instincts, has no inner resources to fall back on. He acts mechanically, as if in a trance. There is no resolution, no catharsis, simply the record of unredeemed suffering.

THE WRECK OF THE GROSVENOR

Type of work: Novel
Author: W. Clark Russell (1844-1911)
Type of plot: Adventure romance
Time of plot: Nineteenth century
Locale: The Atlantic Ocean
First published: 1877

The Wreck of the Grosvenor *is more than a stirring sea romance; with a sure sense of the maritime life, Russell shows his sympathy for the common sailor, often the victim of injustice and miserable exploitation.*

W. Clark Russell's numerous sea novels continue that colorful breed of sea literature in the tradition of James Fenimore Cooper's *The Pilot* and *The Red Rover; The Wreck of the Grosvenor* helped to slake the thirst of the English-speaking public on both sides of the Atlantic for sea yarns. Unlike Cooper, however, Russell specialized in tales of the sea; and his novels were popular in the days when "Britannia ruled the waves." *The Wreck of the Grosvenor* is still one of the more popular of Russell's many novels. Russell wanted the novel to teach a lesson by exposing the meanness of ship owners who turned good sailors bad, bad sailors outrageous, and harmless sailors into criminals. Russell attempted to expose the rascals who sent rotten ships to sea, ships with rotten food as well as rotten timbers. The wrongs done to English sailors were not understood ashore, he believed, hence sailors had few champions. One would have to live, work, and suffer with sailors to appreciate their misery—to go aloft, man pumps, eat salt pork and sea biscuit, drink wormy water, and experience shore temptations such as the harpies who drug and fleece sailors.

Few sea stories are as stirring as *The Wreck of the Grosvenor,* and Russell's works are said almost to comprise a mariner's encyclopedia. It is almost as if Russell communed with the illimitable ocean and took some of its power for his descriptions; the reader sails and lives with the good, bad, and indifferent crew members of the *Grosvenor.* From first page to last the reader suffers the suspense, violence, storm, shipwreck, mutiny, cruelty, pathos, and tragedy that were the lot of the crew, and cannot help but admire the blue-water sailors of the days of "iron men and wooden ships."

Reforms aboard vessels that flew "the red ensign" (traditional bunting of the Merchant Navy, as compared to "the white ensign" of the Royal Navy) were indirectly implemented by Russell's novel. Russell closed his book by lamenting that the battlefield of Waterloo had monuments for officers but not privates, while naval expeditions to the North Pole bred plaques commemorating naval commanders, "But we have little to say about Poor Jack, who dies by scurvy on the North Pole."

WUTHERING HEIGHTS

Type of work: Novel
Author: Emily Brontë (1818-1848)
Type of plot: Impressionistic romance
Time of plot: 1757-1803
Locale: The moors of northern England
First published: 1847

Published under the pseudonym Ellis Bell, this famous novel was once considered such a risk by its publishers that Emily Brontë had to defray the cost of publication until a sufficient number of copies had been sold. Despite some scenes of romantic exaggeration, Wuthering Heights *is an intriguing tale of revenge in which the main figures exist in the more than life-size vitality of their own consuming passions.*

F. R. Leavis, in his influential *The Great Tradition* (1948), calls *Wuthering Heights* a "sport." He cannot find a clear place for the book in his historical scheme of the English novel's development. The novel has eluded classification since its publication, and to this day its characters and ideas perplex and fascinate. The source of its energy lies in the powerful tension between its plot and its characters, between its organization and its themes. Dorothy Van Ghent (*The English Novel,* 1953) observes that in plot and design the book has rigorous "limitation" although its characters are passionately immoderate; as a result the story is constantly explosive. Time and space force their restrictions on spirits straining to be free.

After an initial reading, the reader tends only to remember the most violent or emotional scenes and thinks back on the organization of the novel as a mere string for fiery gems: Lockwood's dream, Cathy and Heathcliff fighting off the dogs of Thrushcross Grange, Heathcliff at Cathy's deathbed, or countless moments of cruelty and ecstasy involving all the characters. On closer analysis, the reader discovers the intricate interweaving of the novel's four parts into the core-story of Catherine and Heathcliff. The scheme can be summarized as follows: the establishment of the violently passionate relationship betwen Catherine and Heathcliff; Catherine's rejection of marriage with Heathcliff, and her marriage to Edgar Linton and death in childbirth; Heathcliff's revenge; and Heathcliff's disintegration and death.

In addition to this four-part design, with its intricate changes in time and relationships among secondary characters, the novel is prescribed by the spatial and social polarity of Wuthering Heights and Thrushcross Grange. Without all these defining and prescriptive forms, the metaphysical revolt that underlies the relationship between Catherine and Heathcliff would not have a sufficient antagonist; to put it another way, the pressures designed to crush them help to make their haunting and demonic challenge to experience credible.

How do Catherine and Heathcliff do it? How does Emily Brontë empower her protagonists to overcome time, space and society? She makes their minds independent of empirical reality. Catherine confides to Ellen Dean that "dreams . . . have stayed with me . . . and changed my ideas; they've gone through and through me, like wine through water, and altered the colour of my mind." Unlike Lockwood, who is terribly frightened by his nightmare, Catherine connects her dreaming with self-definition. In Catherine's dream the angels in Heaven are so offended by her "weeping to come back to earth . . . that they flung" her out "into the middle of the heath on the top of Wuthering Heights," where she wakes "sobbing for joy." Long before she dies physically, Catherine resurrects herself in her imagination; the irony of this religious vision is that it reverses traditional priorities: earth becomes a paradise to Heaven's misery. A "vision" of Nature replaces the phenomenal world of time and space.

Gods are realized in the minds of their worshipers. Catherine has only one worshiper, Heathcliff, but he is powerful enough to substitute for the multitudes. Heathcliff is Catherine's Faith because their souls are interchangeable ("Nelly, I am Heathcliff"); powerless to resist her intensity, Heathcliff is sanctified by her identification with him. The terms are diabolical: " . . . you have treated me infernally," complains Heathcliff to Catherine after his return to Wuthering Heights. In response to Catherine's plea that he refrain from marrying Isabella Linton, Heathcliff lashes back: "The tyrant (and he means Catherine) grinds down his slaves and they don't turn against him, they crush those beneath them." The terms may be diabolical, but the actuality is seraphic. Emily Brontë is similar to William Blake in the way she reverses the values of Heaven and Hell in order to dramatize and release a spiritually revolutionary moral energy.

When Heathcliff learns of Catherine's illness, he tells Ellen Dean that "existence after losing her would be hell." Indeed, the love Heathcliff and Catherine share is a new kind of emotional paradise, despite its pain and destiny of frustration, so that when Catherine lies ill on what will be her deathbed, Heathcliff is literally witness to a crucifixion. Afraid that Heathcliff will be harmed by Linton once he discovers them together, Catherine's words ring with beatific self-denial: "Kiss me again; and don't let me see your eyes. I forgive what you have done to me. I love my murderer—but *yours!* How can I?" When Ellen tells him shortly afterward of Catherine's death, Heathcliff demands that she haunt him to his dying day since life without her is inconceivable. Just as Catherine preferred Nature with Heathcliff to Heaven without him in her dreams, Heathcliff spends the rest of his life rejecting earthly possibilities and directs the track of his spiritual and mental energies toward reunion with Catherine: "I cannot live without my soul!" And when the time comes, he prepares for his death as if it were salvation: "Last night, I was on the threshold of hell. Today, I am within sight of my heaven."

These two lovers literally inhabit a psychic and emotional world entirely their own. Ellen Dean seems an honest observer, but her conventional imagination makes her finally a spiritual stranger to all the facts she so carefully relates. Lockwood is awed by the lovers' story, but he "sees" it at a great distance because of limitations of feeling and perception. Three generations of Lintons and Earnshaws together with the conflicts of class and religious differences embodied in the juxtaposition of "Heights" and "Grange," seem merely an insignificant background to the classless, timeless, and eerily universal passion of these two children of the moor.

Peter A. Brier

THE YEARLING

Type of work: Novel
Author: Marjorie Kinnan Rawlings (1896-1953)
Type of plot: Regional romance
Time of plot: Late nineteenth century
Locale: The Florida scrub country
First published: 1938

A juvenile romance set against an unusually realistic background of struggle and privation on a marginal Florida farm, The Yearling *deals with one year in the life of a twelve-year-old boy, the year in which he passes from adolescence into young manhood.*

The Yearling, a classic of juvenile romantic fiction, appeals to both young and adult readers. As a novel of development, the book treats a "rite of passage" from the carefree pleasures of childhood to the more sober stage of responsibilities that come with growth—a subject that interests as well as educates children. At the same time, Rawlings' careful observation of people and setting in rural Florida entertains mature readers. Life is hard for the Baxters. Although Jody is reared close to nature with a joyous appreciation for beauty and is secure in the affection of his family, his parents have to struggle to make ends meet. Theirs is a marginal existence from a stubborn soil; and Rawlings constantly reminds the reader of the Baxters' empty woodbox, the water barrels that need filling from the sink hole, the privations of the scrub-farmers' toil. Without glossing over the hardships of the Baxters and their neighbors, the author also shows her love for the land and its creatures, her admiration for the rugged honesty and perseverance of the farmers, and her sense of wonder at the beauty of Florida's vanishing wilderness.

The plot of *The Yearling* falls into two main narratives that treat the two important actions: the first is the bear hunt that culminates with the killing of Old Slewfoot; the second is the story of Jody's affection for the fawn Flag, the yearling. The first narrative reminds the reader of Faulkner's novella *The Bear*. Like the Faulkner story, the bear hunt is a ritual involving not only the boy and his family, but also neighbors of all sorts, representing rural society. In both stories, the bear at first escapes from the hunters; in both, a feist—a small aggressive hound—is important either to make the hunt possible or to corner the bear; finally, in Faulkner as well as Rawlings, the bear is considered to be an extremely capable, sly, and dangerous foe. Beyond this point the resemblance between the stories cannot be extended. Faulkner's bear is clearly a metaphysical force as well as an animal; Rawlings' bear is only a powerful creature.

The second narrative concerns Jody's discovery of the fawn, his growing sense of identification with the animal, and his terrible grief when the yearling is slain. This action resembles some parts of the first section of Steinbeck's *The Red Pony* (1937)—"The Gift." In both stories a boy (each named, coincidentally, Jody) receives for his particular care an animal—Flag for Jody Baxter, the pony Gabilan for Jody Tiflin; in both the raising of the animal is difficult yet emotionally rewarding for the boy; in both the animal does not survive, and the boy is heartbroken. To be sure, in Steinbeck's novel the pony is not slain by man. The special poignancy of the conclusion of *The Yearling* is the manner of Flag's death. To protect her corn from the fawn's ravages, Mrs. Baxter has to shoot the animal; when the job is botched, it is Jody who must finish off his beloved pet. This necessary but agonizing chore estranges the boy from his parents. Torn by grief, Jody flees them as betrayers—then returns. By the end of the book Jody has learned to make compromises with reality. It is a bitter lesson, but young readers understand that it is an essential part of one's education in growing up.

THE YEARS

Type of work: Novel
Author: Virginia Woolf (1882-1941)
Type of plot: Domestic chronicle
Time of plot: 1880-1937
Locale: London
First published: 1937

The Years is more than the story of a middle-class family with all its frustrations, ambitions, triumphs, joys, and defeats; in its episodic pattern, it represents an effort to capture and record the process of time passing and to catch in fiction a sudden flash of recognition or a moment of perception that conveys a poetic impression.

In her essay "A Room of One's Own," Virginia Woolf describes a young man and woman getting into a taxi together to exemplify her artistic ideal: the "androgynous mind" which unites both male and female principles. The same symbol—here the two are alighting from a taxi—is found at the end of *The Years* and strikes one of the few hopeful notes in the book.

The novel covers roughly the time period of Virignia Woolf's own life, a sixty-year span which witnessed massive historical changes. It is this period— with its colonial expansion, uneasy days before World War I, the war itself and the ensuing disillusionment, the depression and cynicism of the 1930's— that is narrated through the lives of three generations of Pargiters. Although social milieu is more important than in any previous novel, Woolf does not merely narrate a historical chronicle, but also continues to explore such themes as uniting the one with the many, bringing order to chaos, and seeing with the androgynous vision. The Pargiter family, many and diverse, remain a unit, together again when the infrequent reunions occur.

Eleanor Pargiter is perhaps the most important character, a young woman around twenty at the beginning, an old woman over seventy at the end. From the beginning, during the terminal illness of the mother, she is the element that holds the family together. Throughout the book, Eleanor's thoughts and situation are given more prominence, and she has more contact with the other family members. Her jottings are noted as she moves through life; she makes an "I," with lines radiating from that center. This image suggests the ego at the center of each person's perceptions; different events become known from different characters' perspectives. Only the reader can see the pattern of the whole.

Eleanor typifies the woman who sacrifices her own ambitions and desires for the good of her aged father. Virginia Woolf often commented on this kind of woman, remarking that it was a blessing that her own parents died when she was relatively young, leaving her free to pursue her writing. When Colonel Pargiter dies it is too late for Eleanor to begin her own life.

The themes of earlier books are found in *The Years,* but the imagery has darkened considerably. Characters are often compared to animals or parts of nature that are gross or horrible. Uncle Edward looks like the shell of an insect, Patrick's face looks like a red gooseberry with a few hairs and his hands are like bear paws, Milly's fat arms draped with beads remind North of pale asparagus. The idea of the animal in man is emphasized by observations about people being "nasty creatures" with "uncontrollable lusts." North characterizes marriage as thirty years of "tut-tut-tut and chew-chew-chew." Such radical dehumanization dominates the imagery throughout the book, but is most prevalent in the last "Present Day" section. It suggests a fundamental pessimism about mankind's possibilities: since man is purely animal, "progress" is an illusion.

More importantly, the constant association of progress with death and aging reemphasizes this pessimistic outlook. Nicholas, for example, speaks of a New World in 1917 and expounds a similar idea in 1937. There is a sense in the latter section that optimistic words are empty and meaningless: Nicholas, after his attempted speech, brings his glass down and it shatters; two children sing for the party but their words are incomprehensible; Eleanor realizes that people know nothing, even about themselves. At the end the old Pargiter brothers and sisters are grouped together by a window, the next generation regarding them as "unreal" as statues. True communication, self-knowledge, and human progress all seem to be lacking.

The book's structure reinforces the theme of decay and entropy: people grow old and die and little else changes or improves. The first section is divided into ten parts, each treating a day in a particular year, from 1880 to 1918. Historical events—the death of Parnell or Edward VII, air raids during World War I, Armistice Day—are used as a means for bringing together different characters. Thus, the historical and social situations are always in the background. The second section is entitled "Present Day" and encompasses the final quarter of the book.

Throughout, such natural phenomena as rain, moon, wind, sun, and snow are used to connect places and people. Sometimes these phenomena recur from one year to another, so that each subsequent mention gains associations from the earlier ones. For instance, the way the sunlight shines through the trees is noted both in 1910 and 1914. The same objects and actions are periodically mentioned, giving to the book a large network of recurrences, where everything has a place in an order and where nothing happens by chance. Flames, sparks, and smoke are mentioned so often that they become symbolic, evoking memories of previous thoughts in the characters' minds. The fraying of the wick under the slow teakettle, the spotted ink-stained walrus, the cooing of the pigeons—these are some of the repeated images which provide links between the years.

Eleanor herself finally realizes that some sort of pattern for the whole exists, and that awareness makes her happy. But, she wonders, "Who makes it? Who thinks it?" Eleanor's vision of that pattern sets a note of hope to the ending of the book which counteracts the dark, dehumanized quality of foreboding prevalent in the 1937 section. However, it is questionable whether her final optimistic image of the young couple and the new day overcomes the pessimistic tone that dominates most of the rest of the book.

Margaret McFadden-Gerber

THE YEMASSEE

Type of work: Novel
Author: William Gilmore Simms (1806-1870)
Type of plot: Historical romance
Time of plot: Early eighteenth century
Locale: South Carolina
First published: 1835

The Yemassee *tells a fast-moving story of adventure and love during the days of Indian warfare in Colonial South Carolina. Simms is most effective in his characterization of the Indians, who are neither idealized nor despised, but shown as human beings fated by race to suffer defeat at the hands of the whites.*

In early American frontier novels the Indian was inevitably characterized in one of two ways, either as a "noble savage," a natural primitive untainted by civilization's corrupting influences, or, more commonly, a savage barbarian who took pleasure in cruelty and violence toward innocent white settlers. Even America's most famous author of historical romances, James Fenimore Cooper, divided his Indians into absolutely "good" and "bad" types and developed his novels accordingly. Perhaps only William Gilmore Simms in *The Yemassee* succeeded in creating believable, human Indians with mixed qualities, natures, and potentials; and that is the primary reason why *The Yemassee,* in spite of severe artistic flaws, must be acknowledged as one of the best nineteenth century frontier novels.

Through the first third of the book, the action is seen primarily from the Indian viewpoint. Simms carefully describes the Yemassee tribe as they plan and attempt to execute an uprising against the white settlers. Their motives, however, spring not from innate hostility or cruelty, but from a realization that the powers and needs of the white man make the conflict—and their own ultimate defeat—inevitable. Thus, Simms imports to the Yemassee a kind of doomed, almost tragic grandeur.

But it is in his presentation of the intimate life of the Indian that Simms is most impressive. Unlike Cooper, Simms describes the natives in their own environment and shows their daily routines, tribal mores, rituals, and politics in minute, careful detail. This Indian culture is presented with respect and individual tribe members are presented as fallible, but admirable human beings.

The most vivid portraits are those of Chief Sanutee, his wife, and their son. Sanutee is a proud, intelligent, brave, but flawed leader, who understands and accepts the unavoidable dissolution of his tribe, but who, nevertheless, inspires his men to heroic resistance. His wife, Matiwan, shares her husband's courage and insight, but her compassion elevates her above racial identity to become a kind of "Earth Mother" figure. Their son, Occonestoga, contaminated by contact with the white man's whiskey and promises, finally finds his courage and nobility in a time of crisis, although too late to salvage his tribal status. Few scenes in nineteenth century fiction are as powerful as the one in which, during the ritual that is to strip Occonestoga of his tribal identity, Matiwan kills her own son before the assembled Indians to save his honor and dignity.

Had Simms been able to sustain the insights and intensity of the first third of the book, *The Yemassee* might have been a great novel. But, unfortunately, once the focus of the novel shifts to the white man's world, the characters, both Indians and whites, become stock characters, and the novel degenerates into a clichéd chase-capture-escape romance.

Simms's sympathetic treatment of the Indians, however, does not mean that he considered them the white man's equal. Even Sanutee "well knew that the superior must necessarily be the ruin of the race which is inferior." As a staunch upholder of the Southern position in the pre-Civil War South, Simms firmly believed in racial superiority and what he and others called an "organic society." In Simms's view the Indian was doomed because he was an inferior race and culture and, unlike the black, could not be fit into a useful place in the white man's world. However tragic and seemingly unjust the displacement or destruction of the red man might be, it was, to Simms, the necessary price that had to be paid in order to establish the superior society.

YOU CAN'T GO HOME AGAIN

Type of work: Novel
Author: Thomas Wolfe (1900-1938)
Type of plot: Impressionistic realism
Time of plot: 1929-1936
Locale: New York, England, Germany
First published: 1940

Wolfe's final novel continues the story of George Webber from The Web and the Rock. *A sprawling yet powerful and often lyrical book,* You Can't Go Home Again *examines with realistic detachment the failed promises of America during the Depression, but shows how the dream of freedom, though difficult to establish, is vastly superior to the poisonous promises of Nazi Germany.*

In May, 1938, having broken with his first editor and "mentor" Maxwell Perkins ("Foxhall Edwards" in the novel), Thomas Wolfe deposited an unfinished manuscript of perhaps a million words on the desk of his new editor, Edward C. Aswell of Harper and Brothers, and left for a tour of the West. In Vancouver he contracted pneumonia, in Seattle it worsened, and finally, after he had been moved to Johns Hopkins in Baltimore, it was found that the illness had triggered the release of previously latent tuberculosis bacteria in his lungs which had gone to the brain; he died on September 15, 1938.

Thus, it was left to Aswell to assemble, organize, and edit Wolfe's admittedly unfinished material into publishable fictions. The major results of Aswell's efforts were the two massive novels that chronicle the life and artistic development of George Webber, *The Web and the Rock* (1939) and *You Can't Go Home Again.* Consequently, the episodic, fragmentary, sometimes even arbitrary structure of these books and the unevenness and occasional excessiveness of the writing must in part be the result of the compositional problems—though these flaws also exist in his two prior works. There is no way of knowing what the final form of the novels would have been had Wolfe lived to complete them to his own satisfaction.

It has been said that Thomas Wolfe wrote only one book during his career, a thinly disguised autobiography. In a sense this is true, but, like Walt Whitman, the American author who seems most like him in artistic intention and attitude, Wolfe saw his own experience as the focal point for the experience of a nation in the process of becoming. Thus, as the major character in Wolfe's novels strives for experience, personal meaning, and a means of artistic expression, he is also trying to seize and formalize the nature and direction of nothing less than American society itself.

You Can't Go Home Again is the most external and social of his four major novels. The title sets the theme and action line of the novel. George cannot go "home" to any of the old places, experiences, or ideas that have formed him, because every time he attempts to do so he either finds a corruption that has destroyed the thing he would return to, or he finds that he has gone beyond that particular experience and has neither the need nor the desire to repeat it. Metaphorically, "home" is the naïve, idealized vision of America and of his potential place in it that he had held as a young man, but now learns no longer exists and perhaps never did.

When George returns to his home town of Libya Hill to attend his aunt's funeral, he finds the old rural values gone and a new corrupt speculative fever running rampant. Then he sees the collapse of this greedy dream in the beginnings of the Depression. He cannot go back to his physical home because it no longer exists and he is repelled by what has replaced it. But Libya Hill is only a microcosm, a foreshadowing of what he is to encounter. As America enters into the Depression, George comes into painful contact with both the results of the American economic and social systems as he intimately observes both its victims and its victimizers—and he seeks to disassociate himself from both.

It is Europe and especially Germany, however, that brings George to his final understanding. The notion that artistic success and fame will bring him satisfaction is destroyed by his meeting with the famous novelist Lloyd Mc-Harg (a fictionalized Sinclair Lewis), who finds only bitterness, loneliness, and alcohol in his success. George then completes his education in Germany when he is exposed to the horror of the newly powerful Nazi regime. The Nazi horror, thus, is the logical extension and end result of the greed and corruption George has observed in America, perhaps even the America of the not too distant future.

And yet *You Can't Go Home Again* is not a despairing book. It ends with an exhortation. For all the evil and pessimism he has encountered in his education, George continues to feel that mankind in general and America in particular still have the potential to assert their positive capacities and realize the ideals they once possessed. That is where, as an artist in Whitman's "Bardic" tradition, George sees his place in America to be—as a spokesman for that vision.

YOU KNOW ME AL

Type of work: Epistolary novel
Author: Ring Lardner (1885-1933)
Type of plot: Humorous satire
Time of plot: c. 1915
Locale: Chicago
First published: 1916

Several streams of American comic tradition merge in this satiric portrait of an egotistical, loutish baseball player: the funny letter, the wisecrack, the braggart character, the use of sporting vocabulary and fractured English, and the general debunking mood.

Ring Lardner was the first important American author to write seriously about sports. As a young sportswriter, his constant association with athletes strongly influenced his notions about American character and society. As early as 1914, Lardner understood what other mainstream American writers did not realize until the 1950's and later—the importance of big sports in the emotions, imaginations, and needs of the public and the extent to which it embodies some of the most basic assumptions and "myths" of the culture.

Sports is one area where pursuit of the American dream can still be seen in its purest form. According to this myth, any man with the requisite talent and drive can compete openly and fairly for the best rewards society has to offer: money, status, and adulation of the people. The best man necessarily wins and goes directly and quickly to the "top."

But Lardner also saw the distance between dream and reality, so he chronicled this incongruity in a series of vivid, funny, sad, biting, and often bitter works of fiction—notably "Champion," "Alibi Ike," "My Roomy," and especially *You Know Me Al.* He described the mean, dreary, crude, and often vicious world of professional athletics with humor, honesty, and realism—without sentimentality, but not without compassion. Although he largely abandoned sportswriting as a profession and sports as a subject matter after 1922, these stories still form the backbone of his reptuation.

Jack Keefe is both an exploiter of the American dream and its victim. He imagines himself a hero—invincible on the diamond, shrewd and popular off of it, applauded by fans, adored by women, destined to "greatness." But, in fact, Jack is mocked and taken advantage of by most people he meets: teammates, opponents, employers, women in general, and his wife, Florrie, in particular. For all of his faults—his bragging, his alibiing, his self-indulgence, laziness, stinginess, beer-swilling, and crudity—he is still more sinned against than sinner. It is this ironical distance between Jack's self-image and the reality of his situation that gives *You Know Me Al* its rich humor and poignancy.

Jack is an especially American comic type: the boastful loser who is too naïve and pugnacious to realize that he really is a loser. It is this dogged, optimistic pursuit of his false image and improbable dream that makes Jack Keefe most human and most American.

YOUMA

Type of work: Novel
Author: Lafcadio Hearn (1850-1904)
Type of plot: Exotic romance
Time of plot: The 1840's
Locale: Martinique
First published: 1890

Like much of Hearn's work, Youma is filled with pictures of exotic scenery and life. A story of West Indian slavery, the novel is remarkable for presenting essentially the Negro's point of view in the Martinique rebellion.

Reportedly based on a true incident that occurred during the Martinique rebellion, *Youma* is an example of Hearn's lifelong fascination with the exotic, and his carefully delineated translations of truth into fiction. The story reveals the degree of Youma's attachment to her white foster family.

Orphaned Youma was accorded many of the same privileges as her mistress' daughter during the children's early years. Although Youma was not taught to read and write and was not sent away to school with the daughter, she was well aware that she received far better treatment than most slaves.

However, Youma was unaware that her mistress planned to arrange for her a suitable marriage with a black freedman and then to free her. Thus, she saw no deterrent to a marriage with Gabriel and was stunned when permission was not granted. She might have fled with Gabriel, but her affection for the white family, and especially for Mayotte, to whom she was a foster mother as Madame Peyronette had been to her, outweighed her resentment and prevented such a course of action.

Had Madame Peyronette acceded to the young couple's wishes, Youma and Mayotte would have remained safely on the plantation. Unfortunately, the romance precipitated obedient Youma's return with the child to the city at a time when tensions were running high among slaves fearful that their masters might attempt to prevent black emancipation. The action of one white man then set the stage for Youma's final act of devotion. His cruel punishment of a slave incited the rebellion.

Youma could have lived by abandoning Mayotte. But neither her fear of death, nor her dislike of slavery, nor the prospect of freedom could induce her to leave the child. Martyred in the flames, Youma represents the epitome of altruistic love.

YVAIN

Type of work: Poem
Author: Chrétien de Troyes (c. 1150-c. 1190)
Type of plot: Chivalric romance
Time of plot: Sixth century
Locale: Britain
First transcribed: After 1164

Yvain, ou le Chevalier au Lion *is the most complicated of the chivalric romances written by Chrétien de Troyes. Episodic in plot and rather conventional in moral theme, it derives from various sources: Ovid's* Metamorphoses *and the* Art of Love, *Vergil's* Aeneid, *and the Arthurian materials presented in the* Historia Regum Britanniae *by Geoffrey of Monmouth.*

Chrétien de Troyes' *Yvain,* or *Knight of the Lion,* deals, like his *Erec and Enide,* with problems of married love.

Although many critics see it as a fairly unified story, others consider the romance divided into two distinct parts: first, the winning of his wife, Lady Laudine, and second, losing her and only gaining her back through a process of moral rehabilitation.

After Yvain wins Laudine by killing her lord and becoming in turn defender of the magic spring, he grows excessively proud. On Gawain's insistence he leaves for a year to take part in tournaments, apparently only to prove his reputation. He promises Lady Laudine to return in a year, but Yvain forgets his promise and his duty to defend the spring, loses his moral qualities—even his wife—and exists like a wild animal in the forest.

Although the narrative from this point on seems episodic and at times disconnected, Yvain, with the help of a faithful lion, slowly regains his moral integrity and works his way back to his former status and his lady.

Various interpretations have been given the lion. He has been related to a lion in an ancient Celtic tale that carries the hero on a journey to the Other World. The lion has Christian symbolism as a noble beast, even representing Christ as opposed to the serpent or personification of evil. Some critics think Chrétien de Troyes might have drawn from the classic story of Androcles and the lion.

It is true that Yvain encounters the lion battling with a serpent, and when Yvain is mad in the forest, a hermit prays for him. For some readers these elements make Yvain a Christian hero who wins his lady the second time not only by physical but also by spiritual strength. But whether Yvain is considered a Christian or pagan hero, Chrétien describes in detail the different stages through which Yvain passes to become a rehabilitated hero—one worthy of Lady Laudine.

Yvain is a sophisticated narrative infused with Chrétien de Troyes' characteristic comic and tragic scenes, combinations of natural and supernatural elements, and his careful anatomy of love. Both Laudine and her damsel, Lunete, are drawn with subtle complexity and seem much like real individuals.

In *Yvain,* which he wrote at full maturity, Chrétien shows much more vigor and delight in composition than in *Erec and Enide,* his first Arthurian romance.

ZADIG

Type of work: Novel
Author: François Marie Arouet de Voltaire (1694-1778)
Type of plot: Social satire
Time of plot: Remote antiquity
Locale: Babylon
First published: 1747

Zadig *is the story of an educated, sensible young man who escapes from great difficulties by continuing to be calmly sensible. Like Voltaire's other great comic satire,* Candide, *this tale also shows the philosopher's disdain of the religious dogmas of his time and his preference for a rational and compassionate consideration of the problems of society.*

Voltaire remains one of the central figures of that epoch in the development of Western culture and civilization called the Enlightenment. For contemporary students of the history of Western thought, the Enlightenment (and Voltaire) signify the establishment of human reason and intellect as a dominant value in estimating conduct, religion, politics, and law.

Zadig is clearly rooted in Voltaire's own experience. In his early fifties, Voltaire spent much time at court and was appointed Historiographer-Royal and gentleman of the King's chamber. But he grew disillusioned with the short-sightedness, hypocrisy, and pettiness of French court politics, and left for Germany. In the meantime, however, he had written *Zadig* as an expression both of his feelings about political life and about those values he deemed most important in life.

Although the central ideas in *Zadig* are clear enough, the episodic structure —consisting of short, frequent chapters—divides the story more than it helps the pace. Further, the characterizations are thin and the style, though often pithy, is sometimes abrupt. In short, *Zadig* is not meant to be read as a story but as a series of brief, interrelated, fictionalized essays. The key ideas in *Zadig* are centered around the questions of the determination of ethical conduct and the nature of the just ruler.

For Voltaire, ethical conduct cannot merely be summarized in the teachings of Christianity. Voltaire's hero, Zadig, follows both the precepts of Zoroaster (whom, it may be supposed, can be taken for Christ), and the guidance of his own reason. In a sense, the goals of his conduct (justice, mercy, loyalty) may have been taken from religion, but their application in real life is made with reason. The necessity for moderation, the futility of self-love, and the need for honesty and science are additional values that Voltaire advocates.

But these values and standards are set forth in a strongly political and juridicial atmosphere. Zadig is, until the end, an adviser to kings, princes, and judges. Thus, the question of the just ruler arises again and again in the course of the work. Voltaire seems to take a Platonist or Neoplatonist view of the matter. He puts forward the need for a philosopher king, a ruler who bases his decisions not on superstition or selfish, short-sighted considerations, but on reason, science, and justice. Voltaire's philosopher king obviously embodies the values of the Enlightenment rather than those of ancient Greece; nonetheless, the same sharp desire for a just ruler that informs Plato's *Republic* also defines and gives life to Voltaire's *Zadig*.

ZAÏRE

Type of work: Drama
Author: François Marie Arouet de Voltaire (1694-1778)
Type of plot: Historical tragedy
Time of plot: During the reign of Osman, Sultan of Jerusalem
Locale: Jerusalem
First presented: 1732

In this elevated tragedy in the neoclassic style, Voltaire gives human dimensions to a grand theme of jealousy. Although the drama is not ordinarily regarded as the equal of Othello, *to which it bears a resemblance, it has merits of dignity and restraint in the development of its own story.*

On June 25, 1732, twenty-two days after Voltaire began work on *Zaïre,* he completed the drama, which is generally regarded as his finest verse tragedy in the neo-Classical style. Some three months earlier, on March 7, 1732, his *Eriphyle,* written partly in imitation of *Hamlet,* had failed miserably on the stage. In that play Voltaire had emphasized scenes of terror rather than passion. Stung by the reaction of both audience and critics (notably his old enemy, J. J. Rousseau), he resolved that his next theatrical effort would treat the romantic emotions as fully as possible. To a friend he wrote: "Everyone here reproaches me that I do not put more love into my pieces. There shall be love enough this time, I swear, and not mere gallantry." In his next play, he promised that "there may be nothing so Turkish, so Christian, so amorous, so tender, so infuriate, as that which I am now putting into verse for the pleasure of the public . . . . We shall love, we shall baptize, we shall kill, and I will send you the outline as soon as it is done." With these romantic ingredients, *Zaïre* was hurried into production on August 13, 1732. Although the occasion of its first performance was disappointing—the actors had not prepared their parts effectively—by August 25, Voltaire was able to write his friend Cideville that none of his other plays had pleased the public so well as this one.

In the *Dissertation sur la Tragédie,* which is prefixed to the edition of *Sémiramis,* Voltaire insists that everything in the story of *Zaïre,* even the names of characters, is fictitious. But as a matter of fact, many elements of the play parallel historical events. The background of *Zaïre* concerns the Christian-Muhammedan wars centering around the Second Crusade (1147-1149) under Louis VII and the Sixth Crusade, associated with Louis IX. From the Moslem point of view, the period was famous for the exploits, legendary or real, of Saladin, whose generous spirit serves as the model for the noble Orosmane (Osman). On July 4, 1187, Saladin's armies defeated Christian forces at the battle of Hittin. One of the prisoners of Saladin, Guy of Lusignan, was later released and eventually became King of Cyprus. Voltaire alters some historical details: he places the battle of Hittin (called

Caesarea) after the fall of Jerusalem, not before. In the playwright's version of that battle, the Moslem forces under Noradin, Orosmane's father, capture Lusignan's two children, Nérestan, a boy scarcely four years old, and Zaïre, his infant daughter. As the play begins, twenty years have passed since Cesarea, and another battle is supposed to have taken place at Damascus. Other details of the play are Voltaire's invention, but the historical basis— Lusignan's possible role in the battle of Bouvines, July 27, 1214—gives to French audiences of the tragedy a sense of religious and national pride.

To English or American readers, however, the drama is more interesting because of its parallels to Shakespearean tragedy than for its sources in the history of the Crusades. From the time of its reception, *Zaïre* has been compared with *King Lear* and *Othello*. Lusignan's poignant reconciliation with his daughter recalls, at least somewhat, that of Lear and Cordelia. More persuasive is the similarity between Voltaire's play and *Othello*. Like Shakespeare's jealous Moor, Orosmane is driven by passion to murder his guiltless lover. However, Corasmin, officer of the Sultan, is only a faint copy of the malicious Iago; and Orosmane's jealousy has its roots in pride as much as sexual rivalry.

Indeed, the major contrast between Voltaire's and Shakespeare's tragedy of jealousy is in their opposing concepts of love. Othello is driven to hysterical violence out of a sense of sexual betrayal. Orosmane, less "barbaric" in his elemental desires, loses control of his passions when his sense of honor is offended. His noble pride cannot endure a rival in love. As soon as he learns that Zaïre, whom he has just murdered, had truly loved him, and him alone, he stabs himself to atone for his guilt. Othello also commits suicide because of guilt. He had misjudged Desdemona, not for a trivial offense that would injure his pride, but because he feared—and was mistaken—that she had been sexually unfaithful to him and had violated his sense of "purity" and order in the universe.

The difference in the concept of love extends to a contrast between Voltaire's and Shakespeare's style. To the French poet, Shakespeare (whom he admired in many respects) was in matters of tact a "barbarian" because of his demonstration of the violent passions. Voltaire's tragedy—elevated, sustained, and, to a modern audience, static—shows how the passions are controlled by civilized restraint. The ultimate model for *Zaïre* is not Shakespeare, then, but Racine. Voltaire's Orosmane earns the reader's sympathetic respect because the measure of his suffering may be guessed by the quality of refinement in his character. Although Orosmane, unlike Othello, is nearly without psychological dimensions, he is a figure of awesome dignity, integrity, and honor. Clearly it is the author's intention to show that, even though the Sultan is an enemy to Christians, he is a friend to the civilized virtues: a chivalrous, fine-spirited gentleman. To the satirist in Voltaire, concealing himself in the guise of dramatist, these virtues are superior to the claims of religious fanaticism.

EL ZARCO

Type of work: Novel
Author: Ignacio Manuel Altamirano (1834-1893)
Type of plot: Romantic tragedy
Time of plot: 1861-1863
Locale: Province of Morelos, Mexico
First published: 1901

Completed shortly before the writer's death, El Zarco *appeared posthumously eight years later. The novel is somber, based upon Mexican history, and suffused with the beauty of the landscape. In Nicolas, an Indian, Altamirano sees a bright promise for the future of his nation.*

El Zarco has beauty, action, and clarity. It paints the subtropical mountains of Morelos between 1861 and 1863, when political conditions were chaotic, a potentially rich economy stagnated, and social justice was unknown. We thus see the traditional reasons for Mexico's sluggish progress, which stemmed basically from bad government, but which has been blamed too exclusively on the rich, on bloated landlords, on narrowminded priests, and other prototypes of the oppressor.

El Zarco sketches folklore, human types, and the Mexican psychology of the time. Above all, it clearly depicts the dichotomy between a virtuous social element—as represented by Nicolas, Antonia, and others—and the various corrupt types that were crippling Mexico through laziness, greed, and dishonesty. As in the times of "El Zarco," the negative minority is sometimes in sociopolitical control today while the healthier majority is excluded from the levers of control. The same theme appears often in Mexican literature, implying that Mexican revolutions have often been meaninglessly destructive, and that even some of the glorified patriotic victories (such as the defeat of Spain 1810-1822; the defeat of Maximilian soon after the time of "El Zarco"; and of Porfirio Diaz in 1910-1911) have blocked as well as unleashed progress. This, for example, is a theme of Mariano Azuela's "The Underdogs" ("Los de Abajo"), which, in describing the civil strife that took place half a century after "El Zarco," condemned the *nouveau riche* of a popular revolution as much as it did their opponents.

El Zarco suffers from the inevitable limitations of the nineteenth century in which it was written. Some of its characterizations are somewhat simplistic —Nicolas, for example, seems too faultless and is not presented convincingly, while Antonia, Pilar, and El Tigre are rather one-dimensional figures. Nevertheless, El Zarco himself was presented in greater depth, since his motivations for vengeance and power—that stemmed from his sorry past as a stable boy and menial drudge on large estates—are convincing. Altamirano even makes it clear that El Zarco's menial tasks were given to him because he was too worthlessly lazy to learn higher skills, and that El Zarco simply belonged to that inherently unblessed type of revolutionary who is ever ready to be whistled out of the mesquite at the wave of a sombrero to murder and plunder for "La Causa."

Manuela is initially callous, greedy, spoiled, and even deliberately evil. Sorrow, frustration, and total defeat finally goad her into psychological transformation. Disillusioned and hapless, knowing that she has sinned, she receives the attendant punishment without self-pity as she dies at the foot of El Zarco's corpse.

The real person that Altamirano was in his daily life stalks through the pages of *El Zarco*. The novel reflects his impoverished youth—for which he yearns, oddly enough—and its memories of slights, offenses, and the indifferences of calculating women who were frivolously incapable of seeing in him anything more than an impoverished youth. Yet Altamirano's novels, even while reliving the memories that makes these novels authentic, are not basically autobiographical. Typically, El Zarco's reaction to his humble past is opposite that of Altamirano's, while Nicolas' reaction to life is Altamirano's since he does not live as an abject and servile Indian but as a cultured man dignified by work and conscious of his own personal worth.

Altamirano was one of the most complete men of action and letters of his time in Mexico. He did not view the novel as a pastime for lazy souls, but "as a treasury whose disguises could be penetrated" to find jewels of historical fact, political doctrine, social reality, and character-building morality. He also felt that the novel should be used to present the beliefs of specific political parties or religious denominations, or even other entities. He considered it, in short, the genre par excellence of the masses, comparable to popular music, mass circulation magazines, or the orator's podium.

Altamirano thus used the novel as he used the sword in favor of his liberal political views, which were liberal in a nineteenth century sense. He thus followed the tradition of Argentina's Domingo Sarmiento and Bartolomé Mitre, who were literary presidents of the Argentine Republic. Like them, Altamirano was politically active as a theoretician and campaigner; he also served in three of Mexico's wars—the War of Ayutla, the War of the Reform, and the War of French Intervention during Maximilian's time. He was also a parliamentarian and journalist, pouring the wisdom of his rich experiences into his novels.

Altamirano stated that he finished *El Zarco* at exactly eleven-twenty on the night of April 6th, 1888. He first titled the novel "Episodes of Mexican Life in 1861-63" and had sold it for two hundred dollars when it was barely half-finished. The novel's stated goal was to be a clear mirror of Mexico, and a compass revealing the advisable path, as well as the erroneous one, for his bleeding nation to follow. For this goal, he dedicated the simple fluidity of his style and the wisdom of his years.

William Freitas

ZULEIKA DOBSON

Type of work: Novel
Author: Max Beerbohm (1872-1956)
Type of plot: Romantic satire
Time of plot: Early twentieth century
Locale: Oxford, England
First published: 1911

On one level Zuleika Dobson. *Beerbohm's only novel, is a burlesque of Oxford undergraduate life; on another the fantasy is a spoof on affectation and absurdity wherever they may be found.*

When readers maintained that he had written a satire on upper-class snobbery, Max Beerbohm insisted that his only novel, *Zuleika Dobson,* was merely a fantasy. The Duke of Dorset, with his club of one, is probably the most outrageous portrait of English snobbery since Thackeray's studies of the subject. But we would be wise to take "the incomparable Max" (the nickname Bernard Shaw gave him in the 1890's) at his word: *Zuleika Dobson* does not engage our passions for social criticism; it does tickle our funnybone by following to their ultimate absurdity the enthusiasms of Edwardian gallantry. Like Beerbohm's many literary caricatures, *Zuleika Dobson* deflates the inflated.

It is a fantasy because it rides whimsy to worlds startling and new. Poor Zuleika, who is cursed with such excessive beauty that all men fall in love with her, makes the best of her affliction. She bears up under the aggressive adulation of the entire student population of Oxford by dressing as smartly as she can and by taking every advantage to be seen publicly. How does this alleviate her suffering? All of Oxford literally drowns in the Isis because of her indifference. The best way to get rid of annoying lovers is simply to drive them to suicide. Is it a trick? Of course, but the magic is Beerbohm's. And the trick is done with understatement. "To love and be scorned—does Fate hold for us a greater inconvenience?" asks the Duke. A parody of realism completes Beerbohm's satire: "There were tiny red marks where he had held her. No man had ever dared to lay hands on her. With a sense of contamination, she proceeded to wash her hands thoroughly with soap and water." The Freudian compulsiveness of this, not to mention the Strindbergian defiance, reflects perfectly Beerbohm's ability to turn the most serious emotions into grist for his satiric mill.

Zuleika has all the energy of a knight on a quest. She must find, somewhere, a man who does *not* love her. Beerbohm's greatest joke is to make a fantasy of antiromance. It is indeed fantastic to imagine a world stripped of its greatest illusion: men idolizing what they love. Indirectly, Beerbohm is telling us that the greatest fantasy of all is the assumption that we can live without fantasy itself.

AUTHOR AND TITLE INDEX

I

II

V

VI

AUTHOR AND TITLE INDEX

VII

AUTHOR AND TITLE INDEX

AUTHOR AND TITLE INDEX

XIV

AUTHOR AND TITLE INDEX